# Genetic Transformation and Expression

# Genetic Transformation and Expression

Editors:
## L.O. Butler

*Department of Medical Microbiology,*
*St. George's Hospital Medical School, London, UK*

## Colin Harwood

*Department of Microbiology,*
*University of Newcastle upon Tyne, UK*

## and B.E.B. Moseley

*AFRC Institute of Food Research,*
*Shinfield, Reading, Berks, UK*

Intercept

Andover, Hants

**British Library Cataloguing in Publication Data**

Genetic transformation and expression.

A CIP catalogue record for this book is
available from the British Library.

ISBN 0–946707–18–9

Published in October 1989 by Intercept Limited,
P.O. Box 716, Andover, Hants SP10 1YG, England.

Filmset in 'Linotron' Times by
Ann Buchan (Typesetters), Shepperton, Middlesex.
Printed by Athenaeum Press Ltd, Newcastle upon Tyne.

# Preface

This volume contains contributions presented at the Ninth European Meeting on Genetic Transformation held at the University of Kent at Canterbury in August 1988. These European meetings have expanded their range of topics since the very first meeting was held in Oeiras in 1972, as reflected in the change in title, and no doubt further changes will be seen as the series progresses. However, there is still a strong background of both fundamental and applied aspects of bacterial transformation, but added to this we now have considerations of plasmid stability and recombination, gene expression, DNA repair, particularly as relevant to recombination, and the extension into animal and plant hosts. The rapid progress in genetic manipulation and molecular technology since the European Meetings began has obviously had a great influence on the extent to which topics may now be pursued.

We would like to thank the authors for their co-operation in the prompt and careful preparation of their manuscripts, and Linda Antoniw for magnificent editorial support, and the various sponsors who made the meeting possible.

L.O. BUTLER
C.R. HARWOOD
B.E.B. MOSELEY
March 1989

# Contributors

ALESSANDRA M. ALBERTINI, *Facoltà di Agraria, Università di Udine, Udine, Italy*

A.R. ARCHIBALD, *Microbial Technology Group, Department of Microbiology, The Medical School, Newcastle upon Tyne, NE2 4HH, UK*

STAFFAN ARVIDSON, *Department of Bacteriology, Karolinska Institute, S-104 01 Stockholm, Sweden*

ELISABETH AUBERT, *Unité de Génie Microbiologique, Institut Pasteur, Paris, France*

S. AYMERICH, *Laboratoire de Génétique des Microorganismes, Institut National Agronomique, CBAI, 78850 Thiverval-Grignon, France*

CLAUDIA BARBERIO, *Department of Animal Biology and Genetics, v. Romana 17, 50125 Firenze, Italy*

GERARD J. BARCAK, *Department of Molecular Biology and Genetics, The Johns Hopkins University School of Medicine, 725 North Wolfe Street, Baltimore, MD 21205, USA*

PETER M. BENNETT, *Department of Microbiology, The Medical School, University of Bristol, University Walk, Bristol BS8 1TD, UK*

IRIT BERGER, *Department of Molecular Genetics, The Hebrew University-Hadassah Medical School, Jerusalem, Israel 91010*

D.J. BLACKBOURN, *Microbial Technology Group, Department of Microbiology, The Medical School, Newcastle upon Tyne, NE2 4HH, UK*

S. BONNASSIE, *Centre de Recherche de Biochimie et de Génétique Cellulaires du CNRS, 118 Route de Narbonne, 31062 Toulouse Cedex, France*

P. BREYNE, *Laboratorium voor Genetica, Rijksuniversiteit Gent, K.L. Ledeganckstraat 35, B-9000 Gent, Belgium*

SIERD BRON, *Department of Genetics, University of Groningen, Kerklaan 30, 9751 NN Haren(Gn), The Netherlands*

DOMINIQUE BRUNIER, *Laboratoire de Génétique Microbienne, Institut de Biotechnologie, INRA, Domaine de Vilvert, 78350 Jouy en Josas, France*

L.O. BUTLER, *Bacterial Genetics Laboratory, Department of Medical Microbiology, St. George's Hospital Medical School, Cranmer Terrace, London SW17 0RE, UK*

TIZIANA CARAMORI, *Dipartimento di Biologia, Università di Trieste, Trieste, Italy*

MARK S. CHANDLER, *Department of Molecular Biology and Genetics, The Johns Hopkins University School of Medicine, 725 North Wolfe Street, Baltimore, MD 21205, USA*

CORINNE CLAVÉ, *Centre de Recherche de Biochimie et de Génétique Cellulaires du CNRS, 118 Route de Narbonne, 31062 Toulouse Cedex, France*

JEAN-PIERRE CLAVERYS, *Centre de Recherche de Biochimie et de Génétique Cellulaires du CNRS, 118 Route de Narbonne, 31062 Toulouse Cedex, France*

AMIKAM COHEN, *Department of Molecular Genetics, The Hebrew University-Hadassah Medical School, Jerusalem, Israel 91010*

ANTONELLA COMANDUCCI, *Department of Microbiology, The Medical School, University of Bristol, University Walk, Bristol BS8 1TD, UK*

D. LE COQ, *Laboratoire de Génétique des Microorganismes, Institut National Agronomique, CBAI, 78850 Thiverval-Grignon, France*

R.D. COXON, *Microbial Technology Group, Department of Microbiology, The Medical School, Newcastle upon Tyne, NE2 4HH, UK*

A.M. CRUTZ, *Laboratoire de Génétique des Microorganismes, Institut National Agronomique, CBAI, 78850 Thiverval-Grignon, France*

NADIA DANHASH, *Department of Biochemistry and Applied Molecular Biology, University of Manchester Institute for Science and Technology, PO Box 88, Manchester M60 1QD, UK*

JULIAN DAVIES, *Unité de Génie Microbiologique, Institut Pasteur, Paris, France*

G. DAXHELET, *Microbiology and Genetics Unit, University of Louvain Medical School, ICP-UCL 7449, 75 Avenue Hippocrate, 1200 Brussels, Belgium*

A. DEPICKER, *Laboratorium voor Genetica Rijksuniversiteit Gent, K.L. Ledeganckstraat 35, B-9000 Gent, Belgium*

ASUNCION DIAZ, *Centro de Investigaciones Biológicas, Velazquez, 144-28006 Madrid, Spain*

JAN MAARTEN VAN DIJL, *Department of Genetics, University of Groningen, Kerklaan 30, 9751 NN Haren (Gn), The Netherlands*

HELEN M. DODD, *Department of Microbiology, The Medical School, University of Bristol, University Walk, Bristol BS8 1TD, UK*

C.A.G. VAN EEKELEN, *Royal Gist-brocades N.V., Research and Development, PO Box 1, 2600 MA Delft, The Netherlands*

PER EGNELL, *Center for BioTechnology, F82, Karolinska Institute, Huddinge University Hospital, S-14186 Huddinge, Sweden*

S. DUSKO EHRLICH, *Laboratoire de Génétique Microbienne, Institut de Biotechnologie, INRA, Domaine de Vilvert, 78350 Jouy en Josas, France*

MARGARETA ELIASSON, *Department of Biochemistry and Biotechnology, The Royal Institute of Technology, S-100 44 Stockholm, Sweden*

MANUEL ESPINOSA, *Centro de Investigaciones Biológicas, Velazquez, 144-28006 Madrid, Spain*

ANNE-MARIE ESTEVENON, *UFR des Sciences Pharmaceutiques, Université Paul Sabatier, 35 Chemin des Maraîchers, 31062 Toulouse Cedex, France*

STEFAN FIEDLER, *Lehrstuhl für Mikrobiologie der Universität München, Maria-Ward-Straße 1a, D-8000 München 19, FRG*

J.F. FLINTERMAN, *Royal Gist-brocades N.V., Research and Development, PO Box 1, 2600 MA Delft, The Netherlands*

JAN-INGMAR FLOCK, *Center for BioTechnology, F82, Karolinska Institute, Huddinge University Hospital, S-14186 Huddinge, Sweden*

U. FORSUM, *Department of Clinical Bacteriology, F71, Karolinska Institute, Huddinge University Hospital, S-14186 Huddinge, Sweden*

ANITA FRIESENEGGER, *Lehrstuhl für Mikrobiologie der Universität München, Maria-Ward-Straße 1a, D-8000 München 19, FRG*

ELISABET FRITHZ, *Department of Microbiology, University of Lund, S-223 62 Lund, Sweden*

NOUZHA FTOUHI, *Institut de Microbiologie, Bâtiment 409, Université Paris-Sud, 91405 Orsay Cedex, France*

ALESSANDRO GALIZZI, *Dipartimento di Genetica e Microbiologia, Università di Pavia, Pavia, Italy*

DAVID C.J. GARDNER, *Department of Biochemistry and Applied Molecular Biology, University of Manchester Institute for Science and Technology, PO Box 88, Manchester M60 1QD, UK*

A.M. GASC, *Centre de Recherche de Biochimie et de Génétique Cellulaires du CNRS, 118 Route de Narbonne, 31062 Toulouse Cedex, France*

G. GERRITSE, *Royal Gist-brocades N.V., Research and Development, PO Box 1, 2600 MA Delft, The Netherlands*

G. GHEYSEN, *Laboratorium voor genetica, Rijksuniversiteit Gent, K.L. Ledeganckstraat 35, B-9000 Gent, Belgium*

M.S. GILBERT, *Department of Physiology and Biochemistry, University of Reading, Whiteknights, PO Box 228, Reading, RG6 2AJ, UK*

G. GONZY-TRÉBOUL, *Group Génétique et Membranes, Institut Jacques Monod, tour 43, 2 place Jussieu, 75005 Paris, France*

T.S. GREWAL, *Department of Physiology and Biochemistry, University of Reading, Whiteknights, PO Box 228, Reading, RG6 2AJ, UK*

NANCY GUILLÉN, *Institut de Microbiologie, Bâtiment 409, Université Paris-Sud, 91405 Orsay Cedex, France*

A.J. HAANDRIKMAN, *Department of Genetics, University of Groningen, Kerklaan 30, 9751 NN Haren(Gn), The Netherlands*

PETER HAIMA, *Department of Genetics, University of Groningen, Kerklaan 30, 9751 NN Haren(Gn), The Netherlands*

C.R. HARWOOD, *Microbial Technology Group, Department of Microbiology, The Medical School, Newcastle upon Tyne, NE2 4HH, UK*

x      Contributors

LARS-OLOF HEDÉN, Department of Microbiology, University of Lund, S-223 62 Lund, Sweden

L. HERMAN, Laboratorium voor Genetica, Rijksuniversiteit Gent, K.L. Ledeganckstraat 35, B-9000 Gent, Belgium

H. HESLOT, Laboratoire de Génétique des Microorganismes, Institut National Agronomique, CBAI, 78850 Thiverval-Grignon, France

R.A.C. VAN DER HOEK, Royal Gist-brocades N.V., Research and Development, PO Box 1, 2600 MA Delft, The Netherlands

P. HOET, Microbiology and Genetics Unit, University of Louvain Medical School, ICP-UCL 7449, 75 Avenue Hippocrate, 1200 Brussels, Belgium

CHRISTINA HOLMBERG, Department of Microbiology, University of Lund, Sölvegatan 21, S-223 62 Lund, Sweden

LAURENT JANNIÈRE, Laboratoire de Génétique Microbienne, Institut de Biotechnologie, INRA, Domaine de Vilvert, 78350 Jouy en Josas, France

LARS JANZON, Department of Bacteriology, Karolinska Institute, S-104 01 Stockholm, Sweden

ANNE DE JONG, Department of Genetics, University of Groningen, Kerklaan 30, 9751 NN Haren(Gn), The Netherlands

V.E. KHAZAK, VNII Genetica, Moscow, 113545, Dorozhnyi pr, 1A, USSR

TOBIAS KIESER, John Innes Institute and AFRC Institute of Plant Science Research, Norwich NR4 7UH, UK

J. KISS-BLÜMEL, Microbiology and Genetics Unit, University of Louvain Medical School, ICP-UCL 7449, 75 Avenue Hippocrate, 1200 Brussels, Belgium

J. KOK, Department of Genetics, University of Groningen, Kerklaan 30, 9751 NN Haren (Gn), The Netherlands

JAN KOOISTRA, Department of Genetics, University of Groningen, Kerklaan 30, 9751 NN Haren (Gn), The Netherlands

J. KORNBLUM, The Public Health Research Institute, 455 First Ave., New York, NY 10016, USA

S. KOTHARI, Department of Medicine, University of Cambridge Clinical School, Addenbrooke's Hospital, Hills Road, Cambridge CB2 2QQ, UK

MICHAEL KRAUSE, Institut für Biochemie und Molekulare Biologie, Technische Universität Berlin, Franklinstr. 29, D-1000 Berlin 10, FRG

B. KREISWIRTH, The Public Health Research Institute, 455 First Ave., New York, NY 10016, USA

H. LAAN, Department of Microbiology, University of Groningen, Kerklaan 30, 9751 NN Haren (Gn), The Netherlands

J.C. VAN DER LAAN, Royal Gist-brocades N.V., Research and Development, PO Box 1, 2600 MA Delft, The Netherlands

SANFORD A. LACKS, Biology Department, Brookhaven National Laboratory, Upton, NY 11973, USA

MARIE-HÉLÈNE LEBAS, *Centre de Recherche de Biochimie et de Génétique Cellulaires du CNRS, 118 Route de Narbonne, 31062 Toulouse Cedex, France*

A.M. LEDEBOER, *Unilever Research Laboratorium, Olivier van Noortlaan 120, 3133 AT Vlaardingen, The Netherlands*

K.J. LEENHOUTS, *Department of Genetics, University of Groningen, Kerklaan 30, 9751 NN Haren, The Netherlands*

WOLFGANG LIEBL, *Lehrstuhl für Mikrobiologie, Technische Universität München, Arcisstr. 21, D-8000 München 2, FRG*

PATRICIA M.-J. LIEVENS, *Istituto di Microbiologia, Universita' di Siena, Via laterina, I-53100 Siena, Italy*

GUNNAR LINDAHL, *Department of Medical Microbiology, University of Lund, S-223 62 Lund, Sweden*

SVEN LÖFDAHL, *Department of Bacteriology, National Bacteriological Laboratory, S-105 21 Stockholm, Sweden*

PALOMA LOPEZ, *Centro de Investigaciones Biológicas, Velazquez, 144-28006 Madrid, Spain*

P.J. LOWRY, *Department of Physiology and Biochemistry, University of Reading, Whiteknights, PO Box 228, Reading, RG6 2AJ, UK*

M. MACKETT, *Paterson Institute for Cancer Research, Christie Hospital and Holt Radium Institute, Wilmslow Road, Withington, Manchester, M20 9BX, England*

LESLIE B. McNEIL, *Department of Pathology, Uniformed Services University of the Health Sciences, Bethseda, MD 20814, USA*

SARIT MAOR, *Department of Molecular Genetics, The Hebrew University-Hadassah Medical School, Jerusalem, Israel 91010*

MOHAMED A. MARAHIEL, *Institut für Biochemie und Molekulare Biologie, Technische Universität Berlin, Franklinstr. 29, D-1000 Berlin 10, FRG*

FRANCK MARTIN, *Centre de Recherche de Biochimie et de Génétique Cellulaires du CNRS, 118 Route de Narbonne, 31062 Toulouse Cedex, France*

SUSANA MARTINEZ, *Biology Department, Brookhaven National Laboratory, Upton, NY 11973, USA*

GIORGIO MASTROMEI, *Department of Animal Biology and Genetics, v. Romana 17, 50125 Firenze, Italy*

VINCENT MÉJEAN, *Centre de Recherche de Biochimie et de Génétique Cellulaires du CNRS, 118 Route de Narbonne, 31062 Toulouse Cedex, France*

BÉNÉDICTE MICHEL, *Laboratoire de Génétique, Institut de Biotechnologie, INRA, Domaine de Vilvert, 78350 Jouy en Josas, France*

KENNETH W. MINTON, *Department of Pathology, Uniformed Services University of the Health Sciences, Bethesda, MD 20814, USA*

GERHARD MITTENHUBER, *Institut für Biochemie und Molekulare Biologie, Technische Universität Berlin, Franklinstr. 29, D-1000 Berlin 10, FRG*

M. VAN MONTAGU, *Laboratorium voor Genetica, Rijksuniversiteit Gent, K.L. Ledeganckstraat 35, B-9000 Gent, Belgium*

EVA MORFELDT, *Department of Bacteriology, National Bacteriological Laboratory, S-105 21 Stockholm, Sweden*

D.A. MORRISON, *Laboratory for Cell, Molecular and Developmental Biology, University of Illinois at Chicago, Chicago, IL 60680, USA*

L.J.S.M. MULLENERS, *Royal Gist-brocades N.V., Research and Development, PO Box 1, 2600 MA Delft, The Netherlands*

ROSA MUSMANNO, *Istituto di Microbiologia, Universita' di Siena, Via Laterina, I-53100 Siena, Italy*

R. NOVICK, *The Public Health Research Institute, 455 First Ave., New York, NY 10016, USA*

ANAT NUSSBAUM, *Department of Molecular Genetics, The Hebrew University-Hadassah Medical School, Jerusalem, Israel 91010*

PER-ÅKE NYGREN, *Department of Biochemistry and Biotechnology, The Royal Institute of Technology, S-100 44 Stockholm, Sweden*

MARCO R. OGGIONI, *The Rockefeller University, 1230 York Ave., New York, NY 10021, USA and Istituto di Microbiologia, Universita' di Siena, Via Laterina, I-53100 Siena, Italy*

STEPHEN G. OLIVER, *Manchester Biotechnology Centre and Department of Biochemistry and Applied Molecular Biology, University of Manchester Institute for Science and Technology, PO Box 88, Manchester M60 1QD, UK*

F. PASTA, *Centre de Recherche de Biochimie et de Génétique Cellulaires du CNRS, 118 Route de Narbonne, 31062 Toulouse Cedex, France*

BEN PEETERS, *Department of Genetics, University of Groningen, Kerklaan 30, 9751 NN Haren(Gn), The Netherlands*

AD PEIJNENBURG, *Department of Genetics, University of Groningen, Kerklaan 30, 9751 NN Haren (Gn), The Netherlands*

STEFANIA PISTOLESI, *Department of Animal Biology and Genetics, v. Romana 17, 50125 Firenze, Italy*

MARIO POLSINELLI, *Department of Animal Biology and Genetics, v. Romana 17, 50125 Firenze, Italy*

GIANNI POZZI, *The Rockefeller University, 1230 York Ave., New York, NY 10021, USA and Istituto di Microbiologia, Universita' di Verona, Strada Le Grazie, 1-37134 Verona, Italy*

S. PROJAN, *The Public Health Research Institute, 455 First Ave., New York, NY 10016, USA*

W.J. QUAX, *Royal Gist-brocades N.V., Research and Development, PO Box 1, 2600 MA Delft, The Netherlands*

FATIMA RAGUEH, *Centre de Recherche de Biochimie et de Génétique Cellulaires du CNRS, 118 Route de Narbonne, 31062 Toulouse Cedex, France*

M.C. RAIN-GUION, *Groupe Génétique et Membranes, Institut Jacques Monod, tour 43, 2 place Jussieu, 75005 Paris, France*

ROSEMARY J. REDFIELD, *Department of Molecular Biology and Genetics, The Johns Hopkins University School of Medicine, 725 North Wolfe Street, Baltimore, MD 21205, USA*

R. RICHTER, *Laboratoire de Génétique des Microorganismes, Institut National Agronomique, CBAI, 78850 Thiverval-Grignon, France*

H. ROSS, *The Public Health Research Institute, 455 First Ave., New York, NY 10016, USA*

BLANKA RUTBERG, *Department of Microbiology, University of Lund, Sölvegatan 21, S-223 62 Lund, Sweden*

D. SAVVA, *Department of Physiology and Biochemistry, University of Reading, Whiteknights, PO Box 228, Reading, RG6 2AJ, UK*

KARL HEINZ SCHLEIFER, *Lehrstuhl für Mikrobiologie, Technische Universität München, Arcisstr. 21, D-8000 München 2, FRG*

A.M. SICARD, *Centre de Recherche de Biochimie et de Génétique Cellulaires du CNRS, 118 Route de Narbonne, 31062 Toulouse Cedex, France*

NICOLE SICARD, *Centre de Recherche de Biochimie et de Génétique Cellulaires du CNRS, 118 Route de Narbonne, 31062 Toulouse Cedex, France*

ZIPORA SILBERSTEIN, *Department of Molecular Genetics, The Hebrew University-Hadassah Medical School, Jerusalem, Israel 91010*

ANTHONY J. SINSKEY, *Department of Biology, Massachusetts Institute of Technology, Cambridge, MA 02139, USA*

HAMILTON O. SMITH, *Department of Molecular Biology and Genetics, The Johns Hopkins University School of Medicine, 725 North Wolfe Street, Baltimore, MD 21205, USA*

HILDE SMITH, *Department of Genetics, University of Groningen, Kerklaan 30, 9751 NN Haren (Gn), The Netherlands*

MICHAEL D. SMITH, *Department of Pathology, Uniformed Services University of the Health Sciences, Bethesda, MD 20814, USA*

A.V. SOROKIN, *VNII Genetica, Moscow, 113545, Dorozhnyi pr, 1A, USSR*

. SOZHAMANNAN, *Laboratoire de Génétique Microbienne, Institut de Biotechnologie, INRA, Domaine de Vilvert, 78350 Jouy en Josas, France*

M. STEINMETZ, *Laboratoire de Génétique des Microorganismes, Institut National Agronomique, CBAI, 78850 Thiverval-Grignon, France*

OHAN STUY, *Department of Biological Science, Florida State University, Tallahassee, Florida 32306, USA*

EAN-FRANÇOIS TOMB, *Department of Molecular Biology and Genetics, The Johns Hopkins University School of Medicine, 725 North Wolfe Street,*

*Baltimore, MD 21205, USA*

MARIE-CLAUDE TROMBE, *Centre de Recherche de Biochimie et de Génétique Cellulaires du CNRS, 118 Route de Narbonne, 31062 Toulouse Cedex, France*

MATHIAS UHLÉN, *Department of Biochemistry and Biotechnology, The Royal Institute of Technology, S-100 44 Stockholm, Sweden*

GERARD VENEMA, *Department of Genetics, University of Groningen, Kerklaan 30, 9751 NN Haren (Gn), The Netherlands*

BEN VOSMAN, *Department of Genetics, University of Groningen, Kerklaan 30, 9751 NN Haren(Gn), The Netherlands*

J.M.B.M. VAN DER VOSSEN, *Department of Genetics, University of Groningen, Kerklaan 30, 9751 NN Haren (Gn), The Netherlands*

A.K. WINSTON, *Microbial Technology Group, Department of Microbiology, The Medical School, Newcastle upon Tyne, NE2 4HH, UK*

REINHARD WIRTH, *Lehrstuhl für Mikrobiologie der Universität München, Maria-Ward-Straße 1a, D-8000 München 19, FRG*

EDWINA M. WRIGHT, *Department of Molecular Genetics, Celltech Ltd, 216 Bath Road, Slough, Berkshire, SL1 4EN, UK*

GEOFFREY T. YARRANTON, *Department of Molecular Genetics, Celltech Ltd, 216 Bath Road, Slough, Berkshire, SL1 4EN, UK*

M. ZAGOREC, *Laboratoire de Génétique des Microorganismes, Institut National Agronomique, CBAI, 78850 Thiverval-Grignon, France*

# Contents

# Part I
## Gene Exchange

# 1
# Competence for Genetic Transformation in *Streptococcus pneumoniae*: Molecular Analysis

D. A. MORRISON*

*Laboratory for Cell, Molecular and Developmental Biology, University of Illinois at Chicago, Chicago, IL 60680, USA*

In naturally transformable bacterial species, a complex DNA-processing pathway efficiently transports DNA into the cell interior, and replaces portions of the resident chromosome with parts of strands of the donor molecule. In the most thoroughly studied species, this pathway is active only in cells in a transient special state, termed competence. This discussion focuses on the nature of the competent state and its control in *Streptococcus pneumoniae* (pneumococcus), a species of which many isolates are highly transformable.

## Regulation of competence

The outline of the regulation of competence for genetic transformation in the streptococci was established in a series of studies of the biology of this system of genetic exchange (e.g. Pakula and Walczak, 1963; Tomasz and Hotchkiss, 1964; Tomasz, 1966, 1971). These studies revealed an unusual form of bacterial cell-to-cell communication which provokes competence and consequent genetic exchange in growing cultures at a specific, high cell density. Ottolenghi and Hotchkiss (1962) showed that release of biologically active DNA accompanied the appearance of the capacity for transformation.

The phenomena these early studies described (Tomasz and Hotchkiss, 1964; Tomasz and Mosser, 1966; Tomasz, 1966) indicated the existence of a protein (competence factor, CF) secreted by non-competent cells, whose action, after an autocatalytic accumulation, was to induce the cells in a culture to become competent for transformation. CF stimulated both CF production and the development of competence. CF was shown to pass through membrane filters and activate a second culture. Its properties as observed in extracts are consistent with those of a small basic protein. The activity of CF increases

* *Present address: c/o Bengtake Jaurin, ABC Research Department (FOA4), National Defense Research Institute, S–901 82 Umea, Sweden*

*Genetic Transformation and Expression*
© Intercept Ltd, PO Box 716, Andover, Hants, SP10 1YG, UK

sharply from pH 7 to pH 8. Cells grown in medium adjusted to pH 6·5 did not become competent, while those grown at pH 8 did. In some strains (e.g. R6) CF was found mainly bound to the surface of cells in a culture, and could be extracted from cell walls (Tomasz and Mosser, 1966). In others (e.g. Rx) competence-inducing activity is assayable directly in the culture supernatant (Morrison, 1981; Morrison *et al.*, 1984). The latter provides a readily available source of crude CF (Morrison *et al.*, 1984; Yother, McDaniel and Bailes, 1986; Chandler and Morrison, 1987b), which has been shown to overcome the low transformability characteristic of most encapsulated strains (Ravin, 1959; Yother, McDaniel and Bailes, 1986). A very similar set of phenomena has been described associated with development of competence in other streptococci (Pakula and Walczak, 1963; Dobrzanski and Osowiecki, 1967; Osowiecki, Nalecz and Dobrzanski, 1969; Leonard, Ranhand and Cole, 1970; Leonard and Cole, 1972; Perry, 1973; Ranhand, 1976; Raina and Ravin, 1980); we may expect to find analogous systems in these species at the molecular level.

The population level at which competence is first manifested in a growing culture (critical cell density) varies continuously with the initial pH of the growth medium (Chen and Morrison, 1987a); if it occurs early, a second cycle of competence may occur, usually with a lower proportion of competent cells. The critical cell density for competence induction appears to depend on a delicate balance between the effects of an increasing level of CF and a decreasing specific activity of the CF caused by the slow metabolic acidification of the medium. In two different studies, one physical (Javor and Tomasz, 1968) and one genetic (Porter and Guild, 1969), it was shown that in a highly competent culture essentially 100% of the cells are competent. Morrison *et al.* (1984) described mutants of *S. pneumoniae* defective in competence induction. These mutants are dependent on exogenous CF for competence, as if they are defective in elaboration of extracellular CF. The fact that the amount of exogenous CF required to stimulate competence of these mutants is higher than for wild-type cells is consistent with an interpretation of the model of Tomasz (1966) for a two-stage process of competence induction in which the accumulating CF in a growing culture first induces a more rapid elaboration of additional CF, but the full competence response is induced only by the higher levels of CF that are then achieved.

### The nature of competent cells

In addition to the capacity to bind and process DNA, a variety of new properties associated with the cell surface are characteristic of competent cells. Those reported include: (1) a new surface antigen (Nava, Galis and Beiser, 1963); (2) a new agglutinin (Tomasz and Zanati, 1971); (3) an interruption of cell wall synthesis (Ephrussi-Taylor and Freed, 1964); (4) a susceptibility to lysis in certain buffers (Lacks and Neuberger, 1975; Seto and Tomasz, 1975); (5) an altered cell wall structure, as seen in the electron microscope (Tomasz and Zanati, 1971); and (6) release of biologically active DNA into the culture medium (Ottolenghi and Hotchkiss, 1962).

Metabolic inhibitor studies showed that the development of competence in response to CF required protein and RNA synthesis, but not DNA synthesis (Tomasz, 1970; Vijayakumar and Morrison, 1983), and suggested that at least some new proteins are required for a cell to become competent. Indeed, direct examination of competent cultures by pulse-labelling with radiolabelled amino acids showed that the appearance of competence in response to CF is accompanied by a switch in protein synthesis such that relatively few proteins are made, and that many of these are proteins not observed during normal growth (Morrison and Baker, 1979; Morrison, 1981). The major induced protein (molecular mass 19 500) binds to donor DNA strands in the cell (Morrison, 1977, 1978; Morrison and Baker, 1979; Morrison, Baker and Mannarelli, 1979; Morrison, 1981; Vijayakumar and Morrison, 1983) and protects them from pneumococcal and other nucleases (Morrison and Mannarelli, 1979), but its principal role remains to be established. Competence-specific polypeptides do not form a single structure, but are distributed in native proteins of various sizes and cellular locations (Vijayakumar, 1982; Vijayakumar and Morrison, 1986).

In a system of this complexity, unravelling the mechanisms of DNA transport and recombination and of competence control will be facilitated by genetic analysis.

**Genetic analysis**

Mutations causing a deficiency in transformation in pneumococcus have been obtained after treatment with chemical mutagens. Some affect DNA processing; others appear to affect competence control. Loci (and associated phenotypes affected in mutant strains) in the former class include: *hex* (mismatch repair) (Lacks, 1970; Tiraby, Claverys and Sicard, 1973); *noz* (a membrane nuclease; DNA uptake or degradation) (Lacks, 1970; Lacks, Greenberg and Neuberger, 1975); *ent* (DNA transport); and *rec* (recombination) (Morrison *et al.*, 1983). In the latter class are *trt* (sensitivity to trypsin in the competence medium) and *ntr* (transformability) (Lacks and Greenberg, 1973). During these studies several methods for screening populations for transformation-deficient mutants have been developed (Lacks and Greenberg, 1973; Tiraby, Claverys and Sicard, 1973). These are closely related to methods developed for *Haemophilus influenzae* and *Bacillus subtilis* (Caster, Postel and Goodgal 1970; Fani *et al.*, 1984; Hahn, Albano and Dubnau, 1987), and depend on conditions for transformation of cells while growing in a colony in or on agar, followed by detection of the transformants *in situ*. A system such as that developed by Lacks and Greenberg (1973), in which transformants give rise to visible papillations on the colony, is particularly convenient, as it eliminates the need for one or more replica-plating steps.

Meanwhile, a previously unknown pathway for recombination and insertion of certain chimeric donor DNA molecules during transformation was described by Vasseghi, Claverys and Sicard, (1981), by Mejean *et al.* (1981) and by Niaudet, Goze and Ehrlich (1982), who pointed out that it provides a gene-disruption method for mutagenesis applicable to many naturally transformable species, in the absence of suitable transposons. Briefly, circular chimeric donor molecules containing a small segment homologous to the resident chromosome can be inserted into the chromosome at the site of homology. Although they are relatively rare, the products of such insertions can be recovered by selection for a marker carried in the non-homologous portion of the donor molecule. The insert in usually found as a tandem duplication of the homologous sequence flanking the non-homologous DNA, or as tandem repetitions of this basic unit (Vasseghi and Claverys, 1983; Mannarelli and Lacks, 1984; Pozzi and Guild, 1985). Appropriate chimeric molecules made *in vitro* can thus direct gene-disruption mutagenesis in the form of insertion-duplications.

We have combined insertion-duplication mutagenesis with transformability screening techniques to start cloning some of the loci relevant to competence in pneumococcus. Among mutants obtained in this way, some were characterized as affecting competence control (Morrison *et al.*, 1984). The first fruits of this approach are represented by the cloning in *E. coli* of a 4 kbp locus from pneumococcus that is implicated in competence control (*Figure 1.1*). The first clone, obtained by direct selection in an *E. coli* vector for DNA linked to an erythromycin resistance determinant, *erm*, that had been inserted in the pneumococcus chromosome, contained a 500 bp fragment of *comA*. Additional clones were obtained during short chromosome walks beyond the ends of this fragment. [Some fragments of this locus (Chandler and Morrison, 1987a), and of many other pneumococcal loci (Chen and Morrison, 1987b, 1988), were observed to be unstable in plasmid cloning vectors in *E. coli*, unless flanked by transcriptional terminator signals.] During *in vitro* transcription and translation in *E. coli* extracts, DNA from this locus directs the synthesis of two proteins, which have been mapped to two contiguous genes, *comA* and *comB*, 2·1 kbp and 1·3 kbp in size, respectively. The specific functions of the *comA comB* locus are not yet known. Possibilities would seem to include: (1) proteins involved in CF production or export from the cell; (2) a receptor system involved in the low-threshold CF response; and (3) the production of an inhibitor of competence induction by these gene-disruption mutants, the effect of which is overcome by high levels of CF.

The genetic evidence linking this locus to competence control consists of the phenotypes of a variety of mutations made *in vitro* at known sites throughout the locus, and then transformed into the pneumococcus genome (Chandler and Morrison, 1987b). Mutants with *erm* insertions located in either gene are absolutely defective in transformation under all normal competence-provoking growth regimens examined. However, they become fully competent when exposed to the supernatant of a competent wild-type culture. The mutants in *comA* that were tested also proved to be defective in the elaboration of additional CF when so induced. Thus, mutations at this locus appear to interfere with CF elaboration, or at least with the superinduction of CF normally associated with the second stage of the competence response. Insertions beyond the locus boundaries, and insertion-duplications including either end of the locus, displayed normal transformability and normal competence induction, as shown in *Figure 1.1*.

The physical evidence establishing the approximate locations of *comA* and

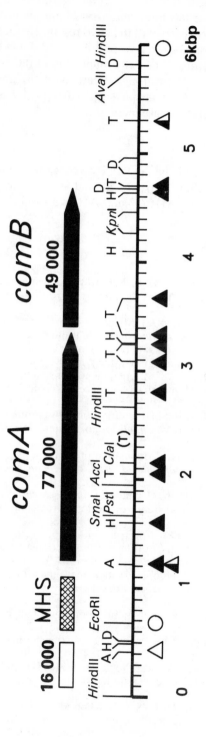

**Figure 1.1** The *com* region of *Streptococcus pneumoniae*. The *comA* and *comB* genes and a third, unidentified, coding sequence, and their protein products are schematically illustrated. A multiple hybridizing sequence (MHS) lies between *comA* and the unidentified gene. The locations and phenotypes of *ermB* insertion mutations created *in vitro* and characterized after transformation into the pneumococcus chromosome (Chandler and Morrison, 1987b) are indicated as follows: ◀, Xfo⁻; △, Xfo⁺; ▲, Xfo⁺/⁻. Also shown are the outer limits for the *com* locus determined by insertion-duplication mutagenesis (○). Restriction enzyme abbreviations: A, *Asu*II; D, *Dra*I; H, *Hpa*II; T, *Taq*I. (Used by permission of the American Society for Microbiology.)

*comB* was obtained by characterizing the *in vitro* protein products made by plasmids containing insertion or truncation mutations of the cloned DNA (Chandler and Morrison, 1988). Truncations of the locus resulted in shortening or loss of the protein products associated with the cloned DNA, while insertions altered the size of the proteins made. Comparison of the observed protein alterations with the known physical map locations of the mutations permitted assignment of gene locations on the physical map of the locus within an estimated error of approximately 250 base pairs.

### Acknowledgement

Research discussed here and carried out at the University of Illinois was supported in part by grant PCM–8021425 from National Science Foundation Genetic Biology Program, and grants AI16783 and AI19875 from the Public Health Service.

### References

CASTER, J.H., POSTEL, E.H. AND GOODGAL, S.H. (1970). Competence mutants: isolation of transformation deficient strains of *Haemophilus influenzae*. *Nature* **227**, 515–517.

CHANDLER, M.S. AND MORRISON, D.A. (1987a). Molecular cloning of a competence control region from *Streptococcus pneumoniae* by use of transcription terminator vectors in *E. coli*. In *Streptococcal Genetics*, (J. Ferretti and R. Curtiss, Eds), pp. 193–196. American Society for Microbiology, Washington, DC.

CHANDLER, M.S. AND MORRISON, D.A. (1987b). Competence for genetic transformation in *Streptococcus pneumoniae*: Molecular cloning of *com*, a competence control locus. *Journal of Bacteriology* **169**, 2005–2011.

CHANDLER, M.S. AND MORRISON, D.A. (1988). Identification of two proteins encoded by *com*, a competence control locus of *Streptococcus pneumoniae*. *Journal of Bacteriology* **170**, 3136–3141.

CHEN, J.D. AND MORRISON, D.A. (1987a). Modulation of competence for genetic transformation in *Streptococcus pneumoniae*. *Journal of General Microbiology* **133**, 1959–1967.

CHEN, J.D. AND MORRISON, D.A. (1987b). Cloning of *Streptococcus pneumoniae* DNA fragments in *Escherichia coli* requires vectors protected by strong transcriptional terminators. *Gene* **55**, 179–187.

CHEN, J.D. AND MORRISON, D.A. (1988). Construction and properties of a new insertion vector, pJDC9, that is protected by transcriptional terminators and useful for cloning of DNA from *Streptococcus pneumoniae*. *Gene* **64**, 155–164.

DOBRZANSKI, W.T. AND OSOWIECKI, H. (1967). Isolation and some properties of the competence factor from group H *Streptococcus* strain *Challis*. *Journal of General Microbiology* **48**, 299–304.

EPHRUSSI-TAYLOR, H. AND FREED, B.A. (1964). Incorporation of thymidine and amino acids into deoxyribonucleic acid and acid-insoluble cell structures in pneumococcal cultures synchronized for competence to transform. *Journal of Bacteriology* **87**, 1211–1215.

FANI, R., MASTROMEI, G., POLSINELLI, M. AND VENEMA, G. (1984). Isolation and characterization of *Bacillus subtilis* mutants altered in competence. *Journal of Bacteriology* **157**, 152–157.

HAHN, J., ALBANO, M. AND DUBNAU, D. (1987). Isolation and characterization of Tn917lac-generated competence mutants of *Bacillus subtilis*. *Journal of Bacteriology* **169**, 3104–3109.

JAVOR, G.T. AND TOMASZ, A. (1968). An autoradiographic study of genetic transformation. *Proceedings of the National Academy of Sciences of the United States of America* **60**, 1216–1222.

LACKS, S. (1970). Mutants of *Diplococcus pneumoniae* that lack deoxyribonucleases and other activities possibly pertinent to genetic transformation. *Journal of Bacteriology* **101**, 373–383.

LACKS, S. AND GREENBERG, B. (1973). Competence for DNA uptake and deoxyribonuclease action external to cells in the genetic transformation of *Diplococcus pneumoniae*. *Journal of Bacteriology* **114**, 152–163.

LACKS, S. AND NEUBERGER, M. (1975). Membrane location of a deoxyribonuclease implicated in the genetic transformation of *Diplococcus pneumoniae*. *Journal of Bacteriology* **124**, 1321–1329.

LACKS, S., GREENBERG, B. AND NEUBERGER, M. (1975). Identification of a deoxyribonuclease implicated in genetic transformation of *Diplococcus pneumoniae*. *Journal of Bacteriology* **123**, 222–232.

LEONARD, C. AND COLE, R. (1972). Purification and properties of streptococcal competence factor isolated from chemically defined media. *Journal of Bacteriology* **110**, 273–280.

LEONARD, C.G., RANHAND, J.M. AND COLE, R.M. (1970). Competence factor production in chemically defined media by noncompetent cells of Group H *Streptococcus* strain Challis. *Journal of Bacteriology* **104**, 674–683.

MANNARELLI, B.M. AND LACKS, S.A. (1984). Ectopic integration of chromosomal genes in *Streptococcus pneumoniae*. *Journal of Bacteriology* **160**, 867–873.

MÉJEAN, V., CLAVERYS, J.-P., VASSEGHI, H. AND SICARD, A.-M. (1981). Rapid cloning of specific DNA fragments of *Streptococcus pneumoniae* by vector integration into the chromosome followed by endonucleolytic excision. *Gene* **15**, 289–293.

MORRISON, D.A. (1977). Transformation in pneumococcus: Existence and properties of a complex involving donor deoxyribonucleate single strands in eclipse. *Journal of Bacteriology* **132**, 576–583.

MORRISON, D.A. (1978). Transformation in pneumococcus: protein content of eclipse complex. *Journal of Bacteriology* **136**, 548–557.

MORRISON, D.A. (1981). Competence-specific protein synthesis in *Streptococcus pneumoniae*. In *Transformation – 1980*, (M. Polsinelli and G. Mazza, Eds), pp. 39–54. Cotswold Press, Oxford.

MORRISON, D.A. AND BAKER, M. (1979). Competence for genetic transformation in pneumococcus depends on the synthesis of a small set of proteins. *Nature (London)* **282**, 215–217.

MORRISON, D.A. AND MANNARELLI, B. (1979). Transformation in pneumococcus: nuclease resistance of deoxyribonucleic acid in eclipse complex. *Journal of Bacteriology* **140**, 655–665.

MORRISON, D.A., BAKER, M. AND MANNARELLI, B. (1979). A protein component of the pneumococcal eclipse complex. In *Transformation – 1978* (S.W. Glover and L.O. Butler, Eds), pp. 43–52, Cotswold Press, Oxford.

MORRISON, D.A., LACKS, S.A., GUILD, W.R. AND HAGEMAN, J.M. (1983). Isolation and characterization of three new classes of transformation deficient mutants of *Streptococcus pneumoniae* that are defective in DNA transport and genetic recombination. *Journal of Bacteriology* **156**, 281–290.

MORRISON, D.A., TROMBE, M.C., HAYDEN, M.K., WASZAK, G.A. AND CHEN, J.D. (1984). Isolation of transformation-deficient *Streptococcus pneumoniae* mutants defective in control of competence, using insertion-duplication mutagenesis with the erythromycin resistance determinant of pAMβ1. *Journal of Bacteriology* **159**, 870–876.

NAVA, G., GALIS, A. AND BEISER, S.M. (1963). Bacterial transformation: an antigen specific for 'competent' pneumococci. *Nature (London)* **197**, 903–904.

NIAUDET, B., GOZE, A. AND EHRLICH, S.D. (1982). Insertional mutagenesis in

*Bacillus subtilis*: mechanism and use in gene cloning. *Gene* **19**, 277–284.

OSOWIECKI, H., NALECZ, J. AND DOBRZANSKI, W.T. (1969). The mechanism of competence in the transformation of streptococci of serological group H: purification and some properties of the competence factor. *Molecular and General Genetics* **105**, 16–20.

OTTOLENGHI, E. AND HOTCHKISS, R.D. (1962). Release of genetic transforming agent from pneumococcal cultures during growth and disintegration. *Journal of Experimental Medicine* **116**, 491–519.

PAKULA, R. AND WALCZAK, W. (1963). On the nature of competence of transformable Streptococci. *Journal of General Microbiology* **31**, 125–133.

PERRY, D. (1973). Isolation of Group H streptococcal competence factor. *Applied Microbiology* **26**, 643–645.

PORTER, R.D. AND GUILD, W.R. (1969). Number of transformable units per cell in *Diplococcus pneumoniae. Journal of bacteriology* **97**, 1033–1035.

POZZI, G. AND GUILD, W.R. (1985). Modes of integration of heterologous plasmid DNA into the chromosome of *Streptococcus pneumoniae. Journal of Bacteriology* **161**, 909–912.

RAINA, J.L. AND RAVIN, A.W. (1980). Switches in macromolecular synthesis during induction of competence for transformation of *Streptococcus sanguis. Proceedings of the National Academy of Sciences of the United States of America* **77**, 6062–6066.

RANHAND, J. (1976). Effect of pH on competence development and DNA uptake in *Streptococcus sanguis. Journal of Bacteriology* **126**, 205–212.

RAVIN, A. (1959). Reciprocal capsular transformations of pneumococci. *Journal of Bacteriology* **77**, 296–309.

SETO, H. AND TOMASZ, A. (1975). Protoplast formation and leakage of intramembrane cell components: induction by the competence activator substance of pneumococci. *Journal of Bacteriology* **121**, 344–353.

TIRABY, G., CLAVERYS, J.-P. AND SICARD, A.M. (1973). Integration efficiency in DNA-induced transformation of pneumococcus. 1. A method of transformation in solid medium and its use for isolation of transformation-deficient and recombination-modified mutants. *Genetics* **75**, 23–33.

TOMASZ, A. (1966). Model for the mechanism controlling the expression of competent state in Pneumococcus cultures. *Journal of Bacteriology* **91**, 1050–1061.

TOMASZ, A. (1970). Cellular metabolism in genetic transformation of pneumococci: requirement for protein synthesis during induction of competence. *Journal of Bacteriology* **101**, 860–871.

TOMASZ, A. (1971). Cell physiology aspects of DNA uptake during genetic transformation in bacteria. In *Informative molecules in biological systems* (L. Ledoux, Ed.), pp. 4–18. North-Holland, Amsterdam.

TOMASZ, A. AND HOTCHKISS, R.D. (1964). Regulation of the transformability of pneumococcal cultures by macromolecular cell products. *Proceedings of the National Academy of Sciences of the United States of America* **51**, 480–486.

TOMASZ, A. AND MOSSER, J.L. (1966). On the nature of the pneumococcal activator substance. *Proceedings of the National Academy of Sciences of the United States of America* **55**, 58–66.

TOMASZ, A. AND ZANATI, E. (1971). Appearance of a protein 'agglutinin' on the spheroplast membrane of pneumococci during induction of competence. *Journal of Bacteriology* **105**, 1213–1215.

VASSEGHI, H. AND CLAVERYS, J.-P. (1983). Amplification of a chimeric plasmid carrying an erythromycin resistance determinant introduced into the genome of *Streptococcus pneumoniae. Gene* **21**, 285–292.

VASSEGHI, H., CLAVERYS, J.-P. AND SICARD, A.-M. (1981). Mechanism of integrating foreign DNA during transformation of *Streptococcus pneumoniae*. In *Transformation – 1980* (M. Polsinelli and G. Mazza, Eds), pp. 137–154. Cotswold Press, Oxford.

VIJAYAKUMAR, M.N. (1982). *Transformation in pneumococcus: identification and properties of competence specific proteins*. Ph.D. Thesis, University of Illinois at Chicago.

VIJAYAKUMAR, M.N. AND MORRISON, D.A. (1983). Fate of DNA in eclipse complex during genetic transformation in *Streptococcus pneumoniae*. *Journal of Bacteriology* **156**, 644–648.

VIJAYAKUMAR, M.N. AND MORRISON, D.A. (1986). Localization of competence-induced proteins in *Streptococcus pneumoniae*. *Journal of Bacteriology* **165**, 689–695.

YOTHER, J., MCDANIEL, L.S. AND BRILES, D.E. (1986). Transformation of encapsulated *Streptococcus pneumoniae*. *Journal of Bacteriology* **168**, 1463–1465.

# 2

# Competence Induction in *Streptococcus Pneumoniae*: A Metabolic Response to Calcium Influx Involving Na$^+$/Ca$^{++}$ Antiport

CORINNE CLAVÉ, FATIMA RAGUEH,
MARIE-HÉLÈNE LEBAS AND MARIE-CLAUDE TROMBE*

*Centre de Recherche de Biochimie et de Génétique Cellulaires du CNRS,
118 Route de Narbonne, 31062 Toulouse Cedex, France*

## Introduction

Competence for genetic transformation corresponds to a specialized physiological state where bacteria exhibit new properties which include specific surface antigens (Nava, Galis and Beiser, 1963), DNA-binding sites (Seto, Lopez and Tomasz, 1975), DNA transport (Lacks, 1977), modulation of gene expression (Morrison and Baker, 1979), accumulation of poly-β-hydroxybutyrate (PHB) (Reusch and Sadoff, 1983; Reusch, Hiske and Sadoff, 1986) and membrane hyperpolarization (Trombe, 1983). So far, the relationship between these different changes, and the mechanism that triggers such changes, are not very well understood.

In *Streptococcus pneumoniae* competence induction can be easily monitored using competence-factor extracts (Tomasz and Hotchkiss, 1964; Morrison, 1981) that induce 100% of the culture to the competent state (Javor and Tomasz, 1968; Porter and Guild, 1969).

In this work, we have focused on the analysis of the ionic and energetic changes at competence in relation to the ionic fluxes under the control of competence-factor addition.

The results show an alkalinization of the cytoplasm in competent bacteria associated with an increased Na$^+$ pool. These ionic changes accompany a stimulation of glycolysis that probably results in an increased ATP level as well as in an accumulation of poly-β-hydroxybutyrate. Moreover, competence induction is triggered by a calcium influx resulting from the activation of an amiloride-sensitive Na$^+$/Ca$^{++}$ antiporter by competence-factor, suggesting that calcium influx is the primary inducer of that physiological state.

---

* Corresponding author.

---

*Genetic Transformation and Expression*
© Intercept Ltd, PO Box 716, Andover, Hants, SP10 1YG, UK

**Material and methods**

CHEMICALS

Nutrients used for growth media were from Difco. A23187 and ethyleneglycol-bis-(β-aminoethyl ether)-$N,N,N',N'$-tetraacetic acid (EGTA) were of analytical grade. $^{22}$NaCl and $^{45}$CaCl$_2$ were from CEA (France). Monensin was provided by Lilly Research (Surrey, England); 3,3',4',5-tetrachloro-salicylanilide (TCS) by Dr I.R. Booth (Aberdeen, Scotland); and amiloride, 2',4'dimethylbenzamil (DMB) and 5-($N,N$-hexamethylene) amiloride (HMA) by Dr E.J. Cragoe, Jr. (Lansdale, USA).

MEDIA AND ORGANISMS

The wild-type strain, Rx, and its derivatives used in this study, as well as competence medium (CTM), are described elsewhere (Morrison, 1977). The mineral medium was a physiological medium for *Streptococcus pneumoniae*, it contained Tris (40 mM), NH$_4$Cl (52 mM), KCl (7·5 mM), MOPS (20 mM) and either sucrose (120 mM) or NaCl (120 mM).

COMPETENCE

Competence was obtained as described by Clavé, Morrison and Trombe (1987). Competence factor (CF) extracts were prepared as described in Morrison (1981) and Lopez *et al.* (1989). Competence was monitored by assaying the appearance of DNA-degrading activity, and by DNA-transport measurement and biological transformation tests, as described by Clavé, Morrison and Trombe (1987).

SPECIAL MATERIAL

Radioactive chromosomal DNA was prepared from a thymidine-requiring strain of *S. pneumoniae*, strain 119, bearing also the Rif$^R$ marker which confers resistance to 1 µg ml$^{-1}$ rifampicin.

The chimeric plasmid pR172, derived from pBR322 (Méjean *et al.*, 1981), bearing the marker *amiA158* belonging to the *ami* locus and conferring resistance to $5 \times 10^{-6}$ M methotrexate, was the source of cloned DNA.

pH$_i$ DETERMINATION

The intracellular pH (pH$_i$) was determined by $^{31}$P NMR combined to the action of TCS (Lopez *et al.*, 1989), and by the bias of $\triangle$pH determination using the weak acid, benzoic acid, as a probe (Lopez *et al.*, 1989).

Na$^+$ AND K$^+$ POOL MEASUREMENTS

Na$^+$ and K$^+$ pools were assayed by flame photometry, while the Na$^+$ pool was also determined by $^{31}$P NMR combined to the action of monensin, both methods are described elsewhere (Lopez *et al.*, 1989).

GLUCOSE CONSUMPTION, ATP AND L-LACTATE DETERMINATIONS

Determinations of glucose consumption, ATP content and L-lactate production were performed as described elsewhere (Lopez *et al.*, 1989).

POLY-β-HYDROXYBUTYRATE EXTRACTION AND ASSAY

Poly-β-hydroxybutyrate (PHB) was extracted as described by Reusch and Sadoff (1983) and was then converted into crotonic acid, which was assayed at 235 nm by spectrophotometry, as described by Law and Slepecky (1961).

$^{22}Na^+$- AND $^{45}Ca^{++}$-FLUXES MEASUREMENT

Sodium- and calcium-fluxes measurements were carried out as described in Clavé, Cragoe and Trombe (submitted).

## Results

ENERGETICS OF COMPETENT CELLS

During competence development, a transient increase in the initial rate of isoleucine uptake with an optimum at the peak of culture transformability, is specifically observed (Trombe, 1983). In our strains of *S. pneumoniae* a single transporter coupled to $\triangle$p is described for isoleucine and the $V_{max}$ of transport is modulated by the value of $\triangle$p (Trombe, Lanéelle and Sicard, 1984). Therefore variations of the initial rate of isoleucine uptake at competence, are likely to reflect modulation in the value of $\triangle$p resulting from modulation of ionic fluxes during competence development.

*Estimation of the components of the proton-motive force at competence*

Both components of the proton-motive force, $\triangle\psi$ and $\triangle$pH, were measured. Determination of the membrane potential value, $\triangle\psi$, using the $\triangle\psi$-probe, $TPP^+$, gave a $\triangle\psi$ value of $138 \pm 5$ mV in competent bacteria, a value similar to previous findings in non-competent bacteria (Trombe, Lanéelle and Sicard, 1984). On the other hand, $\triangle$pH measurements using ($^{14}C$) benzoic acid as a probe, gave a $\triangle$pH $= 0.5$ at $pH_o = 7.8$ showing a net alkalinization of the cytoplasm at competence, since the control exhibited no $\triangle$pH under the same conditions, as already shown in *S. pneumoniae* (Trombe, Lanéelle and Sicard, 1984). That result was confirmed by a method combining $^{31}P$ NMR and the utilization of the protonophore, TCS, giving an estimation of pH, equal to 8.3 in competent bacteria and 7.8 in the control (Lopez *et al.*, 1989).

So competent bacteria exhibit a cytoplasm more alkaline than the control and, consequently, at a given $pH_o$ present a higher $\triangle\mu_{H^+}/F$, resulting from an extra $Z\triangle$pH of 30 mV. This suggests that the increased $\triangle$p-driven isoleucine uptake observed at competence corresponds to an increase in $\triangle$pH. This result also suggests a regulation of proton flux during competence development.

## Na⁺ and K⁺ pools at competence

*Na$^+$ and K$^+$ pools at competence*

Besides protons, sodium and potassium ions are part of the more active circulating cations implicated in bacterial life (Heefner, 1982). The $K^+$ content of the culture during the development of a competence cycle (monitored by flame photometry) showed no significant variation (*Table 2.1*) compared to the control in the absence of CF (in which the $K^+$ content fell to around 250 mM). This suggests no specific regulation of $K^+$ transport during competence development, as previously shown by Tomasz (1969). In contrast, the $Na^+$ values fluctuated with a maximum at 340 mM ($\pm 30\%$) before the start of competence (15 minutes after CF addition), 120 mM at the peak time and 83 mM at the end of the competence wave (*Table 2.1*), the latter value being similar to that determined in non-competent bacteria (not shown). These results were corroborated by determinations using a method where $^{31}$P NMR and monensin utilisation were combined (Lopez *et al.*, 1989). Both approaches showed that competent bacteria exhibit an increased sodium pool when compared to the control.

**Table 2.1**  Bacterial $Na^+$ and $K^+$ content during a competence cycle. Tester cells were incubated at 37°C in the presence of CF (5%, v/v). ($^3$H) DNA was added ($42 \times 10^3$ dpm ml$^{-1}$) to an aliquot and competence development was monitored by assaying DNA–degrading activity. At intervals 10 ml aliquots were filtered and $Na^+$ and $K^+$ were assayed by flame photometry. Under these conditions the competence peak occurs between 25 and 38 minutes

| Time (min) | Na$^+$ (mM) | K$^+$ (mM) | Degradation (dpm ml$^{-1}$ ± 10%) |
|---|---|---|---|
| 5 | 45 ± 10* | 272 ± 2* | 0 |
| 10 | 210 ± 20 | | 0 |
| 15 | 339 ± 39 | 283 ± 2 | 0 |
| 20 | 153 ± 12 | 229 ± 14 | 910 |
| 25 | 121 ± 7 | 250 ± 8 | 3000 |
| 38 | 121 ± 2 | 274 ± 10 | 26940 |
| 50 | 88 ± 6 | 206 ± 19 | 31600 |
| 60 | 78 ± 7 | 223 ± 24 | 31860 |

*    ($\pm$) Standard deviation of four independent determinations.

*Evolution of the ATP pool at competence*

Often, where other bacteria have evolved cation porters powered by the electrochemical proton gradient, the streptococci have developed ATP-powered cation pumps (Heefner, 1982). Regulation of $Na^+$ circulation during competence induction might result in the modulation of the activity of a $Na^+$-ATPase by variations of the ATP pool. We therefore questioned the fate of the ATP content of the bacteria during competence development. ATP measurements in bacterial extracts prepared at different stages of competence expression showed that in competent bacteria the ATP pool reached 9·5 ± 0·5 mM, while it was 6·3 ± 0·5 mM in the control (*Figures 2.1* and *2.2*). This enhanced ATP content probably resulted from glycolysis stimulation as determined by a 30% extra glucose consumption (*Figure 2.2*) and an increase in lactate production during induction (not shown).

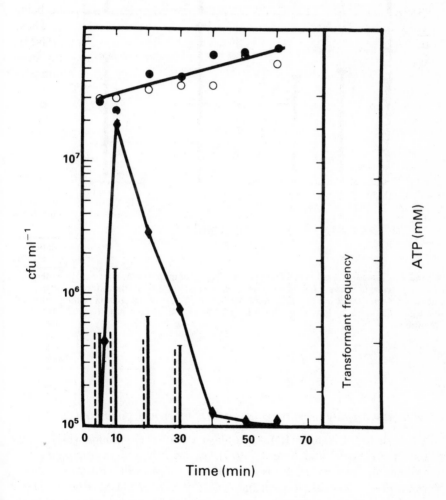

**Figure 2.1** ATP content of the culture during competence development. Tester cells were incubated at 37°C in the presence of CF (5% v/v). At intervals 1 ml aliquots were extracted for ATP determination (bars, +CF; dotted lines, −CF) and 0·1 ml aliquots were incubated for 5 min at 30°C in the presence of pR172 DNA (0·1 μg ml$^{-1}$) bearing the *ami* marker. The frequency of Mtx$^R$ (◆) was determined by plating experiments (○, cfu ml$^{-1}$; ●, cfu ml$^{-1}$ in an induced culture).

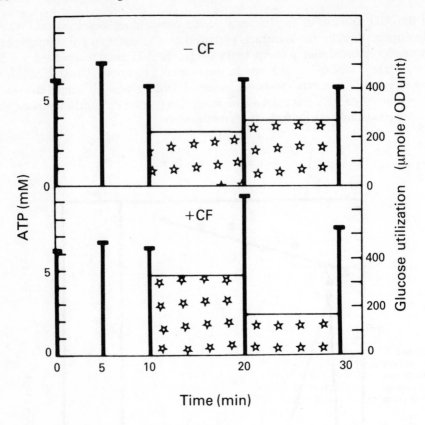

**Figure 2.2**  Glucose utilization in CF-activated cultures compared to the control. The experiment was conducted as in *Figure 2.1*. Glucose consumption was deduced from the difference between the glucose levels of the culture at time 0 and after 20 and 30 minutes incubation in the presence or absence of CF extracts. Bars represent ATP pool levels; ☆, glucose utilization; −CF, control experiment.

*Accumulation of poly-β-hydroxybutyrate in competent* S. pneumoniae

Poly-β-hydroxybutyrate (PHB), a cytoplasmic storage compound widely found in bacteria (Dawes and Senior, 1973), is accumulated at competence in transformable species such as *Azotobacter vinelandii, Bacillus subtilis, Haemophilus influenzae* (Reusch and Sadoff, 1983) and *E. coli* (Reusch, Hiske and Sadoff, 1986). We therefore analysed the PHB content of competent *S. pneumoniae*. The results (*Figure 2.3b*) show that competent cells accumulated PHB compared to non-competent cultures (*Figure 2.3a*), a result that is reminiscent of data on other species. Therefore competent *S. pneumoniae* can be characterized by its high energetic potential resulting in an increase in the proton-motive force and in the chemical energy sources, ATP and PHB.

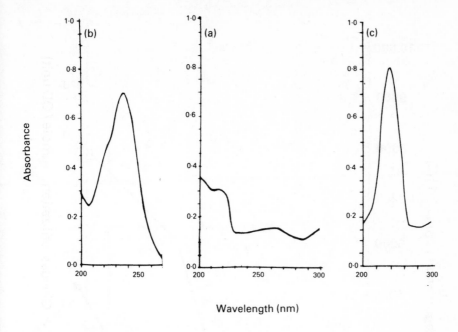

Wavelength (nm)

**Figure 2.3** PHB content of competent *S. pneumoniae*. PHB was extracted from non-competent (a) and competent (b) cultures of *S. pneumoniae* and converted to crotonic acid ($\lambda_{max}$ = 235 nm), which was assayed by spectrophotometry as described by Law and Slepecky (1961). Spectra correspond to spectrophotometric assay of crotonic acid derived from pneumococcal-extracted PHB (a and b) or 7.5 µg of commercial PHB (c).

AMILORIDE-SENSITIVE IONIC FLUXES IN COMPETENCE INDUCTION

Changes in cytoplasmic pH and the $Na^+$ pool in competent bacteria led us to investigate the role of these ionic changes on competence development.

Indeed, the protonophore, TCS, that lowers $pH_i$ inhibited induction by 35%, while the cationophore, monensin, that exchanges $Na^+$ and $H^+$ blocked induction totally, suggesting a predominant role for controlled sodium circulation in the induction process (*Figure 2.4, Table 2.2*).

This was investigated more precisely using pharmacological drugs derived from amiloride and known to inhibit specifically $Na^+$ porters in eukaryotes. The derivatives 2′,4′dimethylbenzamil (DMB) specific to the $Na^+/Ca^{++}$ antiporter (Kaczorowski *et al.*, 1985) and 5-(*N,N*-hexamethylene)amiloride (HMA) specific to the $Na^+/H^+$ antiporter (L'Allemain *et al.*, 1984) reduced competence induction, with a more pronounced effect for DMB than for HMA (*Table 2.2*). Inhibition of induction was not associated with a reduction of expression when the drugs were added to pre-induced bacteria (*Table 2.2*). This suggests that sodium fluxes involving DMB- and HMA-sensitive functions are required for competence induction. Direct measurements of $^{22}Na^+$ fluxes showed a net sodium efflux in the first 3–5 min following CF addition to a culture. Efflux was reduced by DMB and by HMA (*Figure 2.5*). Such a

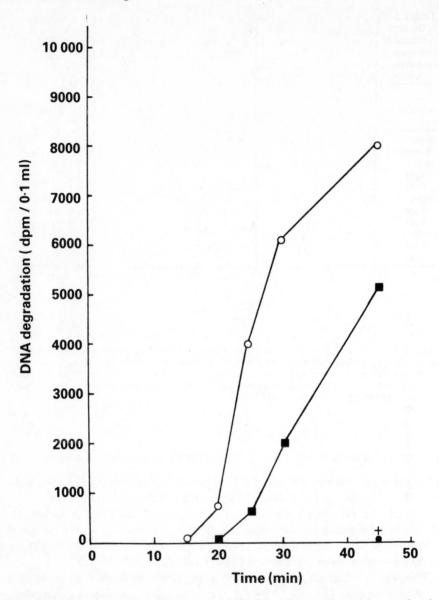

**Figure 2.4** Effect of ionophores on competence induction. Aliquots of bacterial suspensions in transformation medium received 5% (v/v) CF extracts and were incubated at 37°C in the presence of 2μM monensin (+) or 5 μM TCS (■). At 20 min [$^3$H]DNA ($21 \times 10^4$ dpm ml$^{-1}$) was added and competence was monitored by measuring the acid-soluble fraction. ○, control; ●, no CF.

Na$^+$ efflux was concomitant with a calcium influx that was blocked by DMB and reduced by HMA (*Figure 2.6*). As DMB was more efficient in inhibiting competence induction than HMA (*Table 2.2*) it is likely that the calcium influx involving a DMB-sensitive Na$^+$/Ca$^{++}$ antiporter represents the initial and determining event in the induction process.

**Table 2.2**  Specific inhibition of competence induction by DMB and monensin. To test the effects of the different drugs on competence induction, bacterial cultures were induced for 20 min at 37°C in the transformation medium containing 5% (v/v) competence factor extract and the various drugs indicated. The cultures were then spun down and resuspended in a medium free of drugs, containing [$^3$H]DNA. The effect of drugs on competence expression was checked by adding the chemicals after the induction step had been carried out in a drug-free medium

| Addition to competence medium | Competence phase | |
|---|---|---|
| | Induction (% ± 5%) | Expression (% ± 5%) |
| None | 100 | 100 |
| Monensin (2 µM) | 0 | 100 |
| TCS | | |
| 1 µM | 100 | 100 |
| 5 µM | 79 | 90 |
| HMA | | |
| 1 µM | 100 | 100 |
| 5 µM | 80 | 100 |
| DMB | | |
| 1 µM | 70 | 100 |
| 5 µM | 20 | 100 |

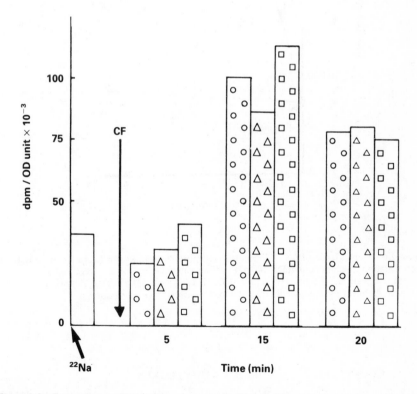

**Figure 2.5**  Dependence of Na$^+$ fluxes upon amiloride-sensitive functions. Three aliquots of bacterial suspensions in transformation medium containing $^{22}$NaCl were incubated at 37°C. 5% (v/v) CF extract was added at 2 min to three samples. Two of these received either 5 µM DMB (△) or 5 µM HMA (□). At intervals, the radioactivity retained by the bacteria was measured. The standard deviation of three independent measurements was 5%. ○, +CF only; unpatterned histogram, before CF addition.

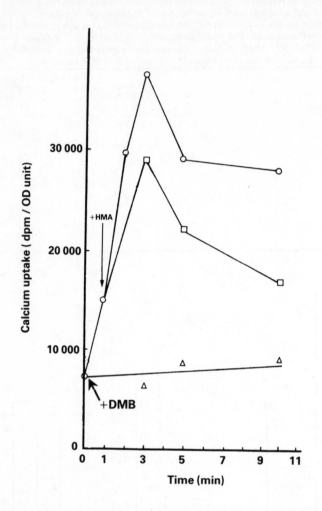

**Figure 2.6** Dependence of $Ca^{++}$ influx on $Na^+$ porters. Aliquots of bacterial suspensions in transformation medium containing 100 μM sodium vanadate and $^{45}Ca^{++}$ received 5% (v/v) CF extracts and were incubated at 37°C. 5 μM DMB ($\triangle$), or 5 μM HMA ($\square$) were added when indicated. At intervals radioactivity retained by the bacteria was determined.

EFFECT OF COMPETENCE FACTOR ON CATION FLUXES

The correlation between these cationic fluxes and CF-activated competence was checked. Results in *Figure 2.7* show a net stimulation of calcium influx and sodium efflux in CF-activated bacteria compared to the control. Therefore it is likely that one of the primary effects of the competence factor is the activation of $Na^+$ and $Ca^{++}$ fluxes via functions sensitive to amiloride derivatives.

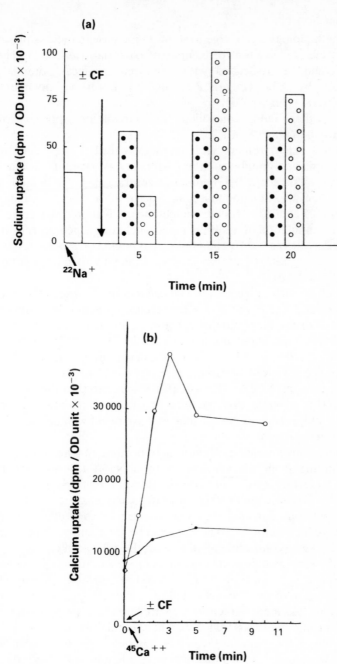

**Figure 2.7** Effect of competence factor on cation fluxes. Aliquots of bacterial suspensions in transformation medium containing either $^{22}$NaCl (a) or $^{45}$CaCl$_2$ (b) were incubated at 37°C with or without 5% (v/v) CF extract. At intervals radioactivity retained by the bacteria was measured as described. The standard deviation of three independent measurements was 5%. (a) Sodium fluxes: +CF, ○; −CF, ●; (b) calcium fluxes: +CF, ○; −CF, ●.

**Conclusion**

Several methodologies converge to show an increase in the cytoplasmic pH as well as in the $Na^+$ content of competent bacteria (*Table 2.1*). These ionic changes could be associated with enhanced chemical potential energy, represented by ATP (*Figure 2.1*) and by a reserve polymer, poly-β-hydroxybutyrate (*Figure 2.3*).

On the other hand, controlled $Na^+$ circulation appears critical for competence induction (*Figure 2.4*).

Ionic fluxes measurement and pharmacological studies using amiloride derivatives known to inhibit sodium porters in eukaryotes (L'Allemain *et al.*, 1984; Kaczorowski *et al.*, 1985) point to a central role in the induction process for a DMB-sensitive function that is likely to be a $Na^+/Ca^{++}$ exchanger (*Table 2.2, Figures 2.5* and *2.6*). Indeed, competence activation by CF corresponds at least to the stimulation of a sodium porter including functions sensitive to the amiloride derivatives, DMB and HMA, that might correspond respectively to $Na^+/Ca^{++}$ and $Na^+/H^+$ exchangers according to their inhibition pattern (*Figures 2.5* and *2.6*).

The result of such an activation is a calcium influx associated to a sodium efflux (*Figures 2.5, 2.6* and *2.7*). Competence induction level appears to be correlated with the amplitude of calcium influx that occurs in the first 3–5 minutes following competence factor addition (*Figure 2.7*) rather than to sodium efflux. Indeed, such an enhanced calcium influx (*Figure 2.7*), detected in the presence of an inhibitor of the $E_1 E_2$ type ATPases, orthovanadate, that blocks the calcium ATPase (Rosen, 1987), is reduced in the absence of the inhibitor. This suggests that the rate of calcium circulation involving the $Na^+/Ca^{++}$ antiporter and the calcium ATPase might well be the determining parameter in induction.

As an integrative model it is tempting to propose that activation of calcium influx resulting from the stimulation of a $Na^+/Ca^{++}$ exchanger by the competence factor constitutes the initial event that triggers competence. Intracellular calcium might then activate some enzyme of the glycolysis pathway and thus enhance the ATP content of the cells as well as the $NAD(P)H_2$ concentration. $NAD(P)H_2$ can be stored through the synthesis of poly-β-hydroxybutyrate while regulation of the ATP pool can be achieved by cellular ATPases, including the calcium ATPase and the $F_1F_0$ ATPase, which export, respectively, calcium (Rosen, 1987) and protons (Kobayashi *et al.*, 1984). Activation of the $F_1F_0$ should tend to shift cytoplasmic pH towards an alkaline value. As a consequence of that cytoplasmic proton 'depletion', an increased proton influx is triggered and this might occur via $H^+$ porters, including the $H^+/Na^+$ exchanger. Thus, competence could be considered as the ultimate response of a homeostatic regulation when bacteria grow in high-calcium-containing media.

Interestingly, induction of competence by competence factor could involve membrane function(s) that are $Na^+/Ca^{++}$ and $Na^+/H^+$ antiporters. According to their inhibition pattern to amiloride derivatives, these functions might well be similar to the corresponding eukaryotic systems (L'Allemain *et al.*, 1984; Kaczorowski *et al.*, 1985). So far they are the first described in prokaryotes.

# References

L'ALLEMAIN, G., FRANCHI, A., CRAGOE, E., JR. AND POUYSSEGUR, J. (1984). Blockade of the $Na^+/H^+$ antiport abolished growth factor-induced DNA synthesis in fibroblasts. Structure-activity relationship in the amiloride series. *Journal of Biological Chemistry* **259**, 4313–4319.

CLAVÉ, C., CRAGOE, E.J., JR. AND TROMBE, M.C. $Na^+$, $Ca^{++}$ fluxes and induction of competence in *Streptococcus pneumoniae*: Involvement of amiloride sensitive functions. Submitted.

CLAVÉ, C., MORRISON, D.A. AND TROMBE, M.C. (1987). Is DNA transport driven by the proton electrochemical potential difference in the naturally transformable bacteria, *Streptococcus pneumoniae*? *Bioelectrochemistry and Bioenergetics* **17**, 269–276.

DAWES, E.A., AND SENIOR, P.J. (1973). Energy reserve polymers in micro-organisms. *Advances in Microbiological Physiology* **14**, 203–266.

HEEFNER, D.L. (1982). Transport of $H^+$, $K^+$, $Na^+$ and $Ca^{++}$ in *Streptococcus*. *Molecular and Cellular Biochemistry* **44**, 81–106.

JAVOR, G.T. AND TOMASZ, A. (1968). An autoradiographic study of genetic transformation. *Proceedings of the National Academy of Sciences of the United States of America* **60**, 1216–1222.

KACZOROWSKI, G.J., BARROS, F., DETHMERS, J.K. AND TRUMBLE, M.J. (1985). Inhibition of $Na^+/Ca^{++}$ exchange in pituitary plasma membrane vesicles by analogues of amiloride. *Biochemistry* **24**, 1394–1403.

KOBAYASHI, H., SUSUKI, T., KINOSHITA, N. AND UNEMOTO, T. (1984). Amplification of the *Streptococcus faecalis* proton-translocating ATPase by a decrease in cytoplasmic pH. *Journal of Bacteriology* **158**, 1157–1160.

LACKS, S.A. (1977). Binding and entry of DNA in bacterial transformation. In *Microbial Interactions* (J. Reissing, Ed.), pp. 179–232. Chapman and Hall, London.

LAW, J.H. AND SLEPECKY, R.A. (1961). Assay of poly-β-hydroxybutyric acid. *Journal of Bacteriology* **82**, 33–36.

LOPEZ, A., CLAVÉ, C., CAPEYROU, R., LAFONTAN, V. AND TROMBE, M.C. (1989). Ionic and energetic changes at competence in the naturally transformable bacterium *Streptococcus pneumoniae*. *Journal of General Microbiology*, in press.

MÉJEAN, V., CLAVERYS, J.-P., VASSEGHI, H. AND SICARD, A.M. (1981). Rapid cloning of specific DNA fragments of *Streptococcus pneumoniae* by vector integration into the chromosome followed by endonucleolytic excision. *Gene* **15**, 289–293.

MORRISON, D.A. (1977). Transformation in pneumococcus: Existence and properties of a complex involving donor deoxyribonucleate single strands in eclipse. *Journal of Bacteriology* **132**, 576–583.

MORRISON, D.A. (1981). Competence specific protein synthesis in *Streptococcus pneumoniae*. In *Transformation – 1980* (M. Polsinelli and G. Mazza, Eds), pp. 39–53. Cotswold Press, Oxford.

MORRISON, D.A., AND BAKER, M.F. (1979). Competence for genetic transformation in pneumococcus depends on synthesis of a small set of proteins. *Nature* **282**, 215–217.

NAVA, G., GALIS, A. AND BEISER, S.M. (1963). Bacterial transformation: An antigen specific for competent pneumococci. *Nature* **197**, 903–904.

PORTER, R.D. AND GUILD, W.R. (1969). Number of transformable units per cell in *Diplococcus pneumoniae*. *Journal of Bacteriology* **97**, 1033–1035.

REUSCH, R.N. AND SADOFF, H.L. (1983). D-(-)-Poly-β-Hydroxybutyrate in membranes of genetically competent bacteria. *Journal of Bacteriology* **156**, 778–788.

REUSCH, R.N., HISKE, T.W. AND SADOFF, H.L. (1986). Poly-β-Hydroxybutyrate membrane structure and its relationship to genetic transformability in *Escherichia coli*. *Journal of Bacteriology* **168**, 553–562.

ROSEN, B.P. (1987). Bacterial calcium transport. *Biochemica et Biophysica Acta* **906**, 101–110.

SETO, H., LOPEZ, R. AND TOMASZ, A. (1975). Cell surface-located deoxyribonucleic acid receptors in transformable pneumococci. *Journal of Bacteriology* **122**, 1339–1350.

TOMASZ, A. (1969). The competent state in genetic transformation. *Annual Review of Genetics* **3**, 217–232.

TOMASZ, A. AND HOTCHKISS, R.D. (1964). Regulation of the transformability of pneumococcal cultures by macromolecular cell products. *Proceedings of the National Academy of Sciences of the United States of America* **51**, 480–487.

TROMBE, M.C. (1983). Altération du transport actif des acides aminés au moment de la compétence chez *Streptococcus pneumoniae*. *Comptes Rendus de l'Académie des Sciences, Paris. Sciences de la vie* **297**, 42–44.

TROMBE, M.C., LANÉELLE, G. AND SICARD, A.M. (1984). Characterization of a *Streptococcus pneumoniae* mutant with altered electric transmembrane potential. *Journal of Bacteriology* **158**, 1109–1114.

# 3

# DNA Uptake in Competent *Streptococcus pneumoniae*: An Insight into Energetics and Mechanism

CORINNE CLAVÉ, FRANCK MARTIN AND
MARIE-CLAUDE TROMBE*

Centre de Recherche de Biochimie et de Génétique Cellulaires du CNRS, 118
Route de Narbonne, 31062 Toulouse Cedex, France

## Introduction

DNA transport across the bacterial cell membrane is the initial event in several genetic exchange systems. In naturally transformable bacteria, DNA uptake is a complex process which occurs only during a specialized physiological state called competence (Lacks, 1979; Morrison, 1981; Smith, Danner and Deich, 1981): double-stranded DNA is bound at the surface of the cells, nicked (Lerman and Tolmach, 1957; Morrison and Guild, 1973; Lacks and Greenberg, 1976) and converted to a single-stranded form during entry (Lacks, 1962; Lacks, Greenberg and Neuberger, 1975; Morrison, 1977; Smith *et al.*, 1984) while oligonucleotides are released in the medium (Lacks and Greenberg, 1973). DNA transfer is linear (Gabor and Hotchkiss, 1966) and directional with a $3' \rightarrow 5'$ polarity (Barany, Kahn and Smith, 1983). Currently, experimental evidence points to the importance of energy (Tomasz, 1970; Lacks and Greenberg, 1973), more precisely of the proton-motive force, in bacterial transformation (Chaustova *et al.*, 1980; Van Nieuwenhoven *et al.*, 1982; Bremer *et al.*, 1984). It has been proposed, as an hypothesis, that the proton-motive force ($\triangle p$) could be the driving force for DNA entry in some bacterial species (Chaustova *et al.*, 1980; Grinius, 1980; Bremer *et al.*, 1984). The chemical gradient ($\triangle pH$) rather than the electrical gradient ($\triangle \psi$) seems to be the driving force for DNA entry in *Bacillus subtilis* (Van Nieuwenhoven *et al.*, 1982). However, in *Streptococcus pneumoniae* previous results based on the analysis of $\triangle \psi^-$ mutants (Sautereau and Trombe, 1986; Trombe, Lanéelle and Sicard, 1984) and on protonophore utilization led us to propose that neither $\triangle \psi$ nor $\triangle pH$ constitute the driving force for DNA uptake in *S. pneumoniae*, but rather that the intracellular pH ($pH_i$) value was critical for

---

* Corresponding author.

*Genetic Transformation and Expression*
© Intercept Ltd, PO Box 716, Andover, Hants, SP10 1YG, UK

uptake (Clavé, Morrison and Trombe, 1987). Interestingly, alkalinization of the cytoplasm and glycolysis stimulation leading to an enhanced ATP pool can be observed in competent bacteria (Lopez *et al.*, 1989).

In the present paper we describe investigations into the involvement of ATP and the ionic requirement of uptake, in conditions where all the cells in a culture become competent for DNA uptake (Porter and Guild, 1969; Lopez *et al.*, 1989), as well as into the nature of the substrate for transport. Our results show that uptake is optimal at alkaline cytoplasmic pH and requires calcium in the medium. They suggest the involvement of a DNA transporter, deriving its energy from ATP, which might use single-stranded DNA as its substrate.

**Materials and methods**

STRAIN AND MEDIA

Wild-type strain and growth media were described in Chapter 2. Strains bearing *ent* mutations were described by Morrison *et al.* (1983). Strain CP1700 was obtained by transformation of the wild type CP1000 with DNA of a strain bearing the mutations *end-5* and *exo-1* (Lacks, 1970).

When required, competence expression was obtained in a mineral medium derived from that previously used for *S. pneumoniae* growth (Trombe, Lanéelle and Sicard, 1984). This medium allows competence expression but not competence induction. It contains Tris (40 mM), $NH_4Cl$ (52 mM), KCl (7·5 mM), and either MOPS (20 mM) or $Na_2HPO_4$ (20 mM). The pH and the NaCl concentration were adjusted as required. Osmolarity was maintained at 240 milliosmoles by addition of KCl.

DEVELOPMENT OF COMPETENCE

Competence was obtained by the method described in Clavé, Morrison and Trombe (1987).

PREPARATION OF CF EXTRACT

Competence factor (CF) extracts were prepared as described elsewhere (Morrison, 1981; Lopez *et al.*, 1989).

ASSAY FOR DNA-DEGRADING ACTIVITY, FOR TRANSPORT AND SELECTION OF TRANSFORMANTS

Assays and selection of transformed bacteria were as described in Clavé, Morrison and Trombe (1987).

GLUCOSE CONSUMPTION, ATP AND L-LACTATE DETERMINATIONS

Glucose consumption, ATP content and L-lactate production determinations are described in Lopez *et al.* (1989).

ARSENATE TREATMENT

For ATP deprivation by arsenate treatment, bacteria were suspended in a phosphate-free medium containing 20 mM sodium arsenate, replaced by 20 mM MOPS in the control culture, and incubated for 5 min at 30°C.

SPECIAL MATERIALS

Chromosomal DNA from strain 119 bearing a $tdr^-$ mutation and the *rif-23* marker which confers resistance to 1 μg ml$^{-1}$ rifampicin was routinely used as a source of [$^3$H]DNA. The chimeric plasmid pR172, derived from pBR322 (Méjean *et al.*, 1981), bearing the marker *ami-258* belonging to the *ami* locus and conferring resistance to $5 \times 10^{-6}$ M methotrexate, was the source of cloned DNA. The chimeric phage M61, constructed by Dr Pedro Garcia (CRBGC, Toulouse), is a M13 derivative where a 1735 bp *Hind*III-*Eco*RI fragment of *S. pneumoniae* DNA bearing the mutation *ami-126* was cloned. It was the source of single-stranded DNA, while its replicative form was used as double-stranded DNA.

3,3',4',5-tetrachlorosalicylanilide (TCS) was kindly provided by Dr I.R. Booth, Department of Microbiology, University of Aberdeen, Aberdeen, Scotland. Monensin was provided by Lilly Research, Surrey, England. The other chemicals were of analytical grade.

## Results

INVOLVEMENT OF THE ELECTROCHEMICAL GRADIENT OF H$^+$ AND OF THE CYTOPLASMIC pH VALUE IN DNA UPTAKE

DNA uptake in bacteria treated with the protonophore TCS, which tends to equilibrate the proton concentration between both sides of the membrane, was measured at different external pHs (pH$_o$). The results plotted in *Figure 3.1* show a linear increase of uptake from pH$_o$ 7 to 8·2 while the untreated control cells exhibited a constant rate of DNA uptake independent of the pH$_o$ value between pH 7 and 8·5. Moreover, at pH$_o$ > 8 the level of uptake was equivalent and optimal either in the presence or absence of TCS (*Figure 3.1*). It was noticed that the nuclease activity which is expressed at competence (Lerman and Tolmach, 1957; Lacks, 1962; Lacks and Greenberg, 1973; Morrison and Guild, 1973; Lacks and Greenberg, 1976) presented a response to pH similar to that of uptake (not shown). This indicates that DNA uptake is independent of $\Delta\mu_{H^+}$ as previously suggested (Clavé, Morrison and Trombe, 1987) but is optimal between pH$_i$ 8·2 and 8·5 (*Figure 3.1*). Indeed, in competent *S. pneumoniae* the pH$_i$ falls to around 8·3 (Lopez *et al.*, 1989), a value where uptake is optimal.

CALCIUM REQUIREMENT FOR UPTAKE

Several authors have proposed a specific calcium requirement for DNA uptake in *S. pneumoniae* (Fox and Hotchkiss, 1957; Lacks, 1962; Seto and Tomasz, 1976) but the mechanism of calcium action is not well understood. Chelating

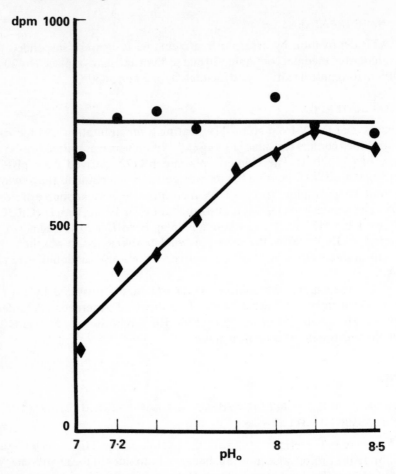

**Figure 3.1** DNA uptake at different $pH_o$ in TCS-treated bacteria. Aliquots of competent bacteria were incubated in competence medium (CTM), at different $pH_o$ containing 10 μM TCS. No TCS was added in the control. [$^3$H] DNA (1 μg, $121 \times 10^3$ dpm ml$^{-1}$) was added. Uptake was measured after 15 minutes incubation at 30°C. ●, Control; ◆, TCS-treated cells.

agents, such as EDTA and EGTA, strongly inhibited nuclease activity and DNA uptake (*Table 3.1*). Calcium was more potent than magnesium in restoring nuclease activity as well as uptake (*Table 3.1*), suggesting that calcium ions are involved in these processes. Moreover, DNA uptake increased with the external calcium concentration up to 0·4 mM (*Figure 3.2*), a concentration twice that required for growth of *S. pneumoniae* (Clavé and Trombe, submitted). This indicates a specific calcium requirement for DNA uptake. A possibility is that calcium ions interact with membrane constituents, either proteins or phospholipids, and activate functions or generate some structures that allow uptake. Such a situation is observed in bacteria where competence is induced by calcium concentrations ranging between 25 and 100 mM (Borovjagin *et al.*, 1987). However, in *S. pneumoniae* the calcium requirement

**Table 3.1** Calcium requirement for DNA uptake and DNA degradation

| Chelating agent* | DNA degradation† (dpm ml⁻¹ ± 10%) ion added‡ | | | | DNA uptake† (dpm ml⁻¹ ± 10%) ion added‡ | | | |
|---|---|---|---|---|---|---|---|---|
| | none§ | $Ca^{++}$ | $Mg^{++}$ | $Ca^{++}$ + $Mg^{++}$ | none§ | $Ca^{++}$ | $Mg^{++}$ | $Ca^{++}$ + $Mg^{++}$ |
| − EDTA | 19310 | 20290 | 19970 | 18750 | 6030 | 7330 | 6260 | 6770 |
| + EDTA | 9760 | 18690 | 12970 | 18770 | 2560 | 5870 | 3100 | 5690 |
| − EGTA | 13830 | 14710 | 13470 | 13600 | 5390 | 5980 | 5620 | 6310 |
| + EGTA | 3820 | 9330 | 4730 | 13480 | 280 | 5130 | 590 | 5850 |

\* Chelating agents as indicated.
† Uptake and degradation were measured after 20 min of incubation with [³H]DNA (1.8 μg, 2 × 10⁵ dpm ml⁻¹), at 30°C.
‡ 0·25 mM $CaCl_2$ and/or $MgCl_2$ were added to the assay.
§ The basic level of $Ca^{++}$ was 0·4 mM as measured by flame photometry.

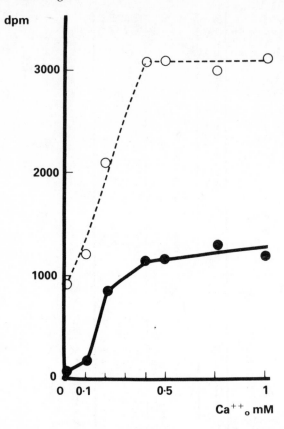

**Figure 3.2** Dose response of DNA degradation and DNA uptake to added calcium. Competent bacteria were suspended in competence medium (CTM) in which endogenous calcium was chelated by 0·5 mM EGTA. Variable amounts of $CaCl_2$ were added; then uptake and degradation of [$^3$H] DNA (1·25 μg, $134 \times 10^3$ dpm ml$^{-1}$) were measured after 20 min incubation at 30°C. ○, DNA degradation; ●, DNA uptake.

is quite low (*Figure 3.2*) and no temperature shift is required to trigger DNA uptake; thus, a different type of mechanism for DNA uptake is likely to be operative. Among other possibilities is that of calcium co-transport with the DNA molecule as a DNA–$Ca^{++}$ complex in response to a $Ca^{++}$ gradient (in<out) generated by a calcium ATPase that pumps out the cation (Kobayashi, Van Brunt and Harold, 1978; Rosen, 1987) or through a specific transporter.

CORRELATION BETWEEN THE ATP POOL AND DNA UPTAKE

*Streptococcus pneumoniae* is a homolactic bacterium (Trombe, Lanéelle and Sicard, 1984). Competence induction results in a stimulation of glycolysis, as shown by the increase in glucose consumption, lactate production and ATP content of the culture (Clavé *et al.*, Chapter 2 this volume; Lopez *et al.*, 1989), with a peak concomitant with the competence peak where the frequency of

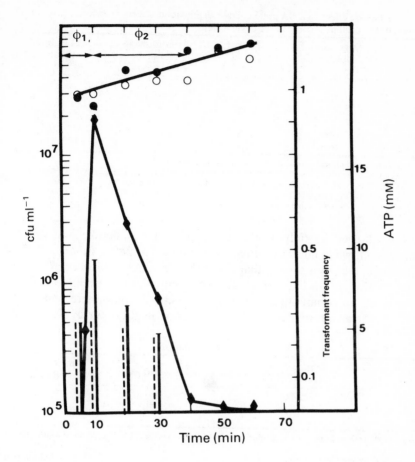

**Figure 3.3** Competence cycle and ATP content of the culture. Tester cells were incubated at 37°C in the presence or absence of CF (5% v/v). Evolution of the number of cfu ml$^{-1}$ with time was followed ($\bigcirc$, −CF; $\bullet$, +CF). At intervals 1 ml aliquots were extracted for ATP determination (bars, +CF; dotted line, −CF) and 0·1 ml aliquots were incubated for 5 min at 30°C in the presence of pR172 DNA (0·1 µg ml$^{-1}$) bearing the *ami-258* marker. Mtx$^R$ frequency ($\blacklozenge$) was determined by plating experiments.

transformants for a cloned genetic marker reaches 0·9 (*Figure 3.3*), attesting that the whole population is competent. Arsenate treatment diminished both the ATP level of the culture and DNA uptake without lethality (*Table 3.2*). The magnitude of reduction in DNA uptake, however, depended on the competence stage of the culture at the time of the treatment. If the bacteria were treated during competence acquisition ($\phi_1$, *see Figure 3.3*), DNA uptake and genetic transformation were reduced by 90% while the nuclease activity specific of competence was only reduced by 35% when the ATP pool shifted by 19%. In contrast, if the treatment was done after the peak time ($\phi_2$, *see Figure 3.3*), where bacteria were losing competence, reduction by 31% of the ATP

**Table 3.2**  Arsenate effect on DNA uptake, DNA degradation, genetic transformation and ATP synthesis at different steps of competence development

|  | Degradation† (dpm ml$^{-1}$ ± 10%) | Uptake† (dpm ml$^{-1}$ ± 10%) | Transformants† (% of the culture ± 10%) | ATP level† reduction (% ± 5%) |
|---|---|---|---|---|
| $\phi_1$* |  |  |  |  |
| − Arsenate | 5000 | 2200 | 0·26 | 0 |
| + Arsenate | 3200 | 100 | 0·03 | 19 |
| $\phi_2$* |  |  |  |  |
| − Arsenate | 16200 | 6500 | 1·7 | 0 |
| + Arsenate | 10000 | 2500 | 0·7 | 31 |

*    $\phi_1$ and $\phi_2$ correspond respectively to 20 min and 30 min inductions by 5% CF.
†    Experiments were conducted in a mineral medium buffered with MOPS (*see* Methods). Either 20 mM arsenate or MOPS was added as indicated, and 5 min incubations were allowed before ATP extraction, then [$^3$H]DNA (20 µg, 230 × 10$^3$ dpm ml$^{-1}$) bearing the genetic marker *rif-23* was added, and degradation, uptake and transformation were allowed for 5 min.

level was followed by only a 60% decrease of DNA uptake and genetic transformation, while nuclease activity was reduced by 38% (*Table 3.2*). This inhibition of uptake by arsenate, that shares the phosphate transporter (Harold and Spitz, 1975), is not likely to result from competition between DNA and arsenate since no competition was observed between phosphate and DNA (*Table 3.3*). As an alternative, arsenate inhibition might occur by the bias of

**Table 3.3**  Absence of competition between phosphate and DNA

| Media† | Degradation* (dpm/10$^8$CFC) | Uptake* (dpm/10$^8$CFC) | Transformants* (% of the culture) |
|---|---|---|---|
| −Phosphate | 22900 | 7790 | 11 |
| +Phosphate 20mM | 17261 | 9205 | 11 |

*    Measurements were made after 30 min incubations with [$^3$H]DNA (1·3 µg, 14 × 10$^4$ dpm ml$^{-1}$) bearing the *rif* marker.
†    Expression was obtained in the minimal medium.

cytoplasmic acidification. However, the differential level of DNA-uptake inhibition in $\phi_1$ and $\phi_2$ for the same arsenate treatment, resulting in a similar ATP level reduction, suggests a more complex role for ATP in uptake. A possibility is that a threshold ATP level is required to trigger the uptake capability of the bacteria at competence, and then ATP could provide energy for uptake directly, if the transporter is a primary transport system, or by the bias of some cation ATPases (Addison and Scarborough, 1982; Rosen, 1987) generating a cation gradient. Such ATPases, including the calcium ATPase, can be characterized by their sensitivity to vanadate (Addison and Scarborough, 1982; Fürst and Solioz, 1986). DNA uptake was not reduced by vanadate up to 0·2 mM (*Table 3.4*) whatever the calcium concentration of the medium. Moreover, for suboptimal free calcium concentration at 1 mM EGTA, when uptake was only 50% of the control (*Table 3.4*), vanadate addition restored 100% uptake. As the calcium ATPase of *S. pneumoniae* is likely to pump out calcium (personal observation) as observed in other streptococci (Kobyashi, van Brunt and Harold, 1978; Rosen, 1987), it is likely that inhibition of calcium export stimulates DNA uptake, suggesting an

**Table 3.4** Effect of vanadate at different calcium concentrations on DNA degradation and uptake

| Vanadate ($\mu$M)* | Assay† | EGTA concentration (mM)‡ | | | |
|---|---|---|---|---|---|
| | | 0 | 0·3 | 0·6 | 1 |
| 0 | DNA degradation | 1036 | 1095 | 1118 | 1128 |
| | DNA uptake | 705 | 692 | 819 | 414 |
| 100 | DNA degradation | 1021 | 954 | 1128 | 1138 |
| | DNA uptake | 763 | nd | 739 | 682 |
| 150 | DNA degradation | 1003 | 1012 | 1130 | 1076 |
| | DNA uptake | 733 | nd | 752 | 777 |
| 200 | DNA degradation | 1110 | 921 | 1075 | 1212 |
| | DNA uptake | 724 | 623 | 815 | 755 |

* Vanadate was added to competent bacteria and maintained throughout incubation.
† DNA transport and DNA degradation of [³H] DNA ($208 \times 10^3$ dpm ml⁻¹) were measured after 5 min incubation at 25°C. Results, expressed in dpm ml⁻¹, are the average of three independent determinations. Standard deviation of the mean was 5%. nd: not determined.
‡ The calcium content of the medium was adjusted by addition of EGTA. In the absence of EGTA it was 1·5 mM.

intracellular role for calcium in the DNA-uptake mechanism. In any case, the inefficiency of vanadate to reduce DNA uptake argues against a transport mechanism coupled to a cation gradient generated by a vanadate-sensitive ATPase. Rather, it might suggest a direct ATP involvement in uptake.

NATURE OF THE DNA MOLECULE SUBSTRATE OF THE UPTAKE MACHINERY

DNA transport might occur via a primary transporter activated at high ATP levels, whose substrate could be single- or double-stranded DNA, or both. To investigate that problem, the wild-type strain, CP1000, and CP1700, an isogenic derivative bearing the mutations (*endo-1, exo-5*) that reduce the membrane endonuclease activity (Lacks, 1970) were used. Transforming DNA were M61 phage DNA and its replicative form (*see* p. 29). The results given in *Table 3.5* show that single-stranded DNA was 40–50 times more transformant

**Table 3.5** Transforming efficiency of single- and double-stranded DNA in strains CP1000 and CP1700

| Strain | DNA* | DNA degradation† (cpm ml⁻¹) | Mtx^R transformants‡ (% of the culture) |
|---|---|---|---|
| CP1000 | ss | 25800 | 0·6 |
| | ds | 22600 | 72 |
| CP1700 | ss | <500 | 25 |
| | ds | 750 | 68 |

* Either phage DNA or its replicative form, both of a concentration of 50 ng ml⁻¹ (50 000 cpm ml⁻¹), were added to competent bacteria and incubated at 32°C for 30 min.
† Degradation was estimated by measuring the acid-soluble radioactive fraction.
‡ Mtx^R frequency was determined by plating experiments.
ss = single-stranded DNA; ds = double-stranded DNA.

in strain CP1700 than in the wild type. As both strains are isogenic but for their nuclease activity, it is likely that the poor efficiency of single-stranded DNA in the wild type resulted from its extensive degradation. In any case it is shown that single-stranded DNA is actively transported in CP1700, supporting the observations of Barany (1982) in wild-type bacteria. Moreover, mutations that reduce uptake without altering competence induction and expression

(Morrison *et al.*, 1983) lowered to a similar level transformation by double-stranded and single-stranded molecules (*Table 3.6*). This suggests that the same function is involved in the transport of both kinds of molecules.

**Table 3.6** Mutations that reduce uptake of double-stranded DNA lower transformation by single-stranded DNA

| Recipient* | MTX$^R$ transformants (% of the culture) | |
| --- | --- | --- |
| | ds – DNA | ss – DNA |
| CP1000 (WT) | 70 | 0·64 |
| CP1214 (ent) | 0·2 | 0·01 |
| CP1211 (ent) | 0·19 | 0·01 |
| CP1217 (ent) | 0·01 | <10$^{-3}$ |
| CP1222 (ent) | 0·01 | <10$^{-3}$ |

* Competent bacteria of each strain received 50 ng of either double-stranded DNA (ds) or the single-stranded form (ss), bearing the *ami-126* marker. After 30 min incubation at 32°C, Mtx$^R$ frequency was determined by plating experiments.

## Conclusion

In contrast to other species (Chaustova *et al.*, 1980; van Nieuwenhoven *et al.*, 1982; Bremer *et al.*, 1984), DNA uptake in competent *Streptococcus pneumoniae* is not coupled to $\Delta\mu_{H^+}$ (*Figure 3.1*). Moreover, resistance of uptake to vanadate (*Table 3.4*), a well-known inhibitor of cation ATPases of the $E_1E_2$ type (Fürst and Solioz, 1986), suggests that cation gradients generated by these ATPases are not involved.

As an alternative it is proposed that specific and transient membrane structures could account for the 'membrane permeability' at competence (Borovjagin *et al.*, 1987). In naturally competent bacteria and in calcium-treated *E. coli*, a good candidate to generate such structures is poly-β-hydroxybutyrate (PHB) (Reusch and Sadoff, 1983; Reusch, Hiske and Sadoff, 1986; Reusch and Sadoff, 1988), a lipid that accumulates at competence. Indeed *S. pneumoniae* contains poly-β-hydroxybutyrate (Clavé *et al.*, Chapter 2 this volume); however, strain CP1212, an uptake⁻ mutant (Morrison *et al.*, 1983), presents the same PHB level as the wild type (Trombe, personal results), suggesting that other parameters are required for uptake.

Interestingly, ATP seems to play a key role in DNA uptake. Reduction of ATP synthesis by arsenate during competence development ($\phi_1$) (*Figure 3.3*), dramatically reduced uptake with a limited effect on DNA degradation and no effect on cell viability (*Table 3.2*) while in $\phi_2$ (*Figure 3.3*) reduction of the ATP pool was comparable to the inhibition level of uptake (*Table 3.2*). To account for this different response of uptake to a similar ATP-level reduction, we propose that a threshold ATP level is first required to trigger uptake by activation of a DNA transport system. Indeed, stimulation of glycolysis leading to an increased ATP pool is observed during competence development (Lopez *et al.*, 1989). Activation might consist of saturation of ATP-binding sites on the transporter or phosphorylation of some protein residue as shown in chemotaxis (Hess *et al.*, 1987) for example. Then DNA transport might derive its energy from either ATP itself or a derivative, and thus behave as a primary transport. During the course of this work results were published showing that DNA uptake by yeast nuclei in an *in vitro* system probably relies upon ATP (Tsuchiya *et al.*, 1988). So if a 'primary transporter' exists for DNA, one might find it in eukaryotes as well as in prokaryotes.

On the other hand, our results show a requirement for calcium (*Figure 3.2*) and an optimum uptake at alkaline $pH_o$ (*Figure 3.1*) in TCS-treated bacteria, while the control is independent toward $pH_o$, suggesting that the $pH_i$ value is determining the rate of DNA uptake. These parameters might correspond to optimal conditions for the activity of the 'transporter', but we cannot exclude the possibility that their influence is on the rate of glycolysis and therefore on ATP production.

On the whole, our results show the strong dependence of DNA uptake on intracellular pH and ATP, properties that are reminiscent of anion transport systems in *Streptococcus faecalis* (Harold and Spitz, 1975). However, it is likely that DNA does not share the route of phosphate transport since no competition could be detected between phosphate and DNA (*Table 3.3*). In any case, as the DNA molecule is a polyanion the model proposed by Harold and Spitz (1975) for anion transport as primary electroneutral exchanges for $OH^-$ driven by ATP, might be suggested for DNA transport. Difficulties in the accurate measurement of cytoplasmic pH at the same time as DNA transport make that model hard to test at the biochemical level. Genetic and molecular studies based on utilization of uptake$^-$ mutants should contribute to a better definition of this process. Indeed, the 10 independent uptake$^-$ mutants tested presented the same profile for their ATP content during competence development (Trombe, personal result) and exhibited no $\Delta \psi$ reduction (Clavé, Morrison and Trombe, 1987) suggesting that their defect in DNA uptake is not due to some energetic failure. A possibility is that these mutants define a 'transporter' for the DNA molecule whose substrate might be single-stranded DNA (*Tables 3.5 and 3.6*). If such a transporter exists, we propose that it should be activated by both high ATP pools and by calcium, and then functions at the expense of ATP to transport single-stranded DNA.

In such a context, the role of the membrane nuclease could be limited to the processing of the DNA molecule when it is double-stranded, as suggested by the high transforming efficiency of single-stranded DNA from M61 in strain CP1700, whose membrane nuclease activity is reduced.

## Acknowledgements

We thank Dr F. Harold for helpful discussion and valuable suggestions during the course of this work, and Drs S. Lacks and I.R. Booth for critical reading of the manuscript.

This work was supported by University Paul Sabatier, Centre National de la Recherche Scientifique LP008201 and ATP microbiologie 1984 no. 953104. Corinne Clavé was supported by a MRT grant.

## References

ADDISON, R. AND SCARBOROUGH, G.A. (1982). Conformational changes of the *Neurospora* plasma membrane H⁺ ATPase during its catalytic cycle. *Journal of Biological Chemistry* **257**, 10421–10426.

BARANY, F. (1982). Transformation of *Streptococcus pneumoniae* by single-stranded plasmid-phage hybrid DNA. In *Microbiology – 1982* (D. Schlessinger, Ed.), pp. 125–129. American Society for Microbiology, Washington, DC.

BARANY, F., KAHN, M.E. AND SMITH, H.O. (1983). Directional transport and integration of donor DNA in *Haemophilus influenzae* transformation. *Proceedings of the National Academy of Sciences of the United States of America* **80**, 7274–7278.

BOROVJAGIN, V.L., SABELNIKOV, A.G., TARAHOVSKY, Y.S., AND VASILENKO, I.A. (1987). Polymorphic behaviour of Gram-negative bacteria membranes. *Journal of Membrane Biology* **100**, 229–242.

BREMER, W., KOOISTRA, J., HELLINGWERF, K.J., AND KONINGS, W.N. (1984). Role of electrochemical proton gradient in genetic transformation of *Haemophilus influenzae*. *Journal of Bacteriology* **157**, 868–873.

CHAUSTOVA, L.P., GRINIUS, L.L., GRINIUVIENE, B.B., JASAïTIS, A.A., KADZIAUSKA, J.P., AND KIAUSINYTE, R.J. (1980). Studies on energy supply for genetic processes. Involvement of membrane potential in genetic transformation of *Bacillus subtilis*. *European Journal of Biochemistry* **103**, 349–357.

CLAVÉ, C., MORRISON, D.A., AND TROMBE, M.C. (1987). Is DNA transport driven by the proton electrochemical potential difference in the naturally transformable bacteria *Streptococcus pneumoniae*? *Bioelectrochemistry and Bioenergetics* **17**, 269–276.

FOX, M.S. AND HOTCHKISS, R.D. (1957). Initiation of bacterial transformation. *Nature* **179**, 1322–1325.

FÜRST, P. AND SOLIOZ, M. (1986). The vanadate-sensitive ATP-ase of *Streptococcus faecalis* pumps potassium in a reconstituted system. *Journal of Biological Chemistry* **261**, 4302–4308.

GABOR, M. AND HOTCHKISS, R.D. (1966). Manifestation of linear organization in molecules of pneumococcal transforming DNA. *Proceedings of the National Academy of Sciences of the United States of America* **56**, 1441–1448.

GRINIUS, L. (1980). Nucleic acid transport driven by ion gradients across the cell membrane. *FEBS Letters* **113**, 1–10.

HAROLD, F.M. AND SPITZ, E. (1975). Accumulation of arsenate, phosphate and aspartate by *Streptococcus faecalis*. *Journal of Bacteriology* **122**, 266–277.

HESS, J.F., OOSAWA, K., MATSUMARA, P. AND SIMON, M.I. (1987). Protein phosphorylation is involved in bacterial chemotaxis. *Proceedings of the National Academy of Sciences of the United States of America* **84**, 7609–7613.

KOBAYASHI, H., VAN BRUNT, J. AND HAROLD, F.M. (1978). ATP-linked calcium transport in cells and membrane vesicles of *Streptococcus faecalis*. *Journal of Biological Chemistry* **253**, 2085–2092.

LACKS, S.A. (1962). Molecular fate of DNA in genetic transformation of pneumococcus. *Journal of Molecular Biology* **5**, 119–131.

LACKS, S.A. (1970). Mutants of *Diplococcus pneumoniae* that lack deoxyribonucleases and other activities possibly pertinent to genetic transformation. *Journal of Bacteriology* **101**, 373–383.

LACKS, S.A. (1979). Steps in the process of DNA binding and entry in transformation. In *Transformation – 1978* (S. W. Glover and L. O. Butler, Eds), pp. 27–39. Cotswold Press, Oxford.

LACKS, S.A. AND GREENBERG, B. (1973). Competence for deoxyribonucleic acid uptake and deoxyribonuclease action external to cells in the genetic transformation of *Diplococcus pneumoniae*. *Journal of Bacteriology* **114**, 152–163.

LACKS, S.A. AND GREENBERG, B. (1976). Single-strand breakage on binding of DNA to cells in the genetic transformation of *Diplococcus pneumoniae*. *Journal of Molecular Biology* **101**, 255–275.

LACKS, S.A., GREENBERG, B. AND NEUBERGER, M. (1975). Identification of a deoxyribonuclease implicated in genetic transformation of *Diplococcus pneumoniae. Journal of Bacteriology* **123**, 222–232.

LERMAN, L.S. AND TOLMACH, L.J. (1957). Genetic Transformation. I. Cellular incorporation of DNA accompanying transformation in pneumococcus. *Biochimica et Biophysica Acta* **26**, 68–82.

LOPEZ, A., CLAVÉ, C., CAPEYROU, R., LAFONTAN, V. AND TROMBE, M.C. (1989). Ionic and energetic changes at competence in the naturally transformable bacterium *Streptococcus pneumoniae. Journal of General Microbiology*, in press.

MÉJEAN, V., CLAVERYS, J.-P., VASSEGHI, H. AND SICARD, A.M. (1981). Rapid cloning of specific DNA fragments of *Streptococcus pneumoniae* by vector integration into the chromosome followed by endonucleolytic excision. *Gene* **15**, 289–293.

MORRISON, D.A. (1977). Transformation in pneumococcus: Existence and properties of a complex involving donor deoxyribonucleate single strands in eclipse. *Journal of Bacteriology* **132**, 576–583.

MORRISON, D.A. (1981). Competence specific protein synthesis in *Streptococcus pneumoniae*. In *Transformation – 1980* (M. Polsinelli and G. Mazza, Eds), pp. 39–53. Cotswold Press, Oxford.

MORRISON, D.A. AND GUILD, W.R. (1973). Breakage prior to entry of donor DNA in pneumococcus transformation. *Biochimica et Biophysica Acta* **299**, 545–556.

MORRISON, D.A., LACKS, S.A., GUILD, W.R. AND HAGEMAN, J.M. (1983). Isolation and characterization of three new classes of transformation deficient mutants of *Streptococcus pneumoniae* that are defective in DNA transport and genetic recombination. *Journal of Bacteriology* **156**, 281–290.

PORTER, R.D. AND GUILD, W.R. (1969). Number of transformable units per cell in *Diplococcus pneumoniae. Journal of Bacteriology* **97**, 1033–1035.

REUSCH, R.N. AND SADOFF, H.L. (1983). D-(-)-Poly-β-hydroxybutyrate in membranes of genetically competent bacteriia. *Journal of Bacteriology* **156**, 778–788.

REUSCH, R.N. AND SADOFF, H.L. (1988). Putative structure and functions of a poly-β-hydroxybutyrate/calcium polyphosphate channel in bacterial plasma membranes. *Proceedings of the National Academy of Sciences of the United States of America* **85**, 4176–4180.

REUSCH, R.N., HISKE, T.W. AND SADOFF, H.L. (1986). Poly-β-hydroxybutyrate membrane structure and its relationship to genetic transformability in *Escherichia coli. Journal of Bacteriology* **168**, 553–562.

ROSEN, B.P. (1987). Bacterial calcium transport. *Biochimica et Biophysica Acta* **906**, 101–110.

SAUTEREAU, A.M. AND TROMBE, M.C. (1986). Electric transmembrane potential mutation and resistance to the cationic and amphiphilic antitumoral drugs derived from pyridocarbazole 2-$N$-methylellipticinium and 2-$N$-methyl-9-hydroxyellipticinium in *Streptococcus pneumoniae. Journal of General Microbiology* **132**, 2637–2641.

SETO, H. AND TOMASZ, A. (1976). Calcium-requiring step in the uptake of deoxyribonucleic acid molecules through the surface of competent pneumococci. *Journal of Bacteriology* **126**, 1113–1118.

SMITH, H.O., DANNER, D.B. AND DEICH, R.A. (1981). Genetic transformation. *Annual Review of Biochemistry* **50**, 41–68.

SMITH, H., WIERSMA, K., VENEMA, G. AND BRON, S. (1984). Transformation in *Bacillus subtilis*: A 75,000 Dalton protein complex is involved in binding and entry of donor DNA. *Journal of Bacteriology* **157**, 733–738.

TOMASZ, A. (1970). Cellular metabolism in genetic transformation of pneumococci: Requirement for protein synthesis during induction of competence. *Journal of Bacteriology* **101**, 860–871.

TROMBE, M.C., LANÉELLE, G. AND SICARD, A.M. (1984). Characterization of a *Streptococcus pneumoniae* mutant with altered electric transmembrane potential. *Journal of Bacteriology* **158**, 1109–1114.

TSUCHIYA, E., SHAKUTO, S., MIYAKAWA, T. AND FUKUI, S. (1988). Characterization of a DNA uptake reaction through the nuclear membrane of isolated yeast nuclei. *Journal of Bacteriology* **170**, 547–551.

VAN NIEUWENHOVEN, M.H., HELLINGWERF, K.J., VENEMA, G. AND KONINGS, W.N. (1982). Role of proton motive force in genetic transformation of *Bacillus subtilis*. *Journal of Bacteriology* **151**, 771–776.

# 4

# DNA Entry in Transformation of *Streptococcus pneumoniae*

VINCENT MÉJEAN AND JEAN-PIERRE CLAVERYS

*Centre de Recherche de Biochimie et de Génétique Cellulaires du CNRS, Université Paul Sabatier, 118 Route de Narbonne, 31062 Toulouse Cedex, France*

## Introduction

DNA-mediated transformation in the Gram-positive bacterium *Streptococcus pneumoniae* is a naturally occurring phenomenon in which DNA in solution is taken up by the cells. Double-stranded DNA is taken up an hundredfold more efficiently than single-stranded DNA (Barany, 1982). The uptake process can be divided into two steps: binding of donor DNA at the cell surface, and entry of the bound DNA. Donor DNA is rendered single-stranded during entry (for review *see* Lacks, 1977). Nicking of the DNA is required for entry. Using labelled donor DNA, it was shown that the length of single strands found within the cells had been reduced to $2 \cdot 2 \times 10^6$ daltons per strand for large donor molecules, whereas for small donor molecules, the median strand length was half that of the donor strands (Morrison and Guild, 1972). These nicks appear to occur within surface-bound DNA prior to entry, since investigation of surface-bound DNA released by NaOH or guanidine-HCl treatment revealed the presence of a double-strand break per 8500 bp (Morrison and Guild, 1973a). This results in a strand length distribution indistinguishable from that of the DNA found inside the cells. Broken DNA released from the cell surface is still active in transformation, implying that the breaks produced outside the cell are not at genetically specific sites (Morrison and Guild, 1973b). One of the two major deoxyribonucleases of *S. pneumoniae*, located in the membrane (Lacks and Neuberger, 1975; Rosenthal and Lacks, 1980), was shown to play a central role in DNA entry (Lacks, Greenberg and Neuberger, 1974, 1975). Use of a nuclease-deficient strain (Lacks and Greenberg, 1976) and of circular donor DNA (Lacks, 1979) led to the conclusion that the first step in the uptake process is the introduction of single-strand breaks in the DNA on binding to the cells. Evidence for a linear entry of DNA was presented by Gabor and Hotchkiss (1966) who observed delayed entry of linked marker pairs relative to single markers.

*Genetic Transformation and Expression*
© Intercept Ltd, PO Box 716, Andover, Hants, SP10 1YG, UK

Together, these results are consistent with a model for entry in which double-stranded donor DNA suffers nicks and double-strand breaks at the cell surface. Entry then proceeds linearly from a newly formed end (Lacks and Greenberg, 1976). The experiments reported here were aimed at elucidating the polarity (if any) of donor DNA entry in transformation of *S. pneumoniae*. Our experiments also give an estimate of the rate of DNA entry.

## Materials and methods

Detailed descriptions of materials and methods used in these studies have been given before (Méjean and Claverys, 1988).

## Polarity of DNA entry

### DESIGN OF THE EXPERIMENT

In order to study the polarity of donor DNA entry in transformation of *S. pneumoniae*, we constructed *in vitro* a series of related molecules specifically labelled either at their 3'- or 5'-end, on one strand only. These molecules were derived from bacteriophage M13mp19 DNA which has no homology within recipient cells. Heterologous DNA can be efficiently taken up by competent pneumococcal cells (for review *see* Lacks, 1977) but cannot integrate into the recipient chromosome as intact pieces of DNA. However, once degraded, donor label can be re-incorporated throughout the genome by *de novo* DNA synthesis. We have shown that this occurs also with homologous DNA when a cloned fragment is used as donor, more than 90% of the donor label being re-incorporated this way (Méjean and Claverys, 1984). Thus, after 10 min contact with donor DNA, competent cells were incubated for a further 15 min at 32°C to allow for re-incorporation of donor label.

### ENTRY OF END-LABELLED DNA MOLECULES

Construction of specifically labelled donor molecules (*Figure 4.1*) has been described (Méjean and Claverys, 1988). Analysis of end-labelled donor DNA molecules indicated that the labelled region was less than 100 bases (data not shown). Inefficient uptake of the 3'-end label was observed when using substrate 1 as donor in transformation, whereas the 5'-end label of substrate 2 entered competent cells efficiently. In the latter case, 20% of the total amount of donor DNA label was taken up by the cells. Such a figure is in good agreement with previous observations using natural donor DNA (Lacks, 1979; Saunders and Guild, 1981; our unpublished results). In contrast, the amount of 3' label retained by the cells was less than 0·5% of the input. After extraction and purification of recipient DNA, no counts above background levels were recovered (data not shown). The inefficient uptake of substrate 1 could be due to inhibition of binding and/or entry by the single-stranded region. Although the efficient uptake of substrate 2, which had a single-stranded region of similar length, argues against this hypothesis, the use of substrates 3 and 4 clearly demonstrated that this is not the case. These two linear double-stranded

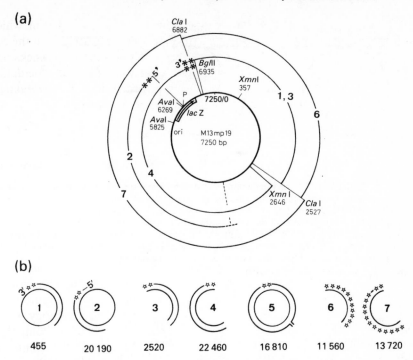

**Figure 4.1** Derivation and configuration of the substrates for study of end-labelled DNA molecules. (a) The various substrates are derived *in vitro* from M13mp19 viral strand DNA as described by Méjean and Claverys (1988). The internal circle represents the viral strand. External portions of circles indicate double-stranded regions. Restriction site positions are numbered according to Yanisch-Perron, Vieira and Messing (1985). P indicates the location of the 17-mer universal primer. Labelling is indicated by (∗). The single-stranded region in substrate 1 is from *Cla*I (2527) clockwise to (close to) *Bgl*II (6935). Substrate 3 is a double-stranded linear fragment retaining only the double-stranded region of substrate 1. Both substrates 1 and 3 are 3′-end labelled. Substrate 5 (not shown) is a fully double-stranded molecule specifically labelled in the immediate vicinity of the *Bgl*II site (6935) and harbouring a panhandle (Lechner, Engler and Richardson, 1983) close to the *Cla*I site (2527) (data not shown). Substrate 4 is a 5′-end labelled linear double-stranded fragment produced by digestion of substrate 5 with *Bgl*II and *Xmn*I (2646). Substrate 2 is 5′-end labelled; its double-stranded region is approximately 2840 bp long, going counterclockwise from the 5′-end of the 17-mer universal primer (6307). Substrates 6 and 7 are linear double-stranded molecules uniformly labelled on one strand. (b) Diagrammatic representation of each substrate. Upper line: substrates used as donors in transformation. Radioactive labelling is symbolized by (☆☆). Lower line: total number of cpm taken up by competent cells and incorporated into the recipient chromosome. 5 ml of competent cells were transformed in parallel experiments with each substrate. Donor DNA concentration was similar for all labelled donor molecules (10–20 ng) corresponding to a total amount of $10^5$ cpm.

molecules are labelled on one strand at the 3′- or 5′-end, respectively (*Figure 4.1*). Substrate 4 entered efficiently (22% uptake) whereas uptake of substrate 3 was only 2·5%. This result not only rules out the possibility of an inhibition of entry resulting from the presence of a long single-stranded region, but confirms that a 3′-end label does not enter the cells. As a last control, we used two linear double-stranded uniformly labelled fragments, substrates 6 and 7, corresponding to the double-stranded region present in substrate 1 (or 3) and substrate 4,

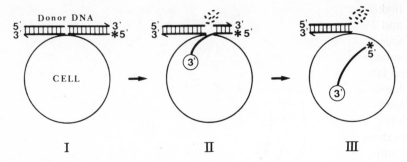

**Figure 4.2** Model for DNA entry in pneumococcal transformation. I: Formation of double-strand breaks upon binding on the cell surface and initiation of entry. II: Entry is initiated from a newly formed 3'-end (encircled) and proceeds linearly toward the 5'-end of the donor fragment. Some degradation (symbolized by small dashes) occurs concomittant with entry (Morrison and Guild, 1973a; Lacks and Greenberg, 1973). III: Entry of the donor strand has been completed and 5'-end label, indicated by ( ∗ ), is found within the cell. The remaining (double-stranded) part of the donor fragment could be released from the cell surface at any time during uptake or, alternatively, one strand could be taken up from its (newly formed) 3'-end.

respectively. Both were efficiently taken up by the cells, indicating that there is no bias against the uptake of the M13mp19 region present in substrates 1 and 3.

Our results, together with those suggesting a linear entry (Gabor and Hotchkiss, 1966) and those showing that donor DNA is broken at the cell surface (for a review *see* Lacks, 1977), lead to the model for entry shown in *Figure 4.2*. In this model, double-stranded donor DNA is nicked on binding at the cell surface. Double-strand breaks are subsequently introduced, possibly by cutting opposite to nicks introduced during binding (Lacks and Greenberg, 1976). Entry of a single strand then proceeds linearly from a newly formed 3'-end to the extremity of the donor fragment. For DNA molecules longer than those used here, the length of single-stranded fragments taken up by the cells is likely to be determined by the spacing between entry sites at the cell surface. This model is similar to the one published by Lacks and Greenberg (1976) except that entry proceeds 3' to 5' instead of 5' to 3'. It is worth noting that the very same polarity has been reported during transformation of the Gram-negative bacterium *Haemophilus influenzae*, at least for exit of donor DNA from the transformasome (a specialized membranous extension involved in DNA transport) into the cell (Barany, Kahn and Smith, 1983). It would be interesting to see if in *Bacillus subtilis*, another naturally transformable Gram-positive bacterium, the entry process shares the same polarity. This would not be surprising in the light of results suggesting similar breakage of donor DNA at the cell surface with linear entry (Lacks, 1977) and the accumulating evidence for the involvement of a nuclease in the uptake mechanism (Vosman *et al.*, 1987).

A prediction of this entry model is that extension of substrate 1 on the 3'-side by DNA synthesis would permit efficient uptake of the label. Indeed, substrate 5, which is directly derived from substrate 1 by synthesis using unlabelled dNTPs, was taken up 37-fold more efficiently than substrate 1 (*Figure 4.1b*).

The higher uptake observed with substrates 2 and 4 as compared to substrates 5, 6 and 7 is also consistent with a linear entry proceeding 3' to 5' from a nick introduced into the donor molecule upon binding. Indeed, any nick introduced into substrates 2 or 4 (on the labelled strand) is expected to lead to uptake of the 5'-end label, whereas for substrates 6 or 7, uptake following random nicking will leave outside the cell all label located 3' to the nick. Moreover, a single, randomly located, nick per molecule is expected to reduce the length average of donor fragments to half its initial value. Uptake counts observed with substrates 6 and 7 are in good agreement with this expectation. For substrate 5, nicks introduced within the region located 5' to the label will also be inefficient for uptake of the label, leading to lower uptake values than with substrates 2 and 4.

The uptake value of the 3'-end label observed with substrate 3, although indicating a rather inefficient entry, corresponded to real counts, incorporated into the recipient DNA (data not shown). This result is surprising in the light of the absence of detectable uptake of substrate 1. An interesting possibility is that for blunt-ended fragments one extremity of the donor DNA contacts an entry site at low frequency making the 3'-end directly available for initiation of uptake. This hypothesis would imply that an intact donor strand is sometimes taken up by the cells.

### Rate of DNA entry

DESIGN OF THE EXPERIMENT

Measurement of the uptake of radioactive material when using a linear donor molecule labelled at the 5'-end, on one strand only, should give an estimate of the rate of DNA entry. Indeed, taking into account that linear molecules shorter than 8 kb suffer a single nick upon binding (Morrison and Guild, 1972, 1973a) and that entry proceeds linearly from the newly introduced 3'-end to the 5'-extremity of the donor molecule (*see Figure 4.2*), the total amount of radioactive label taken up by the cells would be expected to increase linearly with time and reach a plateau value. The phase of linear increase would correspond to the uptake of longer and longer molecules in the population, at a constant rate, i.e. those molecules having suffered a nick closer and closer to the 3'-extremity of the donor. The time of arrival at a plateau would correspond to the time needed for the uptake of the longest molecules, i.e. almost full size donor molecules.

UPTAKE OF 5'-END LABELLED LINEAR MOLECULES

To prepare the 5'-end labelled substrate, a twofold excess of the universal 17-mer primer (6291–6307; United States Biochemical Corporation) was annealed to 0·2 µg of M13mp19 viral strand DNA (7250 nucleotides long) and the mixture was incubated for 5 min at 20°C with 5 units of T7 DNA polymerase (United States Biochemical Corporation), in the presence of 4 µCi of 5'-[$\alpha$-$^{32}$P]dATP (3000 Ci mM$^{-1}$; Amersham) and the three other unlabelled dNTPs (0·1 µM). The reaction was continued for 12 min at 37°C after addition

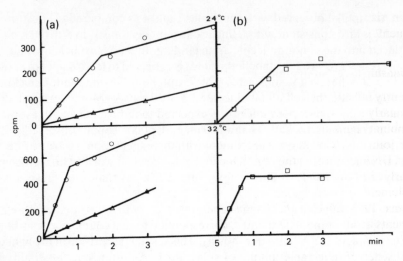

**Figure 4.3** Rate of DNA entry. Top, 24°C; bottom, 32°C. (a) ○, Uptake after contact between cells and DNA for 15 sec; △, uptake upon diluted conditions (*see* text). (b) Curves obtained by subtracting uptake values under diluted conditions from uptake values after 15 seconds' contact (*see* text).

of the four unlabelled dNTPs (20 μM). The product of the reaction was then linearized upon *Bgl*I digestion (unique site at position 6431, *see Figure 4.1a*).

Contact between competent cells and linear 5'-end labelled M13 DNA (2–4 ng ml$^{-1}$) was reduced to 15 sec. The cell suspension was then diluted to one-twentieth and the amount of radioactive label, taken up by the cells in a DNaseI-resistant form, was monitored at various time intervals. Results of experiments performed at 24°C (*Figure 4.3a*, top, ○) or 32°C (*Figure 4.3a*, bottom, ○) exhibit similar biphasic curves: a rapid increase was observed during 45 sec (32°C) or 105 sec (24°C), followed by a slow constant increase.

We interpret the first phase as the rapid uptake of DNA molecules bound to the cells during the 15 seconds' initial contact. We attribute the second phase to the continuous uptake of DNA molecules subsequently bound under one-twentieth diluted conditions. As a control, we measured the radioactive uptake using one-twentieth diluted conditions throughout (*Figure 4.3a*, top and bottom, △). This uptake proceeds linearly, without any plateau, in a strictly parallel fashion to the slow phase observed above. Upon subtraction of uptake values obtained in these control experiments, the curves obtained at both temperatures exhibit an excellent fit to the prediction of a linear increase followed by a true plateau (*Figure 4.3b*). From the time needed to reach the plateau we deduce an entry rate of 70 nucleotides/sec at 24°C and 150 nucleotides/sec at 32°C.

It is worth noting that the value we estimated at 24°C is in very good agreement with the value reported by Morrison and Guild (1973a). They estimated the entry rate to be 80 nucleotides/sec at 25°C by measuring (by sedimentation on alkaline sucrose gradients) the increase with time in the median size of fragments extracted from transformed cells after DNaseI treatment.

## Relationship to recombination

That entry introduces first the 3'-end of donor fragments into recipient cells is particularly interesting in the light of the reported polarity of RecA-catalysed recombination. A free 3'-homologous end has been shown to be required for stable joint molecule formation between linear single-stranded and circular duplex DNA (Konforti and Davis, 1987). In as much as RecA proteins function similarly in Gram-positive and Gram-negative bacteria, as shown by complementation studies between *B. subtilis* and *E. coli* (de Vos, de Vries and Venema, 1983; Love and Yasbin, 1986), the entry process may provide donor fragments in a form immediately available for homologous recombination.

## Acknowledgements

We are grateful to Walter Guild for sharing his unpublished results on the polarity of DNA entry. We thank Michael Chandler for editing the manuscript. This work was supported in part by a Contrat de Recherche Externe no. 861005 from the Institut National de la Santé et de la Recherche Médicale.

## References

BARANY, F. (1982). Transformation of *Streptococcus pneumoniae* by single-stranded plasmid-phage hybrid DNA. In *Microbiology – 1982* (D. Schlessinger, Ed.), pp. 125–129. American Society for Microbiology, Washington, DC.

BARANY, F., KAHN, M.E. AND SMITH, H.O. (1983). Directional transport and integration of donor DNA in *Haemophilus influenzae*. *Proceedings of the National Academy of Sciences of the United States of America* **80**, 7274–7278.

DE VOS, W.M., DE VRIES, S.C. AND VENEMA, G. (1983). Cloning and expression of the *Escherichia coli recA* gene in *Bacillus subtilis*. *Gene* **25**, 301–308.

GABOR, M. AND HOTCHKISS, R.D. (1966). Manifestation of linear organization in molecules of pneumococcal transforming DNA. *Proceedings of the National Academy of Sciences of the United States of America* **56**, 1441–1448.

KONFORTI, B.B. AND DAVIS, R.W. (1987). 3' homologous free ends are required for stable joint molecule formation by the RecA and single-stranded binding proteins of *Escherichia coli*. *Proceedings of the National Academy of Sciences of the United States of America* **84**, 690–694.

LACKS, S.A. (1977). Binding and entry of DNA in bacterial transformation. In *Microbial interactions* (J.L. Reissig, Ed.), pp. 179–232. Chapman and Hall, London.

LACKS, S.A. (1979). Uptake of circular deoxyribonucleic acid and mechanism of deoxyribonucleic acid transport in genetic transformation of *Streptococcus pneumoniae*. *Journal of Bacteriology* **138**, 404–409.

LACKS, S.A. AND GREENBERG, B. (1973). Competence for deoxyribonucleic acid uptake and deoxyribonuclease action external to cells in the genetic transformation of *Diplococcus pneumoniae*. *Journal of Bacteriology* **114**, 152–163.

LACKS, S.A. AND GREENBERG, B. (1976). Single-strand breakage on binding of DNA to cells in the genetic transformation of *Diplococcus pneumoniae*. *Journal of Molecular Biology* **101**, 255–275.

LACKS, S.A. AND NEUBERGER, M. (1975). Membrane location of a deoxyribonuclease implicated in the genetic transformation of *Diplococcus pneumoniae*. *Journal of Bacteriology* **124**, 1321–1329.

LACKS, S.A., GREENBERG, B. AND NEUBERGER, M. (1974). Role of a nuclease in the genetic transformation of *Diplococcus pneumoniae*. *Proceedings of the National Academy of Sciences of the United States of America* **71**, 2305–2309.

LACKS, S.A., GREENBERG, B. AND NEUBERGER, M. (1975). Identification of a deoxyribonuclease implicated in genetic transformation of *Diplococcus pneumoniae*. *Journal of Bacteriology* **123**, 222—232.

LECHNER, R.L., ENGLER, M.J. AND RICHARDSON, C.C. (1983). Characterization of strand displacement synthesis catalyzed by bacteriophage T7 DNA polymerase. *Journal of Biological Chemistry* **258**, 11174–11184.

LOVE, P.E. AND YASBIN, R.E. (1986). Induction of the *Bacillus subtilis* SOS-like response by *Escherichia coli* RecA protein. *Proceedings of the National Academy of Sciences of the United State of America* **83**, 5204–5208.

MÉJEAN, V. AND CLAVERYS, J.P. (1984). Use of a cloned fragment to analyze the fate of donor DNA in transformation of *Streptococcus pneumoniae*. *Journal of Bacteriology* **158**, 1175–1178.

MÉJEAN V. AND CLAVERYS, J.P. (1988). Polarity of DNA entry in transformation of *Streptococcus pneumoniae*. *Molecular and General Genetics* **213**, 444–448.

MORRISON, D.A. AND GUILD, W.R. (1972). Transformation and deoxyribonucleic acid size: extent of degradation on entry varies with size. *Journal of Bacteriology* **112**, 1157–1168.

MORRISON, D.A. AND GUILD, W.R. (1973a). Breakage prior to entry of donor DNA in pneumococcus transformation. *Biochimica et Biophysica Acta* **299**, 545–556.

MORRISON, D.A. AND GUILD, W.R. (1973b). Structure of deoxyribonucleic acid on the cell surface during uptake by pneumococcus. *Journal of Bacteriology* **115**, 1055–1062.

ROSENTHAL, A.L. AND LACKS, S.A. (1980). Complex structure of the membrane nuclease of *Streptococcus pneumoniae* revealed by two-dimensional electrophoresis. *Journal of Molecular Biology* **141**, 133–146.

SAUNDERS, C.W. AND GUILD, W.R. (1981). Pathway of transformation in pneumococcus: open circular and linear molecules are active. *Journal of Bacteriology* **146**, 517–526.

VOSMAN, B., KOOISTRA, J., OLIJVE, J. AND VENEMA, G. (1987). Cloning in *Escherichia coli* of the gene specifying the DNA-entry nuclease of *Bacillus subtilis*. *Gene* **52**, 175–183.

YANISCH-PERRON, C., VIEIRA, J. AND MESSING, J. (1985). Improved M13 phage cloning vectors and host strains: nucleotide sequences of the M13mp18 and pUC19 vectors. *Gene* **33**, 103–119.

# 5

# Isolation and Characterization of *Bacillus subtilis* Genes Involved in Competence*

BEN VOSMAN, JAN KOOISTRA AND GERARD VENEMA

*Department of Genetics, University of Groningen, Kerklaan 30, 9751 NN Haren (Gn), The Netherlands*

## Introduction

In transformation of *Streptococcus pneumoniae* and *Bacillus subtilis*, DNA enters into the cell in a single-stranded form. The uptake of one strand is accompanied by the release of an equal amount of acid-soluble DNA breakdown products, suggesting digestion of the DNA strand complementary to the one which is internalized (Dubnau and Cirigliano, 1972; Morrison and Guild, 1973). Nucleases involved in the entry of donor DNA into competent *S. pneumoniae* and *B. subtilis* cells were identified (Rosenthal and Lacks, 1980; Mulder and Venema, 1982b). Comparison of the nuclease activities present in competent and non-competent wild-type cells, as well as analysis of nuclease activity present in DNA-entry-deficient mutants, led to the identification of at least three competence-specific nuclease activities in *B. subtilis*, with relative molecular masses of 14 kDa, 17 kDa and 28 kDa (Mulder and Venema, 1982a, 1982b; Barberio *et al.*, 1985).

Smith *et al.* (1983, 1984) have isolated a 75 kDa protein complex, which consisted of two subunits of the 17 kDa nuclease and two subunits of an 18 kDa protein. A mutant lacking the 18 kDa protein was found to be DNA-binding deficient (Smith, De Vos and Bron, 1983; Smith *et al.*, 1983). This observation led to the speculation that the 18 kDa protein might be involved in the binding of DNA to competent cells.

To study the involvement of the *B. subtilis* competence-specific nuclease and the 18 kDa protein in transformation, the genes specifying these proteins were cloned. Further, mutants were constructed in which the respective genes were interrupted in order to examine the effect of the 18 kDa protein and nuclease deficiencies on binding and entry of DNA.

---

* Some of the results given here have been published in *Journal of Bacteriology* **170**, 3703–3710.

**Materials and methods**

The materials and methods were as described previously (Vosman *et al.*, 1986, 1987, 1988).

**Results and discussion**

ISOLATION OF COMPETENCE-DEFICIENT MUTANTS

By means of insertional mutagenesis with plasmid pHV60 (Michel, Niaudet and Ehrlich, 1983), *B. subtilis* transformation-deficient mutants were isolated. In a number of these mutants, which were as resistant to mytomycin-C as the wild type, the mutation was linked to the *aroI* marker. Some of these mutants lacked the competence-specific 17 kDa nuclease activity, suggesting that the gene encoding this nuclease was located near to the *aroI* region (Vosman *et al.*, 1987).

CLONING OF THE GENE ENCODING THE 17 kDa NUCLEASE

With the aid of one of the competence-deficient mutants carrying the mutation linked to the *aroI* region, a plasmid was isolated which contained a chromosomal DNA insert of 2·2 kbp (Vosman *et al.*, 1987). This plasmid, designated pGVM465, was used as a probe to screen a *B. subtilis* genome bank in phage λEMBL4. When *Escherichia coli* cells were infected with the recombinant phages, hybridizing with pGVM465, 14 kDa and 17 kDa nuclease activities were detected in the *E. coli* cell extracts, suggesting that the chromosomal DNA insert in the recombinant phages contained the gene encoding the competence-specific 17 kDa nuclease. The 14 kDa nuclease may be derived from the 17 kDa nuclease, as suggested previously (Smith *et al.*, 1984). Subcloning fragments of the chromosomal DNA, into plasmid pGV1 (Vosman *et al.*, 1987), showed that a 700 bp *Eco*RI–*Pst*I fragment specified the 17 kDa nuclease. Further, it was shown that this *Eco*RI–*Pst*I fragment lacked promoter of the nuclease gene, and that the gene was transcribed from the promoter of the *lacZ* gene in pGV1 (Vosman *et al.*, 1987).

In order to clone the 17 kDa nuclease gene preceded by its own promoter, a *Hind*III–*Eco*RI DNA fragment, hybridizing with the 700 bp *Eco*RI–*Pst*I fragment, was subcloned from the recombinant phage into pGV1 in such a way that the nuclease gene was in the opposite orientation to the *lacZ* promoter. This resulted in plasmid pGV290 (*Figure 5.1*). In lysates prepared from strain JM83 (Vieira and Messing, 1982), carrying plasmid pGV290, nuclease activities were present at 14 kDa and 17 kDa positions. This suggested that the additional DNA fragment cloned (the H–B–P–P fragment in *Figure 5.1*) specified promoter activity in *E. coli*.

COMPLEMENTATION AND CHARACTERIZATION OF A NUCLEASE-DEFICIENT MUTANT

A nuclease-deficient mutant was constructed to examine whether a plasmid

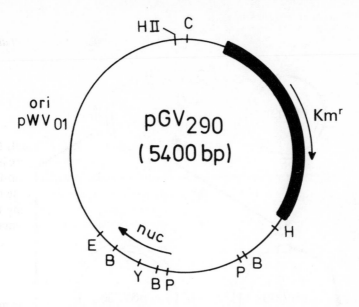

**Figure 5.1** Physical map of plasmid pGV290. Arrows indicate the direction of transcription of the kanamycin resistance (Km^r) and the nuclease (*nuc*) gene, ori = Origin of replication. C, H, HII, B, P, Y and E represent *Cla*I, *Hin*dIII, *Hin*dII, *Bcl*I, *Pst*I, *Bal*I and *Eco*RI sites, respectively.

carrying the nuclease gene could complement this mutant, and to study the effect of nuclease-deficiency on transformation and entry of DNA. The mutant was obtained by transformation of a *B. subtilis* wild-type strain with a linearized plasmid, carrying the nuclease gene. This plasmid was modified, however, by the insertion of a *Dra*I fragment, containing a chloramphenicol resistance (Cm^r) gene derived from pC194, into the *Bal*I site of the nuclease gene (*Figure 5.1*). This plasmid, designated pGV370, can replicate in *E. coli* but not in *B. subtilis*. The integration of the linearized pGV370 into the chromosome, requiring a replacement recombination event, was monitored by Cm^r and resulted in the isolation of a nuclease-deficient transformant designated 8G370 (*Figure 5.2*).

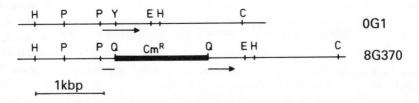

**Figure 5.2** Relevant part of the chromosome of the wild-type (0G1) and mutant 8G370. The mutant was constructed as outlined in the text. The arrows indicate the nuclease gene. H, B, P, Y, E and C represent *Hin*dIII, *Bcl*I, *Pst*I, *Bal*I, *Eco*RI and *Cla*I sites, respectively. Q represents the *Bal*I/*Dra*I fusion resulting from insertion of a *Dra*I fragment containing the chloramphenicol resistance (Cm^r) marker from pC194, into the *Bal*I site of the nuclease gene.

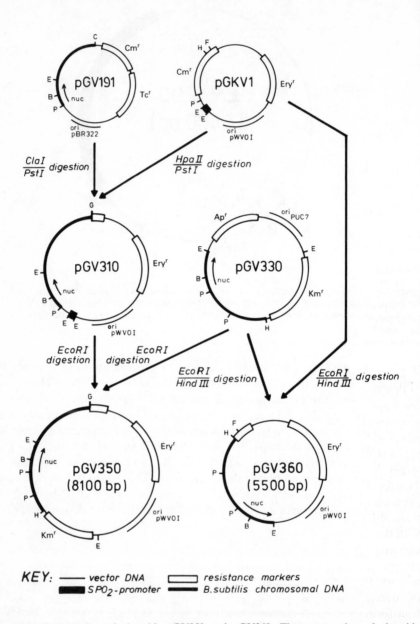

**Figure 5.3** Construction of plasmids pGV350 and pGV360. The construction of plasmids pGV191 and pGV330 has been described previously (Vosman *et al.*, 1987, 1988). Ery^r and Km^r represent erythromycin and kanamycin resistance genes. E, B, P, H and F represent *Eco*RI, *Bal*I, *Pst*I, *Hind*II and *Hpa*II sites, respectively. G indicates the *Cla*I/*Hpa*II fusion point of the chromosomal *Cla*I site with the *Hpa*II site of pGKV1 (Van der Vossen, Kok and Venema, 1985).

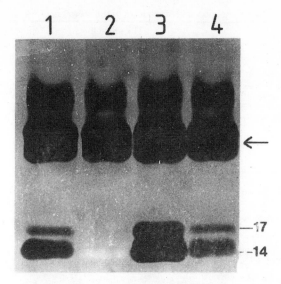

**Figure 5.4** Formation of 14 kDa and 17 kDa nuclease activities in cells carrying the nuclease gene on the plasmids pGV350 and pGV360. The activities were all obtained from membranes of cells subjected to the competence regimen. Lanes: 1, 7G224(pGKV1); 2, 7G370(pGKV1); 3, 7G370(pGV350); 4, 7G370(pGV360). Nuclease activities were detected on gels as described previously (Vosman *et al.*, 1987). 10 μg of protein was applied to the gel. The positions of the 14 kDa and 17 kDa nucleases are indicated. The activity indicated by the arrow is due to DNaseI, routinely added for the isolation of the membrane vesicles.

To examine complementation of 8G370, use was made of the plasmids pGV350 and pGV360 (*Figure 5.3*), both containing a fragment with the nuclease gene. Plasmid pGV350 contains a larger chromosomal DNA fragment downstream of the nuclease gene than pGV360. To preclude the integration of these plasmids directly into the chromosome, the *recE4* mutation was introduced in strain 8G370, giving strain 7G370. The nuclease activities of strain 7G370, carrying plasmids with and without the nuclease gene, were examined on a nuclease detection gel (Vosman *et al.*, 1987). The results, presented in *Figure 5.4*, showed that the 14 kDa and 17 kDa nuclease activities were absent in strain 7G370 but were restored in strains carrying the plasmids with the nuclease gene. *Table 5.1* shows the effect of the presence of a plasmid carrying the nuclease gene, on the nuclease-deficient mutant 8G370. In the absence of the plasmid the mutant still showed 5% residual transforming activity, suggesting that an alternative, minor pathway may exist for the entry of donor DNA. The presence of plasmid pGV350 largely restored transformability and entry of DNA of the mutant (*Table 5.2*).

**Table 5.1**  Transformation frequency of partial diploids

| Strain | Transformation frequency (%)* |
|---|---|
| 8G5(pGKV1) | 1·0 |
| 8G370(pGKV1) | 0·05 |
| 8G370(pGV350) | 0·37 |

* % = (Number of *trp*[+] transformants/total count) × 100. The values are the means of three independent transformations.

**Table 5.2**  Total association, entry and breakdown of transforming DNA

| Strain | $^3$H-radioactivity ($\times 10^6$ cpm/cfu) | | |
| --- | --- | --- | --- |
| | Total association* | Entry† | Breakdown‡ |
| 7G370(pGKV1) | 316 | 9 | 10 |
| 7G370(pGV350) | 164 | 54 | 25 |

\* Total amount of radioactivity associated with cells both sensitive and resistant to DNaseI.
† Amount of DNaseI–resistant radioactivity associated with the cells.
‡ Acid-soluble radioactivity in transformation mixture, derived from transforming DNA.

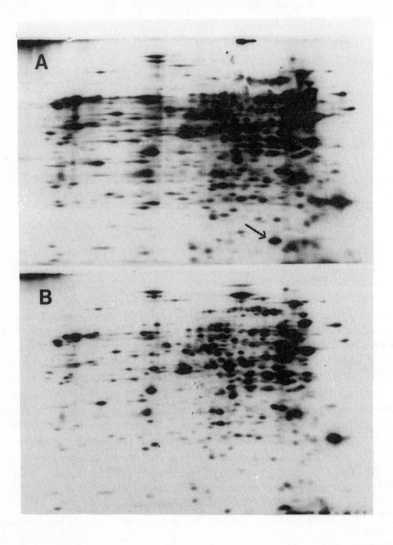

**Figure 5.5**  Two-dimensional gel electrophoresis of [$^{35}$S] methionine-labelled proteins of the wild-type 8G5 strain (A), and mutant 8G370(B). Both strains were subjected to the competence regimen. The 18 kDa protein is marked by the arrow. Isoelectrofocusing (IEF) was from the left (basic) to the right (acidic).

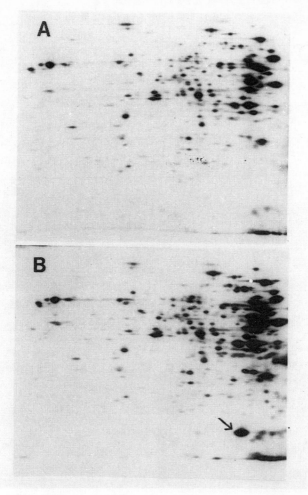

**Figure 5.6**   Two-dimensional gel electrophoresis of [³⁵S] methionine-labelled proteins obtained from competent cultures of strain 7G370 containing plasmids pGKV1 (A) and pGV350 (B). The 18 kDa protein is marked by the arrow. IEF was from the left (basic) to the right (acidic).

CLONING OF THE GENE ENCODING THE 18 kDa PROTEIN

The 18 kDa protein was detected by two-dimensional gel electrophoresis of cell extracts of competent cultures. In *Figure 5.5A*, the arrow indicates the position of the 18 kDa protein. *Figure 5.5B* shows the protein pattern of cell extracts of the nuclease-deficient mutant 8G370. Apparently, interruption of the nuclease gene also prevented the production of the 18 kDa protein, suggesting that the gene encoding the 18 kDa protein is in the same operon as the 17 kDa nuclease gene, and that it is located downstream of the nuclease gene. This was corroborated by the introduction of plasmid pGV350 (*Figure 5.3*), into the nuclease-deficient mutant. As shown in *Figure 5.6*, the presence of pGV350 restores production of the 18 kDa protein, indicating that the chromosomal DNA fragment on pGV350 contained the gene encoding the 18 kDa protein.

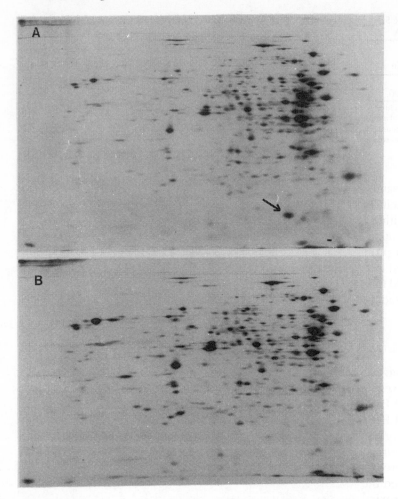

**Figure 5.7** Two-dimensional gel electrophoresis of [³⁵S] methionine-labelled proteins of the wild-type 8G5 strain(A) and the mutant 8G206(B). Both strains were subjected to the standard competence regimen. The 18 kDa protein is marked by an arrow. IEF was from the left (basic) to the right (acidic).

## CONSTRUCTION AND CHARACTERIZATION OF A MUTANT DEFICIENT IN THE 18 kDa PROTEIN

An 18 kDa protein-deficient mutant was constructed by transformation of a 8G5 (wild-type) strain with a linearized plasmid unable to replicate in *B. subtilis* and carrying the chromosomal P–B–E–G fragment present in pGV350 (*Figure 5.3*). An *Eco*RI fragment, containing the kanamycin-resistance (Km$^r$) gene derived from plasmid pPJ1, was inserted into the *Eco*RI site in the chromosomal fragment (Peeters *et al.*, 1988). Transformation with this plasmid resulted in strain 8G206, in which the 18 kDa protein was absent (*Figure 5.7*). The total amount of donor DNA associated with the mutant was approximately

**Table 5.3**  Transformation, total DNA association, DNA entry and breakdown of transforming DNA

| Strain | Transformation(%)* | $^3$H-radioactivity ($\times 10^6$ cpm/cfu) | | |
|---|---|---|---|---|
| | | Total association† | Entry‡ | Breakdown§ |
| 8G5 | 0·80 | 732 | 41 | 44 |
| 8G206 | 0·22 | 672 | 35 | 42 |

\* (Number of *trp*+ transformants/total count) × 100.
† Total amount of radioactivity associated with cells both sensitive and resistant to DNaseI.
‡ Amount of DNaseI–resistant radioactivity associated with the cells.
§ Acid-soluble radioactivity in the transformation mixture, derived from transforming DNA.

the same as with the wild-type strain (*Table 5.3*), indicating that the 18 kDa protein was not involved in donor DNA binding, as was assumed previously (Smith, De Vos and Bron, 1983). The transformation frequency of the mutant was approximately fourfold lower than the wild type, suggesting that the 18 kDa protein may have some function in transformation. Since this protein could inhibit the 17 kDa nuclease (Vosman *et al.*, 1988), the 18 kDa protein could function by protecting the entering donor DNA strand against excessive degradation.

CONSTRUCTION AND USE OF AN 18 kDa PROTEIN-lacZ FUSION

To investigate the expression of the 18 kDa protein in competent cells, a fusion between the N-terminus of this protein and β-galactosidase, specified by pMLB1034 (Silhavy, Bergman and Enquist, 1984), was constructed by cleaving pMLB1034 with *Eco*RI and *Sca*I and ligating it to *Hind*II–*Eco*RI-cleaved pGV290 (*Figure 5.1*). *E. coli* strain MC1000 was transformed with the ligation mixture and Km$^r$ transformants were selected on plates containing 5-bromo-4-chloro-3-indolyl-β-D-galactopyranoside (X-gal). The blue colonies all contained the same plasmid, designated pGV322. MC1000 (pGV322) produced approximately 1250 U β-galactosidase (Miller, 1982). Competent cells of strain 8G5 were transformed with plasmid pGV322, resulting in strain 8G322. Since pGV322 cannot replicate in *B. subtilis*, the plasmid must have been integrated into the chromosome by a Campbell-like mechanism. This was confirmed by Southern hybridization.

No β-galactosidase activity could be detected in colonies of strain 8G322 growing on TY-plates containing X-gal. When the strain was grown in TY-medium, which does not result in competence development, no β-galactosidase was produced. The strain produced β-galactosidase only when it was grown to competence. Separation of the cells by renografin gradient centrifugation (Joenje, Konings and Venema, 1975) showed that cells from the top of the gradient were enriched in β-galactosidase activity (transformation frequency: 0·5%; 74 U β-galactosidase production), whereas cells from the bottom of the gradient (transformation: 0·13%) produced only 26 U β-galactosidase. This indicates that, although the separation of competent from non-competent cells had not been very efficient, the β-galactosidase was produced mainly by the competent fraction.

To obtain further evidence that the fusion protein was competence specific, the mutation present in *B. subtilis* strain E26 which blocks competence development completely (Vosman *et al.*, 1986), was introduced into the 8G322 background, resulting in strain 8G322E26. The mutation in strain E26 strongly reduced the expression of both the 18 kDa protein and the nucleases. When β-galactosidase activity produced in competent cells of strain 8G322 was compared to that in strain 8G322E26, subjected to the competence regimen, it was found that strain 8G322 produced 23 U (transformation: 0·8%), whereas strain 8G322E26 produced only 3·9 U (transformation absent). This result clearly indicates that this mutation, which inhibits competence development, but is not linked to the genes encoding the nuclease and 18 kDa protein (Vosman *et al.*, 1986, 1987), affected the expression of the 18 kDa protein.

## References

BARBERIO, C., COPPOLECCHIA, R., MASTROMEI, G. AND POLSINELLI, M. (1985). Competence proteins in *Bacillus subtilis com* mutants. *Biochimica et Biophysica Acta* **842**, 184–188.

DUBNAU, D. AND CIRIGLIANO, C. (1972). Fate of transforming DNA following uptake by competent *Bacillus subtilis*. *Journal of Molecular Biology* **64**, 9–29.

JOENJE, H., KONINGS, W.M. AND VENEMA, G. (1975). Interactions between exogenous deoxyribonucleic acid and membrane vesicles isolated from competent and non-competent *Bacillus subtilis*. *Journal of Bacteriology* **121**, 771–776.

MICHEL, B., NIAUDET, B. AND EHRLICH, S.D. (1983). Intermolecular recombination during transformation of *Bacillus subtilis* competent cells by monomeric and dimeric plasmids. *Plasmid* **10**, 1–10.

MILLER, J.H.(1982). *Experiments in Molecular Genetics*. Cold Spring Harbor Laboratory. Cold Spring Harbor, New York.

MORRISON, D.A. AND GUILD, W.R. (1973). Breakage prior to entry of donor DNA in *Pneumococcus* transformation. *Biochimica et Biophysica Acta* **299**, 545–556.

MULDER, J.A. AND VENEMA, G. (1982a). Isolation and partial characterization of *Bacillus subtilis* mutants impaired in DNA entry. *Journal of Bacteriology* **150**, 260–268.

MULDER, J.A. AND VENEMA, G. (1982b). Transformation-deficient mutants of *Bacillus subtilis* impaired in competence-specific nuclease activities. *Journal of Bacteriology* **152**, 166–174.

PEETERS, B.P.H., DE BOER, J.H., BRON, S. AND VENEMA, G. (1988). Structural plasmid instability in *Bacillus subtilis:* Effects of direct and inverted repeats. *Molecular and General Genetics* **212**, 450–458.

ROSENTHAL, A.L. AND LACKS, S.A. (1980). Complex structure of the membrane nuclease of *Streptococcus pneumoniae* revealed by two-dimensional electrophoresis. *Journal of Molecular Biology* **141**, 133–146.

SILHAVY, T.J., BERGMAN, M.L. AND ENQUIST, L.W. (1984). *Experiments with Gene Fusions*. Cold Spring Harbor Laboratory. Cold Spring Harbor, New York.

SMITH, H., DE VOS, W.M. AND BRON, S. (1983). Transformation in *Bacillus subtilis*. Properties of DNA-binding-deficient mutants. *Journal of Bacteriology* **153**, 12–20.

SMITH, H., WIERSMA, K., BRON, S. AND VENEMA, G. (1983). Transformation in *Bacillus subtilis*: purification and partial characterization of a membrane-bound DNA-binding protein. *Journal of Bacteriology* **156**, 101–108.

SMITH, H., WIERSMA, K., BRON, S. AND VENEMA, G. (1984). Transformation in *Bacillus subtilis*: a 75,000-dalton protein complex is involved in binding and entry of donor DNA. *Journal of Bacteriology* **157**, 733–738.

VAN DER VOSSEN, J.M.B.M., KOK, J. AND VENEMA, G. (1985). Construction of cloning, promoter-screening, and terminator-screening shuttle vectors for *Bacillus subtilis* and *Streptococcus lactis*. *Applied and Environmental Microbiology* **50**, 540–542.

VIEIRA, J. AND MESSING, J. (1982). The pUC plasmids, an M13 *mp7*-derived system for insertion mutagenesis and sequencing with synthetic universal primers. *Gene* **19**, 259–268.

VOSMAN, B., KOOISTRA, J., OLIJVE, J. AND VENEMA, G. (1986). Integration of vector-containing *Bacillus subtilis* chromosomal DNA by a Campbell-like mechanism. *Molecular and General Genetics* **204**, 524–531.

VOSMAN, B., KOOISTRA, J., OLIJVE, J. AND VENEMA, G. (1987). Cloning in *Escherichia coli* of the gene specifying the DNA-entry nuclease of *Bacillus subtilis*. *Gene* **52**, 175–183.

VOSMAN, B., KUIKEN, G., KOOISTRA, J. AND VENEMA, G. (1988). Transformation in *Bacillus subtilis*: Involvement of the 17-kilodalton DNA-entry nuclease and the competence-specific 18-kilodalton protein. *Journal of Bacteriology* **170**, 3703–3710.

# 6

# Isolation and Characterization of Tn*917*-Generated Competence Mutants of *Bacillus subtilis*

GIORGIO MASTROMEI, CLAUDIA BARBERIO,
STEFANIA PISTOLESI AND MARIO POLSINELLI

*Department of Animal Biology and Genetics, v. Romana 17, 50125 Firenze, Italy*

The genetic transformation of *Bacillus subtilis* requires a physiological state known as competence (Young and Spizizen, 1961). Several competence (*com*) mutants have been identified and partially characterized (Mulder and Venema, 1982; Smith, de Vos and Bron, 1983; Fani *et al.*, 1984; Hahn, Albano and Dubnau, 1987); however, it is likely that many more genes have to be identified. In our work we have isolated and mapped several new competence mutations obtained both by chemical mutagenesis and insertional mutagenesis with the transposon Tn*917*.

In a previous paper (Fani *et al.*, 1984), we described the isolation and characterization of *B. subtilis com* mutants obtained by chemical mutagenesis. The mapping of *com* mutations obtained by this procedure was tedious and in several cases ambiguous results were obtained because of the difficulty of scoring the Com⁻ phenotype. For this reason new mutants were isolated by insertional mutagenesis using the transposon Tn*917* carried by the plasmid pTV1 (Youngman, Perkins and Losick, 1983), which also contains a *cat* gene and a *B. subtilis* temperature-sensitive origin of DNA replication. The transposon carries the *erm* gene and, therefore, the site of insertion can be mapped easily by screening for erythromycin and lincomycin resistance.

The mutants were obtained by selecting for erythromycin resistance at 49°C; at this temperature pTV1 does not replicate and only the cells in which Tn*917* has transposed into the chromosome will grow. The mutants were screened for their capacity to be transformed on solid medium, and 68 transformation-deficient strains were isolated. These strains were further characterized by measuring their transformation and transduction frequencies in liquid medium. By this procedure we isolated 23 *com* mutants with transformation frequencies $10^2$–$10^6$ times lower than the parental strain. Of the 23 *com* mutants isolated, 14 had the transposon inserted between *purB* and *tre12*, as in the case of the *com-14* mutation (*Figure 6.1*). The high number of *com* mutations in this region could be due to the involvement of more than one gene in competence development or to a preferential insertion of Tn*917*.

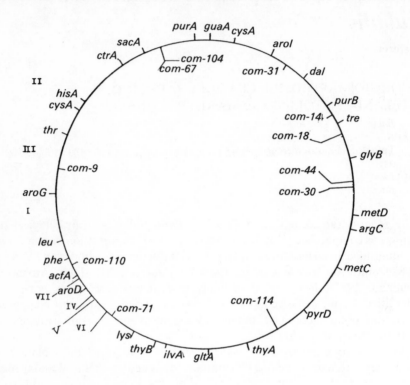

**Figure 6.1** *Bacillus subtilis* chromosome map showing the position of the *com* loci. The numbers from I to VII refer to the different classes of *com* mutations mapped by Hahn, Albano and Dubnau (1987).

Two other new *com* genes have been identified by the *com-18* and *com-114* mutations, while *com-44* and *com-67* mapped in the same area as the previously described *com-30* and *com-104* mutations, respectively (*Figure 6.1*). The *com-110* mutation mapped in a location which might be the same as, or close to, that of the class VII mutants described by Hahn, Albano and Dubnau (1987). However, it must be noted that *com-110* was not cotransduced with the *lys-1* marker and that the colonies were not sticky as in the case of the class VII mutants.

Only two of the mutants, *com-67* and *com-114*, could bind and take up DNA, although less efficiently than the parental strain. This might be expected since these two strains had a transformation frequency higher than that of the other mutants. There are also indications that the *com* genes located between *sacA* and *purA* might be involved in the entry of the transforming DNA.

*Figure 6.1* gives the position of all the known *com* loci which have been mapped (Fani *et al.*, 1984; Hahn, Albano and Dubnau, 1987). All these data concur to give the idea that many genes are involved in competence development and that they are spread all over the chromosome.

## References

FANI, R., MASTROMEI, G., POLSINELLI, M. AND VENEMA, G. (1984). Isolation and characterization of *Bacillus subtilis* mutants altered in competence. *Journal of Bacteriology* **157**, 152–157.

HAHN, J., ALBANO, M. AND DUBNAU, D. (1987). Isolation and characterization of Tn*917lac*-generated competence mutants of *Bacillus subtilis*. *Journal of Bacteriology* **169**, 3104–3109.

MULDER, J.A. AND VENEMA, G. (1982). Isolation and partial characterization of *Bacillus subtilis* mutants impaired in DNA entry. *Journal of Bacteriology* **150**, 260–268.

SMITH, H., DE VOS, W. AND BRON, S. (1983). Transformation in *Bacillus subtilis*: properties of DNA binding deficient mutants. *Journal of Bacteriology* **153**, 12–20.

YOUNG, F.E. AND SPIZIZEN, J. (1961). Physiological and genetic factors affecting transformation of *Bacillus subtilis*. *Journal of Bacteriology* **81**, 823–829.

YOUNGMAN, P.J., PERKINS, J.B. AND LOSICK, R. (1983). Genetic transposition and insertional mutagenesis in *Bacillus subtilis* with *Streptococcus faecalis* transposon Tn*917*. *Proceedings of the National Academy of Sciences of the United States of America*, **80**, 2305–2309.

# 7

# Electroporation: A General Method for Transformation of Gram-negative Bacteria

STEFAN FIEDLER, ANITA FRIESENEGGER
AND REINHARD WIRTH

*Lehrstuhl für Mikrobiologie der Universität München, Maria-Ward-Straße 1a, D-8000 München 19, FRG*

## Introduction

Transformation, i.e. the introduction of plasmid DNA into bacteria, is probably the most important method for genetic analyses of bacteria. To date, however, only a limited number of bacterial species are transformable, either because they show natural competence (e.g. *Haemophilus influenzae, Streptococcus pneumoniae* and *Bacillus subtilis*) or because they are susceptible to special 'treatments' inducing competence (e.g. the $CaCl_2$ method for transformation of *Escherichia coli*, or the polyethylene glycol method for *B. subtilis*). The ability to transform bacteria is, however, still the exception, and not the rule.

An alternative method for transformation might be the use of an electric current to create distortions in the cell membranes, allowing the uptake of DNA. The methods for electric field-induced fusion of membranes—termed electrofusion—and the generation of small localized holes in biological membranes—termed electroporation—were first developed for eukaryotic cells by Zimmermann and colleagues (*see* Zimmermann, 1982). Adaptation of these methods to bacterial systems was undertaken only recently; the available data (*see*, for example, Chassy and Flickinger, 1987; Harlander, 1987; MacNeil, 1987; Fiedler and Wirth, 1988) led us to believe that electroporation should be a very promising alternative method for transformation of bacterial cells. Here we report our data on a systematic evaluation of susceptibility of various Gram-negative bacteria to electroporation. The results indicate that a high proportion of Gram-negative species can be transformed by electroporation.

*Genetic Transformation and Expression*
© Intercept Ltd, PO Box 716, Andover, Hants, SP10 1YG, UK

**Material and methods**

APPARATUS FOR ELECTROPORATION

Throughout this study the Gene Pulser™ electroporation apparatus from Bio-Rad Laboratories was used. This is a capacitor discharge device producing exponential declining pulses of a field strength between 125 and 6250 V cm$^{-1}$. The duration of the pulse depends on the conductivity of the buffer and the choice of capacitor. The time needed for a given pulse to decline to 37% from its initial setting is displayed by the apparatus as the 'time constant'. The pulses are delivered to a sterile, disposable plastic cuvette with the electrodes set 4 mm apart.

BACTERIAL STRAINS AND PLASMID

Strains characterized as wild type were isolated at the University of München in January/February 1988 from natural sources, stored for no longer than 4 weeks at 4°C and then used for electroporation. Strains characterized as lab strains came originally from natural sources and were routinely subcultured in rich media for at least 1 year before use. Strains designated DSM were obtained from the Deutsche Sammlung für Mikroorganismen (DSM, Braunschweig, FRG) and represent in most cases the respective type strain.

The plasmid used throughout our studies was pKT231 (Bagdasarian *et al.*, 1981). This plasmid belongs to the *inc*Q/P4 incompatibility group, has a broad host-range and expresses kanamycin and streptomycin resistance in most Gram-negative bacteria.

ELECTROPORATION PROTOCOL

Bacteria were grown in liquid media at 30°C or 37°C to mid-logarithmic phase (optical density of 0·3 at 600 nm) with shaking, washed once in transformation buffer (300 mM sucrose, 7 mM sodium phosphate pH 7·4, 1 mM MgCl$_2$) and resuspended in transformation buffer to yield $10^9$ cfu ml$^{-1}$. 1 ml of the cell suspension was mixed with 200 ng pKT231 and incubated for 30 min on ice. An aliquot was removed for controls (absolute number of input cells and transformation rate without electroporation) and 800 µl of the mixture subjected to electroporation (one pulse at 6250 V cm$^{-1}$ using the 25 µF capacitor) in a cooled cuvette. The mixture was kept for 20 min on ice, diluted in the original growth medium, incubated at 30°C/37°C for 45 min and various amounts were plated on original medium plates containing 50 µg kanamycin ml$^{-1}$. Growth conditions (media, temperature) were as suggested by DSM. Colony hybridization was performed as described earlier (Maniatis, Fritsch and Sambrook, 1982) using $^{32}$P nick-translated pKT231 DNA and Nytran nylon membrane (Schleicher & Schüll).

**Results and discussion**

The protocol used throughout this study was developed by us (Fiedler and

Wirth, 1988) for *E. coli*. It is an optimized procedure which results in at least the same transformation efficiency, expressed as transformants per µg input plasmid DNA, as the $CaCl_2$ method for *E. coli*. It might well be the case that transformation efficiencies reported below can be increased several orders of magnitude by optimizing the method for the respective strains (indeed our original protocol for *E. coli* yielded $10^3$ transformants per µg pKT231 compared to $10^5$ transformants per µg pKT231 for the optimized protocol). For our purposes, namely testing susceptibility of Gram-negative bacteria to electroporation, such as optimization was not necessary. We would not be surprised if optimized procedures result in much higher transformation efficiencies.

The transformation efficiencies for a variety of Gram-negative bacteria are shown in *Table 7.1*; transformants were identified by their ability to grow on solid media containing 50 µg kanamycin $ml^{-1}$ (the parent strains showed no growth under these conditions). For each experiment, 6–12 randomly chosen

**Table 7.1** Susceptibility of various Gram-negative bacteria to electroporation with plasmid pKT231

| Species | Source | Transformation frequency (cfu $\mu g^{-1}$ pKT231) |
|---|---|---|
| *Escherichia coli* HB101 | lab strain | $1 \cdot 6 \times 10^5$ |
| *Escherichia coli* JM105 | lab strain | $1 \cdot 1 \times 10^5$ |
| *Escherichia coli* WA321 | lab strain | $1 \cdot 8 \times 10^4$ |
| *Escherichia coli* 3132 | wild type (soil) | $1 \cdot 2 \times 10^4$ |
| *Escherichia coli* | wild type (man) | $9 \times 10^2$ |
| *Escherichia coli* | wild type (guinea pig) | $3 \cdot 5 \times 10^3$ |
| *Escherichia coli* | wild type (guinea pig) | $4 \cdot 4 \times 10^4$ |
| *Escherichia coli* | wild type (cat) | $6 \cdot 5 \times 10^3$ |
| *Salmonella typhimurium* LT2 | lab strain | $\leqslant 5$ |
| *Citrobacter freundii* | wild type (water) | $1 \times 10^3$ |
| *Citrobacter freundii* | wild type (cat) | $2 \cdot 7 \times 10^3$ |
| *Citrobacter freundii* | DSM 30039 | $3 \cdot 6 \times 10^3$ |
| *Klebsiella oxytoca* | wild type (dog) | $\leqslant 5$ |
| *Klebsiella pneumoniae* | lab strain | $2 \times 10^2$ |
| *Klebsiella pneumoniae* | DSM 2026 | $2 \times 10^2$ |
| *Enterobacter aerogenes* | lab strain | $5 \times 10^1$ |
| *Erwinia carotovora* | wild type (carrot) | $4 \cdot 1 \times 10^4$ |
| *Erwinia carotovora* | wild type (carrot) | $4 \times 10^5$ |
| *Serratia plymuthica* | wild type (cat) | $1 \cdot 8 \times 10^3$ |
| *Serratia marcescens* | lab strain | $4 \times 10^2$ |
| *Serratia marcescens* | DSM 30121 | $4 \times 10^3$ |
| *Hafnia alvei* | DSM 30163 | $\leqslant 5$ |
| *Edwardsiella tarda* | DSM 30052 | $\leqslant 5$ |
| *Proteus mirabilis* | lab strain | $6 \times 10^3$ |
| *Proteus mirabilis* | DSM 30115 | $4 \cdot 2 \times 10^2$ |
| *Proteus vulgaris* | DSM 2140 | $8 \cdot 7 \times 10^2$ |
| *Pseudomonas oxalaticus* | wild type (soil) | $9 \times 10^2$ |
| *Pseudomonas putida* | lab strain | $9 \times 10^4$ |
| *Pseudomonas putida* KT2440 | lab strain | $3 \cdot 1 \times 10^4$ |
| *Pseudomonas chlororaphis* | DSM 50083 | $7 \cdot 6 \times 10^2$ |
| *Xanthomonas campestris* | DSM 1706 | $8 \times 10^2$ |
| *Agrobacterium tumefaciens* | DSM 30205 | $5 \cdot 1 \times 10^2$ |
| *Rhodospirillum rubrum* | wild type (pond) | $\leqslant 5$ |
| *Rhodospirillum molischianum* | wild type (pond) | $2 \cdot 4 \times 10^3$ |
| *Rhodobacter capsulata* | wild type (pond) | $\leqslant 5$ |
| *Rhodocyclus gelatinosa* | wild type (pond) | $\leqslant 5$ |

transformants were grown overnight together with the parent on non-selective media, the colonies were transferred onto a nylon membrane and colony hybridization was carried out as described above. None of the parental strains showed hybridization to nick-translated pKT231, whereas all transformants showed strong hybridization. For a few selected clones the presence of pKT231 was demonstrated by plasmid preparations and restriction analyses, as well as by colony hybridization (not shown).

The data presented in *Table 7.1* show that we were not able to transform some of the tested species (transformation frequency $\leq 5$ colonies per µg pKT231). Explanations for this might be:

1.  These species are indeed not susceptible to electroporation, i.e. we could not generate small holes in the membranes under the conditions used;
2.  pKT231 does not replicate in these species;
3.  Selective conditions were not appropriate, i.e. kanamycin resistance was lower than 50 µg ml$^{-1}$;
4.  These species harbour plasmids of the same incompatibility group, thus eliminating pKT231 after transformation.

Since we cannot differentiate between these possibilities, a negative result reported here should not be interpreted as indicating that these species are not susceptible to electroporation under appropriate conditions.

The great majority of species and strains tested were susceptible to electroporation, albeit to different degrees. For strains of *E. coli* there was a difference in transformation frequency of more than two orders of magnitude (cf. lines 1 and 5), with lab strains more transformable than wild-type strains. This tendency was found for the other species tested.

Besides *E. coli*, we tested 10 other species of the family Enterobacteriaceae, belonging to eight different genera (Krieg and Holt, 1984). Four species, namely *Salmonella typhimurium*, *Klebsiella oxytoca*, *Hafnia alvei* and *Edwardsiella tarda*, could not be transformed; possible reasons for this are discussed above. All four representatives of the family Pseudomonadaceae were susceptible to electroporation, with transformation frequencies between $10^2$ and $10^4$. We assume that, as for other non-*E. coli* species, optimization would result in much higher transformation efficiency.

In the cases of *E. coli* 3132 and *Pseudomonas putida*, we compared transformation frequencies obtained by the CaCl$_2$ method and by electroporation, because both strains were given to us as being not transformable. Indeed transformation frequencies with the standard procedures were below 20 cfu µg$^{-1}$ for pKT231. The results indicate that, for these two strains at least, electroporation allows reasonable transformation. To our knowledge, transformation of *Serratia plymuthica*, *Pseudomonas oxalaticus* and *Rhodospirillum molischianum* has not been reported previously; therefore we suggest that electroporation is the method of choice if transformation of 'unusual' bacterial species is tried.

Of the four photosynthetic species tested, only *Rhodospirillum molischianum* was susceptible to electroporation under our conditions. This strain could be lysed without difficulty, while the other three strains could not be

lysed with standard procedures used for small-scale rapid plasmid preparations. Furthermore, we noted that electroporation treatment resulted in some
loss of viable cells only in the case of *R. molischianum* (*c.* 60% survival rate). It
is therefore tempting to speculate that rigidity of the cell wall and susceptibility
to electroporation are inversely related; however, we do not have any direct
proof of this.

In conclusion, we have shown that a great variety of Gram-negative
bacteria—15 different species in a total of 11 genera—are susceptible to
transformation by electroporation. This clearly shows the great potential of
electroporation to induce transformation. We are currently expanding our
studies on electroporation, including, in genetic terms, more 'unusual
Gram-negative' and Gram-positive bacteria.

## Acknowledgements

We want to thank those who contributed to this work by providing strains.
Special thanks are due to M. Geier for editorial help. This work was supported
by grant B8 to R.W. in the Sonderforschungsbereich 145 by the DFG.

## References

BAGDASARIAN, M., LURZ, R., BÜCKERT, B., FRANKLIN, F.C.H., BAGDASARIAN,
M.M., FREY, J. AND TIMMIS, K.N. (1981). Specific-purpose plasmid cloning
vectors: Broad host range, high copy number, RSF1010-derived vectors, and a
host–vector system for gene cloning in *Pseudomonas. Gene* **16**, 237–247.
CHASSY, B.M. AND FLICKINGER, J.L. (1987). Transformation of *Lactobacillus casei* by
electroporation. *FEMS Microbiology Letters* **44**, 173–177.
FIEDLER, S. AND WIRTH, R. (1988). Transformation of bacteria with plasmid DNA by
electroporation. *Analytical Biochemistry* **170**, 38–44.
HARLANDER, S.K. (1987). Transformation of *Streptococcus lactis* by electroporation.
In *Streptococcal Genetics* (J.J. Ferretti and R. Curtiss III, Eds), pp. 229–233.
American Society for Microbiology, Washington, DC.
KRIEG, N.R. AND HOLT, J.G. (1984). Bacterial classification. In *Bergey's Manual of
Systematic Bacteriology* (B. Tansill, Ed.), volume 1, pp. 1–18. Williams and
Wilkins, Baltimore.
MACNEIL, D.J. (1987). Introduction of plasmid DNA into *Streptomyces lividans* by
electroporation. *FEMS Microbiology Letters* **42**, 239–244.
MANIATIS, T., FRITSCH, E.F. AND SAMBROOK, J. (1982). *In situ* hybridization of
bacterial colonies or bacteriophage plaques. In *Molecular Cloning* (T. Maniatis,
E.F. Fritsch and J. Sambrook, Eds), pp. 326–328. Cold Spring Harbor Laboratory,
New York.
ZIMMERMANN, U. (1982). Electric field-mediated fusion and related electrical
phenomena. *Biochimica et Biophysica Acta* **694**, 227–277.

# 8

# Transformation by Electroporation of Two Gram-positive Bacteria: *Streptococcus pneumoniae* and *Brevibacterium lactofermentum*

S. BONNASSIE, A.M. GASC AND A.M. SICARD

*Centre de Recherche de Biochimie et de Génétique Cellulaires du CNRS, 118 Route de Narbonne, 31062 Toulouse Cedex, France*

## Introduction

Molecular genetics has undergone a tremendous development as a result of the discovery of novel systems for the exchange of genetic material. The first system to be discovered was that of DNA-induced natural bacterial transformation in *Streptococcus pneumoniae* (Avery, MacLeod and McCarty, 1944). The number of naturally transformable strains being small, several techniques have been devised to introduce DNA into bacteria. The discovery of penetration of DNA into *Escherichia coli* cells by Mandel and Higa (1970) opened the field of genetic engineering. However, this procedure is inefficient for the majority of bacteria. Protoplast transformation is much more generally applicable to most genera (Katsumata *et al.*, 1984; Yeh, Oreglia and Sicard, 1985; Yoshihama *et al.*, 1985), but it is difficult to establish the best conditions of transformation, and is often not reproducible. Moreover, regeneration of protoplasts may require one week, and the efficiency of transformation is always much lower than natural transformation. DNA uptake by electroporation seems to be a much more general system. In this report we describe plasmid transformation of two Gram-positive bacteria by electroporation: *Streptococcus pneumoniae* as a representative of naturally transformable bacteria and *Brevibacterium lactofermentum*, which we have previously transfected and transformed by the protoplast method (Yeh, Oreglia and Sicard, 1985; Yeh *et al.*, 1986).

## Materials and methods

Pneumococcal R6 strains used in this study, R800 and R801, were derived from

*Genetic Transformation and Expression*
© Intercept Ltd, PO Box 716, Andover, Hants, SP10 1YG, UK

Avery's strain R36A. Cells were grown in complete CAT medium (Morrison *et al.*, 1983) at 37°C and harvested in the mid-logarithmic growth phase (OD 0·3–0·4). They were washed twice and concentrated tenfold in the electroporation medium (sucrose 0·5 M, potassium phosphate 7 mM pH 7·5, magnesium chloride 1 mM). A volume of 0·8 ml of cell suspension was poured into the Bio-Rad cuvette. The pSP2 plasmid DNA was added at a concentration of 0·3 μg ml$^{-1}$. The mixture was kept at 0°C for 10 min. The setting of the Bio-Rad apparatus was at its maximum (6·25 KV cm$^{-1}$, 25 μF). One single impulsion was given. Aliquots of 0·1 ml of cells were plated on blood-agar medium (Sicard and Ephrussi-Taylor, 1965) and incubated for 2 h at 37°C. A second layer of agar medium containing erythromycin was then added, to have a final concentration of 4 μg ml$^{-1}$. After an overnight incubation, transformants were scored. When pLS1 plasmid DNA was used, transformants were selected at a concentration of 1·5 μg ml$^{-1}$ of tetracycline.

The same method has been applied to a derivative of *B. lactofermentum* (ATCC 21086), except that the cultures were grown at 32°C with aeration in L broth (LB) medium. After the pulse, the cell suspension was diluted in 1·5 ml of fresh LB medium supplemented with 2% (w/v) glucose and incubated for 3 h at 32°C. Cells were plated on LB agar medium containing the appropriate antibiotic. The pBLA plasmid used in these experiments is a *E. coli/B. lactofermentum* shuttle vector. Transformants were selected on plates containing 25 μg ml$^{-1}$ of kanamycin. The pBLA DNA was isolated by the alkaline lysis method described by Maniatis, Fritsch and Sambrook (1982), except that lysis was obtained by adding lysozyme and penicillin (2 μg ml$^{-1}$). Plasmid DNA was used at a concentration of 0·1 μg ml$^{-1}$.

### Results

After treatment with the electric field as described above, the cell survival of *S. pneumoniae* R801 was slightly reduced (*Table 8.1A*). In the absence of the electric field no transformants were detected by addition of either plasmid pSP2 DNA or chromosomal DNA bearing a marker conferring resistance to streptomycin (R800 *str-r*), which is used in natural transformation as a reference marker. Therefore under these conditions, there was no natural competence. Moreover, there was no spontaneous mutation for either marker. In the presence of the electric field and plasmid DNA, transformants were induced at a frequency of 2–3·6 × 10$^{-5}$ per surviving cell. The efficiency of electroporation was 1·4 × 10$^3$ transformants per μg of DNA. DNA was taken up by the cells during the electric pulse, since the addition of DNase a few seconds after the pulse did not inhibit transformation (*Table 8.1B*). The addition of chromosomal DNA did not give transformants by electroporation.

To test if the plasmid DNA taken inside the cells was double stranded or single stranded we used a shuttle plasmid (pLS1) that replicates in *E. coli* and *S. pneumoniae* (Stassi *et al.*, 1981). As the pneumococcal recipient strain R801 contains restriction enzymes (Lacks and Greenberg, 1977), it should degrade plasmid DNA extracted from *E. coli* if double-stranded DNA penetrates the cells. We have transformed strain R801 by pLS1 plasmid DNA isolated from

**Table 8.1**  Transformation, induced by an electric field, of *Streptococcus pneumoniae* (strain R801)

|   | Viable cells per ml | Electroporation | DNA | *ery-r*/ml | *tet-r*/ml | *str-r*/ml | Frequency |
|---|---|---|---|---|---|---|---|
| A | $3\cdot1 \times 10^7$ | − | − | <1 | <1 | <1 | |
|   | | + | − | <1 | <1 | <1 | |
|   | | − | pSP2 | <1 | | | |
|   | $1\cdot9 \times 10^7(61\%)$ | + | pSP2 | $3\cdot86 \times 10^2$ | | | $2\cdot0 \times 10^{-5}$ |
| B | $3\cdot0 \times 10^7$ | − | − | <1 | | | |
|   | $1\cdot2 \times 10^7(40\%)$ | + | pSP2 | $4\cdot34 \times 10^2$ | | | $3\cdot6 \times 10^{-5}$ |
|   | | + | pSP2 + DNase* | $4\cdot00 \times 10^2$ | | | $3\cdot3 \times 10^{-5}$ |
|   | | − | R800 str | − | − | <1 | |
|   | | + | R800 str | − | − | <1 | |
| C | $1 \times 10^8$ | − | − | | <1 | | |
|   | | − | pLS1 (coli) | | <1 | | |
|   | $5\cdot3 \times 10^7(53\%)$ | + | pLS1 (coli) | | $1\cdot1 \times 10^2$ | | $0\cdot2 \times 10^{-5}$ |
|   | | − | pLS1 (pneu.) | | <1 | | |
|   | $5\cdot8 \times 10^7(58\%)$ | + | pLS1 (pneu.) | | $3\cdot2 \times 10^2$ | | $0\cdot55 \times 10^{-5}$ |

The DNA concentration used in all the experiments was $0\cdot3$ µg ml$^{-1}$. Plasmid pSP2 DNA was prepared from pneumococcal strain R801 carrying this plasmid. Plasmid pLS1 DNA was prepared from *E. coli* LE392 (pLS1 coli) and *S. pneumoniae* R800 (pLS1 pneu.) carrying this plasmid.
\* Pancreatic DNase (1 µg ml$^{-1}$) was added immediately after the electric pulse.

pneumococcal R801 or from *E. coli* strains. The results show that transformants are obtained only when pLS1 is grown in pneumococcus (*Table 8.1C*). The pLS1 plasmid extracted from *E. coli* is also able to transform, although at a reduced frequency. This may be due to a partial restriction. Finally, electroporation has been used by R. Kiewiet in our laboratory to introduce pSP2 plasmid into a naturally poorly transformable strain (endo-14) deficient in the endonuclease gene (Lacks, Greenberg and Neuberger, 1975). The efficiency of plasmid transformation by electroporation was the same as in the wild-type strain.

Transformation of *B. lactofermentum* by an electric pulse was performed as described above. For a cell concentration of $5 \times 10^8$ per ml, survival was 100% and transformant frequency was $5 \times 10^{-5}$ per cell with a concentration of $0\cdot1$ µg DNA/ml. Average transformation efficiency was $1\cdot3 \pm 0\cdot4 \times 10^5$ transformants per µg of DNA. The effect of plasmid DNA concentration on transformation was examined (*Figure 8.1*). The dose response is linear up to $0\cdot8$ µg ml$^{-1}$. At higher doses, saturation is reached. As in pneumococcal experiments, there were no transformants obtained in the absence of the electric field nor spontaneous mutants resistant to kanamycin. Therefore intact cells of *B. lactofermentum* can be easily transformed by the electroporation procedure.

Our results contribute to the generalization of transformation of intact bacteria by an electric field. For *B. lactofermentum*, which occupies a central role for industrial purposes, the advantage is that the procedure is fast, easy and reproducible. Moreover, colonies can be scored after only two overnight incubations. These properties are quite an advantage over the protoplast method. It is likely that better conditions of treatment can be obtained to increase the efficiency of transformation.

In *S. pneumoniae*, electroporation can be used to introduce a plasmid into

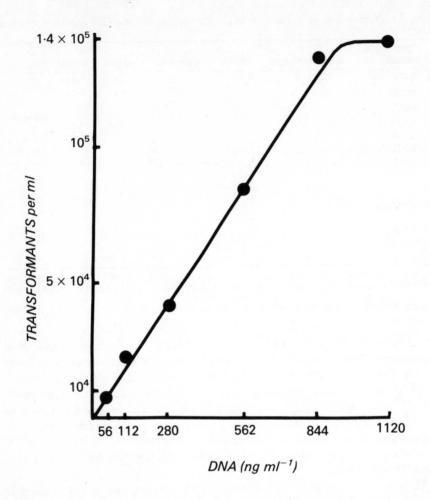

**Figure 8.1** Effect of plasmid DNA concentration on transformation by electroporation of *B. lactofermentum*. pBLA plasmid DNA was added to a concentrated cell suspension. One single impulsion of 6.25 KV cm$^{-1}$, 25 μF was given. Transformants were selected on complete medium containing 25 μg ml$^{-1}$ kanamycin.

poorly competent cells. Although its efficiency per μg of DNA is not high, it is likely that it can be increased by several orders of magnitude at the same level as in *B. lactofermentum*. For instance, higher cell concentrations for the same amount of DNA should improve efficiency. Our results indicate that electroporation is a process quite different from natural competence:

1.  It does not require a specific phase of growth in special media containing albumin, although better results are obtained in an exponential than in a stationary growth phase.
2.  DNA uptake is extremely fast, as if DNA penetration was concomitant with the pulse; this argues for a direct relationship between the electric shock and transport of DNA across the cell envelope.

3. We could not detect transformation for a chromosomal marker. This suggests that one or several recombination conditions, such as single strandedness, induction of a single-strand binding protein and/or recombination enzymes, are not present during electroporation experiments but are induced during natural competence. Thus electroporation would be an elegant procedure to separate DNA uptake from DNA integration into the chromosome.

Therefore electroporation appears to be an useful tool of investigation not only for applied genetic engineering but also for basic molecular genetics.

### Acknowledgements

We are grateful to J. Teissié for helpful discussions and P. Ritzenthaler for the electroporation facilities.

### References

AVERY, O.T., MacLEOD, C.M. AND McCARTY, M. (1944). Studies on the chemical nature of the substance inducing transformation of pneumococcal types. Induction of transformation by a DNA fraction isolated from pneumococcus type III. *Journal of Experimental Medicine* **89**, 137–158.

KATSUMATA, R., OZAKI, A., OKA, T. AND FURUYA, A. (1984). Protoplast transformation of glutamate producing bacteria with plasmid DNA. *Journal of Bacteriology* **159**, 306–311.

LACKS, S. AND GREENBERG, B. (1977). Complementary specificity of restriction endonucleases of *Diplococcus pneumoniae* with respect to DNA methylation. *Journal of Molecular Biology* **114**, 153–168.

LACKS, S.A., GREENBERG, B. AND NEUBERGER, M. (1975). Identification of a deoxyribonuclease implicated in the genetic transformation of *Diplococcus pneumoniae*. *Journal of Bacteriology* **123**, 222–232.

MANDEL, M. AND HIGA, A. (1970). Calcium-dependent bacteriophage DNA infection. *Journal of Molecular Biology* **53**, 159–162.

MANIATIS, T., FRITSCH, E.F. AND SAMBROOK, J. (EDS) (1982). *Molecular Cloning, a laboratory manual*. Cold Spring Harbor Laboratory, New York.

MORRISON, D.A., LACKS, S.A., GUILD, W.R. AND HAGEMAN, J.M. (1983). Isolation and characterization of three new classes of transformation deficient mutants of *Streptococcus pneumoniae* that are defective in DNA transport and genetic recombination. *Journal of Bacteriology* **156**, 281–290.

SICARD, A.M. AND EPHRUSSI-TAYLOR, H. (1965). Genetic recombination in DNA-induced transformation of pneumococcus. II. Mapping the *ami*A region. *Genetics* **52**, 1207–1227.

STASSI, D.L., LOPEZ, P., ESPINOSA, M. AND LACKS, S.A. (1981). Cloning of chromosomal genes in *Streptococcus pneumoniae*. *Proceedings of the National Academy of Sciences of the United States of America* **78**, 7028–7032.

YEH, P., OREGLIA, J. AND SICARD, A.M. (1985). Transfection of *Corynebacterium lilium* protoplasts. *Journal of General Microbiology* **131**, 3179–3183.

YEH, P., OREGLIA, J., PRÉVOTS, F. AND SICARD, A.M. (1986). A shuttle vector system for *Brevibacterium lactofermentum*. *Gene* **47**, 301–306.

YOSHIHAMA, M., HIGASHIRO, K., RAO, E.A., AKEDO, M., STRANABRUCH, W.G., FOLLETTIE, M.T., WALKER, G.C. AND SINSKEY, A.J. (1985). Cloning vector system for *Corynebacterium glutamicum*. *Journal of Bacteriology* **162**, 591–597.

# 9

# Transformation, by Electroporation, of *Bacillus circulans* NRRL B 3312, the Producer of Butirosin

ELISABETH AUBERT AND JULIAN DAVIES

*Unité de Génie Microbiologique, Institut Pasteur, Paris, France*

## Introduction

Butirosin produced by *Bacillus circulans* (Dion *et al.*, 1972) is the only aminocyclitol antibiotic known to be produced by a representative of the *Bacillaceae*. Butirosin is derived biosynthetically from ribostamycin, and yet ribostamycin is produced by micro-organisms unrelated in evolutionary terms to *Bacillus* (*Streptomyces* and *Micromonospora*). Cloning of genes involved in butirosin biosynthesis and resistance (*but*) provides an approach to elucidate structure and regulatory mechanisms, for comparison with aminoglycoside biosynthetic genes from other organisms.

The butirosin-resistance gene has been cloned previously (Courvalin, Weisblum and Davies, 1977) and sequenced (Herbert, Giles and Akhtar, 1983). It encodes for an aminoglycoside phosphotransferase and it is assumed that the resistance gene plays two roles in antibiotic production (Davies, 1986), both as a mechanism to prevent suicide when the organism produces the antibiotic and also a regulatory function. In the latter case, the antibiotic-resistance gene may be induced only when a particular intermediate is produced during growth, and the expression of the resistance gene then activates the remainder of the biosynthetic pathway.

In an attempt to analyse the biosynthesis of butirosin in *B. circulans* and the mechanism by which the biosynthetic pathway is regulated, we wish to identify and clone the biosynthetic genes by complementation of non-butirosin-producing mutants of *B. circulans*. However, to apply recombinant DNA techniques for genetic manipulation, we need an efficient and reliable DNA transformation system.

## Protoplast transformation

Protoplast-mediated transformation methods (Chang and Cohen, 1979) are

*Genetic Transformation and Expression*
© Intercept Ltd, PO Box 716, Andover, Hants, SP10 1YG, UK

well established for a few species of *Bacillaceae* including *B. subtilis 168* (Landman, Ryter and Frehel, 1968) and *B. megaterium* (Fodor, Hadlaczky and Alföldi, 1975). Specific regeneration media have been described for use with individual species: *B. sphaericus* (McDonald and Burke, 1984), *B. popilliae* and *B. larvae* (Bakhiet and Stahly, 1985), *B. stearothermophilus* (Imanaka *et al.*, 1982), *B. thuringiensis* (Alikhanian *et al.*, 1981). Rates of regeneration from protoplasts to bacilli remain poor and variable.

In the case of *B. circulans B3312*, despite many efforts to optimize and control parameters that influence transformation and regeneration, transformation frequencies remained negligible. Problems arise from the mucoidicity of the strain, its resistance to lysozyme and its high sensitivity to mutanolysin or similar enzymes. Moreover, we have been unable to find any transducing bacteriophage that infects the *B. circulans* species we are using, and conjugation was not effective. In this report we describe an approach designed to overcome many of the current limitations in the transformation of 'difficult' bacilli.

## Electroporation of *B. circulans* cells

Zimmermann and co-workers have described the effects of high-voltage electric pulses on the membranes of mammalian, plant and bacterial cells (Scheurich and Zimmermann, 1981; Zimmermann, 1983). Although electroporation has been demonstrated to be extremely effective in enhancing gene transfer in various mammalian and plant systems, there are few references on the application of this technology to *Bacillaceae*. Shivarova used electroporation to transform *B. cereus* protoplasts (Shivarova *et al.*, 1983) and, in comparison with polyethylene glycol (PEG)-induced protoplast transformation, demonstrated an increase in transformation efficiency of one order of magnitude. Transformation using electroporation has been successfully demonstrated with other Gram-positive bacteria: *Enterococcus faecalis* (Fiedler and Wirth, 1988), *Lactobacillus casei* (Chassy and Flickinger, 1987), *Lactobacillus acidophilus, Lactobacillus fermentum, L. casei, Staphylococcus aureus* and *B. cereus* (Luchansky, Muriana and Klaenhammer, 1988).

We were thus interested in the possible usefulness of electroporation for transformation of *B. circulans*.

## Methods

A Gene Pulser™ apparatus (Bio-Rad Laboratories) was used for all electroporation experiments described in this study. *B. circulans* was grown to an optical density of 0·3 at 650 nm in $AM_3$ (Antibiotic Medium No.3, Difco), harvested, washed twice with cold HEPES buffer [272 mM sucrose, 1 mM $MgCl_2$, 7 mM *N*-2-hydroxyethylpiperazine-*N'*-2-ethanesulphonic acid (HEPES), pH 7·3] and suspended to a final concentration of $10^9-3\times10^9$ cells per ml in HEPES buffer. PEB buffer (7 mM $K_2HPO_4-KH_2PO_4$, 1 mM $MgCl_2$, 272 mM sucrose, pH 7·4) was also employed. Approximately $4\times10^8$ cells were used for each trial, and held on ice for 10 min. Plasmid DNA in 10μl of TE (about 300 ng) was thoroughly mixed with 0·8 ml of cell suspension in a chilled Gene Pulser cuvette. Cells were exposed to a single electric pulse (peak voltage, 2·5 kV; capacitance, 25 µF) which generated a peak field strength of 6·25 kV cm$^{-1}$. Immediately after the pulse, 1 ml of SOC medium (2% Bacto Tryptone, 0·5% Bacto yeast extract, 10 mM NaCl, 2·5 mM KCl, 10 mM MgCl$_2$, 10 mM MgSO$_4$, 20 mM glucose) was added. Rapid addition of SOC seems to be important in maximizing the recovery of transformants. Cell suspensions were held at 37°C with agitation for 45 min and then cells were spread on L agar plates and incubated at 37°C. Transformants were selected on media containing 20 µg ml$^{-1}$ of chloramphenicol, 2·5 µg ml$^{-1}$ of erythromycin or 20 µg ml$^{-1}$ of tetracycline, depending on the plasmid being used. All experiments included controls which were permeabilized in the absence of added plasmid DNA. Erythromycin- and tetracycline-resistant clones were never observed, but chloramphenicol-resistant colonies were visible on plates after extended incubation (48–72h).

## Results

The following parameters were varied to optimize conditions for transformation of *B. circulans* by electroporation.

### EFFECT OF VOLTAGE ON SURVIVAL AND TRANSFORMATION

Variation of voltage had an effect on survival and transformation efficiency and frequency. As seen in *Table 9.1* and *Figure 9.1*, using HEPES buffer and a capacitance of 25 µF at 3750 V cm$^{-1}$, 50% of the original colony-forming unit (cfu) count was recovered but the transformation frequency and efficiency

**Table 9.1** Transformation of *Bacillus circulans* by electroporation

| Buffer | Voltage (V cm$^{-1}$) | Time constant (msec) | %survival $\left[\dfrac{cfu_{rec} \times 100}{cfu_{tot}}\right]$ | Frequency ($\times 10^{-5}$) $\left[\dfrac{cfu_{obs}}{cfu_{tot}}\right]$ | Efficiency ($\times 10^3$) $\left[\dfrac{cfu_{obs}}{\mu g\,DNA}\right]$ |
|---|---|---|---|---|---|
| HEPES | 1250 | 31 | 100 | 0·2 | 0·6 |
| | 2500 | 26 | 75 | 0·4 | 1·2 |
| | 3750 | 24 | 50 | 0·8 | 2·7 |
| | 5000 | 24 | 30 | 2 | 6 |
| | 6250 | | 15 | 2·6 | 8 |
| PEB | 1250 | 5·3 | 31 | 1·8 | 6 |
| | 2500 | 4·4 | 20 | 2·6 | 7 |
| | 3750 | 4 | 15 | 2·6 | 7 |
| | 5000 | 3·5 | 8 | 2 | 6·5 |
| | 6250 | | 1·5 | 1 | 4 |

Capacitance: 25 µF was applied.
pMK4 DNA plasmid was used.
Selection was applied for chloramphenicol (20 µg ml$^{-1}$).
cfu$_{tot}$: total colony-forming units used in the electroporation, as determined by dilution and plating on L agar.
cfu$_{rec}$: colony-forming units recovered after electroporation, dilution and plating.
cfu$_{obs}$: colony-forming units observed as antibiotic resistant on selective plates; equals total number of cells transformed by electroporation.

were low. Increasing the voltage to 6250 V cm$^{-1}$ raised the efficiency and frequency while lowering the survival to 15%. Using a lower capacitance (3 µF), no killing was detected but we were not able to obtain any transformants.

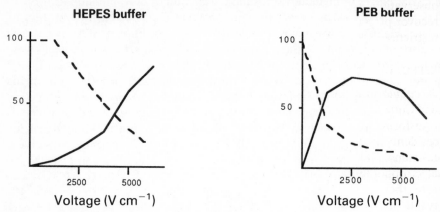

**Figure 9.1** Effect of voltage on survival and transformation efficiency and frequency of *B. circulans*. --, percentage survival of cells; —, number of transformants (×10²).

## EFFECT OF THE LENGTH OF THE TIME CONSTANT ON SURVIVAL AND TRANSFORMATION

The electrical resistance is affected by ionic strength of the electroporation buffer. Two sucrose buffers (PEB and HEPES) were employed in order to obtain different time constants. As shown in *Table 9.1*, the ionic strength of the buffer greatly influences cell survival.

## TRANSFORMATION WITH DIFFERENT PLASMID DNA PREPARATIONS

A variety of plasmid species were transferred to *B. circulans 3312* by electroporation (*Table 9.2*). Acquisition of plasmid DNA in these transfor-

**Table 9.2** Transformation of *Bacillus circulans* by different plasmid DNA

| Plasmid features | Number of transformants | Frequency (× 10$^{-5}$) $\left[\dfrac{\text{cfu}_{obs}}{\text{cfu}_{tot}}\right]$ | Efficiency $\left[\dfrac{\text{cfu}_{obs}}{\text{µg DNA}}\right]$ |
|---|---|---|---|
| pMK4(Cm$^R$)* 5·6 kbp | 200 | 1 | $5 \times 10^3$ |
| pTV1(Em$^R$)* 12·4 kbp | 6 | 0·03 | $5 \times 10^1$ |
| pBC16(Te$^R$)* 4·25 kbp | 18 | 0·1 | $5 \times 10^2$ |
| pUB110(Bleo$^R$)* 4·5 kbp | 0 | 0 | 0 |

* Cm$^R$, Em$^R$, Te$^R$, Bleo$^R$ confer resistance to chloramphenicol, erythromycin, tetracycline and bleomycin, respectively.
kbp: kilobase pairs.

mants was confirmed by both phenotype and plasmid analysis. Nevertheless, the vector pUB110 failed to transform *B. circulans* for bleomycin resistance by electroporation. This result is in good agreement with our previous observations of lack of transformants using this plasmid. The inability to recover pUB110 from *B. circulans* is probably due to the presence of a host restriction system in *B. circulans*.

EFFECT OF ELECTROPORATION ON STABILITY OF A RESIDENT PLASMID

*B. circulans* possesses a cryptic resident plasmid of 48 kbp (pIP850) (Carlier and Courvalin, 1982). Experiments were carried out to determine whether cells transformed by electroporation had an elevated frequency of curing of this resident plasmid. After selection for chloramphenicol or erythromycin resistance, 50 colonies were tested for the presence of pIP850 by electrophoretic analysis. All transformants analysed retained pIP850. Therefore, there is no increase in the frequency of curing the resident plasmid as a result of electroporation. A similar observation has been made by Powell (Powell *et al.*, 1988) working with lactic streptococci. Thus, unlike protoplast-dependent transformation, electroporation does not appear to lead to the curing of resident plasmids (Gasson, 1983).

**Discussion**

For several reasons, most notably the absence of whole-cell transformation and transduction systems and the low efficiency of protoplast transformation, previous efforts to introduce plasmid DNA into the butirosin-producing strain of *B. circulans, NRRL B 3312*, were not successful. In this study plasmid DNA was readily introduced in *B. circulans* via electroporation. There are a number of important advantages to an electric-pulse-induced transformation system. Because high-voltage pulses are capable of permeabilizing both bacterial cell walls and membranes, it is not necessary to prepare protoplasts. Therefore osmotic stabilizing agents are not required and cells transformed by electroporation appeared after 24 h of incubation rather than after the 3 days usually required for protoplast regeneration.

Voltage and buffer strength were examined, to establish conditions for optimal electroporation frequency. The greatest number of transformants were consistently recovered following electroporation of the DNA–cell mixture suspended in HEPES using 6250 V cm$^{-1}$ at 25 µF. At that time, the highest electroporation frequency is $8 \times 10^3$ transformants of *B. circulans* per µg of pMK4 DNA. Modifications in other parameters, such as conditions of growth, DNA concentration, addition of lysozyme or PEG prior to electroporation or cell concentration, should increase the transformation efficiency.

The ability to introduce plasmid molecules at sufficiently high frequency will allow analysis by the direct cloning of *B. circulans* DNA fragments into butirosin-deficient mutants of *B. circulans*. The introduction of plasmid DNA should also facilitate directed-mutagenesis studies of antibiotic biosynthesis in this strain.

## Acknowledgement

This work was supported by Biogen Research Corporation and The Pasteur Institute.

## References

ALIKHANIAN, S.I., RYABCHENKA, N.F., BUKANOV, N.O., AND SAKANYAN, V.A. (1981). Transformation of *Bacillus thuringiensis* subsp. *galleriae* protoplasts by plasmid pBC16. *Journal of Bacteriology* **146**, 7–9.

BAKHIET, H. AND STAHLY, D.P. (1985). Studies on transfection and transformation of protoplasts of *Bacillus larvae, Bacillus subtilis* and *Bacillus popilliae*. *Applied and Environmental Microbiology* **49**, 577–581.

CARLIER, C. AND COURVALIN, P. (1982). A plasmid which does not encode the aminoglycoside phosphotransferase in the butirosin-producing strain of *Bacillus circulans*. *Journal of Antibiotics* **35**, 629–634.

CHANG, S. AND COHEN, S.N. (1979). High frequency transformation of *Bacillus subtilis* protoplasts by plasmid DNA. *Molecular and General Genetics* **168**, 111–115.

CHASSY, B.M. AND FICKINGER, J.L. (1987). Transformation of *Lactobacillus casei* by electroporation. *FEMS Microbiology Letters* **44**, 173–177.

COURVALIN, P., WEISBLUM, B. AND DAVIES, J. (1977). Aminoglycoside-modifying enzyme of an antibiotic-producing bacterium acts as a determinant of antibiotic resistance in *Escherichia coli*. *Proceedings of the National Academy of Sciences of the United States of America* **74**, 999–1003.

DAVIES, J. (1986). A new look at antibiotic resistance. *FEMS Microbiology Reviews* **39**, 363–371.

DION, H.W., WOO, P.W.K., WILLMER, N.E., KERN, D.L., ONAGRA, J. AND FUSARI, S.A. (1972). Butirosin, a new aminoglycosidic antibiotic complex: Isolation and characterization. *Antimicrobial Agents and Chemotherapy* **2**, 84–88.

FIEDLER, S. AND WIRTH, R. (1988). Transformation of bacteria with plasmid DNA by electroporation. *Analytical Biochemistry* **170**, 33–44.

FODOR, K., HADLACZKY, G. AND ALFÖLDI, L. (1975). Reversion of *Bacillus megaterium* protoplasts to the bacillary form. *Journal of Bacteriology* **121**, 390–391.

GASSON, M.J. (1983). Plasmid complements of *Streptococcus lactis* NCDO 712 and other lacti streptococci after protoplast-induced curing. *Journal of Bacteriology* **154**, 1–9.

HERBERT, C.J., GILES, I.G. AND AKHTAR, M. (1983). The sequence of an antibiotic resistance gene from an antibiotic producing bacterium. Homologies with transposon genes. *FEBS Letters* **160**, 67–70.

IMANAKA, T., FUJII, M., ARAMORI, I. AND AIBA, A. (1982). Transformation of *Bacillus stearothermophilus* with plasmid DNA and characterisation of shuttle vector plasmids between *Bacillus stearothermophilus* and *Bacillus subtilis*. *Journal of Bacteriology* **149**, 824–830.

LANDMAN, O.E., RYTER, A. AND FREHEL, C. (1968). Gelatin-induced reversion of protoplasts of *Bacillus subtilis* to the bacillary form: electron microscope and physical studies. *Journal of Bacteriology* **96**, 2154–2170.

LUCHANSKY, J.B., MURIANA, P.M. AND KLAENHAMMER, T.R. (1988). Application of electroporation for transfer of plasmid DNA to *Lactobacillus, Lactococcus, Leuconostoc, Listeria, Pediococcus, Bacillus, Staphylococcus, Enterococcus* and *Propionibacterium*. *Molecular Microbiology* **2**, 637–646.

MCDONALD, K.O. AND BURKE, W.F. (1984). Plasmid transformation of *Bacillus sphaericus* 1593. *Journal of General Microbiology* **130**, 203–208.

POWELL, I.B., ACHEN, M.G., HILLIER, A.J. AND DAVIDSON, B.E. (1988). A simple and rapid method for genetic transformation of lactic streptococci by electroporation. *Applied and Environmental Microbiology* **54**, 655–660.

SCHEURICH, P. AND ZIMMERMANN, U. (1981). Giant human erythrocytes by electric field-induced cell to cell fusion. *Naturwissenschaften* **68**, 45–46.

SHIVAROVA, N., FORSTER, W., JACOB, H.E. AND GRIGOROVA, R. (1983). Microbiological implications of electric field effects. VII. Stimulation of plasmid transformation of *Bacillus cereus* protoplasts by electric field pulses. *Zentroblatt Allogie Mikrobiologie* **23**, 595–599.

ZIMMERMANN, U. (1983). Electrofusion of cells: principles and industrial potential. *Trends in Biotechnology* **1**, 149–155.

# 10

# The *Haemophilus influenzae* Genetic Transformation System

JOHAN H. STUY

*Department of Biological Science, Florida State University, Tallahassee, Florida 32306, USA*

## Introduction

Bergey's Manual describes the bacterial genus *Haemo ·hilus* as minute to medium-sized non-motile Gram-negative cells, which may show marked pleiomorphism. The genus is strictly parasitic and requires either haemin, or nicotinic acid amide adenine dinucleotide (NAD), or both. Cells are aerobic or facultatively anaerobic. *H. influenzae* is described as small rods or filaments requiring haemin and NAD. Pitman (1931) recognized six different capsular (sero)types (Sa, Sb, Sc, Sd, Se and Sf) as well as non-encapsulated strains (so-called non-typable or NT). In my limited experience, those strain differences hold well for phage restriction (Stuy, 1976a) and for type II restriction enzymes (Kelly and Smith, 1970; Smith and Wilcox, 1970). Estimates of the *H. influenzae* chromosome, based on measurements of contour lengths of putative whole chromosomes in electron micrographs (MacHattie, Berns and Thomas, 1965) or the amount of DNA per cell (Zamenhof, Alexander and Leidy, 1953; Berns and Thomas, 1965; Zoon and Scocca, 1975), have given values of 1050–2400 kbp. Recently Lee and Smith (1988) have sized the chromosome by pulse-field agarose gel electrophoresis and obtained values from 1810 to 1878 kbp.

In 1951 Dr Hattie Alexander and co-workers discovered that a certain Sd strain (Garfesius) of *H. influenzae* could transform to different capsular types with DNA from other serotypes (Alexander and Leidy, 1951). Mutant derivatives of this isolate are now used in nearly all laboratories studying *H. influenzae* transformation. When this Rd strain is grown without shaking in 2 ml of Levinthal broth, about one per 100 000 cells becomes competent (about 1000 transformants per ml) when the culture reaches stationary phase (*Figure 10.1*). Studies by Roger Herriott and co-workers (Goodgal and Herriott, 1961; Spencer and Herriott, 1965; Herriott, Meyer and Vogt, 1970), by Leidy, Jaffee and Alexander (1962), and by me (Stuy, 1962) have revealed that with certain competence regimes all cells in a given suspension can become capable of

*Genetic Transformation and Expression*
© Intercept Ltd, PO Box 716, Andover, Hants, SP10 1YG, UK

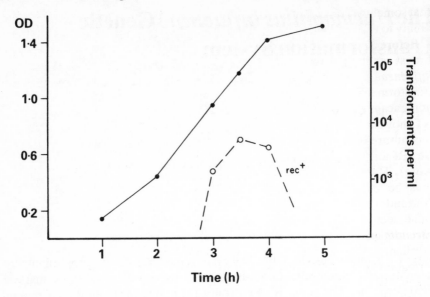

**Figure 10.1**    Appearance of competence in a 2 ml *H. influenzae* Rd culture growing in Levinthal broth at 37°C without shaking. ● turbidity; ○ numbers of transformable cells per ml (low efficiency *novAB* marker).

taking up homologous DNA. That phenomenon made this Rd strain very attractive for studies of genetic transformation.

In evaluating observations made of what happens to DNA taken up by competent recipient Rd cells, one should realize that:

1. The different competence development regimes may yield different results (a concern expressed by Barany and Kahn, 1985, *see also* Setlow and Boling, 1972).
2. The fate of donor DNA is not necessarily sealed by its integration into the cell's chromosome [the mismatch and the *mutB* repair systems may remove some, or most, of the donor DNA after its integration (Steinhart and Herriott, 1968)].
3. Many of the older studies used an Rd strain that carried a defective prophage (Stachura *et al.*, 1969), which is not present (Boling, Allison and Setlow, 1973) in the BC200 strain (Barnhart and Cox, 1968) now in use in most laboratories.

It is customary to distinguish three aspects of genetic transformation: adsorption of the donor DNA, transport of the adsorbed DNA to the chromosome, and integration of it into the cell's chromosome. I will follow that custom here also, but I would like to call the reader's attention to a question that is nearly never asked: Why does this *H. influenzae* Rd strain transform so efficiently (Stuy and Hoffmann, 1970)? Or rather, one might ask: What is the molecular event taking place in (some?) cells when they reach stationary phase that somehow induces in them a process that leads to cell competence, i.e. their ability to take up DNA?

Before beginning to review the basic aspects of *Haemophilus* transformation I must remind the reader that efficient transformation within the species *H. influenzae* is relatively rare. In my hands only four strains are efficiently transformable. Three of these are serotype d; one was isolated as a non-encapsulated culture (Stuy, 1976a). The latter should thus be defined as NT; however, plasmid transfer studies in my laboratory indicate strongly that this culture is an Rd one. I have found all of a considerable number of Ra, Rb, Re, Rf and NT strains to transform at very low efficiencies (down 99% or more). The four Rc strains studied were incapable of DNA uptake; they can thus be classified as *com⁻*. Leidy and co-workers (Leidy, Jaffee and Alexander, 1962) reported that an Rb strain transformed at only 10% of the value seen for Rd. These values were 20% and 5%, respectively, for *H. parainfluenzae* strain (Boss) and *H. aegyptius* strain (#15). A number of excellent review articles have appeared about *Haemophilus* genetic transformation (Stuy, 1970a, 1970b; Notani and Setlow, 1975; Smith, Danner and Deich, 1981; Goodgal, 1982a; Kahn and Smith, 1984). I will therefore restrict myself to more recent developments and give the reader a review that is strongly biased in favour of the transformasome model.

## DNA uptake

### IRREVERSIBLE DNA BINDING

The first step in *H. influenzae* genetic transformation is the uptake of donor DNA. This requires that the cells be competent, i.e. capable of irreversible DNA uptake. Rapidly growing bacteria are unable to do this (Stuy and Hoffmann, 1970), although they may bind DNA reversibly under certain ionic conditions. There are now basically two competence regimes to make *H. influenzae* suspensions fully competent: the widely used MIV method developed by Herriott's group (Herriott, Meyer and Vogt, 1970) and the so-called aerobic–anaerobic–saline method (Leidy, Jaffee and Alexander, 1962; Stuy, 1962). In both regimes rapidly growing cells in a rich medium (supplemented Difco brain–heart infusion (sBHI) or Levinthal broth) are subjected to a nutrient shift-down. In the MIV method the growing cells are centrifuged and resuspended in the (incomplete) MIV medium. Competence develops in about one hour. In the other method, the growing cells are held anaerobically for some 90 min and are then diluted into saline. There is no significant increase in colony-forming units in the latter two phases. Apparently, these shifts-down trigger some event in the cells that leads, under the right conditions, to the development of competence (*see* below). For both regimes competence is rapidly lost when the cells are again incubated in sBHI. Notani and Setlow (1975) have covered extensively the effects of various substances on competence development (*see also* Kahn and Smith, 1984). Suffice it to say here that protein synthesis, but not DNA synthesis, is required.

IONIC CONDITIONS

The ionic conditions for irreversible adsorption of DNA by competent cells have been described (Barnhart and Herriott, 1963; Stuy, 1970a). Not surprisingly, the optimal monovalent ion concentration ($Na^+$) is about 0·1 M. Low concentrations of either $Mg^{++}$ or $Ca^{++}$ are required and they also speed up DNA uptake. There is a broad pH optimum around a value of 7. Uptake is largely reduced in the presence of the metabolic inhibitor dinitrophenol (Stuy, 1962; Barnhart and Herriott, 1963); uptake may thus require energy. The specificity of DNA uptake (*see* below) is reduced at lower salt concentrations. Postel and Goodgal (1966, 1967) have described the (efficient) uptake of single-stranded DNA.

DNA uptake is very much affected by temperature. Already rapid at room temperature, it is faster at 30°C, at 37°C and even at 40°C (unpublished observations). Owing to the quick loss of competency at the two high temperatures, the numbers of transformants observed against time level off early, and they are then lower than those seen at the lower temperatures.

NUMBER OF UPTAKE SITES

How many DNA uptake sites are there per competent cell? In my laboratory it was found that irreversible DNA uptake is extremely rapid: in just 3 sec (at room temperature) significant numbers of transformants were observed (Stuy and Stern, 1964). Uptake was complete in some 90 sec. Kahn and Smith (1984) reported this also. The number of uptake sites was estimated at two per cell from these kinetic experiments. Other estimates are based on the numbers of DNA molecules adsorbed and the assumption that each site acts only once; the numbers range from 3·2 to 14 (Deich and Smith, 1980; Barouki and Smith, 1986) and 40 for very small molecules (Barouki and Smith, 1986).

SPECIFICITY OF DNA UPTAKE

In 1960 Schaeffer and co-workers reported that *H. influenzae* showed a marked specificity for DNA uptake, in that *Haemophilus* DNA was preferentially taken up (Schaeffer, Edgar and Rolfe, 1960). Their conclusions were based on uptake competition experiments. This observation has been confirmed (Newman and Stuy, 1971; Scocca, Poland and Zoon, 1974). Scocca and co-workers reported that competent *H. influenzae* took up about five *H. influenzae* DNA molecules per cell while less than one DNA molecule of *Escherichia coli* DNA was adsorbed per 50 cells (Scocca, Poland and Zoon, 1974). I have studied the kinetics of uptake of radioactively labelled phage HP1 DNA, phage λ DNA and phage T7 DNA (all about the same size). The irreversible uptake of HP1 DNA was three times faster than that for λ DNA and nine times faster than that for T7 DNA. The widely used *recA1* (Setlow *et al.*, 1968) and *rec-2 H. influenzae* Rd (Setlow *et al.*, 1972) mutants behaved exactly the same (unpublished observations). Scocca, Poland and Zoon (1974) suggested that *H. influenzae* or *H. parainfluenzae* DNA carries either a recognizable specific modification pattern or a specific repeated sequence. Sisco and Smith (1979) cloned segments of *H. parainfluenzae* DNA into *E. coli* DNA and demonstrated that these fragments were then preferentially taken up. Danner *et al.* (1980) sequenced a number of such (small) fragments and determined that four of them contained the 11-base sequence 5'-AAGTGCGGTCA. They inferred that this sequence was necessary for preferential DNA uptake. Confirmation of the importance of the 11-base sequence for uptake was obtained by synthesizing the sequence and inserting it into foreign DNA (Sisco and Smith, 1979; Danner, Smith and Narang, 1982). The uptake frequencies of these fragments depended surprisingly on the AT-richness of flanking regions. The estimate is that there are about 600 copies of this sequence in the *H. influenzae* or *H. parainfluenzae* genome, i.e. one per 4 kbp (Sisco and Smith, 1979). Phage λ DNA carries one 10-base sequence matching the 11-base sequence. It is now believed that the (less efficient) uptake of heterologous DNA is explained by the presence of 'incomplete' 11-base sequences (Chung and Goodgal, 1979; Goodgal, 1982b). Competent *Neisseria gonorrhoeae* also shows sequence specificity in DNA uptake (Graves, Biswas and Sparling, 1982).

GENETICS OF COMPETENCE

The genetics of competence development has not yet been determined. A number of investigators have isolated uptake-negative mutants (Caster, Postel and Goodgal, 1970; Beattie and Setlow, 1971; Hoffmann and Stuy, 1972; Kooistra, van Boxel and Venema, 1980). With the exception of some (*see below*) these have not yielded much information about the affected gene(s). Interestingly, one may consider serotype Rc strains as being naturally competence-deficient. *H. influenzae* Rd cells lysogenic for phage N3 (Samuels and Clarke, 1969) are unable to take up DNA (Piekarowicz and Siwinska, 1977). This is also true for Rd cells carrying certain conjugative tetracycline-resistance plasmids (Stuy, 1979). I have phage N3 and plasmid pRI234 mutants which show near-normal DNA uptake (unpublished).

The study of periplasmic or membrane proteins and of phospholipids (Sutrina and Scocca, 1976) in non-competent, competence-deficient and competent suspensions has yielded information about a number of possible competence-related polypeptides (Sutrina and Scocca, 1979). Zoon and Scocca (1975) observed the appearance of three periplasmic polypeptides, of sizes 70, 95 and 120 kDa during competence development. Zoon, Habersat and Scocca (1975a) labelled proteins during competency development and observed related polypeptides of 40·5, 58·5, 64, 78, 80 and 95 kDa. Concino and Goodgal (1981) used surface-specific iodination and observed a competence-specific polypeptide of 29 kDa. In addition, they obtained evidence of several related polypeptides ranging in size from 23 to 88 kDa. These results are difficult to interpret because the make-up of membrane and/or periplasmic proteins may have changed upon the cultures' shifts-down.

DNA BINDING BY TRANSFORMASOMES

An exciting discovery was made in 1979 by Kahn and co-workers that a competence-deficient mutant of *H. parainfluenzae* (*com-10*) shed vesicles during competence induction (Kahn *et al.*, 1979; Deich and Hoyer, 1982). Isolated vesicles possessed DNA-binding activity (Kahn, Maul and Goodgal, 1982). Similar vesicles were found with the *com-51* mutant of *H. influenzae* (Kahn *et al.*, 1979; Concino and Goodgal, 1982). Analysis of peptide composition of the vesicles yielded a 29 kDa polypeptide. The vesicles were enriched for 33 and 42 kDa polypeptides and possibly also for ones of 27 and 36 kDa. The significance of these vesicles lies in the observation that those for *H. parainfluenzae* disappeared from the cells' surface upon the addition of homologous DNA (Kahn, Maul and Goodgal, 1982). The vesicles appeared to move into the periplasmic space and cytoplasm. DNase-resistant membrane–DNA complexes could be recovered from disrupted cells. These observations indicated that donor DNA entered the competent cells in association with the vesicles. The vesicles on the surface of competent *H. influenzae* did not disappear after addition of DNA. This may imply a basic difference in the transport of donor DNA through the competent cell's membranes (Kahn, Maul and Goodgal, 1982). Electron micrographs showed that the vesicles extend some 40 nm from the cell surface. They average some 20 nm in diameter and they have a pore structure with an opening of about 5 nm at the point of attachment to the cell membrane (Kahn, Barany and Smith, 1983). In *H. influenzae*, adsorbed DNA may remain sequestered until it exits through the 5 nm pore into the cell's interior.

This scheme explains why irreversibly bound donor DNA is in a 'protected' state, i.e. resistant to exogenous and endogenous DNases. Sequestered within the transformasomes it does not come into contact with cytoplasmic enzymes (Kahn, Barany and Smith, 1983). Evidence for this sequestering was obtained by re-isolating donor DNA through gentle CsCl–phenol extraction of the recipient cells, which presumably yielded intact transformasomes. Most of the DNA, partitioned into the phenol phase, was found to be resistant to DNaseI and *Eco*RI. After its release by SDS treatment, the DNA had become sensitive to these two enzymes.

In summary, then, induction of competence in *Haemophilus* is associated with the appearance of cell-surface vesicles, now called transformasomes. Donor DNA is believed to bind to these vesicles, to become packaged within them, and to remain there until released into the cytoplasm. The average number of transformasomes (10–12) is about that estimated for DNA uptake sites (4–20). The transformasomes appear to be enriched for a number of competence-related polypeptides.

**DNA transport**

WILD-TYPE *H. INFLUENZAE* CELLS

If donor DNA is adsorbed by competent *H. influenzae* Rd cells by binding to, and packaging in, transformasomes, how is it released from these vesicles and then transported to the chromosomal integration sites? Kahn and co-workers (Barany, Khan and Smith, 1983; Kahn, Barany and Smith, 1983; Kahn and Smith, 1984, 1986) studied these questions by using heavily labelled *E. coli*-grown plasmid DNA that contained a 10 kbp *H. influenzae* Rd DNA fragment. Recipient cells were mixed with linearized plasmid DNA. At various times of incubation, donor DNA was extracted from the cells and processed by agarose gel electrophoresis (to determine sizes) before and after being subjected to *Hind*III digestion (to establish *Hind*III methylation). They observed that after a few minutes the donor DNA could be re-isolated intact from the cells, and that it had not undergone modification (it was still susceptible to *Hind*III). That observation suggested that the DNA was in a 'protected' state and not (yet) in the cytoplasm. At progressively longer incubation times, donor DNA label moved into the chromosomal fraction and was now resistant to *in vitro* cleavage by *Hind*III. The still 'protected' donor DNA had undergone considerable degradation, however, as evidenced by the presence of smears below the donor-label agarose bands. No DNA remained in the protected state after some 40 min. The picture indicated by these results is that linear double-stranded donor DNA molecules were adsorbed by, and packaged inside, transformasomes where they remained in a protected state until they were gradually released into the cells' interiors. One of the two strands was degraded upon exiting the transformasomes (by an exonuclease?). The other strand was trimmed down while 'searching' for a homologous region in the cells' chromosomes.

Linear DNA, sealed at the ends (hairpin ends), exited only slowly from the transformasomes (Barany, Kahn and Smith, 1983). When one sealed end was removed, the DNA was released rapidly again. The authors then constructed linear donor DNA with either both ends free or sealed, or only one end sealed. Only the middle (homologous) fragment, having a *Bst*EII site, was labelled. They extracted the recipient cells' DNA after complete integration of donor DNA (the fragment), digested it with *Bst*EII, and then electrophoresed it. In the first two cases the (labelled) junction fragments were equally represented, but in the third case the 7·0 kbp fragment was almost exclusively observed. The conclusion was that the exit of donor DNA from the transformasomes was directional and that the 5'-strand was preferentially destroyed while the 3'-strand was integrated. It is interesting to compare this recombination scheme with that reviewed for *E. coli* (Smith, 1987, 1988).

Studies with open and closed circular donor DNA also revealed that such DNA molecules without ends remained in the 'protected' state for very much longer than linear molecules (Barany, Khan and Smith, 1983; Khan, Barany and Smith, 1983; Khan and Smith, 1984). It thus appeared that the requirement for DNA molecules to exit transformasomes is the possession of free ends.

### *H. INFLUENZAE rec-2* RECIPIENTS

Setlow and co-workers (1972) isolated a transformation-negative Rd mutant strain (*rec-2*) that had some remarkable properties. It was not UV-sensitive and was normally prophage inducible, but it was incapable of phage recombination.

Plasmid recombination appeared to be normal (McCarthy, 1982). Digitonin treatment of recipient cells selectively released much of the donor DNA from *rec-2* cells but not from those of wild-type or *recA1* cells. Donor DNA never became associated with the chromosome (Setlow *et al.*, 1972). In my laboratory, *rec-2* recipients are normally transfected with vegetative phage DNA but not with prophage DNA. They are normally transformed with plasmid DNA; transfection as well as plasmid transfer show the glycerol effect (*see* below), although chromosomal transformation is not influenced by glycerol. *rec-2* recipients irreversibly adsorbed labelled phage HP1 DNA, *E. coli* phage λ DNA and phage T7 DNA. In all cases only some 3% of the label was solubilized over 20–40 min and excreted into the medium (instead of 20% observed with wild-type or *recA1* cells; unpublished results). It thus appears that the *rec-2* mutation somehow blocks the transport of adsorbed DNA into the recipient cells' interiors.

Barouki and Smith (1985) studied this *rec-2* mutant and observed that adsorbed DNA remained in the 'protected' state for long periods of time. Donor DNA label was never recovered in the chromosome, although it was slowly degraded (within the transformasomes). They concluded that the donor DNA was not translocated out of the transformasomes and they speculated that the protein involved in translocation might also play a role in recombination. They also observed endonuclease and phosphatase activity associated with transformasomes.

McCarthy and Kupfer (1987) observed single-stranded gaps and single-stranded tails in the DNA from competent Rd cells (electron microscope). No single-stranded gaps were seen in DNA from competent *rec-2* cells. They speculated that the gaps may play a crucial role in the translocation of donor DNA out of transformasomes.

McCarthy has very recently cloned the *rec-2* gene; he observed that the plasmid with this gene restored all mutant properties to wild type (personal communication).

FATE OF ADSORBED CHROMOSOMAL DNA

*Physical fate*

I should point out here that most of the observations to be reviewed in the following sections were made before the formulation of the transformasome model.

Because chromosomal donor DNA preparations are, as a rule, very heterodisperse, they are not suitable for finding out what kinds of damage donor DNA may suffer after uptake (Notani, 1971). I therefore developed the phage DNA transformation system (Stuy, 1969) in which the donor DNA is monodisperse vegetative phage DNA and the recipient cells carry prophage-deficiency mutations. Phage DNA transforming markers in this system (wild-type alleles) behave exactly like 'standard' chromosomal markers. Some markers are high-efficiency (HE) ones, most are of low efficiency (LE). The latter become high-efficiency markers when scored on a mismatch repair-deficient recipient (*see* below; Bagci and Stuy, 1979). Phage HP1 (Harm and

Rupert, 1963) DNA molecules are physically and genetically identical (Stuy, 1974b; Fitzmaurice and Scocca, 1983); they are some 32 kbp long. Phage HP3 DNA molecules are also identical (Stuy, 1976a). The advantage of this system is that the phage DNA behaves as transforming DNA when (defectively) lysogenic recipient cells are used (donor DNA is chromosomally integrated), while it behaves as transfecting DNA with non-lysogenic recipients (there is no chromosomal integration). Observed differences in the fate of adsorbed phage DNA between these two systems may therefore relate to the actual integration process.

Labelled phage DNA was added to competent defectively lysogenic and non-lysogenic recipient cells and re-extracted DNA was characterized immediately after uptake and after up to 60 min of incubation of the recipient cells (Stuy, 1985). The following observations were made. First, for both systems about 20% of the donor label appeared in the medium in the first 20 min, after which there was little further increase (Stuy, 1974a). Presumably the breakdown products were those found in an earlier study: inorganic phosphate, deoxyribo-nucleotides and traces of small oligonucleotides (Stuy and van der Have, 1971). This breakdown is probably not associated with chromosomal integration because it occurred in both non-lysogenic and lysogenic recipients. The remaining 70–80% of the donor phage DNA appeared both physically (sucrose gradient centrifugation) and biologically intact (linked transforming activity of three markers spanning nearly the entire phage genome). I concluded that one out of every five adsorbed donor DNA molecules was completely degraded while the remaining 70–80% were virtually unchanged. How is this conclusion to be explained? Either all donor DNA molecules were taken up into transformasomes and one in five of these completely degraded its contents (excreting them into the medium), or one in five DNA molecules was adsorbed at a different site (no transformasomes) and was there completely degraded. The latter explanation is not attractive.

Secondly, re-isolated DNA for both systems at 0 and 20 min of incubation had unaltered sedimentation properties in both neutral and alkaline sucrose density gradients (Stuy, 1975). This implied that the adsorbed DNA had not suffered either single-, or double-strand breaks, and that it remained virtually unaffected until it was processed. The interpretation is now that the DNA stayed sequestered inside transformasomes. After longer periods of incubation, re-extracted donor phage DNA label was found in short, single-stranded and in extensively damaged, short, double-stranded DNA fragments (identified by hydroxyapatite column chromatography). But again, because the observations were made for both kinds of non-lysogenic and lysogenic recipients, I concluded that these fragments were not by-products of the donor DNA integration process.

After 50–60 min of incubation, some donor label had associated with the recipient chromosome, although still quite large amounts of label behaved like unaltered phage DNA molecules.

Notani and Goodgal (1966; *see also* Goodgal and Postel, 1967) have shown that only one donor DNA strand is eventually chromosomally integrated. But, unlike other genetic transformation systems, no long single-stranded donor

DNA molecules were found in re-extracted chromosomal donor DNA, even after up to 60 min of incubation (Stuy, 1965). This observation is now explained by the transformasome model which postulates that exiting single-stranded donor DNA molecules undergo immediate chromosomal integration. The single-strand integration model (Notani and Goodgal, 1966) explains why recipient restriction enzymes do not affect transformation (Gromkova and Goodgal, 1974; Stuy, 1976b).

Muhammed and Setlow (1970, 1974) have elucidated the mechanism of repair of UV-damaged transforming DNA. They postulate that damaged single strands are integrated with their damage into the recipient chromosome. Integration is not very much influenced by the damage. After integration, thymine dimer excision repair acts on the integrated donor DNA, removing the damage.

*Fate of donor DNA in* recA⁻ *recipient cells*

Setlow and co-workers (1968) isolated a transformation-deficient mutant of *H. influenzae* Rd. They showed that this *rec-1* mutant (DB117) was UV- and X-ray-sensitive and that it did not carry out phage recombination (Balganesh and Setlow, 1986). The *rec* locus co-transformed some 25% with the *strA* locus. It was concluded that the mutant was deficient in a protein that controlled homologous recombination. Kooistra and Setlow (1976) described three similar mutations which all mapped in the region of the *rec-1* locus. They mentioned that their mutants resembled *E. coli recA* mutants. Because the mutation has been mapped and because the mutant behaviour is similar to *E. coli recA* behaviour, I will call this mutation *recA1*. The fate of donor DNA in *recA* recipients has been studied extensively (Notani *et al.*, 1972; Kooistra and Venema, 1974; Kooistra, van Boxel and Venema, 1983; Barouki and Smith, 1985). Notani *et al.*, (1972) showed that donor DNA label was incorporated in the *recA1* recipient's chromosome, but they suspected that this label represented random donor DNA breakdown products; later, Barouki and Smith (1985) confirmed this speculation. These latter authors used a heavily labelled *E. coli*-grown *E. coli* plasmid with a 10 kbp *H. influenzae* insert (*see* above). By following the fate of this label, using agarose gel electrophoresis of re-isolated DNA, they were able to show by restriction enzyme analysis that homologous donor DNA integration had occurred only in the wild-type recipients. Junction fragments were not observed in the DNA re-isolated from *recA1* cells. In both cases, translocation of the donor DNA out of the transformasomes had occurred normally; thus, translocation may not be coupled to recombination.

Kooistra and co-workers (Kooistra and Venema, 1980; Kooistra, van Boxel and Venema, 1983) have described a number of recombination-deficient Rd mutants which map in the region of the *recA1* locus. The *ird* mutants transform at 3–10% of wild type and they show normal induction of the HP1c1 prophage. In the HM5 mutant, the replication of the donor–recipient DNA complex is inhibited. Transformation frequencies were increased by preventing protein synthesis during transformation. Kooistra and co-workers showed that Setlow's *recA1* mutant lacked three proteins, called a, b and c. The HM5 mutant also lacked these proteins but it appeared to have an altered b protein. The authors speculated that the altered b protein was responsible for the inhibition of the replication of the donor–recipient DNA complex, presumably by preventing the removal of a hypothetical protein which is normally induced during recombination.

The *recA* gene has been cloned, as DNA fragments of 15 kbp, 10 kbp and 3 kbp, into plasmid pAT4 (in press). The presence of the wild-type *recA* gene was verified by transforming out the *recA4* mutation in a *recA4* strain (Stuy and Walter, 1983). The *recA+* locus from these transformants co-transformed some 25% with the *strA1* locus. Rec plasmid-carrying *recA1* strains transformed normally (but, *see below*); however, their UV- and methyl methanesulphonate (MMS)-resistances were not fully restored. Rec plasmid-carrying wild-type cells, on the other hand, were normally resistant. Single- and double-prophage induction, as well as inter- and intra-chromosomal recombination were also only partly restored (Stuy, Hoffmann and Duket, 1972).

## Size of integrated donor DNA

How long are donor DNA fragements that become integrated in the recipient chromosome? The answer is that in the procedures used in the preparation of competent cells such fragments are quite long. Three linked markers in phage HP1 DNA, about 3/4 genome lengths apart (27 kbp), co-transformed about 30% of the time (Stuy, 1969, 1975). This observation indicates that, on the average, long donor DNA strands are integrated into the recipient chromosome.

## Mismatch repair

*H. influenzae* Rd transforming markers show a wide range of integration efficiencies. The donor–recipient DNA recombination product is a heteroduplex if the donor DNA strand carries a mutation. Bagci and Stuy (1979) have isolated Rd mutator mutants (*hex1, hex2*), which are transformed at equally high efficiencies by LE and HE markers. The *hex* mutants behave exactly like the mismatch repair-deficient mutants of *Streptococcus pneumoniae* and I therefore believe that we have identified the *H. influenzae* mismatch repair system. We have also reported observations which explain why compounds like bromouracil (BU) are not mutagenic for wild-type *H. influenzae* (Bagci and Stuy, 1980). Bromouracil did induce mutations in the *hex1* mutant. We concluded that the (premutational) BU–A mismatches, caused by BU incorporation into the newly replicated DNA instead of thymine, are efficiently recognized as mismatches, and then repaired out in *hex+* cells.

Studies on UV sensitivity of transforming DNA have shown that low-efficiency (LE) markers are much more sensitive than high-efficiency (HE) ones if *hex+* recipients are used. LE markers become UV-resistant when scored on *hex1* recipients (Bagci and Stuy, 1982). By studying DNA repair in *hex* and *uvr* recipients we concluded that recombinational repair of UV lesions in the donor strand and mismatch repair of the recipient strand overlapped and caused double-strand (lethal) interruptions.

## mutB1 *recipients*

Ron Walter has studied a mutator *H. influenzae* Rd mutant (Walter, 1985; Walter and Stuy, 1988). This mutant carries one mapped point mutation as determined by revertant analysis. It appears to be deficient in both excision and recombinational repair. Walter observed that the mutant's behaviour is quite similar to that of *E. coli uvrD* mutants. A most interesting mutant property was that a number of markers transformed the mutant at greatly reduced efficiencies. It appeared that HE markers were down much more than LE ones (*Tables 10.1* and *10.2*). Walter used plasmid DNA in some crosses as an internal marker to ascertain that the various recipients were roughly equally competent (*Table 10.1*). He also observed that HE markers were much more UV-sensitive when assayed on the *mutB1* mutant. *Hex1–mutB1* double mutants behaved like *mutB1* single ones. One explanation is that *mutB1* recipients do not carry out *hex* mismatch repair. Because of their impaired recombinational capability, donor DNA integration is greatly reduced, and markers are more UV-sensitive. A question mark remains, however. Why are the transformation efficiencies reduced more for some markers than for others (*Table 10.2*)?

**Table 10.1** Genetic transformation of wild-type, *hex1* and *mutB1 H. influenzae* recipient cells with the HE marker *novA1*, and the LE marker *rifA2* and, using glycerol, with whole plasmid pJS1867

| Recipient | Transformants per ml | | | | Ratio | | |
|---|---|---|---|---|---|---|---|
| | *novA1* | *rifA2* | *amp23* | Nov/Amp | Rif/Amp | ratio* |
| wild type | $3\cdot0 \times 10^5$ | $7\cdot0 \times 10^4$ | $1\cdot4 \times 10^4$ | 22 | 5 | 0·33 |
| *hex1* | $3\cdot2 \times 10^5$ | $3\cdot7 \times 10^5$ | $3\cdot2 \times 10^4$ | 10 | 12 | 1·2 |
| *mutB1* | $6\cdot0 \times 10^4$ | $5\cdot0 \times 10^4$ | $1\cdot4 \times 10^4$ | 4·3 | 3.6 | 0·33 |

* $\dfrac{\text{Rif/Amp}}{\text{Nov/Amp}}$

**Table 10.2** Genetic transformation of *H. influenzae* wild-type and *mutB1* recipient cells with DNA from a multiply marked donor. Note that linkage between the *novA1* and *rifA2* loci (as defined by double transformants over those for least efficient marker) has not changed

| Recipient | *eryA1* | *nalA1* | *novA1* | *rifA2* | *vioA2* | *novA1, rifA2* |
|---|---|---|---|---|---|---|
| Rd1287 | $1\cdot2 \times 10^6$ | $5\cdot0 \times 10^5$ | $2\cdot0 \times 10^6$ | $3\cdot0 \times 10^5$ | $2\cdot7 \times 10^5$ | $6\cdot0 \times 10^4$ |
| Rd1140 *mutB1* | $3\cdot0 \times 10^5$ | $1\cdot4 \times 10^5$ | $1\cdot6 \times 10^5$ | $3\cdot5 \times 10^5$ | $1\cdot5 \times 10^5$ | $4\cdot0 \times 10^4$ |

## CHROMOSOMAL DNA WITH NON-HOMOLOGOUS SEQUENCES

### Integrated plasmids

Many antibiotic-resistant *H. influenzae* hospital isolates do not carry free plasmids (Stuy, 1980a). Bendler (1978) reported on the transfer of one such resistance by transformation from a serotype b isolate to the common Rd strain. He observed that this was an inefficient phenomenon. The transformation frequency in subsequent Rd to Rd crosses was considerably increased. He speculated that resistance (*amp-r*) was located on a long, non-homologous DNA sequence in the cell's chromosome. I have studied the same Sb strain and found that it, as well as many other isolates, carried an integrated conjugative plasmid (Stuy, 1980a). A scheme was proposed (Stuy, 1980a) for the transformation transfer of such chromosomally located resistance determinants. The plasmid-flanking segments of the single-stranded donor DNA synapse with homologous sequences in the chromosome. The consequence is that the (single-stranded) plasmid DNA segment 'loops out' of the recombinant DNA structure. It may be vulnerable to endonuclease cutting in that stage and then the longer the looped-out segment, the more likely it will be that it is cut and no transformant will be produced. The single-stranded segment becomes double-stranded upon duplication of the chromosome.

*Single prophage DNA*

Harm and Rupert (1963) reported that *H. influenzae* prophage HP1 DNA could transfect competent Rd cells. This has been confirmed by others (Boling, Setlow and Allison, 1972; Stuy, 1980c). My observations have always been that single HP1 or HP3 prophage DNA transfected about 10 times more frequently than did vegetative DNA. The general explanation for this increase has been that in prophage DNA the phage DNA ends (at the joints) are (initially) protected from exonuclease digestion starting from prophage DNA ends (Flock, 1978). It occurred to me that there could be another explanation. The phage genome in the DNA fragment can be viewed simply as a non-homologous DNA segment that is added to the recipient chromosome, as outlined for transfer of integrated plasmids (Stuy, 1980b). The phage genome will then loop out as a single strand. Upon duplication of this segment, the recipient is always induced because it contains no phage repressor. In this scheme the transfection frequency is determined by the length of the phage genome and not by the extent of damage suffered by the prophage DNA upon entering the recipient.

Proof for my hypothesis was obtained by observing that:

1. Transfection with prophage DNA required a functional *recA* gene, while transfection with vegetative DNA did not;
2. UV-damaged prophage DNA was not repairable, while vegetative phage DNA was; and
3. *H. influenzae* prophage DNA did not transfect *H. parainfluenzae* (lack of homology between phage genome-flanking DNA segments and the *H. parainfluenzae* chromosome), while vegetative phage DNA did.

The mechanism offered by Setlow and Boling (1972) is thus probably not correct. The generally used *H. parainfluenzae* strain (Boss) is resistant to phage HP1; the transfection experiment showed that this strain does not restrict phage HP1. Similar observations were made with prophage HP3.

*Double prophage DNA*

Superinfection of *H. influenzae* Rd single lysogens with phage HP1 or HP3 yields about 1% tandem double lysogens (Stuy and Hoffmann, 1971). DNA from such double lysogens transfects about 100 times more efficiently than does single prophage DNA (Stuy, 1980c). I believe that the scheme for additive transformation cannot explain this observation because:

1. The efficiency of prophage transfection should then be lower (the to-be-added segment is twice as long);
2. Double prophage DNA efficiently transfected *H. parainfluenzae* despite the absence of homology between phage genome-flanking regions and chromosome; and
3. CaCl$_2$-generated competent Rd cells were transfected by vegetative phage DNA and by double prophage DNA, but not by single prophage DNA. Such cells are also not transformed by chromosomal DNA and that suggests that they cannot carry out recombination between donor DNA and chromosome (Stuy, 1980c).

The conclusion is therefore that double prophage transfection does not require interaction of the donor DNA with the recipient chromosome. Marker analysis of phage produced by multiply-marked double prophage DNA has provided evidence for the explanation that tandem double prophage DNA undergoes internal recombination (after uptake). That event results in a double-stranded circular phage genome and a single prophage DNA fragment (*see* Stuy and Hoffmann, 1971). The phage produced in transfection originates from the circular phage genome. However, because of the transformasome model for transformation, this scheme has to be modified. The double prophage DNA fragment exits the transformasomes as single strands. DNA duplication begins at the origins of the two phage genomes (Stuy, 1974b), which results in a partially double-stranded DNA molecule. This structure then undergoes internal recombination to yield a circular phage genome. That assumption now explains why repair of UV-damaged double prophage DNA was not observed (Stuy, 1980c): damaged single strands cannot be repaired. It is also clear now why *rec-2* recipients are not transfected by double prophage DNA: the DNA is not translocated out of the transformasomes.

*Additive transformation*

Ron Walter constructed a number of lysogenic Rd strains with non-homologous plasmid pRI234-derived (Stuy, 1979) DNA segments spliced into their HP1 prophages (Stuy and Walter, 1981). The transfer efficiencies of these non-homologous segments were proportional to their UV-sensitivites (Walter and Stuy, 1982b). Walter concluded that transformation efficiencies were measures of insert sizes. The mismatch repair system does not recognize such donor DNA segments. However, just one closely linked point mutation in the recipient chromosome drastically reduced transfer, while such mutations in the donor DNA had much smaller effects (Walter and Stuy, 1982a). Interestingly, this effect was independent of the recipients' mismatch repair phenotype (*hex*⁺ or *hex*). It may be that the looped-out structure interferes with repair of the mismatched base pair. Walter's observations explain why transfer of integrated plasmids is so much more efficient between isogenic strains (*see* above).

Walter also observed that recipients' inserts were very efficiently deleted when using prophage donor DNA without inserts. The *hex* repair system did not influence these deletions. Inserts could be replaced by other inserts, and here the efficiencies observed were those obtained for insert addition. We speculated that heterologous transformation might be similar to insert substitution.

I have recently cloned the *cl* insert which transforms additively with an efficiency of about 0·10 relative to the HE *novA1* marker. The cl insert is 9 kbp long.

VEGETATIVE PHAGE HP1 DNA

Competent Rd cells can be transfected by phage HP1 DNA (Harm and Rupert, 1963; Boling, Setlow and Allison, 1972; Setlow and Boling 1972; Boling, Allison and Setlow, 1973; Stuy, 1975, 1980c, 1986). The physical fate of this DNA has been studied by Jane Setlow and co-workers (Boling, Setlow and Allison, 1972; Setlow and Boling, 1972; Notani, Setlow and Allison, 1973) and by me (Stuy, 1975) with the purpose of understanding why this phenomenon is so inefficient. The *rec-2* Rd mutant is transfected with wild-type efficiency but transfection of the *recA1* mutant is down by some 80% or more. Setlow and co-workers reported that wild-type recipients give a concentration response of less than 2; however, different competency regimes gave different values (Notani, Setlow and Allison, 1973). *recA1* recipients gave a linear response. The authors also reported that dimeric forms of phage DNA, found in some of their preparations, had increased activity per molecule but only on wild-type recipients (Boling, Allison and Setlow, 1973). They observed a fast-sedimenting fraction in phage DNA re-isolated from wild-type recipients but not in DNA re-isolated from *recA1* ones. Notani and co-workers (1973) published electron microscopic evidence for the presence in the re-isolated DNA of covalently closed, twisted DNA molecules and very long molecules. They concluded that recombination between degraded phage DNA molecules (after leaving the transformasomes?) was responsible for concatemer formation, and thus for most of the transfection activity observed in the original transfecting phage DNA. Their assumptions explained the role of the *recA* gene in phage DNA transfection. The low efficiency of transfection was thus, in their view, caused by damage suffered by the phage DNA molecules after uptake.

In my laboratory carefully prepared HP1 DNA preparations show a near-linear transfection response with concentration (between 1·2 and 1·4; Stuy, 1986). Such preparations have a very low transfecting efficiency of about one unit per 100 000 DNA molecules. It is attractive to explain this by assuming that the phage DNA suffers damage upon entering the cell. This damage, however, is neither single-strand nor double-strand interruptions (Stuy, 1975).

The transformasome model postulates that double-stranded DNA molecules are converted to single-stranded ones upon exiting transformasomes and that these single-stranded molecules are trimmed at exiting. One can argue that by chance some completely undamaged single-stranded phage DNA molecules are released into the cells' interiors. These molecules, however, cannot be converted to double-stranded molecules, because phage DNA duplication appears to go in only one direction and the duplication origin is not at an end (Stuy, 1974b). It is more likely that no single-stranded molecules escape trimming (and thus inactivation) while exiting the transformasomes. Because UV-damaged transfecting DNA is repairable (Setlow and Boling, 1972; Stuy, 1980c, 1986), transfecting DNA molecules must enter the recipient cells' interiors as double-stranded molecules. I have explained the repair phenomenon by assuming that a few phage DNA molecules 'leak' out of the transformasomes (Stuy, 1986). This speculation is supported by the observation that treatment of transfected cells with glycerol before plating increased the production of phage-producing transfected recipients by some 25–50 times (Stuy, 1986).

Transfection was studied some 16 years ago in my laboratory. We prepared phage HP1 DNA (often labelled radioactively) and followed its fate after uptake by competent Rd cells. *Figure 10.2b* shows that these preparations did not contain fast-sedimenting biological activity; transforming and transfecting activities co-sedimented. Thus, activity resided in monomeric linear forms of the phage DNA. DNA re-isolated from transfected cells, was centrifuged through neutral sucrose density gradients and fractions were analysed for label, transfecting activity and transforming activity (a single central marker as well as three linked markers spanning two-thirds of the phage genome). Labelled *E. coli* phage T7 was used as a reference marker in most experiments. After 30 min of uptake at room temperature, both transforming activities of the re-isolated DNA co-sedimented at the expected velocities but nearly all of the transfecting activity sedimented ahead of these activities (Rosenthal, 1972; Bacon, 1974). Bacon's results with three different recipients are shown in *Figure 10.2*. His results, obtained with the *recA1* recipient, are significantly different from those observed with the wild-type and with the *rec-2* recipients. We found that even after 20 min of incubation at 37°C of wild-type transfected cells, the transfecting activity sedimented faster than the transforming activity (unpublished). Our observations indicate that:

1. Some 90% of the adsorbed phage DNA had suffered damage rendering it non-transfecting; and
2. A minute portion of the adsorbed DNA had undergone a change which had rendered it 'supertransfecting'. The amounts of this DNA were too small to give measurable label or transforming activities in the sucrose fractions.

Given the recent discovery (Stuy, 1986) that glycerol treatment of transfected cells before plating results in some 25 times more plaque-forming units, I think that the following conclusions can be made:

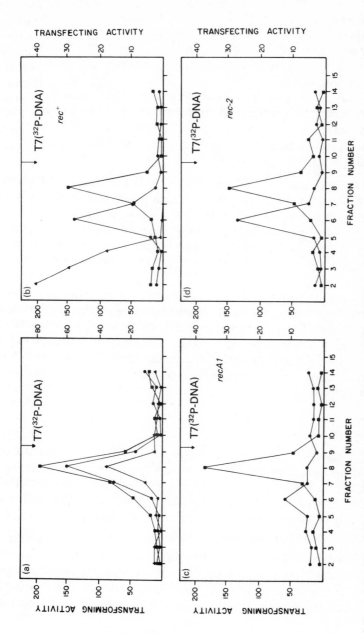

**Figure 10.2** (a) Sucrose density gradient sedimentation of mature phage HP1 DNA; ●, transfecting units. (b) Sedimentation of total DNA isolated from *rec*⁺ competent cells that had taken up phage HP1 DNA for 30 min at room temperature; ●and ■, *see* (a). (c) As (b) but with *recA1* recipients. (d) As (b) but with *rec-2* recipients; ●, transfecting units; ■, NA118⁺ transforming units; ▲, triple marker transforming units; ▲, recipient chromosomal *nov-r* transforming units; ▲, recipient chromosomal *nov-r* transforming units.

1. Damage suffered by the bulk of the adsorbed DNA during uptake is the loss of 5′ terminal phosphate and/or terminal nucleotides; this damage is not affecting transforming activities.
2. Some 10% of the DNA appears to escape this action; it is still monomeric and linear (it sediments with the bulk of the DNA), and glycerol treatment releases these molecules from the transformasomes.
3. The sedimentation velocity of the minute 'supertransfecting' DNA fraction indicates that it is either supercoiled closed circles, or linear dimers, or both.
4. A functional *recA*⁺ gene may be necessary for the formation of this 'supertransfecting' DNA fraction; this fraction is probably formed in the transformasomes because we observed it after only 5 min of DNA uptake at room temperature (unpublished). Transformasomes have ligase activity (Goodgal, 1982a).

Preliminary experiments of both Rosenthal (1972) and Bacon (1974) have shown that the 'supertransfecting' DNA fraction is sensitive to heat and to shear, but resistant to pronase and chloroform treatment. In the light of the discovery that tandem double prophage DNA is in a way also 'supertransfecting', it seems to me that the above vegetative phage DNA fraction consists (mostly) of dimer DNA molecules which transfect as described for double prophage DNA.

In summary, nearly all phage DNA molecules are damaged after uptake into the transformasomes and rendered non-transfecting. Some undamaged molecules 'leak' out of these vesicles as double-stranded (repairable) linear forms; these yield transfected cells. Some undamaged double-stranded molecules are dimerized and become supertransfecting in *rec*⁺ recipients. They exit the transformasomes as (unrepairable) single strands. Dimerization may require a functional *recA* gene.

PLASMID DNA

Efficiencies of plasmid transfer (I prefer this term over transformation) are very low, but no quantitative studies have been published. Large plasmids appear to transfer less efficiently. The concentration response is linear, meaning that one plasmid is sufficient for transfer (Stuy and Walter, 1986a, 1986b). It is important for cloning purposes to know how plasmid transfer efficiencies can be increased. Increases can be realized by three phenomena.

1. It is reasonable to assume (but not proven) that *H. influenzae* plasmids that do not carry the 11-base sequence are poorly taken up. Adsorption can be expected to increase drastically by inserting an 11-base-carrying DNA fragment into the plasmid. Such increases should also be observed with *recA1* recipients.
2. Insertion of a chromosomal DNA fragment into a plasmid will boost transfer but only with *rec*⁺ recipients (Setlow *et al.*, 1981; Stuy and Walter, 1986a). This phenomenon can thus be distinguished from the one described above. The explanation, worked out by researchers using

*Bacillus subtilis* and *Streptococcus pneumoniae*, is that adsorbed plasmid is randomly cut to form inactive linear molecules. When insert plasmids happen to be cut within their inserts, linear single-stranded fragments can synapse their two (insert) ends with the homologous chromosome DNA segment, thereby looping out the plasmid genome. Duplication of this looped-out DNA followed by re-circularization yields the circular insert plasmid genome. This phenomenon is called plasmid reconstitution (for a review, see Stuy and Walter, 1986a). A functional *recA* gene product is required for the synapsis. For cloning purposes one should realize that this reconstitution often results in the transfer of mutations from chromosome to insert, which fact may defeat the purpose of the cloning effort. This phenomenon may also occur between a resident plasmid (instead of the chromosome) and donor plasmid (Stuy and Walter, 1986a; *see also* Balgamesh and Setlow, 1986).

3. The transformasome model postulates that circular DNA molecules can only exit these uptake vesicles as linearized molecules. Linearized plasmids are inactive (Stuy and Walter, 1986a). The fact that *H. influenzae* plasmids are transferable with linear kinetics into both $rec^+$ and *recA1* recipients suggested that the established plasmids might have been ones that had leaked intact out of transformasomes (Stuy and Walter, 1986b). The observations that UV-damaged plasmids are repairable (Stuy, 1980a; Stuy and Walter, 1986b) indicated that the leaked ones had entered the cells' interiors as double-stranded molecules. We speculated that we might increase this leakage by treating recipients (after plasmid DNA uptake) with compounds that would disorganize transformasome membrane-bound proteins, namely those that control the normal exiting of DNA molecules as linear single DNA strands. We found that glycerol and dimethylsulphoxide did cause such increases. The glycerol treatment procedure, now routinely used in my laboratory, can increase plasmid transfer by some 1000 times. Our discovery has enabled the cloning of a number of DNA repair genes, including *recA*.

**Development of competence**

Genetic transformation is a rather rare phenomenon in the world of bacteria. It is my point that even within the genus *Haemophilus* efficient genetic transformation is found with only a few strains or species. There is, to my knowledge, no substantiated evidence that transformation occurs in nature; in fact, what evidence there is says that it is extremely rare (Stuy, 1985). However, Rd strains show efficient transformation (in the laboratory) and (by dogma) this behaviour must have some advantage. I have always frowned upon pure genetic explanations. What remains, then, is speculation centred around DNA repair.

If efficient transformation is a laboratory phenomenon, we must seek answers to its why and how in the methods used to prepare fully competent recipients. The MIV method is basically a nutritional shift-down from supplemented brain–heart infusion to the incomplete MIV medium. Effects of oxygen starvation have been reported (Barnhart and Herriott, 1963; Miller and Huang, 1972). Notani and Setlow (1975), in their monumental review of genetic transformation, have listed all compounds that had an effect on the development of competence. The relevance of these effects is mostly unclear, however. Miller and Huang (1972) reported that a shift-down from a defined medium to MIV required oxygen starvation for development of competence. They argued that some compounds may have repressed the initiation of the development of competence rather than other compounds having induced it. They speculated that relief of catabolite repression might control this phenomenon.

Their speculation was substantiated by the discovery that cyclic adenosine 3', 5'-monophosphate (cAMP) produced a considerable increase in competency (Wise, Alexander and Powers, 1973), although not to maximal levels. Zoon and co-workers (1975b) followed up this discovery. They reported that cAMP did derepress the synthesis of some enzymes, but that it did not yield detectable levels of competence-related envelope proteins. These authors concluded that additional regulatory events had to occur to trigger complete expression of competence.

The aerobic–anaerobic method for making *H. influenzae* fully competent involves two shifts-down: first an oxygen starvation, which is followed by a nutritional shift-down while releasing the oxygen starvation. Joan Hoffmann and I (Stuy and Hoffmann, 1970, 1971) reported that growing cells, anaerobically held cells, or cells that had been diluted in saline without a preceding oxygen starvation treatment, did not take up DNA. Only aerobically–anaerobically saline-incubated (competent) cells did. We answered the question as to whether any of these four groups of cells were internally capable of performing genetic transformation by using defectively lysogenic recipients and infecting them with wild-type phage HP1. We observed that competent defectively monolysogenic cells carried out efficient transformation to wild-type monolysogens. Anaerobically held cells, as well as the saline-incubated ones did so, too, but the growing cells' response was mainly the formation of double lysogens. We concluded that the recombination mechanisms in the former three kinds of cells were fully mobilized as a consequence of either the shift-down in oxygen supply or the nutritional shift-down. The development of the ability to take up DNA, however, required both procedures in the correct order. Unfortunately, neither the catabolite repression hypothesis, nor the events described here, give any clue as to the biochemical nature of the hypothetical event that triggers the development of competence.

I have always believed that the experiment outlined in *Figure 10.1* can tell us something about that triggering event. By incubating a 2 ml broth culture at 37°C without shaking we may impose both an oxygen starvation and a nutrient shift-down upon the cells. But, if so, why do so few cells (1 per 10 000) become competent? It seemed to me that there were two possible answers:

1.  The triggering event occurred in just those few cells, all of which became competent; or
2.  The event occurred in all cells but only a few became competent because a

necessary contributing compound was present in sufficient amounts only in a few cells.

I now have reason to believe that the second answer may be the correct one.

As mentioned, I have cloned the $recA^+$ gene in plasmid pAT4 as 15 kbp, 10 kbp and 3 kbp inserts. When I repeated the experiment in *Figure 10.1* with *rec* plasmid-carrying cultures, either as chromosomally Rec⁺ or Rec⁻, the numbers of competent cells increased dramatically (*Figure 10.3*). In some experiments they even approached the theoretical maximum. To ensure that this phenomenon was not serotype d-specific, I introduced some of the *rec* plasmids in an Rc (Ruggiero) and in an Rb (Santo) strain. Rc strains cannot be made competent. *rec* plasmid-carrying Rc strains could not be made competent either. The Rb strain used is poorly transformable; however, the presence of a *rec* plasmid increased its competence by some 100 times. The stimulation of competence development thus appears to be a general phenomenon.

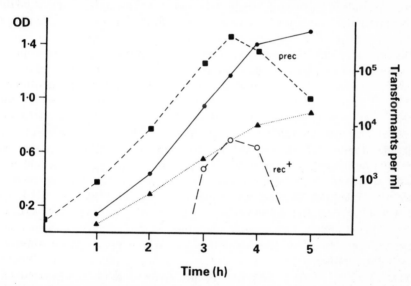

**Figure 10.3** Competency development in wild-type *H. influenzae* without a plasmid and in *recA1* *H. influenzae* carrying the *rec* plasmid pJS2255 during growth in Levinthal broth at 37°C. ●, turbidity of wild-type culture; ▲, same for *rec* plasmid-carrying culture; ○, numbers of potential transformants per ml for wild-type culture; ■, same for *rec* plasmid-carrying culture. Note that the *novAB* marker used has a transformation efficiency of only 0·1.

What can this observation tell us about the nature of the triggering event? It seems to me that the main difference between the regular culture and the *rec* plasmid-carrying one is that the latter contains much more *recA* gene product. That product might be the necessary contributing compound which is present in limiting amounts in normal cultures. It is known that the *recA* gene product interacts with regions of single-stranded DNA. I therefore speculate that shifts-down lead to disorganized replication forks. The absence of oxygen prevents the production of DNA precursor triphosphates, and unwound DNA regions at the replication fork remain single-stranded. DNA regions that happen to undergo repair from spontaneous damage may also remain single-stranded. I have found in preliminary experiments that the incubation of shaken cultures in 2,4-dinitrophenol can, to some degree, replace the anaerobic phase in my competency regime. *rec* plasmid-carrying cultures responded even better. Growing cultures responded similarly to the presence of nalidixic acid or novobiocin. And my observation that additive transformation appears to be more efficient with *rec* plasmid-carrying recipients points to an association of the *recA* gene product with single-stranded DNA segments, namely, the looped out to-be-added DNA segment, thereby protecting it from being cut.

Setlow and co-workers (Leclerc and Setlow, 1975; Sedgwick and Setlow, 1976) have published experiments which showed that competent Rd cells had single-stranded regions in their DNA. McCarthy and Kupfer (1987) examined the DNA from Rd cells by electron microscopy and observed that single-stranded gaps and single-stranded tails formed in DNA during development of competence. They calculated that as much as 4·5% of the cells' genomes existed in a single-stranded state. They also found that *rec-2* mutant cells produced only single-stranded tails. Their speculation was that the gaps are somehow involved in the translocation of the donor DNA out of the transformasomes. They calculated that between 5 and 10 segments of the recipient genome would be available for synapsis with transforming donor DNA. Their speculation requires an extensive turn-over of the gaps so that most of the genome would be exposed within the relatively short time observed for the donor DNA's stay within the transformasomes. Although their speculation has attractive points, the actual link between transformation and single-stranded DNA regions remains unclear. In my speculation, the single-stranded DNA regions are simply a general signal, like the one found in *E. coli* SOS repair. In the case of *H. influenzae*, the genes to be derepressed by the single-stranded DNA–recA protein complex may well include the competence genes. This derepression may only be non-specifically affected by catabolite repression.

The purpose of transformation is not made evident, of course, by my hypothesis. I believe that we must first find out where in nature, and under what conditions, genetic transformation occurs. Perhaps then, this purpose may become clear.

## References

ALEXANDER, H.E. AND LEIDY, G. (1951). Determination of inherited traits of *Haemophilus influenzae* by deoxyribonucleic acid fractions isolated from type-specific cells. *Journal of Experimental Medicine* **93**, 345–359.

BACON, W. (1974). Master's Degree Thesis, Florida State University.

BAGCI, H. AND STUY, J.H. (1979). A *hex* mutant of *Haemophilus influenzae*. *Molecular and General Genetics* **175**, 175–179.

BAGCI, H. AND STUY, J.H. (1980). Bromouracil-induced mutagenesis in a mismatch-repair-deficient strain of *Haemophilus influenzae*. *Mutation Research* **73**, 15–19.

BAGCI, H. AND STUY, J.H. (1982). Repair of ultraviolet-damaged transforming DNA in a mismatch repair-deficient strain of *Haemophilus influenzae*. *Photochemistry and Photobiology* **35**, 331–335.

BALGANESH, M. AND SETLOW, J.K. (1986). Plasmid-to-plasmid recombination in *Haemophilus influenzae*. *Journal of Bacteriology* **165**, 308–311.

BARANY, F. AND KAHN, M.E. (1985). Comparison of transformation mechanisms of *Haemophilus parainfluenzae* and *Haemophilus influenzae*. *Journal of Bacteriology* **161**, 72–79.

BARANY, F., KAHN, M.E. AND SMITH, H.O. (1983). Directional transport and integration of donor DNA in *Haemophilus influenzae* transformation. *Proceedings of the National Academy of Sciences of the United States of America* **80**, 7274–7278.

BARNHART, B.J. AND COX, S.H. (1968). Radiation-sensitive and radiation-resistant mutants of *Haemophilus influenzae*. *Journal of Bacteriology* **96**, 280–282.

BARNHART, B.J. AND HERRIOTT, R.M. (1963). Penetration of deoxyribonucleic acid into *Haemophilus influenzae*. *Biochimica et Biophysica Acta* **76**, 25–39.

BAROUKI, R. AND SMITH, H.O. (1985). Reexamination of the phenotypic defects in the *rec-1* and *rec-2* mutants of *Haemophilus influenzae* Rd. *Journal of Bacteriology* **163**, 629–634.

BAROUKI, R. AND SMITH, H.O. (1986). Initial steps in *Haemophilus influenzae* transformation. *Journal of Biological Chemistry* **261**, 8617–8623.

BEATTIE, K.L. AND SETLOW, J.K. (1971). Transformation-defective strains of *Haemophilus influenzae*. *Nature* **231**, 177–179.

BENDLER, J.W. (1978). Physical size of the donor locus and transmission of *Haemophilus influenzae* ampicillin resistance genes by deoxyribonucleic acid-mediated transformation. *Journal of Bacteriology* **125**, 197–204.

BERNS, K.I. AND THOMAS, C.A. (1965). Electron microscopy of DNA from *Haemophilus influenzae*. *Journal of Molecular Biology* **11**, 476–490.

BOLING, M.E., ALLISON, D.P. AND SETLOW, J.K. (1973). Bacteriophage of *Haemophilus influenzae*. III. Morphology, DNA homology, and immunity properties of HP1c1, S2, and the defective bacteriophage from strain Rd. *Journal of Virology* **11**, 585–591.

BOLING, M.E., SETLOW, J.K. AND ALLISON, D.P. (1972). Bacteriophage of *Haemophilus influenzae*. I. Differences between infection by whole phage, extracted phage DNA, and prophage DNA extracted from lysogenic cells. *Journal of Molecular Biology* **63**, 335–348.

CASTER, J.H., POSTEL, E.H. AND GOODGAL, S.H. (1970). Competence mutants: Isolation of transformational deficient strains of *Haemophilus influenzae*. *Nature* **227**, 515–517.

CHUNG, B.C. AND GOODGAL, S.H. (1979). The specific uptake of cloned *Haemophilus* DNA. *Biochemistry and Biophysics Research Communications* **88**, 208–214.

CONCINO, M.F. AND GOODGAL, S.H. (1981). *Haemophilus influenzae* polypeptides involved in deoxyribonucleic acid uptake detected by cellular surface protein iodination. *Journal of Bacteriology* **148**, 311–318.

CONCINO, M.F. AND GOODGAL, S.H. (1982). Partial characterization and properties of *Haemophilus influenzae* com-51 and vesicles produced during incubation in MIV nongrowth medium. *Journal of Bacteriology* **152**, 441–450.

DANNER, D.B., SMITH, H.O. AND NARANG, S.A. (1982). Construction of DNA recognition sites active in *Haemophilus* transformation. *Proceedings of the National Academy of Sciences of the United States of America* **79**, 2393–2397.

DANNER, D.B., DEICH, R.A., SISCO, K.L. AND SMITH, H.O. (1980). An eleven-base-pair sequence determines the specificity of DNA uptake in *Haemophilus* transformation. *Gene* **11**, 311–318.

DEICH, R.A. AND HOYER, L.C. (1982). Generation and release of DNA-binding vesicles by *Haemophilus influenzae* during induction and lose of competence. *Journal of Bacteriology* **152**, 855–864.

DEICH, R.A. AND SMITH, H.O. (1980). Mechanism of homospecific DNA uptake in

*Haemophilus influenzae* transformation. *Molecular and General Genetics* **177**, 369–374.

FITZMAURICE, W.P. AND SCOCCA, J.J. (1983). Restriction map and location of mutations on the genome of bacteriophage HPIc1 of *Haemophilus influenzae* Rd. *Gene* **24**, 29–35.

FLOCK, J.-I. (1978). Transfection with replicating DNA from the temperate *Bacillus* bacteriophage φ105 and with T4-ligase treated φ105 DNA: the importance in transfection of being longer than genome-length. *Molecular and General Genetics* **163**, 7–15.

GOODGAL, S.H. (1982a). DNA uptake of *Haemophilus* transformation. *Annual Review of Genetics* **16**, 169–192.

GOODGAL, S.H. (1982b). Specificity of DNA uptake by *Haemophilus*. In *Genetic Exchange* (U. N. Streips, S.H. Goodgal, W.R. Guild and G.A. Wilson, Eds), pp. 187–196. Dekker, New York.

GOODGAL, S.H. AND HERRIOTT, R.M. (1961). Studies of transformation of *Haemophilus influenzae*. I. Competence. *Journal of General Physiology* **44**, 1201–1227.

GOODGAL, S.H. AND POSTEL, E.H. (1967). On the mechanism of integration following transformation with single-stranded DNA of *Haemophilus influenzae*. *Journal of Molecular Biology* **28**, 261–273.

GRAVES, J.F., BISWAS, G.D. AND SPARLING, P.F. (1982). Sequence-specific DNA uptake in transformation of *Neisseria gonorrhoeae*. *Journal of Bacteriology* **152**, 1071–1077.

GROMKOVA, R. AND GOODGAL, S.H. (1974). On the role of restriction enzymes of *Haemophilus* in transformation and transfection. In *Oak Ridge Symposium on Mechanism of Recombination*, pp. 309–316. Plenum Publishing, New York.

HARM, H. AND RUPERT, C.S. (1963). Infection of transformable cells of *Haemophilus influenzae* by bacteriophage and by bacteriophage DNA. *Zeitschrift für Verenbungslehre* **94**, 336–348.

HERRIOTT, R.M., MEYER, E.M. AND VOGT, M. (1970). Refined nongrowth media for stage II development of competence in *Haemophilus influenzae*. *Journal of Bacteriology* **101**, 517–524.

HOFFMANN, J.F. AND STUY, J.H. (1972). Prophage recombination in transformation-negative mutants of *Haemophilus influenzae*. *Biochemical and Biophysical Research Communications* **46**, 1388–1393.

KAHN, M.E. AND SMITH, H.O. (1984). Transformation in *Haemophilus*: a problem in membrane biology. *Journal of Membrane Biology* **81**, 89–103.

KAHN, M.E. AND SMITH, H.O. (1986). Role of transformasomes in *Haemophilus influenzae* Rd transformation. *Branbury Report 24: Antibiotic resistance genes: Ecology, Transfer, and Expression*, pp. 143–152. Cold Spring Harbor Laboratory, New York.

KAHN, M.E., BARANY, P. AND SMITH, H.O. (1983). Transformasomes: specialized membranous structures that protect DNA during *Haemophilus* transformation. *Proceedings of the National Academy of Sciences of the United States of America* **80**, 6927–6931.

KAHN, M.E., MAUL, G. AND GOODGAL, S.H. (1982). Possible mechanism for donor DNA binding and transport in *Haemophilus*. *Proceedings of the National Academy of Sciences of the United States of America* **79**, 6370–6374.

KAHN, M., CONCINO, M., GROMKOVA, R. AND GOODGAL, S.H. (1979). DNA binding activities of vesicles produced by competence-deficient mutants of *Haemophilus*. *Biochemical and Biophysical Research Communications* **87**, 764–772.

KELLY, T.J. AND SMITH, H.O. (1970). A restriction enzyme from *Haemophilus influenzae*. II. Base sequence of the recognition site. *Journal of Molecular Biology* **51**, 393–409.

KOOISTRA, J. AND SETLOW, J.K. (1976). Similarity in properties and mapping of the three *rec* mutants of *Haemophilus influenzae*. *Journal of Bacteriology* **127**, 327–333.

KOOISTRA, J. AND VENEMA, G. (1974). Fate of donor deoxyribonucleic acid in a highly transformation-deficient strain of *Haemophilus influenzae*. *Journal of Bacteriology* **119**, 705–717.

KOOISTRA, J. AND VENEMA, G. (1980). Properties of *Haemophilus influenzae* mutants that are slightly recombination deficient and carry a mutation in the *rec-1* region. *Journal of Bacteriology* **142**, 829–835.

KOOISTRA, J., VAN BOXEL, T. AND VENEMA, G. (1980). Deoxyribonucleic acid binding properties and membrane protein composition of a competence-deficient mutant of *Haemophilus influenzae*. *Journal of Bacteriology* **144**, 22–27.

KOOISTRA, J., VAN BOXEL, T. AND VENEMA, G. (1983). Characterization of a conditionally transformation-deficient mutant of *Haemophilus influenzae* that carries a mutation in the *rec-1* gene region. *Journal of Bacteriology* **153**, 852–860.

LECLERC, J.E. AND SETLOW, J.K. (1975). Single-strand regions in the deoxyribonucleic acid of competent *Haemophilus influenzae*. *Journal of Bacteriology* **122**, 1091–1102.

LEE, J.J. AND SMITH, H.O. (1988). Sizing of *Haemophilus influenzae* Rd genome by pulse-field agarose gel electrophoresis. *Journal of Bacteriology* **170**, 4402–4405.

LEIDY, G., JAFFEE, I. AND ALEXANDER, H. (1962). Emergence of competence (for transformation) of three *Haemophilus* species in a chemically defined environment. *Proceedings of the Society of Experimental and Biological Medicine* **111**, 648–649.

MCCARTHY, D.(1982). Plasmid recombination in *Haemophilus influenzae*. *Journal of Molecular Biology* **157**, 577–596.

MCCARTHY, D. AND KUPFER, D.M. (1987). Electron microscopy of single-stranded structures in the DNA of competent *Haemophilus influenzae* cells. *Journal of Bacteriology* **169**, 565–571.

MACHATTIE, L.A., BERNS, K.I. AND THOMAS, C.A. (1965). Electron microscopy of DNA from *Haemophilus influenzae*. *Journal of Molecular Biology* **11**, 648–649.

MILLER, D.H. AND HUANG, P.C. (1972). Identification of competence repressing factors during log-phase growth of *Haemophilus influenzae*. *Journal of Bacteriology* **109**, 560–564.

MUHAMMED, A. AND SETLOW, J.K. (1970). Ultraviolet-induced decrease in integration of *Haemophilus influenzae* transforming deoxyribonucleic acid in sensitive and resistant cells. *Journal of Bacteriology* **101**, 444–448.

MUHAMMED, S. AND SETLOW, J.K. (1974). Integration and repair of ultraviolet-irradiated transforming deoxyribonucleic acid in *Haemophilus influenzae*. *Journal of Bacteriology* **118**, 514–522.

NEWMAN, C.M. AND STUY, J.H. (1971). Fate of bacteriophage lambda after adsorption by *Haemophilus influenzae*. *Journal of General Microbiology* **65**, 153–159.

NOTANI, N.K. (1971). Genetic and physical properties of unintegrated donor DNA molecules during *Haemophilus* transformation. *Journal of Molecular Biology* **59**, 223–226.

NOTANI, N.K. AND GOODGAL, S.H. (1966). On the nature of recombinants formed during transformation of *Haemophilus influenzae*. *Journal of General Physiology* **49**, 197–209.

NOTANI, N.K. AND SETLOW, J.K. (1975). Mechanisms of bacterial transformation and transfection. *Progress in Nucleic Acid Research and Molecular Biology* **14**, 39–99.

NOTANI, N.K., SETLOW, J.K. AND ALLISON, D.P. (1973). Intracellular events during infection by *Haemophilus influenzae* phage and transfection by its DNA. *Journal of Molecular Biology* **75**, 581–599.

NOTANI, N.K., SETLOW, J.K., JOSHI, R.V. AND ALLISON, D.P. (1972). Molecular basis for the transformation defects in mutants of *Haemophilus influenzae*. *Journal of Bacteriology* **110**, 1171–1180.

PIEKAROWICZ, A. AND SIWINSKA, M. (1977). Inhibition of transformation and transfection in *Haemophilus influenzae* Rd9 by lysogeny. *Journal of Bacteriology* **122**, 22–29.

PITMAN, M. (1931). Variation and type specificity in the bacterial species *Haemophilus influenzae*. *Journal of Experimental Medicine* **53**, 471–492.

POSTEL, E.H. AND GOODGAL, S.H. (1966). Uptake of single-stranded DNA in *Haemophilus influenzae* and its ability to transform. *Journal of Molecular Biology* **16**, 317–327.

POSTEL, E.H. AND GOODGAL, S.H. (1967). Further studies on transformation with single-stranded DNA of *Haemophilus influenzae*. *Journal of Molecular Biology* **18**, 247–259.

ROSENTHAL, A. (1972). Master's Degree Thesis, Florida State University.

SAMUELS, J. AND CLARKE, K.J. (1969). New bacteriophage of *Haemophilus influenzae*. *Journal of Virology* **4**, 797–798.

SCHAEFFER, P., EDGAR, R.S. AND ROLFE, R. (1960). Sur l'inhibition de la transformation bacterienne par des desoxyribonucleates de composition variées. *Comptes Rendus des Sciences de la Société de Biologie et de ses Filliales* **154**, 1978–1983.

SCOCCA, J.J., POLAND, R.L. AND ZOON, K.C. (1974). Specificity in deoxyribonucleic acid uptake by transformable *Haemophilus influenzae*. *Journal of Bacteriology* **118**, 169–173.

SEDGWICK, B. AND SETLOW, J.K. (1976). Single-stranded regions in transforming deoxyribonucleic acid after uptake by competent *Haemophilus influenzae*. *Journal of Bacteriology* **125**, 588–596.

SETLOW, J.K. AND BOLING, M.E. (1972). Bacteriophage of *Haemophilus influenzae*. II. Repair of ultraviolet-irradiated phage DNA and the capacity of irradiated cells to make phage. *Journal of Molecular Biology* **63**, 349–362.

SETLOW, J.K., BROWN, D.C., BOLING, J.E., MATTINGLY, A. AND GORDON, M.P. (1968). Repair of deoxyribonucleic acid in *Haemophilus influenzae*. X-ray-sensitivity of ultraviolet-sensitive mutants and their behavior as hosts to ultraviolet-irradiated bacteriophage and transforming deoxyribonucleic acid. *Journal of Bacteriology* **95**, 546–558.

SETLOW, J.K., BOLING, M.E., BEATTIE, K.L. AND KIMBALL, R.F. (1972). A complex of recombination and repair genes in *Haemophilus influenzae*. *Journal of Molecular Biology* **68**, 361–378.

SETLOW, J.K., NOTANI, N.K., MCCARTHY, M. AND CLAYTON, N.-L. (1981). Transformation of *Haemophilus influenzae* by plasmid RSF0885 containing a cloned segment of chromosomal deoxyribonucleic acid. *Journal of Bacteriology* **148**, 804–811.

SISCO, K.L. AND SMITH, H.O. (1979). Sequence-specific DNA uptake in *Haemophilus influenzae*. *Proceedings of the National Academy of Sciences of the United States of America* **76**, 972–976.

SMITH, G.R. (1987). Mechanism and control of homologous recombination in *Escherichia coli*. *Annual Review of Genetics* **21**, 179–201.

SMITH, G.R. (1988). Homologous recombination in procaryotes. *Microbiological Reviews* **52**, 1–28.

SMITH, H.O. AND WILCOX, W. (1970). A restriction enzyme from *Haemophilus influenzae*. I. Purification and general properties. *Journal of Molecular Biology* **51**, 379–391.

SMITH, H.O., DANNER, D.B. AND DEICH, R.A. (1981). Genetic transformation. *Annual Review of Biochemistry* **50**, 41–68.

SPENCER, H.T. AND HERRIOTT, R.M. (1965). Development of competence of *Haemophilus influenzae*. *Journal of Bacteriology* **90**, 911–920.

STACHURA, I., MCKINLEY, F.W., LEIDY, G. AND ALEXANDER, H. (1969). Incomplete bacteriophage-like particles in ultraviolet-irradiated *Haemophilus influenzae*. *Journal of Bacteriology* **98**, 818–820.

TEINHART, W.L. AND HERRIOTT, R.M. (1968). Genetic integration in the heterospecific transformation of *Haemophilus influenzae* cell by *Haemophilus parainfluenzae* deoxyribonucleic acid. *Journal of Bacteriology* **96**, 1725–1731.

TUY, J.H. (1962). Transformability of *Haemophilus influenzae*. *Journal of General Microbiology* **29**, 537–549.

TUY, J.H. (1965). Fate of transforming DNA in the *Haemophilus influenzae* transformation system. *Journal of Molecular Biology* **13**, 554–570.

TUY, J.H. (1969). Prophage mapping by transformation. *Virology* **38**, 567–572.

TUY, J.H. (1970a). Bacterial transformation, surface phenomena. In *Uptake of Informative Molecules by Living Cells* (L. Ledoux, Ed.), pp. 99–112. Mol, Belgium.

TUY, J.H. (1970b). Bacterial transformation, integration of donor DNA. In *Uptake of Informative Molecules by Living Cells* (L. Ledoux, Ed.), pp. 113–121. Mol, Belgium.

TUY, J.H. (1974a). Acid-soluble breakdown of homologous deoxyribonucleic acid adsorbed by *Haemophilus influenzae*: its biological significance. *Journal of Bacteriology* **120**, 917–922.

TUY, J.H. (1974b). Origin and direction of *Haemophilus* bacteriophage HP1 DNA replication. *Journal of Virology* **13**, 757–759.

TUY, J.H. (1975). Fate of transforming bacteriophage HP1 deoxyribonucleic acid in *Haemophilus influenzae* lysogens. *Journal of Bacteriology* **122**, 1038–1044.

TUY, J.H. (1976a). On the nature of nontypable *Haemophilus influenzae*. *Antonie van Leeuwenhoek Journal of Microbiology and Serology* **44**, 367–376.

TUY, J.H. (1976b). Restriction enzymes do not play a significant role in *Haemophilus* homospecific or heterospecific transformation. *Journal of Bacteriology* **128**, 212–220.

TUY, J.H. (1979). Plasmid transfer in *Haemophilus influenzae*. *Journal of Bacteriology* **139**, 520–529.

TUY, J.H. (1980a). Chromosomally integrated conjugative plasmids are common in antibiotic-resistant *Haemophilus influenzae*. *Journal of Bacteriology* **142**, 925–930.

TUY, J.H. (1980b). Mechanism of additive genetic transformation in *Haemophilus influenzae*. *Journal of Bacteriology* **144**, 999–1002.

TUY, J.H. (1980c). Mechanism of *Haemophilus influenzae* transfection by single and double prophage deoxyribonucleic acid. *Journal of Bacteriology* **144**, 1003–1008.

TUY, J.H. (1985). Transfer of genetic information within a colony of *Haemophilus influenzae*. *Journal of Bacteriology* **162**, 1–4.

TUY, J.H. (1986). Effect of glycerol on *Haemophilus influenzae* transfection. *Journal of Bacteriology* **166**, 285–289.

TUY, J.H. AND HOFFMANN, J.F. (1970). A motive for bacterial transformation. In *Uptake of Informative Molecules by Living Cells* (L. Ledoux, Ed.), pp. 28–37. Mol, Belgium.

TUY, J.H. AND HOFFMANN, J.F. (1971). Influence of transformability on the formation of superinfection double lysogens in *Haemophilus influenzae*. *Journal of Virology* **7**, 127–136.

TUY, J.H. AND STERN, D. (1964). The kinetics of DNA uptake by *Haemophilus influenzae*. *Journal of General Microbiology* **35**, 391–400.

TUY, J.H. AND VAN DER HAVE, B. (1971). Degradation of adsorbed transforming DNA by *Haemophilus influenzae*. *Journal of General Microbiology* **65**, 147–152.

TUY, J.H. AND WALTER, R.B. (1981). Addition, deletion, and substitution of long nonhomologous deoxyribonucleic acid segments by genetic transformation of *Haemophilus influenzae*. *Journal of Bacteriology* **148**, 565–571.

TUY, J.H. AND WALTER, R.B. (1983). Repair of ultraviolet-irradiated transforming DNA in a *recA* mutant of *Haemophilus influenzae*. *Photochemistry and Photobiology* **37**, 391–394.

TUY, J.H. AND WALTER, R.B. (1986a). Homology-facilitated plasmid transfer in *Haemophilus influenzae*. *Molecular and General Genetics* **203**, 288–295.

STUY, J.H. AND WALTER, R.B. (1986b). Effect of glycerol on plasmid transfer in genetically competent *Haemophilus influenzae*. *Molecular and General Genetics* **203**, 296–299.

STUY, J.H., HOFFMANN, J.F. AND DUKET, L.H. (1972). Chromosomal recombination in *Haemophilus influenzae*. *Genetics* **71**, 507–520.

SUTRINA, S.L. AND SCOCCA, J.J. (1976). Phospholipids of *Haemophilus influenzae* Rd during exponential growth and following the development of competence for genetic transformation. *Journal of General Microbiology* **92**, 410–412.

SUTRINA, S.L. AND SCOCCA, J.J. (1979). *Haemophilus influenzae* periplasmic proteins which bind DNA: properties and possible participation in genetic transformation. *Journal of Bacteriology* **139**, 1021–1027.

WALTER, R.B. (1985). *DNA repair in* Haemophilus influenzae: *Isolation and characterization of an ultraviolet-sensitive mutator mutant*. PhD thesis, Florida State University.

WALTER, R.B. AND STUY, J.H. (1982a). Effect of linked point mutations on additive transformation in *Haemophilus influenzae*. In *Genetic Exchange* (U.N. Streips, S.H. Goodgal, W.R. Guild and G.A. Wilson, Eds), pp. 176–186. Dekker, New York.

WALTER, R.B. AND STUY, J.H. (1982b). Ultraviolet sensitivity of the addition, deletion, and substitution of long nonhomologous DNA segments by genetic transformation of *Haemophilus influenzae*. *Photochemistry and Photobiology* **35**, 337–341.

WALTER, R.B. AND STUY, J.H. (1988). Isolation and characterization of an ultraviolet-sensitive mutator mutant (*mutB1*) of *Haemophilus influenzae*. *Journal of Bacteriology* **170**, 2537–2542.

WISE, E.M., ALEXANDER, S.P. AND POWERS, M. (1973). Adenosine 3'5'-cyclic monophosphate as a regulator of bacterial transformation. *Proceedings of the National Academy of Sciences of the United States of America* **70**, 471–474.

ZAMENHOF, S., ALEXANDER, H.E. AND LEIDY, G. (1953). Studies on the chemistry of the transforming activity. *Journal of Experimental Medicine* **98**, 378–397.

ZOON, K.C. AND SCOCCA, J.J. (1975). Constitution of the cell envelope of *Haemophilus influenzae* in relation to competence for genetic transformation. *Journal of Bacteriology* **123**, 666–677.

ZOON, K.C., HABERSAT, M. AND SCOCCA, J.J. (1975a). Synthesis of envelope peptides by *Haemophilus influenzae* during development of competence for genetic transformation. *Journal of Bacteriology* **127**, 545–554.

ZOON, K.C., HABERSAT, M. AND SCOCCA, J.J. (1975b). Multiply regulatory events in the development of competence for genetic transformation in *Haemophilus influenzae*. *Journal of Bacteriology* **124**, 1607–1609.

# 11

# Isolation of Transformation-Deficient Mutants of *Haemophilus influenzae* Rd Generated by Transposon Mutagenesis

JEAN-FRANÇOIS TOMB, GERARD J. BARCAK,
MARK S. CHANDLER, ROSEMARY J. REDFIELD AND
HAMILTON O. SMITH

*Department of Molecular Biology and Genetics, The Johns Hopkins University School of Medicine, 725 North Wolfe Street, Baltimore, MD 21205, USA*

## Introduction

The natural transformation system of *Haemophilus influenzae*, a Gram-negative bacterium, has been extensively studied (for reviews, *see* Goodgal, 1982; Kahn and Smith, 1984). The development of competence, the transport of donor DNA into the cell and the integration of the DNA into the chromosome are genetically determined. In an attempt to analyse the transformation pathway, several investigators have isolated and characterized transformation-deficient mutants. Caster, Postel and Goodgal (1970) used nitrosoguanidine mutagenesis and screened for mutants using a DNA-dependent plate assay for transformation. They identified four classes of mutants based on their ability to bind, take up, and/or transform with native or denatured donor DNA. Some of these mutant strains were also sensitive to ultraviolet irradiation. Beattie and Setlow (1971) enriched for transformation-deficient mutants by multiple rounds of transformation with lethal donor DNA from *H. parainfluenzae* and obtained mutants deficient in DNA uptake, homologous recombination and DNA repair. Kooistra and Venema (1970) isolated transformation-deficient strains of *H. influenzae* while screening for clones sensitive to the DNA-damaging agent mitomycin C. Despite the efforts of these investigators, a systematic genetic analysis of the transformation pathway has not yet been achieved, in part due to the lack of good methods for genetic analysis in *Haemophilus*.

In this chapter, we describe the use of mini-Tn*10kan* transposon mutagenesis for isolation of transformation-deficient mutants. This method yields non-leaky, non-reverting mutants and also permits cloning of the mutated genes. Since a system for transposon mutagenesis in *H. influenzae* is not

*Genetic Transformation and Expression*
© Intercept Ltd, PO Box 716, Andover, Hants, SP10 1YG, UK

available, the mutagenesis was carried out on a plasmid library of *H. influenzae* *Pst*I DNA fragments in *Escherichia coli*. The mini-Tn*10kan* system of Way *et al.* (1984) was used for the mutagenesis. In this system, the 2 kbp mini-Tn*10kan* element is carried on phage lambda along with the Tn*10* transposase under *tac* promoter control. On infection of the library clones in a *lacI* background the transposase is induced and very high levels of transposition are achieved. After the transposon mutagenesis had occurred in our library population, the pooled kanamycin-resistant plasmids were isolated, cut with *Pst*I, and the mutated library fragments used to transform wild-type *H. influenzae* cells. From among a large number of kanamycin-resistant clones, 54 transformation-deficient (Tfo⁻) strains were isolated by screening with DNA plate-transformation assays. A preliminary characterization and grouping of these mutants is presented. A similar approach has recently been used to isolate and characterize competence mutants of the Gram-positive organism, *Bacillus subtilis* (Hahn, Albano and Dubnau, 1987).

## Materials and methods

### REAGENTS AND ENZYMES

Haemin (equine), β-nicotinamide adenine dinucleotide (NAD), DNaseI and all antibiotics were from Sigma. Adenosine 3′,5′-cyclic monophosphate (cAMP) was from Aldrich. Restriction enzymes and T4 DNA ligase were from New England Biolabs or Pharmacia and were used according to manufacturer's specifications. Deoxycytidine 5′-[α-$^{32}$P]triphosphate (3000 Ci mmol⁻¹) and [methyl-³H]thymidine (42 Ci mmol⁻¹) were from Amersham. Nitrocellulose (BA–85) and nylon (NYTRAN) filters were from Schleicher and Schuell.

### BACTERIAL, PHAGE AND PLASMID STRAINS

*H. influenzae* Rd strain KW20 is wild type and KW26 is Strʳ Novʳ Vioʳ Thy⁻ (Wilcox and Smith, 1975). *H. influenzae* Rd strains DB117 *rec-1* (Beattie and Setlow, 1971) and MAP7 Strʳ Nalʳ Kanʳ Novʳ Stvʳ Spcʳ Vioʳ, and Eryˢ derivative of strain MAP (Catlin, Bendler and Goodgal, 1972), were obtained from J. Setlow. Strains designated JG followed by an isolation number are transformation-deficient derivatives of KW20, each carrying a single mini-Tn*10kan* insertion giving a Tfo⁻ phenotype (*see Table 11.1*). *Escherichia coli* strain MC1060 Δ (*lacI-Y*)74 galE15 galK16 λ⁻ relA1 rpsL150 spoT1 hsdR2 (Casadaban and Cohen, 1980) was obtained from the *E. coli* genetic stock centre.

Phage λ1105 carrying the 2 kbp mini-Tn*10kan* element and the Tn*10* transposase under *tac* promoter control has been described by Way *et al.* (1984). The low copy number plasmid pGB2, which confers resistance to spectinomycin (Churchward, Belin and Nagamine, 1984), was obtained from S. Friedman. Plasmid pUC71K was the source of the *nptI* (*kan*) gene probe (Vieira and Messing, 1982). Plasmid pGJB103 is a derivative of pHVT1 (Danner and Pifer, 1982) and confers resistance to tetracycline and ampicillin.

ts construction will be described in a later publication; but briefly, the region in HVT1 between the *Ava*I and *Sph*I sites was deleted and a *Bgl*II linker was aserted at the *Ssp*I site in the untranslated leader region of the $bla^+$ gene. The DALK plasmids are pGJB103 derivatives containing cloned *Pst*I fragments of *I. influenzae* Rd DNA bearing mini-Tn*10kan* insertions. Each pDALK lasmid has an isolation number corresponding to the JG strain from which its *st*I fragment insert is derived. The pDAL plasmids correspond to the pDALK lasmids except that they have lost the mini-Tn*10kan* insertion by *in vivo* ecombination with the wild-type chromosomal gene (*see* below).

ACTERIAL GROWTH AND COMPETENCE DEVELOPMENT

*I. influenzae* cells were grown in brain–heart infusion (BHI) broth upplemented with 2 µg ml$^{-1}$ NAD and 100 µg ml$^{-1}$ haemin, and were made ompetent by the MIV medium procedure of Herriott, Meyer and Vogt (1970). Antibiotics were used at the following final concentration (µg ml$^{-1}$): :anamycin 20 or 35; streptomycin, 250 or 500; novobiocin, 2·5; tetracycline, 5. 'lasmid pGB2 was maintained in *E. coli* by selection with 50 µg ml$^{-1}$ pectinomycin.

:HROMOSOMAL AND PLASMID DNA PREPARATION

:hromosomal DNA was prepared from *H. influenzae* cells grown to saturation n supplemented BHI according to Silhavy, Berman and Enquist (1984) with he omission of lysozyme. The concentration of DNA was determined photometrically (1 µg ml$^{-1}$ = 0·02 absorbance units at 260 nm). [$^3$H]DNA approximately $10^5$ cpm µg$^{-1}$) was prepared from KW26 cells grown for everal generations to a concentration of $10^9$ colony-forming units per ml in upplemented heart infusion (HI) broth containing 25 µCi ml$^{-1}$ of $^3$H]thymidine. Plasmid DNA was prepared from *H. influenzae* according to Vicard *et al.* (1985) with the omission of the column chromatography step, and rom *E. coli* by the alkaline lysis method (Silhavy, Berman and Enquist, 1984).

OUTHERN HYBRIDIZATION

:hromosomal DNA (3–5 µg) from JG strains was digested with either *Pst*I, :la I or *Eco*RI and subjected to electrophoresis through an 0·8% or 1% agarose el in TAE buffer (Maniatis, Fritsch and Sambrook, 1982). DNA bands were plotted onto nitrocellulose or NYTRAN filters and hybridized with the $^2$P-labelled *Bam*HI fragment of pUC71K containing the *npt*I (*kan*) gene, as lescribed by Maniatis, Fritsch and Sambrook (1982). The probe DNA was $^2$P-labelled to about $10^8$ cpm µg$^{-1}$ by the random primer method of Feinberg nd Vogelstein (1983).

:ONSTRUCTION OF A PLASMID LIBRARY OF *H. INFLUENZAE* Rd DNA AND 'RANSPOSON MUTAGENESIS

'lasmid pGB2 DNA (5 µg) was digested to completion with *Pst*I and dephosphorylated with calf intestine alkaline phosphatase (Boehringer Mannheim) using standard reaction conditions (Maniatis, Fritsch and Sambrook, 1982). The vector DNA (2·5 μg) was then ligated to *Pst*I-cleaved KW20 DNA (0·4 μg) in a 200 μl reaction under standard conditions using 2 units of T4 DNA ligase for 20 h at 15°C. Additional *Haemophilus* DNA (1·2 μg) and ligase (2 units) were added and the reaction continued for 5 h, after which the reaction was heat inactivated at 65°C for 10 min. Samples of the ligation mixture (equivalent to about 0·5 μg of vector DNA) were then used to transform 0·2 ml aliquots of competent calcium chloride-treated *E. coli* MC1060 cells using standard methods (Maniatis, Fritsch and Sambrook, 1982). The spectinomycin-resistant transformants (about 6300) were scraped off the plates and pooled, and 1 ml was diluted into 200 ml of L broth containing spectinomycin and 0·4% maltose and grown for 2 h. The cells were harvested by centrifugation and resuspended in 12·5 ml of broth (approximately $2 \times 10^{10}$ cells per ml). Cell samples (1 ml) were then infected with phage λ1105 (multiplicity of infection of about 0·4), incubated 30 min at 30°C, centrifuged, washed and resuspended in 1 ml of fresh broth containing 50 μg ml$^{-1}$ of spectinomycin and incubated at 37°C for 2 h with shaking, after which 0·1 ml samples were plated on TY agar containing 100 μg ml$^{-1}$ kanamycin and 50 μg ml$^{-1}$ spectinomycin. Each plate contained 10 000–20 000 colonies after overnight incubation at 42°C. Approximately 300 000 total transductants were pooled and used for subsequent steps.

SCREENING FOR Tfo⁻ PHENOTYPES BY THE cAMP DNA REPLICA-PLATE METHOD

Plasmid DNA was extracted from the pooled transductant colonies and 3 μg was digested with *Pst*I and used to transform 1 ml of competent KW20 cells (Herriott, Meyer and Vogt, 1970). About 20 000 Kan$^r$ transformants (300–400 per plate) were obtained. These were replica-plated onto supplemented BHI agar containing 1 mM cAMP, on the surface of which had been spread 50 μg of *H. influenzae* MAP7 DNA (Wise, Alexander and Powers, 1973). After overnight incubation at 37°C, colonies were further replica-plated onto supplemented BHI agar with and without streptomycin or novobiocin. Colonies appearing on drug-free plates, but not on antibiotic-containing plates, were chosen as potential Tfo⁻ strains. In control tests, KW20 colonies transform well on the DNA plates and give rise to greater than 99% drug-resistant colonies on replica-plating. However, in our screening about 5% of Tfo⁺ colonies were falsely scored as Tfo⁻ with this assay (false negatives), possibly due to other phenotypic alterations.

CLONING OF Tfo⁻ MUTATIONS

To clone each mutation, chromosomal DNA from the respective JG strain was digested with *Pst*I and the fragments were ligated into *Pst*I-cleaved pGJB103 DNA using standard reaction conditions (Maniatis, Fritsch and Sambrook, 1982). The ligation mixture was used to transform DB117 cells by the glycerol shock procedure of Stuy and Walter (1986), and clones containing the mini-Tn*10kan* element were selected on plates containing 35 μg ml$^{-1}$ kanamycin. Restriction analysis was used to confirm that the kanamycin-resistant DB117 clones carried a pDALK plasmid with the expected insertion. Conversion of the pDALK insertion plasmids to the corresponding pDAL plasmids was achieved with high efficiency by recombinational exchange of the mutated locus with the wild-type chromosomal locus (Setlow, Cabrera-Juarez and Griffin, 1984). Accordingly, competent KW20 cells were transformed with each of the pDALK plasmids and tetracycline-resistant colonies were selected and tested for sensitivity to 35 μg ml$^{-1}$ kanamycin. Plasmids were isolated from the Tet$^r$ Kan$^s$ clones and subjected to restriction analysis to confirm loss of the mini-Tn*10kan* element and replacement by the wild-type *H. influenzae* Rd *Pst*I DNA insert.

DNA UPTAKE AND TRANSFORMATION ASSAYS

A 1 μg sample of [$^3$H]DNA was added to 1 ml of competent cells at 37°C. After 30 min, a 0·1 ml sample was withdrawn, diluted 1 to 10 in supplemented HI and incubated at 37°C for 1 h, to allow expression before plating on supplemented BHI agar with and without 250 μg ml$^{-1}$ streptomycin. At the same time a 0·2 ml sample was withdrawn and incubated with DNaseI (50 μg ml$^{-1}$) at 0°C. After 5 min the sample was brought to 0·5 M NaCl, centrifuged, and washed once with 1 ml of MIV medium containing 0·5 M NaCl. The pellet was resuspended in MIV medium, transferred to a glass fibre filter, dried, and the radioactivity determined in Omnifluor (New England Nuclear) in a liquid scintillation counter.

## Results

PREPARATION OF TRANSFORMATION-DEFICIENT MUTANTS BY TRANSPOSON MUTAGENESIS

The library of *Pst*I fragments of KW20 DNA that was to be subjected to transposon mutagenesis was carried on the low-copy plasmid vector, pGB2, in *E. coli* strain MC1060 and consisted of about 6300 primary spectinomycin-resistant transformants (*see* p. 115–116). Random screening of small-scale plasmid preparations by agarose gel electrophoresis revealed that about 70% of these contained inserts averaging about 5 kbp in size. We calculated that the number of recombinant clones required to represent any *Pst*I fragment of the *H. influenzae* genome with 99% probability was 1700 (Maniatis, Fritsch and Sambrook, 1982). The primary transformants were pooled and subjected to transposon mutagenesis (*see* p. 116). Approximately 300 000 Kan$^r$ transductant colonies were pooled and the plasmid DNA isolated. Based on the known frequency of transposition of the mini-Tn*10kan* element in this system, we estimate that about 1 or 2% of the plasmids carried mutations within their *H. influenzae* DNA inserts.

The next step was to introduce the mutated library inserts back into wild-type

*H. influenzae* cells to produce mutated *Haemophilus* clones which could be screened for transformation defects. The pooled plasmid DNA was cleaved with *Pst*I and used to transform KW20 cells. The transformants were then screened for the Tfo⁻ phenotype using the DNA replica-plate method (*see* p 116). About 1000 potential Tfo⁻ strains were identified in this first screening. To eliminate false negatives, these were then rescreened by the replica-plate method and a total of 116 putative Tfo⁻ clones were identified and assigned insertion numbers. Twelve of these were lost during propagation, 26 proved to be Tfo⁺ when examined for competence by the MIV procedure, and 16 displayed a 'sticky' phenotype and were not included in the study. The insertions in the remaining 62 Tfo⁻ strains were then characterized by Southern hybridization and molecular cloning.

EACH Tfo⁻ STRAIN CARRIES A SINGLE INSERTION

Chromosomal DNA from each of the 62 Tfo⁻ strains was digested with *Pst*I or *Eco*RI and then analysed by Southern hybridization using the *npt1* gene as the labelled probe to detect the mini-Tn*10kan* element (*Figure 11.1*). Since neither restriction enzyme cuts in the element, the number of labelled bands should correspond to the number of elements in the chromosome. With each of the 62 mutant strains only a single band was observed.

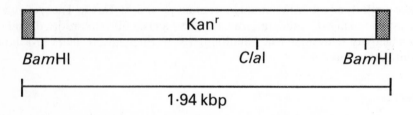

**Figure 11.1** Structure of the mini-Tn*10kan* element used for insertional mutagenesis. The shaded ends are derived from IS*10*R. There are no *Eco*RI or *Pst*I sites in the element.

CLASSIFICATION OF Tfo⁻ STRAINS AND LINKAGE OF THE MUTANT
PHENOTYPES TO THE MINI-Tn*10kan* INSERTION

The insertions in different strains can be related as follows:

1.  Insertions into different *Pst*I fragments;
2.  Insertions into the same *Pst*I fragment but at different locations; and
3.  Insertions into the same *Pst*I fragment and into the same apparent location.

To determine the relationships of the 62 mutants, they were subjected to restriction and Southern hybridization analysis. For this analysis they were arbitrarily divided into two groups of 31. Examples of the distribution of *Pst*I fragment sizes in the first group of 31 are shown in *Figure 11.2A*. To determine whether co-migrating *Pst*I fragments were identical (*Figure 11.2A*, compare lanes 7 and 8) and to map the point of the mini-Tn*10kan* insertion, the

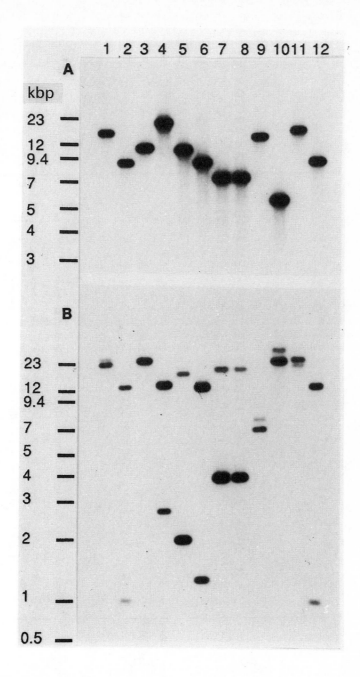

**Figure 11.2** Southern hybridization analysis of chromosomal DNA from Tfo⁻ strains using a labelled *npt1* gene probe. (A) Chromosomal DNAs were cut with *Pst*I. Lanes 1–12 correspond to strains JG1, 4, 16, 38, 40, 45, 49, 50, 55, 58, 76 and 98. (B) Chromosomal DNAs were cut with *Cla*I. The lanes correspond to the same JG strains as in (A). In lane 3 the apparent single band is a doublet.

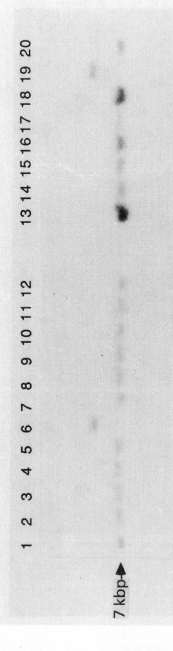

**Figure 11.3**    Southern hybridization analysis of *Pst*I-digested chromosomal DNAs of Tto⁻ strains using a labelled pDAL98 probe. Lanes 1–20 correspond to strains JG13, 19, 21, 22, 24, 26, 30, 31, 32, 36, 37, 56, 57, 59, 62, 65, 68, 70, 72 and 73. The probe hybridizes to a *Pst*I fragment corresponding to itself in all lanes except 6 and 19. In these lanes the labelled band is shifted to a 2 kbp larger size due to insertion of the mini-Tn*10kan* element in the *Pst*I fragment.

chromosomal DNAs were digested with *Cla*I (*Figure 11.2B*). This enzyme cleaves asymmetrically within the mini-Tn*10kan* element. In each case two bands were seen when hybridized to the labelled *nptI* probe. Two strains showing apparently identical bands were assumed to have insertions at the same location. These probably arose from the pooling steps in the isolation procedure. From this analysis, we identified 16 distinct insertions into 11 different *Pst*I fragments.

Analysis of the second group of 31 mutants yielded 13 different *Pst*I fragments, of which nine had occurred in the first group and four were new. An additional comparison between the *Pst*I fragments in groups 1 and 2 is illustrated in *Figure 11.3*. In this experiment, pDAL98, the wild-type version of pDALK98 (*see* next section), was used as a labelled probe in Southern hybridizations against the various *Pst*I-cleaved JG strain chromosomal DNAs of group 2. The probe hybridizes to the 7 kbp wild-type *Pst*I fragment in each lane, except when the strain carries the mini-Tn*10kan* insertion in this fragment, increasing its size by 2 kbp. From *Figure 11.3* it can be seen that JG26 and JG72 carry insertions in the same *Pst*I fragment as the JG98 strain from which the probe was derived. Similar experiments were done for each of the strains of groups 1 and 2 that appeared to be mutated in identical *Pst*I fragments.

To establish that the Tfo$^-$ phenotypes were a direct result of the insertion of mini-Tn*10kan* elements, 1 ml of competent KW20 cells were transformed with 50 ng or less of DNA extracted from each JG strain. From each experiment, five Kan$^r$ transformants were tested for the Tfo$^-$ phenotype by the cAMP DNA plate method and at least one was tested for the relevant phenotypes, that is, binding and uptake of DNA and transformation after the MIV treatment. In five strains, JG12, JG15, JG46, JG66 and JG103, the mutant phenotype was found not to be linked to kanamycin resistance. These five strains were then eliminated from further study. In summary, we have isolated 24 distinct insertions in 10 different *Pst*I fragments (*Table 11.1*). These fragments ranged in size from 3·5 to 12·8 kbp.

The transformation phenotypes (DNA uptake and transformation frequency) associated with each insertion were determined by transformation of MIV-treated cultures with $^3$H-labelled KW26 DNA (*Table 11.1*). Most strains were defective both for DNA uptake (<1% of wild type) and for transformation frequency ($<10^{-6}$ to $10^{-2}$ of wild type); however, two mutants, JG37 and JG56, took up donor DNA at wild-type levels but transformed at $<10^{-5}$ of the wild-type level. Three other mutants, JG108, JG88 and JG112, took up nearly normal amounts of donor DNA and transformed at about $10^{-2}$ of the wild-type level.

## CONVERSION OF pDALK PLASMIDS TO pDAL PLASMIDS BY EXCHANGE OF TRANSPOSON-MUTAGENIZED GENES FOR WILD-TYPE GENES

Competent KW20 cells were transformed with each of the pDALK plasmids and the Tet$^r$ clones were scored for kanamycin sensitivity. In each case, 30–90% of the Tet$^r$ colonies were Kan$^s$. All of the plasmids from the Kan$^s$ clones were found by restriction analysis to have lost the mini-Tn*10kan* insert

**Table 11.1**   Transformation-deficient mutants of *H. influenzae*

| Strain* | DNA uptake† | Transformation frequency‡ |
|---|---|---|
| KW20(Tfo⁺) | 0·61 | $2 \times 10^{-3}$ |
| JG1 | <0·001 | $<10^{-9}$ |
| JG7 | <0·001 | $<10^{-9}$ |
| JG48 (52, 61) | <0·001 | $<10^{-9}$ |
| JG56 | 0·58 | $6·5 \times 10^{-8}$ |
| JG76 (96) | 0·003 | $1·1 \times 10^{-8}$ |
| JG45 (92, 106) | 0·004 | $2 \times 10^{-7}$ |
| JG72 | 0·003 | $2·9 \times 10^{-8}$ |
| JG98 (4, 26) | <0·001 | $<10^{-9}$ |
| JG6 | 0·005 | $2·2 \times 10^{-6}$ |
| JG40 | 0·007 | $5·5 \times 10^{-6}$ |
| JG63 | 0·013 | $5·4 \times 10^{-7}$ |
| JG59 | 0·009 | $6 \times 10^{-7}$ |
| JG84 | 0·005 | $4·1 \times 10^{-6}$ |
| JG101 | 0·036 | $3 \times 10^{-5}$ |
| JG115 | 0·007 | $5·3 \times 10^{-6}$ |
| JG108 (57) | 0·54 | $7 \times 10^{-5}$ |
| JG88 (73) | 0·42 | $2·9 \times 10^{-5}$ |
| JG112 | 0·34 | $5·5 \times 10^{-6}$ |
| JG16 (17, 24, 70, 82 83, 85, 90, 102) | <0·001 | $<10^{-9}$ |
| JG27 | 0·005 | $1·5 \times 10^{-6}$ |
| JG37 | 0·57 | $<10^{-9}$ |
| JG46 | 0·009 | $2·9 \times 10^{-7}$ |
| JG49 (13, 14, 19, 33, 34 42, 43, 50, 99, 105) | 0·010 | $2·5 \times 10^{-5}$ |
| JG58 (31, 62) | 0·005 | $<10^{-9}$ |
| JG87 (89) | <0·001 | $<10^{-9}$ |

* Mutant strains whose insertions mapped to the same *Pst*I fragment are grouped together. The strain numbers of any apparently identical isolates are given in parentheses.
† DNA uptake is the ratio of DNaseI-resistant cpm to total input cpm.
‡ Transformation frequency is the ratio of antibiotic-resistant cfu to total cfu.

without undergoing any other detectable deletion or rearrangement within the *Pst*I fragment.

## Discussion

We have successfully produced a variety of Tfo⁻ mutations in *H. influenzae* Rd using mini-Tn*10kan* (Way *et al.*, 1984). Perhaps the most important advantage of this method of mutagenesis is that the Kan^r marker on the element provides a convenient selection for subsequent cloning of the (mutated) gene. Additional advantages of *Haemophilus* are the ability to transfer insertions generated in *E. coli* into the *Haemophilus* chromosome by transformation, and the ability to readily exchange cloned mutated fragments for their wild-type homologues by *in vivo* recombination.

There were a few disadvantages to our approach. By carrying out the transposition in *E. coli*, we introduced the possibility that certain genes would be selected against and possibly lost from the *Haemophilus* library. To minimize this we used the low copy number vector pGB2. Because the insertion-bearing plasmids were propagated and pooled before transformation into *Haemophilus*, independent transformants sometimes received identical insertions. Because transposon mutations are rarely leaky, insertions in essential genes would not be represented.

Despite the few disadvantages, we identified 24 Tfo⁻ mutations distributed among 10 *Pst*I DNA fragments in this initial application of the method. Thus we have identified at least 10 non-essential genes involved in transformation. An important question, requiring additional investigation, is whether all of these genes code for actual components of the membrane transport and recombination machinery, or whether some genes are transformation-related only in some secondary, perhaps physiological, fashion. For example, one could imagine that a non-transformation-specific membrane protein might operationally affect the induction or function of the transformation-related membrane pathway without being an actual component. The fact that most of the mutants are extremely defective in transformation argues that most are directly involved in the process. Our future work is directed toward mapping the mutants, studying their regulation, investigating the properties of the gene products and studying their cellular location.

### Acknowledgements

We thank B. Bachmann, S. Friedman, N. Kleckner and J. Setlow for their gifts of bacterial strains, phages and plasmids. We thank Mildred Kahler for expert typing of this manuscript. This work was supported by National Institutes of Health Grant 5-PO1-CA16519. M. Chandler is supported by National Institutes of Health Training Grant 5–T32–CA09139. G. Barcak is a Monsanto Postdoctoral Fellow. R. Redfield is supported by a postdoctoral fellowship from the Medical Research Council of Canada. H.O.S. is an American Cancer Society Research Professor.

### References

BEATTIE, K.L. AND SETLOW, J.K. (1971). Transformation-defective strains of *Haemophilus influenzae*. *Nature New Biology* **231**, 177–179.

CASADABAN, M.J. AND COHEN, S.N. (1980). Analysis of gene control signals by DNA fusion and cloning in *Escherichia coli*. *Journal of Molecular Biology* **138**, 179–207.

CASTER, J.H., POSTEL, E.H. AND GOODGAL, S.H. (1970). Competence mutants: Isolation of transformation deficient strains of *Haemophilus influenzae*. *Nature* **227**, 515–517.

CATLIN, B.W., BENDLER, J.W., III AND GOODGAL, S.H. (1972). The type b capsulation locus of *Haemophilus influenzae*: Map location and size. *Journal of General Microbiology* **70**, 411–422.

CHURCHWARD, G., BELIN, D. AND NAGAMINE, Y. (1984). A pSC101-derived plasmid which shows no sequence homology to other commonly used cloning vectors. *Gene* **31**, 165–171.

DANNER, D.B. AND PIFER, M.L. (1982). Plasmid cloning vectors resistant to ampicillin and tetracycline which can replicate in both *E. coli* and *Haemophilus* cells. *Gene* **18**, 101–105.

FEINBERG, A.P. AND VOGELSTEIN, B. (1983). A technique for radiolabelling DNA restriction endonuclease fragments to high specific activity. *Analytical Biochemistry* **132**, 6–13.

GOODGAL, S.H. (1982). DNA uptake in *Haemophilus* transformation. *Annual Review of Genetics* **16**, 169–192.

HAHN, J., ALBANO, M. AND DUBNAU, D. (1987). Isolation and characterization of Tn*917lac*-generated competence mutants of *Bacillus subtilis*. *Journal of Bacteriology* **169**, 3104–3109.

HERRIOTT, R.M., MEYER, E.M. AND VOGT, M. (1970). Defined nongrowth media for stage II development of competence in *Haemophilus influenzae*. *Journal of Bacteriology* **101**, 517–524.

KAHN, M.E. AND SMITH, H.O. (1984). Transformation in *Haemophilus*: A problem in membrane biology. *Journal of Membrane Biology* **81**, 89–103.

KOOISTRA, J. AND VENEMA, G. (1970). Fate of donor DNA in some poorly transformable strains of *Haemophilus influenzae*. *Mutation Research* **9**, 245–253.

MANIATIS, T., FRITSCH, E.F. AND SAMBROOK, J. (1982). *Molecular Cloning: A Laboratory Manual*. Cold Spring Harbor Laboratory, New York.

MICARD, D., SOBRIER, M.L., COUDERC, J.L. AND DASTUGUE, B. (1985). Purification of RNA-free plasmid DNA using alkaline extraction followed by ultrogel A2 column chromatography. *Analytical Biochemistry* **148**, 121–126.

SETLOW, J.K., CABRERA-JUAREZ, E. AND GRIFFIN, K. (1984). Mechanism of acquisition of chromosomal markers by plasmids in *Haemophilus influenzae*. *Journal of Bacteriology* **160**, 662–667.

SILHAVY, T.J., BERMAN, M.L. AND ENQUIST, L.W. (1984). *Experiments with Gene Fusions*, pp. 137–139. Cold Spring Harbor Laboratory, New York.

STUY, J.H. AND WALTER, R.B. (1986). Effect of glycerol on plasmid transfer in genetically competent *Haemophilus influenzae*. *Molecular and General Genetics* **203**, 296–299.

VIEIRA, , J. AND MESSING, J. (1982). The pUC plasmids, an M13mp7-derived system for insertion mutagenesis and sequencing with synthetic universal primers. *Gene* **19**, 259–268.

WAY, J.C., DAVIS, M.A., MORISATO, D., ROBERTS, D.E. AND KLECKNER, N. (1984). New Tn*10* derivatives for transposon mutagenesis and for construction of *lacZ* operon fusions by transposition. *Gene* **32**, 369–379.

WILCOX, K.W. AND SMITH, H.O. (1975). Isolation and characterization of mutants of *Haemophilus influenzae* deficient in an adenosine 5'-triphosphate-dependent deoxyribonuclease activity. *Journal of Bacteriology* **122**, 443–453.

WISE, E.M., JR., ALEXANDER, S.P. AND POWERS, M. (1973). Adenosine 3':5'-cyclic monophosphate as a regulator of bacterial transformation. *Proceedings of the National Academy of Sciences of the United States of America* **70**, 471–474.

# 12
# Plasmid Genetics and Gene Expression in *Deinococcus radiodurans*

MICHAEL D. SMITH, LESLIE B. MCNEIL AND
KENNETH W. MINTON

*Department of Pathology, Uniformed Services University of the Health
Sciences, Bethesda, MD 20814, USA*

## Introduction

*Deinococcus radiodurans* is extremely resistant to ionizing and ultraviolet
(UV) radiation by virtue of efficient and non-mutagenic repair (for reviews *see*
Moseley, 1983; Moseley, 1984). Natural transformation of *D. radiodurans* is
very efficient (Moseley and Setlow, 1968; Tirgari and Moseley, 1980) and
heterologous DNA can be introduced to *D. radiodurans* by duplication
insertion (Smith *et al.*, 1988). The kanamycin resistance (Km$^r$) determinant
*aphA* from Tn*903* and the chloramphenicol resistance (Cm$^r$) determinant *cat*
from Tn*9* are expressed in *D. radiodurans* when introduced by duplication
insertion and amplified to many copies per cell (Smith *et al.*, 1988).

D. *radiodurans* strain R1 contains a cryptic plasmid species (pS16) present in
very low amounts per cell (Smith *et al.*, 1988). *D. radiodurans* strain Sark
contains two cryptic plasmids present in higher amounts per cell, pUE10 (37
kbp) and pUE11 (45 kbp) (Mackay, Al-Bakri and Moseley, 1985). We have
now inserted an *E. coli* plasmid into both pUE10 and pUE11 and characterized
the resulting recombinant plasmids pS28 and pS19.

## Results and discussion

### GENERATION OF SHUTTLE PLASMIDS pS19 AND pS28

Plasmid DNA fragments from *D. radiodurans* strain Sark (which contains both
pUE10 and pUE11) were cloned into pUC19 (Yanisch-Perron, Viera and
Messing, 1985) using *Eco*RI and *Hin*dIII (*Figure 12.1*). One recombinant
plasmid (pS15) contained a 12·5 kbp *Eco*RI–*Hin*dIII insert from pUE11. Near
the middle of the insert was a single *Eco*RV site, into which was cloned an *E.
coli* plasmid (pS27) which confers kanamycin resistance (*Figure 12.1*). In the
resulting construction (pS18), pS27 was present as a simple insertion in the 12·5

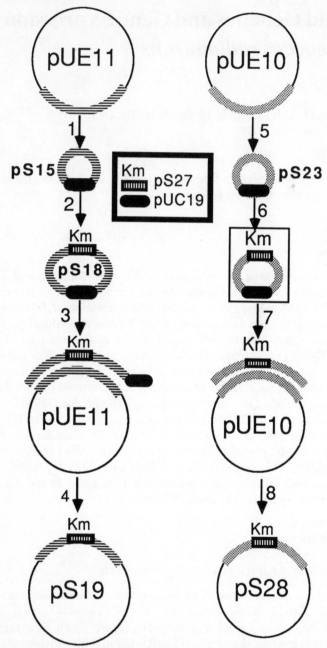

**Figure 12.1** Construction of pS19 and pS28. pS27 is the larger of the two *Eco*RV fragments of pMK20 and contains the ColE1 replicon and the *aphA* gene from Tn*903*. 1, An *Eco*RI-*Hin*dIII fragment of pUE11 was inserted into pUC19; 2, pS27 was inserted into an *Eco*RV site in pS15 and transformed into *E. coli*; 3, Sark recipients were transformed to Km$^r$ by pS18; 4, DNA from Sark transformants was transformed into *E. coli* and characterized; 5, an *Eco*RI-*Hin*dIII fragment of pUE10 was subcloned into pUC19; 6, pS27 was ligated into a filled-in *Nco*I site in pS23; 7, Sark recipients were transformed with the ligation mixture—the box between 6 and 7 signifies that the intermediate is hypothetical; 8, DNA from a Sark transformant was transformed into *E. coli* and characterized.

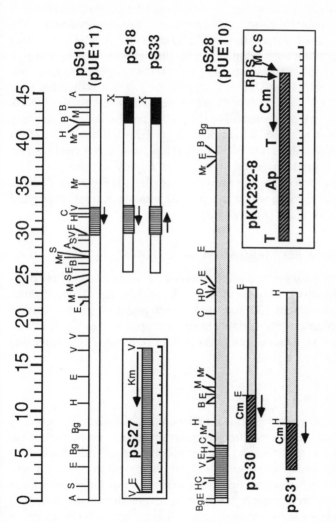

**Figure 12.2**  Restriction maps of pS19 and pS28, and diagrams of other plasmids. A, *Apa*I; B, *Bam*HI; Bg, *Bgl*II, C, *Cla*I; D, *Dra*I; E, *Eco*RI; H, *Hind*III; M, *Mlu*I, Mr, *Mra*I; P, *Pst*I; S, *Sal*I, V, *Eco*RV; X, *Xba*I; RBS, ribosome binding site; MCS, multiple cloning site; T, transcription terminator. White boxes, pUE11; black boxes, pUC19; vertical stripes, pS27; diagonal stripes, pKK232–8. Arrows indicate the direction of *aphA* or *cat* transcription. The pS27 sequences in pS28 appear to be in a rearranged form spanning 6 kbp which has not been observed to amplify, but has not been further defined. The top scale, in kbp, does not apply to pS27 (2·9 kbp) or pKK232–8 (5·4 kbp). pKK232–8 derivatives contain pUE10 fragments produced with *Eco*RI (pS30, which has the two largest pKK232–8 *Eco*RI fragments), *Hind*III (pS31) or *Bcl*I (pS32, linked at the pKK232–8 *Bam*HI site, not shown).

kbp pUE11 fragment. The results described below show that transformation of *D. radiodurans* strain Sark with pS18 resulted in $Km^r$ transformants via a double crossover which allowed integration of pS27 into the 45 kbp recipient plasmid pUE11 (*Figure 12.1*).

pS18 transformed *D. radiodurans* strain Sark recipients to $Km^r$ at a high frequency (70 000 $Km^r$ $\mu g^{-1}$). Linearization of pS18 with *Xba*I (which cleaves pS18 once within the pUC19 sequences) decreased the transformation frequency somewhat (10 000 $Km^r$ $\mu g^{-1}$). Two Sark transformants from each donor (circular and linear pS18) were characterized, and all contained pS19, which was 48 kbp, much larger than pS18 (*Figure 12.2*). pS19 was also generated by transforming Sark recipients with the ligation mixture that was used to generate pS18. pS19 transformed *E. coli* DH5α recipients to $Km^r$, but not to $Ap^r$. Plasmid DNA from DH5α, Sark/pS19 and Sark was digested with *Eco*RI and *Eco*RV, and Southern blots were probed with pS19. Plasmid DNA from untransformed Sark contained all of the pS19 *Eco*RI–*Eco*RV fragments except for pS27 (not shown). pS19 hybridized to pUE11, but not pUE10 (not shown). Other restriction digests of pS19 and Sark plasmid DNA confirm that pS19 is pUE11 with a simple insertion of pS27 at an *Eco*RV site (not shown).

A similar series of experiments was used to clone pUE10 (*Figure 12.1*). Sark transformants contained pS28, which was pUE10 with a permutation of pS27 inserted at a filled-in *Nco*I site (*Figure 12.2*).

## $Km^r$ EXPRESSION IN SARK REQUIRED A SPECIFIC ORIENTATION

pS33 is identical to pS18 except that pS27 is inverted (*Figure 12.2*). While pS18 transforms Sark recipients at a high frequency (70 000 $Km^r$ $\mu g^{-1}$), transformation by pS33 was infrequent (30 $Km^r$ $\mu g^{-1}$) and probably by duplication insertion since the colonies were variable in size and appeared only after three days (Smith *et al.*, 1988). This suggests that pUE11 sequences are promoting expression of the pS27 *aphA* gene.

## SUBCLONING pUE10 WITH A PROMOTOR PROBE

Three plasmids, two of which are shown in *Figure 12.2*, were constructed by inserting Sark plasmid fragments directly upstream from a promotorless *cat* gene in pKK232–8 and transforming R1 recipients to $Cm^r$. All three were pUE10 derivatives and none expressed the $Cm^r$ phenotype in *E. coli*. These results demonstrate that signals sufficient for expression of the promotorless *cat* in *D. radiodurans* were unable to promote expression in *E. coli*. The ribosome binding site in the promotor probe directly upstream from *cat* in pKK232–8 is GGAGG (Brosius, 1984); the ribosome binding site for the only *Deinococcus* gene that has been fully sequenced appears to be GGAGG (Peters *et al.*, 1988), and the 3'-OH terminus of *Deinococcus radiodurans* rRNA contains the sequence CCUCC (Brooks *et al.*, 1980). Thus it appears that the differences in expression between *E. coli* and *D. radiodurans* may be at the level of transcription.

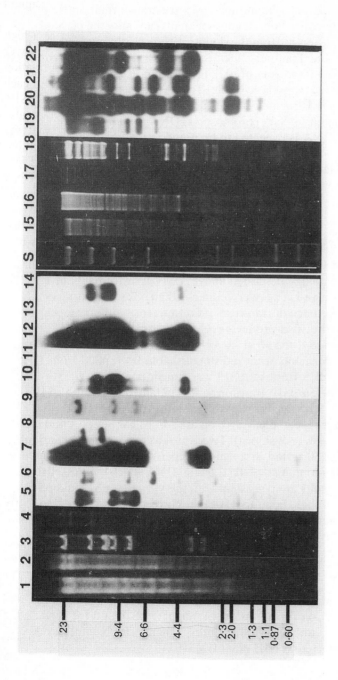

**Figure 12.3** Agarose gel electrophoresis of *Eco*RI digests of chromosomal (chr) or plasmid (cc) DNA followed by staining with ethidium bromide (dark backgrounds), blotting, hybridization and autoradiography (light backgrounds). Size standards in kilobases are indicated in the left-hand gel and are included in right-hand gel. 1, Sark chr; 2, R1 chr; 3, Sark cc; 4, R1 cc; 5–8, lanes 1–4 probed with pS19; 9, Sark cc probed with pS19, exposed briefly; 10–13, lanes 1–4 probed with pS28; 14, Sark cc probed with pS28, exposed briefly; S, size standards; 15, Sark chr; 16, R1 chr; 17, R1 cc; 18, Sark cc; 19–22, lanes 15–18 probed with R1 cc.

HOMOLOGY BETWEEN pS19 AND pS16

In *Bacillus subtilis* and *Streptococcus pneumoniae*, homology between donor plasmids and the recipient genome increases the transformation frequency, and recombination between homologous segments can cause the plasmid in the transformant to be different from the donor plasmid (Contente and Dubnau, 1979; Bron, Luxen and Trautner, 1980; Lopez *et al.*, 1982). pS28 hybridized weakly to two *Eco*RI fragments of pUE11, and not at all to the cryptic R1 plasmid pS16 (*Figure 12.3*). pS19 hybridized to the two major *Eco*RI fragments of pS16, several *Eco*RI fragments of strain R1 chromosomal DNA, and to several *Eco*RI fragments of Sark chromosomal DNA (*Figure 12.3*). Since open and linear plasmid DNA is expected to be found in the 'chromosomal' DNA fraction, homology to chromosomal fragments is deduced from hybridization to fragments not found in plasmid digests. pS16 hybridized to *Eco*RI fragments of strain R1 chromosomal DNA, Sark chromosomal DNA and Sark plasmid DNA (*Figure 12.3*).

INTRODUCTION OF pS19 AND pS28 TO STRAIN R1

Plasmid DNA from *E. coli* hosts was used to transform *D. radiodurans* strain R1. Despite the homology described above, pS19 transformants of R1 (100 Km$^r$ µg$^{-1}$) were observed at a lower frequency than pS28 transformants (1000 Km$^r$ µg$^{-1}$). The difference in transformation frequency did not appear to be due to restriction by the *Mra*I-producing R1 recipients (Wani *et al.*, 1982), since each plasmid contained three *Mra*I sites (*Figure 12.2*). *Eco*RI digests of pS28 from R1/pS28 transformants were indistinguishable from pS28 from DH5α/ pS28 (not shown). pS19 from R1/pS19 was transformed into *E. coli* DH5α recipients. These DH5α/pS19 transformants contained authentic pS19 (not shown). Sark and R1 transformants containing pS19 retained the Km$^r$ phenotype even after repeated passages on drug-free agar plates, but the yield of pS19 from R1 was low (not shown). Two Km-sensitive variants of Sark/pS28 were found among 250 tested in a similar experiment. Both were cured of pUE10, because they contained pUE11, but no DNA which hybridized to pS28 (not shown). The results are consistent with the view that pS16 and pS19 are related episomes that share homology with the chromosome and are frequently in the integrated state, especially in strain R1. This hypothesis is far from proven, however.

**Acknowledgements**

We thank B.E.B. Moseley for strains, unpublished results, procedures, and advice; R. Abrahamson for her effort in mapping pS28 and for reading the manuscript; and E. Lennon, I. Masters and V. Manners for helpful discussions. This work was supported by NIH grant GM39933.

# References

BROOKS, B.W., MURRAY, R.G.E., JOHNSTON, J.L., STACKEBRANDT, E., WOESE, C.R. AND FOX, G.E. (1980). Red-pigmented micrococci: a basis for taxonomy. *International Journal of Systematic Bacteriology* **30**, 627–646.

BRON, S., LUXEN, E. AND TRAUTNER, T.A. (1980). Restriction and modification in *B. subtilis*: the role of homology between donor and recipient DNA in transformation and transfection. *Molecular and General Genetics* **179**, 111–117.

BROSIUS, J. (1984). Plasmid vectors for the selection of promotors. *Gene* **27**, 151–160.

CONTENTE, S. AND DUBNAU, D. (1979). Marker rescue transformation by linear plasmid DNA in *Bacillus subtilis. Plasmid* **2**, 555–571.

LOPEZ, P., ESPINOZA, M., STASSI, D.L. AND LACKS, S.A. (1982). Facilitation of plasmid transfer in *Streptococcus pneumoniae* by chromosomal homology. *Journal of Bacteriology* **150**, 692–701.

MACKAY, M.W., AL-BAKRI, G.H. AND MOSELEY, B.E.B. (1985). The plasmids of *Deinococcus* spp. and the cloning and restriction mapping of the *D. radiophilus* plasmid pUE1. *Archives of Microbiology* **141**, 91–94.

MOSELEY, B.E.B. (1983). Photobiology and radiobiology of *Micrococcus (Deinococcus) radiodurans. Photochemical and Photobiological Reviews* **7**, 223–274.

MOSELEY, B.E.B. (1984). Radiation damage and its repair in non-sporulating bacteria. In *The Revival of Injured Microbes* (M.H.E. Andrew and A.D. Russell, Eds), pp. 147–174. Academic Press, New York.

MOSELEY, B.E.B. AND SETLOW, J. (1968). Transformation in *Micrococcus radiodurans* and the ultraviolet sensitivity of its DNA. *Proceedings of the National Academy of Sciences of the United States of America* **61**, 176–183.

PETERS, J., PETERS, M., LOTTSPEICH, F., SCHAFTER, W. AND BAUMEISTER, W. (1988). Nucleotide sequence analysis of the gene encoding the *Deinococcus radiodurans* surface protein, derived amino acid sequence, and complementary protein chemical studies. *Journal of Bacteriology* **169**, 5216–5223.

SMITH, M.D., LENNON, E., McNEIL, L.B. AND MINTON, K.W. (1988). Duplication insertion of drug resistance determinants in the radioresistant bacterium *Deinococcus radiodurans. Journal of Bacteriology* **170**, 2126–2135.

TIRGARI, S. AND MOSELEY, B. (1980). Transformation in *Micrococcus radiodurans*: measurement of various parameters and evidence for multiple, independently segregating genomes per cell. *Journal of General Microbiology* **119**, 287–296.

WANI, A.A., STEPHENS, R.E., D'AMBROSIO, S.M. AND HART, R.W. (1982). A sequence specific endonuclease from *Micrococcus radiodurans. Biochemica et Biophysica Acta* **697**, 178–184.

YANISCH-PERRON, C., VIEIRA, J. AND MESSING, J. (1985). Improved M13 phage cloning vectors and host strains: Nucleotide sequences of the M13mp18 and pUC19 vectors. *Gene* **33**, 103–119.

# 13

# Plasmid Transformation and Maintenance in Yeast

STEPHEN G. OLIVER*[†], NADIA DANHASH[†] AND
DAVID C.J. GARDNER[†]

* Manchester Biotechnology Centre and [†] Department of Biochemistry and
Applied Molecular Biology, University of Manchester Institute for Science and
Technology, PO Box 88, Manchester M60 1QD, UK

## Introduction

The discovery by Beggs (1978) and by Hinnen, Hicks and Fink (1978) that the baker's and brewer's yeast, *Saccharomyces cerevisiae* could be genetically transformed by plasmid DNA has revolutionized the genetics of the organism (Botstein and Davis, 1982) and made it the eukaryotic model of choice for the molecular and cell biologist. The genetics of yeast had previously been analysed in great detail using classical techniques. The organism may be grown in either the haploid or diploid phase and this facilitates both the isolation of mutants and the definition of genes by complementation testing. Diploid cells may readily be induced to undergo meiosis, and the technique of microdissection permits the culture of separate clones from each of the four ascospores. In this way all four products of individual meiotic events may be determined and genes mapped with great precision using tetrad analysis (Mortimer and Schild, 1985).

The linkage groups defined by such classical techniques represent chromosomes whose DNA component consists of a single double-helical molecule (Petes, Byers and Fangman, 1973). These chromosomes are very small (240–2600 kbp; Carle and Olson, 1984) and may be physically separated from one another using pulse field gel electrophoresis techniques such as OFAGE (orthogonal-field-alternation gel electrophoresis; Carle and Olson, 1984) and CHEF (contour-clamped homogeneous electric field; Chu, Vollrath and Davis, 1986). A CHEF separation of yeast chromosomes is shown in *Figure 13.1*.

A large number of yeast genes has now been cloned and sequenced (Sharp, Tuohy and Mosuraki, 1986) and it is likely that a complete chromosome and even the entire genome will be sequenced in the not-too-distant future. This laboratory and that of C.S. Newlon have made a significant start in this

*Genetic Transformation and Expression*
© Intercept Ltd, PO Box 716, Andover, Hants, SP10 1YG, UK

1  2  3  4  5  6  7  8  9  10  11

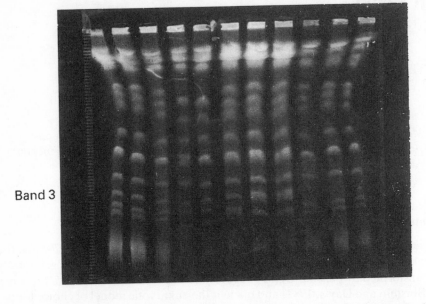

Band 3

**Figure 13.1**   CHEF separation of yeast chromosomes from several strains of *S. cerevisiae*. Tracks 9–11 contain chromosome III ring strains and band 3, which corresponds to the linear form of the chromosome, is missing. The ring form of the chromosome remains in the well. (Photograph courtesy of M. Richards, UMIST.)

direction by collaborating on the DNA sequence analysis of chromosome III, one of the smallest yeast chromosomes (see Warmington *et al.*, 1985, 1986, 1987; Palzkill, Oliver and Newlon, 1986).

The great strength of yeast as a molecular genetic system lies in the ease with which functional analysis may be carried out to provide a biological context for sequence data. Such analyses may be performed on two levels, and the development of a transformation system for the organism was essential for both techniques.

The first approach to the functional analysis of a cloned yeast gene is the technique known as 'one-step gene disruption' (Rothstein, 1983). In this technique, a fragment of a gene is incorporated into a non-replicative plasmid vector (a YIp or yeast integrative plasmid; Parent, Fenimore and Bostian, 1985). Integration of such a plasmid into the gene of interest on a yeast chromosome is facilitated by linearizing the plasmid by a restriction cut within the gene fragment (Orr-Weaver, Szostak and Rothstein, 1981). By this means the plasmid is accurately and efficiently targeted to the gene of interest. This exploits another useful feature of the yeast system—namely its strict requirement for homology in genetic recombination. This feature does not obtain in either the filamentous fungi or mammalian cells. Integration of the YIp plasmid bearing the gene fragment (*Figure 13.2*) effectively produces a null

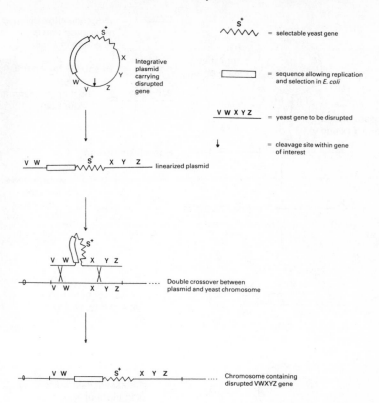

**Figure 13.2** One-step gene disruption in yeast.

mutation since the gene is disrupted by the vector sequence, two incomplete duplicate copies of the gene being produced by the Campbell-type integration event. By this means a phenotype may be obtained for a gene which has been isolated by cloning and which has not been identified previously by mutation analysis. The battery of tests which should be applied to search for a phenotype of such disruption or 'knock-out' mutants has yet to be formalized. However, Goebl and Petes (1986), using a random disruption technique, have determined that as large a proportion as 60% of yeast genes are not essential for growth on complex media. A detailed analysis of two chromosomes—I (Crowley and Kaback, 1984; Coleman *et al.*, 1986; Wickner *et al.*, 1987) and III (Symington and Petes, 1988 a, b; Warmington *et al.*, 1986, 1987)—has also revealed a high number of non-essential genes.

The second technique which may be applied in such functional analyses is that of gene replacement. This is an extension of the gene-disruption protocol and a complete copy, rather than a fragment, of the gene of interest is incorporated into the integrative plasmid. The integration event then duplicates the gene on the chromosome and a second recombination event may excise the plasmid, bearing either its original copy of the gene or the chromosomal copy (*Figure 13.3*). This technique may be used to clone a mutant copy of the gene from the chromosome or, more importantly, to replace a

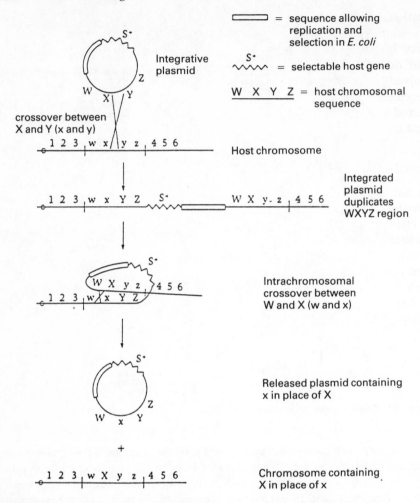

**Figure 13.3** Gene replacement in yeast (from Oliver and Ward, 1985; with permission).

wild-type copy of the gene with a mutant copy. This mutant copy is exactly positioned in the gene's normal chromosomal site. This is of particular importance in the study of gene regulation where, in eukaryotes, position effects (which may involve the higher order structure of the chromosome) can be very important. The gene replacement technique has been applied by Rudolph, Koenig-Rauseo and Hinnen (1985) in their careful dissection of the promoters of the *PHO5* gene (for a recent review of yeast transcription, *see* Oliver and Warmington, 1988).

The exquisite precision of the gene replacement technique rests on the assumption that the only change that has been made to the cell is the specific mutation that was introduced into the gene of interest *in vitro*. In particular, this assumes that the process of transformation (which, in the absence of transducing viruses, is the only convenient means of introducing DNA into yeast) is entirely neutral. In the rest of this chapter, we wish to discuss some data which indicate that the transformation process may have deleterious effects by inducing, or selecting for, some lesion in the host organism. These ideas derive from experiments carried out in our laboratory which have involved a comparison of the induced and spontaneous loss of plasmid molecules. For this reason, we must make a brief excursion into the topic of plasmid stability in yeast before returning to our major theme of yeast transformation.

## Plasmid stability in yeast—a prelude

The nuclei of nearly all laboratory and industrial strains of *Saccharomyces cerevisiae* contain a double-stranded circular DNA plasmid of size 2 μm (6318 bp; Hartley and Donelson, 1980). The plasmid contains two inverted repeat sequences of 599 bp in length. Intramolecular recombination events between the two repeats 'flip' the plasmid between two conformations, the A and B forms (Guerineau, Grandchamp and Slonimski, 1976; Gubbins *et al.*, 1977), which differ in the relative orientation of the two unique regions (*Figure 13.4*). In most yeast strains, the A and B forms of the molecule are present in equimolar amounts.

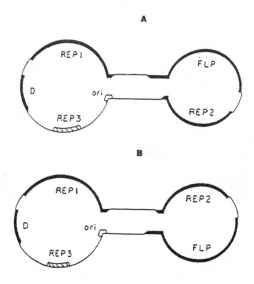

**Figure 13.4** The A and B forms of the 2 μm plasmid.

The intramolecular recombination event which interconverts the A and B forms of the 2 μm circle is catalysed by a plasmid gene product designated *FLP* (Blanc *et al.*, 1979; Broach and Hicks, 1980). The *FLP* protein is a site-specific recombinase which recognizes a region within the inverted repeat sequence known as the *FRT* site (*FLP* Recombination Target) which consists of two 13 bp inverted repeats separated by an 8 bp spacer (Broach, Guarascio and

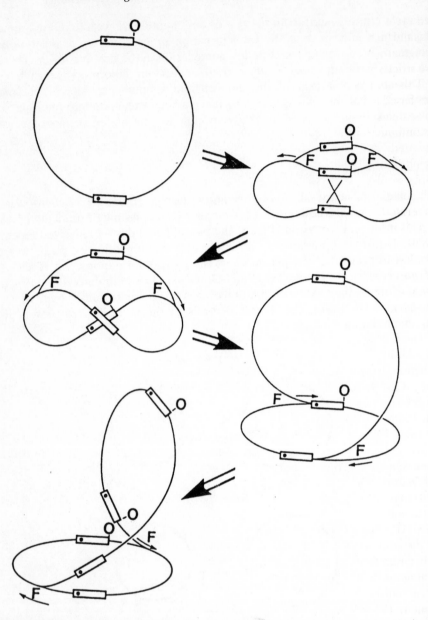

**Figure 13.5**   The Futcher model for 2 μ amplification: O, origin of replication; F, replication fork; X, recombination event; ▭, inverted repeat. The dot shows sequence orientation (from Futcher, 1988; with permission).

Jayaram, 1982; Andrews *et al.*, 1985; Jayaram, 1985; Senecoff, Bruckner and Cox, 1985). This elaborate and highly specific system of plasmid sequence rearrangement plays an essential role in copy-number amplification (Futcher, 1986, 1988). Plasmid replication, like that of yeast chromosomes, is under strict cell cycle control. The 2 μm circle is only replicated in the S-phase and each plasmid molecule replicates only once per cell cycle (Zakian, Brewer and Fangman, 1979). In contrast to bacterial DNA replication, re-initiation events are strictly prohibited.

This control system poses the question of how the copy number of a 2 μm-based plasmid is increased from *c*. 1 immediately following transformation to a steady-state value of *c*. 50. Futcher's (1986) model postulated that a recombination event between a replicated and an unreplicated copy of the inverted repeat would produce a situation where replication switched from being bidirectional to unidirectional (*see Figure 13.5*). The two replication forks would follow one another round the circle and generate a multimeric molecule. In this way several genomes' worth of 2 μm plasmid could be generated from a single initiation event.

This model has now been proved in all its essentials (Volkert and Broach, 1986). It probably represents a general mechanism for eukaryotic plasmid amplification since the plasmids of a wide variety of yeast species (*Zygosaccharomyces rouxii*, Araki *et al.*, 1985; *Z. bisporus*, Toh–E and Utatsu, 1985; *Kluyveromyces drosophilarum*, Chen *et al.*, 1986; and *Z. bailii*, *Z. fermentati*, Utatsu *et al.*, 1987) all have an inverted repeat structure and a *FLP*-type recombination system.

The *S. cerevisiae* 2 μm plasmid sequence contains three open reading-frames in addition to *FLP* (Hartley and Donelson, 1980) and these all represent functional genes involved in plasmid maintenance and partition (Kikuchi, 1983; Cashmore *et al.*, 1988). These proteins, REP1, REP2 and D act together with a *cis*-acting locus called *STB* to ensure that 2 μm plasmid molecules are partitioned approximately equally between mother and daughter cells at division. The way in which they achieve this has recently been summarized by Murray (1987). This property of equipartition is essential to the stability of the 2 μm molecule. It contrasts with recombinant plasmids based on chromosomal replicators, or *ARS* fragments (Williamson, 1985). These show a marked maternal bias in their segregation (Murray and Szostak, 1983) and are extremely unstable, even under selective conditions. *ARS*-based plasmids or YRps (Parent, Fenimore and Bostian, 1985) may have their stability improved by the addition of a *STB* sequence. This *cis*-acting element contains five and a half direct tandem repeats of a 62 bp sequence and has been considered as analogous to both the centromere of eukaryotic chromosomes (for review, *see* Fitzgerald-Hayes, 1987) and the *PAR* locus of *E. coli* plasmids (Meacock and Cohen, 1980). Its mechanism of action is far from clear and one popular suggestion, that it is involved in attaching the 2 μm plasmid to the membrane or some other structure within the nucleus, need not necessarily have the desired stabilizing effect (*see* below).

## Maintenance of the 2 μm plasmid, and its derivatives in yeast populations

So far this chapter has discussed the molecular components involved in 2 μm plasmid partition in yeast. However, there is a second major contribution to plasmid stability in microbial populations and that is selection. The most reliable method of studying the contributions of segregation and selection to overall plasmid stability during mitotic growth is to use continuous culture. This is because cells may be kept in a constant physical and chemical environment which avoids effects due to fluctuations in nutrient concentration, pH or growth phase.

A particular advantage of continuous culture during serial subculture in batch for the study of plasmid stability during a large number of generations is that it avoids spurious selection effects due to 'jack-potting'. This phenomenon results from the fact that a very small sample of one batch culture is taken to inoculate the next culture. If, by chance, a particular variant is present in that sample it will be over-represented in the cell population of the new culture compared to its incidence in the donor culture. The fortuitous selection of the variant is equivalent to hitting the jack-pot in a game of chance. In continuous culture, the only way a variant can increase or decrease its representation in the population is as a direct consequence of its selective fitness. Since continuous culture can maintain the population in exponential growth over long periods, even quite small changes in relative selective fitness may be detected.

In the case of plasmid stability, we can assume that once a cell has lost the plasmid it is unable to regain it. There is no equivalent to reversion as found in the study of mutations. We have thus been able to simplify the equations developed by Moser (1958) in order to model plasmid loss from chemostat populations of yeast (Walmsley, Gardner and Oliver, 1983). Three situations can be distinguished: (1) the presence of the plasmid is selectively neutral; (2) plasmid loss is a selective advantage to the cell; and (3) plasmid loss is a selective disadvantage. *Figure 13.6* presents the relevant equations as well as graphs describing the kinetics of plasmid loss in each of these three cases. In our original study of the stability of 2 μm-based recombinant plasmids (or YEps. Parent, Fenimore and Bostian, 1985) we found that two closely related plasmids gave strikingly different kinetics of loss from a population of haploid yeast cells maintained in a glucose-limited chemostat (Walmsley, Gardner and Oliver, 1983). The parent plasmid, pJDB219 (Beggs, 1978) was lost from the population with the kinetics expected of a plasmid which conferred a selective advantage on its host (*Figure 13.6*). This occurred in spite of the fact that it reduced the growth rate of its host yeast cell by 21%. In contrast, pSLe1 (a derivative of pJDB219 which contains only yeast, and no bacterial, DNA sequences) was lost with the exponential kinetics expected of a plasmid which conferred a 28% growth rate disadvantage on its host. Plasmid loss was monitored by screening for the expression of nutritional marker gene, *LEU2* Derivatives which were *leu2*⁻ proved to be of three types: some had lost the recombinant plasmid but retained the native 2 μm circle, some contained plasmids which appeared to be recombination products between the YEp and the native plasmid, while others contained no plasmid molecules at all. We will return to these plasmid-free [*cir*⁰] derivatives later since they are central to the argument that transformation is not entirely neutral in *S. cerevisiae*.

The conflicting data obtained from two such closely related 2 μm-based recombinant plasmids was obviously unsatisfactory and so we decided to examine the stability of the native 2 μm circle directly. On the face of it, this

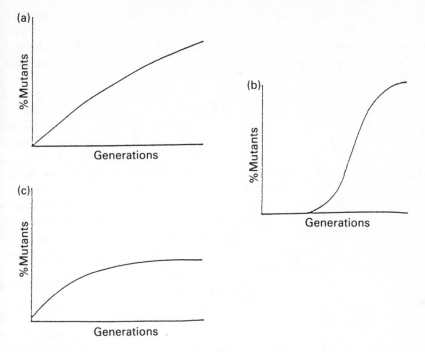

**Figure 13.6** Idealized curves predicting the pattern of accumulation of plasmid-free cells in chemostat culture. The presence of the plasmid is considered to be either (a) selectively neutral, as determined by the equation $f = 1 - (1-f_0)(1-M)^t$; (b) a selective disadvantage, as determined by the equation

$$f = \frac{f_0 + \dfrac{M}{S} - \dfrac{M}{S}(1-f_0)e^{-St}}{f_0 + \dfrac{M}{S} + (1-f_0)e^{-St}};$$

or (c) a selective advantage, as determined by the equation

$$f = \frac{M}{|S|} - \left[\frac{M-f_0}{|S|}\right]e^{-|S|t}.$$

The equations in (b) and (c) were adapted by Walmsley, Gardner and Oliver (1983) from Moser (1958). $f$ = concentration of plasmid-free cells; $f_0$ = initial concentration of plasmid-free cells; $t_0$ = start time; $t$ = generations elapsed since $t_0$; $M$ = mutation (segregation) rate; $S$ = selection pressure = (growth rate of parent) − (growth rate of mutant).

seemed a bizarre thing to do since the 2 μm circle was well known to be completely stable in a wide range of yeast strains (Broach, 1981). However, we felt that the power of continuous culture in these kinds of studies was sufficient to detect even a low level of instability. The problem was that there was no facile method to measure loss of the native 2 μm circle, since it is a cryptic plasmid which confers no overt phenotype on its host cell. For this reason, we had to resort to colony hybridization to detect plasmid loss.

These studies (Mead, Gardner and Oliver, 1986a) revealed that the 2 μm circle was not absolutely stable in glucose-limited chemostat populations of

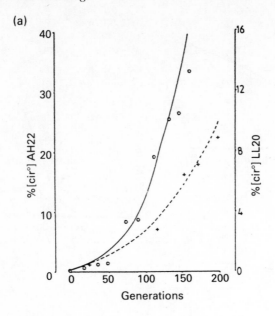

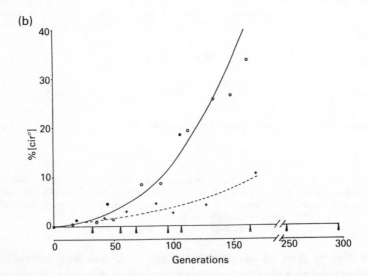

**Figure 13.7** (a) Kinetics of 2 μ loss in haploid strains of *S. cerevisiae* grown in a glucose-limited chemostat. O–O, AH22; +–+ LL20. The continuous line represents the model of loss assuming a segregation rate ($M$) of 0·025% per generation and a growth rate advantage ($S$) of 2·5% to the [*cir*$^0$] segregants. The dashed line is the model for LL20 assuming $M = 0·01%$ and $S = 1·5%$. (b) The effects of growth rate, stationary phase and ploidy on 2μ stability. Accumulation of [*cir*$^0$] cells in AH22 culture grown at a dilution rate ($D$) of 0·24h$^{-1}$ (O–O); $D = 0·1$ h$^{-1}$ (●–●); and when the culture was allowed to pass into stationary phase for 18 h every 54 h (+–+). Accumulation of [*cir*$^0$] cells in a diploid culture grown at $D = 0·23$ h$^{-1}$ (△–△) and $D = 0·255$ h$^{-1}$ (▲–▲). (From Mead, Gardner and Oliver, 1986a; with permission.)

east but was lost with apparently exponential kinetics (*Figure 13.7*). These kinetics conform to the model in which plasmid-free cells are at a selective advantage over their plasmid-bearing progenitors (*see Figure 13.6*). We used our derivatives of Moser's equations (Walmsley, Gardner and Oliver, 1983) to calculate that spontaneous circle-free ($[cir^0-s]$) segregants had a growth rate advantage of 1·5–3% over their $[cir^+]$ parents, according to strain. This was confirmed by carrying out competition experiments between $[cir^+]$ and $[cir^0]$ versions of the same strain. Indeed, the growth rate differences between the two is so small that it cannot be measured directly, even by wash-out (Pirt, 1976; Esener *et al.*, 1981) from a chemostat (*see* Mead, Gardner and Oliver, 1986a, 1987).

The fact that $[cir^0-s]$ segregants of yeast strains grow more rapidly than their $cir^+]$ parents mark the 2 μm molecule as one of that class of DNA molecules which have been described as 'selfish' (Dawkins, 1976; Doolittle and Sapienza, 1980; Orgel and Crick, 1980). This rather emotive term is meant to indicate that a DNA sequence confers no selective advantage on the organism in which it is found or even, as is the case with the yeast 2 μm circle, imposes a small selective penalty. Selfish DNA molecules avoid the seemingly inevitable consequences of selection by having highly efficient mechanisms for their own replication and spread. In the case of the 2 μm plasmid, there appear to be at least three components to its survival strategy (Mead, Gardner and Oliver, 1986a; Futcher, Reid and Hickey, 1988) all of which exploit the organism's life-cycle.

The continuous culture apparatus is a rather unnatural environment for the yeast cell and in the wild, the brewery or winery, or in the laboratory, yeast populations are subjected to cycles of feed and famine. When such a cyclical life-cycle was artificially reproduced by periodically switching off the medium feed to our chemostat culture, it was found that the rate of plasmid loss was reduced significantly (*Figure 13.7*, and Mead, Gardner and Oliver, 1986a). The basis of this effect of stationary phase on plasmid stability is not understood; one possibility is that plasmid multimers accumulate during exponential growth and are resolved by homologous recombination during stationary phase.

The yeast 2 μm plasmid is not an infective agent and it may only be spread from cell to cell via the mating process (Livingston, 1977). The diploid progeny of a $[cir^0] \times [cir^0]$ are $[cir^+]$ and contain at least twice the number of copies of the plasmid as a $[cir^+]$ haploid (Mead, Gardner and Oliver, 1986a; Futcher, Reid and Hickey, 1988; Spalding and Tuite, 1989). The 2 μm circle appears to be absolutely stable in diploid cells and we have never isolated a $[cir^0-s]$ segregant from $[cir^+]$ diploid cells. The crossing of two $[cir^0-s]$ haploids to produce a 'derived' $[cir^0-s]$ diploid has permitted the demonstration that such cells are at a selective advantage over $[cir^+]$ diploids (Mead, Gardner and Oliver, 1986a) and so it must be concluded that such segregants do not arise at any measurable frequency, probably due to the high copy number of the plasmid in diploid cells. A similar stability for 2 μm-based recombinant plasmids has been demonstrated in both diploids and cells of higher ploidy (Mead, Gardner and Oliver, 1986b; Spalding and Tuite, 1989).

Circle-free segregants of haploid cells arise with a frequency of c. $10^{-4}$ per generation (Erhart and Hollenberg, 1983; Futcher and Cox, 1984; Mead,

Gardner and Oliver, 1986a). This is the frequency expected if an element with a copy number of 10 were segregating at random, whereas the actual copy number of the plasmid is 50–70 2μm genome equivalents per cell (Mead, Gardner and Oliver, 1986a). It may be that the number of segregating units of 2 μm DNA is considerably less than the genome copy number, perhaps due to the accumulation of multimers via the Flp-mediated amplification process. Multimerization is known to be a major determinant of the stability of bacterial plasmids (Sherratt, 1986). Another way of viewing the problem is that all but 10 copies of the plasmid are sequestered in the mother nucleus such that they are not free to segregate into the bud. They may, for instance, be attached to the nuclear membrane or the nuclear cage. The 10 free copies then segregate at random between mother and bud. In the case of a diploid cell, the number of free copies would be 50–90 and the corresponding segregation frequency, $10^{-15}$–$10^{-27}$. Such a frequency of plasmid loss is, for all practical purposes, undetectable.

Diploid cells represent, therefore, a stable reservoir of 2 μm molecules in yeast populations. On sporulation, these cells pass the plasmid to all four of their meiotic progeny. Thus a mating event between a $[cir^+]$ and a $[cir^0]$ haploid, followed by meiosis of the $[cir^+]$ diploid so formed, results in the production of four $[cir^+]$ haploid cells, thus doubling the frequency of $[cir^+]$ cells in the population. This theory of the sexual transmission of the plasmid through a population in spite of the selection against it has been verified experimentally (Futcher, Reid and Hickey, 1988).

## Phenotype differences between $[cir^0]$ cells and the consequences of transformation

The preceding account has demonstrated that 2 μm plasmid-free $[cir^0]$ strains of *S. cerevisiae* may be derived in two ways. They may be isolated as spontaneous segregants from cells grown in continuous culture (Mead, Gardner and Oliver, 1986a); these we term $[cir^0-s]$ derivatives where 's' stands for 'spontaneous'. They may also be isolated by transforming yeast with a 2 μm-based recombinant plasmid, selecting for the expression of a plasmid-borne gene such that the recombinant plasmid displaces the resident native 2 μm circles, and then isolating plasmid-free segregants (Dobson, Futcher and Cox, 1980; Erhart and Hollenberg, 1983; Walmsley, Gardner and Oliver, 1983). These we term $[cir^0-i]$ derivatives, where the 'i' stands for induced since plasmid loss has been induced by transformation with a competing plasmid. Superficially, at least, if the only difference between $[cir^0-s]$ and $[cir^0-i]$ cells is the manner of plasmid loss, we would expect them to be both genotypically and phenotypically identical. In fact, there are significant phenotype differences between the two kinds of plasmid-free cells (Walmsley, Gardner and Oliver, 1983; Mead, Gardner and Oliver, 1987). We have seen already that $[cir^0-s]$ cells grow slightly faster than their $[cir^+]$ progenitors although this difference is so small that it can only be detected by competition experiments. The $[cir^0-i]$ type, on the other hand, grows more slowly than its $[cir^+]$ forebears (*see Table 13.1* and Mead, Gardner and Oliver, 1987).

**Table 13.1**    Growth rates of induced and spontaneous [$cir^0$] strains

| | Strain | $Td^*$ (h±SEM) | Change in $Td$ (%) | Level of significance | Growth phenotype |
|---|---|---|---|---|---|
| | AH22[$cir^+$] | 2·59±0·05 | — | — | normal |
| | AH22[$cir^0$−s] | 2·54±0·07 | − 2·7 | NS | normal |
| | AH22[$cir^0$−i] | 2·90±0·06 | +12·0 | >99% | slow |
| | ALD1[$cir^+$] | 2·62±0·06 | — | — | normal |
| (a) | ALD1[$cir^0$−s] | 2·59±0·05 | − 1·1 | NS | normal |
| | ALD1[$cir^0$−i] | 3·47±0·17 | +32·4 | >99·9% | slow |
| (b) | ALD1[$cir^0$−is] | 3·88±0·03 | +48·0 | >99·9% | slow |
| (c) | ALD1[$cir^0$−sc] | 3·32±0·09 | +26·7 | >99% | slow |
| (d) | ALD1[$cir^0$−120] | 3·73±0·13 | +42·3 | >95% | slow |

\* Doubling times ($Td$) with standard error of the mean (SEM), of different isolates of a haploid yeast strain (AH22) and a diploid strain (ALD1) at their maximum specific growth rates in glucose-limited chemostats. The levels of significance were determined using Student's $t$-test; levels of significance <90% were considered not significant (NS).
a) ALD1[$cir^0$−s] was produced by mating two [$cir^0$−s] haploids.
b) was produced by mating a [$cir^0$−i] haploid with a [$cir^0$−s] haploid.
c) was produced by subjecting ALD1[$cir^0$−s] cells to a mock curing process with a YEp.
d) was produced by subjecting ALD1[$cir^0$−s] cells to a mock curing process with a YRp.

This slow-growth phenotype is produced whether the competing plasmid is introduced into the [$cir^+$] yeast by the transformation of protoplasts (Hinnen, Hicks and Fink, 1978) or via whole cell transformation using the lithium acetate procedure of Ito *et al.* (1983). Transformation of haploid yeast cells can produce cells of higher ploidy by cell fusion events (Harashima, Takagi and Oshima, 1984; Karpova *et al.*, 1984). However, all the [$cir^0$−i] derivatives studied have been demonstrated to be still in the haploid state (Mead, Gardner and Oliver, 1987). If a [$cir^+$] diploid is cured by transformation, then the [$cir^0$−i] derivatives show a slow-growth phenotype which is even more marked than that observed in haploid cells (*Table 13.1*). The result implies that if (and it is by no means proven) the slow-growth phenotype is the result of a genetic mutation, then the mutant allele must be a dominant one. This has been confirmed by crossing a [$cir^0$−i] with a [$cir^0$−s] strain and demonstrating that the resultant diploid exhibits slow growth (*Table 13.1*, Danhash, Gardner and Oliver, unpublished). The genetic analysis has not been extended to the meiotic progeny of this diploid since the effect of the segregation of the forcing markers in the cross complicates the growth rate determinations.

The slow-growth phenotype cannot be due to the loss of the 2 μm plasmid *per se* since it is not exhibited by the spontaneous, [$cir^0$−s], segregants. It would seem, therefore, that it must be a result of the curing process or of genetic transformation itself. To further test this idea, [$cir^0$−s] cells were put through a mock curing regime in which they were transformed with either a 2 μm-based recombinant plasmid or an *ARS*-based YRp plasmid, and plasmid-free segregants isolated. In both cases, the slow-growth phenotype was produced (*Table 13.1*, and Danhash, Gardner and Oliver, unpublished). Therefore it is not the curing process which is involved but DNA-mediated transformation. It is now important to determine whether transformation is inducing, or selecting for, a particular class of mutants or whether it is promoting some genetic or epigenetic transition. So far we have excluded the idea that the small proportion of competent cells in a yeast population is some mutant class which

**Table 13.2**    Transformation frequencies of spontaneous circle-free strains

| | Percentage transformants per µg DNA per viable cell | | |
| --- | --- | --- | --- |
| | ALD1[$cir^0$−s] | ALD1[$cir^0$−sc] | Percentage difference |
| (a) | $1.7 \times 10^{-4}$ | $4.4 \times 10^{-4}$ | +61·3 |
| (b) | $3.9 \times 10^{-4}$ | $2.4 \times 10^{-4}$ | −38·4 |
| (c) | $1.4 \times 10^{-3}$ | $1.8 \times 10^{-3}$ | +22·2 |
| (d) | $4 \times 10^{-6}$ | $4.1 \times 10^{-6}$ | + 2·4 |
| (e) | $3.9 \times 10^{-6}$ | $3.6 \times 10^{-6}$ | −7·6 |

A comparison of the transformation frequency in cells which have not previously been transformed (ALD1[$cir^0$−s]), and cells which have been transformed but no longer contain the transforming DNA (ALD1[$cir^0$−sc]). The results of repeated trials failed to reveal a definite trend in transformability. In trials (a)–(c), yeast protoplasts were transformed, while in trials (d) and (e) whole cells were transformed after treatment with lithium acetate.

is, of necessity, selected during genetic transformation. Cells which have been successfully transformed once do not transform at any higher frequency in subsequent trials (*Table 13.2* and Danhash, Gardner and Oliver, unpublished). It may be that transformation triggers some genetic transition, perhaps analogous to phase variation in enteric bacteria (Simon *et al.*, 1980). On the other hand, we could be producing some heritable change to the yeast cell which is not DNA-mediated. For instance, transformation might produce some alteration in the cell wall which is propagated through subsequent generations. Others have noted that transformed yeast cells may show alterations in their flocculation ability (J.R. Johnston, personal communication). The structural inheritance of cell surface patterns has been well documented in protozoa (Aufderheide, Frankel and Williams, 1980). *Figure 13.8* presents a cartoon of the sort of concept we have in mind. Much investigation remains to be done

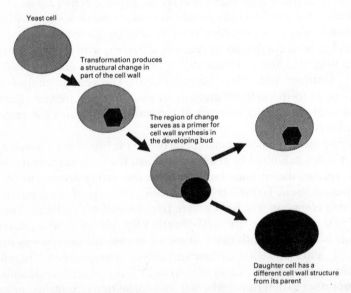

**Figure 13.8**    Physical inheritance of cell surface patterns in *S. cerevisiae*. In our proposed model transformation causes a structural alteration at the yeast cell wall (represented by the shaded area). The altered region serves as a primer for cell wall synthesis in the developing bud giving rise to a daughter cell with a different cell wall structure.

>efore we will understand fully how the slow-growth phenotype is produced. Vhat is certain is that we can no longer be confident that the only change which )NA-mediated transformation produces in a yeast cell is the introduction of a pecific gene or set of genes.

## cknowledgements

)ur investigations have benefited from stimulating discussions with a number )f colleagues including David Mead, Richard Walmsley, Bill Greenhalf, John Zullum and Alan Eddy of UMIST and Mike Dawson of Glaxo. Work on 2 μm )lasmid stability and the slow-growth phenotype in our laboratory is supported )y the SERC Biotechnology Directorate and by Glaxo Group Research.

## References

ANDREWS, B.J., PROTEAU, G.A., BEATTY, L.G. AND SADOWSKI, P.D. (1985). The FLP recombinase of the 2 μ circle DNA of yeast: Interaction with its target sequences. *Cell* **40**, 795–803.

ARAKI, H., JEARNPIPATKUL, A., TATSUMI, H., SAKURAI, T., USHIO, K., MUTA, T. AND OSHIMA, Y. (1985). Molecular and functional organization of yeast plasmid pSR1. *Journal of Molecular Biology* **182**, 191–203.

AUFDERHEIDE, K.J., FRANKEL, J. AND WILLIAMS, N.E. (1980). Formation and positioning of surface-related structures in protozoa. *Microbiological Reviews* **44**, 252–302.

BEGGS, J.D. (1978). Transformation of yeast by a replicating hybrid plasmid. *Nature* **275**, 104–109.

BLANC, H., GERBAUD, C., SLONIMSKI, P.P. AND GUERINEAU, M. (1979). Stable yeast transformation with chimeric plasmids using a 2 μm-circular DNA-less strain as a recipient. *Molecular and General Genetics* **176**, 335–342.

BOTSTEIN, D. AND DAVIS, R.W. (1982). Principles and practice of recombinant DNA research in yeast. In *The Molecular Biology of the Yeast Saccharomyces* (J.N. Strathern, E.W. Jones and J.R. Broach, Eds), pp. 607–637. Cold Spring Harbor Laboratory, Cold Spring Harbor, New York.

BROACH, J.R. (1981). The yeast plasmid 2μ circle. In *The Molecular Biology of the Yeast Saccharomyces: Life Cycle and Inheritance* (J.N. Strathern, E.W. Jones and J.R. Broach, Eds), pp. 445–470. Cold Spring Harbor Laboratory, Cold Spring Harbor, New York.

BROACH, J.R. AND HICKS, J.B. (1980). Replication and recombination functions associated with the yeast plasmid, 2μ circle. *Cell* **21**, 501–508.

BROACH, J.R., GUARASCIO, V.R. AND JAYARAM, M. (1982). Recombination within the yeast plasmid 2μ circle is site-specific. *Cell* **29**, 227–234.

CARLE, G.F. AND OLSON, M.V. (1984). Separation of chromosomal DNA molecules from yeast by orthogonal-field-alternation gel electrophoresis. *Nucleic Acids Research* **12**, 5647–5664.

CASHMORE, A.M., ALBURY, M.S., HADFIELD, C. AND MEACOCK, P.A. (1988). The 2 μm D region plays a role in yeast plasmid maintenance. *Molecular and General Genetics* **212**, 426–431.

CHEN, X.J., SALIOLA, M., FALCONE, C., BIANCHI, M.M. AND FUKUHARA, H. (1986). Sequence organization of the circular plasmid pKD1 from the yeast *Kluyveromyces drosophilarum*. *Nucleic Acids Research* **14**, 4471–4481.

CHU, G., VOLLRATH, D. AND DAVIS, R.W. (1986). Separation of large DNA molecules by contour-clamped homogeneous electric fields. *Science* **234**, 1582–1585.

COLEMAN, K.G., STEENSMA, H.Y., KABACK, D.B. AND PRINGLE, J.R. (1986). Molecular cloning of Chromosome I DNA from *Saccharomyces cerevisiae*: Isolation and characterization of the *CDC24* gene and adjacent regions of the chromosome. *Molecular and Cellular Biology* **6**, 4516–4525.

CROWLEY, J.C. AND KABACK, D.B. (1984). Molecular Cloning of Chromosome I DNA from *Saccharomyces cerevisiae*: isolation of the *ADE1* gene. *Journal of Bacteriology* **154**, 413–417.

DAWKINS, R. (1976). *The selfish gene*. Oxford University Press, Oxford.

DOBSON, M.J., FUTCHER, A.B. AND COX, B.S. (1980). Loss of 2 μm DNA from *Saccharomyces cerevisiae* transformed with the chimaeric plasmid pJDB219. *Current Genetics* **2**, 201–205.

DOOLITTLE, W.F. AND SAPIENZA, C. (1980). Selfish genes, the phenotype paradigm and evolution. *Nature* **284**, 604–607.

ERHART, E. AND HOLLENBERG, C.P. (1983). The presence of a defective *LEU2* gene on 2μ DNA recombinant plasmids of *Saccharomyces cerevisiae* is responsible for curing and high copy number. *Journal of Bacteriology* **156**, 625–635.

ESENER, A.A., ROELS, J.A., KOSSEN, N.W.F. AND ROOZENBURG, J.W.H. (1981). Description of microbial growth behaviour during the wash-out phase: determination of the maximum specific growth rate. *European Journal of Applied Microbiology and Biotechnology* **13**, 141–144.

FITZGERALD-HAYES, M. (1987). Yeast centromeres. *Yeast* **3**, 187–200.

FUTCHER, A.B. (1986). Copy number amplification of the 2 μm circle plasmid of *Saccharomyces cerevisiae*. *Journal of Theoretical Biology* **119**, 197–204.

FUTCHER, A.B. (1988). The 2 μm circle plasmid of *Saccharomyces cerevisiae*. *Yeast* **4**, 27–40.

FUTCHER, A.B. AND COX, B.S. (1984). Copy number and the stability of 2 μm circle-based artificial plasmids of *S. cerevisiae*. *Journal of Bacteriology* **157**, 283–290.

FUTCHER, A.B., REID, E. AND HICKEY, D.A. (1988). Maintenance of the 2 μm circle plasmid of *S. cerevisiae* by sexual transmission: An example of a selfish DNA. *Genetics* **118**, 411–415.

GOEBL, M.G. AND PETES, T.D. (1986). Most of the yeast genomic sequences are not essential for cell growth and division. *Cell* **46**, 983–992.

GUBBINS, E.J., NEWLON, C.S., KANN, M.D. AND DONELSON, J.E. (1977). Sequence organization and expression of a yeast plasmid. *Gene* **1**, 185–207.

GUERINEAU, M., GRANDCHAMP, C. AND SLONIMSKI, P. (1976). Circular DNA of a yeast episome with two inverted repeats: Structural analysis by a restriction enzyme and electron microscopy. *Proceedings of the National Academy of Sciences of the United States of America* **73**, 3030–3034.

HARASHIMA, S., TAKAGI, A. AND OSHIMA, Y. (1984). Transformation of protoplasted yeast cells is directly associated with cell fusion. *Molecular and Cellular Biology* **4**, 771–778.

HARTLEY, J.L. AND DONELSON, J.E. (1980). Nucleotide sequence of the yeast plasmid. *Nature* **286**, 860–865.

HINNEN, A., HICKS, J.B. AND FINK, G.R. (1978). Transformation of yeast. *Proceedings of the National Academy of Sciences of the United States of America* **75**, 1929–1933.

ITO, H., FUKUDA, Y., MURATA, K. AND KIMURA, A. (1983). Transformation of intact yeast cells treated with alkali cations. *Journal of Bacteriology* **153**, 163–168.

JAYARAM, M. (1985). Two-micrometer circle site-specific recombination: The minimal substrate and the possible role of flanking sequences. *Proceedings of the National Academy of Sciences of the United States of America* **82**, 5875–5879.

KARPOVA, T.A., GORDENIN, D.A., KOZINA, T.N., ANDRIANOVA, V.M., LARIONOV V.L. AND INGE-VECHTOMOV, S.G. (1984). Rapid genetic test for discrimination between haploids and polyploid transformants in *Saccharomyces*. *Current Genetic* **8**, 341–344.

KIKUCHI, Y. (1983). Yeast plasmid requires a *cis*-acting locus and two plasmid protein for its stable maintenance *Cell* **35**, 487–493.

LIVINGSTON, D.M. (1977). Inheritance of the 2 µm DNA plasmid from *Saccharomyces*. *Genetics* **86**, 73–84.

MEACOCK, P.A. AND COHEN, S.N. (1980). Partitioning of bacterial plasmids during cell division: a *cis*-acting locus that accomplishes stable inheritance. *Cell* **20**, 529–542.

MEAD, D.J., GARDNER, D.C.J. AND OLIVER, S.G. (1986a). The yeast 2 µ plasmid: strategies for the survival of a selfish DNA. *Molecular and General Genetics* **205**, 417–421.

MEAD, D.J., GARDNER, D.C.J. AND OLIVER, S.G. (1986b). Enhanced stability of a 2 µm based recombinant plasmid in diploid yeast. *Biotechnology Letters* **8**, 391–396.

MEAD, D.J., GARDNER, D.C.J. AND OLIVER, S.G. (1987). Phenotypic differences between induced and spontaneous 2 µm-free segregants of *S. cerevisiae*. *Current Genetics* **11**, 415–418.

MORTIMER, R.K. AND SCHILD, D. (1985). Genetic map of *Saccharomyces cerevisiae*, Edn 9. *Microbiological Reviews* **49**, 181–212.

MOSER, H. (1958). The dynamics of bacterial populations maintained in the chemostat. *Carnegie Institute of Washington Publication No. 614.*

MURRAY, A.W. AND SZOSTAK, J.W. (1983). Pedigree analysis of plasmid segregation in yeast. *Cell* **34**, 961–970.

MURRAY, J.A.H. (1987). Bending the rules: the 2 µ plasmid of yeast, *Molecular Microbiology* **1**, 1–14.

OLIVER, S.G. AND WARD, J.M. (1985). *A Dictionary of Genetic Engineering*. Cambridge University Press, Cambridge.

OLIVER, S.G. AND WARMINGTON, J.R. (1988). Transcription. In *The Yeasts, Vol. 3*, (A.H. Rose and J.S. Harrison, Eds), pp. 117–160. Academic Press, London.

ORGEL, L.E. AND CRICK, F.H.C. (1980). Selfish DNA: The ultimate parasite. *Nature* **284**, 604–607.

ORR-WEAVER, T.L., SZOSTAK, J.W. AND ROTHSTEIN, R.J. (1981). Yeast transformation: A model system for the study of recombination. *Proceedings of the National Academy of Sciences of the United States of America* **78**, 6354–6358.

PALZKILL, T.G., OLIVER, S.G. AND NEWLON, C.S. (1986). DNA sequence analysis of *ARS* elements from chromosome III of *Saccharomyces cerevisiae*: identification of a new conserved sequence. *Nucleic Acids Research* **14**, 6247–6264.

PARENT, S.A., FENIMORE, C.M. AND BOSTIAN, K.A. (1985). Vector systems for the expression, analysis and cloning of DNA sequences in *S. cerevisiae*. *Yeast* **1**, 83–138.

PETES, T.D., BYERS, B. AND FANGMAN, W.L. (1973). Size and structure of yeast chromosomal DNA. *Proceedings of the National Academy of Sciences of the United States of America* **70**, 3072–3076.

PIRT, S.J. (1976). *Principles of microbe and cell culture*. Blackwell Scientific Publications, Oxford.

ROTHSTEIN, R.J. (1983). One-step gene disruption in yeast. *Methods in Enzymology* **101**, 228–245.

RUDOLPH, H., KOENIG-RAUSEO, I. AND HINNEN, A. (1985). One-step gene replacement in yeast by co-transformation. *Gene* **36**, 87–95.

SENECOFF, J.F., BRUCKNER, R.C. AND COX, M.M. (1985). The FLP recombinase of the yeast 2 µm plasmid: Characterisation of its recombination site. *Proceedings of the National Academy of Sciences of the United States of America* **82**, 7270–7274.

SHARP, P.M., TUOHY, T.M.F. AND MOSURSKI, K.R. (1986). Codon usage in yeast: cluster analysis clearly differentiates highly and lowly expressed genes. *Nucleic Acids Research* **14**, 5125–5143.

SHERRATT, D. (1986). Control of plasmid maintenance. In *Regulation of gene expression – 25 years on* (I.R. Booth and C.F. Higgins, Eds), pp. 239–250. Cambridge University Press, Cambridge.

SIMON, M., ZIEG, J., SILVERMAN, M., MANDELL, G. AND DOOLITTLE, R. (1980). Phase variation: evolution of a controlling element. *Science* **209**, 1370–1374.

SPALDING, A. AND TUITE, M.F. (1989). Host-plasmid interactions in *Saccharomyces cerevisiae*: Effect of host ploidy on plasmid stability and copy number. *Journal of General Microbiology* **135**, 1037–1045.

SYMINGTON, L.S. AND PETES, T.D. (1988a). Meiotic recombination within the centromere of a yeast chromosome. *Cell* **52**, 237–240.

SYMINGTON, L.S. AND PETES, T.D. (1988b). Expansions and contractions of the genetic map relative to the physical map of yeast chromosome III. *Molecular and Cellular Biology* **8**, 595–604.

TOH-E, A. AND UTATSU, I. (1985). Physical and functional structure of a yeast plasmid pSB3, isolated from *Zygosaccharomyces bisporus*. *Nucleic Acids Research* **13** 4267–4283.

UTATSU, I., SAKAMOTO, S., IMARU, T. AND TOH-E, A. (1987). Yeast plasmid resembling 2 μm DNA: Regional similarities and diversities at the molecular level. *Journal of Bacteriology* **169**, 5537–5545.

VOLKERT, F.C. AND BROACH, J.R. (1986). Site-specific recombination promotes plasmid amplification in yeast. *Cell* **46**, 541–550.

WALMSLEY, R.M., GARDNER, D.C.J. AND OLIVER, S.G. (1983). Stability of a cloned gene in yeast grown in chemostat culture. *Molecular and General Genetics* **192** 361–365.

WARMINGTON, J.R., WARING, R.B., NEWLON, C.S., INDGE, K.J. AND OLIVER, S.G (1985). Nucleotide sequence characterization of Tyl–17, a class II transposon from yeast. *Nucleic Acids Research* **13**, 6679–6693.

WARMINGTON, J.R., ANWAR, R., NEWLON, C.S., WARING, R.B., DAVIES, R.W. AND OLIVER, S.G. (1986). A 'hot spot' for Ty transposition on the left arm of yeast chromosome III. *Nucleic Acids Research* **14**, 3475–3485.

WARMINGTON, J.R., GREEN, R.P., NEWLON, C.S. AND OLIVER, S.G. (1987) Polymorphisms on the right arm of yeast chromosome III associated with Ty transposition and recombination events. *Nucleic Acids Research* **15**, 8963–8982.

WICKNER, R.B., KOH, T.J., CROWLEY, J.C., O'NEIL, J. AND KABACK, D.B. (1987) Molecular cloning of chromosome I DNA from *S. cerevisiae*: Isolation of the *MAK 16* gene and analysis of an adjacent gene essential for growth at low temperatures *Yeast* **3**, 51–57.

WILLIAMSON, D.H. (1985). The yeast *ARS* element six years on: A progress report *Yeast* **1**, 1–14.

ZAKIAN, V.A., BREWER, B.J. AND FANGMAN, W.L. (1979). Replication of each copy of the yeast 2 micron DNA plasmid occurs during the S-phase. *Cell* **17**, 923–934.

# 14

# *Agrobacterium tumefaciens* as a Tool for the Genetic Transformation of Plants

G. GHEYSEN, L. HERMAN, P. BREYNE, M. VAN MONTAGU AND
A. DEPICKER

Laboratorium voor Genetica, Rijksuniversiteit Gent, K.L. Ledeganckstraat 35,
B–9000 Gent, Belgium

## Transformation of plant cells by *Agrobacterium tumefaciens*

THE *AGROBACTERIUM* SYSTEM

The use of *Agrobacterium tumefaciens* as a natural system to construct transgenic plants is based on the finding that during the interaction of agrobacteria with wounded plant tissues a well-defined segment of the Ti plasmid, called T-DNA (*Figure 14.1*), is transferred to the plant cell and integrated into the nuclear genome (for a review of the *Agrobacterium* system, *see* Gheysen *et al.*, 1985). The virulence region is defined as the DNA segment of the Ti plasmid that codes for the gene products required for the T-DNA transfer from *Agrobacterium* to the plant cell (*Figure 14.1*). The T-DNA contains a number of genes that encode enzymes involved in the synthesis of phytohormones and specific metabolites, called opines, the most common of which are octopine and nopaline. As a consequence of expression of these T-DNA genes, the transformed plant cells form tumorous 'crown gall' tissues, capable of growing on hormone-free medium and excreting opines that can be metabolized by the inciting bacteria. *Agrobacterium* has a very wide host range, including some monocotyledonous plants (De Cleene and De Ley, 1976). However, *Agrobacterium*-mediated transformation of Gramineae, especially of the important cereal crops, has yet to be achieved.

TRANSFORMATION VECTORS BASED ON THE Ti PLASMID

A wide variety of *Agrobacterium* vector systems has been developed (Zambryski *et al.*, 1983; Bevan, 1984; An *et al.*, 1985; Deblaere *et al.*, 1985, 1987; Fraley *et al.*, 1985; Klee, Yanofsky and Nester, 1985; van den Elzen *et al.*, 1985a; Simoens *et al.*, 1986; Rogers *et al.*, 1987). They allow convenient cloning of foreign genes and mobilization in a single step from *Escherichia coli* to

*Genetic Transformation and Expression*
© Intercept Ltd, PO Box 716, Andover, Hants, SP10 1YG, UK

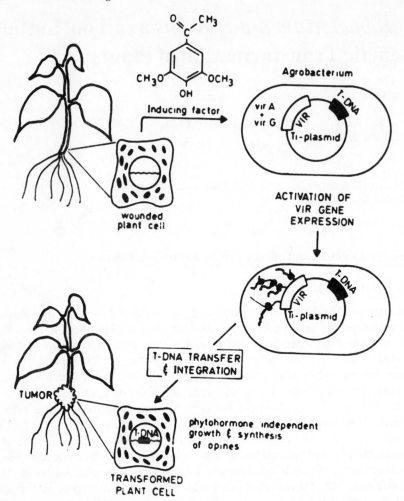

**Figure 14.1** The *Agrobacterium*/plant cell interaction. Upon induction by wounded plant cell exudates, e.g. acetosyringone, the *Agrobacterium vir* genes are induced and their products mediate T-DNA transfer to the plant cell. *virA* and *virG* are the two components of a regulatory system which activates the *virB*, *virC*, *virD*, *virE* and *virG* genes. After transfer and stable integration in the plant cell, the T-DNA-encoded genes are expressed. The transformed cells form tumorous 'crown gall' tissues excreting opines which can be metabolized by the inciting bacteria.

*Agrobacterium.* Four observations allowed the design of the presently used Ti plasmid vectors:

1. The T-DNA genes responsible for phytohormone-independent tumorous growth of crown gall cells (the 'oncogenes') are not required for T-DNA transfer or integration (Leemans *et al.*, 1982; Joos *et al.*, 1983).

2. The 25 bp direct repeats flanking the T-DNA (the 'T-DNA borders') (Yadav *et al.*, 1982; Zambryski *et al.*, 1982) are essential in *cis* for T-DNA transfer.

3.  Chimeric constructs consisting of a plant promoter sequence and a bacterial antibiotic resistance gene can be used as efficient marker genes to select transformed plant cells (Herrera-Estrella *et al.*, 1983a, 1983b; De Block *et al.*, 1984).
4.  The virulence genes (*vir*) that lie outside the T-DNA on the Ti plasmid (Holsters *et al.*, 1980; Stachel and Nester, 1986) encode the functions mediating T-DNA transfer. These *vir* genes can act in *cis*, i.e. when the T-DNA and the *vir* genes are on the same plasmid, or in *trans*, i.e. when the T-DNA and the *vir* genes are on separate plasmids, to initiate the events that form a T-DNA intermediate which is subsequently transferred to the plant cells.

SELECTABLE MARKERS FOR TRANSFORMED PLANT CELLS

Plant cells are sensitive to many of the antibiotics that inhibit ribosome function. This is easily explained since bacterial and chloroplast ribosomes are evolutionarily related. Plant cell resistance to antibiotics that inhibit prokaryotic ribosomes could thus be obtained by fusing the coding sequences of the corresponding antibiotic-inactivating genes, isolated from prokaryotes, to appropriate plant expression signals. In this way several selectable markers were obtained that can be used for the selection of genetically transformed plant cells.

The first developed, and still most widely used, selection marker is the resistance to a number of aminoglycoside antibiotics, such as neomycin, kanamycin, gentamycin, and G418, which is obtained by the expression of the neomycin phosphotransferase II gene (*npt-II*) (Herrera-Estrella *et al.*, 1983b; Bevan, Flavell and Chilton, 1983). The reaction involves transfer of the γ-phosphate group of ATP to the antibiotic molecule. This addition detoxifies the antibiotic by preventing its interaction with the organelle ribosomes. Besides its properties as a selectable marker, the *npt-II* gene expression can easily be quantified (down to 1 ng of enzyme) by an enzymatic test. After electrophoretic separation of the NPT-II enzyme from interfering proteins, the activity of the enzyme is assayed by *in situ* phosphorylation of kanamycin (Reiss *et al.*, 1984). In this way, an idea of the levels of expression of different plant promoter sequences can be obtained by analysing plants transformed with a hybrid gene, consisting of the *npt-II*-coding sequence fused to the plant promoters to be tested.

Other selectable markers for plant cell transformation have been developed from different prokaryotic antibiotic-resistance genes. Frequently used markers are the hygromycin phosphotransferase gene (*hpt*) (van den Elzen *et al.*, 1985b; Waldron *et al.*, 1985), methotrexate- (De Block *et al.*, 1984), bleomycin- (Hille *et al.*, 1986), streptomycin- (Jones *et al.*, 1987a) and glyphosate-resistance genes (Fillatti *et al.*, 1987), the chloramphenicol acetyltransferase (*cat*) (De Block *et al.*, 1984) and the phosphinothricin acetyltransferase (*bar*) genes (De Block *et al.*, 1987; Thompson *et al.*, 1987); the latter two selection markers also allow enzymatic quantification of the corresponding gene expression.

METHODS FOR PLANT CELL TRANSFORMATION USING *AGROBACTERIUM*

Once an appropriate *Agrobacterium* vector has been constructed with a particular gene combination in the T-DNA, transformed plant cells can be obtained by co-cultivation of the engineered *Agrobacterium* with leaf discs (Horsch *et al.*, 1985) or other wounded plant organs, e.g. roots (Valvekens, Van Montagu and Van Lijsebettens, 1988), or with plant cell protoplasts.

The isolation of single-leaf-cell protoplasts and their subsequent infection with a particular *Agrobacterium* strain is a transformation method which was first published by Márton *et al.* (1979) to isolate clonal tumour lines. Later, De Block *et al.* (1984) applied this method in combination with antibiotic selection to obtain transgenic plant regenerates. The main requirements for obtaining transgenic plants after co-cultivation of protoplasts are that the transformed cells can reform cell walls, proliferate *in vitro* and differentiate into mature plants. Although the tissue-culture manipulations are rather complicated compared to the leaf-disc infections, the protoplast system has its advantages. The high transformation frequency (easily up to 20% for SR1 tobacco cells; Depicker *et al.*, 1985) makes selectable markers dispensable. Furthermore, the large number of transformants allows selection for rare events. By this method, plant promoter sequences could be isolated by screening a pool of random DNA fragments for ones that transcribed a selectable marker in plant cells (Herman, Van Montagu and Depicker, 1986). Moreover, the large number of transformants allows quantitative data to be obtained about the relative importance of the left and right T-DNA border sequences and about the frequency of aberrant T-DNA insertions (unpublished results).

THE 'EARLY EVENTS' IN THE TRANSFORMATION PROCESS

*The* Agrobacterium/*plant cell contact*

*Agrobacterium tumefaciens* attaches to plant cells in a polar way as a single bacterium or in clusters. The attachment is mediated by chromosomal virulence loci, which are expressed in a constitutive fashion (Douglas *et al.*, 1985; Cangelosi *et al.*, 1987; Matthysse, 1987; Thomashow *et al.*, 1987; Zorreguieta *et al.*, 1988). It is not known whether *Agrobacterium* preferentially attaches to particular plant cell wall structures, but experimental evidence suggests that primary cell walls of rapidly dividing cells are preferred. This observation is exploited in the transformation technique of co-cultivation with plant protoplasts and infection of leaf discs, root systems or other organ explants.

The preference for actively dividing cells is probably due to the release of chemotactically active substances in the plant exudates. It was shown that only actively growing plant cells (wounded plant cells) release acetosyringone and α-hydroxy-acetosyringone in the exudates (Bolton, Nester and Gordon, 1986). In turn, these phenolic compounds specifically induce the *vir* functions in *Agrobacterium* (*Figure 14.1*); (Stachel, Nester and Zambryski, 1986; Stachel and Zambryski, 1986). It has been found that besides functioning as a specific inducer of *vir* gene expression, acetosyringone also attracts *Agrobacterium* chemotactically at a concentration of $10^{-7}$ M, which is one hundredfold lower than the concentration for maximal *vir* induction (Ashby, Watson and Shaw, 1987). This suggests a biological system in which acetosyringone, at low concentrations, acts as a chemo-attractant for *Agrobacterium*. The bacterium moves up the concentration gradient towards the wounded plant cells. Then, at higher concentrations, acetosyringone activates *vir* gene expression. This suggests that the T-DNA transfer system in *Agrobacterium* is only activated in the presence of plant cells which are susceptible for transformation.

Some hours after induction, site-specific DNA nicks are found after the third or fourth base of the 25 bp right and left border repeat (Wang *et al.*, 1987). At the same time, a linear single-stranded molecule (T-strand) is synthesized, which corresponds to the bottom strand of the T-region, the 5' and 3' ends of which map at the right and left T-DNA border, respectively (Stachel, Timmerman and Zambryski, 1986; Albright *et al.*, 1987; Veluthambi, Ream and Gelvin, 1988).

Border nicking and T-strand production are analogous to nicking of *oriT* and replacement strand synthesis in the processing of plasmid DNA for interbacterial conjugation (for a review, *see* Willetts and Wilkins, 1984). This suggests that the mechanism of T-DNA transfer to plant cells by *A. tumefaciens* is an evolutionary adaptation of a pre-existing process, namely bacterial conjugation. Recent molecular data on the virulence proteins further strengthen this hypothesis.

*The role of the virulence genes*

The induction of the *Agrobacterium vir* genes (*Figures 14.1, 14.2*) in response to plant wound-specific phenolics implies that there must be a bacterial recognition system to detect the plant signal and transmit the information inside the bacterial cell. This process appears to be mediated by the products of *virA* and *virG*. VirA is homologous to EnvZ, NtrB, and various other transmembrane chemoreceptor proteins (Leroux *et al.*, 1987), while VirG is closely related to the proteins encoded by the *ompR* and the *ntrC* genes and several other proteins that are thought to function as positive regulatory elements (Winans *et al.*, 1986). Therefore, it is believed that the VirA protein, which has been localized in the bacterial inner membrane (Leroux *et al.*, 1987) may be able to sense the presence of wound-induced plant phenolics. After receiving this signal, VirA could transform VirG from an inactive form to an active form capable of promoting transcription of the plant-inducible *vir* genes. A similar two-component, regulatory system has been proposed for the control of nitrogen-regulated genes by NtrB and NtrC (Nixon, Ronson and Ausubel, 1986). Recently, Shaw *et al.* (1988) have shown that VirA and VirG are also the only plasmid-encoded functions necessary for chemotaxis. This suggests a multifunctional role for the VirA–VirG system: at low acetosyringone concentrations, it would mediate chemotaxis, whereas at higher concentrations, it causes induction of *vir* gene expression.

After recognition of and attachment to a susceptible plant cell, the next step in the transformation process is the production of a T-DNA transfer

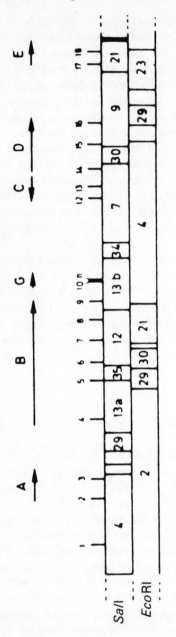

**Figure 14.2** Transcriptional organization of the *vir* region of the octopine plasmid pTiA6 (Stachel and Nester, 1986). The length and orientation of the *vir* transcripts are shown as arrows above the restriction map. Numbers 1 to 18 indicate the position of some *vir* mutants.

intermediate. Nicking of the border repeats and T-strand production are involved in this T-DNA processing. Yanofsky *et al.* (1986) have shown that the 5' end of the *virD* operon encodes a site-specific endonuclease that cleaves the border repeat. Complementation studies indicated that the products of both *virD1* and *virD2* are required for this nicking activity (Jayaswal *et al.*, 1987). Several activities other than a border endonuclease are expected to be essential for T-strand synthesis. Nevertheless, none of the chromosomal *chv* and Ti plasmid *vir* mutant strains were found to be deficient in T-strand production alone (Stachel, Timmerman and Zambryski, 1987). This suggests that the other activities of T-strand synthesis (such as helicase, polymerase, etc.) might be essential bacterial functions encoded by the *A. tumefaciens* chromosome.

By analogy with bacterial conjugation, one would expect that the T-strand is transferred as a protein–DNA complex. Indeed, it has been found that the VirD2 protein is covalently attached to the 5' end of T-strands (Herrera-Estrella *et al.*, 1988; Young and Nester, 1988). Furthermore, the *virE2* gene encodes a single-stranded DNA-binding protein which is shown to be associated with T-strand molecules (Gietl, Koukolíková-Nicola and Hohn, 1987; Christie *et al.*, 1988; Citovsky, De Vos and Zambryski, 1988; Das, 1988). It is therefore tempting to imagine the transfer intermediate as a multiple protein–DNA complex consisting of the single-stranded T-DNA molecule with the VirD2 protein covalently attached to the 5' end and the VirE2 protein covering the rest of the DNA molecule. The hydrophilic nature of the VirE2 protein (Hirooka, Rogowsky and Kado, 1987; Winans *et al.*, 1987), its abundancy in induced agrobacteria (Engström *et al.*, 1987), and the fact that *virE* mutant strains can be complemented by co-infection with wild-type strains (Otten *et al.*, 1984) are consistent with an extracellular structural function, potentially as part of a transferable T-DNA–protein complex.

The nucleotide sequence analysis of the largest *vir* operon, *vir B*, revealed 11 open reading-frames, most of them probably encoding secreted or membrane-associated proteins (Thompson *et al.*, 1988; Ward *et al.*, 1988). Indeed, many of the major induced proteins in *Agrobacterium*, including three identified *virB* products, have been specifically localized in the cell envelope (Engström *et al.*, 1987). The abundance and localization of these proteins suggest that they may participate in the formation of a structural element on the bacterial surface, potentially a transmembrane structure through which a T-DNA–protein complex might be exported and delivered into the plant cell. It is interesting that a potential ATP-binding site is present in VirB4 and in VirB11 (Thompson *et al.*, 1988). The presence of an ATP-binding subunit is reported to be a common feature of the components from different periplasmic transport systems (Higgins *et al.*, 1986).

## Structural properties of the T-DNAs in transformed plant cells

INTEGRITY OF THE T-DNA

Transformation with *Agrobacterium* has the advantage that the DNA segment integrated in the plant cell usually has the same structure as the copy originally engineered in the bacterium. The right T-DNA border is very precise, meaning that the junction with plant DNA occurs within 10 bp of the right-border repeat (this has been estimated by characterizing six different T-DNA junctions); the left junction is less precise and varies over a stretch of 200 bp inside of the left-border sequence (Gheysen *et al.*, 1985).

Besides these normal T-DNA integrations, several experiments report the occurrence of truncated, scrambled and rearranged T-DNAs (Hepburn *et al.*,

1983a; Kwok, Nester and Gordon, 1985; Peerbolte *et al.*, 1986; Spielmann and Simpson, 1986; Van Lijsebettens *et al.*, 1986; Jorgensen, Snyder and Jones, 1987). The frequency of these truncated T-DNAs varies between 1/100 and 1/10 of normal T-DNA insertions. There seems to be no correlation between the length of the T-DNA and the frequency of truncation, nor does it seem that the truncation sites represent pseudoborder sequences, imperfectly recognized by the transfer enzymes (unpublished results). Therefore, we presume that truncation occurs primarily during integration.

In contrast to the *Agrobacterium*/plant cell transformation, the direct gene transformation methods (naked DNA transformation by PEG treatment or electroporation) have in common that the transferred DNA is integrated as a random sequence without specific ends, often disrupting the genes that must be expressed. Also, integration is not very efficient (for a discussion, *see* Czernilofsky *et al.*, 1986a, 1986b).

PLANT DNA TARGET SITES FOR T-DNA INTEGRATION

Genomic characterization of many T-DNA insertions convincingly showed the occurrence of many different plant–T-DNA junctions. *In situ* hybridization (Ambros, Matzke and Matzke, 1986) and genetic analysis (Chyi *et al.*, 1986) demonstrates that T-DNA insertions can be found on every chromosome. Moreover, sequence analysis of different left and right T-DNA–plant junction sequences proved that all are different and that no preference for a unique site or particular sequence motif can be demonstrated.

The plant DNA which is found at the junction with the T-DNA borders can be unique or repetitive. Early studies on T-DNA integration sites in tobacco (Thomashow *et al.*, 1980; Zambryski *et al.*, 1980, 1982; Yadav *et al.*, 1982), indicated that the T-DNA is usually attached to repetitive plant sequences. Recent publications contradict this thesis. Gene tagging experiments in *Nicotiana plumbaginifolia* indicate that one in 10 of the T-DNAs integrates into transcriptionally active, presumably non-repetitive regions (André *et al.*, 1986). Analogous conclusions can be drawn from gene-fusion experiments in *N. tabacum* (Herman, Van Montagu and Depicker, 1987).

The fact that most of the plant–T-DNA junctions hybridize to repetitive plant DNA sequences is not surprising. Since at least 55% of the nuclear DNA of *N. tabacum* is organized in a pattern consisting of single-copy sequences, on average about 1400 bp long, alternating with repetitive sequences approximately 300 nucleotides long (Zimmerman and Goldberg, 1977), it is expected that many of the utilized plant probes have at least one copy of a repeated sequence. Therefore, when the T-DNA border junctions hybridize to repetitive plant DNA, it does not necessarily mean that the T-DNA is directly adjacent to or within the repeat.

By cloning and sequence analysis of plant DNA target sequences and comparison with the plant DNA flanking the left and right sides of the T-DNA, it was demonstrated that T-DNA integration can be accompanied by sequence rearrangements (Gheysen, Van Montagu and Zambryski, 1987). The most conspicuous rearrangement is the duplication of a 158 bp sequence which flanks the T-DNA in a direct repeat at its left and right side after integration. Moreover, a small deletion of 27 bp at the outer end of the duplication at the right side, and the insertion of a 33 bp filler sequence at the left side suggest that these changes in the plant target DNA sequence are the result of DNA recombination–repair activities. This may not be a unique case, since the DNA between tandem T-DNAs (Zambryski *et al.*, 1982; Holsters *et al.*, 1983) or flanking other T-DNA–plant junctions (Simpson *et al.*, 1982) also contains scrambled, rearranged T-DNA sequence motifs.

These results demonstrate that T-DNA integration does not occur by a simple recombination, breaking and joining process, but is accompanied by replication and repair activities, probably by plant-encoded enzymes.

STABILITY AND INHERITANCE OF THE T-DNA IN TRANSGENIC PLANTS

The inheritance of genes introduced by the T-DNA in plants can be studied by the techniques of classical genetics. Segregation data allow the determination of the number and the stability of the introduced loci in the transformed clones. In this way, it was shown that the T-DNAs are stably maintained and that the encoded markers strictly follow the Mendelian rules through several sexual generations without selective pressure (Chyi *et al.*, 1986; Müller *et al.*, 1987).

The segregation of the kanamycin-resistance gene in 44 transformed clones, obtained by co-cultivation of regenerating protoplasts with agrobacteria harbouring a chimeric *nos–npt-II* gene has been determined (Budar *et al.*, 1986). In this experiment, most of the plants contained only one expressing T-DNA locus. It is important to remember, however, that a single T-DNA or a number of closely linked inserts can be present at each locus. In other transformation experiments both by protoplast or leaf-disc infection, the majority of regenerated plants contains two or more segregating T-DNA loci (Herman, Van Montagu and Depicker, 1986; Spielmann and Simpson, 1986; Jones *et al.*, 1987b). It is not known yet what governs the multiplicity of T-DNA insertions. It might be correlated with infection conditions, the transformation frequency and/or the *Agrobacterium* strain used.

## Expression of transferred genes in transgenic plants

STUDY OF PLANT GENES

Although plant transformation for crop improvement (*see* later) has attracted much of the attention, one should not forget its major impact on fundamental research in plant molecular biology. Plant biologists are no longer restricted to the passive study of physiological and biochemical processes because the introduction of native or modified genes allows a more directed analysis. The use of chimeric gene fusions in all its aspects has expanded enormously the knowledge of plant gene function, expression and regulation.

Promoter and 3' sequences of various plant genes have been characterized by fusion to the coding sequence of quantifiable markers (for a review on the regulation of gene expression in higher plants, *see* Kuhlemeier, Green and Chua, 1987).

As already described, the *npt-II* gene can be used to measure promoter activities. Another marker gene which is becoming very important for the quantification and localization of enzyme activities in plant cells or tissues is β-glucuronidase (GUS; EC 3.2.1.31). β-Glucuronidase catalyses the cleavage of a wide variety of β-glucuronides of which many are available as spectrophotometric or fluorometric substrates (Jefferson, Kavanagh and Bevan, 1987). It offers a gene-fusion system that is easy to quantitate and is highly sensitive. It is also possible to use this reporter enzyme in histochemical assays for the localization of gene activity in particular cell types.

Some examples of tissue-specifically, environmentally or developmentally regulated plant sequences studied in transgenic plants are: the regulatory sequences of the small subunit of the ribulose-1,5-bisphosphate carboxylase (Broglie *et al.*, 1984; Herrera-Estrella *et al.*, 1984; Nagy *et al.*, 1985; Fluhr and Chua, 1986; Kuhlemeier *et al.*, 1988), the chlorophyll a/b-binding protein (Simpson *et al.*, 1985, 1986), the soybean-seed lectin (Okamuro, Jofuku and Goldberg, 1986) and the proteinase inhibitor II gene (Thornburg *et al.*, 1987).

Also partial or complete plant gene coding sequences have been used in gene-fusion experiments. In this way it was shown that the transit peptide from the small subunit of ribulose-1,5-bisphosphate carboxylase when fused to the *npt-II*-coding sequence was sufficient to target the NPT-II protein to chloroplasts (Van den Broeck *et al.*, 1985). Experiments in which a coding sequence in 'sense' (Smigocki and Owens, 1988) or 'antisense' orientation (van der Krol *et al.*, 1988) is fused to a strong promoter may become a widely used method to study plant gene function.

VARIATION OF GENE EXPRESSION

The level of expression of a particular gene varies in different transgenic plants. This variation of gene expression of a particular hybrid gene in different transgenic plants can be observed even when these transgenic plants were obtained with the same gene construct (Hain *et al.*, 1985; Jones, Dunsmuir and Bedbrook, 1985; Nagy *et al.*, 1985; Czernilofsky *et al.*, 1986b; Eckes *et al.*, 1986). This means that the position of the T-DNA insert in the plant chromosome influences the expression of the T-DNA-linked genes and this has been called 'position effect'. Most of the variation is seen in the magnitude of gene expression and not in the pattern of gene expression.

The variation of expression can have several reasons: a different T-DNA copy number in different transgenic plants, *cis*-acting elements such as silencers and enhancers in the T-DNA target site, transcriptional interference of T-DNA- and target-expression units, and the general chromatin structure produced by nearby heterochromatic DNA. This variation in expression between different transgenic plants can, in fact, be used by the geneticists to their advantage, e.g. transgenic plants can be screened for position effects which increase the expression of a particular T-DNA-linked gene (Vaeck *et al.*, 1987). However, we want to caution the reader against misinterpretations of data: genetically identical transgenic plants can show different levels of expression of the reporter gene, probably because of different physiological conditions (Czernilofsky *et al.*, 1986b; Jones *et al.*, 1987b).

## The T-DNA copy number

The number of T-DNA copies generally varies between 1 and 10, and in some studies, a positive correlation has been found between the number of T-DNA inserts and the level of T-DNA-linked gene expression (Stockhaus *et al.*, 1987). On the other hand, transgenic plants with a high copy number sometimes show a rather low level of expression (Jones *et al.*, 1987b).

Several authors found that a homozygous transgenic plant can contain twice the expression of a hemizygous plant (Potrykus *et al.*, 1985; Czernilofsky *et al.*, 1986b); this would suggest that the expression of a particular locus is characteristically dosage-dependent. This observation has been confirmed in the Laboratory of Genetics (Gent, Belgium) for several T-DNA inserts and several hybrid genes (unpublished results).

## Cis-*acting elements*

Plant DNA sequences, such as enhancers and silencers in the regions flanking the T-DNA, could also strongly influence the expression of the T-DNA genes, especially of the outermost genes. Indeed, transcription regulatory elements can influence the recognition of promoter sequences over long distances when fused in *cis* at the 5' or 3' end of the gene, and in this way the expression of a T-DNA gene may be modulated by the surrounding plant DNA elements.

## Chromatin structure and methylation

The insertion of the T-DNA in heterochromatin or euchromatin, assuming that both occur, could influence the level of expression; for instance by altering the accessibility to transcriptional complexes or by imposing a certain methylation pattern onto the T-DNA insert. Partial or complete inactivation of T-DNA genes by methylation has been demonstrated elegantly by Van Lijsebettens *et al.* (1986). These authors rescued *Agrobacterium*-transformed calli which expressed the *onc* genes only transiently. In the derived hormone-dependent lines, they found up to five full-length T-DNA copies but these sequences contained more than the normal level of *C*-methylation. Other researchers found that the methylation pattern can be removed by growing cells with the methylation inhibitor azacytidine, and that this is correlated with the reappearance of T-DNA gene expression (Hepburn *et al.*, 1983b; Van Slogteren, Hooykaas and Schilperoort, 1984).

### Genetic transformation for crop improvement

GENE TRANSFER AS A NEW TOOL IN PLANT BREEDING

One of the difficulties in a breeder's programme has always been that in order to add one characteristic to a plant variety, the complete genotypes of two varieties have to be mixed and then back-crossed repeatedly in order to remove heterogeneity for all but the desired new character. Therefore, control over the addition (or deletion) of specific characteristics in a certain species would be both advantageous and economical. To achieve this, the most important requirements are (1) the characterization of a given phenotype and the ability to isolate the corresponding genetic information, i.e. DNA fragment(s); (2) the possibility to reintroduce it into plant cells; and (3) the regeneration of transgenic plants.

The isolation of the genetic information for a certain phenotype is very laborious, and often practically impossible, when it concerns a trait which is coded by several genes dispersed over different chromosomes. Moreover, even when a trait is encoded by a single locus it is very difficult to make the link between a particular DNA fragment and the characteristic it encodes. To date, the methods used mostly are gene tagging with a transposon, or screening an expression library for the presence of the protein by an antibody or a well-defined biochemical reaction.

The most widely used method to introduce DNA into plant cells is based on natural engineering by *Agrobacterium tumefaciens*. However, the host range of *Agrobacterium* is limited and cereals, which constitute the most important group of plants for human nutritional needs, have remained unresponsive. Yet, 'direct gene transfer' methods are now available (for a review, *see* Potrykus *et al.*, 1987). Microinjection (Steinbiss *et al.*, 1985), polyethylene glycol treatment (Paszkowski *et al.*, 1984) and electroporation (Fromm, Taylor and Walbot, 1985, 1986) have been used successfully for the introduction of DNA into protoplasts, including those of monocotyledonous plants (Fromm, Taylor and Walbot, 1985, 1986; Uchimiya *et al.*, 1986; Rhodes *et al.*, 1988).

However, the next problem in the production of transgenic monocots is related to requirement (3): most of the important cereal and grass crops have generally proved to be very recalcitrant to regeneration from protoplasts. The discovery and exploitation of embryogenic tissue cultures, in which plant regeneration takes place by the formation of embryos from single somatic cells, has led to the development of efficient procedures for plant regeneration from many monocotyledonous crop plants (for a review, *see* Vasil, 1988). These new improved methods for the regeneration of plants, together with recently developed techniques for the introduction of DNA into intact cells and tissues (Klein *et al.*, 1988; McCabe *et al.*, 1988), may be very beneficial for further progress towards the genetic transformation of Gramineae.

Although the first engineered plants were reported only a few years ago (Zambryski *et al.*, 1983; De Block *et al.*, 1984), we are already witnessing the practical use of the genetic transformation methods for agricultural applications. Examples of this are the production of genetically engineered plants for insect, virus, and herbicide resistance.

INSECT RESISTANCE BY GENETIC TRANSFORMATION

For a long time spore preparations of *Bacillus thuringiensis* (BT) have been used as a spray against the larvae of *Lepidopterae* (Carlton and González, 1986). This is because the bacteria synthesize a protein which is toxic when ingested by these larvae (the biological significance is that *B. thuringiensis* can grow in dead bodies of *Lepidopterae*). The gene coding for this protein has been isolated from the *B. thuringiensis* genome (Höfte *et al.*, 1986) and has been fused with plant expression signals. The hybrid gene construct was subsequently cloned into a T-DNA vector and introduced into tobacco (Vaeck *et al.*, 1987) and tomato (Fischhoff *et al.*, 1987) via the *Agrobacterium* vector system. The resulting transgenic plants showed significant resistance to the larvae of *Manduca sexta* (these larvae feed only on tobacco leaves). During the first few days, larvae started to feed on both BT-transgenic and normal control plants. After some days, the larvae had eaten most of the leaf material of normal tobacco plants, while the larvae on the transgenic plants were killed and the plants showed only some marks of the initial feeding (Vaeck *et al.*, 1987). The insect-resistance trait was shown to be stably inherited over several generations. The first field tests of BT toxin production in some commercial tobacco varieties occurred in 1986 with good results. Currently, industrial researchers are trying to broaden the action spectrum of the BT protein for toxicity in other insect genera.

In an analogous way, the gene encoding a cowpea trypsin inhibitor has been introduced into tobacco plants. The resulting transgenic plants showed enhanced resistance to the tobacco budworm (Hilder *et al.*, 1987).

VIRUS RESISTANCE BY GENETIC TRANSFORMATION

Several groups have presented data which suggest that an increased level of virus resistance can be obtained by the introduction of certain genetic information. One of the approaches has been to introduce and express the gene for a coat protein in plants (Abel *et al.*, 1986; Loesch-Fries *et al.*, 1987; Nelson *et al.*, 1988). The idea behind this strategy is that the incoming viral RNA is inactivated by encapsidation before an infection cycle can start (Tumer *et al.*, 1987) or that the coat protein interferes with early events in RNA infection by a different mechanism (Hemenway *et al.*, 1988).

Another strategy has been to introduce a satellite virus DNA unit. Such satellite RNAs are dependent on the viral infection cycle to reproduce and in this way they compete with the virus for rate-limiting factors and consequently suppress the effects of a super-infecting pathogenic virus strain (Gerlach, Llewellyn and Haseloff, 1987; Harrison, Mayo and Baulcombe, 1987).

Another approach, which has not yet been proven very effective, concentrates on the use of antisense RNA to inactivate or reduce the expression of viral genomes (Cuozzo *et al.*, 1988).

HERBICIDE RESISTANCE BY GENETIC TRANSFORMATION

Several companies have attempted to combine the use of a herbicide with the introduction of the corresponding resistance gene in the crop to be protected. This combined application of herbicide and herbicide-resistant crop does not only increase the specificity of protection but also allows the use of new herbicides with a higher efficiency. Importantly, this new set of herbicides

**Figure 14.3** Herbicide-resistant sugar beet. Sugar beet (*Beta vulgaris* ssp. *saccharissima*) was transformed with a chimeric *bar* gene. Transgenic and control plants were treated with the herbicide phosphinothricin (Basta®, Hoechst). The picture was taken 6 days after treatment (6 D.A.T.). The transformed plants are clearly much more resistant to the herbicide than the controls (Dr K. D'Halluin, unpublished results; ©Plant Genetic Systems N.V.).

could be less toxic for animals and the environment. The resistance gene can be obtained in two different ways; either the gene for a resistant target protein, or the gene for a herbicide-modifying enzyme can be isolated from resistant organisms.

The first approach has been followed in several industrial laboratories. The target site for sulphonylurea and imidazolinone herbicides is the enzyme acetolactate synthase (ALS), the first common enzyme in the biosynthesis of the amino acids isoleucine, valine and leucine. Resistant *als* genes have been isolated from resistant microbes and from higher plants which had become insensitive to the herbicide (Chaleff and Ray, 1984; Shaner and Anderson, 1985). These resistance genes can be combined with expression regulatory sequences and introduced into plants via the *Agrobacterium* vector system (Haughn *et al.*, 1988). An analogous approach was followed to obtain glyphosate resistance. A mutant form of the bacterial *aroA* gene was expressed in transgenic tomato (Fillatti *et al.*, 1987), petunia (Della-Cioppa *et al.*, 1987) and tobacco (Comai *et al.*, 1985) plants. Because the herbicide-resistant enzyme is dominant to the herbicide-sensitive target enzyme (glyphosate blocks the synthesis of aromatic amino acids; Jaworski, 1972), higher levels of glyphosate tolerance were obtained in the transgenic plants than in unmodified lines. Other investigators have overproduced the plant target enzyme, i.e. the normal 5-enol-pyruvyl-shikimate-3-phosphate synthase, to confer glyphosate tolerance in transgenic petunia plants (Shah *et al.*, 1986).

The second approach has been described by De Block *et al.* (1987). It is based on the principle that the introduction of a herbicide-modifying enzyme will confer resistance to the corresponding herbicide in the same way as the expression of an antibiotic-modifying enzyme will confer resistance to the corresponding antibiotics. The herbicides phosphinothricin (PPT) (Basta®, Hoechst AG) and bialaphos (Herbrace®, Meiji Sheika Ltd) are potent inhibitors of glutamine synthetase (Murakami *et al.*, 1986). Inhibition of glutamine synthetase by PPT causes rapid accumulation of ammonia which leads to death of the plant cell. The PPT resistance gene (*bar*) from *Streptomyces hygroscopicus* (synthesizes bialaphos) has been cloned (Thompson *et al.*, 1987) and a hybrid *bar* gene has been transferred to several crop plants. The resulting transgenic tobacco, potato, tomato and sugar beet (*Figure 14.3*) plants are resistant to a dose 10 times higher than the concentration that is normally used in agriculture (De Block *et al.*, 1987).

**Conclusion**

*Agrobacterium*-mediated plant cell transformation is one of the most thoroughly studied bacteria–plant interactions. Many questions about the mechanism of T-DNA transfer and integration still remain unanswered but as new data are emerging, many parts of the puzzle fall into place.

Even before anything was known about how the *vir* loci mediate T-DNA transfer, *Agrobacterium* was adapted as a vector system for the genetic engineering of plants cells. Initially, this efficient transformation method was one of the major reasons for the rapid development of plant molecular biology and, even though its use for real improvement of agriculturally important crops may not be that straightforward, the mere existence of the first transgenic crop plants is exciting and promising.

## Acknowledgements

We gratefully acknowledge Dr Kan Wang for advice and Ms Martine De Cock and Stefaan Van Gijsegem for preparing the manuscript. This work has been supported by grants from the 'ASLK-Kankerfonds', the 'Fonds voor Geneeskundig Wetenschappelijk Onderzoek' (FGWO 3.0001.82), and the Services of the Prime Minister (OOA 12.0561.84 and I.U.A.P. 120C0187). L.H. was a Research Assistant of the National Fund for Scientific Research (Belgium) and P.B. is indebted to the IWONL for a fellowship.

## References

ABEL, P.P., NELSON, R.S. DE, B., HOFFMAN, N., ROGERS, S.G., FRALEY, R.T. AND BEACHY, R.N. (1986). Delay of disease development in transgenic plants that express the tobacco mosaic virus coat protein gene. *Science* **232**, 738–743.

ALBRIGHT, L.M., YANOFSKY, M.F., LEROUX, B., MA, S. AND NESTER, E.W. (1987). Processing of the T-DNA of *Agrobacterium tumefaciens* generates border nicks and linear, single-stranded T-DNA. *Journal of Bacteriology* **169**, 1046–1055.

AMBROS, P.F., MATZKE, A.J.M. AND MATZKE, M.A. (1986). Localization of *Agrobacterium rhizogenes* T-DNA in plant chromosomes by *in situ* hybridization. *EMBO Journal* **5**, 2073–2077.

AN, G., WATSON, B.D., STACHEL, S., GORDON, M.P. AND NESTER, E.W. (1985). New cloning vehicles for transformation of higher plants. *EMBO Journal* **4**, 277–284.

ANDRÉ. D., COLAU, D., SCHELL, J., MONTAGUE, M. VAN AND HERNALSTEENS, J.-P. (1986). Gene tagging in plants by a T-DNA insertion mutagen that generates APH(3′)II-plant gene fusions. *Molecular and General Genetics* **204**, 512–518.

ASHBY, A.M., WATSON, M.D. AND SHAW, C.H. (1987). A Ti-plasmid determined function is responsible for chemotaxis of *Agrobacterium tumefaciens* towards the plant wound product acetosyringone. *FEMS Microbiology Letters* **41**, 189–192.

BEVAN, M. (1984). Binary *Agrobacterium* vectors for plant transformation. *Nucleic Acids Research* **12**, 8711–8721.

BEVAN, M.W., FLAVELL, R.B. AND CHILTON, M.-D. (1983). A chimaeric antibiotic resistance gene as a selectable marker for plant cell transformation. *Nature (London)* **304**, 184–187.

BOLTON, G.W., NESTER, E.W. AND GORDON, M.P. (1986). Plant phenolic compounds induce expression of the *Agrobacterium tumefaciens* loci needed for virulence. *Science* **232**, 983–985.

BROGLIE, R., CORUZZI, G., FRALEY, R.T., ROGERS, S.G., HORSCH, R.B., NIEDERMEYER, J.G., FINK, C.L., FLICK, J.S. AND CHUA, N.-H. (1984). Light-regulated expression of a pea ribulose-1,5-bisphosphate carboxylase small subunit gene in transformed plant cells. *Science* **224**, 838–843.

BUDAR, F., THIA-TOONG, L., MONTAGU, M. VAN AND HERNALSTEENS, J.-P. (1986). *Agrobacterium* mediated gene transfer results mainly in transgenic plants transmitting the T–DNA as a single Mendelian factor. *Genetics* **114**, 303–313.

CANGELOSI, G.A., HUNG, L., PUVANESARAJAH, V., STACEY, G., OZGA, D.A., LEIGH, J.A. AND NESTER, E.W. (1987). Common loci for *Agrobacterium tumefaciens* and *Rhizobium meliloti* exopolysaccharide synthesis and their roles in plant interactions. *Journal of Bacteriology* **169**, 2086–2091.

CARLTON, B.C. AND GONZÁLEZ, J.M., JR (1986). Biocontrol of insects – *Bacillus thuringiensis*. In *Biotechnology for Solving Agricultural Problems* (P.C. Augustine, H.D. Danforth and M.R. Bakst, Eds), pp. 253–272. Martinus Nijhoff Publishers, Dordrecht.

CHALEFF, R.S. AND RAY, T.B. (1984). Herbicide-resistant mutants from tobacco cell cultures. *Science* **223**, 1148–1151.

CHRISTIE, P.J., WARD, J.E., WINANS, S.C. AND NESTER, E.W. (1988). The *Agrobacterium tumefaciens virE2* gene product is a single-stranded-DNA-binding protein that associates with T-DNA. *Journal of Bacteriology* **170**, 2659–2667.

CHYI, Y.-S., JORGENSEN, R.A., GOLDSTEIN, D., TANKSLEY, S.D. AND LOAIZA-FIGUEROA, F. (1986). Locations and stability of *Agrobacterium*-mediated T–DNA insertions in the *Lycopersicon* genome. *Molecular and General Genetics* **204**, 64–69.

CITOVSKY, V., VOS, G. DE AND ZAMBRYSKI, P. (1988). Single-stranded DNA binding protein encoded by the *virE* locus of *Agrobacterium tumefaciens*. *Science* **240**, 501–504.

COMAI, L., FACCIOTTI, D., HIATT, W.R., THOMPSON, G., ROSE, R.E. AND STALKER, D.M. (1985). Expression in plants of a mutant *aroA* gene from *Salmonella typhimurium* confers tolerance to glyphosate. *Nature (London)* **317**, 741–744.

CUOZZO, M., O'CONNELL, K.M., KANIEWSKI, W., FANG, R.-X., CHUA, N.-H AND TUMER, N.E. (1988). Viral protection in transgenic tobacco plants expressing the cucumber mosaic virus coat protein or its antisense RNA. *Bio/technology* **6**, 549–557.

CZERNILOFSKY, A.P., HAIN, R., HERRERA-ESTRELLA, L., LÖRZ, H., GOYVAERTS, E., BAKER, B.J. AND SCHELL, J. (1986a). Fate of selectable marker DNA integrated into the genome of *Nicotiana tabacum*. *DNA* **5**, 101–113.

CZERNILOFSKY, A.P., HAIN, R., BAKER, B. AND WIRTZ, U. (1986b). Studies on the structure and functional organization of foreign DNA integrated into the genome of *Nicotiana tabacum*. *DNA* **5**, 473–482.

DAS, A. (1988). *Agrobacterium tumefaciens virE* operon encodes a single-stranded DNA-binding protein. *Proceedings of the National Academy of Sciences of the United States of America* **85**, 2909–2913.

DE BLOCK, M., HERRERA-ESTRELLA, L., MONTAGU, M. VAN, SCHELL, J. AND ZAMBRYSKI, P. (1984). Expression of foreign genes in regenerated plants and their progeny. *EMBO Journal* **3**, 1681–1689.

DE BLOCK, M., BOTTERMAN, J., VANDEWIELE, M., DOCKX, J., THOEN, C., GOSSELÉ, V., MOVVA, R., THOMPSON, C., MONTAGUE, M. VAN AND LEEMANS, J. (1987). Engineering herbicide resistance in plants by expression of a detoxifying enzyme. *EMBO Journal* **6**, 2513–2518.

DE CLEENE, M. AND LEY, J. DE (1976). The host range of crown-gall. *Botanical Reviews* **42**, 389–466.

DEBLAERE, R., BYTEBIER, B., GREVE, H. DE, DEBOECK, F., SCHELL, J., MONTAGU, M. VAN AND LEEMANS, J. (1985). Efficient octopine Ti plasmid-derived vectors for *Agrobacterium*-mediated gene transfer to plants. *Nucleic Acids Research* **13**, 4777–4788.

DEBLAERE, R., REYNAERTS, A., HÖFTE, H., HERNALSTEENS, J.-P., LEEMANS, J. AND MONTAGU, M. VAN (1987). Vectors for cloning in plant cells. In *Methods in Enzymology, Volume 153: Recombinant DNA, part D* (R. Wu and L. Grossman, Eds), pp. 277–292. Academic Press, New York.

DELLA-CIOPPA, G., BAUER, S.C., TAYLOR, M.L., ROCHESTER, D.E., KLEIN, B.K., SHAH, D.M., FRALEY, R.T. AND KISHORE, G.M. (1987). Targeting a herbicide-resistant enzyme from *Escherichia coli* to chloroplasts of higher plants. *Bio/technology* **5**, 579–584.

DEPICKER, A., HERMAN, L., JACOBS, A., SCHELL, J. AND MONTAGU, M. VAN (1985). Frequencies of simultaneous transformation with different T-DNAs and their relevance to the *Agrobacterium*/plant cell interaction. *Molecular and General Genetics* **201**, 477–484.

DOUGLAS, C.J., STANELONI, R.J., RUBIN, R.A. AND NESTER, E.W. (1985). Identification and genetic analysis of an *Agrobacterium tumefaciens* chromosomal virulence region. *Journal of Bacteriology* **161**, 850–860.

ECKES, P., ROSAHL, S., SCHELL, J. AND WILLMITZER, L. (1986). Isolation and characterization of a light-inducible, organ-specific gene from potato and analysis of its expression after tagging and transfer into tobacco and potato shoots. *Molecular and General Genetics* **205**, 14–22.

ENGSTRÖM, P., ZAMBRYSKI, P., MONTAGU, M. VAN AND STACHEL, S. (1987). Characterization of *Agrobacterium tumefaciens* virulence proteins induced by the plant factor acetosyringone. *Journal of Molecular Biology* **197**, 635–645.

FILLATTI, J.J., KISER, J., ROSE, R. AND COMAI, L. (1987). Efficient transfer of a glyphosate tolerance gene into tomato using a binary *Agrobacterium tumefaciens* vector. *Bio/technology* **5**, 726–730.

FISCHHOFF, D.A., BOWDISH, K.S., PERLAK, F.J., MANONE, P.G., MCCORMICK, S.M., NIEDERMEYER, J.G., FEAN, D.A., KUSANO-KRETZMER, K., MAYER, E.J., ROCHESTER, D.E., ROGERS, S.G. AND FRALEY, R.T. (1987). Insect tolerant transgenic tomato plants. *Bio/technology* **5**, 807–813.

FLUHR, R. AND CHUA, N.-H. (1986). Developmental regulation of two genes encoding ribulose-bisphosphate carboxylase small subunit in pea and transgenic petunia plants: phytochrome response and blue-light induction. *Proceedings of the National Academy of Sciences of the United States of America* **83**, 2358–2362.

FRALEY, R.T., ROGERS, S.G., HORSCH, R.B., EICHHOLTZ, D.A., FLICK, J.S., FINK, C.L., HOFFMANN, N.L. AND SANDERS, P.R. (1985). The SEV system: a new disarmed Ti plasmid vector system for plant transformation. *Bio/technology* **3**, 629–635.

FROMM, M., TAYLOR, L.P. AND WALBOT, V. (1985). Expression of genes transferred into monocot and dicot plant cells by electroporation. *Proceedings of the National Academy of Sciences of the United States of America* **82**, 5824–5828.

FROMM, M.E., TAYLOR, L.P. AND WALBOT, V. (1986). Stable transformation of maize after gene transfer by electroporation. *Nature (London)* **319**, 791–793.

GERLACH, W.L., LLEWELLYN, D. AND HASELOFF, J. (1987). Construction of a plant disease resistance gene from the satellite RNA of tobacco ringspot virus. *Nature (London)* **328**, 802–805.

GHEYSEN, G., MONTAGU, M. VAN AND ZAMBRYSKI, P. (1987). Integration of *Agrobacterium tumefaciens* transfer DNA (T-DNA) involves rearrangements of target plant DNA sequences. *Proceedings of the National Academy of Sciences of the United States of Emerica* **84**, 6169–6173.

GHEYSEN, G., DHAESE, P., MONTAGU, M. VAN AND SCHELL, J. (1985). DNA flux across genetic barriers: the crown gall phenomenon. In *Advances in Plant Gene Research, Volume 2: Genetic flux in plants* (B. Hohn and E.S. Dennis, Eds), pp. 11–47. Springer Verlag, Wien.

GIETL, C., KOUKOLÍKOVÁ-NICOLA, Z. AND HOHN, B. (1987). Mobilization of T-DNA from *Agrobacterium* to plant cells involves a protein that binds single-stranded DNA. *Proceedings of the National Academy of Sciences of the United States of America* **84**, 9006–9010.

HAIN, R., STABEL, P., CZERNILOFSKY, A.P., STEINBISS, H.H., HERRERA-ESTRELLA, L. AND SCHELL, J. (1985). Uptake, integration, expression and genetic transmission of a selectable chimaeric gene to plant protoplasts. *Molecular and General Genetics* **199**, 161–168.

HARRISON, B.D., MAYO, M.A. AND BAULCOMBE, D.C. (1987). Virus resistance in transgenic plants that express cucumber mosaic virus satellite RNA. *Nature (London)* **328**, 799–802.

HAUGHN, G.W., SMITH, J., MAZUR, B. AND SOMERVILLE, C. (1988). Transformation with a mutant *Arabidopsis* acetolactate synthase gene renders tobacco resistant to sulfonylurea herbicides. *Molecular and General Genetics* **211**, 266–271.

HEMENWAY, C., FANG, R.-X., KANIEWSKI, W.K., CHUA, N.-H. AND TUMER, N.E.

(1988). Analysis of the mechanism of protection in transgenic plants expressing the potato virus X coat protein or its antisense RNA. *EMBO Journal* 7, 1273–1280.

HEPBURN, A.G., CLARKE, L.E., BLUNDY, K.S. AND WHITE, J. (1983a). Nopaline Ti plasmid, pTiT37, T-DNA insertions into a flax genome. *Journal of Molecular and Applied Genetics* 2, 211–224.

HEPBURN, A.G., CLARKE, L.E., PEARSON, L. AND WHITE, J. (1983b). The role of cytosine methylation in the control of nopaline synthase gene expression in a plant tumor. *Journal of Molecular and Applied Genetics* 2, 315–329.

HERMAN, L.M.F., MONTAGU, M. VAN AND DEPICKER, A.G. (1986). Isolation of tobacco DNA segments with plant promoter activity. *Molecular and Cellular Biology* 6, 4486–4492.

HERMAN, L., MONTAGU, M. VAN AND DEPICKER, A. (1987). Insertional activation of a T-DNA marker gene in plant cells. *Archives Internationales de Physiologie et Biochimie* 95, B130.

HERRERA-ESTRELLA, L., DEPICKER, A., MONTAGU, M. VAN AND SCHELL, J. (1983a). Expression of chimaeric genes transferred into plant cells using a Ti-plasmid-derived vector. *Nature (London)* 303, 209–213.

HERRERA-ESTRELLA, L., BLOCK, M. DE, MESSENS, E., HERNALSTEENS, J.-P., MONTAGU, M. VAN AND SCHELL, J. (1983b). Chimeric genes as dominant selectable markers in plant cells. *EMBO Journal* 2, 987–995.

HERRERA-ESTRELLA, L., BROECK, G. VAN DEN, MAENHAUT, R., MONTAGU, M. VAN, SCHELL, J., TIMKO, M. AND CASHMORE, A. (1984). Light-inducible and chloroplast-associated expression of a chimaeric gene introduced into *Nicotiana tabacum* using a Ti plasmid vector. *Nature (London)* 310, 115–120.

HERRERA-ESTRELLA, A., CHEN, Z., MONTAGU, M. VAN AND WANG, K. (1988). The 5′ termini of T-strand molecules of *Agrobacterium tumefaciens* are covalently linked to protein. *EMBO Journal* 7, 4055–4062.

HIGGINS, C.F., HILES, I.D., SALMOND, G.P.C., GILL, D.R., DOWNIE, J.A., EVANS, I.J., HOLLAND, I.B., GRAY, L., BUCKEL, S.D., BELL, A.W. AND HERMODSON, M.A. (1986). A family of related ATP-binding subunits coupled to many distinct biological processes in bacteria. *Nature (London)* 323, 448–450.

HILDER, V.A., GATEHOUSE, A.M.R., SHEERMAN, S.E., BARKER, R.F. AND BOULTER, D. (1987). A novel mechanism of insect resistance engineered into tobacco. *Nature (London)* 300, 160–163.

HILLE, J., VERHEGGEN, F., ROELVINK, P., FRANSSEN, H., KAMMEN, A. VAN AND ZABEL, P. (1986). Bleomycin resistance: a new dominant selectable marker for plant cell transformation. *Plant Molecular Biology* 7, 171–176.

HIROOKA, T., ROGOWSKY, P.M. AND KADO, C.I. (1987). Characterization of the *virE* locus of *Agrobacterium tumefaciens* plasmid pTiC58. *Journal of Bacteriology* 169, 1529–1536.

HÖFTE, H., GREVE, H. DE, SEURINCK, J., JANSENS, S., MAHILLON, J., AMPE, C., VANDEKERCKHOVE, J., VANDERBRUGGEN, H., MONTAGU, M. VAN, ZABEAU, M. AND VAECK, M. (1986). Structural and functional analysis of a cloned crystal protein of *Bacillus thuringiensis* berliner 1715. *European Journal of Biochemistry* 161, 273–280.

HOLSTERS, M., SILVA, B., VLIET, F. VAN, GENETELLO, C., BLOCK, M. DE, DHAESE, P., DEPICKER, A., INZÉ, D., ENGLER, G., VILLARROEL, R., MONTAGU, M. VAN AND SCHELL, J. (1980). The functional organization of the nopaline *A. tumefaciens* plasmid pTiC58. *Plasmid* 3, 212–230.

HOLSTERS, M., VILLARROEL, R., GIELEN, J., SEURINCK, J., GREVE, H. DE, MONTAGU, M. VAN AND SCHELL, J. (1983). An analysis of the boundaries of the octopine TL–DNA in tumors induced by *Agrobacterium tumefaciens*. *Molecular and General Genetics* 190, 35–41.

HORSCH, R.B., FRY, J.E., HOFFMANN, N.L., EICHHOLTZ, D., ROGERS, S.G. AND FRALEY, R.T. (1985). A simple and general method for transferring genes into plants. *Science* 227, 1229–1231.

JAWORSKI, E. (1972). The mode of action of N-phosphonomethylglycine: inhibition of aromatic amino acid biosynthesis. *Journal of Agricultural and Food Chemistry* **20**, 1195–1198.

JAYASWAL, R.K., VELUTHAMBI, K., GELVIN, S.B. AND SLIGHTOM, J.L. (1987). Double-stranded cleavage of T–DNA and generation of single-stranded T-DNA molecules in *Escherichia coli* by a *vir*D-encoded border-specific endonuclease from *Agrobacterium tumefaciens*. *Journal of Bacteriology* **169**, 5035–5045.

JEFFERSON, R.A., KAVANAGH, T.A. AND BEVAN, M.W. (1987). GUS fusions: β-glucuronidase as a sensitive and versatile gene fusion marker in higher plants. *EMBO Journal* **6**, 3901–3907.

JONES, J.D.G., DUNSMUIR, P. AND BEDBROOK, J. (1985). High level expression of introduced chimeric genes in regenerated transformed plants. *EMBO Journal* **4**, 2411–2418.

JONES, J.D.G., SVAB, Z., HARPER, E.C., HURWITZ, C.D. AND MALIGA, P. (1987a). A dominant nuclear streptomycin resistance marker for plant cell transformation. *Molecular and General Genetics* **210**, 86–91.

JONES, J.D.G., GILBERT, D.E., GRADY, K.L. AND JORGENSEN, R.A. (1987b). T-DNA structure and gene expression in petunia plants transformed by *Agrobacterium tumefaciens* C58 derivatives. *Molecular and General Genetics* **207**, 478–485.

JOOS, H., INZÉ, D., CAPLAN, A., SORMANN, M., MONTAGU, M. VAN AND SCHELL, J. (1983). Genetic analysis of T-DNA transcripts in nopaline crown galls. *Cell* **32**, 1057–1067.

JORGENSEN, R., SNYDER, C. AND JONES, J.D.G. (1987). T-DNA is organized predominantly in inverted repeat structures in plants transformed with *Agrobacterium tumefaciens* C58 derivatives. *Molecular and General Genetics* **207**, 471–477.

KLEE, H.J., YANOFSKY, M.F. AND NESTER, E.W. (1985). Vectors for transformation of higher plants. *Bio/technology* **3**, 637–642.

KLEIN, T.M., GRADZIEL, T., FROMM, M.E. AND SANFORD, J.C. (1988). Factors influencing gene delivery into *Zea mays* cells by high-velocity microprojectiles. *Bio/technology* **6**, 559–563.

KUHLEMEIER, C., GREEN, P.J. AND CHUA, N.-H. (1987). Regulation of gene expression in higher plants. *Annual Review of Plant Physiology* **38**, 221–257.

KUHLEMEIER, C., CUOZZO, M., GREEN, P.J., GOYVAERTS, E., WARD, K. AND CHUA, N.-H. (1988). Localization and conditional redundancy of regulatory elements in *rbcS-3A*, a pea gene encoding the small subunit of ribulose-bisphosphate carboxylase. *Proceedings of the National Academy of Sciences of the United States of America* **85**, 4662–4666.

KWOK, W.W., NESTER, E.W. AND GORDON, M.P. (1985). Unusual plasmid DNA organization in an octopine crown gall tumor. *Nucleic Acids Research* **13**, 459–471.

LEEMANS, J., DEBLAERE, R., WILLMITZER, L., GREVE, H. DE, HERNALSTEENS, J.-P., MONTAGU, M. VAN AND SCHELL, J. (1982). Genetic identification of functions of TL-DNA transcripts in octopine crown galls. *EMBO Journal* **1**, 147–152.

LEROUX, B., YANOFSKY, M.F., WINANS, S.C., WARD, J.E., ZIEGLER, S.F. AND NESTER, E.W. (1987). Characterization of the *virA* locus of *Agrobacterium tumefaciens*: a transcriptional regulator and host range determinant. *EMBO Journal* **6**, 849–856.

LOESCH-FRIES, L.S., MERLO, D., ZINNEN, T., BURHOP, L., HILL, K., KRAHN, K., JARVIS, N., NELSON, S. AND HALK, E. (1987). Expression of alfalfa mosaic virus RNA 4 in transgenic plants confers virus resistance. *EMBO Journal* **6**, 1845–1851.

MCCABE, D.E., SWAIN, W.F., MARTINELL, B.J. AND CHRISTOU, P. (1988). Stable transformation of soybean (*Glycine max*) by particle acceleration. *Bio/technology* **6**, 923–926.

MÁRTON, L., WULLEMS, G.J., MOLENDIJK, L. AND SCHILPEROORT, R.A. (1979). *In vitro* transformation of cultured cells from *Nicotiana tabacum* by *Agrobacterium tumefaciens*. *Nature (London)* **277**, 129–130.

MATTHYSSE, A.G. (1987). Characterization of nonattaching mutants of *Agrobacterium tumefaciens*. *Journal of Bacteriology* **169**, 313–323.

MÜLLER, A.J., MENDEL, R.R., SCHEEMANN, J., SIMOENS, C. AND INZÉ, D. (1987). High meiotic stability of a foreign gene introduced into tobacco by *Agrobacterium*-mediated transformation. *Molecular and General Genetics* **207**, 171–175.

MURAKAMI, T., ANZAI, H., IMAI, S., SATOH, A., NAGAOKA, K. AND THOMPSON, C.J. (1986). The bialaphos biosynthetic genes of *Streptomyces hygroscopicus*: molecular cloning and characterization of the gene cluster. *Molecular and General Genetics* **205**, 42–50.

NAGY, F., MORELLI, G., FRALEY, R.T., ROGERS, S.G. AND CHUA, N.-H. (1985). Photoregulated expression of a pea *rbcS* gene in leaves of transgenic plants. *EMBO Journal* **4**, 3063–3068.

NELSON, R.S., McCORMICK, S.M., DELANNAY, X., DUBÉ, P., LAYTON, J., ANDERSON, E.J., KANIEWSKA, M., PROKSCH, R.K., HORSCH, R.B., ROGERS, S.G., FRALEY, R.T. AND BEACHY, R.N. (1988). Virus tolerance, plant growth, and field performance of transgenic tomato plants expressing coat protein from tobacco mosaic virus. *Bio/technology* **6**, 403–409.

NIXON, B.T., RONSON, C.W. AND AUSUBEL, F.M. (1986). Two-component regulatory systems responsive to environmental stimuli share strongly conserved domains with the nitrogen assimilation regulatory genes *ntrB* and *ntrC*. *Proceedings of the National Academy of Sciences of the United States of America* **83**, 7850–7854.

OKAMURO, J.K., JOFUKU, K.D. AND GOLDBERG, R.B. (1986). Soybean seed lectin gene and flanking nonseed protein genes are developmentally regulated in transformed tobacco plants. *Proceedings of the National Academy of Sciences of the United States of America* **83**, 8240–8244.

OTTEN, L., GREVE, H. DE, LEEMANS, J., HAIN, R., HOOYKAAS, P.J.J. AND SCHELL, J. (1984). Restoration of virulence of Vir region mutants of *Agrobacterium tumefaciens* strain B6S3 by coinfection with normal and mutant *Agrobacterium* strains. *Molecular and General Genetics* **195**, 159–163.

PASZKOWSKI, J., SHILLITO, R.D., SAUL, M., MANDÁK, V., HOHN, T., HOHN, B. AND POTRYKUS, I. (1984). Direct gene transfer to plants. *EMBO Journal* **3**, 2717–2722.

PEERBOLTE, R., LEENHOUTS, K., HOOYKAAS-VAN SLOGTEREN, G.M.S., WULLEMS, G.J. AND SCHILPEROORT, R.A. (1986). Clones from a shooty tobacco crown gall tumor II: irregular T-DNA structures and organization, T-DNA methylation and conditional expression of opine genes. *Plant Molecular Biology* **7**, 285–299.

POTRYKUS, I., PASZKOWSKI, J., SAUL, M.W., PETRUSKA, J. AND SHILLITO, R.D. (1985). Molecular and general genetics of a hybrid foreign gene introduced into tobacco by direct gene transfer. *Molecular and General Genetics* **199**, 169–177.

POTRYKUS, I., PASZKOWSKI, J., SHILLITO, R.D. AND SAUL, M.W. (1987). Direct gene transfer to plants. In *Advances in Plant Gene Research, Volume 3: Plant DNA infectious agents* (Th. Hohn and J. Schell, Eds), pp. 230–247. Springer-Verlag, Wien.

REISS, B., SPRENGEL, R., WILL, H. AND SCHALLER, H. (1984). A new sensitive method for qualitative and quantitative assay of neomycin phosphotransferase in crude cell extracts. *Gene* **30**, 211–218.

RHODES, C.A., PIERCE, D.A., METTLER, I.J., MASCARENHAS, D. AND DETMER, J.J. (1988). Genetically transformed maize plants from protoplasts. *Science* **240**, 204–207.

ROGERS, S.G., KLEE, H.J., HORSCH, R.B. AND FRALEY, R.T. (1987). Improved vectors for plant transformation: expression cassette vectors and new selectable markers. In *Methods in Enzymology, Volume 153: Recombinant DNA, part D* (R. Wu and L. Grossman, Eds), pp. 253–277. Academic Press, New York.

SHAH, D.M., HORSCH, R.B., KLEE, H.J., KISHORE, G.M., WINTER, J.A., TUMER, N.E., HIRONAKA, C.M., SANDERS, P.R., GASSER, C.S., AYKENT, S., SIEGEL, N.R., ROGERS, S.G. AND FRALEY, R.T. (1986). Engineering herbicide tolerance in transgenic plants. *Science* **233**, 478–481.

172     *Gene Exchange*

SHANER, D.L. AND ANDERSON, P.C. (1985). Mechanism of action of the
imidazolinones and cell culture selection of tolerant maize. In *Biotechnology in
plant science. Relevance to agriculture of the eighties* (M. Zaitlin, P. Day and A
Hollaender, Eds), pp. 287–299. Academic Press, New York.
SHAW, C.H., ASHBY, A.M., BROWN, A., ROYAL, C., LOAKE, G.J. AND SHAW, C.H.
(1988). *virA* and *virG* are the Ti-plasmid functions required for chemotaxis of
*Agrobacterium tumefaciens* towards acetosyringone. *Molecular Microbiology* **2**
413–417.
SIMOENS, C., ALLIOTTE, TH., MENDEL, R., MÜLLER, A., SCHIEMANN, J.,
LIJSEBETTENS, M. VAN, SCHELL, J., MONTAGU, M. VAN AND INZÉ, D. (1986). A
binary vector for transferring genomic libraries to plants. *Nucleic Acids Research*
**14**, 8073–8090.
SIMPSON, R.B., O'HARA, P.J., KWOK, W., MONTOYA, A.L., LICHTENSTEIN, C.,
GORDON, M.P. AND NESTER, E.W. (1982). DNA from the A6S/2 crown gall tumor
contains scrambled Ti-plasmid sequences near its junctions with the plant DNA.
*Cell* **29**, 1005–1014.
SIMPSON, J., TIMKO, M.P., CASHMORE, A.R., SCHELL, J., MONTAGU, M. VAN AND
HERRERA-ESTRELLA, L. (1985). Light-inducible and tissue-specific expression of a
chimaeric gene under control of the 5'-flanking sequence of a pea chlorophyll
*a/b*-binding protein gene. *EMBO Journal* **4**, 2723–2729.
SIMPSON, J., SCHELL, J., MONTAGU, M. VAN AND HERRERA-ESTRELLA, L. (1986).
Light-inducible and tissue-specific pea *lhcp* gene expression involves an upstream
element combining enhancer- and silencer-like properties. *Nature (London)* **323**,
551–554.
SMIGOCKI, A.C. AND OWENS, L.D. (1988). Cytokinin gene fused with a strong
promoter enhances shoot organogenesis and zeatin levels in transformed plant
cells. *Proceedings of the National Academy of Sciences of the United States of
America* **85**, 5131–5135.
SPIELMANN, A. AND SIMPSON, R.B. (1986). T-DNA structure in transgenic tobacco
plants with multiple independent integration sites. *Molecular and General Genetics*
**205**, 34–41.
STACHEL, S.E. AND NESTER, E.W. (1986). The genetic and transcriptional organization
of the *vir* region of the A6 Ti plasmid of *Agrobacterium tumefaciens*. *EMBO
Journal* **5**, 1445–1454.
STACHEL, S.E. AND ZAMBRYSKI, P. (1986). *Agrobacterium tumefaciens* and the
susceptible plant cell: a novel adaptation of extracellular recognition and DNA
conjugation. *Cell* **47**, 155–157.
STACHEL, S.E., NESTER, E.W. AND ZAMBRYSKI, P.C. (1986). A plant cell factor
induces *Agrobacterium tumefaciens vir* gene expression. *Proceedings of the
National Academy of Sciences of the United States of America* **83**, 379–383.
STACHEL, S.E., TIMMERMAN, B. AND ZAMBRYSKI, P. (1986). Generation of
single-stranded T-DNA molecules during the initial stages of T–DNA transfer
from *Agrobacterium tumefaciens* to plant cells. *Nature (London)* **322**, 706–712.
STACHEL, S.E., TIMMERMAN, B. AND ZAMBRYSKI, P. (1987). Activation of
*Agrobacterium tumefaciens vir* gene expression generates multiple single-stranded
T-strand molecules from the pTiA6 T-region: requirements for 5' *virD* gene
products. *EMBO Journal* **6**, 857–863.
STEINBISS, H.-H., STABEL, P., TÖPFER, R., HIRTZ, R.D. AND SCHELL, J. (1985).
Transformation of plant cells by microinjection of DNA. In *The experimental
manipulation of ovule tissues* (G.P. Chapman, S.H. Mantell and R.W. Daniels,
Eds), pp. 64–75. Longman, New York.
STOCKHAUS, J., ECKES, P., BLAU, A., SCHELL, J. AND WILLMITZER, L. (1987)
Organ-specific and dosage-dependent expression of a leaf/stem specific gene from
potato after tagging and transfer into potato and tobacco plants. *Nucleic Acid.
Research* **15**, 3479–3491.
THOMASHOW, M.F., NUTTER, R., MONTOYA, A.L., GORDON, M.P. AND NESTER

E.W. (1980). Integration and organisation of Ti-plasmid sequences in crown gall tumors. *Cell* **19**, 729–739.

THOMASHOW, M.F., KARLINSEY, J.E., MARKS, J.R. AND HURLBERT, R.E. (1987). Identification of a new virulence locus in *Agrobacterium tumefaciens* that affects polysaccharide composition and plant cell attachment. *Journal of Bacteriology* **169**, 3209–3216.

THOMPSON, C.J., ROA MOVVA, N., TIZARD, R., CRAMERI, R., DAVIES, J.E., LAUWEREYS, M. AND BOTTERMAN, J. (1987). Characterization of the herbicide-resistance gene *bar* from *Streptomyces hygroscopicus*. *EMBO Journal* **6**, 2519–2523.

THOMPSON, D.V., MELCHERS, L.S., IDLER, K.B., SCHILPEROORT, R.A. AND HOOYKAAS, P.J.J (1988). Analysis of the complete nucleotide sequence of the *Agrobacterium tumefaciens virB* operon. *Nucleic Acids Research* **16**, 4621–4636.

THORNBURG, R.W., AN, G., CLEVELAND, T.E., JOHNSON, R. AND RYAN, C.A. (1987). Wound-inducible expression of a potato inhibitor II – chloramphenicol acetyltransferase gene fusion in transgenic tobacco plants. *Proceedings of the National Academy of Sciences of the United States of America* **84**, 744–748.

TUMER, N.E., O'CONNELL, K.M., NELSON, R.S., SANDERS, P.R., BEACHY, R.N., FRALEY, R.T. AND SHAH, D.M. (1987). Expression of alfalfa mosaic virus coat protein gene confers cross-protection in transgenic tobacco and tomato plants. *EMBO Journal* **6**, 1181–1188.

UCHIMIYA, H., FUSHIMI, T., HASHIMOTO, H., HARADA, H., SYONO, K. AND SUGAWARA, Y. (1986). Expression of a foreign gene in callus derived from DNA-treated protoplasts of rice (*Oryza sativa* L.). *Molecular and General Genetics* **204**, 204–207.

VAECK, M., REYNAERTS, A., HÖFTE, H., JANSENS, S., BEUCKELEER, M. DE, DEAN, C., ZABEAU, M., MONTAGU, M. VAN AND LEEMANS, J. (1987). Transgenic plants protected from insect attack. *Nature (London)* **328**, 33–37.

VALVEKENS, D., MONTAGU, M. VAN AND LIJSEBETTENS, M. VAN (1988). *Agrobacterium tumefaciens*-mediated transformation of *Arabidopsis* root explants using kanamycin selection. *Proceedings of the National Academy of Sciences of the United States of America* **85**, 5536–5540.

VAN DEN BROECK, G., TIMKO, M.P., KAUSCH, A.P., CASHMORE, A.R., MONTAGU, M. VAN AND HERRERA-ESTRELLA, L. (1985). Targeting of a foreign protein to chloroplasts by fusion to the transit peptide of ribulose 1,5-bisphosphate carboxylase. *Nature (London)* **313**, 358–363.

VAN DEN ELZEN, P., LEE, K.Y., TOWNSEND, J. AND BEDBROOK, J. (1985a). Simple binary vectors for DNA transfer to plant cells. *Plant Molecular Biology* **5**, 149–154.

VAN DEN ELZEN, P.J.M., TOWNSEND, J., LEE, K.Y. AND BEDBROOK, J.R. (1985b). A chimaeric hygromycin resistance gene as a selectable marker in plant cells. *Plant Molecular Biology* **5**, 299–302.

VAN DER KROL, A.R., LENTING, P.E., VEENSTRA, J., MEER, I.M. VAN DER, KOES, R.E., GERATS, A.G.M., MOL, J.N.M. AND STUITJE, A.R. (1988). An anti-sense chalcone synthase gene in transgenic plants inhibits flower pigmentation. *Nature (London)* **333**, 866–869.

VAN LIJSEBETTENS, M., INZÉ, D., MONTAGU, M. VAN AND SCHELL, J. (1986). Transformed cell clones as a tool to study T-DNA integration mediated by *Agrobacterium tumefaciens*. *Journal of Molecular Biology* **188**, 129–143.

VAN SLOGTEREN, G.M.S., HOOYKAAS, P.J.J. AND SCHILPEROORT, R.A. (1984). Silent T–DNA genes in plant lines transformed by *Agrobacterium tumefaciens* are activated by grafting and by 5-azacytidine treatment. *Plant Molecular Biology* **3**, 333–336.

VASIL, I.K. (1988). Progress in the regeneration and genetic manipulation of cereal crops. *Bio/technology* **6**, 397–402.

VELUTHAMBI, K., REAM, W. AND GELVIN, S.B. (1988). Virulence genes, borders, and overdrive generate single-stranded T-DNA molecules from the A6 Ti plasmid of

*Agrobacterium tumefaciens. Journal of Bacteriology* **170**, 1523–1532.

WALDRON, C., MURPHY, E.B., ROBERTS, J.L., GUSTAFSON, G.D., ARMOUR, S.L. AND MALCOLM, S.K. (1985). Resistance to hygromycin B: a new marker for plant transformation studies. *Plant Molecular Biology* **5**, 103–108.

WANG, K., STACHEL, S., TIMMERMAN, B., MONTAGU, M. VAN AND ZAMBRYSKI, P. (1987). Site-specific nick in the T-DNA border sequence following *vir* gene expression in *Agrobacterium*. *Science* **235**, 587–591.

WARD, J.E., AKIYOSHI, D.E., REGIER, D., DATTA, A., GORDON, M.P. AND NESTER, E.W. (1988). Characterization of the *virB* operon from an *Agrobacterium tumefaciens* Ti plasmid. *Journal of Biological Chemistry* **263**, 5804–5814.

WILLETTS, N. AND WILKINS, B. (1984). Processing of plasmid DNA during bacterial conjugation. *Microbiological Reviews* **48**, 24–41.

WINANS, S.C., EBERT, P.R., STACHEL, S.E., GORDON, M.P. AND NESTER, E.W. (1986). A gene essential for *Agrobacterium* virulence is homologous to a family of positive regulatory loci. *Proceedings of the National Academy of Sciences of the United States of America* **83**, 8278–8282.

WINANS, S.C., ALLENZA, P., STACHEL, S.E., MCBRIDE, K.E. AND NESTER, E.W. (1987). Characterization of the *virE* operon of the *Agrobacterium* Ti plasmid pTiA6. *Nucleic Acids Research* **15**, 825–837.

YADAV, N.S., VANDERLEYDEN, J., BENNETT, D.R., BARNES, W.M. AND CHILTON, M.-D. (1982). Short direct repeats flank the T-DNA on a nopaline Ti plasmid. *Proceedings of the National Academy of Sciences of the United States of America* **79**, 6322–6326.

YANOFSKY, M.F., PORTER, S.G., YOUNG, C., ALBRIGHT, L.M., GORDON, M.P. AND NESTER, E.W. (1986). The *virD* operon of *Agrobacterium tumefaciens* encodes a site-specific endonuclease. *Cell* **47**, 471–477.

YOUNG, C. AND NESTER, E.W. (1988). Association of the VirD2 protein with the 5' end of T strands in *Agrobacterium tumefaciens*. *Journal of Bacteriology* **170**, 3367–3374.

ZAMBRYSKI, P., HOLSTERS, M., KRUGER, K., DEPICKER, A., SCHELL, J. MONTAGU, M. VAN AND GOODMAN, H.M. (1980). Tumor DNA structure in plant cells transformed by *A. tumefaciens*. *Science* **209**, 1385–1391.

ZAMBRYSKI, P., DEPICKER, A., KRUGER, K. AND GOODMAN, H. (1982). Tumor induction by *Agrobacterium tumefaciens*: analysis of the boundaries of T-DNA. *Journal of Molecular and Applied Genetics* **1**, 361–370.

ZAMBRYSKI, P., JOOS, H., GENETELLO, C., LEEMANS, J., MONTAGU, M. VAN AND SCHELL, J. (1983). Ti plasmid vector for the introduction of DNA into plant cells without alteration of their normal regeneration capacity. *EMBO Journal* **2**, 2143–2150.

ZIMMERMAN, J.L. AND GOLDBERG, R.B. (1977). DNA sequence organization in the genome of *Nicotiana tabacum*. *Chromosoma* **59**, 227–252.

ZORREGUIETA, A., GEREMIA, R.A., CAVAIGNAC, S., CANGELOSI, G.A., NESTER, E.W. AND UGALDE, R.A. (1988). Identification of the product of an *Agrobacterium tumefaciens* chromosomal virulence gene. *Molecular Plant–Microbe Interactions* **1**, 121–127.

# 5

# Genetic Recombination Analysis of *Bacillus subtilis* by Protoplast Fusion

NANCY GUILLÉN AND NOUZHA FTOUHI

*Institut de Microbiologie, Bâtiment 409, Université Paris-Sud, 91405 Orsay Cedex, France*

## Introduction

In the Gram-positive bacterium *Bacillus subtilis*, the diploid state necessary to accomplish genetic recombination is obtained either partially by transformation and transduction, or totally by protoplast fusion. Fusion of *B. subtilis* protoplasts, first shown by Schaeffer, Cami and Hotchkiss (1976), results in the formation of different cellular products:

1. Diploid clones, which are represented by two types: complementing diploids, which exhibit genetic complementation (Lévi-Meyrueis, Sanchez-Rivas and Schaeffer, 1980), and non-complementing diploids, which carry the two parental chromosomes but express only one of them (Hotchkiss and Gabor, 1980; Guillén, Amar and Hirschbein, 1985).
2. Recombinant clones, which show novel combinations of markers derived from both auxotrophic parental lines (Schaeffer, Cami and Hotchkiss, 1976).

During the heterozygous diploid state created by protoplast fusion, the recombinants are obtained either soon after cellular wall regeneration, or many generations later among the progeny of diploid cells (Hotchkiss and Gabor, 1980; Lévi-Meyrueis, Sanchez-Rivas and Schaeffer, 1980). In previous work, the phenotypic analysis of recombinants has shown that the genetic exchanges necessary for recombinant production occur in diverse regions of the bacterial chromosome. Although a stimulation of recombination was found in areas surrounding the origin and the terminus of chromosomal replication, the DNA–membrane attachment was suggested to be responsible for such stimulation (Sanchez-Rivas *et al.*, 1982; Gabor and Hotchkiss, 1983).

The potentialities of the protoplast fusion system have not yet been exploited to study bacterial genetic recombination. We are interested in exploring the mechanisms and regulatory interactions involved in genetic recombination in *B. subtilis* using protoplast fusion. For example, there is no information about

*Genetic Transformation and Expression*
© Intercept Ltd, PO Box 716, Andover, Hants, SP10 1YG, UK

the gene products involved in this recombination pathway. It is not known precisely if there are any hot spots of recombination in particular areas of the chromosome, nor the influence of a genetic exchange on the production of other exchanges in the same diploid cell. Also, the influence of chromosomal functions, such as replication and transcription, have not been investigated.

Studies were undertaken on genetic recombination following fusion of *B. subtilis* protoplasts. Specifically, we attempted to elucidate the role of the *recE* gene product in this system. The RecE protein is the equivalent of *Escherichia coli* RecA (Love and Yasbin, 1986), and is required for homologous recombination during transformation and transduction.

We have constructed polymarked bacterial strains that permit the analysis of recombination in different chromosomal regions in the same fusion experiment. As a function of their genetic markers, we have defined 10 genetic intervals. Here we report an analysis of the cellular products of fusion that reveals the number and chromosomal distribution of crossover events.

## Material and methods

### BACTERIAL STRAINS

The *B. subtilis* strains used in this work were constructed in our laboratory and are listed in *Table 15.1*.

**Table 15.1**   *B. subtilis* strains used in this work

| Strain | Genotype | Phenotype |
|---|---|---|
| S6 | *thr5 ura1 trpF7 rfm-486* | $T^- U^- O^- R^R$ |
| MO501 | *argA metB5 pheA2 purA16 trpC2 rplV1* | $a^- M^- P^- A^- O^- E^R$ |
| MO507 | *argA3 metB5 pheB12 purA16 trpC2 recE4 rplV1 spcB1* | $a^- M^- P^- A^- O^- Rec^- S^R$ |
| MO508 | *thr5 ura1 trpF7 rfm-486 recE4 spcB1* | $U^- O^- T^- R^R Rec^- S^R$ |

All of these strains are constructed in our laboratory. Their genetic markers were checked before each fusion experiment.
Abbreviations: A, Adenosine; a, arginine; E, erythromycin; L, leucine; M, methionine; O, tryptophan; P, phenylalanine; R, rifamicin; S, spectinomycin; T, threonine; U, uridine; Rec, recombination.

### MEDIA

For fusion experiments, bacteria were cultured in nutrient broth (Schaeffer, Millet and Aubert, 1965) and protoplasts were reverted to bacillary form in a rich regeneration agar medium (R medium) of high tonicity (Wyrick and Rogers, 1973). For recombinants, minimal medium (Anagnostopoulos and Spizizen, 1961), supplemented with selection agents and growth factors, was used.

### FUSION EXPERIMENTS

Fusion experiments were performed according to Schaeffer, Cami and

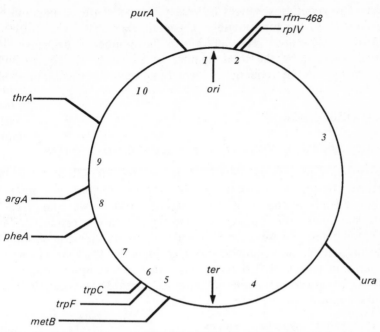

**Figure 15.1**  Simplified genetic map of *Bacillus subtilis*. The markers present in the strains are placed in the map. Distances between the markers are proportional to map units and define the genetic intervals tested for recombination in fusion experiments. *ori* and *ter* are respectively the origin and terminus of replication.

Hotchkiss (1976). After regeneration of protoplasts to the bacillary form, well-isolated colonies were transferred to rich agar medium. After growth, the colonies were replica plated onto 15 different types of minimal media supplemented with factors permitting the growth of recombinant, biparental and parental colonies. Two of these 15 media types permit the identification of complementary phenotypes occurring after recombination into genetic intervals 1 and 10 (*Figure 15.1, Table 15.2*). The phenotype of an exfusant product was determined according to its differential growth in the assorted

**Table 15.2**  Size of the genetic intervals tested for recombination in the fusion crosses

| Interval | Markers concerned | Estimate of the size of the DNA in kbp |
|---|---|---|
| 1 | *purA–rfm-468(rpoB)* | 210 |
| 2 | *rfm-468(rpoB)–rplV* | 10 |
| 3 | *rplV–ura* | 1685 |
| 4 | *ura–metB* | 855 |
| 5 | *metB–trpF* | 60 |
| 6 | *trpF–trpC* | 1 |
| 7 | *trpC–pheA* | 660 |
| 8 | *pheA–argA* | 140 |
| 9 | *argA–thrA* | 310 |
| 10 | *thrA–purA* | 1074 |

We have defined the different sizes of the genetic intervals according to the genetic map of *B. subtilis* (Piggot and Hoch, 1985). The chromosome has an estimated size of 5000 kbp and the map is organized in 360°. One unit is equivalent to 13·8 kbp. The replication origin is in interval 1 and the terminus in interval 4.

media. The genetic exchanges necessary to produce each phenotype wer
determined and the total number of genetic exchanges in the recombinan
population was scored. The addition of the number of exchanges in eacl
interval, divided by the total number of exchanges in the recombinan
population, gives the frequency of recombination in a particular interval.

## Results and discussion

### PRODUCT OF FUSION CROSSES BETWEEN STRAINS MO501 AND S6

A mixture of protoplasts derived from strains MO501 and S6, markee
genetically by mutation in multiple chromosome regions, was treated witl
polyethylene glycol and the wall-regenerated products were analysed (*Tabl*
*15.3*). We found the classical proportions of fusion products: 7·6% o
wall-regenerated cells were phenotypically biparental clones generating eithe
stable or unstable non-complementing diploids; 70·4% were phenotypicall
parental and represented parents and stable non-complementing diploids
finally 22% were recombinants containing a mixture of markers from the twe
parental strains.

**Table 15.3**  Fusion of MO501 and S6 strains

| Percentage cell wall regeneration | Percentage phenotype recovered | | |
|---|---|---|---|
| | Biparental | Recombinant | Parental |
| 20·0 | 7·6 | 22·0 | 70·4 |

Fusion crosses were carried out as indicated (p. 176) and were followed by wall regeneration on R Medium. The
colonies were transferred with toothpicks onto rich medium and then replicated onto selective media for
phenotypic classification. Percentage of wall regeneration was calculated taking into account the number of
protoplasts mixed in the fusion ($4 \times 10^8 ml^{-1}$). The criteria for detecting a biparental phenotype were as
previously published (Guillén, Amar and Hirschbein, 1985).

### COMPLEXITY IN SINGLE COLONIES PRODUCING RECOMBINANTS

The recombinants were counted from isolated colonies that were transferred to
growth in rich medium and subsequently replica plated on the different

**Table 15.4**  Distribution of genetic exchanges on the chromosome, obtained by protoplast fusion

| Interval | Number of exchanges | Percentage |
|---|---|---|
| 1 | 111 | 36·7 ± 5·4 |
| 2 | 58 | 19·2 ± 4·4 |
| 3 | 18 | 5·9 ± 2·6 |
| 4 | 34 | 11·2 ± 3·5 |
| 5 | 1 | 0·3 |
| 6 | 2 | 0·6 |
| 7 | 2 | 0·6 |
| 8 | 5 | 1·65 |
| 9 | 35 | 11·5 ± 3·5 |
| 10 | 36 | 11·9 ± 3·6 |

Total number of crossovers: 302
Total number of recombinants: 114
Number of phenotypes found: 13
Number of colonies analysed: 520

Percentage recombination was calculated as described above. The statistical variance test was carried out with
95% confidence limits.

elective media to determine their phenotypes. The different recombination frequencies are shown in *Table 15.4*.

The results shown represent the classical analysis conducted in several experiments. Of a total of 520 exfusant colonies studied, a total of 114 recombinants were scored. These recombinants were distributed among 13 different phenotypes resulting from 302 genetic exchanges.

At least two genetic exchanges are necessary to obtain a recombinant from protoplast fusion. Some recombinants with complex phenotypes were seen, indicating that there had been multiple genetic exchanges in a diploid cell. Among the recombinants, 66% resulted from two crossovers, 24% of the recombinants were the products of four crossovers and 10% of six crossovers. Finding more than two crossovers in the same recombinant shows that multiple opportunities for recombination often occur. However, at present the influence of a crossover event on the production of other such events is unknown. Single recombination events, presumably occurring before any genome replication, are also common, since an appreciable proportion of colonies consisted of a single recombinant genotype. Specifically, 86 of the 114 colonies analysed contained only one type of recombinant, while 14 colonies gave the complementary phenotype resulting from recombination in intervals 1 and 10. This finding reinforces the results of our previous work in which it was shown that fused protoplasts of *B. subtilis* produce a completely diploid cell (Guillén, Amar and Hirschbein, 1985). The presence of reciprocal recombinants growing from the same parental diploid bacteria, confirms the frequent reciprocality of recombination after fusion observed by Gabor and Hotchkiss (1983).

CHROMOSOMAL SITES OF CROSSOVERS OCCURRING AFTER FUSION OF
*B. SUBTILIS* PROTOPLASTS

The frequency of recombination in each genetic interval was calculated by the ratio of the number of exchanges in the interval and the total number of exchanges in the recombinant population. The values are summarized in *Table 15.4*. Recombination was observed in the whole chromosome. Moreover, a high proportion (68%) of crossovers occurred in the intervals surrounding the origin of chromosomal replication (intervals 1, 2 and 10). The interval comprising the terminus of DNA replication showed a significant frequency of recombination, 11·2% of the total events. The other intervals had similar frequencies of recombination, between 0·5% and 2%.

Our findings support previous observations of increased recombination at or near the origin or terminus of DNA replication. However, in the present work we used only a couple of polyauxotrophic strains and analysed a large population of recombinants. The previous results (Gabor and Hotchkiss, 1983) were obtained by multiple crosses and found an enhanced recombination in the terminus of replication. In addition, we also used markers close to the replication origin, allowing us to conclude that the origin of DNA replication is the most recombinogenic region in the *B. subtilis* chromosome, as found by protoplast fusion.

ROLE OF THE RecE PROTEIN IN RECOMBINATION INDUCED BY FUSION OF *B. SUBTILIS* PROTOPLASTS

The RecE protein is necessary for intermolecular recombination in *B. subtilis*. The RecE is analogous to RecA in *E. coli* and similarly promotes exchange between DNA strands *in vivo* and *in vitro* (Lovett and Roberts, 1985). The *recE4* mutation was introduced in the same pair of strains used in the preceding experiment and the resulting bacteria used in fusion experiments.

The protoplasts of two Rec$^-$ strains (MO507 and MO508) were fused according to the Schaeffer experimental conditions (Schaeffer, Cami and Hotchkiss, 1976). Wall-regenerated colonies were analysed in the same way as the exfusants of the Rec$^+$ crosses. We analysed 409 colonies in two independent experiments. The classical phenotypes of cellular fused products were recovered: 2% of colonies were biparentals, 49% had a parental phenotype and 49% of colonies were recombinants. Analysis of these 201 recombinants showed that they had one unique and stable phenotype: A$^-$U$^-$O$^-$R$^R$ that resulted from two crossovers, one into interval 1 and the second into interval 10. Any recombinant with the reciprocal phenotype that could appear by the reciprocal exchange in the same intervals was detected. Thus, unexpected recombination events are produced only in areas comprising the origin of chromosome replication. They are asymmetrical.

It is clear from these results that the chromosomes of diploid bacteria can recombine at the origin of DNA replication in the absence of a functional RecE protein. Whether this recombination can occur between non-replicating molecules or whether it is concomitant with replication remains to be discovered. In fact, it is not clear if DNA replication occurs in the protoplasts. The proportion of recombinants recovered from the fusion of *recE* strains was higher that the total recombination observed in a Rec$^+$ background and only one phenotype was obtained. With the exception of the 'origin-specific' recombination described, all other instances of genetic exchange were inhibited in crosses of two Rec$^-$ strains. This finding could indicate that the RecE protein is an inhibitor of illegitimate intermolecular recombination and is a positive factor necessary for homologous recombination.

### Acknowledgements

This work was supported by grants from the Centre National de la Recherche Scientifique and from the Fondation pour la Recherche Medicale.

### References

ANAGNOSTOPOULOS, C. AND SPIZIZEN, J. (1961). Requirements for transformation in *Bacillus subtilis*. *Journal of Bacteriology* **81**, 741–746.

GABOR, M.H. AND HOTCHKISS, R.D. (1983). Reciprocal and non reciprocal recombination in diploid clones from *Bacillus subtilis* protoplast fusion Association with the replication origin and terminus. *Proceedings of the Nationa Academy of Sciences of the United States of America* **80**, 1426–1430.

GUILLÉN, N., AMAR, M. AND HIRSCHBEIN, L. (1985). Stabilised non-complementing diploids (Ncd) from fused protoplast products of *Bacillus subtilis*. *EMBO Journal* **4**, 1333–1338.

HOTCHKISS, R.D. AND GABOR, M.H. (1980). Biparental products of bacterial protoplasts fusion showing unequal parental chromosome expression. *Proceedings of the National Academy of Sciences of the United States of America* **77**, 3553–3557.

LÉVI-MEYRUEIS, C., SANCHEZ-RIVAS, C. AND SCHAEFFER, P. (1980). Formation de bactéries diploides stables par fusion de protoplastes de *Bacillus subtilis*. *Comptes Rendus des Seances de l'Academie des Sciences, Paris D* **291**, 67–70.

LOVE, P.E. AND YASBIN, R.E. (1986). Induction of the *Bacillus subtilis* S.O.S. like response by *Escherichia coli* RecA protein. *Proceedings of the National Academy of Sciences of the United States of America* **83**, 5204–5208.

LOVETT, C.M. AND ROBERTS, J.W. (1985). Purification of a RecA protein analogous from *Bacillus subtilis*. *Journal of Biological Chemistry* **260**, 3305–3313.

PIGGOT, P. AND HOCH, J. (1985). Revised genetic linkage map of *Bacillus subtilis*. *Microbiological Reviews* **49**, 158–179.

SANCHEZ-RIVAS, C., LEVI-MEYRUEIS, C., LAZARD-MONIER, F. AND SCHAEFFER, P. (1982). Diploid state of phenotypically recombinant progeny arising after protoplast fusion in *Bacillus subtilis*. *Molecular and General Genetics* **188**, 272–278.

SCHAEFFER, P., CAMI, B. AND HOTCHKISS, R.D. (1976). Fusion of bacterial protoplasts. *Proceedings of the National Academy of Sciences of the United States of America* **73**, 2151–2155.

SCHAEFFER, P., MILLET, J. AND AUBERT, J.P. (1965). Catabolic repression of bacterial sporulation. *Proceedings of the National Academy of Sciences of the United States of America* **54**, 504–711.

WYRICK, P.B. AND ROGERS, H.J. (1973). Isolation and characterization of cell wall defective variants of *Bacillus subtilis* and *Bacillus licheniformis*. *Journal of Bacteriology* **116**, 456–465.

# 16

# Gene Exchange in Streptococci: The Conjugative Chromosomal Element Ω6001 as the Vector of Recombinant DNA Molecules

GIANNI POZZI*, ROSA A. MUSMANNO[†] AND
MARCO R. OGGIONI[†]

Istituto di Microbiologia, Universita' di Verona, Strada Le Grazie, I–37134
Verona, Italy and [†]Istituto di Microbiologia, Universita' di Siena, Via Laterina,
I–53100 Siena, Italy

## Introduction

Plasmid conjugation can be used to transfer recombinant DNA molecules among streptococci. In particular, the capability of the broad-host-range plasmid pIP501 and its derivatives to mobilize small plasmid vectors has been exploited for this purpose (Smith and Clewell, 1984; Scott *et al.*, 1986; Romero *et al.*, 1987). When a recombinant plasmid is to be introduced in a non-transformable streptococcus, the conjugative mobilization of a plasmid vector is a valuable alternative to protoplast transformation or electroporation.

Chromosomal integration of recombinant DNA is possible in naturally competent streptococci, since it has been shown that heterologous DNA can be integrated into the chromosome during transformation (Shoemaker, Smith and Guild, 1979; Vasseghi, Claverys and Sicard, 1981; Mannarelli and Lacks, 1984; Morrison *et al.*, 1984; Pozzi and Guild, 1985). If the heterologous sequences are flanked on either side by DNA homologous to the recipient chromosome, stable integration of heterologous DNA can be achieved (Pozzi and Guild, 1985).

Here we describe a gene transfer system that allows integration of recombinant DNA molecules into the chromosome of transformable and non-transformable streptococci. The system exploits the properties of Ω(*cat tetM*) 6001 (Ω6001), a genetic element originally found in a clinical strain of *Streptococcus pneumoniae* (pneumococcus), which is capable of conjugal transfer from the chromosome of a donor strain to the chromosome of a recipient in intra- and interspecific matings (Shoemaker, Smith and Guild, 1979; Guild, Smith and Shoemaker, 1982). Ω6001 is 65·5 kbp in size and has

*Genetic Transformation and Expression*
© Intercept Ltd, PO Box 716, Andover, Hants, SP10 1YG, UK

183

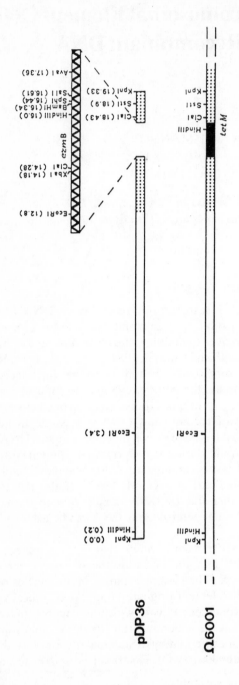

**Figure 16.1**  Restriction map of the insertion vector pDP36 and of the homologous region of Ω6001. pDP36 is linearized at its single *Kpn*I site. The 14·4 kbp *Kpn*I fragment of Ω6001 containing *tetM* (Vijayakumar, Priebe and Guild, 1986) is present in pDP36 where it is interrupted by 5·9 kbp of heterologous DNA (▨) belonging to *E. coli* plasmid pVA891 (Macrina *et al.*, 1983). At the site of insertion of pVA891 in pDP36 there is a 1·1 kbp deletion (■) in *tetM*. Upon transformation of an Ω6001-containing streptococcus with pDP36, integration of the heterologous sequences (▨) into the 5·0 kbp *Hinc*II fragment containing *tetM* (▤) produces a 1·1 kbp deletion (■), which inactivates the tetracycline-resistance marker.

one specific insertion site in the pneumococcal chromosome (Vijayakumar, Priebe and Guild, 1986; Vijayakumar *et al.*, 1986). Ω6001 integrated into the chromosome of naturally transformable strains of *S. pneumoniae* and *Streptococcus sanguis* was used as target for integration of heterologous DNA during transformation. Ω6001 carrying the heterologous DNA could then be transferred by conjugation to the chromosomes of transformable and non-transformable streptococci.

In this system the *Escherichia coli* plasmid pDP36 was used as integration vector; pDP36 was capable of inserting into Ω6001 5·9 kbp of heterologus DNA carrying a selectable *erm* gene (*Figure 16.1*). The inactivation of the *tetM* gene of Ω6001 indicated stable integration of the heterologous DNA.

## Chromosomal integration of heterologous DNA

pDP36 efficiently transformed competent streptococcal cells containing Ω6001: the dose response for transformation of *S. pneumoniae* DP1322 with pDP36 showed detectable transforming activity with DNA at 1 pg ml$^{-1}$ of

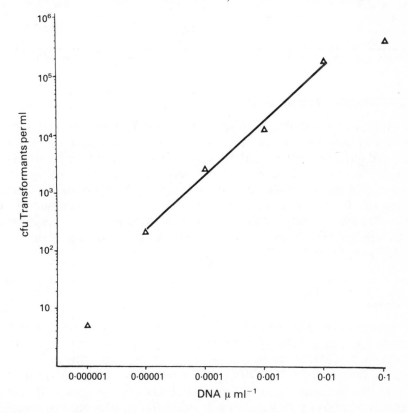

**Figure 16.2**   Dose response for transformation of *S. pneumoniae* DP1322 (Ω6001) with pDP36. Erythromycin-resistant transformants are expressed as colony-forming units (cfu) per ml of competent cells. Competent cells of DP1322 were at a concentration of 6·2 × 10$^7$ cfu ml$^{-1}$. The dose response shows one-hit kinetics; the line drawn has a slope calculated according to the experimental values obtained with DNA concentrations from 0·00001 to 0·01 µg ml$^{-1}$.

competent cells (*Figure 16.2*). Selection of transformants was for erythromycin (Em) resistance; genetic analysis showed that in a fraction of the Em-resistant transformants the integration via flanking homology of the heterologous DNA caused inactivation of the *tetM* determinant of Ω6001 (*Figure 16.1*). Results of typical transformation experiments are reported in *Table 16.1*. Analysing the stability of the resistance markers, it was found that stable integration of heterologous DNA was achieved only in the Em-resistant, tetracycline (Tc)-sensitive transformants (Pozzi *et al.*, 1988).

**Table 16.1**　Transformation of streptococcal recipients containing Ω6001

| | Recipients | |
|---|---|---|
| | *S. pneumoniae* DP1322 | *S. sanguis* GP201 |
| Donor DNA | pDP36 | pDP36 |
| DNA concentration | 0·01 | 0·01 |
| (μg ml$^{-1}$ of competent cells) | | |
| Competent cells | $1·5 \times 10^7$ | $2·4 \times 10^8$ |
| (cfu ml$^{-1}$) | | |
| Selection | Em | Em |
| Transformants | $1·2 \times 10^5$ | $8·8 \times 10^4$ |
| (cfu ml$^{-1}$) | | |
| Genetic analysis | 87% Em$^r$, Tc$^s$ | 24% Em$^r$, Tc$^r$ |
| (300 transformants) | 13% Em$^r$, Tc$^s$ | 76% Em$^r$, Tc$^s$ |

Abbreviations: cfu, colony-forming units; Em, erythromycin; Tc, tetracycline; r, resistant; s, sensitive.

**Conjugal transfer of Ω6001-*ermB***

Conjugal transfer of Ω6001 carrying heterologous DNA was checked using as donors Em-resistant, Tc-sensitive streptococcal strains with *ermB* stably integrated into Ω6001. We could detect conjugal transfer of the heterologous sequences to strains of *S. pneumoniae, S. sanguis, S. faecalis* and *S. pyogenes* (Pozzi *et al.*, 1988). Preliminary results of Southern blot hybridization analysis indicate that Ω6001-*ermB* has a single insertion site in the chromosome of all transconjugants (Pozzi, Pelosi and Oggioni, in preparation), as already established for the pneumococcal chromosome (Vijayakumar, Priebe and Guild, 1986).

**Discussion**

We have shown that heterologous DNA can be integrated into the chromosomal element Ω6001 during transformation of a naturally competent streptococcus, and then can be transferred by conjugation to the chromosome of other streptococci. The Ω6001–pDP36 host–vector system opens new possibilities for gene transfer in streptococci. By this method cloned streptococcal DNA can be returned to its original host, allowing complementation tests and fine physiological studies to be performed with recombinant DNA molecules integrated in the chromosome rather than on plasmids. Also, this system allows genetic manipulation of non-transformable streptococci; it can be used for studying competence-defective mutants of naturally competent bacteria, capsulated strains of *S. pneumoniae*, or other pathogenic streptococci (Oggioni and Pozzi, Chapter 17 this volume).

A key feature of this host–vector system is that recombinant DNA molecules can be subcloned into the region of pDP36 which is heterologous with respect to Ω6001; upon transformation of a streptococcal strain containing Ω6001, stable integration can be scored for by selecting erythromycin-resistant, tetracycline-sensitive transformants (Oggioni and Pozzi, Chapter 17 this volume). It should be pointed out also that, since heterologous DNA of pDP36 is integrated into the *tetM* gene (*Figure 16.1*), the flexibility of this system could be improved by using other *tetM*-carrying conjugative genetic elements (conjugative transposons) with a broader host-range (Clewell, 1981; Guild, Smith and Shoemaker, 1982; Clewell and Gawron-Burke, 1986; Pozzi *et al.*, 1986).

## Acknowledgements

This work was supported by grants 87.00600.52 and 87.00642.52 from the Consiglio Nazionale delle Ricerche. Participation at the 9th European Meeting on Genetic Transformation was possible thanks to the generous support of the University of Verona.

## References

CLEWELL, D.B. (1981). Plasmid, drug resistance, and gene transfer in the genus *Streptococcus*. *Microbiological Reviews* **45**, 409–436.

CLEWELL, D.B. AND GAWRON-BURKE, C. (1986). Conjugative transposons and the dissemination of antibiotic resistance in streptococci. *Annual Review of Microbiology* **40**, 635–659.

GUILD, W.R., SMITH, M.D. AND SHOEMAKER, N.B. (1982). Conjugative transfer of chromosomal R determinants in *Streptococcus pneumoniae*. In *Microbiology-1982* (D. Schlessinger, Ed.), pp. 88–92. American Society for Microbiology, Washington, DC.

MACRINA, F.L., EVANS, R.P., TOBIAN, J.A., HARTLEY, D.L., CLEWELL, D.B. AND JONES, K.R. (1983). Novel shuttle plasmid vehicles for *Escherichia–Streptococcus* transgeneric cloning. *Gene* **25**, 145–150.

MANNARELLI, B.M. AND LACKS, S.A. (1984). Ectopic integration of chromosomal genes in *Streptococcus pneumoniae*. *Journal of Bacteriology* **160**, 867–873.

MORRISON, D.A., TROMBE, M.-C., HAYDEN, M.K., WASZAK, G.A. AND CHEN, J.-D. (1984). Isolation of transformation-deficient *Streptococcus pneumoniae* mutants defective in control of competence, using insertion–duplication mutagenesis with the erythromycin resistance determinant of pAMβ1. *Journal of Bacteriology* **159**, 870–876.

POZZI, G. AND GUILD, W.R. (1985). Modes of integration of heterologous plasmid DNA into the chromosome of *Streptococcus pneumoniae*. *Journal of Bacteriology* **161**, 909–912.

POZZI, G., STELLINI, M., MARRI, L. AND MOLINA, A.M. (1986). Transformation as a tool for studying the epidemiology of *tet* determinants in *Streptococcus pneumoniae*. *European Journal of Epidemiology* **2**, 90–94.

POZZI, G., MUSMANNO, R.A., RENZONI, E.A., OGGIONI, M.R. AND CUSI, M.G. (1988). Host–vector system for integration of recombinant DNA into chromosomes of transformable and nontransformable streptococci. *Journal of Bacteriology* **170**, 1969–1972.

ROMERO, D.A., SLOS, P., ROBERT, C., CASTELLINO, I. AND MERCENIR, A. (1987). Conjugative mobilization as an alternative vector delivery system for lactic streptococci. *Applied and Environmental Microbiology* **53**, 2405–2413.

SCOTT, J.R., GUENTHNER, P.C., MALONE, L.M. AND FISCHETTI, V.A. (1986). Conversion of an M− group A Streptococcus to M+ by transfer of a plasmid containing an M6 gene. *Journal of Experimental Medicine* **164**, 1641–1651.

SHOEMAKER, N.B., SMITH, M.D. AND GUILD, W.R. (1979). Organization and transfer of heterologous chloramphenicol and tetracycline resistance genes in pneumococcus. *Journal of Bacteriology* **139**, 432–441.

SMITH, M.D. AND CLEWELL, D.B. (1984). Return of *Streptococcus faecalis* DNA cloned in *Escherichia coli* to its original host via transformation of *Streptococcus sanguis* followed by conjugative mobilization. *Journal of Bacteriology* **160**, 1109–1114.

VASSEGHI, H., CLAVERYS, J.-P. AND SICARD, A.M. (1981). Mechanisms of integrating foreign DNA during transformation of *Streptococcus pneumoniae*. In *Transformation 1980* (M. Polsinelli and G. Mazza, Eds), pp. 137–153. Cotswold Press, Oxford.

VIJAYAKUMAR, M.N., PRIEBE, S.D. AND GUILD, W.R. (1986). Structure of a conjugative element in *Streptococcus pneumoniae*. *Journal of Bacteriology* **166**, 978–984.

VIJAYAKUMAR, M.N., PRIEBE, S.D., POZZI, G., HAGEMAN, J.H. AND GUILD, W.R. (1986). Cloning and physical characterization of chromosomal conjugative elements in Streptococci. *Journal of Bacteriology* **166**, 972–977.

# 17
# Ω6001-Mediated Conjugative Mobilization of the Cloned M6 Protein Gene to the Chromosomes of Different Strains of *Streptococcus pyogenes*

MARCO R. OGGIONI*† AND GIANNI POZZI*‡


*The Rockefeller University, 1230 York Ave., New York, NY 10021, USA, †Istituto di Microbiologia, Universita' di Siena, Via Laterina, I–53100 Siena, Italy and ‡Istituto di Microbiologia, Universita' di Verona, Strada Le Grazie, I–37134 Verona, Italy*

## Introduction

Group A streptococci (*Streptococcus pyogenes*) are human pathogens which infect primarily at the skin or nasopharynx. The M protein is a surface molecule which is composed of two alpha-helical polypeptide chains which fold to form a coiled-coil dimer extending approximately 60 nm from the cell wall (Fischetti *et al.*, 1988). Because of its profound antiphagocytic capacity, the M molecule is considered a major virulence factor for the streptococcus (Lancefield, 1962). Because this molecule undergoes antigenic variation (Hollingshead, Fischetti and Scott, 1987) there are now more than 80 immunologically distinct M proteins identified from nature. The M protein gene from type 6 streptococci (*emm-6·1*) was cloned in *Escherichia coli* (Scott and Fischetti, 1983) and its complete nucleotide sequence determined (Hollingshead, Fischetti and Scott, 1986).

The host–vector system Ω6001–pDP36 allows recombinant DNA molecules to be exchanged among chromosomes of transformable and non-transformable streptococci (Pozzi *et al.*, 1988; Pozzi, Musmanno and Oggioni, Chapter 16 this volume). This genetic exchange system is based on the conjugative properties of the chromosomal element Ω6001 (Vijayakumar *et al.*, 1986; Vijayakumar, Priebe and Guild, 1986) originally found in a clinical strain of *Streptococcus pneumoniae* (Shoemaker, Smith and Guild, 1979). Stable chromosomal

*Genetic Transformation and Expression*
©Intercept Ltd, PO Box 716, Andover, Hants, SP10 1YG, UK

integration of heterologous DNA via flanking homology (Pozzi and Guild, 1985) is achieved during transformation of a competent streptococcus carrying the Ω6001 element. The host–vector system Ω6001–pDP36 was used to transfer the cloned M6 protein gene to strains of *S. pyogenes*, isogenic and non-isogenic, to *S. pyogenes* D471, the strain from which *emm-6·1* was originally cloned. The strategy consisted essentially of two steps:

1. *emm-6·1*, subcloned into pDP36, was integrated into the chromosomal element Ω6001, by transformation of an intermediate host (*S. pneumoniae*); and
2. Ω6001 containing *emm-6.1* was transferred by conjugation from *S. pneumoniae* to the chromosomes of M+ and M− *S. pyogenes* strains.

### Integration of *emm-6·1* into Ω6001

The 2·8 kbp *Bam*HI-*Sph*I fragment of pJRS50 (Scott *et al.*, 1986) containing *emm-6·1* was subcloned in pDP36 (Pozzi *et al.*, 1988; Pozzi, Musmanno and Oggioni, Chapter 16 this volume) cut at *Bam*HI and *Sph*I. The recombinant plasmid pRMB20 contained *emm-6·1* integrated into those DNA sequences of pDP36 which are heterologous with respect to Ω6001 and contain the erythromycin-resistance determinant *ermB* (*Figure 17.1*).

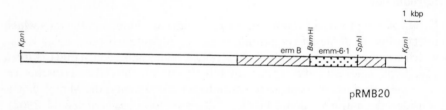

pRMB20

**Figure 17.1**    Map of plasmid pRMB20 linearized at *Kpn*I. The DNA sequences of streptococcal chromosomal element Ω6001 are interrupted by a DNA segment carrying *emm-6·1* and *ermB*.☐, DNA from Ω6001;▨, DNA of *E. coli* plasmid pVA891;▥, DNA from the chromosome of *S. pyogenes* D471 (*emm-6·1*).

pRMB20 was used to transform DP1322, a *S. pneumoniae* strain containing Ω6001. DNA sequences of pRMB20 homologous to Ω6001 led to the integration of the heterologous DNA containing *emm-6·1* and *ermB* into the chromosome of DP1322. pRMB20 transforming DNA (0·5 μg ml$^{-1}$ of competent cells) yielded $1·4 \times 10^5$ erythromycin-resistant transformants per ml, 6% of which had lost resistance to tetracycline. GP97 is the prototype of those transformants in which integration of heterologous DNA produced a 1·1 kbp deletion in the *tetM* determinant of Ω6001, inactivating the tetracycline-resistance marker (Pozzi *et al.*, 1988; Pozzi, Musmanno and Oggioni, Chapter 16 this volume). As expected from previous results (Pozzi and Guild, 1985; Pozzi *et al.*, 1988), the heterologous DNA segment containing *emm-6·1* and *ermB* proved to be stably integrated into the chromosome of GP97.

## Conjugation experiments

*S. pneumoniae* GP97 was used as the donor in filter matings where different strains of *S. pyogenes* were recipients. It was possible to transfer Ω6001–*emm-6·1* from GP97 to several streptomycin-resistant strains of *S. pyogenes*, using erythromycin plus streptomycin for selection of transconjugants (*Table 17.1*). By this method *emm-6·1*, complete with about 400 bp upstream from its translation initiation codon, was integrated into the chromosome of:

1. two strains derived from D471 (the group A streptococcus from which *emm-6·1* was cloned;
2. a strain where the M28 protein gene was deleted (M−); and
3. strains producing different M proteins (M5, M17).

**Table 17.1**   Conjugal transfer of Ω6001–*emm6–ermB* *

| Recipient<br>*S. pyogenes* | Transfer<br>frequency† | Representative<br>transconjugant |
|---|---|---|
| GP411<br>(△*emm–28* Str-r) | 3·6 × 10⁻⁷ | GP413 |
| J17E/165/S<br>(*emm-17* Str-r) | 6·9 × 10⁻⁸ | GP417 |
| B788/S<br>(*emm-5* Str-r) | 2·0 × 10⁻⁷ | GP418 |
| D471/D9/A10<br>(*emm-6·3* Str-r) | 1·2 × 10⁻⁷ | GP419 |
| D471/F1<br>(M−Str-r) | 2·9 × 10⁻⁷ | GP420 |

* Donor was *S. pneumoniae* GP97. △*emm-28*, the M28 protein gene is deleted; *emm-17* and *emm-5*, M17 and M5 protein genes, respectively; *emm-6·3*, mutated *emm-6·1* encoding for production of M6·3, a shorter M6 protein; Str-r, high-level resistance to streptomycin; M−, no production of M protein.
† Colony-forming units (cfu) of transconjugants divided by cfu of donors.

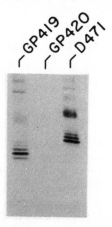

**Figure 17.2**   Western blot analysis of lysin extracts of streptococcal isogenic strains D471 (type M6) and transconjugants GP419 and GP420. Blots were processed for the identification of M protein with a monoclonal antibody reactive with M6 protein. Transconjugant GP419 produces its homologous M protein (M6·3, which is shorter than that of D471) and does not express an M protein equivalent to that of D471. GP420, a transconjugant where Ω6001–*emm-6·1* is integrated into the chromosome of the spontaneous M− mutant D471/F1, also does not produce any M6·1 protein from the integrated *emm-6·1* gene.

**Analysis of transconjugants**

All *S. pyogenes* transconjugants (*Table 17.1*) were resistant to erythromycin, chloramphenicol and streptomycin, sensitive to tetracycline, and contained *emm-6·1* integrated into the chromosome within the $\Omega$6001 element, as judged by Southern blot analysis (data not shown). However, no expression of M6 protein could be detected by Western blot analysis when $\Omega$6001–*emm-6·1* was integrated into the chromosome of such transconjugants, whereas M6 protein was expressed in the *E. coli* strain harbouring pRMB20. Data concerning expression of M6 protein in the isogenic strains D471 and GP419 are shown in *Figure 17.2*. The cloned *emm-6·1* gene is not expressed in an isogenic genetic background (GP419) in which a shorter M6 protein (M6·3) is actively synthesized. It is also not expressed in an isogenic strain which is defective in M6·1 production (GP420) (*Figure 17.2*).

Evidence for a positive regulation of gene expression at the level of transcription was found for *emm-6·1* (Caparon and Scott, 1987) and for *emm-12* (Robbins *et al.*, 1987). A DNA region upstream from the transcription starting site appears to be involved in this regulation. Caparon and Scott (1987) call this regulatory element *mry* (M protein RNA yield) and suggest it may encode for a *trans*-acting factor. We find no evidence of a *trans*-acting mechanism in any of the transconjugants in this study, some of which were able to effectively produce other M proteins (M5, M17, M6·3) but did not produce M6·1. Particularly notable is the case of GP419, where, in a fully isogenic genetic background, a shorter M6 protein (M6·3) is produced from *emm-6·3* but no expression of M6·1 protein is observed from the *emm-6·1* gene integrated elsewhere in the chromosome (*Figure 17.3*). Further investigations are needed to determine the nature of the control of M protein gene expression.

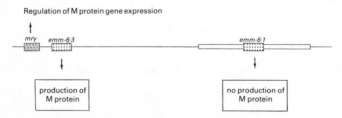

**Figure 17.3**   Schematic representation of the chromosome of *S. pyogenes* GP419. *emm-6·3* is expressed and a shorter M6 protein is synthesized, whereas *emm-6·1*, integrated into the chromosome within $\Omega$6001, is not expressed. *mry* appears to allow expression of *emm-6·3*, but seems to be unable to affect *emm-6·1* integrated elsewhere in the chromosome.

**Acknowledgements**

The authors wish to thank Vincent A. Fischetti for scientific advice and financial support, and Alexander Tomasz for graciously allowing some of these studies to be performed in his laboratory. This work was supported in part by US Public Health Service grant AI11822 and AI20723 to VAF, and by grant 87.00600.52 from the Consiglio Nazionale delle Ricerche.

References

CAPARON, M.G. AND SCOTT, J.R. (1987). Identification of a gene that regulates expression of M protein, the major virulence determinant in group A streptococci. *Proceedings of the National Academy of Sciences of the United States of America* **84**, 8677–8681.

FISCHETTI, V.A., PARRY, D.A.D., TRUS, B.L., HOLLINGSHEAD, S.A., SCOTT, J.R. AND MANJULA, B.N. (1988). Conformational characteristic of the complete sequence of group A streptococcal M6 protein. *Proteins: Structure, Function, and Genetics* **3**, 60–69.

HOLLINGSHEAD, S.K., FISCHETTI, V.A. AND SCOTT, J.R. (1986). Complete nucleotide sequence of type 6 M protein of the group A streptococcus. *Journal of Biological Chemistry* **261**, 1677–1686.

HOLLINGSHEAD, S.K., FISCHETTI, V.A. AND SCOTT, J.R. (1987). Size variation in group A streptococcal M protein is generated by homologous recombination between intragenic repeats. *Molecular and General Genetics* **207**, 196–203.

LANCEFIELD, R.C. (1962). Current knowledge of the type specific M antigens of group A streptococci. *Journal of Immunology* **89**, 307–313.

POZZI, G. AND GUILD, W.R. (1985). Modes of integration of heterologous plasmid DNA into the chromosome of *Streptococcus pneumoniae*. *Journal of Bacteriology* **161**, 909–912.

POZZI, G., MUSMANNO, R.A., RENZONI, E.A., OGGIONI, M.R. AND CUSI, M.G. (1988). Host vector system for integration of recombinant DNA into chromosomes of transformable and non-transformable streptococci. *Journal of Bacteriology* **170**, 1969–1972.

ROBBINS, J.C., SPANIER, J.G., JONES, S.J., SIMPSON, W.J. AND CLEARY, P.P. (1987). *Streptococcus pyogenes* type 12 M protein gene regulation by upstream sequences. *Journal of Bacteriology* **169**, 5633–5640.

SCOTT, J.R. AND FISCHETTI, V.A. (1983). Expression of streptococcal M protein in *Escherichia coli*. *Science* **221**, 758–760.

SCOTT, J.R., GUENTHNER, P.C., MALONE, L.M. AND FISCHETTI, V.A. (1986). Conversion of an M− group A streptococcus to M+ by transfer of a plasmid containing an M6 gene. *Journal of Experimental Medicine* **164**, 1641–1651.

SHOEMAKER, N.B., SMITH, M.D. AND GUILD, W.R. (1979). Organization and transfer of heterologous chloramphenicol and tetracycline resistance genes in pneumococcus. *Journal of Bacteriology* **139**, 432–441.

VIJAYAKUMAR, M.N., PRIEBE, S.D. AND GUILD, W.R. (1986). Structure of a conjugative element in *Streptococcus pneumoniae*. *Journal of Bacteriology* **166**, 978–984.

VIJAYAKUMAR. M.N., PRIEBE, S.D., POZZI, G., HAGEMAN, J.M. AND GUILD, W.R. (1986). Cloning and physical characterization of chromosomal conjugative elements in streptococci. *Journal of Bacteriology* **166**, 972–977.

# Part II

## Recombination, Transposition and Plasmid Stability

# 18
# Recombination in Bacterial Plasmids and Chromosomes

S. DUSKO EHRLICH*, DOMINIQUE BRUNIER*, BEN PEETERS[†],
SIERD BRON[†], LAURENT JANNIÈRE*, BÉNÉDICTE MICHEL* AND
S. SOZHAMANNAN*

*Laboratoire de Génétique Microbienne, Institut de Biotechnologie, INRA,
Domaine de Vilvert, 78350 Jouy en Josas, France and [†] Department of Genetics,
University of Groningen, Kerklaan 30, 9751 NN Haren(Gn), The Netherlands

## Introduction

Rearrangements of *in vitro* constructed plasmids were observed soon after the advent of DNA cloning. For example, in the first instance of heterospecific cloning of a biosynthetic gene (the *Bacillus subtilis* thyP gene in *Escherichia coli*) three of the four clones obtained harboured rearranged plasmids (Ehrlich et al., 1976). The frequency of the phenomenon, soon named plasmid structural instability (segregational instability was used to describe the loss of the entire plasmid from its host; Primrose and Ehrlich, 1981), was unexpectedly high. It pointed to the need for understanding, and possibly controlling, the underlying molecular processes, if DNA cloning technology was to be used optimally. This view was strengthened by the development of cloning procedures in organisms other than *E. coli*. The best characterized example is that of *B. subtilis*, historically the first such organism (Ehrlich, 1977, 1978) where the plasmid structural instability is a frequent event (cf. Ehrlich et al., 1986 for a review).

Plasmid rearrangements are most often due to recombination between sequences of short or no homology. It has been argued that such recombination, termed illegitimate (Franklin, 1971), may correspond to errors of various proteins which interact with DNA (Ehrlich, 1989). The underlying mechanisms are, however, not well characterized. The present manuscript focuses on mechanisms of recombination between short homologous sequences.

## Recombination between short repeats

Deletions are the most extensively studied type of plasmid rearrangements. They frequently result from recombination between short, directly repeated sequences (Farabaugh *et al.*, 1978; Albertini *et al.*, 1982; Jones, Primrose and Ehrlich, 1982; Lopez *et al.*, 1984), and sometimes also from recombination between non-homologous sequences (Peijnenburg *et al.*, 1988; Bron *et al.*, Chapter 19 this volume). A model system used to study recombination between short repeats is precise excision of transposons such as Tn*5* or Tn*10* (Egner and Berg, 1981; Foster *et al.*, 1981). These elements duplicate 9 bp of the target genome sequence upon insertion, and can excise by recombination between the duplications. Excision does not require the transposon-encoded functions. It can restore the activity of a gene and therefore be detected by a simple phenotypic test.

Several observations indicate that single-stranded (ss) DNA synthesis stimulates transposon excision. Tn*5* excises much more frequently (100–1000 times) from genomes which replicate via a ss intermediate, such as ssDNA phages and plasmids or conjugating *E. coli* plasmid F', than from plasmids which replicate as double-stranded (ds) molecules, such as non-conjugating F' and certain *B. subtilis* plasmids (Schaller, 1978; Berg, Egner and Lowe, 1983; Syvanen *et al.*, 1986; Jannière and Ehrlich, 1987; Jannière, Bruand and Ehrlich, 1989). This low frequency is similar to that observed for Tn*5* excising from the *B. subtilis* chromosome (Jannière and Ehrlich, 1987). Furthermore, excision of a transposon derived from Tn*10* can be greatly stimulated by induction of ssDNA synthesis in a dsDNA plasmid. This was shown with pBR322 carrying the replication origin of phage M13. Activation of the phage origin by the cognate replication protein generates ssDNA. Such activation stimulated the excision of a Tn*10*-derived transposon about $10^6$ times (Brunier, Michel and Ehrlich, 1988).

Frequency of transposon excision upon induction of ssDNA synthesis was high enough to allow using a biochemical approach for studying the mechanism of the process (Brunier, Michel and Ehrlich, 1988). Cellular DNA was radioactively labelled under conditions restrictive for excision; labelling was discontinued and the excision was simultaneously induced. After three generations of cell growth, plasmid DNA was extracted and analysed by gel electrophoresis. It contained 30% parental Tn-carrying molecules, and 70% recombinant Tn-free molecules. Only the parental molecules were labelled. This result shows that Tn-free plasmids were synthesized *de novo* during cell growth in the non-radioactive medium, which indicates that transposon excision occurs by a copy-choice recombination (cf. Lederberg, 1955, for an early proposal of such a process). Presumably, this recombination involves slippage of the replication machinery on the ssDNA template from the duplication preceding the transposon to the duplication which follows it, without copying the transposon sequence. From the resulting heteroduplex, which consists of one Tn-carrying and one Tn-free DNA strand, a recombinant molecule can be generated in a subsequent round of replication (Egner and Berg, 1981; Foster *et al.*, 1981; Albertini *et al.*, 1982; Brunier, Michel and Ehrlich, 1988).

How general may copy-choice illegitimate recombination be? To answer this question it is useful first to consider DNA sequences which play a role in transposon excision. The recombining 9 bp direct repeats are adjacent to transposon ends, which are inverted repeats. It is known that the transposon excision frequency is affected by the presence and the length of inverted repeats (Egner and Berg, 1981; Foster *et al.*, 1981; Peeters *et al.*, 1988). These may form hairpin structures in ssDNA, which could facilitate copy-choice recombination in two ways: by bringing the recombining duplications into close proximity and by temporarily arresting DNA replication (cf. Ehrlich, 1989). To determine whether the proximity of inverted repeats affects the mechanism of recombination between short direct repeats we constructed several synthetic duplications, which flanked inverted repeats of 300 bp or 8 bp, or flanked no inverted repeats (cf. Peeters *et al.*, 1988, for the construction strategy). The 9 bp duplications recombined efficiently by a copy-choice process, irrespective of the presence of inverted repeats, as judged by the absence of transfer of radioactivity from the parental to recombinant molecules upon induction of recombination.

Slightly longer duplications, 18 and 27 bp were also tested. Interestingly, they recombined by a break–join mechanism, as deduced from a massive transfer of radioactivity from the parental to the recombinant molecules. Still longer duplications of 200 bp recombined in a similar way. This suggests that legitimate' homologous recombination takes place between duplications which are equal to, or longer than, 18 bp.

## Functions affecting recombination between short repeats

To identify the host functions involved in recombination between short repeats two types of mutants were examined. The first, represented by *recA*, suppresses homologous recombination, whereas the second, represented by *uvrD*, stimulates transposon excision (Lundblad and Kleckner, 1984). The results are shown in *Table 18.1*. Recombination between 9 bp duplications was not affected by the *recA* mutation, while that between 18 bp was affected. Both types of recombination were stimulated by *uvrD* mutation. Interestingly, in *uvrD* cells the *recA* mutation did not reduce the recombination frequency of either duplication. These results may be most simply explained as follows.

**Table 18.1** Recombination of short repeated sequences in *E. coli*

| | Length of duplication* | | | |
| | 9 bp | | 18 bp | |
| Phenotype | Recombination frequency | Recombinant specific activity[+] | Recombination frequency | Recombinant specific activity |
|---|---|---|---|---|
| Wild type | 1[‡] | $<10^{-3}$ | 10 | 0·64 |
| recA | 1 | ND[§] | 1[‡] | ND |
| uvrD | 100 | $<10^{-3}$ | 100 | 0·10 |
| recA uvrD | 100 | $<10^{-3}$ | 100 | $<10^{-3}$ |

No inverted repeats were adjacent to duplications.
Expressed relative to parental plasmid.
This value corresponds to $10^{-8}$ recombinants in a population of cells carrying plasmids in a ds form.
Not determined.

Copy-choice recombination, represented schematically in *Figure 18.1* does not require the RecA protein. The intermediate, generated by slippage of the replication machinery, can be destroyed by the *uvrD* gene product, which is called helicase II. This enzyme might unwind the short duplex region resulting from slippage, and thus allow restoration of the pre-slippage configuration. Helicase II would therefore act as an anti-recombinase in the copy-choice recombination pathway.

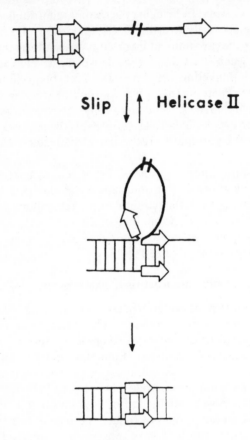

**Slip** ↓↑ **Helicase II**

**Figure 18.1**  Copy-choice recombination. Replication slippage between the direct repeats (open arrows) occurs on a ssDNA template. A recombination intermediate is formed, in which a ssDNA loop is flanked by a long duplex region on one side, and a short duplex region on the other side. Helicase II unwinds the short duplex region and thus allows the pre-slippage configuration to be restored. If the helicase does not act, further replication of the recombination intermediate generates a recombinant molecule lacking the region between the repeats.

Breakage and reunion recombination of the Meselson–Radding type requires RecA protein. It is therefore not surprising that the absence of that protein reduced frequency of recombination between duplications of 18 bp. However, the effect of the *uvrD* mutation, which stimulated recombination between these duplications and rendered it independent of the RecA protein (*Table 18.1*) suggested that they might also undergo copy-choice recombination.

To test this hypothesis, we studied transfer of radioactivity from parental to recombinant plasmid upon induction of recombination in different mutant hosts (*Table 18.1*). In control experiments, no transfer was detected with 9 bp duplications, which shows that copy-choice recombination can take place in all strains. With 18 bp duplications massive transfer was detected in wild-type cells, since the specific activity of recombinant plasmids approached that of parental plasmids. Breakage–reunion recombination is therefore a dominant process in these cells. Less transfer was observed in *uvrD* mutants, which indicates that they can support both breakage–reunion and copy-choice recombination. No transfer occurred in *uvrD recA* cells, which shows that only the copy-choice recombination pathway is functional in these mutants.

Similar results were obtained for longer duplications (27 bp and about 200 bp), which recombined by a breakage–reunion process in wild-type cells, and by copy choice in the double mutant *recA uvrD*. This shows that:

1. Two mutations, *recA* and *uvrD*, are necessary and sufficient to change the mechanism of homologous recombination from breakage–reunion to copy choice in *E. coli*;
2. Helicase II acts as an anti-recombinase in recombination between repeated plasmid sequences. Interestingly, helicase II acts as an anti-recombinase in other types of homologous recombination, such as conjugation (Feinstein and Low, 1986) or recombination between chromosomal duplications (Konrad, 1977). It was suggested that it might destroy intermediates while acting to correct mismatched bases possibly present in the resulting heteroduplexes (Radman, 1988).

### Stabilization of the cloned genes

The observations reported in the above section indicate that ssDNA is a highly recombinogenic species. Genes cloned on vectors which generate little or no ss-DNA during replication should therefore rearrange infrequently. Two lines of evidence support this hypothesis.

First, genes integrated in the *B. subtilis* chromosome can be maintained stably for many generations, even when present in multiple copies (up to 50; Jannière *et al.*, 1985). It is known that recombination between short and long repeated sequences is low in the *B. subtilis* chromosome (Niaudet, Jannière and Ehrlich, 1984; Jannière *et al.*, 1985; Jannière and Ehrlich, 1987; Vagner and Ehrlich, 1988; Young and Ehrlich, 1989). Presumably, little ssDNA is generated during chromosomal replication.

Secondly, large DNA segments (up to 40 kbp) were efficiently cloned and stably maintained (for up to 150 generations) on plasmids which generate no detectable ssDNA during replication (Jannière and Ehrlich, 1989). In contrast, only small DNA segments (<10 kbp) could be cloned on plasmids which generate large amounts of ssDNA (Michel *et al.*, 1980; Jannière and Ehrlich, 1989). Most of the cloning vectors used in *B. subtilis*, and in other Gram-positive bacteria, derive from such plasmids (cf. Gruss and Ehrlich, 1989, for a review), which may explain frequent rearrangements of genes carried on these vectors.

## Conclusions

The understanding of various processes which rearrange genetic material is crucial for the optimal utilization of DNA cloning technology. Characterization of the mechanisms underlying recombination between short homologous sequences has already allowed us to maintain foreign genes stably for many generations in a bacterial host. The approach which was followed, using vectors which generate little or no ssDNA during replication, is probably general, and could be used in any host. However, further work is needed to ascertain this point. Further work is also needed to characterize various processes which recombine non-homologous sequences, and which play a major role in the instability of certain genetic constructs. Given the importance of genome rearrangements, not only for DNA cloning but also for evolution and medicine, this effort seems fully justified.

## References

ALBERTINI, A.M., HOFER, M., CALOS, M.P. AND MILLER, J.M. (1982). On the formation of spontaneous deletions: the importance of short sequence homologies in the generation of large deletions. *Cell* **29**, 319–328.

BERG, D.E., EGNER, C. AND LOWE, J.B. (1983). Mechanism of F factor-enhanced excision of transposon Tn*5*. *Gene* **22**, 1–7.

BRUNIER, D., MICHEL, B. AND EHRLICH, S.D. (1988). Copy choice illegitimate DNA recombination. *Cell* **52**, 883–892.

EGNER, C. AND BERG, D.E. (1981). Excision of transposon Tn*5* is dependent on the inverted repeats but not on the transposase function of Tn*5*. *Proceedings of the National Academy of Sciences of the United States of America* **78**, 459–463.

EHRLICH, S.D. (1977). Replication and expression of plasmids from *Staphylococcus aureus* in *Bacillus subtilis*. *Proceedings of the National Academy of Sciences of the United States of America* **74**, 1680–1682.

EHRLICH, S.D. (1978). DNA cloning in *Bacillus subtilis*. *Proceedings of the National Academy of Sciences of the United States of America* **75**, 1433–1436.

EHRLICH, S.D. (1989). Illegitimate recombination. In *Mobile DNA* (D.E. Berg and M. Howe, Eds), pp. 797–830. ASM Publications.

EHRLICH, S.D., BURSZTYN-PETTEGREW, H., STROYNOWSKI, I. AND LEDERBERG, J. (1976). Expression of the thymidylate synthetase gene of the *Bacillus subtilis* bacteriophage Phi-3-T in *Escherichia coli*. *Proceedings of the National Academy of Sciences of the United States of America* **73**, 4145–4149.

EHRLICH, S.D., NOIROT, PH, PETIT, M.A., JANNIÈRE, L., MICHEL, B. AND TE RIELE, H. (1986). Structural instability of *Bacillus subtilis* plasmids. In *Genetic Engineering, Volume 8* (J.K. Setlow and A. Hollaender, Eds), pp. 71–83. Plenum, New York.

FARABAUGH, P.J., SCHMEISSNER, U., HOFER, M. AND MILLER, J.H. (1978). Genetic studies of the *lac* repressor. VII. On the molecular nature of spontaneous hotspots in the *lac*I gene of *Escherichia coli*. *Journal of Molecular Biology* **126**, 847–863.

FEINSTEIN, S.I. AND LOW, K.B. (1986). Hyper-recombining recipient strains in bacterial conjugation. *Genetics* **113**, 13–33.

FOSTER, T.J., LUNDBLAD, V., HANLEY-WAY, S., HALLING, S.M. AND KLECKNER, N. (1981). Three Tn*10*-associated excision events: relationship to transposition and role of direct and inverted repeats. *Cell* **23**, 215–227.

FRANKLIN, N. (1971). Illegitimate recombination. In *The bacteriophage lambda* (A.D. Hershey, Ed), pp. 175–194. Cold Spring Harbor Press, New York.

GRUSS, A. AND EHRLICH, S.D. (1989). The family of highly interrelated ss DNA plasmids. *Microbiological Reviews* **53**, in press.

JANNIÈRE, L. AND EHRLICH, S.D. (1987). Recombination between short repeated sequences is more frequent in plasmids than in the chromosome of *Bacillus subtilis*. *Molecular and General Genetics* **210**, 116–121.

JANNIÈRE, L., BRUAND, C. AND EHRLICH, S.D. (1989). Structurally stable DNA cloning vectors, submitted.

JANNIÈRE, L., NIAUDET, B., PIERRE, E. AND EHRLICH, S.D. (1985). Stable gene amplification in the chromosome of *Bacillus subtilis*. *Gene* **40**, 47–55.

JONES, I.M., PRIMROSE, S.B. AND EHRLICH, S.D. (1982). Recombination between short direct repeats in a RecA host. *Molecular and General Genetics* **188**, 486–489.

KONRAD, E.B. (1977). Method for the isolation of *Escherichia coli* mutants with enhanced recombination between chromosomal duplications. *Journal of Bacteriology* **130**, 167–172.

LEDERBERG, J. (1955). Recombination mechanisms in bacteria. *Journal of Cellular and Comparative Physiology* **45**, 75–107.

LOPEZ, P., ESPINOSA, M., GREENBERG, B. AND LACKS, S.A. (1984). Generation of deletions in pneumococcal *mal* genes cloned in *Bacillus subtilis*. *Proceedings of the National Academy of Sciences of the United States of America* **81**, 5189–5193.

LUNDBLAD, V. AND KLECKNER, N. (1984). Mismatch repair mutations of *Escherichia coli* K12 enhance transposon excision. *Genetics* **109**, 3–19.

MICHEL, B., PALLA, E., NIAUDET, B. AND EHRLICH, S.D. (1980). DNA cloning in *Bacillus subtilis*. III. Efficiency of random-segment cloning and insertional inactivation vectors. *Gene* **12**, 147–154.

NIAUDET, B., JANNIÈRE, L. AND EHRLICH, S.D. (1984). Recombination between repeated DNA sequences occurs more often in plasmids than in the chromosome of *Bacillus subtilis*. *Molecular and General Genetics* **197**, 46–54.

PEETERS, B.P.H., DE BOER, J.H., BRON, S. AND VENEMA, G. (1988). Structural plasmid instability in *Bacillus subtilis*: effect of direct and inverted repeats. *Molecular and General Genetics* **212**, 450–458.

PEIJNENBURG, A.A.C.M., BREED, P.V., BRON, S. AND VENEMA, G. (1988). Plasmid deletion formation in *rec*E4 and *add*B72 mutants of *Bacillus subtilis*. *Plasmid* **20**, 23–32.

PRIMROSE, S.B. AND EHRLICH, S.D. (1981). Isolation of plasmid deletion mutants and study of their instability. *Plasmid* **6**, 193–201.

RADMAN, M. (1988). Mismatch repair and genetic recombination. In *Genetic Recombination* (R. Kucherlapati and G.R. Smith, Eds), pp. 169–192. ASM Publications, Washington, DC.

SCHALLER, H. (1978). The intergenic region and the origins for filamentous phage DNA replication. *Cold Spring Harbor Symposium of Quantitative Biology* **43**, 401–408.

SYVANEN, M., HOPKINS, J.D., GRIFFIN, T.J. IV, LIANG, T.-Y., IPPEN-IHLER, K. AND KOLODNER, R. (1986). Stimulation of precise excision and recombination by conjugal proficient F' plasmids. *Molecular and General Genetics* **203**, 1–7.

WAGNER, V. AND EHRLICH, S.D. (1988). Efficiency of homologous DNA recombination varies along the *Bacillus subtilis* chromosome. *Journal of Bacteriology* **170**, 3978–3982.

YOUNG, M. AND EHRLICH, S.D. (1989). Stability of reiterated sequences in the *Bacillus subtilis* chromosome. *Journal of Bacteriology* **171**, 2653–2656.

# 9

# Cloning and Plasmid (In)Stability in Bacillus subtilis

SIERD BRON, AD PEIJNENBURG, BEN PEETERS,
PETER HAIMA AND GERARD VENEMA

Department of Genetics, University of Groningen, Kerklaan 30, 9751 NN
Haren(Gn), The Netherlands

## Introduction

In *Bacillus subtilis* two types of plasmid instability have been observed frequently (Dubnau, 1983; Bron and Luxen, 1985; Ehrlich *et al.*, 1986; Bron, Luxen and Swart, 1988). *Segregational instability* refers to the loss of the entire plasmid population from the cell, and *structural instability* to plasmid rearrangements, most frequently deletions (Ehrlich *et al.*, 1986).

Significant progress in the understanding of plasmid instability in Gram-positive bacteria has recently been made. A key observation was that many plasmids of staphylococcal origin, such as pC194, pE194 and pUB110, replicate via single-stranded rolling-circle intermediates (te Riele, Michel and Ehrlich, 1986). In particular, the frequently observed deletions between short direct repeats (3–20 bp) have been considered to result from replication errors in single-stranded DNA by a template-switching mechanism during which part of the template is not copied (Ehrlich *et al.*, 1986; Peeters *et al.*, 1988; Ehrlich *et al.*, Chapter 18 this volume). Deletions between sequences other than direct repeats are not explained by this mechanism.

The rolling-circle mode of replication of many plasmids of Gram-positive origin may also affect segregational plasmid stability. Gruss, Ross and Novick (1987) speculated that the inefficient conversion of single-stranded replication intermediates of several *Staphylococcus* plasmids, such as pC194, pE194 and pT181, may be a major cause of their instability in *B. subtilis*. Support for the idea that this may be a more common problem with plasmids in *B. subtilis* is presented in this paper.

In our group several aspects of plasmid (in)stability in *B. subtilis*, both structural and segregational, are being studied. The results, summarized in the following sections, emphasize the significance of rolling-circle replication in plasmid stability.

*Genetic Transformation and Expression*
© Intercept Ltd, PO Box 716, Andover, Hants, SP10 1YG, UK

**Results and discussion**

DELETION FORMATION BETWEEN SHORT DIRECTLY REPEATED SEQUENCES

We have studied the effects of several variables on deletion formation between short direct repeats (DRs). DRs of 9, 18 and 27 bp were generated in the *Nco*I site of the chloramphenicol-resistance (Cm$^r$) gene of plasmid pHP3Ff using synthetic oligonucleotides (*Figure 19.1*). As a consequence, the Cm$^r$ gene was inactivated. Deletion by recombination at the DRs will restore the original sequence, which can be quantified by the frequency of Cm$^r$ cells. The effects of the distance between the DRs on the deletion frequencies were studied by placing a 1·4 kbp insert between the DRs (*Figure 19.1 Bb*). Finally, a series of plasmids was constructed (*Figure 19.1 Bc*) which allowed the analysis of the effects of flanking inverted repeats (IRs) on deletions generated between the short DRs. Inverted repeats of variable length were taken from transposon Tn*5*.

The results (*Table 19.1*) can be summarized as follows:

1. The deletion frequencies increased with the size of the DRs: by a factor of 100 to 1000 upon an increase from 9 to 18 bp; and by another factor of 5 upon a further increase to 27 bp.
2. Comparison of columns (a) and (b) shows that close proximity of the DRs stimulated the deletion frequencies; the separation of the DRs by a 1·4 kbp insert reduced the frequency of Cm$^r$ cells by about twentyfold.
3. Flanking inverted repeats stimulated deletion formation about one hundred- to one thousandfold [columns (b) and (c)]. The level of stimulation was rather constant with IRs ranging from about 300 to 1500 bp. Only when the IRs became relatively small (185 bp) was a reduction by about a factor of ten in the level of stimulation observed (results not shown).

**Table 19.1** Effects of the length of direct and inverted repeats on deletion frequencies in plasmid pHP3Ff

| Length DR (bp) | Frequency of Cm$^r$ cells* | | |
| | (a) (no insert) | (b) 1·4 kbp insert | (c) (IRs + insert) |
| --- | --- | --- | --- |
| 9 | $1 \cdot 1 \times 10^{-6}$ | $<10^{-8}$ | $3 \cdot 7 \times 10^{-6}$ |
| 18 | $0 \cdot 9 \times 10^{-4}$ | $5 \cdot 7 \times 10^{-6}$ | $4 \cdot 7 \times 10^{-3}$ |
| 27 | $4 \cdot 8 \times 10^{-4}$ | $2 \cdot 7 \times 10^{-5}$ | $2 \cdot 6 \times 10^{-2}$ |

\* The frequency of Cm$^r$ cells, taken as a relative measure of deletion frequencies, was determined in colonies after approximately 25 generations of growth in the absence of chloramphenicol.
The results in columns (a), (b) and (c) correspond to the structures shown in *Figure 19.1Ba, b* and *c*, respectively

These results are entirely consistent with models implicating slipped-mispairing/template-switching errors during replication (Albertini *et al.*, 1982; Ehrlich *et al.*, 1986). The latter authors speculated that single-stranded rolling-circle intermediates are particularly prone to such errors. We tested this prediction in two ways. First, by replacing the pTA1060 moiety of pHP327FX containing a 27 bp DR and 300 bp flanking IR, with replication functions from

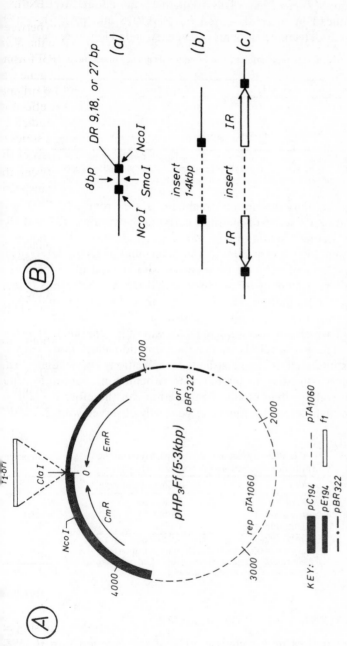

**Figure 19.1** (A) pHP3Ff contains the replication functions of pTA1060. It replicates in *B. subtilis* and *E. coli*. Synthetic oligonucleotides were inserted in the *Nco*I site of the Cm$^r$ gene (*see* text). (After Peeters, *et al.*, 1988.) (B) The DNA region flanking the *Nco*I site in pHP3Ff is shown schematically: (a) synthetic oligonucleotides creating 9, 18 or 27 bp DRs, respectively, were inserted in the *Nco*I site; the repeats were separated by 8 bp, containing a *Sma*I site; (b) the DRs were separated by a 1·4 kbp DNA fragment inserted in the *Sma*I site; (c) IRs of variable length and containing the 1·4 kbp insert, were inserted in the *Sma*I site.

plasmids generating different amounts of single-stranded DNA. A correlation was observed between the levels of single-stranded DNA and the frequency of deletion formation (*Table 19.2*). This frequency was about fifty- to five-hundredfold reduced in plasmids based on pTA1015 and pAMβ1, which produce low or non-detectable amounts of single-stranded DNA, respectively.

**Table 19.2**  Effects of different replication functions on the frequency of deletions based on short direct repeats

| Replication function | % ss DNA | Copy no. | Frequency of Cm$^r$ cells |
|---|---|---|---|
| pE194 | 30 | 5 | $6·4 \times 10^{-3}$ |
| pTA1060 | 30 | 5 | $1·8 \times 10^{-2}$ |
| pTA1015 | 5 | 3 | $1·3 \times 10^{-4}$ |
| pAMβ1 | 0 | 2 | $5·1 \times 10^{-5}$ |

The pTA1060-based replication functions of pHP327FX, containing a 27 bp DR, 300 bp IR and 1·4 kbp spacer region between the IRs, was replaced by the replication functions of the plasmids indicated. In the case of pTA1015, the entire plasmid was inserted. Frequencies of Cm$^r$ cells were determined as described in *Table 19.1*.

Secondly, the stability-promoting fragment, *stab*, from pTA1060 was introduced in the pHP3 series of plasmids carrying the various DRs and IRs described above. In one orientation, the *stab* fragment reduced the amount of single-stranded pHP3 DNA from 30% to non-detectable levels (*see* later). This enabled a comparison of deletion frequencies with related plasmids under conditions of different amounts of single-stranded DNA. The results (*Table 19.3*) showed that in orientation A *stab* caused a 32-fold reduction in deletion frequencies. In this orientation no single-stranded DNA was detected. In orientation B, in which single-stranded DNA was still generated, *stab* had much less effect. These results indicate that the formation of deletions between short DRs is stimulated if single-stranded replication intermediates can accumulate. This is consistent with a template-switching mechanism for their generation. The rolling-circle mode of replication can therefore explain, at least in part, the high deletion frequencies generally observed with *B. subtilis* plasmids.

**Table 19.3**  Effect of *stab* from pTA1060 on the formation of deletions between direct repeats

| *stab* | Frequency of Cm$^r$ cells |
|---|---|
| absent | $1·8 \times 10^{-2}$ |
| orientation A | $5·6 \times 10^{-4}$ |
| orientation B | $3·7 \times 10^{-3}$ |

pHP327FX, containing a 27 bp DR, 300 bp IR and 1·4 kbp insert between the IRs, analogous to situation (c) in *Figure 19.1B*, was used. Frequencies of Cm$^r$ cells were determined as described in *Table 19.1*.

DELETIONS BETWEEN NON-REPEATED SEQUENCES

Non-repeated sequences may comprise 50% of the deletion targets in *B. subtilis* (Lopez *et al.*, 1984). Such deletions are not easily explained by replication errors in single-stranded DNA. How, then, are these deletions generated, and is their formation stimulated by rolling-circle replication? To approach these questions, we selected many deletions in plasmid pGP1

(Peijnenburg, Bron and Venema, 1987) in which expression of a cloned *E. coli lacZ* gene is dependent on a N-terminally fused *B. licheniformis penP* gene. Nearly all deletions in the *penP–lacZ* region, isolated from cells producing white colonies on plates containing 5-bromo-4-chloro-3-indolyl-β-D-galactopyranoside (X-gal), appeared to have one end point (defined as 'left') located in a rather narrow region (700 bp) containing the *penP* transcription/translation signals (Peijnenburg, Bron and Venema, 1988). Sequence analysis of 28 randomly chosen fusion points showed that only one deletion had occurred between DRs (10 bp). This deletion may have resulted from template-switching during replication. The other deletions are not easily explained by this mechanism. At the left end points a strong preference for T–T–T, or the complementary A–A–A sequences was observed (15 of 28 cases, $P<0.003$). Of the left end points, 80% were located in potentially stable stem-loop structures. This, together with the preference for T–T–T (or A–A–A) sequences, makes it attractive to speculate that topoisomerase I was involved. The rationale behind this idea is that topoisomerase I from *E. coli* was reported to have similar (*in vitro*) properties (Kirkegaard, Pflugfelder and Wang, 1984). Other investigators (Lopez *et al.*, 1984) have suggested that topoisomerase II (DNA gyrase) might be involved in deletion formation at non-repeated sequences in *B. subtilis*. Evidence for this idea is lacking, however. Our results did not allow speculations about how the right deletion end points may be specified.

To study whether these deletions might be affected by the mode of replication, the *penP–lacZ* fusion was introduced in a related set of plasmids producing different amounts of single-stranded DNA. Replication functions were taken from pAMβ1, pGP1 and pTA1060. Preliminary results (*Table 19.4*)

**Table 19.4**  Effects of different amounts of single-stranded DNA on deletion in *penP–lacZ*

| Replication function | Copy no. | Relative deletion efficiency* | | |
|---|---|---|---|---|
| | | wild-type | *recE4* | *addB72* |
| pAMβ1 | 1–2 | 1·0 | 0·0 | 8·0 |
| pGP1 | 5 | 3·5 | 0·0 | 25·0 |
| pTA1060 | 5 | 3·8 | 0·0 | 21·0 |

* Relative deletion efficiencies are expressed as the percentages of cells yielding white progeny on X-gal plates after 40 generations of growth in the presence of selective antibiotics. The high values obtained are partly caused by the selective growth advantage of cells carrying deleted instead of the original plasmids.

showed that in the wild-type strain, plasmids based on pAMβ1 generated deletions at a high frequency (only a factor 3–4 lower than in plasmids based on pGP1 or pTA1060). This difference may, at least in part, be accounted for by the lower copy number of pAMβ1. Also, in the highly deletogenic *addB72* mutant, the pAMβ1-based and the other plasmids differed only by a factor of 3–4. Also in the *recE4* mutant, pAMβ1-based plasmids behaved like the others: no deletions were detected. Restriction analysis indicated that the deletions in the pAMβ1-based plasmid were similar to those obtained with pGP1. Since pAMβ1 does not seem to generate single-stranded replication intermediates (Jannière and Ehrlich, personal communication) these results suggest that deletion formation between non-repeated sequences in the *penP–lacZ* fusion is not significantly stimulated by rolling-circle replication.

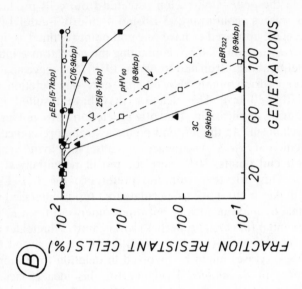

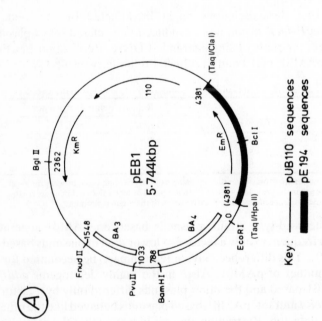

**Figure 19.2** (A) pEB1 is the entire pUB110, containing the Em$^r$ gene of pE194 at position 4381. (B) Segregational stabilities were measured during 100 generations of growth in non-selective media, by plating on selective agars. ●——●, pEB1; ○--○, pEB1-1C; ■——■, pEB1-2S; ▲——▲, pEB1-3C; △--△, pUB110/pHV60; □--□, pUB110/pBR322. (After Bron, Luxen and Swart, 1988.)

SEGREGATIONAL (IN)STABILITY OF pUB110 AND pTA1060

We studied segregational instability in *B. subtilis* with two plasmids; the commonly used *S. aureus*-derived pUB110, and the cryptic *B. subtilis* plasmid pTA1060 (Uozumi *et al.*, 1980).

### Size-dependent instability of pUB110 plasmids

To study the effect of cloning on segregational stability, DNA fragments of various sizes were inserted at several positions in pUB110. pEB1 (*Figure 19.2A*), 5·74 kbp, carries the erythromycin-resistance (Em$^r$) gene of pE194 at position 4381 (coordinates of pUB110 are according to McKenzie *et al.*, 1986). The *E. coli* DNA fragments 1C (1·2 kbp) and 3C (4·2 kbp), and the *B. subtilis* DNA fragment 2S (2·4 kbp) were inserted in the *Bgl*II site (position 2362) of pEB1, yielding plasmids of 6·9, 9·9 and 8·1 kbp, respectively. Plasmids pHV60 and pBR322 were fused to pUB110 at positions 1548 (*Eco*RV/*Fnu*dII fusion), and 788 (*Bam*HI/*Bam*HI fusion), yielding plasmids of 8·8 and 8·9 kbp, respectively. The segregational stabilities (*Figure 19.2B*) indicate that irrespective of the site of insertion, and irrespective of the nature of the insert, these plasmids were unstable in a size-dependent way. Whereas the smaller plasmids were rather stable during 100 generations of growth in non-selective medium, plasmids carrying inserts of more than about 3 kbp were poorly maintained. This may render pUB110 unsuitable for the cloning of large inserts, particularly if no selective pressure can be applied.

The plasmid copy numbers (monomeric forms were measured) were strongly negatively correlated with plasmid size (*Figure 19.3*). This suggests that the reduction in copy numbers is a possible explanation for the impaired stabilities of the larger plasmids. An alternative explanation is based on recent observations from two other laboratories. Gruss and Ehrlich (1988) observed that hybrid pUB110 plasmids, analogous to the ones studied here, generate large amounts of aberrant, high molecular weight (HMW) replication products in *B subtilis*. Viret and Alonso (1987), using rearranged pUB110 derivatives, also observed HMW plasmid DNA. The presence of this material was conceived to be deleterious to the cells (Viret and Alonso, 1987; personal communication) and could thus explain the segregational instabilities observed in certain mutants (Alonso, Viret and Tailor, 1987), and possibly also in wild-type strains.

### A stability function on the BA3 fragment of pUB110 may be the priming site for lagging strand synthesis

The membrane-binding areas BA3 (coordinates 1033–1548) and BA4 (coordinates 0–788) were deleted separately from pEB1–1C, and the effects on stability were determined. The results (*Figure 19.4*) show that the removal of BA3 (or BA3 plus BA4, coordinates 0–1548) reduced the stability of pEB1–1C considerably. Deletion of BA4 from this plasmid had no detectable effect. Apparently, the BA3 fragment, which is not part of the minimal pUB110 replicon, carries a stability determinant.

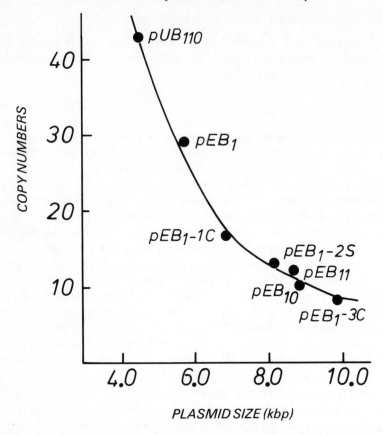

**Figure 19.3**    Copy numbers were determined in radioactively labelled log-phase cultures grown under selective pressure. The ratios of radioactivities in plasmid and chromosomal DNA were used to calculate plasmid copy numbers per chromosome equivalent.

The removal of BA3 also had a profound effect on the levels of single-stranded DNA. Whereas only 5% of pEB1 was found to be single-stranded, 80% of all molecules lacking BA3 were present in the single-stranded state (Bron, Luxen and Swart, 1988). Deletion of BA4 had no effect. These results show that BA3 contains a determinant for the conversion of single- to double-stranded DNA in *B. subtilis*. Results obtained by Viret and Alonso (1988), and Gruss (personal communication) also suggest the presence of a priming site for lagging-strand synthesis (minus origin) on the BA3 fragment. These results altogether suggest that the stability-promoting activity of BA3 is in fact the minus origin activity. Inefficient priming of rolling-circle replication intermediates, therefore, seems to cause segregational plasmid instability.

Inefficient priming, or absence of active minus origins, may well be a rather general cause of segregational plasmid instability in *B. subtilis*. The putative minus origins of pE194, pC194 and pT181 (Gruss, Ross and Novick, 1987), and the *Streptococcus* plasmid pLS1 (Del Solar, Puyet and Espinosa, 1987) do not

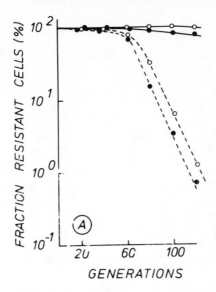

GENERATIONS

**Figure 19.4**   The segregational stabilities of pEB1–1C (O—O) plasmids lacking BA3 (O– –O), BA4 (●—●) or both (●– –●) were determined as described for *Figure 19.2* (after Bron, Luxen and Swart, 1988).

seem to function in *B. subtilis*. These plasmids have been reported to be unstable in this organism.

## Segregational stability of pTA1060-derived plasmids

We reasoned that endogenous *Bacillus* plasmids might be more stable than pUB110 which originally was obtained from *S. aureus*. pTA1060 (8·6 kbp, five copies per chromosome equivalent, Uozumi *et al.*, 1980; Bron *et al.*, 1987) was chosen as a candidate. The segregational stability of pBB2, a genetically marked derivative (11·3 kbp), was superior to that of pUB110 (compare *Figures 19.2B* and *19.5B*). Even relatively large inserts, like the 3C fragment (4·2 kbp) which had a dramatic effect on pUB110, affected the stability of pBB2 only slightly. The reasons for the high stability of pTA1060 hybrids are unknown at present. Of relevance may be that, unlike pUB110, pTA1060 plasmids did not show a size-dependent reduction in copy number. Preliminary results also suggested that pTA1060 hybrids generated relatively little HMW DNA.

In contrast to pBB2, pBB3, which lacks the 1·5 kbp *Cla*I fragment denoted as *stab*, was unstable. This indicates that the *stab* fragment contains a stability determinant which is not part of the minimal replicon. Like BA3 of pUB110, *stab* seems to contain an initiation site for lagging-strand synthesis. This was concluded from the observation that *stab* reduced the amount of single-stranded pHP3Ff DNA from 30% to non-detectable levels in one orientation, but not in the other (results not shown). As described above, the frequency of deletions based on DRs was markedly affected by the *stab* fragment.

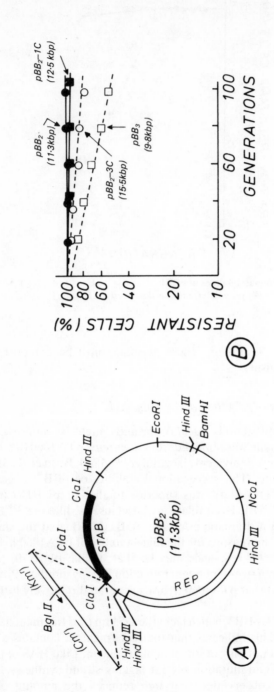

**Figure 19.5** (A) pBB2 consists of the entire pTA1060 into which Cm[r] and Km[r] markers were introduced. The replication functions are indicated as REP; the stability determinant as STAB. (B) The segregational stabilities of pBB2 (●——●), pBB2–1C (■——■), pBB2–3C (○– –○) and pBB3 (□– –□) are indicated (after Bron *et al.*, 1987).

The above results suggest that, like many *S. aureus* plasmids, pTA1060 replicates via single-stranded rolling-circle intermediates. Also, the presence in this plasmid of the minus origin of replication seems to be required for optimal segregational stability. The stability function *par* of the cryptic *B. subtilis* plasmid pLS11, described by Chang, Chang and Gray (1987), is likely to be similar, if not identical to *stab* of pTA1060. The stability determinant of the *Bacillus* plasmid pBAA1 (Devine *et al.*, 1988) is also likely to be a minus origin. It is, therefore, attractive to assume that all stability functions which are not part of the minimal replicon, described so far for plasmids in *B. subtilis*, are priming sites for lagging-strand synthesis.

To characterize the BA3 and *stab* functions further, potential stable intrastrand secondary structures were searched for with the ASRNA program on a VAX computer. A high degree of hyphenated dyad symmetry was found in the segments shown in *Figure 19.6*, allowing several stable secondary structures to be formed. It is of interest that the *palA* sequences described for pE194, pC194 and related plasmids (Gruss, Ross and Novick, 1987) are also rich in hyphenated dyad symmetry, which may reflect a similar function. However, sequence similarities between *palA* and BA3 or *stab* were not found.

Although the most stable structures of BA3 and *stab* show certain similarities (most notably in the stem-loops III and IV), no similarities were found at the sequence level. For a better understanding of the function of these stem-loops, if any, the minus origin and plasmid stability functions will have to be more precisely delimited. Deletion analysis in conjunction with site-directed mutagenesis may also aid in the better understanding of these functions.

## Cloning in vectors based on pTA1060

The observation that pBB2 was segregationally stable, even with the 3C (4·2 kbp) insert, prompted us to study the value of pTA1060-based vectors for shotgun cloning in *B. subtilis*. For this purpose the *B. subtilis*/*E. coli* shuttle plasmid pHP13 (*Figure 19.7*) was constructed, which carries the pTA1060 and pBR322 replication functions (Haima, Bron and Venema, 1987). Shotgun cloning of *E. coli* DNA in pHP13 was highly efficient using *B. subtilis* competent cells lacking the *Bsu*M restriction system (*Table 19.5*). Clones comprised 36% of all transformants. The average insert length was high (3·6 kbp), and inserts up to 10–15 kbp were detected with relative ease. In these properties pHP13 is superior to most other plasmids used in *B. subtilis*. If restriction-proficient recipients were used, the fraction of large inserts was under-represented. This could be attributed to the higher frequency of CTCGAG (*Xho*I) sequences in these fragments, which constitute targets for *Bsu*M restriction (Bron, Jannière and Ehrlich, 1988).

**Table 19.5**  Cloning in competent *B. subtilis* $r_M^-$ with plasmid pHP13

| Clones/µg DNA | Frequency of recombinant clones | Average length of insert | Range of inserts |
|---|---|---|---|
| $10^4$ | 36% | 3·6 kbp | 0·2–16 kbp |

pHP13 is described in the text. *E. coli* DNA (from a *dam⁻ dcm⁻* strain) was digested with *Bcl*I and shotgun-cloned in *Bcl*I-cleaved pHP13. Competent, non-restricting *B. subtilis* cells were used as recipients in transformation. Insert lengths were determined by restriction analysis.

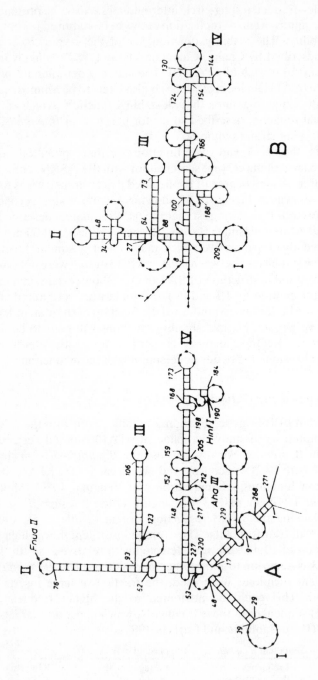

**Figure 19.6** Potential stable secondary structures were predicted using the VAX computer program ASRNA. (A) Part of BA3. The nucleotide numbering from 1 to 271 corresponds to coordinates 1359–1626 on the map of McKenzie *et al.* (1986). (After Bron, Luxen and Swart, 1988.) (B) The central part of the *stab* fragment is shown.

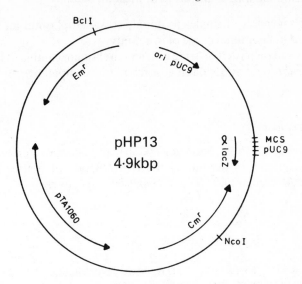

**Figure 19.7**   pHP13 contains the replication functions of pTA1060 and most of pBR322. The unique *Bcl*I site in the Em$^r$ gene was used for cloning in *B. subtilis* (after Haima, Bron and Venema, 1987).

## Conclusions

A major determinant in plasmid deletion formation between short direct repeats (DRs) was the size of the DRs. The formation of these deletions was, moreover, stimulated about one thousandfold by the presence of flanking inverted repeats, and about twentyfold by close proximity of the DRs. The accumulation of rolling-circle intermediates strongly stimulated deletion formation between DRs. These results are entirely consistent with models in which errors in the replication of single-stranded DNA, as a consequence of template-switching, underlie deletion formation.

Deletions based on DRs were rare in a plasmid carrying a *penP–lacZ* fusion. In almost all deletions one end point was located in a short region, such that the transcription/translation signals of the fusion had been removed. This suggests that expression of the fusion favoured the generation (or selection) of deletions. T–T–T, or the complementary A–A–A, triplets were favoured at these end points, which were frequently located in potentially stable stem-loop structures. These results favour the idea that topoisomerase I may be involved in the formation of these deletions by a break-and-join mechanism. This deletion event did not seem to be stimulated by rolling-circle replication.

pUB110 hybrids were segregationally unstable in a size-dependent way. Size-dependent reductions in copy numbers, or the production of aberrant replication products may be the cause. A stability determinant on the BA3 fragment seems to function as a priming site for lagging-strand synthesis.

Hybrids of the *B. subtilis* plasmid pTA1060 were superior to pUB110 with respect to segregational stability. A stability determinant on pTA1060 is also likely to be a priming site for lagging-strand synthesis. It was assumed that inefficient conversion of single- to double-stranded plasmid molecules in *B. subtilis* is a rather common cause of instability.

Vectors based on pTA1060 were efficient in shotgun cloning of heterologous DNA in *B. subtilis*, in particular if non-restricting competent cells were used as recipients.

**Acknowledgements**

We thank Academic Press, San Diego (Cal.), and Springer Verlag, Heidelberg (BRD) for courtesy in permitting the reproduction of figures published in *Plasmid* and *Molecular and General Genetics*, respectively.

**References**

ALBERTINI, A.M., HOFER, M., CALOS, M.P. AND MILLER, J.H. (1982). On the formation of spontaneous deletions: the importance of short sequence homologies in the generation of large deletions. *Cell* **9**, 319–328.
ALONSO, J.C., VIRET, J.-F. AND TAILOR, R.H. (1987). Plasmid maintenance in *Bacillus subtilis* recombination-deficient mutants. *Molecular and General Genetics* **208**, 349–352.
BRON, S. AND LUXEN, E. (1985). Segregational instability of pUB110-derived recombinant plasmids in *Bacillus subtilis*. *Plasmid* **14**, 235–244.
BRON, S., JANNIÈRE, ,L. AND EHRLICH, S.D. (1988). Restriction and modification in *Bacillus subtilis* Marburg 168: target sites and effects on plasmid transformation. *Molecular and General Genetics* **211**, 186–189.
BRON, S., LUXEN, E. AND SWART, P. (1988). Instability of recombinant pUB110 plasmids in *Bacillus subtilis*: Plasmid-encoded stability function and effects of DNA inserts. *Plasmid* **19**, 231–241.
BRON, S., BOSMA, P., VAN BELKUM, M. AND LUXEN, E. (1987). Stability function in the *Bacillus subtilis* plasmid pTA1060. *Plasmid* **18**, 8–15.
CHANG, S., CHANG, S.-Y. AND GRAY, O. (1987). Structural and genetic analysis of a *par* locus that regulates plasmid partition in *Bacillus subtilis*. *Journal of Bacteriology* **169**, 3952–3962.
DEL SOLAR, G.H., PUYET, A. AND ESPINOSA, M. (1987). Initiation signals for the conversion of single stranded to double stranded DNA forms in the streptococcal plasmid pLS1. *Nucleic Acids Research* **15**, 5561–5580.
DEVINE, K.M., HOGAN, S.T., HIGGINS, D.G. AND MCCONNELL, D.J. (1988). Replication and segregational stability of the *Bacillus* plasmid pBAA1. *Journal of Bacteriology* **171**, 1166–1172.
DUBNAU, D. 1983. Molecular cloning in *Bacillus subtilis*. In *Experimental Manipulation of Gene Expression* (M. Inouye, Ed.), pp. 33–51. Academic Press, Orlando.
EHRLICH, S.D., NOIROT, P.H., PETIT, M.A., JANNIÈRE, L., MICHEL, B. AND TE RIELE, H. (1986). Structural instability of *Bacillus subtilis* plasmids. In *Genetic Engineering* (J.K. Setlow and A. Hollaender, Eds), Volume 8, pp. 71–83. Plenum Press, New York.
GRUSS, A.D. AND EHRLICH, S.D. (1988). Insertion of foreign DNA into plasmids from Gram-positive bacteria induces formation of high molecular weight plasmid multimers. *Journal of Bacteriology* **170**, 1183–1190.
GRUSS, A.D., ROSS, H.F. AND NOVICK, R.P. (1987). Functional analysis of a palindromic sequence required for normal replication of several staphylococcal plasmids. *Proceedings of the National Academy of Sciences of the United States of America* **84**, 2165–2169.

HAIMA, P., BRON, S. AND VENEMA, G. (1987). The effect of restriction on shotgun cloning and plasmid stability in *Bacillus subtilis* Marburg. *Molecular and General Genetics* **209**, 335–342.

KIRKEGAARD, K., PFLUGFELDER, G. AND WANG, J.C. (1984). The cleavage of DNA by type-I DNA topoisomerases. *Cold Spring Harbor Symposia on Quantitative Biology* **49**, 411–419.

LOPEZ, P., ESPINOSA, M., GREENBERG, B. AND LACKS, S.A. (1984). Generation of deletions in pneumococcal *mal* genes cloned in *Bacillus subtilis*. *Proceedings of the National Academy of Sciences of the United States of America* **81**, 5189–5193.

MCKENZIE, T., HOSHINO, T., TANAKA, T. AND SUEOKA, N. (1986). The nucleotide sequence of pUB110: some salient features in relation to replication and its regulation. *Plasmid* **15**, 93–103.

PEETERS, B.P.H., DE BOER, J.H., BRON, S. AND VENEMA, G. (1988). Structural plasmid instability in *Bacillus subtilis*: effect of direct and inverted repeats. *Molecular and General Genetics* **212**, 450–458.

PEIJNENBURG, A.A.C.M., BRON, S. AND VENEMA, G. (1987). Structural plasmid instability in recombination- and repair-deficient strains of *Bacillus subtilis*. *Plasmid* **17**, 167–170.

PEIJNENBURG, A.A.C.M., BRON, S. AND VENEMA, G. (1988). Plasmid deletion formation in *Bacillus subtilis*. *Plasmid* **20**, 23–32.

TE RIELE, H., MICHEL, B. AND EHRLICH, S.D. (1986). Are single-stranded circles intermediates in plasmid replication? *EMBO Journal* **5**, 631–637.

UOZUMI, T., OZAKI, A., BEPPU, T. AND ARIMA, K. (1980). New cryptic plasmid of *Bacillus subtilis* and restriction analysis of other plasmids found by general screening. *Journal of Bacteriology* **142**, 315–318.

VIRET, J.-F. AND ALONSO, J.C. (1987). Generation of linear multi-genome-length plasmid molecules in *Bacillus subtilis*. *Nucleic Acids Research* **15**, 6349–6367.

VIRET, J.-F. AND ALONSO, J.C. (1988). A DNA sequence outside the minimal replicon is required for normal replication in *Bacillus subtilis*. *Nucleic Acids Research* **16**, 4389–4406.

# 20
# Structural Plasmid Stability in *Bacillus subtilis*

AD PEIJNENBURG, GERARD VENEMA AND SIERD BRON

*Department of Genetics, University of Groningen, Kerklaan 30, 9751 NN Haren(Gn), The Netherlands*

## Introduction

From the onset of DNA cloning in *Bacillus subtilis*, hybrid plasmids have been reported frequently to be structurally unstable (for a review *see* Ehrlich *et al.*, 1986). Structural plasmid instability refers to the rearrangement of DNA sequences, usually deletions (Primrose and Ehrlich, 1981). This most often results from illegitimate recombination, i.e. recombination between sequences of little or no homology (for a review *see* Anderson, 1987). Sequence analysis of novel junction points has revealed that at least two categories of sequences are involved in illegitimate recombination in *B. subtilis*: short direct repeats (Lopez *et al.*, 1984; Saunders *et al.*, 1984), and non-repeated sequences. Errors of replication of single-stranded plasmid DNA, resulting from template switching at the direct repeats (Ehrlich *et al.*, 1986; Peeters *et al.*, 1988), may well explain deletions based on direct repeats.

Relatively little is known about mechanisms that underlie deletions based on non-repeated sequences. It has been speculated that break-and-join enzymes, such as topoisomerases, are involved in these deletion events (Lopez *et al.*, 1984). Also, little is known about other host functions involved in structural plasmid instability.

The aims of these studies were twofold. In the first place, we analysed a great number of deletion junctions to study whether specific sequence patterns were involved in deletion formation. In the second place, we attempted to gain an insight into the host functions involved in deletion formation by comparing plasmid stabilities in various *B. subtilis* mutants deficient in functions known to play a role in general recombination and/or DNA repair (Mazza and Galizzi, 1978; Alonso, Tailor and Lüder, 1988).

*Genetic Transformation and Expression*
© Intercept Ltd, PO Box 716, Andover, Hants, SP10 1YG, UK

**Results**

CHARACTERISTICS OF PLASMID pGP1

To monitor structural plasmid instability in *B. subtilis* a system was set up based on plasmid pGP1 (*Figure 20.1*). This plasmid consists of pGK13 with a 5·5 kbp *Bam*HI insert containing a fusion between the *Bacillus licheniformis* 749/C penicillinase gene (*penP*) and the *Escherichia coli* β-galactosidase gene (*lacZ*).

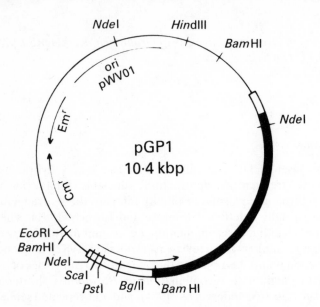

**Figure 20.1**    Structure of plasmid pGP1. ☐, *penP* sequences; ■, *lacZ* sequences; Cm$^r$, chloramphenicol-resistance gene; Em$^r$, erythromycin-resistance gene. Arrows represent directions of transcription. (After Peijnenburg, Bron and Venema, 1987.)

Plasmid pGK13 (Cm$^r$, Em$^r$, 4·9 kbp) is based on the cryptic *Streptococcus cremoris* plasmid pWV01 (Kok, van der Vossen and Venema, 1984) and replicates in *E. coli*, *B. subtilis* and lactic acid streptococci. In pGP1 the expression of *lacZ* is dependent on *penP* regulatory signals. Rearrangements that affected β-galactosidase activity were selected from white *B. subtilis* colonies on plates containing the chromogenic indicator substrate X-gal (5-bromo-4-chloro-3-indolyl-β-D-galactopyranoside). The levels of structural plasmid instability were determined as follows. Cells containing pGP1 were grown for approximately 20 generations on plates supplemented with Cm, Em and X-gal. Subsequently, 20 blue colonies were grown separately for 15–20 generations in liquid media with appropriate antibiotics. The percentage of cells containing rearranged plasmids in each of the 20 cultures was determined by plating on selective agars containing X-gal. In the recombination- and repair-proficient *B. subtilis* strain 8G5 (Bron and Venema, 1972), denoted as the wild type, pGP1 was relatively stable (*Figure 20.2*, first block); about 2% of all cells yielded white colonies. Since, without exception, pGP1 derivatives isolated from white colonies appeared to have undergone deletions, the frequency of white colonies was taken as a measure of relative deletion frequencies.

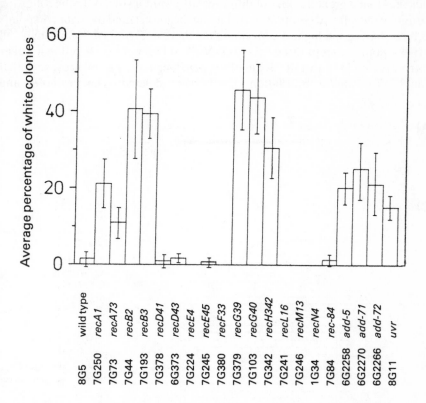

**Figure 20.2** Structural instability of pGP1 in isogenic recombination- and repair-deficient *B. subtilis* strains. Twenty blue colonies of each strain were analysed for the presence of cells producing white progeny on X-gal plates. Cells were grown at 37°C, unless noted otherwise. Bars indicate standard deviation in the frequencies of white colonies. (After Peijnenburg, Bron and Venema, 1987.)

STABILITY OF pGP1 IN RECOMBINATION- AND REPAIR-DEFICIENT STRAINS

To study the effects of various cellular functions on structural plasmid instability in *B. subtilis*, the relative deletion frequencies of pGP1 (frequencies of white colonies) were determined in an isogenic set of recombination- and repair-deficient strains. *Figure 20.2* shows that the levels of stability were markedly affected by many host mutations. Three classes could be distinguished: (1) mutants in which pGP1 was highly stable (*recE, recF, recL, recM*); (2) mutants in which pGP1 was moderately stable (the wild type, *recD, rec-84*); and (3) strains in which pGP1 was highly unstable (*recA, recB, recG, recH, add, uvr*).

DELETIONS GENERATED IN THE WILD-TYPE STRAIN

Restriction analysis of 60 pGP1 derivatives carrying deletions in the *penP–lacZ* region, independently obtained from *B. subtilis* 8G5 (pGP5 plasmids), showed that at least 46 different deletions could be distinguished (*Figure 20.3*). This indicates that a great number of different sites were involved. In the following we define the left end points as those having the lowest, and the right end points as those having the highest coordinate numbers in *Figure 20.3*. Strikingly, all left end points, except three (pGP5–115/–49/–111), were clustered in a rather narrow region in or just upstream of the *penP* regulatory sequences, such that transcription and/or translation signals were deleted. The promoter and

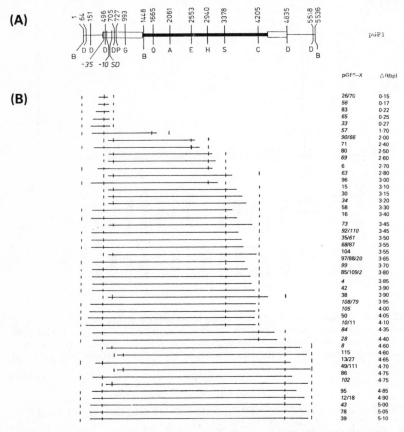

**Figure 20.3**   Location of deletions in the *penP–lacZ* region of pGP1. The upper part of the figure (A) shows the 5·5 kbp *Bam*HI insert of pGP1. Numbers correspond to positions (in bp), the first nucleotide of the insert being 1. Restriction sites are indicated as follows: A, *Aat*II; B, *Bam*HI; C, *Acc*I; D, *Dra*I; E, *Eco*RI; G, *Bgl*II; H, *Bss*HII; O, *Oxan*I; P, *Pst*I; S, *Sac*I. In the lower part of the figure (B), the deleted regions in the various derivatives, denoted as pGP5 with a suffix, are indicated with horizontal lines. Vertical dashes correspond to the restriction sites used for the fine-mapping of the deletion end points. The numbers in italics represent deletions of which the junction points were sequenced. □ , *penP* sequences; ■ , *lacZ* sequences; —— , *B. licheniformis* chromosomal DNA. The promoter and Shine–Dalgarno sequence of *penP* are designated as −35, −10 and SD, respectively. (Reproduced courtesy of Academic Press, Inc., from Peijnenburg, Bron and Venema, 1988.)

Shine–Dalgarno sequences are located around positions 510 and 670, respectively (*Figure 20.3*). Most right end points were found in *lacZ* or downstream sequences.

To examine whether specific sequence patterns were present in the surroundings of the deletion termini, the novel junction points of 28 arbitrarily chosen pGP5 plasmids, shown in italics in *Figure 20.3*, were sequenced. The sequences at the left and right end points are shown in *Figure 20.4*. The data can be summarized as follows.

```
┌LEFT ──────────────────────────────┐RIGHT ────────────────────────────
                      TTT                                GGGGAAAA    mis-
     pGP5-            AAA            pGP5-                CCC TTTG    match
     ---------------------------     ----------------------------------
     108   154-AAAGCGCCTTTTTTAATGAGGCGCA      69   3102-CAGTATCCCCGTTTACAGGGCG    0
      99   361-AGGTTTGCCATTTTAAGAAGTCAAT      92   3803-CGACATTGGCGTAAGTGAAGCG    0
      28   101-TTTCGTCTATATTTTGGTGtgtaAAC    110   3803-CGACATTGGCGTAAGTGAAGCG    0
     105   101-TTTCGTCTATATTTGGTGtgtaAAC      68   3958-AGCATCAGGGGAAAACCTTATT     0
       4   101-TTTCGTCTATATTTGGTGtgtaAAC      73   3958-AGCATCAGGGGAAAACCTTATT     0
      20   101-TTTCGTCTATATTTGGTGtgtaAAC      61   3979-TTATCAGCCGGAAAACCTACCG     0
      65   353-CTCATTATAGGTTTGCCATTTTAAG       2   3979-TTATCAGCCGGAAAACCTACCG     0
      57   291-CGCATCAGAGATTTGAGGTATTTTT       4   3991-AAACCTACCGGATTGATGGTAG     0
      69   522-CAAAGACTACAITtgtaAGATTTGA      108   4063-ATCCGGCGCGGATTGGCCTGAA     0
      34   653-ATCAAATATTCAAACGGAGGGAGAC       10   4063-ATCCGGCGCGGATTGGCCTGAA     0
      63   653-ATCAAATATTCAAACGGAGGGAGAC      105   4103-AGCAGAGCGGGTAAACTGGCTC     0
       2   111-ATTTGGTGtgtaAACGAAAACCCGT       79   4103-AGCAGAGCGGGTAAACTGGCTC     0
      10    46-GTTCCATtgtaAAACCGGTTTAAAA       43   5385-GAGATTACGGGAAAAGGAACCG     0
      43   330-CCTATACTTACAAAtgtaATACTCT       28   4529-CGTATTTCGCGTAAGGAAATCC     0
      84     9-ATCATTCTCCAAAAAGTTTAATAGA      102   5351-GCGGGATGCCGAATGAAGCTGT     0

      90   608-ACACtgtaGGGATAGTGGAAAGAGT       65   608-ACACtgtaGGGATAGTGGAAAG     1
       8   608-ACACtgtaGGGATAGTGGAAAGAGT       12   5164-CAAGGGGCCGGCAAAATTAGCCG    1
      56   335-ACTTACAAAtgtaATACTCTCATTA       57   2032-ATATGTGGCCGATGAGCGGCAT    1
      33   229-TTAATTACCTCATTTGGTATTGATCG       20   3788-TGCACCGCTGGATAACGACATT    1
      66   497-TTAAATCTTACATAtgtaATACTTT       
      73   497-TTAAATCTTACATAtgtaATACTTT       34   3842-CGCCTGGGTCGAACGCTGGAAG    2
      92   326-TCATCCTATACTTACAAAtgtaATA       63   3457-GTAAACAGTTGATTGAACTGCC    2
     110   326-TCATCCTATACTTACAAAtgtaATA       99   4087-GCCAGCTGGCGCAGGTAGCAGA    2
                                              90   2677-AAACCCACGGCATGGTGCCAAT    2
      68   451-CCGGTGGAAACGAGGTCATCATTTC       66   2651-GTATGTGGTGGATGAAGCCAAT    2
     102   602-GCCATAACACtgtaGGGATAGTGGA        8   5312-GTCTGTTGTGGACAATGGCGCC    2
      12   255-AGAATGCTTCCAGATGACTTTCATC       84   4325-GCAACTGATGGAAACCAGCCAT    3
      61   442-CATTTGTCCCCGGTGGAAACGAGGT       33   503-CTTACATAtgtaATACTTTCAA     3
      79   165-TTTAATGAGGCGCAGCATGGTTTGG       56   503-CTTACATAtgtaATACTTTTCAA    3
```

**Figure 20.4** Nucleotide sequences (5' to 3') near deletion termini. The left and right sequences represent the regions flanking the left and right deletion termini, respectively. Arrows indicate breakage points. Directly repeated sequences at the end points are boxed. Breakage may have occurred at any position within the boxes. T–G–T–A sequences are shown in small characters. Trinucleotides T–T–T or A–A–A, and the octanucleotide consensus sequence are shaded. The sequences were aligned according to these boxes. Nucleotide positions correspond to those in *Figure 20.3*. (After Peijnenburg, Bron and Venema, 1988.)

1.  Deletion between sequence homologies of more than 3 bp had occurred only once (pGP5–56). A 10 bp perfect direct repeat was present at the end points of pGP5–56, which can be extended to 21 bp if two mismatches are allowed. Within this repeat an inverted repeat of 12 bp (including one mismatch) is present (*Figure 20.4*, horizontal arrows). The low frequency of deletions between direct repeats in this system was unexpected, since in

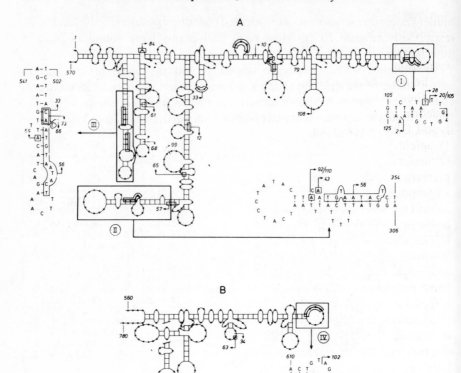

**Figure 20.5**  Optimal DNA folding in the 5' region of the 5·5 kbp *Bam*HI fragment of pGP1, as predicted by computer analysis. The positions of the deletion termini are indicated with arrows. The tetranucleotide T–G–T–A is shaded. (A) Positions 1–570; (B) positions 560–780. I, II, III, IV, deletogenic regions with multiple deletion end points at positions 112–116; 339–347; 507–514 and 615–622, respectively. (Reproduced from Peijnenburg, Bron and Venema, 1988, courtesy of Academic Press, Inc.)

other systems, both in *E. coli* and *B. subtilis*, such deletions have been described to occur more frequently (Jones, Primrose and Ehrlich, 1982; Glickman and Ripley, 1984; Lopez *et al.*, 1984).

2.  The sequence 5'–T–T–T–3', or the 5'–A–A–A–3' complement thereof, was present at 15 left cleavage points ($P<0·003$), which suggests a preference for these sequences at these sites.

3.  In 16 cases, the tetranucleotide 5'–T–G–T–A–3' was found within 10 bp from the left end point ($P<0·005$), which suggests that these sequences also play a role in deletion formation.

4.  A loose sequence motif 5'–G/C–G/C–G/C–G–A/T–A/T–A/T–A/G–3' could be identified near 15 right termini.

The region of DNA in which the left end points were clustered, was also characteristic, in that potentially it could form stable intrastrand secondary structures: region 1–570 (*Figure 20.5A*), $\triangle G = -127·3$ kcal mol$^{-1}$; and region

560–780 (*Figure 20.5B*), $\triangle G = -42.3$ kcal mol$^{-1}$. Deletions occurred frequently near the tops of stem-loop structures (indicated as I–IV in *Figure 20.5*), suggesting that secondary structures play a significant role in deletion formation.

These results suggest that particular sequence patterns (T–T–T or A–A–A), together with DNA secondary structures, specified at least the majority of left deletion termini. This cleavage specificity is very reminiscent to that of the type-I DNA topoisomerases of *E. coli* and *Micrococcus luteus* (Kirkegaard, Pflugfelder and Wang, 1984; Kirkegaard and Wang, 1985). Moreover, the sequences 5′–Py–T–T–3′ and 5′–A–A–Pu have been considered to be preferred cleavage sites for eukaryotic DNA topoisomerase I (Bullock, Champoux and Botchan, 1985). It is therefore tempting to speculate that the *B. subtilis* topoisomerase I was involved in the generation of the deletions studied in the present work.

The observation that nearly all left end points were located in a region involved in transcriptional control, raises the question whether active transcription might stimulate the deletion events. The region upstream of the *penP* promoter contains the *penI* repressor gene, which is transcribed in a direction opposite to that of *penP* (Himeno, Imanaka and Aiba, 1986; Nicholls and Lampen, 1987). As outlined by Liu and Wang (1987), in a plasmid with two divergently transcribed genes, strong negative supercoiling will occur between the two promoters, and positive supercoiling in the downstream regions. Since pGP1 encodes inactive (truncated) PenI repressor, expression of both *penI* and *penP* will be constitutive. The expected increase of negative superhelicity in the *penP* regulatory region could be envisaged to stimulate the generation of secondary structures, such as depicted in *Figure 20.5*. These could be considered to increase the susceptibility to topoisomerase I, since this enzyme preferentially removes negative supercoils.

DELETION FORMATION IN *recE4* AND *addB72* MUTANTS

Restriction mapping of 25 pGP4 and 28 pGP7 plasmids, generated in the *recE4* and *addB72* strains, respectively, also revealed a great variety of deletions: at least 22 different pGP4, and 26 different pGP7 plasmids were found. As in the wild type, nearly all left deletion end points appeared to be located in the narrow regulatory region between nucleotides 1 and 705. Also similar to the wild type, the majority of the right end points occurred in or downstream of the *lacZ* coding region in both strains.

Deletion junction points of 10 pGP4 and 13pGP7 plasmids were chosen randomly for sequence analysis. The results (not shown) can be summarized as follows:

1.  Deletions between direct repeats (>3 bp) were not observed in the *recE4* mutant, but comprised nearly half of the total in the *addB72* strain.
2.  Irrespective of the genetic background, the sequences 5′–T–T–T–3′ or 5′–A–A–A–3′ were, as in the wild type, frequently found at left cleavage sites. This confirms the idea expressed above that these sequences are preferred targets for deletion formation. Likewise, the T–G–T–A motif

228     *Recombination, Transposition, Plasmid Stability*

was frequently observed near left end points of deletions generated in *recE4* and *addB72* strains.

3.  Loose sequence patterns, related to those found in the wild type, were also observed near the right end points of deletions generated in the *recE4* and *addB72* mutants. The significance, if any, of these patterns for deletion formation is not clear at present.

In the *recE4* and *addB72* strains, the left end points occurred frequently near the tops of the same stem-loop structures as in the wild type. This observation and those presented above suggest that, despite the considerable differences observed between the three strains with respect to deletion frequencies, similar mechanisms underlie deletion formation in the wild type, *recE4* and *addB72* strains. We assume that the Add and RecE proteins affect deletion formation in an indirect way. The ATP-dependent helicase activity of the Add complex is believed to interfere with secondary structure formation, thus explaining increased deletion frequencies in its absence (*add* strains). Stimulation of folding by the RecE protein might explain the higher deletion frequencies observed in wild type compared to *recE4* strains. Alternatively, it is conceivable that RecE exerts an unknown effect on deletion formation via its central role in the SOS-like response of *B. subtilis*.

**Acknowledgements**

We are grateful to Academic Press, Inc., San Diego (CA) for permission to reproduce figures published in *Plasmid*.

**References**

ALONSO, J.C., TAILOR, R.H. AND LÜDER, G. (1988). Characterization of recombination-deficient mutants of *Bacillus subtilis*. *Journal of Bacteriology* **170**, 3001–3007.
ANDERSON, P. (1987). Twenty years of illegitimate recombination. *Genetics* **115**, 581–584.
BRON, S. AND VENEMA, G. (1972). Ultraviolet inactivation and excision repair in *Bacillus subtilis*. I. Construction and characterization of a transformable eightfold auxotrophic strain and two ultraviolet-sensitive derivatives. *Mutation Research* **15**, 1–10.
BULLOCK, P., CHAMPOUX, J.J. AND BOTCHAN, M. (1985). Association of crossover points with topoisomerase I cleavage sites: a model for nonhomologous recombination. *Science* **230**, 954–958.
EHRLICH, S.D., NOIROT, P.H., PETIT, M.A., JANNIÈRE, L., MICHEL, B. AND TE RIELE, H. (1986). Structural instability of *Bacillus subtilis* plasmids. In *Genetic Engineering, Volume 8* (J.K. Setlow and A. Hollaender, Eds), pp. 71–83. Plenum Press, New York.
GLICKMAN, B.W. AND RIPLEY, L.S. (1984). Structural intermediates of deletion mutagenesis: a role for palindromic DNA. *Proceedings of the National Academy of Sciences of the United States of America* **81**, 512–516.
HIMENO, T., IMANAKA, T. AND AIBA, S. (1986). Nucleotide sequence of the penicillinase repressor gene *penI* of *Bacillus licheniformis* and regulation of *penP* and *penI* by the repressor. *Journal of Bacteriology* **168**, 1128–1132.

JONES, I.M., PRIMROSE, S.B. AND EHRLICH, S.D. (1982). Recombination between short direct repeats in a *recA* host. *Molecular and General Genetics* **188**, 486–489.

KIRKEGAARD, K. AND WANG, J.C. (1985). Bacterial topoisomerase I can relax positively supercoiled DNA containing a single-stranded loop. *Journal of Molecular Biology* **185**, 625–637.

KIRKEGAARD, K., PFLUGFELDER, G. AND WANG, J.C. (1984). The cleavage of DNA by type-I DNA topoisomerases. *Cold Spring Harbor Symposia on Quantitative Biology* **49**, 411–419.

KOK, J., VAN DER VOSSEN, J.M.B.M. AND VENEMA, G. (1984). Construction of plasmid cloning vectors for lactic streptococci which also replicate in *Bacillus subtilis* and *Escherichia coli*. *Applied and Environmental Microbiology* **48**, 726–731.

LIU, L.F. AND WANG, J.C. (1987). Supercoiling of the DNA template during transcription. *Proceedings of the National Academy of Sciences of the United States of America* **84**, 7024–7027.

LOPEZ, P., ESPINOSA, M., GREENBERG, B. AND LACKS, S.A. (1984). Generation of deletions in pneumococcal *mal* genes cloned in *Bacillus subtilis*. *Proceedings of the National Academy of Sciences of the United States of America* **81**, 5189–5193.

MAZZA, G. AND GALIZZI, A. (1978). The genetics of DNA replication, repair and recombination in *Bacillus subtilis*. *Microbiologica* **1**, 111–135.

NICHOLLS, N.J. AND LAMPEN, J.O. (1987). Repressor gene, *blaI*, for *Bacillus licheniformis* 749 β-lactamase. *FEBS Letters* **221**, 179–183.

PEETERS, B.P.H., DE BOER, J.H., BRON, S. AND VENEMA, G. (1988). Structural plasmid instability in *Bacillus subtilis*: effect of direct and inverted repeats. *Molecular and General Genetics* **212**, 450–458.

PEIJNENBURG, A.A.C.M., BRON, S. AND VENEMA, G. (1987). Structural plasmid instability in recombination- and repair-deficient strains of *Bacillus subtilis*. *Plasmid* **17**, 167–170.

PEIJNENBURG, A.A.C.M., BRON, S. AND VENEMA, G. (1988). Plasmid deletion formation in *Bacillus subtilis*. *Plasmid* **20**, 23–32.

PRIMROSE, S.B. AND EHRLICH, S.D. (1981). Isolation of plasmid deletion mutants and study of their instability. *Plasmid* **6**, 193–201.

SAUNDERS, C.W., SCHMIDT, B.J., MIROT, M.S., THOMPSON, L.D. AND GUYER, M.S. (1984). Use of chromosomal integration in the establishment and expression of *blaZ*, a *Stapylococcus aureus* beta-lactamase gene, in *Bacillus subtilis*. *Journal of Bacteriology* **157**, 718–726.

# 21
# Plasmid Double-Strand Ends: Origin and Role in Recombination

AMIKAM COHEN, ANAT NUSSBAUM, SARIT MAOR, IRIT BERGER AND ZIPORA SILBERSTEIN

Department of Molecular Genetics, The Hebrew University–Hadassah Medical School, Jerusalem, Israel 91010

## The role of exonucleases in plasmid recombination

Plasmids are maintained in wild-type *Escherichia coli* cells primarily as supercoiled circles, and as such they resist digestion by exonucleases. Nevertheless, several exonucleases affect plasmid recombination. RecBCD nuclease, the *recBreccCrecD* gene product, which is essential for conjugational recombination by the major recombination pathway in wild-type cells (Emmerson and Howard-Flanders, 1967; Emmerson, 1968), inhibits plasmid recombination in every genetic background tested (*Table 21.1*). Its effect in wild-type cells is minor (Fishel, James and Kolodner, 1981; Laban and Cohen, 1981). However, in genetic backgrounds where the RecE, RecF and λ Red recombination pathways are functional, plasmid recombination is RecBCD sensitive (Cohen and Laban, 1983; Nussbaum and Cohen, 1988). The RecE recombination pathway is active in cells where exonuclease VIII synthesis is derepressed by *sbcA* mutations (Kushner, Nagaishi and Clark, 1974). Plasmids recombine in these cells at high frequency and recombination is *recA* independent (Fishel, James and Kolodner, 1981; Laban and Cohen, 1981). High recombination frequency and independence of *recA* activity are observed in RecBCD⁻ but not in RecBCD⁺ cells. The RecF recombination pathway that is functional in *sbcB* mutants is also RecBCD sensitive (Nussbaum and Cohen, 1988). This pathway is also sensitive to exonuclease I, which digests single-strand DNA in a 3' to 5' direction (Lehman and Nussbaum, 1964). Expression of λ *red* genes, *exo* and *bet*, in *E. coli* cells, activates the Red recombination pathway. Like recombination by the RecE and RecF pathways, plasmid recombination by the Red pathway is RecBCD sensitive (Nussbaum and Cohen, 1988).

Four exonucleases affect recombination frequency in the RecE, RecF and Red pathways: exonuclease I, exonuclease VIII, λ *red* exonuclease and RecBCD nuclease. Since none of these enzymes can use circular DNA as a

*Genetic Transformation and Expression*
© Intercept Ltd, PO Box 716, Andover, Hants, SP10 1YG, UK

**Table 21.1**   The effect of exonucleases on recombination activity of bacterial plasmids

| Bacterial relevant genotype (strain) | RecBCD | Relevant phenotype ExoI | ExoVIII | RecA | Relative recombinant frequency* |
|---|---|---|---|---|---|
| rec⁺ (AB1157) | + | + | − | + | 1 |
| recBrecC (JC5519) | − | + | − | + | 3 |
| sbcB (JC11451) | + | − | − | + | 1 |
| recBrecCsbcB (JC7623) | − | − | − | + | ND† |
| sbcA (JC11445) | + | + | + | + | 1 |
| recBrecCsbcA (JC5879) | − | + | + | + | 32 |
| recAsbcA (JC15503) | + | + | + | − | 0·02 |
| recArecBrecCsbcA (JC9604) | − | + | + | − | 33 |

\* Relative plasmid recombinant frequencies were calculated from results by Fishel, James and Kolodner (1981), Laban and Cohen (1981), Cohen and Laban (1983) and unpublished results.

† Recombinant frequencies could not be determined in recBrecCsbcB mutants due to the poor maintenance of plasmid in this genetic background. Plasmid instability appears to be due to a recombination related process, since recA, recJ and recF mutations restore plasmid stability in these mutants (Ream, Crisona and Clark, 1978).

substrate, their effect on plasmid recombination frequency must imply that plasmid-DNA ends are available in the cell, and that these ends are active in recombination. A role for DNA ends in recombination in *recBrecCsbcA* and in *recBrecCsbcB* cells is suggested also by the finding that linearized plasmid dimers are more active as intramolecular recombination substrates in these mutants than circular dimers, and that ends of linear substrates are recombinogenic (Symington, Morrison and Kolodner, 1986; Luisi-Deluca and Kolodner, unpublished results).

*In vivo*, circular DNA molecules may yield DNA ends either by endonucleolytic digestion or by a rolling-circle type of replication. We have demonstrated that in certain genetic backgrounds, plasmid mode of replication is diverted from θ-type mechanism to rolling-circle replication (Cohen and Clark, 1986), and that mutual dependence exists between the latter mode of replication and recombination by the RecE, RecF and Red recombination pathways (Nussbaum and Cohen, 1988).

### Synthesis of plasmid linear multimers

Plasmid linear multimers (PLM) were first observed in *recBrecCsbcB* cells (Cohen and Clark, 1986). In an attempt to determine the reason for the instability of ColE1-type plasmids in these cells, the distribution of plasmid molecular species in total DNA preparations was analysed by the Southern hybridization procedure (Southern, 1975). Two electrophoretic bands, hybridizable to plasmid DNA, were observed in DNA preparations of *recBrecCsbcB* mutants but not in preparations of wild-type cells. One co-migrated with chromosomal DNA, while the other was non-migratory. Plasmid DNA in the former band was sensitive to RecBCD nuclease and yielded a 'ladder' of linear plasmid oligomers upon partial hydrolysis by restriction endonucleases that have unique sites on the plasmid. These findings, together with electron microscopic examination, lead to the conclusion that this band consists primarily of plasmid linear multimers (Cohen and Clark, 1986). Samples of the non-migratory DNA were eluted from the gel

and subjected to analysis by electron microscopy. Results indicated that this
band consisted of highly branched molecular structures and of single branched
circles (σ-shaped molecules) (*Figure 21.1*). Length measurement of several
molecules revealed that in most σ-shaped molecules the circle domain was of
one plasmid unit length. The length of the linear domain varied, but in most
molecules it was more than five plasmid unit lengths. The identification of
linear plasmid multimers and of σ-shaped molecules in *recBrecCsbcB* cells
suggested that inhibition or elimination of RecBCD nuclease and exonuclease I
allows plasmid replication by a rolling-circle mechanism to yield plasmid linear
multimers. Further studies have demonstrated that this mode of plasmid
replication is active also in *recBrecCsbcA* cells. It is active also in *recBrecC* or in
*sbcB* cells following expression of λ *red* activities (Maor, 1988).

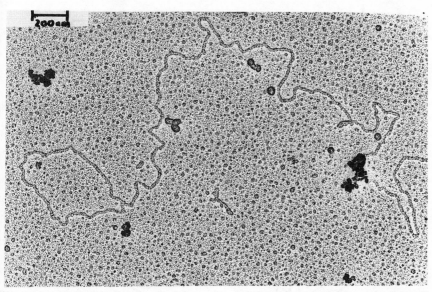

**Figure 21.1** Rolling-circle replication intermediates of plasmids expressing λ *gam* in *sbcB* cells.
Total cellular DNA from *sbcB* mutants harbouring plasmids expressing λ *gam* was subjected to
agarose gel electrophoresis. Non-migratory DNA was eluted from the agarose gel, spread by the
Kleinschmidt technique (1968) and visualized in the electron microscope.

## The dependence of plasmid recombination on replication

Genetic analysis of PLM synthesis and plasmid recombination revealed a
striking similarity between the conditions that divert plasmid mode of
replication from θ to rolling-circle mechanism and the conditions that facilitate
recombination by the RecE, RecF and Red recombination pathways. Both
plasmid recombination and PLM synthesis are enhanced by *red* functions in
*recBrecC* and in *sbcB* mutants (Maor, 1988; Nussbaum and Cohen, 1988).
These two activities depend on λ *gam* activity, which inhibits RecBCD nuclease
(Karu *et al.*, 1975), in *sbcA* and *sbcB* mutants (Cohen and Clark, 1986;
Nussbaum and Cohen, 1988; Cohen and Silberstein, unpublished). Neither

*gam* nor *red* expression affect recombination activity or PLM synthesis in RecBCD$^+$ExoI$^+$ cells (Nussbaum and Cohen, 1988; Maor, 1988). When induced by Gam, both recombination and PLM synthesis are *rec*A-dependent and when induced by Red both are *rec*A-independent (Cohen and Clark, 1986; Maor, 1988; Nussbaum and Cohen, 1988).

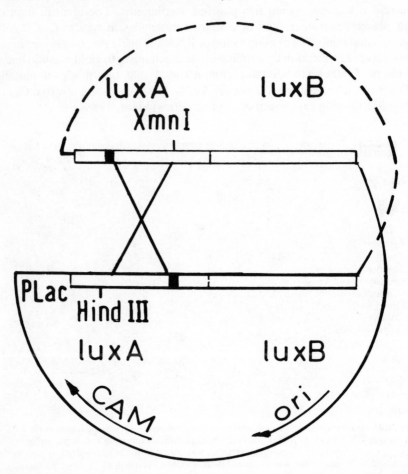

**Figure 21.2**   A plasmid substrate for the bioluminescence intramolecular recombination assay (pAC604). Homology is indicated by parallel lines; relevant restriction sites are indicated and mutations are marked by heavy vertical lines; the broken line indicates linkage.

The close correlation between the conditions that facilitate plasmid recombination by the RecE, RecF and Red pathways and the conditions that divert the plasmid mode of replication from θ to rolling circle, suggest a role for the latter type of replication in plasmid recombination by these pathways. Specifically, we propose that ends of plasmid linear multimers or intermediates of plasmid rolling-circle replication serve as substrates for a double-strand break–repair (DSBR) type of recombination by the RecE, RecF and Red

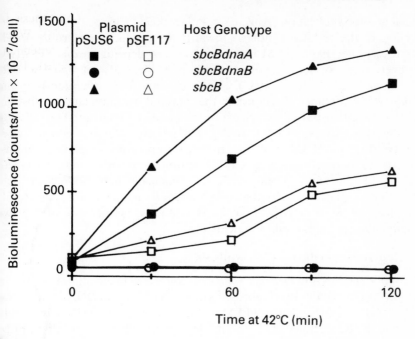

**Figure 21.3**    The effect of *dnaA46* and *dnaB558* mutations on Red- and Gam-mediated plasmid recombination. Cells of the indicated genotype harbouring pAC604 (*Figure 21.2*) and either pSJS6 (Sandler, 1985), which expresses *red* from $p_L p_R$ promoters under $cI^{857}$ repressor control, or pSF117, which expresses *gam* under $cI^{857}$ repressor control (Friedman and Hays, 1986), were transferred from 28°C to 42°C for the indicated period of time. Bioluminescence was measured by a liquid scintillation spectrometer as described by Nussbaum and Cohen (1988) and is presented as counts per minute.

pathways. It follows from this proposal that plasmid recombination by these pathways should depend on replication. To test this prediction the effect of thermal inactivation of temperature-sensitive *dnaA* and *dnaB* products on Red- and Gam-mediated plasmid recombination in *sbcB* mutants was investigated.

Recombination activity is commonly assayed by scoring viable recombinants. Since viability depends on DNA synthesis, such an assay may not be used for determining the role of DNA replication in recombination. To overcome this problem, a plasmid recombination assay system, which determines recombination activity by measuring expression of transcribable recombination products, was developed. The assay substrate is a plasmid, carrying a tandem duplication of *Vibrio fischeri luxA* bioluminescence gene. Each repeat is mutated at a different restriction endonuclease site (*Figure 21.2*). An intramolecular recombination event yields a functional *luxA* gene, the activity of which is conveniently measured by determination of light intensity. This assay system and controllable expression of λ *red* and *gam* genes from *E. coli* plasmids allow the investigation of the dependence of plasmid recombination in *sbcB* mutants on DNA synthesis (*Figure 21.3*). Thermal inactivation of *dnaA^{ts}* product leads to substantial reduction in the rate of normal plasmid replication (Abe, 1980; Polaczek and Ciesla, 1983) and to the direction of the residual synthesis towards the production of rolling-circle structures (Abe, 1980). PLM synthesis does not depend on *dnaA* activity However, like normal plasmid replication, it depends on *dnaB* activity (Silberstein and Cohen, 1987). Cultures of *sbcB*, *sbcBdnaA46* and *sbcBdnaB558* mutants, harbouring the plasmid recombination substrate pAC604 and either pSF117 which expresses *gam* (Freidman and Hays, 1986) or pSJS6, which expresses *red* (Sandler, 1985), both under $cI^{857}$ control, were transferred from 28°C to 42°C. In the temperature-sensitive mutants temperature shift-up derepresses $cI^{857}$-controlled activities and also inacti- vates *dnaA* or *dnaB* products. Results indicate that both *gam*- and *red*-mediated plasmid recombination in *sbcB* mutants are completely dependent on *dnaB* activity. Like PLM synthesis, neither one of the two recombination systems is *dnaA* dependent.

### The role of recombination in PLM synthesis

Most of plasmid DNA in *recBrecCsbcB* cells consists of linear multimers, but in *recArecBrecCsbcB* cells PLM represents only 1% of plasmid DNA (Cohen and Clark, 1986). The dependence of PLM synthesis on *recA* activity indicates a role for one of the RecA functions in this mode of plasmid DNA replication. PLM synthesis may depend on RecA-mediated recombination. However, RecA may also be involved in this mode of plasmid replication as a regulatory protein, or in stabilizing replication intermediates. To further investigate the role of homologous recombination in PLM synthesis, the effects of *recF* and *recJ* mutations and of λ *bet* activity on PLM synthesis were investigated. *gam* expression was derepressed in *sbcB*, *recAsbcBrecFsbcB* and *recJsbcB* mutants harbouring pSF117 by thermal inactivation of $cI^{857}$ repressor and the effect of *gam* expression on the ratio of PLM to total plasmid DNA was determined. Results (*Figure 21.4*) indicate that *recA*, *recF* and *recJ* activities are involved in Gam-mediated PLM synthesis in *sbcB* cells.

β protein is one of the two λ *red* products. It is a helix-destabilizing protein which can also promote one type of homologous pairing reaction—the annealing of complementary single-strand DNA (Kmiec and Holloman, 1981; Muniyappa and Radding, 1986). RecA, on the other hand, catalyses two types of homologous pairing reactions: single-strand DNA annealing and invasion of duplex DNA by a homologous single strand (Weinstock, McEntee and Lehman, 1979; Radding, 1982).

The independence of Red-mediated PLM synthesis in *sbcB* mutants of *recA* activity suggests that, in this system, *bet* protein may catalyse the homologous pairing reaction (Maor, 1988). In such a case *bet* activity should suppress *recA* mutations in Gam-mediated PLM synthesis in *sbcB* mutants. To test this prediction, cultures of *recAsbcB* cells harbouring pIB507, which expresses *gam* and *bet* under $cI^{857}$ repressor control, were transferred from 28°C to 42°C, and the effect of *gam* and *bet* expression on the distribution of plasmid molecular species was determined. Control cultures were of *recAsbcB* cells harbouring plasmids which conditionally express *gam* (pSF117) or *bet* (pIB509) alone (*Figure 21.5*). PLM synthesis is observed in *recAsbcB* cells following *gam* and

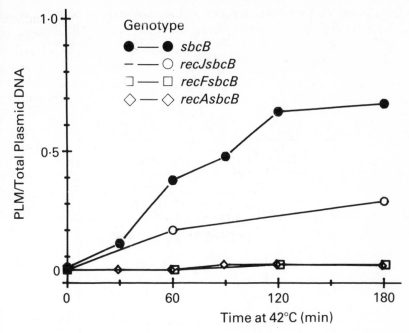

**Figure 21.4** The effect of *recA*, *recF* and *recJ* mutations on accumulation of plasmid linear multimers in *sbcB* cells. Cells of the indicated genotypes, harbouring pSF117, were transferred from 28°C to 42°C for the indicated period of time. Total DNA preparations were subjected to Southern hybridization analysis, using plasmid DNA as a probe. The ratio of PLM to total plasmid DNA monomers was determined by microdensitometry (Silberstein and Cohen, 1987).

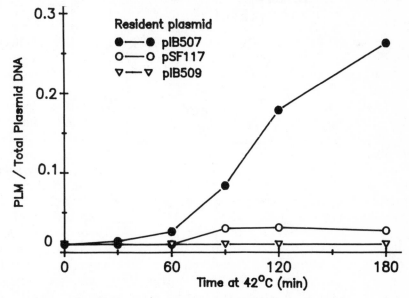

**Figure 21.5** Suppression of RecA deficiency in Gam-mediated PLM synthesis by β protein activity. *recAsbcB* cells harbouring plasmids which express λ functions under $cI^{857}$ temperature-sensitive repressor control were transferred from 28°C to 42°C and the effect of λ genes expression on the ratio of PLM to total plasmid DNA was determined. pIB507 expresses *gam* and *bet*. pIB509 expresses *bet* and pSF117 expresses *gam*.

*bet* expression. This synthesis depends on the expression of both λ function since it is not observed in cells harbouring either pSF117 or pIB509 alone.

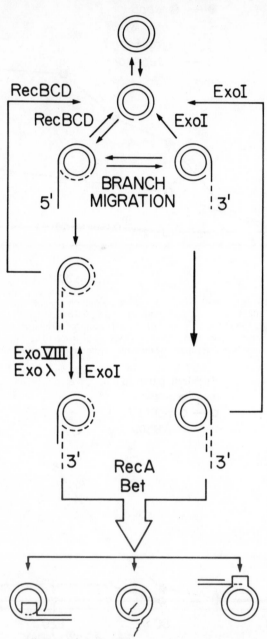

**Figure 21.6** Relationship of plasmid replication and recombination. The proposed role of RecBCD nuclease (RecBCD), exonuclease I (ExoI), λ *red* exonuclease (Exo λ), exonuclease VIII (Exo VIII), RecA and β protein (Bet) in controlling plasmid mode of replication and recombination is presented. A 3′ single-strand end of a rolling-circle structure in RecBCD⁻ExoI⁻, RecBCD⁻ExoVIII⁺, or in RecBCD⁻Red⁺ cells, may serve as a substrate for a β protein or RecA-mediated recombination leading to recombinant formation and PLM synthesis.

## Conclusion: Relationship between plasmid recombination and mode of replication

Results presented above and elsewhere (Cohen and Clark, 1986; Silbertstein and Cohen, 1987; Nussbaum and Cohen, 1988) indicate mutual dependence of plasmid recombination by the RecE, RecF and Red pathways and PLM synthesis. The genetic and physiological requirements of the two activities are similar. Plasmid recombination by these pathways depends on *dnaB* activity, and PLM synthesis depends on several functions which are normally involved in recombination. To rationalize these findings we present a hypothesis which relates the plasmid mode of replication to recombination (*Figure 21.6*). Rolling-circle replication by circular replicons is inhibited in wild-type cells by RecBCD nuclease which degrades single- and double-strand DNA ends. Mutations in *recBrecCrecD* genes or *gam* activity allow rolling-circle-type replication which is initiated at a 3'-OH end of the nicked strand. This recombination-independent mechanism, which is very efficient in linear multimer synthesis by λ phage DNA (Better and Freifelder, 1983) and by λdv replicons (Silberstein and Cohen, unpublished), allows only a low rate of PLM synthesis. However, it yields DNA ends which may be converted to 3' single-strand DNA ends. The 3' single-strand end appears to play a major role in recombination-dependent PLM synthesis, and in recombination by the RecE, RecF and Red pathways. The displaced 5' single-strand end may be converted to a 3' single-strand end by either one of two alternative mechanisms: (1) formation of a double-strand end by lagging-strand synthesis, and then conversion to a 3' single-strand end by a 5' to 3' exonucleolytic digestion, catalysed by exonuclease VIII or by λ *red* exonuclease; (2) the σ-shaped molecule, with a 5' single-strand end may be converted to a σ-shaped molecule with a 3' single-strand end by a process of branch migration. Since a 3' single-strand end is susceptible to degradation by exonuclease I, it would be stabilized by *sbcB* mutations. The 3' single-strand end may serve as a substrate in an intermolecular or intramolecular homologous pairing reaction, catalysed by RecA or by β protein. This reaction is proposed to play a major role both in DSBR type of recombination and in priming PLM synthesis at a 3' OH single-strand end.

The hypothesis presented in *Figure 21.6* is consistent with:

1. The observed inhibitory effect of RecBCD nuclease and exonuclease I on PLM synthesis and on plasmid recombination;
2. The enhancing effect of exonuclease VIII and λ *red* exonuclease on the two systems;
3. The dependence of PLM synthesis on recombination functions;
4. The dependence of plasmid recombination by the RecE, RecF and Red pathways on concurrent DNA replication; and
5. The demonstrated role of replicon ends in recombination by plasmids and λ DNA by these pathways.

## Acknowledgements

We thank A.J. Clark for stimulating discussions and advice, R. Kolodner for communicating results before publication, J.B. Hays, S.J. Sandler and A.J. Clark for plasmids and bacterial strains, and A. Maschler for assistance in preparing this manuscript.

This investigation was supported by the US–Israel Binational Foundation and by The Basic Research Foundation of The Israel Academy of Science and Humanities.

## References

ABE, M. (1980). Replication of ColE1 plasmid deoxyribonucleic acid in thermosensitive *dna*A mutants of *Escherichia coli*. *Journal of Bacteriology* **141**, 1024–1030.

BETTER, M. AND FREIFELDER, D. (1983). Studies on the replication of *Escherichia coli* phage λ DNA. The kinetics of DNA replication and requirements for the generation of rolling circles. *Virology* **126**, 168–182.

COHEN, A. AND CLARK, A.J. (1986). Synthesis of linear plasmid multimers in *Escherichia coli* K-12. *Journal of Bacteriology* **167**, 327–335.

COHEN, A. AND LABAN, A. (1983). Plasmidic recombination in *Escherichia coli* K-12: the role of *rec*F gene function. *Molecular and General Genetics* **189**, 471–474.

EMMERSON, P.T. (1968). Recombination deficient mutants of *Escherichia coli* K-12 that map between *thy*A and *arg*A. *Genetics* **60**, 19–30.

EMMERSON, P.T. AND HOWARD-FLANDERS, P. (1967). Cotransduction with *thy* of a gene required for genetic recombination in *Escherichia coli*. *Journal of Bacteriology* **93**, 1729–1731.

FISHEL, R.A., JAMES, A.A. AND KOLODNER, R. (1981). *rec*A-independent general genetic recombination of plasmids. *Nature* **294**, 184–186.

FRIEDMAN, S.A. AND HAYS, J.B. (1986). Selective inhibition of *Escherichia coli* RecBC activities by plasmid-encoded *gam*S functions of phage lambda. *Gene* **43**, 255–263.

KARU, A., SAKAKI, Y., ECHOLS, H. AND LINN, S. (1975). The protein *gam* specified by bacteriophage λ: Structure and inhibitory activity for *rec*BC enzyme of *Escherichia coli*. *Journal of Biological Chemistry* **250**, 7377–7387.

KLEINESCHMIDT, A. (1968). Monolayer techniques in electron microscopy of nucleic acid molecules. In *Methods in Enzymology* (L. Grossman and K. Moldave, Eds), pp. 361–377. Academic Press, New York.

KMIEC, E. AND HOLLOMAN, W.K. (1981). Beta protein of bacteriophage lambda promotes renaturation of DNA. *Journal of Biological Chemistry* **256**, 12636–12639.

KUSHNER, S.R., NAGAISHI, H. AND CLARK, A.J. (1974). Isolation of exonuclease VIII: the enzyme associated with the *sbc*A indirect suppressor. *Proceedings of the National Academy of Science of the United States of America* **71**, 3593–3597.

LABAN, A. AND COHEN, A. (1981). Interplasmidic and intraplasmidic recombination in *Escherichia coli* K-12. *Molecular and General Genetics* **184**, 200–207.

LEHMAN, I.R. AND NUSSBAUM, A.L. (1964). The deoxyribonucleases of *Escherichia coli*. V. On the specificity of exonuclease I (phosphodiesterase). *Journal of Biological Chemistry* **239**, 2628–2636.

MAOR, S. (1988). M.Sc. thesis, The Hebrew University of Jerusalem, Israel.

MUNIYAPPA, K. AND RADDING, C.M. (1986). The homologous recombination system of phage lambda. Pairing activities of beta protein. *Journal of Biological Chemistry* **261**, 7472–7478.

NUSSBAUM, A. AND COHEN, A. (1988). The use of bioluminescence gene reporter for the investigation of Red-dependent and Gam-dependent plasmid recombination in *Escherichia coli* K-12. *Journal of Molecular Biology* **203**, 391–402.

POLACZEK, P. AND CIESLA, Z. (1983). Rifampicine-induced replication of the plasmid pBR322 in *Escherichia coli* strains carrying *dna*A mutations. *Molecular and General Genetics* **190**, 326–330.

ADDING, C.M. (1982). Homologous pairing and strand exchange in genetic recombination. *Annual Review of Genetics* **16**, 405–437.

EAM, L.W., CRISONA, N.Y. AND CLARK, A.J. (1978). ColE1 plasmid stability in *exoI⁻exoV⁻* strains of *Escherichia coli* K-12. In *Microbiology—1978* (D. Schlessinger, Ed.), pp. 78–80. American Society for Microbiology, Washington, DC.

ANDLER, S.J. (1985). Ph.D. Thesis, The University of California, Berkeley, California.

ILBERSTEIN, Z. AND COHEN, A. (1987). Synthesis of linear multimers of *ori*C and pBR322 derivatives in *Escherichia coli* K-12: Role of recombination and replication functions. *Journal of Bacteriology* **169**, 3131–3137.

OUTHERN, E.M. (1975). Detection of specific sequences among DNA fragments separated by gel electrophoresis. *Journal of Molecular Biology* **98**, 503–517.

YMINGTON, L.S., MORRISON, P. AND KOLODNER, R. (1986). Intramolecular recombination of linear DNA catalyzed by the *Escherichia coli* RecE recombination pathway. *Journal of Molecular Biology* **186**, 515–525.

EINSTOCK, G.M., MCENTEE, K. AND LEHMAN, I.R. (1979). ATP-dependent renaturation of DNA catalyzed by the *rec*A protein of *E. coli*. *Proceedings of the National Academy of Science of the United States of America* **76**, 126–130.

22

# Marker-Rescue of *Bacillus subtilis* Phage 2C Mutants by Cloned Viral DNA: Unique Features of the Terminal Redundancies of the Phage Genome

I. KISS-BLÜMEL* AND P. HOET

*Microbiology and Genetics Unit, University of Louvain Medical School, ICP-UCL 7449, 75 Avenue Hippocrate, 1200 Brussels, Belgium*

## Introduction

Phage 2C causes a lytic infection of *Bacillus subtilis*. Its DNA (100 MDa) contains hydroxymethyluracil instead of thymine. This abnormal base is synthesized by viral-encoded enzymes. Large direct repeats (10 MDa) at both ends of the genome were revealed by cross-hybridization of specific restriction fragments (Coene, Hoet and Cocito, 1983). Homologous sequences were found in the related phages SP01, SP82 and φe (Hoet, Coene and Cocito, 1983).

Autonomous replication of plasmids was provided by viral sequences, originating from the terminal redundancies and from unique sequences close to the right end of the genome (Lannoy, Hoet and Cocito, 1985). During infection by the related phage SP01, most early functions are carried by the terminal repeat sequences (Curran and Stewart, 1985; Perkus and Shub, 1985). A cascade-type of regulation might control the temporal expression of early, middle and late SP01 genes (Losick and Pero, 1981; Geiduschek and Ito, 1982).

This chapter describes work in which molecular cloning techniques were applied in order to relate the genetic map of phage 2C (Kiss-Blümel, 1987) with the physical structure of its genome. This approach will provide the tools to study phage genes and their products, only a few of which have been characterized in SP01 (Yehle and Ganesan, 1973; Constanzo and Pero, 1983; Perkus and Shub, 1985; Greene *et al.*, 1986).

In addition, exchanges between plasmid-borne phage sequences and infecting phage DNA during the lytic cycle were analysed, and suggest the involvement of different recombinational systems.

* Present address: Department of Biochemistry, Medical School, University of Valparaiso, Chile.

*Genetic Transformation and Expression*
© Intercept Ltd, PO Box 716, Andover, Hants, SP10 1YG, UK

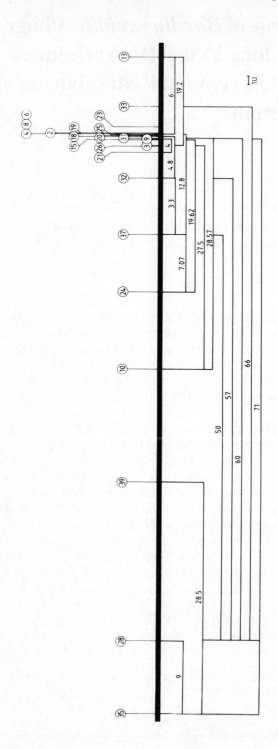

**Figure 22.1**  Genetic map of phage 2C. Thermosensitive mutants (encircled numbers) on top. Below, recombination frequencies between mutants.

**Materials and methods**

Phage 2C infection of *B. subtilis*, phage purification and titration have been described (Coene, Hoet and Cocito, 1983).

Thermosensitive phage mutants were isolated after nitrous acid, nitroso-guanidine or hydroxylamine treatment (Meynell and Meynell, 1970).

Plasmid extraction, cloning and hybridizations were performed according to established procedures (Southern, 1975; Maniatis, Fritsch and Sambrook, 1982).

**Results**

GENETIC MAP OF PHAGE 2C

Thermosensitive mutants were characterized by a decrease of their infectious titre ($10^{-4}$ to $10^{-7}$) at the non-permissive temperature ($47^{\circ}$C).

The distance between mutations carried by two phage genomes, leading to wild-type progeny, was proportional to the frequency of recombination between them. Recombination frequencies were thus determined after pairwise infection of *B. subtilis* by 28 independently isolated mutants. These recombination frequencies, spanning 71 recombination units, were used in an originally designed computer program in order to derive a precise genetic map. (Kiss-Blümel, 1987).

It can be seen (*Figure 22.1*) that the mutations were evenly distributed, except for a clustering towards the right end of the genetic map. In order to ascertain whether the isolated mutants did indeed cover the whole of the genome, the correspondence of the genetic and physical map of phage 2C was studied by recombination of mutated genes with wild-type sequences of known location, carried by plasmids.

SHOTGUN CLONING OF PHAGE 2C-DNA AND MAPPING OF PLASMID-BORNE VIRAL FRAGMENTS

Plasmid pHV33 (Ehrlich, 1978), with a unique *Bam*HI site, expresses chloramphenicol resistance (Cm$^r$) in *B. subtilis*. 2C-DNA, partially restricted with *Sau*3AI, yields fragments of 100–1000 bp, whose ends were compatible with the *Bam*HI-generated cohesive ends on the vector. After ligation, transformants of *B. subtilis* SB202 were selected on Cm plates (10 µg ml$^{-1}$).

Out of 1000 transformants, 10 colonies hybridizing with nick-translated $^{32}$P-labelled 2C-DNA, were chosen for further study. Two recombinant clones (4 and 16) had a molecular mass in excess (by 3·6 and 0·3 MDa, respectively) of the cloning vector. The other recombinant plasmids were smaller than pHV33, having deleted vector sequences while inserting viral sequences of unknown size.

In order to locate cloned fragments on the available restriction map of phage 2C (Hoet, Coene and Cocito, 1983; Lannoy, Hoet and Cocito, 1985), recombinant plasmids were extracted, $^{32}$P-labelled by nick-translation and hybridized to restricted 2C-DNA (*Eco*RI, *Sal*I + *Hae*III, *Bgl*II), previously transferred to nitrocellulose membranes (Southern, 1975).

Most recombinant plasmids gave similar hybridization patterns. *Figure 22.2B* summarizes the hybridization data and allows the localization of the cloned fragments on the available restriction map of 2C-DNA (*Figure 22.2A*). *Figure 22.2C* emphasizes the extent of the terminal redundancy (10 kbp), and the specific hybridization pattern of the clones 12, 13, 14 and 16: they hybridized to the overall structure of the right terminal redundancy, but recognized only the left part of the homologous region on the left end of the genome (open bars). We concluded that these clones contained unique sequences that originated from the right terminal redundancy.

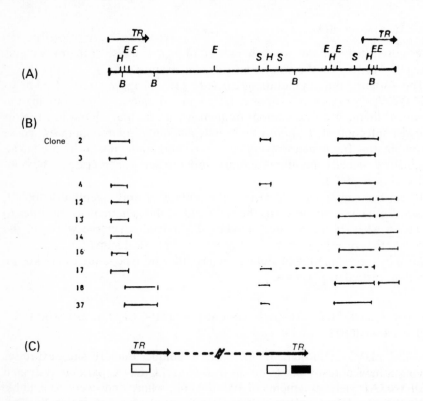

**Figure 22.2** Location of cloned fragments on the 2C restriction map. (A) Restriction map of phage 2C-DNA. E, *Eco*RI; S, *Sal*I; B, *Bgl*II; TR, terminal redundancy. (B) Hybridization pattern of pHV33–2C recombinant plasmids. (C) Hybridization (indicated by boxes) of clones 12, 13, 14 and 16 with left and right terminal redundancies (TR), indicated by arrows.

GENETIC RECOMBINATION BETWEEN MUTATED PHAGES AND CLONED FRAGMENTS OF 2C-DNA

*B. subtilis* strains, containing one of the pHV33 recombinant plasmids (described in the previous section) were each infected at permissive temperature by the 39 thermosensitive phage mutants. Lysates were titrated at permissive (37°C) and non-permissive (47°C) temperatures. Control experiments consisted of parallel infections of *B. subtilis* bearing native pHV33, subsequently titrated at both temperatures (*Table 22.1*). In comparison with these control values, an increase in the proportion of wild-type phages will result from recombinational integration of plasmid-borne wild-type sequences in a mutated phage genome. This was the case for a limited number of the 390 combinations. As reported in *Table 22.1* (for a few chosen combinations) mutant 9 was rescued by three recombinant clones, which were thus assumed to carry the corresponding viral sequences. Recombinant plasmids 4 and 37, in addition, provided wild-type sequences to mutant 10. These plasmids were not identical, however, since they rescued different mutants (mutants 3, 4 and 15).

**Table 22.1**   Plating efficiency of 2C thermosensitive mutants on plasmid-carrying *B. subtilis*

| 2C strain | pHV33 (cloning vector) | Plating efficiency: $\dfrac{\text{titre at } 47°C}{\text{titre at } 37°C}$ Recombinant pHV33–2C clones | | |
| | | 3 | 4 | 37 |
|---|---|---|---|---|
| wild type | 0·5 | 0·5 | 0·5 | 0·5 |
| TS   3 | $1\cdot5 \times 10^{-7}$ | | $2\cdot2 \times 10^{-4}$ | |
| 4 | $1\cdot0 \times 10^{-7}$ | | $1\cdot6 \times 10^{-4}$ | |
| 9 | $6\cdot0 \times 10^{-6}$ | $2\cdot4 \times 10^{-3}$ | $9\cdot2 \times 10^{-4}$ | $2\cdot6 \times 10^{-4}$ |
| 10 | $2\cdot0 \times 10^{-8}$ | | $1\cdot2 \times 10^{-2}$ | $6\cdot5 \times 10^{-4}$ |
| 15 | $5\cdot2 \times 10^{-6}$ | | | $2\cdot8 \times 10^{-4}$ |

*B. subtilis* SB202 ($5 \times 10^8$ cells/ml), carrying pHV33 or pHV33–2C recombinant plasmids, were infected at 37°C by 2C (wild type or thermosensitive mutant) at a multiplicity of 6. Lysates were titrated at 37°C and 47°C.

## COLINEARITY OF THE GENETIC AND RESTRICTION MAPS OF PHAGE 2C

Having at our disposal the location of plasmid-borne restriction fragments, which could recombine with mutated genomes, these data could be compared with the genetic map. Mutant 10, located in the middle of the genetic map, recombined with hybrid plasmids 2, 4 and 37 (*Table 22.1*), all three of which contained sequences hybridizing to the central part of the genome (*Figure 22.2*). In addition, mutants 3, 4 and 15 are close on the genetic map. Marker-rescue of these mutants was shown to occur with recombinant plasmids 4 and 37 (*Table 22.1*), which both hybridized to the same restriction fragments at the right end of the genome (*Figure 22.2*). This analysis allowed us to align the physical and genetic maps of phage 2C (*Figure 22.3*). According to these data, mutants 13 and 33 have a unique location within the right terminal redundancy. This suggests that both ends of the genome, displaying overall homologies, might contain unique sequences.

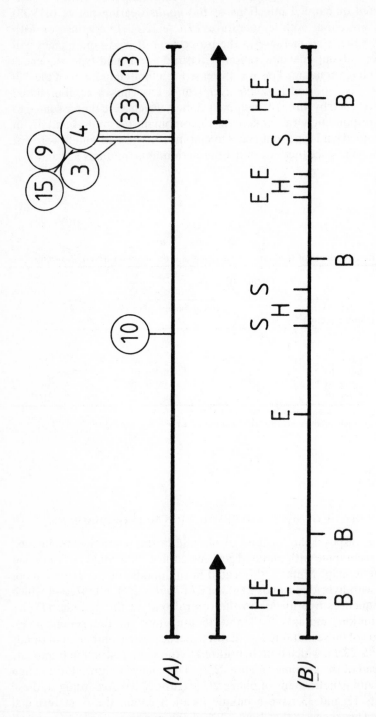

**Figure 22.3**  Integration of physical and genetic maps of phage 2C. (A)  Genetic location of mutants recombining with hybrid pHV33–2C plasmids (*Table 22.1* and *Figure 22.2*). Numbers in circles correspond to the thermosensitive mutants. (B)  Restriction map of phage 2C. H, *Hae*III; E, *Eco*RI; B, *Bgl*II; S, *Sal*I; →, terminal redundancy.

MARKER-RESCUE OF GENETIC MUTATIONS DURING THE LYTIC CYCLE

Since recombinations occurred between phage and plasmid sequences, the fate of the genetic marker was followed during the lytic cycle. *B. subtilis*, harbouring recombinant plasmids 4 and 37, was infected at 37°C by thermosensitive mutants, as indicated in *Figure 22.4*. Samples, taken at different times after infection, were treated with lysozyme and subsequently titrated at 37°C and 47°C. The results (*Figure 22.4*) showed three distinct patterns:

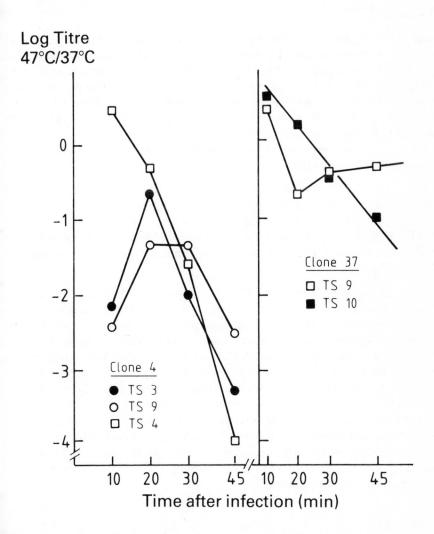

**Figure 22.4** Marker-rescue as a function of time after infection. *B. subtilis* SB202, carrying pHV33–2C recombinant plasmids 4 and 37, was infected at 37°C by thermosensitive mutants (TS) of phage 2C, as indicated (multiplicity of infection = 10). At different times after infection, samples were taken, centrifuged, resuspended in the presence of lysozyme (10 min, 37°C) and titrated at 37°C and 47°C.

1. The titre of wild-type recombinants decreased steadily during the infectious cycle (clone 4, infected by mutant 9; clone 37 infected by mutant 10);
2. The titre of wild-type recombinants increased during the eclipse phase and decreased during maturation and lysis of the host cell (clone 4, infected by mutants 3 and 4);
3. Biphasic pattern, with a decrease of wild-type recombinants during the first half of the lytic cycle, followed by a plateau throughout the second part of the cycle.

## Discussion

Fragments of phage 2C have been cloned in *B. subtilis* by using plasmid pHV33. The cloned sequences originated from three limited regions of the viral genome (*Figure 22.2*): (1) the terminal redundancy; (2) unique sequences adjacent to the right terminal redundancy; and (3) the central portion of the genome. These sequences might confer a selective advantage to the cloning plasmid (e.g. segregational stability); this could explain the bias of the cloning procedure towards specific viral sequences.

Two sets of data suggested that unique sequences were present in the right terminal redundancy of 2C:

1. Shotgun cloning resulted in the insertion of viral sequences that hybridized to the right terminal redundancy, but not to the homologous sequences at the left end of the genome (*Figure 22.2C*).
2. By aligning the physical and genetic map of phage 2C, two mutants were located uniquely in the right terminal redundancy (*Figure 22.3*; mutants 33 and 13).

Data in *Figure 22.4* illustrate the recombination of hybrid plasmids with infecting phages as a function of the lytic cycle. Recombination may occur at the beginning of the lytic infection, suggesting the involvement of the host recombinational system. In other combinations, recombination increased during maturation. This pattern could depend on viral-coded recombinational enzymes (distinct from the host enzymes) shown to appear after viral DNA synthesis had started (10 min after infection) (Hoet and Cocito, 1982). In only one combination (clone 37, infected by TS mutant 10) were the wild-type recombinants shown to be stably established in the vegetative progeny pool. In all other combinations, the proportion of wild-type recombinants dropped in the second half of the lytic cycle, suggesting that plasmid replication was inhibited during phage infection, thus limiting the integration of wild-type sequences in the phage genome.

## References

Coene, M., Hoet, P. and Cocito, C. (1983). Physical map of virus 2C-DNA: evidence for the existence of large redundant ends. *European Journal of Biochemistry* **132**, 69–75.
Constanzo, M. and Pero, J. (1983). Structure of a *Bacillus subtilis* bacteriophage

SP01 gene encoding a RNA polymerase factor. *Proceedings of the National Academy of Sciences of the United States of America* **80**, 1236–1240.

CURRAN, J.F. AND STEWART, C.R. (1985). Cloning and mapping of the SP01 genome. *Virology* **142**, 78–97.

EHRLICH, S.D. (1978). DNA cloning in *Bacillus subtilis*. *Proceedings of the National Academy of Sciences of the United States of America* **75**, 1433–1436.

GEIDUSCHEK, E.P. AND ITO, J. (1982). Regulatory mechanisms in the development of lytic bacteriophages in *Bacillus subtilis*. In *The Molecular Biology of the Bacilli* (D.A. Dubnau, Ed.), pp. 230–240. Academic Press, New York.

GREENE, J.R., MORRISSEY, L.M., FOSTER, L.M. AND GEIDUSCHEK, E.P. (1986). DNA binding by the bacteriophage SP01-encoded type II DNA-binding protein, transcription factor 1. Formation of nested complexes at a selective binding site. *Journal of Biological Chemistry* **261**, 12820–12827.

HOET, P. AND COCITO, C. (1982). Replication and recombination of the viral genome during lytic infection of *Bacillus subtilis* by phage 2C. In *Genetic Exchange* (M. Dekker, Ed.), pp. 275–282. Academic Press, New York.

HOET, P., COENE, M. AND COCITO, C.M. (1983). Comparison of the physical map and redundant ends of the chromosome of viruses 2C, SP01, SP82 and φe. *European Journal of Biochemistry* **132**, 63–67.

KISS-BLÜMEL, J. (1987). Carte génétique et clonage de fragments génomiques du virus 2C de *Bacillus subtilis*. Ph.D. Thesis, University of Louvain, Louvain-La-Neuve.

LANNOY, N., HOET, P. AND COCITO, C. (1985). Cloning of DNA segments of phage 2C, which allows autonomous plasmid replication in *Bacillus subtilis*. *European Journal of Biochemistry* **152**, 137–142.

LOSICK, R. AND PERO, J. (1981). Cascades of sigma factors. *Cell* **25**, 582–584.

MANIATIS, T., FRITSCH, E.F. AND SAMBROOK, J. (1982). *Molecular cloning: a laboratory manual*. Cold Spring Harbour Laboratory, New York.

MEYNELL, G.G. AND MEYNELL, E. (1970). *Theory and practice in experimental bacteriology*. Cambridge University Press, Cambridge.

PERKUS, M.E. AND SHUB, D.A. (1985). Mapping the genes in the terminal redundancy of bacteriophage SP01 with restriction endonucleases. *Journal of Virology* **56**, 40–48.

SOUTHERN, E.M. (1975). Detection of specific sequences among DNA fragments separated by gel electrophoresis. *Journal of Molecular Biology* **98**, 503–517.

YEHLE, C.O. AND GANESAN, A.T. (1973). Deoxyribonucleic acid synthesis in bacteriophage SP01-infected *B. subtilis*. *Journal of Biological Chemistry* **248**, 7456–7463.

# 23
# Stable Chromosomal Gene Amplification in *Bacillus*

J.C. VAN DER LAAN, C.A.G. VAN EEKELEN, G. GERRITSE,
R.A.C. VAN DER HOEK, J.F. FLINTERMAN, L.J.S.M. MULLENERS
AND W.J. QUAX

*Royal Gist-brocades N.V., Research and Development, PO Box 1, 2600 MA Delft, The Netherlands*

## Introduction

Bacilli have been used widely for the production of industrially important enzymes such as α-amylase (EC 3.2.1.1.), neutral protease (EC 3.4.24.4.) and alkaline or serine proteases (EC 3.4.21.14.) (Debabov, 1982). Improving the production of *Bacillus* enzymes can be achieved both by classical genetic techniques and by modern molecular biological techniques. In the latter case, one approach is to increase the copy number of the gene in question. Amplification is primarily achieved by inserting the gene into a multicopy plasmid. However, a significant problem with this approach has been the instability of the plasmid, particularly under large-scale production conditions.

More stable ways of gene amplification can be obtained by chromosomal integration (Jannière *et al.*, 1985). The serine protease gene of an alcalophilic *Bacillus* strain (van Eekelen *et al.*, 1987) and the thermostable α-amylase gene of *B. licheniformis* (Sanders *et al.*, 1985) have been cloned and characterized. These genes have been used to increase enzyme production, using gene amplification in the original producer strain. When introduced on a multicopy plasmid, the recombinant strains were unstable: under production conditions plasmid segregation occurred. More stable gene amplification was obtained by chromosomal integration. This was achieved in both strains by homologous recombination, resulting in strains with two tandemly arranged genes and, by illegitimate recombination, resulting in strains with a second copy of the gene in question not adjacent to the originally present gene. Stability and production of both types of gene amplification were studied.

*Genetic Transformation and Expression*
© Intercept Ltd, PO Box 716, Andover, Hants, SP10 1YG, UK

## Materials and methods

Integration vectors pMax-4 and pELatB were constructed using the temperature-sensitive origin of replication of pEl94 (Iordanescu *et al.*, 1978). The integration vectors are shown in *Figure 23.1*.

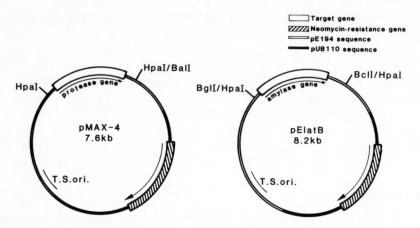

**Figure 23.1**    Structure of the integration vectors pMax-4, containing the serine protease gene of *B. alcalophilis*, and pElatB, containing the α-amylase gene of *B. licheniformis*.

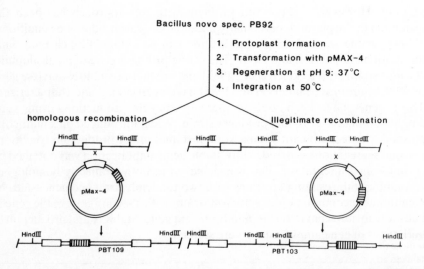

**Figure 23.2**    The strategy used to develop strains containing an additional protease gene in the chromosome. A schematic drawing of the recombinations observed is included. ☐, protease gene;⎯, chromosomal DNA;══, plasmid DNA; ⅢⅢ, neomycin-resistance gene. Integrants were characterized using (*Hin*dIII) restriction-enzyme analysis, as indicated in the drawings.

For both strains, modified transformation procedures, based on the protoplast transformation as described (Chang and Cohen, 1979), were developed. Transformants were isolated and characterized. Selection for integrants was performed by inoculating transformants into a neomycin-containing medium and increasing the temperature to a level such that plasmid replication was prevented. To check whether, and in which way, integration took place, chromosomal DNA maps were made using restriction-enzyme digestions followed by Southern blotting and hybridization. *Figure 23.2* shows the two different types of integration that were observed with pMax-4.

For pElatB a slightly different strategy was chosen. In order to eliminate homologous recombination, a strain with a deleted α-amylase gene was used as depicted in *Figure 23.3*.

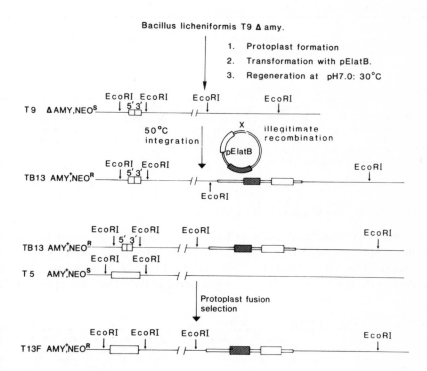

**Figure 23.3** The strategy used to develop a strain with an additional α-amylase gene located at a site distal to the originally present gene. Because a strain containing two α-amylase genes located in a tandem array was already present, a different strategy was chosen. Integration of the additional α-amylase gene was performed in a strain with a deleted α-amylase gene(T9). An α-amylase gene-containing integrant (TB13) was isolated at random. To develop a double gene integrant, strain TB13 was fused (Sanders *et al.*, 1985) to the original wild-type strain T5. ☐, α-amylase gene; ——, chromosomal DNA; ══, plasmid DNA; ▨, neomycin-resistance gene. Integrants were characterized using (*Eco*RI) restriction enzyme analysis as indicated.

Stability of the plasmids under the production conditions of the strains concerned was determined by measuring the percentage of neomycin-resistant colonies after fermentation (Eschweilers or shake flasks). In the case of PBT108 and T13F (random integrants) additional controls were performed to exclude the possibility of deletion of one of the amplified genes without concomitant loss of neomycin resistance.

## Results and conclusions

### STABILITY OF DUPLICATED PROTEASE GENES

The double gene strains PBT109 (tandem) and PBT108 (random) were compared to the wild-type *B. alcalophilis* strain PB92 and to the wild-type strain transformed with plasmid pMAX-4. The relative levels of protease production and stability of the neomycin-resistant phenotype were determined. Results are shown in *Table 23.1*.

**Table 23.1**    Stability of duplicated protease genes

| Strain | % Neo$^r$ cells after fermentation | Relative production of protease* in Eschweiler fermenters |
|---|---|---|
| PB92 control | — | 100% |
| PB92+ pMax-4 | 50 | 105–115% |
| PBT109 | 75–95 | 115–120% |
| PBT108[†] | 100 | 120% |

\*    Protease activity was assayed using dimethyl casein as the substrate.
[†]    100 individual colonies were checked for level of production. After fermentation 100 neomycin-resistant colonies were taken at random and individually tested on their ability to produce protease. All 100 colonies produced protease at a level consistant with the possession of two genes, indicating that no recombination without concomitant loss of neomycin resistance had occurred.
Abbreviation: Neo$^r$, neomycin resistance

### STABILITY OF DUPLICATED α-AMYLASE GENES

The randomly integrated single (TB13) and double (T13F) α-amylase gene strains were compared with T390, a tandemly integrated double α-amylase strain (Sanders *et al.*, 1985). Furthermore, wild-type *B. licheniformis* T5 and wild-type *B. licheniformis* T5 carrying plasmid pGB33 (Sanders *et al.*, 1985)

**Table 23.2**    Stability of duplicated amylase genes

| Strain | % Neo$^r$ cells after fermentation | Relative production of amylase* in shake flasks |
|---|---|---|
| T5 control | — | 100% |
| T5 pGB33 | 0 | 95% |
| TB13 | 100 | 20% |
| T390[†] | 88 | 200% |
| T13F[‡] | 100 | 120% |

\*    Amylase activity was assayed using starch as the substrate. Iodide was used as an indicator.
[†]    T390 is a strain with two tandomly arranged amylase genes originating from pGB33 (Sanders *et al.*, 1985).
[‡]    After fermentation, 20 neomycin-resistant colonies were selected at random and their chromosomal DNA isolated and characterized. All colonies tested contained two amylase genes.
Abbreviation: Neo$^r$, neomycin resistance

were tested. The relative α-amylase production and the stability of the neomycin-resistant phenotype were determined. Results are shown in *Table 23.2*. It can be seen that the randomly integrated strain TB13 displays absolute stability. However, the production level of the double gene strain T13F is not as high as the production level of the tandem double gene strain T390. It is possible that the localization of the second gene copy within the chromosome does not promote an optimal expression in the case of T13F. The low expression level of TB13 is in agreement with this hypothesis.

## Conclusions

All strains with chromosomally amplified genes showed increased production and were more stable than the plasmid-containing strain. Absolute stability was only found with strains containing non-tandem duplications. This method of gene amplification circumvents stability problems often encountered when using plasmids or tandemly arranged genes in the chromosome. Our results show the broad applicability of this method to achieve stable gene amplification.

## Acknowledgements

This work was supported by International Bio-Synthetics, Rijswijk, The Netherlands.

## References

CHANG, S. AND COHEN, S.N. (1979). High frequency transformation of *Bacillus subtilis* protoplasts by plasmid DNA. *Molecular and General Genetics* **168**, 111–115.

DEBABOV, V.G. (1982). The Industrial use of Bacilli. In *The Molecular Biology of the Bacilli* (P.A. Dubnau, Ed.), volume 1, pp. 331–370. Academic Press, New York.

IORDANESCU, S., SURDEANCE, M., LATTA, P.D. AND NOVICK, R. (1978). Incompatibility and molecular relationships between small staphylococcal plasmids carrying the same resistance marker. *Plasmid* **1**, 468–479.

JANNIÈRE, L., NIAUDET, B., PIERRE, E. AND EHRLICH, S.D. (1985). Stable gene amplification in the chromosome of *Bacillus subtilis*. *Gene* **40**, 47–55.

SANDERS, J.P.M., VAN DEN BERG, J.A., ANDREOLI, P.M., VOS, Y.J., VAN EE, J.H. AND MULLENERS, L.J.S.M. (1985). *Molecular Cloning and Expression in Industrial Microorganism Species*. European Patent Application 0134048.

VAN EEKELEN, C.A.G., VAN DER LAAN, J.C., GERRITSE, G., VAN DER HOEK, R.A.C. AND MULLENERS, L.J.S.M. (1987). Stable chromosomal gene amplification in an alcalophilic *Bacillus* strain to increase the production of alcaline protease. In *The Fourth International Conference of Genetics and Biotechnology of Bacilli. 21–24 June 1987, San Diego*, p. 76.

# 24

# *Bacillus thuringiensis kurstaki* Hybrid Endotoxin Genes Generated by *In Vivo* Recombination

TIZIANA CARAMORI*, ALESSANDRA M. ALBERTINI†
AND ALESSANDRO GALIZZI‡

*Dipartimento di Biologia, Università di Trieste, Trieste, Italy, †Facoltà di Agraria, Università di Udine, Udine, Italy and ‡Dipartimento di Genetica e Microbiologia, Università di Pavia, Pavia, Italy*

## Introduction

The entomopathogenic activity of the *Bacillus thuringiensis* parasporal crystal is due to its composition: in the case of the *B. thuringiensis* subspecies specifically active against Lepidopteran larvae, it is composed of 130–160 kDa protoxin polypeptides. Different subspecies, and often individual strains of the same subspecies, produce endotoxins having a characteristic spectrum of insect toxicity (Whiteley and Schnepf, 1986; Andrews *et al.*, 1987).

Cloning and sequencing of the structural genes for the protoxin production from distinct strains of *B. thuringiensis kurstaki* revealed that different related genes are responsible for the synthesis of the large polypeptides. These differences are evident not only among genes from different strains but also among the multiple copies of the protoxin gene in the same strain (Andrews *et al.*, 1987). The *kurstaki* HD-1 Dipel protoxin gene (Schnepf, Wong and Whiteley, 1985) and the *kurstaki* HD-73 protoxin gene (Adang *et al.*, 1985) show an homology of 85% at the primary DNA sequence level. K-1 type and K-73 type crystals show distinct toxic activity against different insect species (Jaquet, Hutter and Luthy, 1987). Optimal alignment of the DNA sequences and of the deduced polypeptide sequences of these two genes and of other *B. thuringiensis* genes reveals that the differences are clustered in the amino-terminal halves of the molecules, i.e. between amino-acid residues 280 and 640 in the case of HD-1 Dipel and HD-73 genes. This region is defined as the hypervariable region, since it shows the maximum variation in other protoxin genes also (Geiser, Schweitzer and Grimm, 1986; Wabiko, Raymond and Bulla, 1986; Andrews *et al.*, 1987).

*Genetic Transformation and Expression*
© Intercept Ltd, PO Box 716, Andover, Hants, SP10 1YG, UK

The clustering of the variable subdomains in these proteins strongly suggests that this region is important in conferring toxic and insect-host range diversity among different *B. thuringiensis* subspecies.

The residual homology of the hypervariable region (in the case of HD-1 Dipel and HD-73 reduced to about 60% at the DNA level) should be enough to promote *in vivo* recombination. A similar approach has been utilized to generate in *Escherichia coli* recombinants between human leucocyte interferon genes (Weber and Weissmann, 1983) and for *Bacillus* α-amylase genes (Rey *et al.*, 1986). In this report we investigate the possibility of generating new hybrid genes and corresponding hybrid polypeptides, with potential different toxic specificity, by *in vivo* recombination between HD-1 Dipel and HD-73 genes.

## Methods

The source of the HD-1 Dipel gene portion was the plasmid pESAC, a derivative of pES1 (ATCC 31995) described by Schnepf and Whiteley (1981). The HD-73 gene portion was derived from pJWK20 plasmid (ATCC 31997) described by Kronstad and Whiteley (1984). pBS19 is an *E. coli–B.subtilis* shuttle vector derived from pBS42 (Wells *et al.*, 1983; Greg and Gray, unpublished).

*Escherichia coli* strains 294 (*endA, thi, pro, hsdR, hsdM, hsm*) and its *recA* derivative were used for transformation following the Hanahan (1985) method of competent-cell preparation. The medium for antibiotic selection (10 μg ml$^{-1}$ for chloramphenicol and 12·5 μg ml$^{-1}$ for tetracycline) was LA (Luria agar). LB (Luria broth) was used in culture growth for plasmid production.

Plasmid DNA preparation was by the alkaline lysis method adapted to larger samples and followed, for sequencing, by a PEG precipitation. Restriction enzyme digestions, ligations and other treatments during plasmid constructions were carried out following the suggested protocols of the enzyme suppliers.

For sequencing, Sequenase was used according to the recommendations of the supplier (USB Corp., Cleveland, Ohio USA). Western blot analysis of stationary-phase cell extracts (5 μl aliquots of culture samples of 10 ml, concentrated 100 ×) resolved by SDS-PAGE electrophoresis was performed with polyclonal antibodies raised against purified crystal proteins of the *B. thuringiensis* HD-73 strain (strain 4D4 of the BGSC, Ohio State University, Ohio, USA).

## Results

### PLASMID CONSTRUCTION

pT is a pBS19 derivative: a 1424 bp *Eco*RI/*Ava*I (blunted in *Ava*I) fragment of pBR322 bearing tetracycline resistance was inserted in pBS19 digested with *Eco*RI and *Sac*I (blunted). pT73 is a pT derivative obtained by inserting in the *Eco*RI site of the pT an *Eco*RI fragment of approximately 5400 bp obtained from pJWK20 (*Figure 24.1*). The fragment comprises the last two-thirds of the HD73 toxin gene, starting from residue 1383 of the sequenced region (Adang *et* *al.*, 1985). pT1 was obtained as follows: pT was digested to completion with *Sma*I, partially with *Bam*HI and ligated to a fragment of approximately 1900 bp derived from pESAC and corresponding to the first portion of the HD-1 Dipel toxin gene from residue 291 to residue 2215 of the sequenced region (Schnepf, Wong and Whiteley, 1985). The fragment was obtained by digestion of pESAC with *Hin*dIII, followed by treatment with Klenow fragment to make it blunted and then by restriction with *Bam*HI.

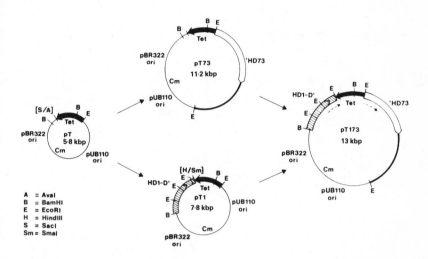

**Figure 24.1**   Construction of pT173 plasmid. pT is a derivative of pBS219 able to express chloramphenicol resistance (Cm) and tetracycline resistance (Tet, heavy black arrow) in *E. coli* and *B. subtilis*. The open box is the HD-73 toxin-coding sequence, starting from residue 1383. The direction of transcription is indicated. The heavy line represents the HD-73 sequences downstream from the toxin gene. The striped box represents the HD-1 Dipel sequence, from residue 291 to residue 2215. The direction of transcription is indicated. The dashed arrows indicate the region of partial homology.

pT173, the plasmid used for the *in vivo* construction of recombinant genes, derived from the insertion in pT73 of the 2500 bp *Bam*HI–*Bam*HI fragment of pT1, comprising the first part of the HD-1 Dipel gene and the last two-thirds of the tetracycline gene. pT73 was completely cleaved with *Bam*HI, thus releasing a fragment of 1200 bp, containing the last two-thirds of the tetracycline gene, and dephosphorylated with pancreatic phosphatase to avoid the re-insertion of the original *Bam*HI fragment (*Figure 24.1*). Tet$^r$ and Cm$^r$ transformants obtained in *E. coli* 294 *recA* strain were examined by plasmid extraction and restriction analysis. Plasmids pT1, pT73 and pT173 were not able to direct the synthesis of a complete endotoxin polypeptide since, in all cases, the gene is truncated. pT1 and pT173 were able to direct the synthesis of a polypeptide of 65–68 kDa that immunoreacted with antibodies raised against the pure toxic crystal (data not shown). The tetracycline-resistance gene was inserted in inverted orientation to ensure that the HD-73 truncated sequences could not be expressed from external expression control regions in pT73 and pT173.

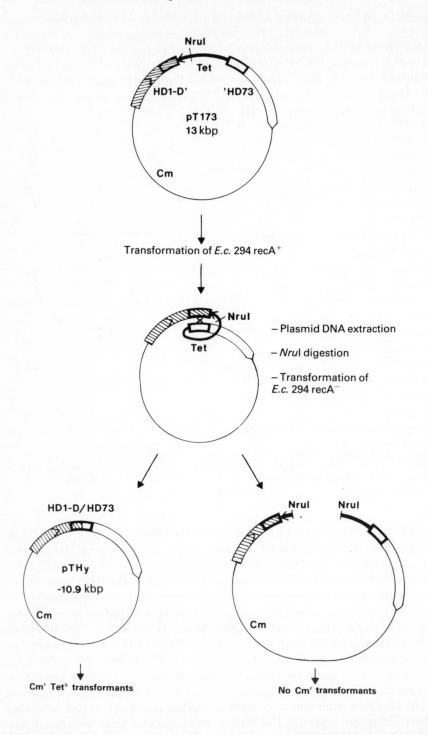

**Figure 24.2**   Scheme of the protocol for generation of the hybrid genes. The heavy closed boxes represent the partially homologous regions, open for HD-73, striped for HD-1 Dipel.

GENERATION OF HYBRID GENES

The sequences of HD-1 Dipel and HD-73 genes in pT173 share a region of homology, i.e. the last 696 bp of the HD-1 Dipel sequence and the first 707 bp of the HD-73 sequence. Between these partial direct repeats there is the tetracycline-resistance determinant, characterized by the unique *Nru*I site. *Figure 24.2* represents the protocol we followed to generate the recombinant plasmids with the hybrid toxin genes. The pT173 plasmid was introduced in a recombination proficient background by transformation of *E. coli* 294 competent cells. A single Tet$^r$ and Cm$^r$ colony was inoculated in LB (supplemented with chloramphenicol) and grown for about 40 generations. Plasmid DNA extracted from the cells was digested with *Nru*I. In this way the molecules not subjected to recombination and having the intact tetracycline gene were linearized. Only circular molecules could replicate and transform the 294 *recA* competent cells to Cm$^r$.

The Cm$^r$ transformants were screened for sensitivity to tetracycline with the aim of obtaining recombinants between the partially homologous regions of the truncated toxin genes (boxed in *Figure 24.2*). In this way we expected to reconstitute an entire hybrid gene, with the first third of the amino-terminal region of the HD-1 Dipel gene and two-thirds from the carboxy-terminal region of the HD-73 gene. The hypervariable region was expected to be a different hybrid region for each clone, able to express a polypeptide immunoreacting with specific antibodies. We isolated 13 Cm$^r$ Tet$^s$ clones, examined them for the production of a polypeptide immunoreacting with polyclonal antibodies raised against HD-73 toxic crystals and for the presence of recombinant plasmids (pTHy). *Figure 24.3* shows the immunoblotting (panel A) and SDS-PAGE (panel B) analysis of cell extracts obtained from the seven cultures producing a polypeptide antigen having electrophoretic mobility similar to the pure HD-73 crystal protein (sample 9).

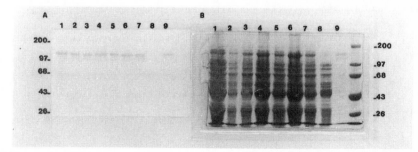

**Figure 24.3** SDS-PAGE electrophoresis Coomassie staining (panel B) and immunoblotting (panel A). Samples numbered 1 to 7 are cell extracts of *E. coli* 294 *recA* containing plasmids from pTHy1 to pTHy7, respectively. Sample 8 is the same strain containing pT173. Sample 9 is a purified sample of crystal antigen from *B. thuringiensis* HD-73.

SEQUENCING OF THE RECOMBINANT REGION

Direct sequence analysis of the putative region of recombination has been performed for three of the seven recombinant genes generated *in vivo*. Two *Eco*RV sites present in both the HD-1 Dipel and the HD-73 sequences have been used to obtain a fragment of approximately 670 bp from pTHy2, pTHy5

```
HD 1 Dipel gene                                              LIMITS:  1521  2215
HD 73 gene                                                   LIMITS:  1383  2091

                                         6
1521    AATTCGCATTCCCTTTATTTGGGAATGCGGGGAATGCAGCTCCACCCGTACTTGT  CTC
        :::: : ::  ::   :: : ::::: :::  ::::::::::::::::::::::::::
1383    ATTCACTTTTCCGCTATATGGAACTATGGGAAATGCAGCTCCACAACAACGTATTGTTG

1579    ATTAACT GGTTTGGGGATTTTTAGAACATTATCTTCACCTTTATATAGAAGAATTATAC
        : ,::: ::: ::: : :::::::::::: ::  ::::::::::::: ::  : :
1442    CTCAACTAGGTCAGGGCGTGTATAGAACATTATCGTCCACTTTATATAGAAGACCT T

1638    TTGGTTCAGGCCCAAATAATCAGGAACTGTTTGTCCTTGATGGAACGGAGTTTTCTTTTG
        :: :: :: ::::::::: :::: : ::: ::::: :: :: :: :: ::
1499    TTAATATAGGGATAAATAATCAACAACTATCTGTTCTTGACGGGACAGAATTTGCTTATG

1695    CCTCCCTAACGACCAACTTGCCTTCCACTATATATAGACAAAGGGGTACAGTCGATTCAC
        ::: : :: ::::: ::: :: :::: ::: :::: :: :: ,: ::::: :
1559    GAACCT   CCTCAAATTTGCCATCCGCTGTATACAGAAAAAGCGGAACGGTAGATTCGC
                                 5                 2
1755    TAGATGTAATACCGCCACAGGATAATAGTGTACCACCTCGTGCGGGATTTAGCCATCGAT
        : :::::: ::::::::::: ::::::::: : ::::::: :: :::::::::::::::::
1616    TGGATGAAATACCGCCACAGAATAACAACGTGCCACCTAGGCAAGGATTTAGTCATCGAT

1815    TGAGTCATGTTACAATGCTGAG CCAAGC    AGCTGGAGCAGTTTA  CACCTTGAGAG
        : ::: :::::: :::::: :    : :: :    ::  :: ::: ::     :  : ::::
1676    TAAGCCATGTTTCAATGTTTCGTTCAGGCTTTAGTAATAGTAGTGTAAGTATAATAAGAG

1872    CTCCAACGTTTTCTTGGCAGCATCGCAGTGCTGAATTTAATAATATAATTCCTTCATCAC
        :::: ::: :: :::::::: :::: :::::::::::::::::::::::: :::: ::
1736    CTCCTATGTTCTCTTGGATACATCGTAGTGCTGAATTTAATAATATAATTGCATCGGATA

1932    AAATTACACAAATACCTTTAACAAAATCTACTAATCTTGGCTCTGGAACTTCTGTCGTTA
        ::::: :::::: ::: ::: :  :: ::::  ::  ::::  :: :
1796    GTATTACTCAAATCCCTGCAGTGAAGGGAAACTTTCTTTTTAATGG    TTCTGTAATTT

1992    AAGGACCAGGATTTACAGGAGGAGATATTCTTCGAAGAACTTCACCTGGCCAGA  TTTC
        :::::::::::::::::: :: ::: ::::::::: ::::::::: ::   ::: : :
1553    CAGGACCAGGATTTACTGGTGGGGACTTAGTTAGATTAAATAGTAGTGGAAATAACATTC

2050    AACCTTAAGAGTAAAT A  TT   ACTGCA   CCAT  TATCACAAAGATATCGGG
        :  : :  ::: ::: :: :  ::  : :::   ::::   :::  : ::::::::: :
1913    AGAATAGAGGGTATATTGAAGTTCCAATTCACTTCCCATCGACATCTACCAGATATCGAG

2097    TAAGAATTCGCTACGCTTCTACTACAAATTTACAATTCCATACATCAATTGACGGAA  G
        : ,  : :  : ::: ::  :: ::: :: :: :  ::: :: :: :::::: ::
1973    TTCGTGTACGGTATGCTTCTGTAACCCCGATTCACCT CA ACGTTAATTGGGGTAATTC

2155    ACCTATTAATCAGGGTAATTTTTCAGCAAC TATGAGTAGTGGGAGTAAATTTACAGTCCG
        : :: ::: :       :: :: :   ::::: :     :  :  :: ::::: :::: ,:
2031    ATCCATTTTTTCCAATACAGTACCAGCTACAGCTACGTCATTAGA TAATCTACAATCAA

2214    GA
        :
2090    GT
```

```
Matches = 456    Mismatches = 226    Unmatched = 40
Length = 722     Matches/length =  63.2 percent
```

**Figure 24.4** Optimal alignment of HD-1 Dipel and HD-73 genes in the regions of partial homology directly repeated in the pT173 plasmid. Vertical dashed lines indicate matches, boxes indicate the crossover regions used for the generation of the hybrid genes Hy6, Hy5 and Hy2.

and pTHy6 recombinant plasmids. This fragment has been subcloned in pGem4z and sequenced on both strands, revealing the crossover region between the two partially homologous sequences as indicated in *Figure 24.4*.

In the Figure the two sequences are aligned to maximize the matches (represented by vertical lines). The regions of crossover are indicated by a box. The three recombinants analysed so far use a different region of crossover. Only in the case of pTHy5 is the crossover located in a region of relative homology; in the other two cases the crossovers are located in regions of only three or two base pairs of uninterrupted homology.

*Figure 24.5* represents the optimal alignment of the deduced polypeptide products of the parental and recombinant genes. As can be seen, the three recombinants create hybrid hypervariable regions, without gaps or insertions or new amino-acid substitutions.

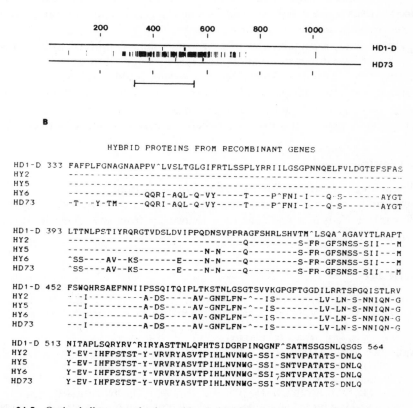

**A**

```
            200        400        600        800       1000
             I          I          I          I          I
                                                                     HD1-D

                                                                     HD73
```

**B**

HYBRID PROTEINS FROM RECOMBINANT GENES

```
HD1-D 333  FAFPLFGNAGNAAPPV^LVSLTGLGIFRTLSSPLYRRIILGSGPNNQELFVLDGTEFSFAS
HY2        ------------------------------------------------------------
HY5        ------------------------------------------------------------
HY6        --------------QQRI-AQL-Q-VY-----T----P^FNI-I---Q-S-------AYGT
HD73       -T---Y-TM-----QQRI-AQL-Q-VY-----T----P^FNI-I---Q-S-------AYGT


HD1-D 393  LTTNLPSTIYRQRGTVDSLDVIPPQDNSVPPRAGFSHRLSHVTM^LSQA^AGAVYTLRAPT
HY2        -----------------------------Q---------S-FR-GFSNSS-SII---M
HY5        ----------------------N-N----Q---------S-FR-GFSNSS-SII---M
HY6        ^SS----AV--KS-------E----N-N----Q---------S-FR-GFSNSS-SII---M
HD73       ^SS----AV--KS-------E----N-N----Q---------S-FR-GFSNSS-SII---M


HD1-D 452  FSWQHRSAEFNNIIPSSQITQIPLTKSTNLGSGTSVVKGPGFTGGDILRRTSPGQISTLRV
HY2        ---I----------A-DS-----AV-GNFLFN-^--IS--------LV-LN-S-NNIQN-G
HY5        ---I----------A-DS-----AV-GNFLFN-^--IS--------LV-LN-S-NNIQN-G
HY6        ---I----------A-DS-----AV-GNFLFN-^--IS--------LV-LN-S-NNIQN-G
HD73       ---I----------A-DS-----AV-GNFLFN-^--IS--------LV-LN-S-NNIQN-G


HD1-D 513  NITAPLSQRYRV^RIRYASTTNLQFHTSIDGRPINQGNF^SATMSSGSNLQSGS 564
HY2        Y-EV-IHFPSTST-Y-VRVRYASVTPIHLNVNWG-SSI-SNTVPATATS-DNLQ
HY5        Y-EV-IHFPSTST-Y-VRVRYASVTPIHLNVNWG-SSI-SNTVPATATS-DNLQ
HY6        Y-EV-IHFPSTST-Y-VRVRYASVTPIHLNVNWG-SSI₇SNTVPATATS-DNLQ
HD73       Y-EV-IHFPSTST-Y-VRVRYASVTPIHLNVNWG-SSI-SNTVPATATS-DNLQ
```

**Figure 24.5** Optimal alignment of polypeptides deduced from the sequences of HD-1 Dipel and HD-73 genes. In panel A (modified after Geiser, Schweitzer and Grimm, 1986) is represented schematically the alignment of the entire polypeptides: a vertical line represents an unmatched residue, short bars near the horizontal lines are deletions. Panel B represents the amino-acid sequences aligned for the region corresponding to the partial homology region, at the DNA sequence level, used for the recombination in pT173. The sequence indicated in B corresponds to the region underlined in panel A. An amino-acid residue identical in HD-1 Dipel and in HD-73 or in the hybrid products is denoted by a bar. ^ represents an amino-acid residue deleted to obtain the maximum alignment.

## Conclusions

The experimental protocol we describe in this report to generate hybrid recombinants between different *B. thuringiensis* genes can be applied to other couples of *B. thuringiensis* genes or to different recombinant products, generating new polypeptides possibly having spectra of toxic activity different from that of the parental products. *In vitro* construction of toxin genes with new hypervariable regions is limited by the number and position of the restriction sites and by rounds of site-directed mutagenesis. We performed the *in vivo* recombination using the two toxin genes that showed the least homology (63.2% in the region where we restricted the recombination events) and the most differentiated toxic activity for the corresponding product, among the sequenced determinants of entomopathogenic protoxin (Andrews *et al.*, 1987).

The recombination was forced in the hypervariable region and in this way generated new amino-acid combinations in the protein domain supposed to be the determinant of the toxic specificity. Preliminary results indicate specific toxic activity against *Ostrinia nubilalis* larvae (European corn borer) of the toxin coded by some of the hybrid genes.

Direct sequence analysis of other recombinants combined with assays of toxicity against different Lepidopteran targets could allow us to identify new toxins. A larger sample of recombinant plasmids could clarify whether there is a hot-spot of recombination. The generation of the large number of different toxin genes present among the *B. thuringiensis* strains could be ascribed to analogous recombination events between partially homologous sequences.

## Acknowledgements

We thank F. Scoffone for expert technical assistance. This research was supported, in part, by grants from the Ministero della Pubblica Istruzione (Roma). T.C. was a recipient of a fellowship from the 'Area di Ricerca, Trieste'.

## References

ADANG, M.J., STAVER, M.J., ROCHELEAU, T.A., LEIGHTON, J., BARKER, R.F. AND THOMPSON, D.V. (1985). Characterized full-length and truncated plasmid clones of the crystal protein of *B. thuringiensis* subsp. *kurstaki* HD-73 and their toxicity to *Manduca sexta*. *Gene* **36**, 289–300.

ANDREWS, R.S., FAUST, R.M., WABIKO, H., RAYMOND, K.C. AND BULLA, L.A. (1987). The biotechnology of *Bacillus thuringiensis*. *CRC Critical Reviews in Biotechnology* **6**, 163–232.

GEISER, M., SCHWEITZER, S. AND GRIMM, C. (1986). The hypervariable region in the genes coding for entomopathogenic crystal protein of *B. thuringiensis*: nucleotide sequence of the *kurhd1* gene of subsp. *kurstaki* HD1. *Gene* **48**, 109–118.

JAQUET, F., HUTTER, R. AND LUTHY, P. (1987). Specificity of *B. thuringiensis* δ-endotoxin. *Applied and Environmental Microbiology* **53**, 500–504.

HANAHAN, D. (1985). Techniques for transformation of *E. coli*. In *DNA cloning* (D.M. Glover, Ed.), volume 1, pp. 109–132. IRL Press, Oxford.

KRONSTAD, J.W. AND WHITELEY, H.R. (1984). Inverted repeat sequences flank a *B. thuringiensis* crystal protein gene. *Journal of Bacteriology* **160**, 95–102.

REY, M.W., REQUADT, C., MAINZER, S.E., LAMSA, M.H., FERRARI, E., LAD, P.J. AND GRAY, G.L. (1986). Homologous α-amylases of *Bacillus* and generation of their hybrids *in vivo*. In *Bacillus Molecular Genetics and Biotechnology Applications* (A.T. Ganesan and J.A. Hoch, Eds), pp. 229–239. Academic Press, Orlando.

SCHNEPF, H.E. AND WHITELEY, H.R. (1981). Cloning and expression of the *B. thuringiensis* crystal protein gene in *E. coli*. *Proceedings of the National Academy of Sciences of the United States of America* **78**, 2893–2897.

SCHNEPF, H.E., WONG, H.C. AND WHITELEY, H.R. (1985). The amino acid sequence of a crystal protein from *B. thuringiensis* deduced from the DNA base sequence. *The Journal of Biological Chemistry* **260**, 6264–6272.

WABIKO, H., RAYMOND, K.C. AND BULLA, L.A. (1986). *Bacillus thuringiensis* entomocidal protoxin gene sequence and gene product. *DNA* **5**, 305–314.

WEBER, H. AND WEISSMANN, C. (1983). Formation of genes coding for hybrid proteins by recombination between related, cloned genes in *E. coli*. *Nucleic Acid Research* **11**, 5661–5669.

WELLS, J.A., FERRARI, E., HENNER, D.J., ESTELL, D.A. AND CHEN, E.Y. (1983). Cloning, sequencing, and secretion of *B. amyloliquefaciens* subtilisin in *B. subtilis*. *Nucleic Acid Research* **11**, 7911/7925.

WHITELEY, H.R. AND SCHNEPF, H.E. (1986). The molecular biology of parasporal crystal body formation in *Bacillus thuringiensis*. *Annual Review of Microbiology* **40**, 549–576.

# 25
# Structure of pSM19035 Replication Region and MLS-Resistance Gene

A.V. SOROKIN AND V.E. KHAZAK

VNII Genetica, Moscow, 113545, Dorozhnyi pr, 1A, USSR

## Introduction

The 27·5 kbp MLS-resistant plasmid pSM19035 was isolated from *Streptococcus pyogenes* (Behnke *et al.*, 1979). Very long inverted repeats were found in the plasmid by electron microscopy and restriction mapping (Behnke *et al.*, 1979; Boitsov *et al.*, 1979; Behnke and Klaus, 1983). Deletion derivatives of the plasmid having an increased copy number (Behnke and Klaus, 1983), have been introduced by transformation into *B. subtilis* and are used as vector molecules in these cells (Boitsov and Golubkov, 1980; Rabinovich *et al.*, 1985). The replication region of pSM19035 was isolated by molecular cloning in *B. subtilis* (Rabinovich *et al.*, 1985; Sorokin *et al.*, 1986). When comparing the restriction map of this region with replication region maps of the streptococci plasmids, pIP501 and pAMβ1 (Behnke and Klaus, 1983; Le Blanc and Lee, 1984) (*Figure 25.1*), we found that they are similar. So, it is possible that these plasmids are very closely related and mechanisms of their replication similar. The plasmid pAMβ1 is conjugative and is used for genetic transfer between different Gram-positive micro-organisms, such as *B. thuringiensis, C. thermobutilicum* and others (Lereclus *et al.*, 1984). So, the knowledge of structural organization an understanding of replication regulation of these plasmids are of interest. Here we present the nucleotide sequence of the smallest region of pSM19035 still able to replicate autonomously in *B. subtilis*.

## Open reading-frame in pSM19035 replication region

As a source of DNA to be sequenced we used plasmids pCB30 and pCB20, shown in *Figure 25.2* which we use as vectors for *B. subtilis*. The replication region of these plasmids, which is located between *Bam*HI and *Pst*I sites, is identical to that of plasmid pKB8, construction of which has been described previously (Sorokin *et al.*, 1986).

*Genetic Transformation and Expression*
© Intercept Ltd, PO Box 716, Andover, Hants, SP10 1YG, UK

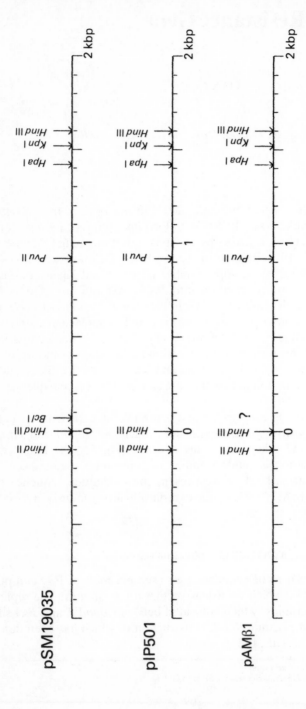

**Figure 25.1** Comparison of restriction maps of replication regions from plasmids pSM19035 (Behnke and Klaus, 1983), pIP501 (Behnke and Klaus, 1983) and pAMβ1 (LeBlanc and Lee, 1984). The presence of the *Bcl*I site on pAMβ1 is undetermined.

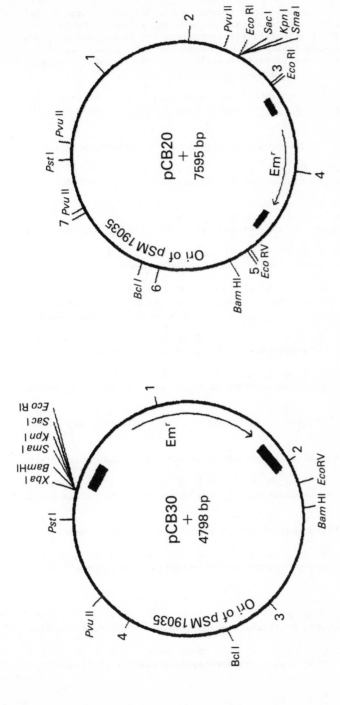

**Figure 25.2** Restriction maps of plasmids pCB30 and pCB20. *Pst*I–*Bam*HI fragments of these plasmids, containing the pSM19035 replication region, and *Hind*III fragments containing the MLS-resistance region, were used as a source of DNA for M13 cloning and sequencing. Inverted repeats around the MLS-resistance gene are shown as black bars.

```
  1 cgtacgtcaattgttgtaaccgatccaaccataaaaacactagaacaaattgcaaagtta      60
                 ^Hpa 1
                 ^HinD2
 61 actaactcaacgctagtagtggatttaatcccaaatgagccaacagaaccagaatcagaa     120
121 caagtaacattggatttagaaatggaagaagaaaaaagcaatgatttcgtgtaaaaaatg     180
181 cacgaaatcattgcttattttttttaaaagcgatatactagatataacgaaacaacgaact     240
241 gaataaagaatacaaaaaaagagccacgaccaacttattttccgccaagaaaataagttg     300
301 cgagccttaattgattaccaccaatcaattaaagaagtcgagacccaaaatttggtaaag     360
         ggtggttagttaatttcttcagctctgg

361 tatttaattactttattaatcagatacttaaatatctgtaaacccattatatcgggtttt     420
421 tgaggggatttcaagtctttaagaagatacccaggcaatcaattaagaaaaacttagttg     480

                 -35                          -10
481 attgccttttttgttgtgattcaactttgatcgtagcttctaactaattaattttcgtaa     540

         S.D.              M  N  I  P  F  V  V  E  T  V  L  H  D  G      15
541 gaaaaggagaacagctgaatgaatatcccttttgttgtagaaactgtgcttcatgacggct     600
         ^Pvu 2

      L  L  K  Y  K  F  K  N  S  K  I  R  S  I  T  T  K  P  G  K      35
601 tgttaaagtacaaatttaaaaatagtaaaattcgctcaatcactaccaagccaggtaaaa     660

      S  K  G  A  I  F  A  Y  R  S  K  K  S  M  I  G  G  R  G  V      55
661 gcaaaggggctattttttgcgtatcgctcaaaaaaaaagcatgattggcggacgtggcgttg     720

      V  L  T  S  E  E  A  I  H  E  N  Q  D  T  F  T  H  W  T  P      75
721 ttctaacttccgaagaagcgattcacgaaaatcaagatacatttacgcattggacaccaa     780
         tttagttctatgtaaatgcgtaacctgtgg

      N  V  Y  R  Y  G  T  Y  A  D  E  N  R  S  Y  T  K  G  H  S      95
781 acgtttatcgttatggtacgtatgcagacgaaaaccgttcatacactaaaggacattctg     840

      E  N  N  L  R  Q  I  N  T  F  F  I  D  F  D  I  H  T  E  K     115
841 aaaacaatttaagacaaatcaataccttctttattgattttgatattcacacggaaaaag     900

      E  T  I  S  A  S  D  I  L  T  T  A  I  D  L  G  F  M  P  T     135
901 aaactatttcagcaagcgatattttaacaacagctattgatttaggttttatgcctacgt     960

      L  I  I  K  S  D  K  G  Y  Q  A  Y  F  V  L  E  T  P  V  Y     155
961 taattatcaaatctgataaaggttatcaagcatattttgtttagaaacgccagtctatg    1020

      V  T  S  K  S  E  F  K  S  V  K  A  A  K  I  I  S  Q  N  I     175
1021 tgacttcaaaatcagaatttaaatctgtcaaagcagccaaaataatctcgcaaaatatcc    1080

      R  E  Y  F  G  K  S  L  P  V  D  L  T  C  N  H  F  G  I  A     195
1081 gtgaatattttggaaagtctttgccagttgatctaacgtgcaatcattttgggattgctc    1140

      R  I  P  R  T  D  N  V  E  F  F  D  P  N  Y  R  Y  S  F  K     215
1141 gtataccaagaacggacaatgtcgaattttttgatcccaattaccgttattctttcaaag    1200
     ^Sna 1
     ^Acc 1

      E  W  Q  D  W  S  F  K  Q  T  D  N  K  G  F  T  R  S  S  L     235
1201 aatggcaagattggtctttcaaacaaacagataataagggctttactcgttcaagtctaa    1260

      M  V  L  S  G  T  E  G  K  K  Q  V  D  E  P  W  F  N  L  L     255
1261 tggttttaagcggtacagaaggcaaaaaacaagtagatgaaccctggtttaatctcttat    1320
                                                          (continued)
```

:ontinued

```
       L  H  E  T  K  F  S  G  E  K  G  L  V  G  R  N  S  V  M  F        275
1321 tgcacgaaacgaaattttcaggagaaaagggtttagtagggcgtaatagcgttatgttta        1380

       T  L  S  L  A  Y  F  S  S  G  Y  S  I  E  T  C  E  Y  N  M        295
1381 ccctctctttagcctactttagttcaggctattcaatcgaaacgtgcgaatataatatgt        1440

       F  E  F  N  N  R  L  D  Q  P  L  E  E  K  E  V  I  K  L  V        315
1441 ttgagtttaataatcgattagatcaacccttagaagaaaaagaagtgatcaaacttgtta        1500
                                  ^Bcl1

       R  S  A  Y  S  E  N  Y  Q  G  A  N  R  E  Y  I  T  I  L  C        335
1501 gaagtgcctactcagaaaactatcaaggggctaatagggaatacattaccattctttgca        1560

       K  A  W  V  S  S  D  L  T  S  K  D  L  F  V  R  Q  G  W  F        355
1561 aagcttgggtatcaagtgatttaaccagtaaagatttatttgtccgtcaagggtggttta        1620
     ^HinD3

       K  F  K  K  K  R  S  E  R  Q  R  V  H  L  S  E  W  K  E  D        375
1621 aattcaagaaaaaaagaagtgaacgtcaacgtgttcatttgtcagaatggaaagaagatt        1680
                         ^HinD2

       L  M  A  Y  I  S  E  K  S  D  V  Y  K  P  Y  L  V  T  T  K        395
1681 taatggcttatattagcgaaaaaagcgatgtatacaagccttatttagtgacgaccaaaa        1740
                                 ^Sna 1
                                 ^Acc 1

       K  E  I  R  E  A  L  G  I  P  E  R  T  L  D  K  L  L  K  V        415
1741 aagagattagagaagcgctaggcattcctgaacgtacgctagataagctattgaaggtat        1800

       L  K  A  N  Q  E  I  F  F  K  I  K  S  G  R  N  G  G  I  Q        435
1801 taaaagcgaatcaagaaatcttctttaagattaaatcaggaagaaatggtggcattcaac        1860

       L  A  S  V  K  S  L  L  L  S  I  I  K  V  K  K  E  E  K  R        455
1861 ttgctagtgttaaatcattgttgctatcgatcattaaagtaaaaaaagaagaaaaagaa        1920

       K  L  Y  K  G  A  D  K  F  F  &                                   465
1921 agctatataaaggcgctgacaaattcttttgacttagagcatacattcattcaagagact        1980

1981 ttaaacaagctagcagaacgccctaaacggacacacaactcgatttgtttagctatgata        2040
        <----  ----  --                              --  ----  --
2041 caggctgaaaataaaacccgcactatgccattacatttatatctatgatacgtgtttgtt        2100
        --->
2101 tttctgtgctgtttagtgaatgattagcagaaatatagagagtaagattttaattaatta        2160
2161 ttaggggggagaaggagagagtagcccgaaaactttttagttggcttggactgaacgaagtg      2220
2221 agggaaaggctactaaaacgtcgaggggcagtgagagcgaagcgaacacttgatctttta        2280
                                                     -35
2281 agttgctatcttttataggtcaatagagtatacttatttgtcctattgattagatagcag        2340
                         ^Sna 1
                         ^Acc 1
          -10                                S.D.
2341 tataatagctttatagagtaggtcatttaagttgagcataataggaggatc              2391
```

Figure 25.3  Nucleotide sequence of the pSM19035 replication region. The position of the first nucleotide corresponds to the first nucleotide after the *Pst*I recognition sequence from plasmids pCB30 and pCB20. Some rarely occurring restriction sites are shown. The amino-acid sequence of ORF A is given above. Underlined are potential promoters and ribosome-binding sites. Two fragments of coding strand, homologous to phage M13 gene II protein-recognition sequence are shown below, underlined. Inverted repeats are indicated by dashed arrows.

274     *Recombination, Transposition, Plasmid Stability*

The primary structure of the *PstI–Bam*HI fragment, determining the abilit
of pCB20 and pCB30 to replicate in *B. subtilis*, is shown in *Figure 25.3*. Th
structure was determined by the dideoxy terminators method (Sanger, Nickle
and Coulson, 1977), after cloning of appropriate fragments into M13tg130 o
M13tg131 phages (Kieny, Lathe and Lecocq, 1983).

Analysis of the primary structure of the pSM19035 replication regio
revealed a potential open reading-frame for a protein with molecular mass 53·8
kDa (ORF A). We have compared the structure of some proteins, essential fo
replication of plasmids in Gram-positive bacteria—repC from pT181 (Novic
*et al.*, 1982), repB from pUB110 (McKenzie *et al.*, 1986), repD from pC22
(Brenner and Shaw, 1985) and repF from pE194 (Villafane *et al.*, 1987)—wit
ORF A. No essential homology was found between these proteins and ORF A.

**Possible role of ORF A as Rep19035**

We have calculated the secondary structure of ORF A, using methods of Cho
and Fasman (1974) and of Garnier, Osguthorpe and Robson (1978). Th
results are shown in *Figure 25.4*. Usually, proteins specifically interacting wit
DNA have in their structure a specific pattern of two α-helices with rathe
conservative amino acids in their vicinities. We have analysed ORF A for th
presence of such features. Two regions were found, shown in *Figure 25.5A*
The first region, located near residue 130 does not fit the rule by its secondary
structure, although this region has striking homology with the DNA
interacting region of phage λ Cro protein. The second region is placed nea
residue 400, and has all the necessary features. This second region ma
correspond to a DNA-recognizing portion of ORF A and shares homology wit
the replication proteins of φX174, pC194 and pUB110 (*Figure 25.5B*)
indicating the possibility that this protein may be covalently linked to DNA
(Van Mansveld, Baas and Janzs, 1984). Thus, there are indications that ORF A
is a protein essential for pSM19035 replication, and therefore we call thi
protein Rep19035. This sequence contains a potential ribosomal-binding
sequence, AGGAGAA, upstream of the ATG start codon at position 558, anc
potential promoters, TTGATC and TAATTT.

As mentioned above, Behnke and Klaus (1983) described a mutant of the
plasmid pSM19035 with an increased copy number. This mutant has a deletior
upstream of the *Pvu*II site, shown on *Figure 25.3*. We propose that a weak
promoter of Rep19035 mRNA was replaced in this mutant by a stronge
promoter. This is a preliminary indication that Rep19035 is a positive regulato
of pSM19035 replication.

**Other features of the pSM19035 replication region**

Plasmid pSM19035 has a copy number of about 2–3 per chromosome
(Rabinovich *et al.*, 1985). Cloning of DNA into the *Eco*RI site of this plasmid
does not influence the copy number (our unpublished data, see also
Rabinovich *et al.*, 1985). Nevertheless, small deletion derivatives of this
plasmid have increased copy numbers, up to 30–50 per chromosome

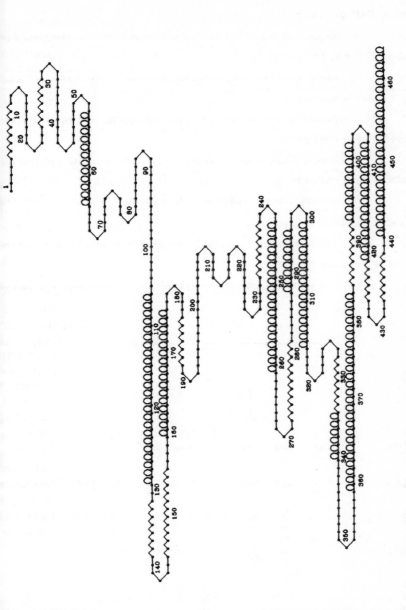

**Figure 25.4**  Secondary structure of protein encoded by ORF A, predicted according to the rules of Chou and Fasman (1974) and of Garnier, Osguthorpe and Robson (1978) by the computer package 'DNASUN' (Mironov *et al.*, unpublished). Each tenth residue is numbered.

**A**

pUB110 protein α

     AsnTrpArgArgAlaMetLysHisGlyIleGlnSerGlnLysValValAlaGluValIle

E.coli CAP-protein

     ArgGlnGluIleIleGlyGlnIleValGlyCysSerArgGluThrValGlyArgIleLeuLys

Lambda CI-repressor

     GlnGluSerValAlaAspLysMetGlyMetGlyGlnSerGlyValGlyAlaLeuPheAsn

E.coli lac-repressor

     LeuTyrAspValAlaGluTyrAlaGlyValSerTyrGlnThrValSerArgValValAsn

E.coli trp-repressor

     GlnArgGluLeuLysAsnGluLeuGlyAlaGlyIleAlaThrIleThrArgGlySerAsn

Lambda cro-protein

     GlnThrLysThrAlaLysAspLeuGlyValTyrGlnSerAlaIleAsnLysAlaIleHis

rep19035 residue No.130

     IleLeuThrThrAlaIleAspLeuGlyPheMetProThrLeuIleIleLysSerAspLys

rep19035 residue No.400

     LysLysGluIleIleArgGluAlaLeuGlyIleProGluArgThrLeuAspLysLeuLeuLys

    helix 2          helix 3

**B**

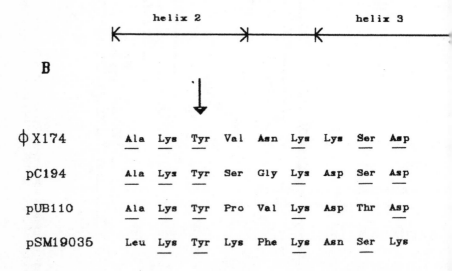

| | | | | | | | | |
|---|---|---|---|---|---|---|---|---|
| φX174 | Ala | Lys | Tyr | Val | Asn | Lys | Lys | Ser | Asp |
| pC194 | Ala | Lys | Tyr | Ser | Gly | Lys | Asp | Ser | Asp |
| pUB110 | Ala | Lys | Tyr | Pro | Val | Lys | Asp | Thr | Asp |
| pSM19035 | Leu | Lys | Tyr | Lys | Phe | Lys | Asn | Ser | Lys |

**Figure 25.5** Comparison of ORF A (Rep19035) with some DNA-interacting proteins. (A) Potential DNA-binding sequences in Rep19035 compared to some DNA-binding proteins. DNA-binding sequences from proteins other than Rep19035 are from (Sueoka *et al.*, 1986). (B) Homology of Rep19035 to replication proteins of phage and staphylococcal plasmids. The arrow indicates tyrosine in φX174 Rep protein, covalently linked to DNA. Sequences from proteins other than Rep19035 are from Gros, te Riele and Ehrlich (1987). The most conservative residues are underlined.

Rabinovich *et al.*, 1985). This increased copy number does not reduce when ong DNA fragments (up to 20 kbp) are cloned in these derivatives. From this ve can conclude that there are some structures in pSM19035 DNA which may e responsible for copy-number control, making it 2–3 per chromosome.

It was suggested recently that some plasmids, originated from Gram-positive acteria, replicate as a rolling circle, similar to the *E. coli* single-stranded DNA hages (Gros, te Riele and Ehrlich, 1987). Essential features of this kind of eplication are the presence of a plasmid-encoded replication protein that has a pecific nicking activity, together with the presence of a conservative sequence n the plasmid DNA recognizable by the protein, as exemplified by the nteraction between such a protein and corresponding DNA investigated in the ase of the gene II protein of the filamentous phage f1 (Greenstein and Ioriuchi, 1987).

We have undertaken a computer search for such sequences in the structure of he replication region of pSM19035, and found two, shown in *Figure 25.3* and *Figure 25.6*. The presence of two potential nicking sites in t'ie replication region f pSM19035 may suggest a rolling-circle mechanism of re )lication for plasmids f this group.

It is interesting also to note the lack of evident inverted repeats around the ossible nicking sites of pSM19035. This indicates that Rep19035 probably emains bound to DNA during synthesis, as does the gene *A* protein of φX174, ut not the gene II protein of M13.

Several structures resembling bacilli vegetative promoters were also found in he vicinity of the *Bam*HI site, for example, TTGTCC at position 2318 and ATAAT at 2341 (*Figure 25.3*). Besides, the AGGAGG overlapping the

5'- TTCTTTCTTATCTTG ATAATAAGGGTAACT    pC194

5'- TGCTCCCCCAACTTG ATATTAATAACACTA    φX174

5'- AAAACCGGCTACTCT AATAGCCGGTTGGAC    pT181

5'- GAGTCCACGTTCTTT AATAGTGGACTCTTG    M13

5'- CGACTTCTTTAATTG ATTGGTGGTAATCAA    pSM19035–position 330

5'- CGTAAATGTATCTTG ATTTTCGTGAATCGC    pSM19035–position 750

**Figure 25.6** Comparison of sequences, found by a homology search of the pSM19035 replication egion with the phage M13 protein II recognition region, and sequences around the nick site (*) of ome plasmids and phages. Sequences, other than of pSM19035, are from Gros, te Riele and hrlich (1987). Nucleotides, often occurring in such sites, are underlined.

```
aagcttgcagccacctacaccaccaataccaaacacctaaacttccaggtatttaaac    60

cttaaaaaagaaaagagtagttaccaaaaaacggtaactactcttttttataaaaaca   120

tttcctcatgtggggtccgagcgcctacgaggaattgtatcgataagaaatagattt   180

aaaaatttcgctgttattttgtacatttaacttgacggtgacatctctctattgtgagtt   240

attagtggtacagttttcaaccgtttaattataaaaagtggtgcattttaaattggc    300

.....  MLS-resistance gene  ..... tttttgtaaatttggaaagttacacgtta  1530

ctaaagggaatgtagataaattattaggtataggcactctaataactaccaattaattc  1590

acctcaaaatgaaattagaaaaaaacagcgaaattttaaatctatttcttatcgataca  1650

aattcctcgtaggcgctcgggacccaacatgaggaatgtttttataaaaaggaagta   1710

gttaccgtttttggtaactactctttttcctttttaaggtttaaatacctgggagttta  1770

ggtgttttgggtattggtggtatgtataggtgctgccaagctt              1810
```

**Figure 25.7** Nucleotide sequence of inverted repeats (underlined) surrounding the MLS-resistance gene of pSM19035. Sequences homologous to terminal 38 bp repeats of Tn917 are in bold-face type (Shaw and Clewell, 1985). Sequences homologous to the *res* site of the same

3amHI recognition sequence can be used as a Shine–Dalgarno sequence (SD) or Gram-positive cells. We checked both promoters and SD, by appropriate probes (data not shown), and found that they can both be used efficiently, at east in *B. subtilis*. So, one can consider the plasmids pCB20 and pCB30, shown n *Figure 25.2*, as expression vectors for Gram-positive bacteria.

## The structure of the MLS-resistance gene of pSM19035

The structure of the pCB30–*Hin*dIII fragment, containing the MLS-resistance gene, was also determined in this study. Sequences of the regulatory region of this gene and of rRNA methylase are not distinguished from the similar gene of ransposon Tn*917* of *Streptococcus* (Shaw and Clewell, 1985). The only differences are the inverted repeats surrounding the gene. Their primary structures are shown in *Figure 25.7*. We have compared the structural organization of this *Hin*dIII fragment with other streptococcal MLS-resistance genes with known primary structures (*Figure 25.8*). All these structures are very closely related to Tn*917*. In the case of pSM19035 we can speculate that he long inverted repeats and MLS-resistance gene originated from ransposition of Tn*917* between two identical replicons, and that the cointegrate structure originating during transposition was not properly resolved; this would be possible because Tn*917* has two resolving sites (Shaw and Clewell, 1985) and cointegrate structures with the pSM19035 replicon could possibly have long lives (Bidnenko and Haykinson, 1988). Following recombination, plasmids such as pSM19035, pSM22095 or ERL1 (Behnke *et al.*, 1979) were obtained. These plasmids are not completely structurally stable,

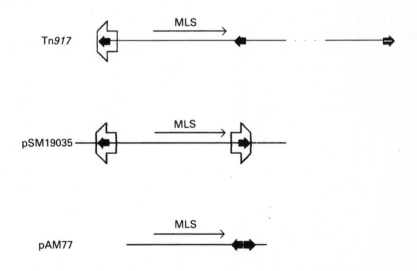

**Figure 25.8**  Homologous regions of Tn*917* (Shaw and Clewell, 1985), pAM77 (Horinouchi, Byeon and Weisblum, 1983) and pSM19035. Black arrows represent sequences homologous to terminal 38 bp repeats of Tn*917*. White arrows represent 103 bp inverted repeats surrounding the MLS-resistance gene of pSM19035, homologous to the left end of Tn*917*.

as is shown by their introduction through genetic transformation into *B. subtili* (Haykinson, Rabinovich and Stepanov, 1982) or streptococcal cells (Behnke Tomich and Clewell, 1980).

## Conclusion

The primary structures of *Streptococcus pyogenes* plasmid pSM1903! replication region and MLS-resistance gene have been determined. An oper reading-frame was found encoding a protein with molecular mass 53·8 kDa which is suggested as the replication protein of pSM19035. Two potentia nicking sites were also found in the replication region. Several bacilli vegetative promoters and a SD-sequence, overlapping the *Bam*HI recognition site, make derivatives of pSM19035 convenient expression vectors. Comparison of the sequence of the MLS-resistance gene from pSM19035 and its inverted repeat with the structure of Tn*917* leads us to suppose that long inverted repeats o plasmids of this group originated from abortive transposition of Tn*917*.

## Acknowledgements

We are grateful to Drs A.A. Mironov and L.S. Lunovskaya-Gurova for the gif of the preliminary version of the DNASUN computer package. The interes and helpful discussions relevant to this work from Professor D. Behnke, Dr A.S. Boitsov, M.Ya. Haykinson, V.E. Bidnenko and R. Breitling are also appreciated.

## References

BEHNKE, D. AND KLAUS, S. (1983). Double or triple sets of replication functions a inverted and direct repeats on *in vitro* reconstructed streptococcal MLS-resistance plasmids. *Zeitschrift für Allgemeine Mikrobiologie* **23**, 539–547.

BEHNKE, D., TOMICH, P.K. AND CLEWELL, D.B. (1980). Electron microscopi mapping of deletions on a streptococcal plasmid carring extraordinarily long inverted repeats. *Plasmid* **4**, 139–147.

BEHNKE, D., GOLUBKOV, V.I., MALKE, H. AND TOTOLIAN, A. (1979). Restriction endonuclease analysis of group A streptococcal plasmids determining resistance t macrolide, lincosamide and streptogramin-B antibiotics. *FEMS Microbiolog Letters* **6**, 5–9.

BIDNENKO, V.E. AND HAYKINSON, M. YA. (1988). Recombination of plasmids witl inverted repeats in *Bacillus subtilis*. *Molekulyarnaya Genetika, Mikrobiologiya Virusologiya* **5**, 17–23.

BOITSOV, A.S. AND GOLUBKOV, V.I. (1980). Transformation of *Bacillus subtilis* by Streptococci plasmids. *Diklady Academii Nauk SSSR* **254**, 490–492.

BOITSOV, A.S., GOLUBKOV, V.I., IONTOVA, I.M., ZAITSEV, E.N., MALKE, H. ANI TOTOLIAN, A.A. (1979). Inverted repeats on plasmids determining resistance t MLS antibiotics in Group A Streptococci. *FEMS Microbiology Letters* **6**, 11–14.

BANNER, D.G. AND SHAW, W.V. (1985). The use of synthetic oligonucleotides witl universal templates for rapid DNA sequencing: results with staphylococca replicon pC221. *EMBO Journal* **4**, 561–568.

CHOU, P.Y. AND FASMAN, G.D. (1974). Prediction of protein conformation *Biochemistry* **13**, 222–245.

GARNIER, J., OSGUTHORPE, D.J. AND ROBSON, B. (1978). Analysis of the accuracy and implications of simple methods for predicting the secondary structure of globular proteins. *Journal of Molecular Biology* 120, 97–120.

GREENSTEIN, D. AND HORIUCHI, K. (1987). Interaction between the replication origin and the initiator protein of the filamentous phage f1. Binding occurs in two steps. *Journal of Molecular Biology* 197, 157–174.

GROS, M.F., TE RIELE, H. AND EHRLICH, S.D. (1987). Rolling circle replication of single-stranded DNA plasmid pC194. *EMBO Journal* 6, 3863–3869.

HAYKINSON, M.YA., RABINOVICH, P.M. AND STEPANOV, A.I. (1982). Role of direct and inverted repeats in transformation of *B. subtilis* by plasmid DNA. *Doklady Academii Nauk SSSR* 265, 975–978.

HORINOUCHI, S., BYEON, W.-H. AND WEISBLUM, B. (1983). A complex attenuator regulates inducible resistance to macrolides, lincosamides, and streptogramin type B antibiotics in *Streptococcus sanguis*. *Journal of Bacteriology* 154, 1252–1262.

KIENY, M.P., LATHE, R. AND LECOCQ, J.P. (1983). New versatile cloning and sequencing vectors based on bacteriophage M13. *Gene* 26, 91–99.

LE BLANC, D.J. AND LEE, L.N. (1984). Physical and genetic analysis of streptococcal plasmid pAMβ1 and cloning of its replication region. *Journal of Bacteriology* 157, 445–453.

LERECLUS, D., RIBIER, J., KLIER, A., MENOU, G. AND LECADET, M.-M. (1984). A transposon-like structure related to the δ-endotoxin gene of *Bacillus thuringiensis*. *EMBO Journal* 3, 2561–2567.

MCKENZIE, T., HOSHINO, T., TANAKA, T. AND SUEOKA, N. (1986). The nucleotide sequence of pUB110: some salient features in relation to replication and its regulation. *Plasmid* 15, 93–103.

NOVICK, R.P., ADLER, G.K., MAJUMDER, S., KHAN, S.A., CARLETON, S., ROSENBLUM, W. AND IORDANESCU, S. (1982). Coding sequence for the pT181 *repC* product: a plasmid-coded protein uniquely required for replication. *Proceedings of the National Academy of the United States of America* 79, 4108–4112.

RABINOVICH, P.M., HAYKINSON, M.YA., ARUTYUNOVA, L.S., JOMANTAS, YU.V. AND STEPANOV, A.I. (1985). The structure and source of plasmid DNA determine the cloning properties of vectors for *Bacillus subtilis*. In *Plasmids in Bacteria* (D.R. Helinski, S.N. Cohen, D.B. Clewell, D.A. Jackson and A. Hollaender, Eds), pp. 635–656. Plenum Press, New York.

SANGER, F., NICKLEN, S. AND COULSON, A.R. (1977). DNA sequencing with chain-terminating inhibitors. *Proceedings of the National Academy of Sciences of the United States of America* 74, 5463–5467.

SHAW, J.H. AND CLEWELL, D.B. (1985). Complete nucleotide sequence of macrolide, lincosamide and streptogramin B-resistance transposon Tn*917* in *Streptococcus faecalis*. *Journal of Bacteriology* 164, 782–796.

SOROKIN, A.V., AVAKOV, A.S., BAYEV, V.B. AND KOZLOV, YU.I. (1986). Cloning of *Bacillus subtilis* promoters with the help of alpha-amylase secretion gene. In *Bacillus Molecular Genetics and Biotechnology Application* (A.T. Ganesan and J.A. Hoch, Eds), pp. 447–456. Academic Press, Orlando.

SUEOKA, N., HOSHINO, T., MCKENZIE, T. AND SONIS, D. (1986). Membrane binding and regulation of replication initiation of pUB110 in *Bacillus subtilis*. In *Bacillus Molecular Genetics and Biotechnology Application* (A.T. Ganesan and J.A. Hoch, Eds), pp. 47–54. Academic Press, Orlando.

VAN MANSVELD, A.B.M., BAAS, P.D. AND JANZS, H.S. (1984). Gene A protein of bacteriophage φX174 is a highly specific single-stranded nuclease and binds via a tyrosyl residue to DNA after cleavage. In *Proteins Involved in DNA Replication* (U. Hübscher and S. Spadari, Eds), pp. 221–229. Plenum Press, New York.

VILLAFANE, R., BECHHOFER, D.H., NARAYANAN, C.S. AND DUBNAU, D. (1987). Replication control genes of plasmid pE194. *Journal of Bacteriology* 169, 4822–4829.

# 26
# Bacterial Transposons and Transposition: Flexibility and Limitations

PETER M. BENNETT

Department of Microbiology, The Medical School, University of Bristol, University Walk, Bristol BS8 1TD, UK

## Introduction

Transpositions are genetic rearrangements that proceed via mechanisms that require neither extensive DNA homology nor a functional host-encoded recombination system. The consequence of a transposition is the insertion of a DNA sequence into a new site, usually one that bears little or no homology to that of the original site of insertion or to the transposed sequence. Transposable elements are, therefore, simple discrete DNA sequences that transpose, i.e. the structure of the element is conserved from one transposition event to the next.

The first bacterial transposable elements to be characterized were insertion sequences, now termed IS elements. Their discovery arose from investigations of unusual strong polar mutations mapping in the *lac* and *gal* operons of *Escherichia coli* (Starlinger and Saedler, 1972). By a combination of elegant genetic and physical analysis the investigators were able to show that the mutations were due to the insertion of extra DNA into one of the early genes of the particular operon. Three different IS elements, IS1, IS2 and IS3, were described in these early experiments.

Although these revelations were of interest to bacterial geneticists and an analogy with the mobile genetic elements of maize described by Barbara McClintock (1956) was recognized, the discovery of IS elements did not excite undue interest and the full impact of their molecular genetic significance could only be guessed.

The second, and decisive, breakthrough came from recombination studies involving plasmid-borne antibiotic-resistance genes. Hedges and Jacob (1974) reported that an ampicillin-resistance determinant of the plasmid RP4, obtained from a clinical isolate of *Pseudomonas aeruginosa*, could become associated with other, apparently unrelated resistance plasmids. Recombination of the ampicillin-resistance gene into other plasmids appeared to be

*Genetic Transformation and Expression*
© Intercept Ltd, PO Box 716, Andover, Hants, SP10 1YG, UK

specific in that neither of the other two antibiotic-resistance determinants of RP4 displayed a similar behaviour. Recombinant plasmids were larger than the particular recipient plasmid and in each case the increase in size was more or less the same. Accordingly, the involvement of a discrete element called a transposon was proposed and designated Tn*A*, since redesignated Tn*1* (Campbell *et al.*, 1979).

The accelerated pace of investigation thereafter stemmed primarily from two considerations. First, if the ampicillin-resistance determinant of RP4 was transposable, why not other antibiotic-resistance genes, so providing an explanation for the rather bewildering speed with which new patterns of multiple antibiotic resistance emerged and spread? Secondly, the discovery of a transposable element with a marker offered a much more easily investigated system than the IS elements, the presence of which can be detected phenotypically only when a mutation results from the insertion. The importance of the discovery of Tn*1* was very quickly consolidated by the discovery of several other transposable antibiotic-resistance determinants (Tn*5*, Berg *et al.*, 1975; Tn*10*, Kleckner *et al.*, 1975; Tn*7*, Barth *et al.*, 1976).

Retrospectively, it is now appreciated that the IS elements were not the first bacterial transposable elements to have been discovered. This distinction really belongs to bacteriophage Mu, or μ (Taylor, 1963), which is now known to replicate by transposition (Toussaint and Résibois, 1983).

**Transposable elements**

Transposable elements range in size from below 1 kbp to 30 kbp or greater. The smallest are the IS elements with sizes normally in the range 1–2 kbp. Of these, IS1 at 768 bp is the smallest independent element yet described (Ohtsubo and Ohtsubo, 1978). Transposons are, in general, 4–5 kbp or larger.

Not including transposing bacteriophages such as μ, most transposable elements appear to conform to one of three basic structures (*Figure 26.1*), although exceptions have been reported (Murphy, 1988). The simplest structures are those of the IS elements. These short sequences are delineated by short terminal inverted repeated sequences (IR sequences) and they encode only functions necessary for transposition. Although many IS elements have a similar genetic arrangement, these seem to have been arrived at independently as there is little evidence for ancestral relationships between the majority of IS elements.

Second, in order of complexity, are the composite transposons. These are built up from IS elements and some other DNA. Each composite structure comprises a unique central section flanked by two copies of the same IS element (*Figure 26.1*). While these may be direct or inverted repeats, the latter conformation appears to be more common. The IS elements provide transposition functions while the central section accommodates the gene(s) responsible for the distinctive phenotype conferred by the element. In many cases the individual IS elements retain the capacity for independent transposition.

The third type of structure is typified by Tn*1* (*Figure 26.1*). This is the

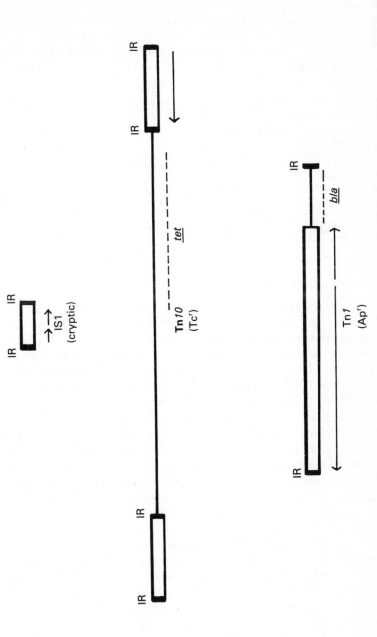

**Figure 26.1**   Representative transposable elements. Transposition functions are represented by boxes, other functions by single lines. Short inverted repeats (IR) are represented by thick vertical bars. Arrows indicate the approximate locations and directions of transcription of transposition genes. *tet*, Tetracycline-resistance gene; *bla*, TEM β-lactamase gene (conferring ampicillin resistance). Elements are drawn to scale.

archetype and many elements with this form of genetic arrangement belong to a family of ancestrally related elements (Grinsted, 1986), in which the transposition functions are evolutionarily related but not necessarily interchangeable.

From studies of several transposable elements a number of generalizations regarding the elements themselves and their activities can be made. These are listed in *Table 26.1*. The majority of transposable elements will conform to most, if not all, of these criteria.

**Table 26.1**   Transposable elements

| |
|---|
| 1. Discrete DNA sequences |
| 2. Delimited by short, terminal inverted repeats |
| 3. Mediate *recA*-independent recombinations |
| 4. Recombination events are site-specific with respect to the ends of the element BUT |
| 5. Recombination is random (more or less) with respect to the site of insertion (target) THEREFORE |
| 6. Recombination has no requirement for DNA–DNA homology |
| 7. The recombination generates short, target-site duplications, usually of a specific length: these occur as short direct repeats flanking the transposed sequence |
| 8. Transposition requires specific function(s) normally encoded by the element |

**Mechanisms of transposition**

Superficially the behaviour of transposable elements is similar, irrespective of the element. Hence, initially, models of transposition attempted to reconcile data from different sources. In due course this was seen to be mistaken and two generally accepted models have emerged. The first relates to IS elements and their composites. These elements transpose primarily in a conservative manner (*Figure 26.2A*) in that the original element is moved, in its entirety, to a new site. Two double-stranded cuts are made at the ends of the element, as defined by the IR sequences, and a short staggered double-strand cut is made at the prospective target site. It is not known if these are independent or interdependent events, but it is assumed that the events are mediated by element-encoded enzymes. The excised element, which may have a circular form (Morisato and Kleckner, 1987), is then ligated into the staggered cut leaving two small gaps on opposing strands of the DNA, one at each end of the insertion. These gaps are then filled and the continuity of both strands restored. The result is a transposon insertion flanked by short direct repeats of the target site, as observed for most, if not all, transposon insertions.

The second model of transposition applies to Tn*1* and related elements and to μ. In these cases transposition is primarily a semiconservative replication process that specifically duplicates the transposable element. The mechanism involves two stages: the first effects transposon replication while the second releases the transposition product (*Figure 26.2B*).

Two single-strand cuts are made on opposing strands at opposite ends of the element and a short staggered double-stranded cut is again made at the prospective target site. Again it is not known if these cleavage events are interdependent, although there is evidence to suggest that the two

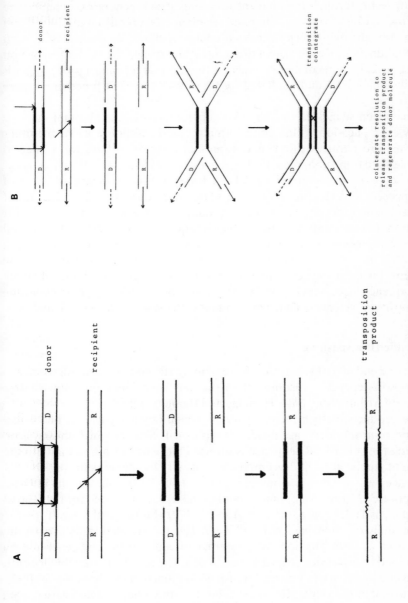

**Figure 26.2**   Models of transposition. (A)   Conservative (direct) transposition (after Berg, 1983; Weinert *et al.*, 1984); (B)   replicative transposition (after Arthur and Sherratt, 1979; Shapiro, 1979). Transposon sequences are indicated by bold lines. Arrowheads indicate points of strand cleavage. Zigzag lines indicate gap-repair DNA synthesis.

transposon-specific cleavages are co-ordinated (Craigie *et al.*, 1988). The free ends created at the ends of the transposon are ligated to those available at the target site. When the transposon and target site are on different DNA molecules this creates a 'joint' molecule, termed a Shapiro intermediate, with potential replication forks at both ends of the transposon. Replication from one, or both, through the element replicates it and generates a cointegrate structure in which both the donor and recipient DNA replicons are joined and which contains two directly repeated copies of the transposon, one at each replicon junction. Resolution of the cointegrate to yield the final transposition product occurs by recombination across these direct repeats, a process that is usually site-specific and mediated by transposon-encoded functions (*Figure 26.2B*).

It has been suggested that the two apparently different mechanisms, one involving replication, cointegrate formation and resolution while the other involves direct transposition, may represent alternative fates for a Shapiro intermediate (Ohtsubo *et al.*, 1981; Craigie *et al.*, 1988).

These generally accepted models of transposition recognize the role of site-specific DNA cleavage at the ends of the transposon, as well as cleavage of the recipient replicon, apparently at random, to generate the target for insertion. In both models the role of the IR sequences is crucial to delineate and preserve the element's integrity. They permit a single enzyme, transposase, accurately to recognize and mediate precise cleavages at both ends of the element, the events which define the transposable sequence. Removal of one IR sequence necessarily destroys the transposon, but, surprisingly, some transposition systems remain active, albeit with greatly reduced activity.

**One-ended transposition**

When one end of Tn*1* is deleted, the remaining IR sequence can still mediate a transposon-dependent recombination that has been called 'one-ended transposition (Arthur *et al.*, 1984; Heritage and Bennett, 1985).

The products of such recombinations, which obviously cannot be normal transposition products, are primarily replicon fusions in which the replicon carrying the solitary IR sequence is inserted more or less at random into the recipient replicon. The recombination is strictly dependent on the IR sequence, which always forms one junction of the fusion, and its cognate transposase (*Figure 26.3*). Similar findings have been reported for the related transposons Tn*21* (Avila *et al.*, 1984) and Tn*1721* (Motsch and Schmitt, 1984).

The analyses involving Tn*21* and Tn*1721* were extended to determine the sequences at both junctions of a number of replicon fusions generated by one-ended transposition (Motsch *et al.*, 1985). The results showed that for each fusion one junction was a normal transposition junction involving precisely the outside end of the single IR sequence but that the other junction varied from one recombinant to another. All insertions were flanked by 5 bp direct repeats of the target site, as found for normal transposition events involving Tn*21* and Tn*1721*, consistent with the dependence on transposition functions. In some replicon fusions the insertion into the recipient was slightly larger than the unit

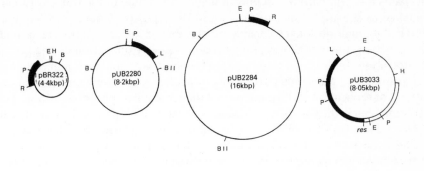

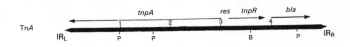

| Plasmids in donor strain | | | Frequency of plasmid A–plasmid B transposition fusions |
|---|---|---|---|
| A | B | C | |
| pUB3033 | pUB307 | | $5.5 \times 10^{-6}$ |
| pUB3078 | pUB307 | pUB3033 | — |
| pUB2280 | pUB307 | | — |
| pUB2280 | pUB307 | pUB3033 | $1 \times 10^{-6}$ |
| pUB2284 | pUB307 | | — |
| pUB2284 | pUB307 | pUB3033 | $1 \times 10^{-7}$ |
| pUB3033 | R388 | | $2.5 \times 10^{-7}$ |
| pBR322 | R388 | pUB3033 | $3 \times 10^{-7}$ |

**Figure 26.3** Transposition mediated by single IR sequences from Tn*1/3* (Tn*A*). Tn*A* sequences are indicated by the bold lines. L and R, IR sequences from the left and right arms of Tn*A*, respectively. Restriction enzyme sites are: B, *Bam*HI; E, *Eco*RI; H, *Hind*III; P, *Pst*I; *tnpA*, transposase; *tnpR*, resolvase; *res*, sequence required for site-specific resolution; *bla*, TEM β-lactamase; IR, inverted repeat. Frequency of fusion formation was determined as the ratio of the number of transconjugants that acquired the antibiotic-resistance markers of both plasmids to the number that acquired pUB307.

length of the replicon with the IR sequence. These insertions had duplications that extended for different distances into and beyond the IR sequence. The duplications formed terminal direct repeats, distinct from the 5 bp target site duplication, indicating that this atypical form of transpositional recombination also involves replication.

Neither of the conventional schemes of transposition (*Figure 26.2*) can explain these findings, since each is constructed to accommodate the fact that transposable elements are delineated by inverted repeats and these are treated indistinguishably. One-ended transposition systems obviously lack the symmetry of intact transposons. Accordingly, another model that also incorporates a replication step is needed. One such model, originally conceived as an explanation for normal transposition events, proposed that one end of a transposon is ligated to the target site to create a replication fork. From here replication proceeds through the element by way of a looped-out rolling-circle mechanism. Termination of replication and completion of the transposition is signalled by the appearance of the second IR sequence (Galas and Chandler, 1981). Although no longer considered credible as an explanation of normal transposition, this model has great attraction as an explanation of one-ended transposition. In this case, termination of replication would be signalled by the reappearance of the solitary IR sequence as the 'donor' replicon turns in the process of replication and completion of the recombination would follow. The variation seen in the sites of termination suggest that this part of the mechanism is less rigorously controlled than the initiation stage via the IR sequence. Indeed, the role of the IR sequence in the terminal stages of one-ended transposition is presumptive rather than proven. The evidence is circumstantial, specifically that the majority of insertions are of near unit length, i.e. the variable end of the majority of insertions is near or within the IR sequence. Indeed, the finding that some insertions are somewhat shorter than unit length argues that the involvement of the IR sequence in the terminal stages of one-ended transposition is not obligatory.

The IR sequence of Tn*1* has been demonstrated to be a binding site for the cognate transposase (Wishart, Broach and Ohtsubo, 1985). It would seem reasonable to suggest that such a protein–DNA complex might present an impediment to the progress of the replication fork and that the impediment might trigger the terminal stages of the transposition. The effect might be potentiated if the transposase–IR complex somehow interacts with the initial recombination junction comprising the IR sequence and the target, causing an extended pause of replication so enhancing the probability that replication will be terminated. However, any similar impediment might be expected to have the same effect, depending on its longevity, thus accounting for insertions that do not approximate to unit length.

If the conclusions drawn as to the possible mechanism of one-ended transposition are correct, then an obvious corollary is that DNA sequences flanked by direct repeats of the Tn*1* IR sequence will transpose.

## Transposition of DNA sequences flanked by direct repeats of the Tn*1* IR sequence

Plasmid pUB3729 was constructed so as to have two antibiotic-resistance determinants, encoding resistance to ampicillin and tetracycline, separated by a pair of directly repeated IR sequences from Tn*1*, and a functional *tnpA* gene encoding Tn*1* transposase (*Figure 26.4*). Transposition of the two resistance genes to a target plasmid, R388, was then investigated.

Both resistance markers transposed to R388. Approximately one-third of plasmid recombinants recovered carried the markers of both plasmids and were indistinguishable from replicon fusions generated by one-ended transposition. Both IR sequences on pUB3729 gave rise to these products.

The remainder of the recombinants recovered comprised R388 and parts of pUB3729. Two classes were found. One class of recombinant plasmids conferred resistance to trimethoprim and ampicillin, while those of the other conferred resistance to trimethoprim and tetracycline. Recombinant plasmids

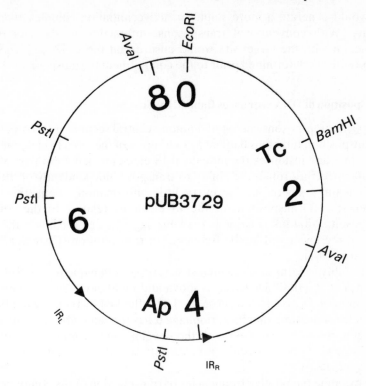

**Figure 26.4**   Map of pUB3729. IR$_L$ and IR$_R$, IR sequences derived from the left and right arms of TN$I$ and Tn$3$, respectively. The arrowheads indicate the orientation of the IR sequence.

of the former type all had approximately 1 kbp from pUB3729 inserted in different positions on R388, while the latter type consisted of R388 and most of pUB3729, specifically all of pUB3729 barring the ampicillin-resistance gene, again inserted at different sites on R388 in different recombinants. These two classes of insertions are what would result from transposition of the markers flanked by the direct repeats of the Tn$I$ IR sequence.

These data indicate that marker(s) flanked by direct repeats of the Tn$I$ IR sequence can transpose. The findings can be considered to be a logical extension of one-ended transposition and add weight to the proposal that the IR sequence is instrumental not only in initiation of the process, but also, in some way, in the majority of termination events.

One interesting additional feature of the results was that the frequency of one-ended transposition from pUB3729 was approximately tenfold higher than from pUB3033, a plasmid that has only one IR sequence (*Figure 26.3*). One possibility suggested by this degree of enhancement is that each copy of the IR sequence can 'sense' the presence of the other. This would pertain if, normally, the two copies of IR interact with each other, as well as with transposase, to produce an initiation complex that is more active than that generated from transposase and a single IR sequence. Further, the inverted configuration of

IRs would generate a more stable or active initiation complex than direct repeats. With conventional transposons, interaction of the IRs prior to interaction with the target site would ensure that the DNA sequence to be transposed was determined prior to the commitment to transpose.

**Transposition of DNA sequences flanked by Tn*1***

Composite transposons consist of a unique central section of DNA possessing no transposition functions flanked by two copies of the same IS element (*Figure 26.1*). In many instances the individual IS elements that form part of such a modular structure retain the ability to transpose independently of the rest of the structure. There is, however, little information about the relative efficiencies of transposition of the IS elements relative to the composite transposon. What information is available suggests that the larger the central segment the lower will be the frequency of transposition (Chandler, Clerget and Caro, 1981).

The ability to form such modular structures is not unique to the IS elements. Dobritsa *et al.* (1981; Dobritsa, Ivanova and Fedoseeva, 1983) reported that two copies of Tn*1* could transpose the DNA flanked by them, and it has been known for some time that bacteriophage μ has the same ability, a finding that has been elegantly exploited with the development of mini-μ and its use in mobilizing genes on to plasmids for easier study and manipulation (Faelen and Toussaint, 1976).

To examine the relative frequencies of transposition of the components of a modular system based on Tn*1* we developed a derivative transposon, Tn*835*, by replacing the *bla* gene of the former with a *cat* gene (*Figure 26.5*). Hence, Tn*835* confers resistance to chloramphenicol rather than to ampicillin. Both elements were transposed to a deletion derivative of R388, pUB3078, generated by circularizing the small *Bgl*II fragment of R388 (Heritage and Bennett, 1985), to create a set of recombinant plasmids with different arrangements of the two transposons. pUB2398 (*Figure 26.5*), which confers resistance to trimethoprim (Tp), ampicillin (Ap) and chloramphenicol (Cm), is representative.

pUB2398 was introduced, by transformation, into a *recA* strain of *E. coli* carrying pUB307, a conjugative R plasmid that confers resistance to kanamycin and tetracycline (Bennett, Grinsted and Richmond, 1977). (pUB3078 is non-conjugative and is not mobilized by pUB307.) The double plasmid strain was crossed with a second *recA* strain of *E. coli* and transconjugants were selected for resistance to either ampicillin (Tn*1*) or chloramphenicol (Tn*835*) and subsequently screened to determine which other markers had been acquired. The results are tabulated in *Figure 26.5*.

As expected, the individual transposons, Tn*1* and Tn*835*, transposed to pUB307 as determined initially by the acquisition of the single resistance genes, *bla* (Ap$^r$) or *cat* (Cm$^r$) respectively, and then by restriction enzyme analysis of the recombinant plasmids. In addition, two combinations of markers were transposed from pUB2398 to pUB307, namely, ApCm and ApCmTp. These correspond to the marker combinations on the two possible composite

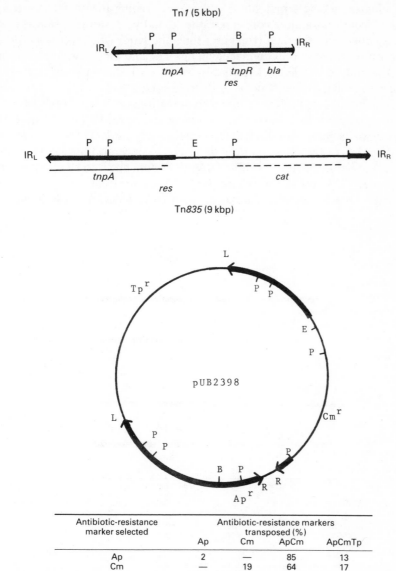

**Figure 26.5**   Transposition of antibiotic resistance genes from pUB2398. Abbreviations used are as in *Figure 26.3*. In addition: *cat*, chloramphenicol acetyltransferase; Ap$^r$, ampicillin resistance; Cm$^r$, chloramphenicol resistance; Tp$^r$, trimethoprim resistance.

elements generated by the presence of both Tn*1* and Tn*835* on pUB2398. Unexpectedly, one of these, that conferring resistance to ApCm, not only transposed efficiently but did so more frequently than either of its component transposons. Indeed, the 'wild-type' element was transposed least frequently.

The data are most easily explained by models that propose that the two ends of a transposon 'find' each other and then act co-operatively to join both ends of the element to the target site. Further, the coming together of the ends probably occurs by random collision, rather than by a systematic search from one IR sequence to the next (tracking) since the latter would be expected to favour transposition of the original elements, Tn*1* and Tn*835*, which is not the case. The random collision hypothesis would also allow pseudo initiation complexes involving direct repeats of IR to be established.

The results indicate that the different combinations of IR sequences, in pairs, are not equally effective in that the different structures delineated by them transpose with significantly different frequencies (*Figure 26.5*). The differences cannot be due to the IR sequences themselves, since all four are identical. Further, the size of the transposable DNA does not appear to be of overriding importance, since it was the second largest structure that transposed most frequently. Hence, sequences adjacent to an IR sequence must influence its activity.

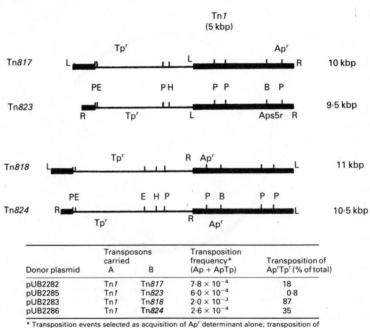

| Donor plasmid | Transposons carried A | B | Transposition frequency* (Ap + ApTp) | Transposition of Ap$^r$Tp$^r$ (% of total) |
|---|---|---|---|---|
| pUB2282 | Tn*1* | Tn*817* | $7·8 \times 10^{-4}$ | 18 |
| pUB2285 | Tn*1* | Tn*823* | $6·0 \times 10^{-4}$ | 0·8 |
| pUB2283 | Tn*1* | Tn*818* | $2·0 \times 10^{-3}$ | 87 |
| pUB2286 | Tn*1* | Tn*824* | $2·6 \times 10^{-4}$ | 35 |

\* Transposition events selected as acquisition of Ap$^r$ determinant alone; transposition of Tp$^r$ determinant detected as a non-selected co-inherited marker.

**Figure 26.6**   Transposition of Tn*1* and its derivatives, Tn*817*, Tn*818*, Tn*823* and Tn*824*, to pUB307. Abbreviations as in *Figures 26.3* and *26.5*.

The set of transposons illustrated in *Figure 26.6* represents a series of composite elements based on Tn*1*. However, instead of each structure being flanked by two functional transposons, each comprises a sequence encoding resistance to trimethoprim flanked on one side by an intact copy of Tn*1* and on the other by just one end of Tn*1*. The four structures represent the four possible arrangements.

With one exception, the Tn*1* component transposes more frequently than

he composite structure of which it is a part, and the frequency of transposition
of Tn*1* in every case is approximately the same. The one notable exception is
Tn*818* which transposes approximately ten times more frequently than its
component Tn*1*. Significantly, Tn*818* is delineated by sequences both of which
are derived from the left arm of Tn*1*, as is the composite structure on pUB2398
encoding resistance to ApCm (*Figure 26.5*) that proved to be the most active
transposon on the plasmid. In contrast, Tn*823*, which is delineated by
sequences both of which are derived from the right arm of Tn*1*, transposes at
only 1% of the frequency of its component Tn*1*.

These data suggest that transposase has a greater affinity for the IR sequence
on the left arm of Tn*1* than that on the right. The difference may not be great in
that it is only apparent in 'competition' experiments such as those described.
When artificial elements are constructed with inverted repeats of either the left
arm of Tn*1* or the right arm, these are found to transpose at more or less the
same frequency, which is not greatly different from that of Tn*1* itself (Arthur *et
al.*, 1984). In the experiments described above, elements defined by inverted
repeats of the left arm of Tn*1* consistently transposed more frequently than any
other, irrespective of their location. Given that the IR sequence itself is
indistinguishable from that on the right, then it is concluded that sequences
adjacent to the IR sequence and derived from Tn*1* must be responsible for the
effect. Either those on the left arm enhance the interaction of transposase with
the IR sequence, or those on the right arm interfere.

The frequency of transposition recorded for a particular element appears to
be determined not only by its current location but also by the potential target.
Kretschmer and Cohen (1977) reported that Tn*3* transposed more readily into
a bacterial plasmid than into the bacterial chromosome, despite the much
greater size of the latter. Similar results have been found in my laboratory.
λ::Tn*1* derivatives were used to introduce the transposon into a *recA* strain of
*E. coli* that was a λ lysogen and carried the IncW R plasmid R388.
Transductants resistant to ampicillin were selected and were obtained at
frequencies of approximately $10^{-6}$. 80% of the transductants carried the
acquired Tn*1* on R388 (A. Batt and P. Bennett, unpublished results). Hence
the plasmid apparently constituted a more attractive target than the
chromosome, despite the fact that it comprised less than 10% of the DNA of
the cell. The reason for this is unknown.

## Control of transposition

Despite the fact that many transposable elements are essentially promiscuous,
the genomes of most bacteria are not overweighted with any particular
elements. This argues that some form of control is exerted upon their activity
and, indeed, it is observed that for some elements e.g. Tn*10*, that as the copy
number per cell rises so the transposition frequency declines. From the genome
viewpoint it is desirable to limit the proliferation of transposable elements
because, not only can they induce damage by inserting within genes, but also
multiple copies provide a basis for more extensive genetic damage in the form
of deletions.

Various mechanisms that act to reduce the transposition activity of a particular element have been described. In the case of Tn*10*, production of transposase appears to be regulated post-transcriptionally by an antisense mRNA that can form a partial duplex with the transposase mRNA and prevent its translation (Kleckner, 1986). In the case of Tn*5*, control is thought to be exerted post-translationally by production of a transposition inhibitor that is a truncated version of the Tn*5* transposase (Berg *et al.*, 1988). Control of production of transposase by these and other IS elements also appears to be regulated by the *dam* methylation system, in that the levels of transposition in *dam* mutants are significantly higher than in *dam+* strains. In the cases of Tn*5* and Tn*10*, sequence analysis has indicated the presence of *dam* methylation sites within or near the promoters of the transposase genes (Kleckner, 1986; Berg *et al.*, 1988). One additional feature of these systems is that transposase would appear to act much more efficiently on IR sequences near the transposase gene and in *cis*. Complementation in *trans* by these enzymes is very inefficient.

Elements such as Tn*1/3* appear also to regulate transposition by a number of mechanisms. In the first instance, production of transposase is controlled by a transcriptional repressor (product of *tnpR, Figure 26.5*), a second activity displayed by the resolvase protein. Secondly, these and related transposons display a behaviour pattern termed transposition immunity, whereby transposition of a second copy of the element to a replicon that already has one is virtually eliminated under normal conditions, i.e. for elements with wild-type transposition functions (Robinson, Bennett and Richmond, 1977). The components of the immunity system are those needed for normal transposition, namely, the IR sequence and transposase.

Transposition immunity is conferred by a single copy of the element's IR sequence (Huang *et al.*, 1986), but its effectiveness in preventing transposition can be overridden (Wallace, Ward and Richmond, 1981; Heritage and Bennett, 1984). Hence, it was found that while a sequence of approximately 1 kbp from the left arm of Tn*1*, terminating in the IR sequence, exerted strong immunity, a sequence of approximately 500 bp from the right arm conferred only weak immunity. Given that the IR sequences in the two cases are identical, then the strength of the immunity reaction must reflect the context of the IR sequence.

It has been reported that phage μ shows a similar behaviour that can be attributed to one of the phage-encoded transposition proteins (B protein) binding more stably to target replicons that lack μ terminal sequences than to replicons that contain either μ or one end of the phage. B protein-target DNA destabilization requires phage A protein (transposase) and ATP (Adzuma and Mizuuchi, 1988).

Hence, it would seem, transposable elements have evolved to control their own movement. The result is that their distribution can be optimized while imposing least genetic stress on the hosts to which they ultimately owe their survival.

In only a few cases is the distribution of transposon insertions into a particular replicon truely random. Bacteriophage μ and Tn*5* may constitute

xceptions, at least in *E. coli*. One set of data serves to illustrate the point.
hree transposons, Tn*1*, Tn*7* and Tn*501*, were transposed on to pUB307.
'lones containing recombinant plasmids were chosen at random, their
lasmids isolated and the sites of transposon insertion determined. The results
early indicate clustering of insertions in various regions of the plasmid, rather
an a more or less random distribution (*Figure 26.7*). Similar results were
:ported by Kretschmer and Cohen (1977). Certainly, some regions would not
e expected to sustain an insertion and survive. However, the proportion of
lasmid RP1, the progenitor of pUB307, devoted to essential functions is
:latively small (Thomas and Smith, 1987) and cannot account for the
istribution seen. The phenomenon may not even be sequence specific, in that
particular sequence may prove to be an attractive target or a poor one
epending upon where on the replicon it is located (Grinsted *et al.*, 1978). This
ggests that considerations more important than DNA sequence may govern
e establishment of a transposon–target site complex.

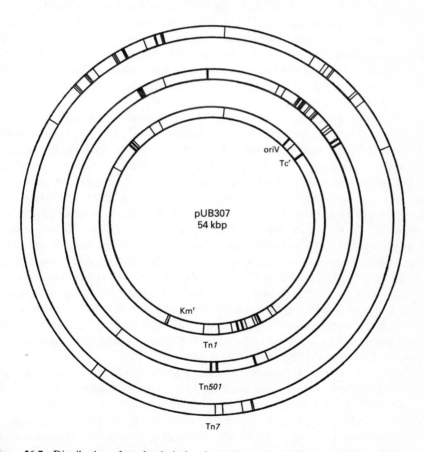

**ure 26.7** Distribution of randomly isolated transposon insertions in pUB307. pUB307 is a
letion derivative of the IncP plasmid RP1 (Bennett, Grinsted and Richmond, 1977). The bars
thin the concentric circles represent points of insertion of Tn*1* (inner), Tn*501* (middle) and Tn*7*
iter). Data taken from Grinsted *et al.* (1978) and Grinsted and Bennett (unpublished). *oriV*,
gin of replication; Tc^r, Km^r, resistance determinants for tetracycline and kanamycin.

Most, if not all, transposable elements seem to display some degree of insertional specificity, but, in general, the basis is unknown. Hence Tn3 has been reported to favour insertion into AT-rich sequences (Tu and Cohen 1980), a bias also observed for IS1 (Meyer, Iida and Arber, 1980). Indeed, Tn may have a tendency to insert close to sequences that are similar to the IR sequence of the element (Tu and Cohen, 1980). However, insertions into plasmids that have intact IR sequences do not cluster round such sequence (Bennett, unpublished results).

A more specific target has been suggested for the composite transposon Tn10. An analysis of many sites of insertion has indicated a preference for site that show some similarity to the sequence 5' GCTNAGC 3', where N identifie any base (Halling and Kleckner, 1982). The more similar the sequence, the greater the probability it will be used as a site of insertion, i.e. hot-spots of insertion are seen at sites that approximate closely to the consensus sequence A similar analysis of Tn5 insertions indicated that G/C pairs are present at the first and ninth base pairs of target duplications at five hot-spots and at about half the sites used infrequently. That these bases were an important feature of the hot-spots was demonstrated by altering them. The altered site ceased to be a hot-spot (Berg, Schmandt and Lowe, 1983; Berg *et al.*, 1988). However given the large number of 9 bp sequences with terminal G/C pairs which are rarely, if ever, used, then some other feature of the DNA must direct the transposon to insertion sites.

Other elements appear to select their target sites much more rigorously, IS4 which generates *gal* mutants in *E. coli* has been found to insert at only one site in the *galT* gene and at a limited number of other sites on the *E. coli* chromosome (Klaer *et al.*, 1981) and a derivative of IS2 was found to insert at single site in bacteriophage λ (Saint-Girons *et al.*, 1981), although the *E. coli* chromosome contains several copies of the parent element. When Tn transposes to a bacterial plasmid it displays a similar degree of specificity to Tn (*Figure 26.7*). However, when it transposes into the *E. coli* chromosome displays a very strict specificity and all insertions are at the same point and in the same orientation. The frequency of the site-specific insertion considerably higher than that of non-specific insertion. Both events are distinct in that, as well as core transposition functions, each also requires its own particular transposon function (Lichtenstein and Brenner, 1982; Rogers *et al.* 1986). Interestingly, most insertions of Tn7 into pUB307 are in the same orientation, unlike those of Tn1 and Tn501 which appear to be more or less random. The basis for the Tn7 bias is not known.

Tn7 seems to be representative of a small set of transposons that are distinct from IS elements and their composites and from the Tn1 family of transposons

Site-specific transposons have also been discovered in Gram-positive bacteria. Tn554, which encodes resistance to erythromycin, is one such. inserts preferentially at a single site in the chromosome of *Staphylococci aureus* and in one preferred orientation (Phillips and Novick, 1979). The transposon is unusual also in that it has asymmetric ends, i.e. no terminal IR sequences, and its insertion does not generate target-site duplication (Murphy, 1988). In contrast, another transposon encoding resistance to erythromycin, Tn*551*, shows no such behaviour. This element is notable because the IR sequences of this Gram-positive element are clearly related to those of Tn*1*, an archetypal Gram-negative transposon (Kahn and Novick, 1980).

## pUB2380

The foregoing has concentrated on conventional transposition systems. However, information is now emerging to indicate that not all transposition systems operate in this manner. One such is that encoded by pUB2380 (*Figure 26.8*), a small R plasmid discovered in a veterinary isolate of *E. coli*. pUB2380 encodes resistance to kanamycin. The *aph* gene responsible for this phenotype is essentially the same as that encoded by the composite transposon Tn*903* (Grindley and Joyce, 1980). The *aph* gene can be transposed from pUB2380 to R388. However, in contrast to conventional systems, the recombinants generated do not all have insertions of the same size, although the sites of

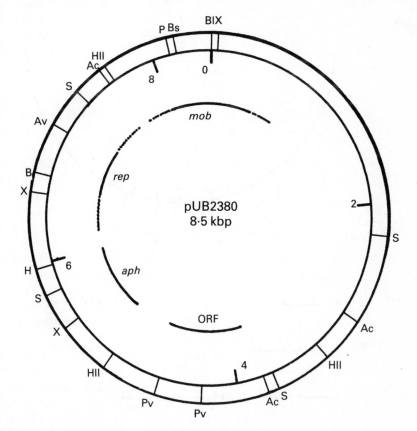

**Figure 26.8** Map of pUB2380. *mob*, Region needed for mobilization by R388; *rep*, region needed for replication; *aph*, aminoglycoside phosphotransferase (APH-3' type 1); ORF, open reading-frame in region necessary for transposition. Restriction sites: Ac, *Acc*I; B, *Bam*HI; Bl, *Bgl*I; Bs, *Bst*EII; HII, *Hind*II; H, *Hind*III; Pv, *Pvu*II; S, *Sma*I; X, *Xho*I. Plasmid coordinates start arbitrarily at the single *Bgl*I site.

insertion vary as in conventional systems (*Figure 26.9*). All insertions are related in that they have a common end, and so form a nested series, and some are larger than the unit length of the plasmid (Bennett *et al.*, 1986). These findings are reminiscent of the artificial one-ended systems generated from Tn*1* and related plasmids. DNA hybridization studies have indicated that the transposition system of pUB2380 is not related to that of Tn*1* and, furthermore, the pattern of behaviour is different in that few replicon fusions are generated. Derivative plasmids that carry two copies of the common terminus, both as direct repeats and inverted repeats, have been constructed. Preliminary data indicates that transposition of markers from these derivatives is essentially the same as from pUB2380, i.e. the system does not respond to terminal inverted repeats. Hence, pUB2380 represents a new form of transposition that naturally utilizes a single specific site, rather than two, and which, as a consequence, effects the transposition of variable lengths of DNA.

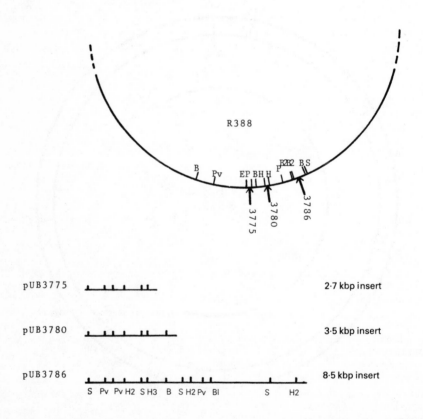

**Figure 26.9**    Transposition of the Km[r] determinant of pUB2380 on to R388. Part of the recipient plasmid R388 is indicated. Arrows indicate points of insertion of pUB2380 sequences into R388. The numbers designate the particular plasmid recombinants and the inserts in these are illustrated in the bottom half of the figure.

eferences

DZUMA, K. AND MIZUUCHI, K. (1988). Target immunity of Mu transposition reflects a differential distribution of Mu B protein. *Cell* 53, 257–266.

RTHUR, A. AND SHERRATT, D. (1979). Dissection of the transposition process: a transposon-encoded site-specific recombination system. *Molecular and General Genetics* 175, 267–274.

RTHUR, A., NIMMO, E., HETTLE, S. AND SHERRATT, D. (1984). Transposition and transposition immunity of transposon Tn*3* derivatives having different ends. *EMBO Journal* 3, 1723–1730.

VILA, P., DE LA CRUZ, F., WARD, E. AND GRINSTED, J. (1984). Plasmids containing one inverted repeat of Tn*21* can fuse with other plasmids in the presence of Tn*21* transposase. *Molecular and General Genetics* 195, 288–293.

ARTH, P.T., DATTA, N., HEDGES, R.W. AND GRINTER, N.J. (1976). Transposition of a deoxyribonucleic acid sequence encoding trimethoprim and streptomycin resistances from R483 to other replicons. *Journal of Bacteriology* 125, 800–810.

ENNETT, P.M., GRINSTED, J. AND RICHMOND, M.H. (1977). Transposition of Tn*A* does not generate deletions. *Molecular and General Genetics* 154, 205–211.

ENNETT, P.M., HERITAGE, J., COMANDUCCI, A. AND DODD, H.M. (1986). Evolution of R plasmids by replicon fusion. *Journal of Antimicrobial Chemotherapy* 18 (Supplement C), 103–111.

ERG, D.E. (1983). Structural requirement for IS*50*-mediated gene transposition. *Proceedings of the National Academy of Sciences of the United States of America* 80, 792–796.

ERG, D.E., SCHMANDT, M.A. AND LOWE, J.B. (1983). Specificity of transposon Tn*5* insertion. *Genetics* 105, 813–828.

ERG, D.E., DAVIES, J., ALLET, B. AND ROCHAIX, J.-D. (1975). Transposition of R factor genes to bacteriophage λ. *Proceedings of the National Academy of Sciences of the United States of America* 72, 3628–3632.

ERG, D.E., KAZIC, T., PHADNIS, S.H., DODSON, K.W. AND LODGE, J.K. (1988). Mechanism and regulation of transposition. In *Transposition: Symposium 43 of The Society for General Microbiology* (A.J. Kingsman, K.F. Chater and S.M. Kingsman, Eds), pp. 107–129. Cambridge University Press, Cambridge.

AMPBELL, A., STARLINGER, P., BERG, D.E., BOTSTEIN, D., LEDERBERG, E.M., NOVICK, R.P. AND SZYBALSKI, W. (1979). Nomenclature of transposable elements in prokaryotes. *Plasmid* 2, 466–473.

HANDLER, M., CLERGET, M. AND CARO, L. (1981). IS*1* promoted events associated with drug resistance plasmids. *Cold Spring Harbor Symposium on Quantitative Biology* 45, 157–165.

RAIGIE, R., MIZUUCHI, M., ADZUMA, K. AND MIZUUCHI, K. (1988). Mechanism of the DNA strand transfer step in transposition of Mu DNA. In *Transposition: Symposium 43 of The Society for General Microbiology* (A.J. Kingsman, K.F. Chater and S.M. Kingsman, Eds), pp. 131–148. Cambridge University Press, Cambridge.

OBRITSA, A.P., IVANOVA, Z.A. AND FEDOSEEVA, V.B. (1983). Transposition of DNA fragments flanked by two inverted Tn*1* sequences: translocation of the plasmid RP4::Tn*1* region harboring the Tc^r marker. *Gene* 22, 237–243.

OBRITSA, A.P., DOBRITSA, S.V., POPOV, E.I. AND FEDOSEEVA, V.B. (1981). Transposition of a DNA fragment flanked by two inverted Tn*1* sequences. *Gene* 14, 217–225.

AELEN, M. AND TOUSSAINT, A. (1976). Bacteriophage Mu-1, a tool to transpose and to localize bacterial genes. *Journal of Molecular Biology* 104, 525–539.

ALAS, D.J. AND CHANDLER, M. (1981). On the mechanism of transposition. *Proceedings of the National Academy of Sciences of the United States of America* 78, 4858–4862.

RINDLEY, N.D.F. AND JOYCE, C.M. (1980). Genetic and DNA sequence analysis of the kanamycin resistance transposon Tn903. *Proceedings of the National Academy of Sciences of the United States of America* **77**, 7176–7180.

GRINSTED, J. (1986). Evolution of transposable elements. *Journal of Antimicrobial Chemotherapy* **18** (Supplement C), 77–83.

GRINSTED, J., BENNETT, P.M., HIGGINSON, S. AND RICHMOND, M.H. (1978). Regional preference of insertion of Tn501 and Tn801 into RP1 and its derivatives. *Molecular and General Genetics* **166**, 313–320.

HALLING, S.M. AND KLECKNER, N. (1982). A symmetrical six-base-pair target site sequence determines Tn10 insertion specificity. *Cell* **28**, 155–163.

HEDGES, R.W. AND JACOB, A.E. (1974). Transposition of ampicillin resistance from RP4 to other replicons. *Molecular and General Genetics* **132**, 31–40.

HERITAGE, J. AND BENNETT, P.M. (1984). The role of TnA transposase in transposition immunity. *Plasmid* **12**, 218–221.

HERITAGE, J. AND BENNETT, P.M. (1985). Plasmid fusions mediated by one end of TnA. *Journal of General Microbiology* **131**, 1131–1140.

HUANG, C.-J., HEFFRON, F., TWU, JR.-S., SCHLOEMER, R.H. AND LEE, C.-H. (1986). Analysis of Tn3 sequences required for transposition and immunity. *Gene* **41**, 23–31.

KAHN, S.A. AND NOVICK, R.P. (1980). Terminal nucleotide sequences of Tn551, a transposon specifying erythromycin resistance in *Staphylococcus aureus*: homology with Tn3. *Plasmid* **4**, 148–154.

KLAER, R., KUHN, S., FRITZ, H.-J., TILLMANN, E., SAINT-GIRONS, I., HABERMANN, P., PFEIFER, D. AND STARLINGER, P. (1981). Studies on transposition mechanisms and specificity of IS4. *Cold Spring Harbor Symposium on Quantitative Biology* **45**, 215–224.

KLECKNER, N. (1986). Mechanism and regulation of Tn10 and IS10 transposition. In *Regulation of Gene Expression, 25 Years On: Symposium 39 of The Society for General Microbiology* (I.R. Booth and C.F. Higgins, Eds), pp. 221–237. Cambridge University Press, Cambridge.

KLECKNER, N., CHAN, R.K., TYE, B.-K. AND BOTSTEIN, D. (1975). Mutagenesis by insertion of a drug resistance element carrying an inverted repetition. *Journal of Molecular Biology* **97**, 561–575.

KRETSCHMER, P.J. AND COHEN, S.N. (1977). Selected translocation of plasmid genes: frequency and regional specificity of translocation of the Tn3 element. *Journal of Bacteriology* **130**, 888–899.

LICHTENSTEIN, C. AND BRENNER, S. (1982). Unique insertion site of Tn7 in the *E. coli* chromosome. *Nature* **297**, 601–603.

MCCLINTOCK, B. (1956). Controlling elements and the gene. *Cold Spring Harbor Symposium on Quantitative Biology* **21**, 197–216.

MEYER, J., IIDA, S. AND ARBER, W. (1980). Does the insertion element IS1 transpose preferentially into A+T-rich DNA segments. *Molecular and General Genetics* **178**, 471–473.

MORISATO, D. AND KLECKNER, N. (1987). Tn10 transposition and circle formation in vitro. *Cell* **51**, 101–111.

MOTSCH, S. AND SCHMITT, R. (1984). Replicon fusion mediated by a single-ended derivative of transposon Tn1721. *Molecular and General Genetics* **195**, 281–287.

MOTSCH, S., SCHMITT, R., AVILA, P., DE LA CRUZ, F., WARD, E. AND GRINSTED, J (1985). Junction sequences generated by 'one-ended transposition'. *Nucleic Acids Research* **13**, 3335–3342.

MURPHY, E. (1988). Transposable elements in *Staphylococcus*. In *Transposition. Symposium 43 of The Society for General Microbiology* (A.J. Kingsman, K.F. Chater and S.M. Kingsman, Eds), pp. 59–89. Cambridge University Press, Cambridge.

OHTSUBO, H. AND OHTSUBO, E. (1978). Nucleotide sequence of an insertion element, IS1. *Proceedings of the National Academy of Sciences of the United States of America* **75**, 615–619.

)HTSUBO, E., ZENILMAN, M., OHTSUBO, H., MCCORMICK, M., MACHIDA, C. AND MACHIDA, Y. (1981). Mechanism of insertion and cointegration mediated by IS*1* and Tn*3*. *Cold Spring Harbor Symposium on Quantitative Biology* **45**, 283–295.

HILLIPS, S. AND NOVICK, R.P. (1979). Tn*554* – a site-specific repressor-controlled transposon in *Staphylococcus aureus*. *Nature* **278**, 476–478.

.OBINSON, M.K., BENNETT, P.M. AND RICHMOND, M.H. (1977). Inhibition of Tn*A* translocation by Tn*A*. *Journal of Bacteriology* **129**, 407–414.

.OGERS, M., EKATERINAKI, N., NIMMO, E. AND SHERRATT, D. (1986). Analysis of Tn*7* transposition. *Molecular and General Genetics* **205**, 550–555.

AINT-GIRONS, I., FRITZ, H.-J., SHAW, C., TILLMANN, E. AND STARLINGER, P. (1981). Integration specificity of an artificial kanamycin transposon constructed by the *in vitro* insertion of an internal Tn*5* fragment into IS2. *Molecular and General Genetics* **183**, 45–50.

HAPIRO, J.A. (1979). Molecular model for the transposition and replication of bacteriophage mu and other transposable elements. *Proceedings of the National Academy of Sciences of the United States of America* **76**, 1933–1937.

TARLINGER, P. AND SAEDLER, H. (1972). Insertion mutations in microorganisms. *Biochimie* **54**, 177–185.

'AYLOR, A.L. (1963). Bacteriophage-induced mutation in *Escherichia coli*. *Proceedings of the National Academy of Sciences of the United States of America* **50**, 1043–1051.

'HOMAS, C.M. AND SMITH, C.A. (1987). Incompatibility group P plasmids: genetics, evolution and use in genetic manipulation. *Annual Review of Microbiology* **41**, 77–101.

'OUSSAINT, A. AND RÉSIBOIS, A. (1983). Phage Mu: transposition as a life-style. In *Mobile Genetic Elements* (J.A. Shapiro, Ed.), pp. 105–158. Academic Press, London.

.U, C.-P. AND COHEN, S.N. (1980). Translocation specificity of the Tn*3* element: characterization of sites of multiple insertions. *Cell* **19**, 151–160.

VALLACE, L.J., WARD, J.M. AND RICHMOND, M.H. (1981). The location of sequences of Tn*A* required for the establishment of transposition immunity. *Molecular and General Genetics* **184**, 80–86.

VEINERT, T.A., DERBYSHIRE, K.M., HUGHSON, F.M. AND GRINDLEY, N.D.F. (1984). Replicative and conservative transpositional recombination of insertion sequences. *Cold Spring Harbor Symposium on Quantitative Biology* **49**, 251–260.

VISHART, W.L., BROACH, J.R. AND OHTSUBO, E. (1985). ATP-dependent specific binding of Tn*3* transposase to Tn*3* inverted repeats. *Nature* **314**, 556–558.

# pUB2380: An R Plasmid Encoding a Unique, Natural One-Ended Transposition System

ANTONELLA COMANDUCCI, HELEN M. DODD AND
PETER M. BENNETT

Department of Microbiology, The Medical School, University of Bristol,
University Walk, Bristol BS8 1TD, UK

## Introduction

pUB2380 is an 8·5 kbp R-plasmid that confers resistance to kanamycin by virtue of production of an aminoglycoside phosphotransferase (APH-3'-type). The plasmid was obtained from *Escherichia coli* SE53, a strain isolated from slurry waste from a commercial calf-rearing unit on a farm in the south-west of England (Linton and Hinton, 1984).

Preliminary investigations indicated that the plasmid is ColE1-like in that it will not establish in a DNA polymerase I-deficient strain of *E. coli*. Subsequent DNA hybridization experiments have demonstrated homology between the replication regions of the two plasmids (R. Heard and P. Bennett, unpublished results). Nonetheless, it is compatible with both pBR322 and pACYC184. pUB2380 can be mobilized by a wide variety of plasmids from many different Inc groups and will assist conjugal transfer of pBR322 mediated by the majority of these at a transfer freqency similar to its own (A. Chalker and P. Bennett, unpublished results).

The kanamycin-resistance gene was initially located by insertional inactivation using Tn*1* from pMR5 (Robinson *et al.*, 1980) and was shown to have strong homology with the kanamycin-resistance gene of Tn*903* (Oka, Sugisaki and Takanami, 1981). Sequencing studies have shown the two genes to be virtually identical and the gene products differ in only two amino acid residues (Dodd and Bennett, unpublished results). Sequences on pUB2380 needed for mobilization were also located by insertional inactivation, using the transposons Tn*1725* and Tn*1732* (Ubben and Schmitt, 1986). Our current knowledge of pUB2380 is summarized in *Figure 27.1*.

*Genetic Transformation and Expression*
© Intercept Ltd, PO Box 716, Andover, Hants, SP10 1YG, UK

305

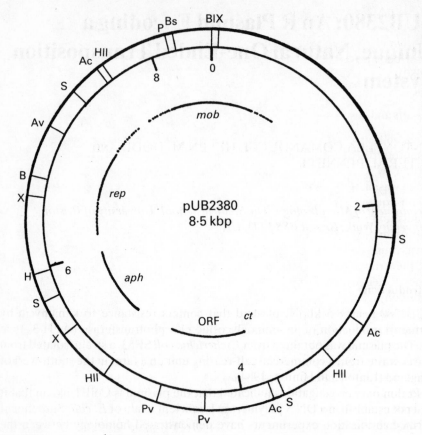

**Figure 27.1**  Map of pUB2380. *mob*, Region needed for mobilization by R388; *rep*, region needed for replication; *aph*, aminoglycoside phosphotransferase (APH-3′-type 1); ORF, open reading-frame in region necessary for transposition. Restriction sites: Ac, *Acc*I; B, *Bam*HI; Bl, *Bgl*I; Bs, *Bst*EII; HII, *Hin*dII; H, *Hin*dIII; Pv, *Pvu*II; S, *Sma*I; X, *Xho*I. Plasmid coordinates start arbitrarily at the single *Bgl*I site, *ct*, the constant terminus of 'one-ended' transposition maps to coordinate 3·5.

Kanamycin-resistance genes, particularly those encoding and APH-3′-type 1 are found on a variety of transposons (Bennett, 1987), so it was of interest to determine if the kanamycin-resistance determinant of pUB2380 is transposable, particularly since small plasmids encoding resistance to aminoglycosides other than streptomycin (Korfmann *et al.*, 1983) appear to be uncommon.

**Methods**

BACTERIAL STRAINS AND PLASMIDS

*E. coli* strains used were: UB5201 (Pro⁻Met⁻NalʳRecA⁻) (Sanchez, Bennett and Richmond, 1982); UB2272 (Trp⁻Met⁻Lys⁻StrʳRifʳPolA⁻) (Jenkins and Bennett, 1976). Plasmids used were: R388 (IncW Tp Su) (Ward and Grinsted,

)78); pACYC184 (CmTc) (Chang and Cohen, 1978); pUB2380 (Km) (this aper).

All *in vivo* and *in vitro* plasmid manipulations were performed essentially as escribed in Grinsted and Bennett (1988) or in Maniatis, Fritsch and Sambrook 1982).

## esults and discussion

UB2380 and the IncW plasmid R388, which encodes resistance to both imethoprim and sulphonamides, were introduced into *E. coli* UB5201, the ormer by transformation and the latter by conjugation. The double-plasmid train was, in turn, outcrossed with *E. coli* UB2272, which is *polA* and which, as consequence, will not maintain pUB2380. Transconjugants, selected for cquisition of kanamycin resistance, were obtained at a frequency of pproximately $10^{-6}$. When these were, in their turn, used as resistance donors was found that the kanamycin-resistance determinant of pUB2380 was linked o the trimethoprim-resistance determinant of R388 in all cases tested. Jnexpectedly, when the sizes of recombinant plasmids from different ransconjugants were examined by agarose gel electrophoresis, instead of them ll having the same size, consistent with acquisition by R388 of a anamycin-resistance transposon from pUB2380, they showed considerable ize variation. Further no particular size class appeared to be dominant.

Several recombinants were isolated and examined by restriction endonuc-ease analysis. The results indicated that each recombinant had a unique nsertion of pUB2380 DNA into R388, both with respect to the length of the nsertion and its location on R388 (*Table 27.1*). The insertions necessarily ormed an overlapping series of fragments in that all had been selected for their bility to confer resistance to kanamycin. Detailed analysis indicated further hat all inserts belonged to a nested series each with one common end, lesignated *ct* (common terminus), a sequence located on pUB2380 between he *Hin*dII site at coordinate 3·3 and the *Acc*I site at 3·85 (*Figure 27.1*). Inserts ranged in size from 2·7 kbp to greater than 10 kbp, i.e. larger than the size of the plasmid monomer (*Table 27.1*). Inserts larger than unit plasmid size were all

**Table 27.1**   R388::pUB2380 derivatives generated by 'one-ended' transposition

| R388::pUB2380 derivative | Length of pUB2380 DNA inserted (kbp) | Location of insertion on R388 |
|---|---|---|
| pUB3780 | 3·5 | 0·4 |
| pUB3778 | 3·3 | 0·9 |
| pUB3786 | 8·6 | 1·5 |
| pUB3775 | 2·8 | 2·1 |
| pUB4421 | 10·0 | 2·55 |
| pUB4426 | 2·8 | 2·6 |
| pUB4423 | 3·2 | 2·7 |
| pUB3781 | 3·7 | 2·8 |
| pUB3783 | 6·8 | 6·4 |
| pUB3776 | 2·8 | 8·8 |
| pUB3779 | 3·5 | 9·0 |
| pUB3777 | 2·9 | 9·6 |

R388 coordinates are according to Avila and de la Cruz (1988).

found to consist of pUB2380 in linear array, from *ct*, with direct termina repeats, the size of which determined the increase in size over unit length. Th lower limit detected represents the smallest sequence, commencing at *ct*, tha can accommodate an intact copy of the kanamycin-resistance gene. Hence, w believe this lower limit is imposed by the selection employed, rather tha being the smallest sequence that can be transposed.

Several recombinants were tested to determine if the pUB2380 sequence transposed on to R388 could mediate further transposition events. Th recombinants were transferred, by conjugation, to *E. coli* UB5201 containin the non-mobilizable artificial plasmid, pACYC184. Double-plasmid strain were then crossed with *E. coli* UB2272. Transconjugants, selected fo resistance to chloramphenicol, were all found to contain new plasmi recombinants comprising one of the original R388–pUB2380 recombinan plasmids inserted into pACYC184, as judged by the fact that the trimethoprim and kanamycin-resistance markers were linked to the resistance markers o pACYC184 (CmTc). Limited restriction endonuclease analysis of one or tw such recombinants confirmed that they comprised R388–pUB2380 recom binant sequences inserted into pACYC184. Control experiments with R38: itself and pACYC184 did not generate such recombinants.

The smallest R388–pUB2380 recombinant tested was pUB3775, whicl carries a 2·7 kbp insert of pUB2380. This recombinant mobilized pACYC18 markers to *E. coli* UB2272 at a frequency of approximately $10^{-7}$. Given tha approximately 1 kbp of the pUB2380 insert represents the kanamycin resistance determinant and that this is located to one end of the insert, then the transposition functions acquired by pUB3775 must be located between the other end of the insert, *ct*, and the start of the kanamycin-resistance determinant, namely, between pUB2380 coordinates 3·5 and 5·2 (*Figure 27.1*) Transposon insertions in this region of pUB2380 eliminate the ability to transpose the kanamycin-resistance determinant.

To determine more accurately the end points of transposed sequences insertions within the trimethoprim-resistance gene of R388, the sequence o which was known (Swift, McCarthy and Heffrom, 1981), were sought. Severa independent insertions were recovered. One of these, pUB4421, has been usec to determine the pUB2380 sequences at the junctions with R388. The result obtained are illustrated in *Figure 27.2*. The pUB2380 sequences on pUB442 are flanked by 4 bp direct repeats of the R388 target DNA, consistent with the formation of the recombinant by a transposition mechanism (Grindley and Reed, 1985). However, in contrast to conventional transposition systems, the ends of the inserted DNA show no evidence of inverted repeated (IR sequences. Indeed, the sequences at *ct* and those at the opposite end of the insertion appear to bear no homology whatsoever.

The sequence at *ct* has been compared to the IR sequences of a variety o different transposable elements, including transposons and IS elements, but no homology with any published sequence has been detected.

The transposition system of pUB2380 represents, therefore, a novel natura system. The evidence for transposition is that the recombination mechanisn inserts one DNA sequence into another in the absence of a functional *recA*

GGGTAGGCAGTCAGAGTTCGATTTGCTTGTCGCCATAATAG
CCCATCCGTCAGTCTCAAGCTAAACGAACAGCGGTATTATC

R388

GGGTAGGCAGTCAGAGTTCACGTATAGGAAATTGAAAAACCAGTCGATACC-----------
CCCATCCGTCAGTCTCAAGTGCATATCCTTTAACTTTTTGGTCAGCTATGG-----------

R388        pUB2380—constant end (*ct*)

---------TTTTCAATTTGCAGCCGCCCAGGCTGCCGTGGTTCGATTTGCTTGTCGCCATAATAG
---------AAAAGTTAAACGTCGGCGGGTCCGACGGCACCAAGCTAAACGAACGGGTATTATC

pUB2380—variable end        R388

**Figure 27.2** Junction sequences of the R388::pUB2380 transposition recombinant pUB4421. Sequences over- and underlined represent those derived from R388. Other sequences are derived from pUB2380. The four base pairs highlighted by the bold underlining are the R388 target sequence duplication generated by the transpositional insertion.

gene product and does not require any obvious DNA–DNA homolog
between the recombination site on pUB2380, namely *ct*, and the putative site (
insertion, but does generate target-site duplications. Conversely, th
transposition does not involve a conventional transposon, in that no define
element is transposed. It remains to be seen if this system has been derive
from a conventional transposon or represents a totally novel mechanism
Whatever, the system has not been derived from one of the well-studied I
elements or class 2 transposons.

The transposition system encoded by pUB2380 represents the first natur;
one-ended transposition system. The nearest equivalent would appear to b
the one-ended transposition systems derived from the class 2 transposons Tn*1/*
(Arthur *et al.*, 1984; Heritage and Bennett, 1985), Tn*21* (Avila *et al.*, 1984) an
Tn*1721* (Motsch and Schmitt, 1984). This system differs from those, howeve
in that the recombinants generated by pUB2380 show considerable variation i
size whereas those generated by one-ended variants of class 2 transposons ar
predominantly of one size, equivalent to the fusion of the donor and recipier
replicons. One suggestion for this is that the solitary IR sequence on thes
derivatives not only initiates the transposition event but also initiates i
termination (Motsch *et al.*, 1985). That, clearly, cannot be the case fc
pUB2380 where putative termination points are located all round the DN/
molecule.

The evidence collected to date suggests that pUB2380 encodes a nov
system capable of mediating transpositional recombination of varying length
of a circular DNA molecule. The finding that the lengths of some insertion
exceed that of the donor plasmid suggests that the mechanism may involv
DNA synthesis and, given the form of the duplication on these inserts,
variation of 'rolling-circle' replication is indicated. Indeed, such a model wa
originally proposed to explain conventional transposition (Galas an
Chandler, 1981) and has been proposed as the mechanism of transposition c
one-ended derivatives of class 2 transposons generated *in vitro*.

### Acknowledgement

PMB gratefully acknowledges the award of an MRC project grant for part o
the work reported.

### References

ARTHUR, A., NIMMO, E., HETTLE, S. AND SHERRATT, D. (1984). Transposition an
    transposition immunity of transposon Tn*3* derivatives having different ends
    *EMBO Journal* **3**, 1723–1730.
AVILA, P. AND DE LA CRUZ, F. (1988). Physical and genetic map of the IncW plasmi
    R388. *Plasmid* **20**, 155–157.
AVILA, P., DE LA CRUZ, F., WARD, E. AND GRINSTED, J. (1984). Plasmids containin
    one inverted repeat of Tn*21* can fuse with other plasmids in the presence of Tn*2*
    transposase. *Molecular and General Genetics* **195**, 288–293.
BENNETT, P.M. (1987). Genetic basis of the spread of antibiotic resistance genes
    *Annali dell'Istituto Superiore di Sanita* **23**, 819–826.
CHANG, A.C.Y. AND COHEN, S.N. (1978). Construction and characterisation o

amplifiable multicopy DNA cloning vehicles derived from the P15A cryptic miniplasmid. *Journal of Bacteriology* **134**, 1141–1156.

ȝALAS, D.J. AND CHANDLER, M. (1981). On the molecular mechanism of transposition. *Proceedings of the National Academy of Sciences of the United States of America* **78**, 4858–4862.

ȝRINDLEY, N.D.F. AND REED, R.R. (1985). Transpositional recombination in prokaryotes. *Annual Reviews of Biochemistry* **54**, 863–896.

ȝRINSTED, J. AND BENNETT, P.M. (Eds) (1988). *Methods in Microbiology, Volume 21: Plasmid technology*, 2nd edn. Academic Press, London.

ȝERITAGE, J. AND BENNETT, P.M. (1985). Plasmid fusions mediated by one end of Tn*A*. *Journal of General Microbiology* **131**, 1131–1140.

ENKINS, S.T. AND BENNETT, P.M. (1976). Effect of mutations in deoxyribonucleic acid repair pathways on the sensitivity of *Escherichia coli* K-12 strains to nitrofurantoin. *Journal of Bacteriology* **125**, 1214–1216.

ȝORFMANN, G., LÜDTKE, W., VAN TREEK, V. AND WIEDEMANN, B. (1983). Dissemination of streptomycin and sulphonamide resistance by plasmid pBP1 in *Escherichia coli*. *European Journal of Clinical Microbiology* **2**, 463–468.

ȝINTON, A.H. AND HINTON, M.H. (1984). The ecology of R plasmids in *Salmonella typhimurium* and associated bacteria. In *Agriculture: Priority aspects of salmonellosis research* pp. 275–286. Commission of the European Communities, EUR 9197 EN.

MANIATIS, T., FRITSCH, E.F. AND SAMBROOK, J. (1982). *Molecular Cloning. A Laboratory Manual*. Cold Spring Harbor, New York.

MOTSCH, S. AND SCHMITT, R. (1984). Replicon fusion mediated by a single-ended derivative of transposon Tn*1721*. *Molecular and General Genetics* **195**, 281–287.

MOTSCH, S., SCHMITT, R., AVILA, P., DE LA CRUZ, F., WARD, E. AND GRINSTED, J. (1985). Junction sequences generated by 'one-ended transposition'. *Nucleic Acids Research* **13**, 3335–3342.

OKA, A., SUGISAKI, H. AND TAKANAMI, M. (1981). Nucleotide sequence of the kanamycin resistance transposon Tn*903*. *Journal of Molecular Biology* **147**, 217–226.

ROBINSON, M.K., BENNETT, P.M., FALKOW, S. AND DODD, H.M. (1980). Isolation of a temperature-sensitive derivative of RP1. *Plasmid* **3**, 343–347.

SANCHEZ, J., BENNETT, P.M. AND RICHMOND, M.H. (1982). Expression of *elt*-B, the gene encoding the B subunit of the heat-labile enterotoxin of *Escherichia coli*, when cloned in pACYC184. *FEMS Microbiology Letters* **14**, 1–5.

SWIFT, G., MCCARTHY, B.J. AND HEFFRON, F. (1981). DNA sequence of a plasmid-encoded dihydrofolate reductase. *Molecular and General Genetics* **181**, 441–447.

UBBEN, D. AND SCHMITT, R. (1986). Tn*1721* derivatives for transposon mutagenesis, restriction mapping and DNA sequence analysis. *Gene* **41**, 145–152.

WARD, J.M. AND GRINSTED, J. (1978). Mapping of functions in the R-plasmid R388 by examination of deletion mutants generated *in vitro*. *Gene* **3**, 87–95.

# 28
# Tn7-like Transposon in the Gonococcus

S. KOTHARI* AND L.O. BUTLER

Bacterial Genetics Laboratory, Department of Medical Microbiology, St.
George's Hospital Medical School, Cranmer Terrace, London SW17 ORE, UK

## Introduction

In recent years, some clinical isolates of penicillinase-producing *Neisseria gonorrhoeae* have shown resistance to spectinomycin. A spectinomycin-resistant gonococcus had been examined in the 1970s and shown by the Sparling laboratory to possess a chromosomal gene mediating the spectinomycin resistance, the gene exhibiting some 30% linkage with the chromosomally located streptomycin-resistance determinant (Sarubbi, Blackman and Sparling, 1974). We have previously reported studies on a recent isolate (known as strain F29) and shown that the spectinomycin-resistance determinant possessed by the strain was not chromosomally located but was associated with the gonococcal conjugative plasmid, which could be transferred into *Escherichia coli* HB101 by transformation and by conjugation, and was responsible for the coding of an enzyme having the properties of AAD3"/9, the product of the *aadA* gene carried by Tn7 (Butler and Kothari, 1984; Kothari and Butler, 1986). We are now able to report on the molecular analysis of the spectinomycin determinant of the strain F29 with the conclusion that the determinant has very close homology with that forming part of the complex transposon Tn7.

## Results and discussion

### EVIDENCE FOR TRANSPOSON NATURE

Transformation into *E. coli* HB101, using as donor DNA either a total DNA preparation of strain F29 or the modified conjugative plasmid of 27·5 MDa separated by electrophoresis on an agarose gel, gave rise to spectinomycin-resistant transformants possessing a larger plasmid of 48·5 MDa (*Figure 28.1*).

* Present address: Department of Medicine, University of Cambridge Clinical School, Addenbrooke's Hospital, Hills Road, Cambridge CB2 2QQ, UK

*Genetic Transformation and Expression*
© Intercept Ltd, PO Box 716, Andover, Hants, SP10 1YG, UK

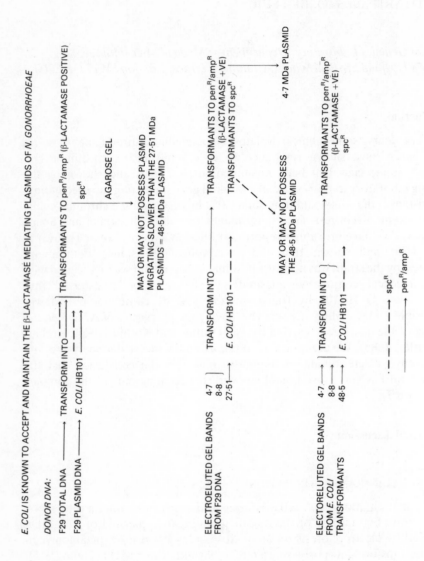

**Figure 28.1**    Summary of transformation with donor DNA derived from *N. gonorrhoeae* strain F29 into *E. coli* HB101.

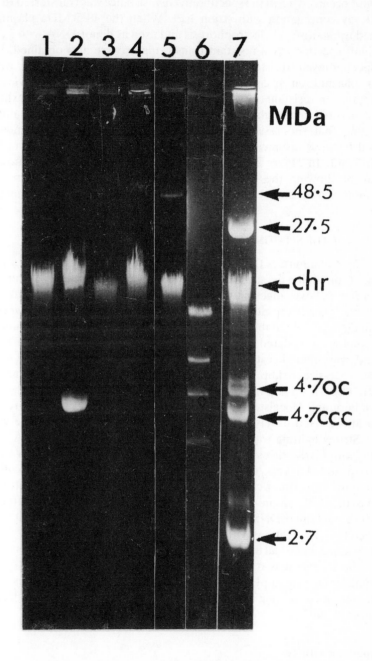

**Figure 28.2** Plasmid profiles shown by electrophoresis in 0·6% (w/v) agarose gel of *N. gonorrhoeae* F29 and of various *E. coli amp*^R and *spc*^R conjugants derived from F29. Lane 1, *E. coli* J53-2, total DNA; lane 2, *E. coli amp*^R conjugant, total DNA; lane 3, *E. coli* HB101, total DNA; lane 4, *E. coli spc*^R conjugant, total DNA; lane 5, *E. coli* J53-2 conjugant (2 step), total DNA; lane 6, lambda DNA/*Hin*dIII digest; lane 7, *N. gonorrhoeae* F29, total DNA.

This also occurred when the spectinomycin resistance was transferred to *E. coli* HB101 by conjugation with strain F29. When the 48·5 MDa plasmid was isolated by agarose gel electrophoresis and used as donor DNA with *E. coli* as recipient, spectinomycin-resistant transformants were also obtained. Hence, the spectinomycin-resistance determinant had become associated with this larger plasmid on transmission to the *E. coli* recipient. However, the spectinomycin-resistant transformants or conjugants did not always exhibit this larger plasmid although the antibiotic resistance was stably maintained, indicating that the resistance determinant might well be chromosomally located in those instances. This would indicate a transposon nature for the determinant. In *Figure 28.2*, lane 5 is DNA from a spectinomycin-resistant conjugant showing the 48·5 MDa plasmid, while lane 4 is from another spectinomycin-resistant conjugant not exhibiting the 48·5 MDa plasmid.

CLONING OF THE SPECTINOMYCIN-RESISTANCE DETERMINANT

*Figure 28.3* summarizes the steps taken in leading to the cloning of a 1·3 kbp fragment containing the spectinomycin determinant. A total DNA preparation from strain F29 was digested with the restriction enzyme *Ava*I giving several fragments. These were cloned into pUC8 and transformed into *E. coli* HB101, and challenged for double resistance to spectinomycin and ampicillin. One such colony was isolated and the cloned plasmid designated pLOB207. This plasmid was then digested with *Eco*RI, giving five fragments. One such fragment of size 6 kbp (in pUC8) gave rise to spectinomycin resistance (pLOB208). This 6 kbp fragment was labelled by the oligonucleotide method of Feinberg and Vogelstein (1984) and used as a probe on denatured DNA preparations fixed on Hybond-Nylon membranes (Amersham International PLC). Strong lighting was obtained with *Eco*RI-digested Tn7 DNA, weaker lighting with *Eco*RI-digested Tn*554* DNA, while three bands, of sizes 1·04 kbp, 0·72 kbp and 0·5 kbp, of a *Hin*fI digest of DNA from an *E. coli* J53–2 spectinomycin-resistant conjugant derived from a primary conjugation of *E. coli* HB101 with strain F29, also gave strong lighting. This latter DNA therefore contained DNA derived from the gonococcal strain F29 that had survived two conjugations with *E. coli*.

The 6 kbp gonococcal insert in pLOB208 was then digested with *Ava*I to give a 1·3 kbp fragment that carried the spectinomycin-resistance determinant, shown after cloning in pUC8 (pLOB209). This was then labelled as a probe, which gave good lighting with the 0·72 kbp fragment derived from the *E. coli* J53–2 conjugant.

**Comparison with Tn7**

The molecular characteristics of the spectinomycin-resistance determinant contained in Tn7 has been well documented by Fling, Kopf and Richards (1985). The *aadA* structural gene was found to be 786 bases long, which compares well with the size of the *Hin*fI fragment having homology with the probe from pLOB209. The *Ava*I–*Eco*RI fragment of 1·3 kbp containing the

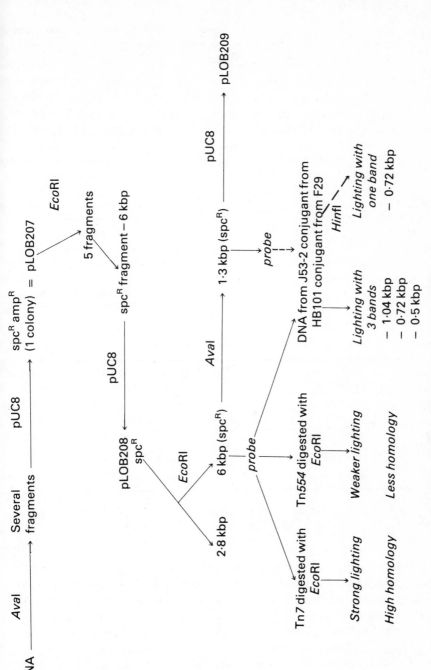

**Figure 28.3** Summary of cloning and hybridization strategies.

# pLOB209

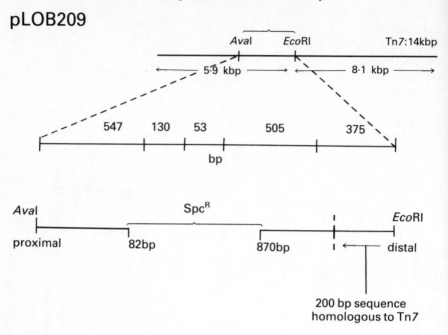

**Figure 28.4**  Comparison of the *Hpa*II digest fragments of the 1·3 kbp *Ava*I–*Eco*RI insert of pLOB209 with the equivalent fragment from Tn7 as published by Fling, Kopf and Richards (1985).

spectinomycin-resistant fragment from pLOB209 was digested with *Hpa*II so that the fragments produced could be compared to those deduced from the sequence data of this fragment determined by Fling and her co-workers. The results given in *Figure 28.4* shows that good agreement was obtained, considering that our results are from gel electrophoresis data while those of Fling, Kopf and Richards are from sequence data. Furthermore, sequencing of the first 204 bp of the 1·3 kbp fragment of pLOB209 starting from the *Eco*RI site has been carried out with the valuable assistance of Dr Ishtiaq Qadri (then of Imperial College, London), giving the results shown in *Table 28.1*. Comparison with the sequence published by Fling, Kopf and Richards (1985) for Tn7 shows that the two sequences corresponded almost perfectly, there being only 5 bases that were different: an addition of adenine at 1523, and deletions of guanine at 1503, cytosine at 1513, adenine at 1554 and thymine at 1555. It can be concluded therefore, that the 1·3 kbp *Ava*I–*Eco*RI fragment in pLOB209 containing the spectinomycin-resistant determinant derived from the gonococcal strain F29 has very close homology with the *Ava*I–*Eco*RI fragment of Tn7.

**Table 28.1** Sequence of 204 base pairs of the right-hand part of the 1·3 kbp *Ava*I–*Eco*RI fragment from *N. gonorrhoeae* strain F29 DNA inserted in pLOB209, with comparison to the equivalent sequence in Tn7 published by Fling, Kopf and Richards (1985)

A A A T G G C A A T T T T C G C T T G C C C C T G A C A G A T A A C G G C
1400           1410

T G A G A T C A T G T A T C T A A G C A A C T A G C C T G C T C T C T A A
1420     1430     1440     1450

T A A A A T G T T A G G C C T C A A C A T C T A G T C G C A A G C T G A G
1460     1470     1480

G G G A A C C A C T A G T (G) T C A T A C G A A (C) C T C C A A G A G(A)
1490     1500     1510     1520

C G G T T A C A C A A A C G G G T A C A T T G T T G A T G T C (A) (T) G
1530     1540     1550

T A T G A C A A T C G C C C A A G T A A G T A T C C A G C T
1560     1570     1580     1586

Numbers refer to base positions in Tn7 fragment.
Brackets represent base deletions in the 204 bp sequence of cloned 1·4 kbp *Ava*I–*Eco*RI fragment which are present in the sequence of the 1·6 kbp fragment of Tn7.
(A), Represents insertion of base, A, absent in Tn7.

## The gene product

The spectinomycin-resistant determinant contained in the 1·3 kbp fragment cloned in pLOB209 was transferred into *E. coli* strain CSR603, and the gene product visualized by autoradiography of incorporated $^{35}$S-methionine, using the protocol of Savva and Butler (1983). The resultant autoradiograph is shown in lane 2 of *Figure 28.5*. Three protein bands are discernable: band (a) of 31·5 kDa corresponds to the precurser of the β-lactamase encoded by the pUC8 vector; band (c) of 29·0 kDa corresponds to the β-lactamase protein itself; while band (b) of 30 kDa, absent in both the control lanes 1 and 4, corresponds to the product of the spectinomycin-resistance determinant. This agrees well with the size 30 kDa of the *aadA* gene product AAD3″/9 synthesized in minicells by Fling and Elwell (1980), and from the predicted molecular mass of 29 207 Da calculated from the polypeptide sequences of 262 amino acids as determined from the size of the structural gene.

The molecular evidence therefore strongly supports the genetic and biochemical evidence that the spectinomycin-resistance determinant of

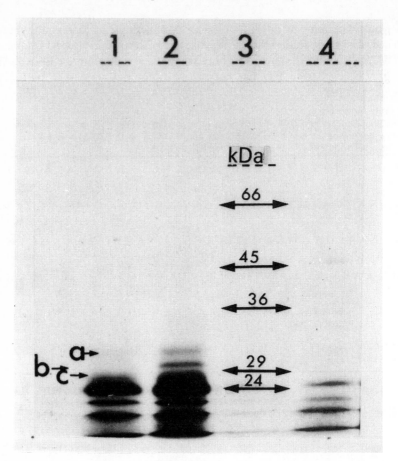

**Figure 28.5** Autoradiograph of [35]S-methionine-labelled proteins encoded by pUC8 and pLOB209 in the maxicells of *E. coli* CSR603. Lane 1, pUC8 transferred into *E. coli* CSR603; lane 2, pLOB209 transformed into *E. coli* CSR603; lane 3, protein molecular weight markers as traced from Coomassie blue stained gel; lane 4, plasmid-free *E. coli* CSR603. a, precursor of β-lactamase, molecular mass 31·5 kDa; b, product of 1·3 kbp insert, molecular mass 30 kDa; c, β-lactamase, molecular mass 29 kDa.

*Neisseria gonorrhoeae* strain F29 is located in a transposon, and that this transposon is either Tn7 itself or very closely related to Tn7.

## References

BUTLER, L.O. AND KOTHARI, S. (1984). Has spectinomycin become plasmid mediated in the gonococcus? *Abstracts of the 7th European Meeting on Genetic Transformation, Paris*, pp. 141–143.

FEINBERG, A.D. AND VOGELSTEIN, B. (1984). A technique for radio labelling DNA restriction endonuclease fractions to high specific activity. *Analytical Chemistry* **137**, 266–267.

FLING, M.E. AND ELWELL, L.P. (1980). Protein expression in *Escherichia coli* minicells containing recombinant plasmids specifying trimethoprim-resistant dihydrofolate reductases. *Journal of Bacteriology* **141**, 779–785.

FLING, M.E., KOPF, J. AND RICHARDS, C. (1985). Nucleotide sequence of the transposon Tn7 gene encoding an aminoglycoside-modifying enzyme, 3″(9)-*O*-nucleotidyl transferase. *Nucleic Acids Research* **13**, 7095–7106.

KOTHARI, S. AND BUTLER, L.O. (1986). Transposon-like behaviour of the spectinomycin-resistance determinant in *Neisseria gonorrhoeae*. *Abstracts of the 8th European Meeting on Genetic Transformation, Uppsala*, p. 46.

SARUBBI, F.A., BLACKMAN, E. AND SPARLING, P.F. (1974). Genetic mapping of linked antibiotic resistance loci in *Neisseria gonorrhoeae*. *Journal of Bacteriology* **120**, 1284–1292.

SAVVA, D. AND BUTLER, L.O. (1983). A protein coded by a cryptic plasmid of *Neisseria gonorrhoeae*. *Microbiology Letters* **23**, 145–147.

# Part III
## DNA Repair

# 29
# Generalized DNA Mismatch Repair: Its Molecular Basis in *Streptococcus pneumoniae* and Other Organisms

SANFORD A. LACKS

*Biology Department, Brookhaven National Laboratory, Upton, NY 11973, USA*

## Introduction

Mismatches in DNA are local deviations from the complementary base pairing (A/T and G/C) normally found in double-stranded DNA. They can be either base mispairs, such as A/G or G/T or insertion–deletion loopouts, in which one strand is missing one or more nucleotides present in the other strand. In nature, these mismatches arise either from errors in replication or from processes of genetic exchange that bring together strands of different genotypes to form a heteroduplex structure. If an error in replication is not corrected, it gives rise to a mutation. If a genetic heteroduplex is corrected, it can appear to be a gene conversion.

Although its role in mutation avoidance may be of paramount importance for a living cell, mismatch repair was first revealed by its effects on genetic exchanges. A correction or repair system was shown to have a marked effect on genetic transformation efficiencies in *S. pneumoniae* (Ephrussi-Taylor, Sicard and Kamen, 1965; Ephrussi-Taylor and Gray, 1966; Lacks, 1966; Lacks, 1970). Subsequently, genetic defects in the repair system were found to exert mutator effects (Tiraby and Fox, 1973). This repair system, called Hex, was shown to be a generalized mismatch correction system that could recognize and remove a variety of mismatches. Similar generalized repair systems have been found in *Escherichia coli* and *Saccharomyces cerevisiae* (for a review, *see* Claverys and Lacks, 1986).

Several instances of specialized mismatch repair systems have come to light. In these cases only a single base mispair is recognized, and it is always one particular base in the mispair that is corrected. Thus, mechanisms for correcting G/T or G/A to G/C in specific sequences of *E. coli* (Lieb, 1987) or *S. pneumoniae* (Mostachfi and Sicard, 1987), respectively, have been observed. Also, *E. coli* can correct A/G to A/T by a specialized system depending on *mutT* (Yanofsky, Cox and Horn, 1966; Lu and Chang, 1988). These specialized

*Genetic Transformation and Expression*
© Intercept Ltd, PO Box 716, Andover, Hants, SP10 1YG, UK

systems will not be considered further here. Rather, the generalized Hex system of *S. pneumoniae* will be reviewed and compared to generalized repair systems in other species, in particular the Mut system of *E. coli*. Emphasis will be placed on the mechanisms of targeting the strand for correction and on the effects of UV-irradiation damage on strand targeting. Components of the generalized systems from different species will be compared at the molecular level, and a scheme for the possible evolution of these repair systems will be proposed.

### Hex system of *S. pneumoniae*

MISMATCH REPAIR AFTER TRANSFORMATION

In the genetic transformation of Gram-positive bacteria, the DNA from a donor cell is converted to single-strand segments on entry into a recipient cell (for a review, *see* Lacks, 1988). These donor segments then replace homologous segments in the recipient chromosome, so that a genetic difference between donor and recipient gives rise to heteroduplex DNA containing a mismatch. Depending on the mutation that gave rise to the genetic difference, or marker, the resulting mismatch is recognized more or less well by the repair system and the donor contribution is correspondingly eliminated. This results in characteristic transformation efficiencies for markers depending on the particular mismatches that they produce, as indicated in *Table 29.1*. Integration efficiencies are measured as the ratio of transformants for the marker in question, here corresponding to the wild-type allele of *malM* mutations, to transformants for a reference marker, here corresponding to a high-efficiency marker conferring sulphonamide resistance. Markers corresponding to some transversion mutations, such as *malM594*, give rise to mismatches that are not recognized by the Hex system, and show a high integration efficiency, approximately 1·0 (*Table 29.1*). Transition mutations, such as *malM567*, give well-recognized mismatches and hence low integration efficiency, approximately 0·05.

**Table 29.1** Base changes at mutated sites and integration efficiency (data taken from Lacks, Dunn and Greenberg, 1982)

| *malM* mutation | Sequence location | DNA change | Integration efficiency* | Base mismatches *l* | *r* |
|---|---|---|---|---|---|
| *564* | 2710–2802 | *del*93 | 0·83 | — | — |
| *594* | 3042 | GC→TA | 0·98 | AGA TAT | ATA TCT |
| *567* | 2722 | GC→AT | 0·04 | GGC CTG | GAC CCG |
| *582* | 2722 | GC→CG | 0·50 | GGC CGG | GCC CCG |

* Ratio of Mal⁺ to Sulʳ transformants with DNA from a *mal⁺*, *sul-d* strain.

Several important aspects of the Hex system were deduced from genetic analysis. Reciprocal crosses (that is, transformation of a *mal⁺* recipient by *mal⁻* donor DNA and vice versa) generally give the same efficiency, be it high, low or intermediate (Lacks, 1966). This shows that either base of a mispair is subject to elimination and that it is always the donor contribution which is eliminated. Low-efficiency markers exclude nearby high-efficiency markers, and the extent of exclusion depends on distance (Lacks, 1966). This dependence indicates that a donor strand segment of 1–2 kilobases in average length is eliminated together with the mismatched base. This length corresponds to the average segment normally integrated.

The existence of a cellular repair system to correct mismatches between donor and recipient DNA was proposed by Ephrussi-Taylor and Gray (1966). Isolation of *hex* mutants, which lacked the repair system, supported this notion (Lacks, 1970). Two loci, *hexA* and *hexB*, were found; the genes were cloned and their products, HexA and HexB, identified as polypeptides of 95 and 83 kDa, respectively (Claverys *et al.*, 1984; Balganesh and Lacks, 1985; Martin, Prats and Claverys, 1985; Prats, Martin and Claverys, 1985).

STRAND TARGETING AND EFFECTS OF UV DAMAGE

An interesting question in generalized mismatch repair is how the system recognizes the target strand, that is, the strand to be corrected. Inasmuch as the Hex system acts at an early stage in transformation (Ghei and Lacks, 1967; Shoemaker and Guild, 1974), it was suggested that breaks at the ends of the donor strand segment prior to complete integration mark the donor contribution for elimination (Guild and Shoemaker, 1976). This is consistent with the loss of the entire donor segment that would have been integrated. A possible model for the action of the Hex system in transformation is shown in *Figure 29.1* (*1–5*). The Hex system monitor, presumably a complex of the HexA and HexB proteins, recognizes a single-strand break (nick) in DNA, perhaps retaining hold of the DNA at that point, and scans the DNA for a mismatch. If it encounters a mismatch that it can recognize, it becomes activated, continues until the next break, where it reverses course and degrades the nicked DNA strand back to its starting point. Repair synthesis on the recipient strand template completes the process. Variants of this model are possible (reviewed in Claverys and Lacks, 1986), but the essential points are conjoint recognition of the mismatch and of at least one strand break in the target strand. Ligation of the donor segment prior to action of the Hex system would preclude repair (*Figure 29.1*, in brackets), which could account for the residual transformation efficiency (0·05) observed for low-efficiency markers.

For some time it has been known that low-efficiency markers are very sensitive to UV-irradiation of the donor DNA (Litman, 1961). This is evident in *Table 29.2*, where it is seen that survival of the *malM567* marker is reduced to 1% by a dose that only reduces survival of a high-efficiency marker to 32%. Both markers show high survival in a Hex⁻ recipient strain. A strain containing *uvr-1*, which renders the cells defective in repair of UV damage, shows reduced survival for the high-efficiency marker but no difference for the low-efficiency marker. Apparently, a *uvr*⁺ strain can repair photoproducts, such as thymine dimers, that are introduced along with a high-efficiency marker. Low-efficiency markers, however, do not appear to benefit from this repair process.

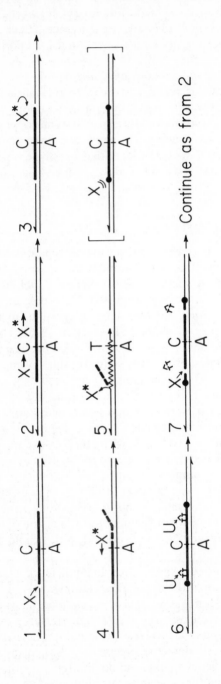

**Figure 29.1** Model for action of Hex mismatch repair after transformation and effect of UV-irradiation of donor DNA. (1) Entry of Hex monitor at 5' end of donor segment in an integration product with a C/A mismatch, prior to covalent joining. (2) Monitor travels relative to DNA and is triggered by the mismatch. (3) Triggered monitor reverses course at subsequent break. (4) Associated exonuclease activity degrades donor DNA. (5) Exonuclease halts at initial break and gap is repaired by replication with recipient strand as template. Brackets enclose situation where prior ligation of the integration product prevents Hex action. (6) With UV-irradiated donor DNA, a UV-endonuclease can act on pyrimidine dimers after ligation. (7) Action of the UV-endonuclease produces new nicks that can allow entry of the Hex monitor. Symbols: thin line, original chromosomal DNA; heavy line, donor DNA; sawtooth line, repair replication; dashed line, exonucleolytic degradation; X, Hex system monitor; X*, triggered monitor with or without associated exonuclease; U, UV-endonuclease; ⌢ᴛ, thymine dimer.

A plausible explanation for the lack of UV-damage repair in this case is that the process of such repair involves excision of the thymine dimer, which reintroduces a break in the donor strand and subjects the marker once more to elimination by the Hex system. This is shown schematically in *Figure 29.1 (6,7)*. The UV effect, therefore, supports a role for strand breaks in strand targeting by the Hex system.

**Table 29.2** Absence of repair of UV-damaged donor DNA in low-efficiency marker transformation

| Recipient strain | | Donor DNA* | | Transformants/ml | | Marker survival[‡] |
|---|---|---|---|---|---|---|
| Number | Genotype | Marker | Efficiency | Unirradiated | Irradiated[†] | |
| 175 | *malM567, uvr⁺, hex⁺* | Sul$^r$ | (1·00) | 186 000 | 5880 | 0·32 |
| | | Mal⁺ | 0·07 | 13 200 | 150 | 0·011 |
| 468 | *malM567, uvr-1, hex⁺* | Sul$^r$ | (1·00) | 88 000 | 7250 | 0·082 |
| | | Mal⁺ | 0·17 | 14 600 | 253 | 0·017 |
| 140 | *malM567, uvr-1, hex-1* | Str$^r$ | (1·00) | 24 200 | 5550 | 0·23 |
| | | Mal⁺ | 1·15 | 27 900 | 9050 | 0·32 |

\* From strain 96; contains Mal⁺, Str$^r$ and Sul$^r$ markers.
† Irradiated with a dose of 720 J m$^{-2}$.
‡ Ratio of transformants with irradiated and unirradiated DNA.

MUTATION AVOIDANCE

Hex⁻ cells show high rates of spontaneous mutation, approximately 100-fold higher than Hex⁺ cells; this is true for both *hexA* and *hexB* mutants (for review, *see* Claverys and Lacks, 1986). Could the nascent strand of DNA that must be corrected to eliminate a potential mutation also be targeted by single-strand breaks? During *in vitro* synthesis of DNA the lagging strand is laid down in an interrupted fashion as 1–2 kilobase fragments; however, the leading strand is continuously synthesized (for review, *see* Kornberg, 1980). Nevertheless, during *in vivo* replication, nascent DNA of both strands is found in such 'Okazaki' fragments (for review, *see* Alberts and Sternglanz, 1977). The single-strand interruptions that give rise to these fragments on denaturation could serve to target nascent DNA repair by the Hex system.

The mechanism of fragmentation of the leading strand of nascent DNA *in vivo* is not known. It was shown that incorporation into that strand of uracil from dUTP, followed by removal of uracil by a glycosylase and nuclease-mediated cleavage of the apyrimidinic DNA, could cause such breaks (Tye *et al.*, 1978). However, the amount of Okazaki fragments was not reduced in a mutant lacking DNA-uracil glycosylase (Tye *et al.*, 1978), hence there may be other mechanisms for producing these breaks. If replication errors can occur with equal frequency in the leading and lagging strands, reduction of mutations by more than a factor of two would require both nascent strands to be targeted by the Hex system. *Figure 29.2A* depicts a possible scheme for Hex system action in mutation avoidance. One strand is synthesized with interruptions and the other incorporates uracil, which is then removed to give breaks. Current work in our laboratory with J.-D. Chen is directed to testing this hypothesis. Subsequently, the Hex system would act on the mismatched DNA just as it does after transformation.

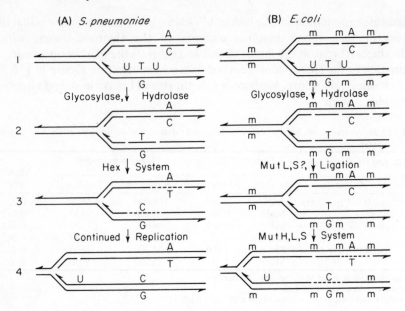

**Figure 29.2**    Possible mechanisms of mutation avoidance by mismatch repair in *S. pneumoniae* and *E. coli*. (A) *S. pneumoniae*: 1, Okazaki fragments formed during replication of lagging strand, uracil incorporation into both nascent strands; 2, removal of uracil by glycosylase and action of an apyrimidinic endonuclease (hydrolase) at such sites produce nicks in the leading strand (other mechanisms for producing such nicks are possible); 3, the Hex system recognizes the mismatch and removes a segment of the nicked nascent DNA strand containing the potential mutation, and repair replication restores the parental genotype; 4, ligation of the fragments precludes further repair. (B) *E. coli*: 1, as in (A), except that parental DNA but not nascent DNA is methylated (m) at GATC sites; 2, nicks are present in both strands as in (A); 3, the Mut system may correct mismatches prior to ligation with nascent-strand targeting by nicks as in (A), but some mismatches may escape its action; 4, persistent mismatches are removed from nascent DNA following formation of nicks at unmethylated sites.

## Mismatch repair in other organisms

### THE Mut SYSTEM OF *E. COLI*

A DNA mismatch repair system in *E. coli* has been shown to be composed of the products of genes *mutH, mutL, mutS* and *uvrD* (for reviews, *see* Claverys and Lacks, 1986; Radman and Wagner, 1986; Modrich, 1987; Meselson, 1988). Defects in these genes increase spontaneous mutation frequencies approximately 1000-fold over wild type (for review, *see* Cox, 1976). This system has been shown to correct artificially constructed heteroduplexes both *in vivo* and *in vitro*. Certain mispairs are recognized better than others, and whenever a mismatch is corrected an entire tract of one strand averaging 1–2 kilobases in length is eliminated. Thus, with respect to differential recognition of mispairs and extensive strand elimination, the Mut and Hex systems appear to be similar.

In one important respect the Mut system differs from Hex. Methylation of *E. coli* DNA at GATC sites (Lacks and Greenberg, 1977) has been implicated in strand targeting; that is, with hemimethylated DNA, the unmethylated strand is prone to correction (Pukkila *et al.*, 1983). The Hex system operates in strains of *S. pneumoniae* that have very little DNA methylation, and it operates on donor DNA that would be as fully methylated as recipient DNA. In the case of Hex, strand targeting appears to depend only on strand breaks. It has been proposed that the Mut system also recognizes single-strand breaks and that methylation-directed repair depends on the formation of such breaks at unmethylated sites in DNA (Lacks, Dunn and Greenberg, 1982). Supporting this hypothesis is the finding that *dam* mutants, which totally lack GATC methylation (Marinus and Morris, 1973; Lacks and Greenberg, 1977), are only partially elevated in spontaneous mutation frequency compared to Mut⁻ strains (Glickman and Radman, 1980), as if mismatch repair can still act, albeit less effectively, in the absence of methyl-directed strand targeting. More directly supporting the hypothesis is the finding that the *mutH* product can produce single-strand breaks in the unmethylated strand of hemimethylated DNA (Welsh, Lu and Modrich, 1987).

The proposed action of the Mut system in mutation avoidance in *E. coli* is shown schematically in *Figure 29.2B*. Here, again, uracil incorporation and removal is shown to produce breaks in the leading strand, although it is likely that a different mechanism produces such breaks (Tye *et al.*, 1978). The Mut system either acts at these breaks or at breaks formed at unmethylated sites in the nascent DNA to remove strand segments that contain a mismatch. Thus, both the Hex and Mut systems may act similarly on the molecular level to recognize strand breaks together with a mismatch lying between them. The Mut system, which could still correct nascent DNA after its Okazaki fragments were ligated together, would be more efficient in mutation avoidance.

MEIOTIC RECOMBINATION IN *S. CEREVISIAE*

One of the earliest recognized manifestations of mismatch repair was the gene conversion that gave rise to unexpected genotypic ratios in genetic crosses of fungi (Mitchell, 1955). Heteroduplex DNA is apparently formed during the recombinatory processes of meiosis and, in *S. cerevisiae*, its persistence in the four-ascospore product (tetrad) of meiosis results in ascospores from which two different genotypes segregate. Repair of the heteroduplex prior to ascospore formation would give rise to a tetrad in which none of the ascospores showed such post-meiotic segregation, but which was aberrant because ascospore genotypes would give a ratio of 3 : 1 rather than 2 : 2, as expected from Mendelian considerations. Analysis of post-meiotic segregation in *S. cerevisiae* by Fogel and his colleagues has provided the strongest evidence to date for a generalized DNA mismatch repair system in eukaryotic cells.

White, Lusnak and Fogel (1985) found that some markers gave more post-meiotic segregation than others. These markers presumably corresponded to base mispairs that were not well recognized by a correction system so that the heteroduplex persisted. Recognizable mispairs were converted to a homoduplex configuration prior to ascospore germination. Mutations in a gene called *PMS1* prevented repair, so that all markers showed post-meiotic segregation. These mutants also gave high spontaneous mutation frequencies (Williamson, Game and Fogel, 1985). This yeast gene is therefore similar to a *hex* or *mut* gene in bacteria. It is apparently part of a generalized mismatch repair system of *S. cerevisiae* that we can call Pms.

## Comparison of mismatch repair in different species

MISMATCH RECOGNITION SPECTRUM

A striking parallel is observed in the abilities of the Hex, Mut and Pms systems to repair particular mismatches. *Table 29.3* shows that transition mispairs, G/T and A/C, are well recognized in all three systems. Similarly, mispairs A/A and T/T that arise from AT→TA transversions are almost as well recognized. With GC→CG transversions, only G/G and not C/C is recognized. Mispairs from AT→CG transversions are generally poorly recognized. These data come from a variety of measurements: single-strand and combined marker transformation efficiency in two different loci of *S. pneumoniae*, frequency of mixed plaques arising from two different heteroduplex phage DNA systems in *E. coli*, extent of restriction site restoration in heteroduplex DNA by an *E. coli* extract in vitro, and post-meiotic segregation frequency (relative to total aberrant tetrads) in *S. cerevisiae*.

**Table 29.3**  Mismatch correction spectrum in different species

| Species | Reference | G/T | A/C | A/A | T/T | G/G | C/C | A/G | C/T |
|---|---|---|---|---|---|---|---|---|---|
| *S. pneumoniae* | a | LE 0·05 +++ | | | | IE 0·5 + | | HE, IE 1·0, 0·2 −,++ | |
| *S. pneumoniae* | b | 0·06 +++ | 0·06 +++ | 0·2 ++ | 0·2 ++ | 0·06 +++ | 1·0 | (+) + | (−) + |
| *E. coli* | c | <1% +++ | | 5–25% ++ | >50% − | <1% +++ | >50% − | 25–50% + | >50% − |
| *E. coli* | d | 6% +++ | 10% ++ | 12% ++ | 7% +++ | 6% +++ | 39% + | 73% − | 80% − |
| *E. coli* | e | 137 +++ | 120 +++ | 70 + | 96 ++ | 96 ++ | 12 − | 36 ± | 62 + |
| *S. cerevisiae* | f | 4% +++ | | 5% +++ | | 33% + | | | |

a  Lacks, Dunn and Greenberg (1982); integration efficiencies in transformation.
b  Claverys et al. (1981, 1983); integration efficiencies in transformation.
c  Kramer, Kramer and Fritz (1984); frequencies of mottled plaques with M13 heteroduplex.
d  Dohet, Wagner and Radman (1985); frequencies of mixed plaques with lambda heteroduplex.
e  Su et al., (1988); in vitro repair of fl heteroduplex, fmol mg$^{-1}$ protein.
f  White, Lusnak and Fogel (1985); post-meiotic segregation frequency.

The three generalized mismatch repair systems also show similar behaviour toward insertion–deletion mismatches (*Table 29.4*). Thus, one- or two-nucleotide deletions (or insertions) are fairly well recognized. As with base mispairs, there is no preference for eliminating either the insertion or the deletion. Rather the eliminated component is determined by which strand is

argeted as 'donor' or 'nascent'. Mismatches six nucleotides or longer in length
re not recognized at all. Intermediate lengths show intermediate recognition
nd elimination.

**Table 29.4** Mismatch correction spectrum in different species

| Species | Reference | Insertion–deletion mismatches* | | | | | | |
|---|---|---|---|---|---|---|---|---|
| | | 1/0 | 2/0 | 3/0 | 4/0 | 5/0 | 6/0 | >30/0 |
| S. pneumoniae | a | | | | | | | 1·0 − |
| S. pneumoniae | b | | | | | | 1·0 − | |
| S. pneumoniae | c | 0·12 ++ | 0·12 ++ | 0·3 + | 0·5 ± | 0·9 − | | |
| E. coli | d | ++ | ++ | ± | − | | | |
| E. coli | e | | | | | | | 50% − |
| S. cerevisiae | f | 0% +++ | | | | | | 54% − |

* Number of nucleotides present in insertion or missing in deletion/0 = deletion.
Lacks (1966); Claverys *et al.* (1981); Lacks, Dunn and Greenberg (1982); transformation efficiency.
Lopez *et al.* (1987); transformation efficiency.
Gasc *et al.* (1987); transformation efficiency.
H.J. Fritz and B. Kramer (personal communication); mottled plaques with M13 heteroduplex.
Dohet *et al.* (1987); mixed plaques with lambda heteroduplex; identical percentage found for *mutL* strain.
White, Lusnak and Fogel (1985); post-meiotic segregation frequency.

The similarities in mismatch recognition between the three systems suggests
that they depend on a common physical mechanism for identifying mismatches.
It further suggests that the systems may have a common ancestral origin.

SIMILARITIES AND DIFFERENCES IN STRAND TARGETING

As indicated above, an average length of 1–2 kilobases is removed from the
targeted strand by both the Hex and Mut systems. This presumably represents
the average distance between nicks in the transformation heteroduplex
intermediate and between unmethylated GATC sites in the partially
methylated λ phage DNA heteroduplexes used in the Hex and Mut system
analyses, respectively. Although these two systems differ in the use of DNA
adenine methylation in strand targeting, the ultimate basis for the targeting
may be strand breaks in both systems. In *S. cerevisiae* the Pms system
presumably depends only on strand breaks for targeting, inasmuch as DNA of
this species shows no adenine and relatively little cytosine methylation
(Hattman *et al.*, 1978).

COMPARISON OF HexA AND MutS PROTEINS

The similarity in properties of the Hex system of *S. pneumoniae* and the Mut
system of *E. coli* lends interest to a comparison of components of the system at
the molecular level. In *Figure 29.3* the protein sequences of *S. pneumoniae*
HexA (Priebe *et al.*, 1988) and *E. coli* MutS (P. Stanley and K.A. Stacey,
personal communication), deduced from the DNA sequences of the genes

```
HexA: ------MAIEKLSPGMQOQYVDIKKQYPDAFLLFRMGDFYELFYEDAVNAAQILELSLTSRNKNADNPIPMAGVPYHSAQQYIDVLIEQGYKVAIAEQMED  100
MutS: --MSGIENFDAHTPMMQQYLRLKAQHPEILLFYRMGDFYELFYDDAKRASOLLDISLTKRGASAGEPIPMAGIPYHAVENYLAKLVNQGESVAICEQIGD
       *         *  *  *  *   **  *********** **    *  *  *  ****  *****  ***  *   *       * *   *  *

PKQAVGVVKREVVQVITPGTVVDSSKPDS-QNNFLVSIDREGNQFGLAYMDLVTGDFYVTGLLDFTLVCGEIRNLKAREVVLGYDLSEE---EEQILSRQ  200
PATSKGPVERKVVRIVTPGTISDEALLOERQDNLLAAIWQDSKGFGYATLDISSGRFRLSEPADRETMAAELQRTNPAELLYAEDFAEMSLIEGRRAVRR
   *    **  ***  ***** *        **  *         *      *        *      *     *     *  *     *

MNLVLSYEKESFEDLHLL----DLRLATVEQT-----ASSKLLQVHRTQMRELNHLKPVIRYEIKDFLQMDYATKASLDLVENARSGKKQGSLFWLDE  300
RPLWEFEIDTARHELNLQFGTRDLVGFGVENAPRGLCAAGCLLQYAKDTQRTTLPHIRSITMEREQDSIIMDAATRRNLEITQNLAGGAENT-LASVLDC
   * *    *  *           *             *   **          *   *        *     *                   *   **

TKTAMGMRLLRSWIHRPLIDKERIVORQEVVQVFLDHFFERSDLTDSLKGVYDIERLASRVSFGKTNPKDLLQLATTLSSVPRIRAILEGMEQPTLAYLI  400
TVTPMGSRMLKRWLHMPVRDTRVLLERQQTIGALQDFTAG---LQPVLRQVGDLERILARLALRTARPRDLARMRHAFQQLPELRAQLETVDSAPVQALR
*  * * *  * *                    *       *  *   *    **   * **     *                      *

AQLDAIPELESLISAAIAPEAPHVITDGGIIRTGFDETLDKYRCVLREGTSWIAEIEAKERENSGISTLKIDYNKKDGYYFHVTNSQLGNVPAHFFRKAT  500
EKMGEFAELRDLLERAIIDTPPVLVRDGGVIASGYNEELDEWRALADGATDYLERLEVRERERTGLDTLKVGFNAVHGYYIQISRGQSHLAPINYMRROT
      * *          * *   *  **  *         *      *        *  *  *   ***       *             *

LKNSERFGTEELARIEGDMLEAREKSANLEYEIFMRIREEVGKYIORLQALAQGIATVDVLQSLAVVAETQHLIRPEFGQDSQIDIRKGRHAVVEKVMGA  600
LKNAERYIIPELKEYEDKVLTSKGKALALEKQLYEELFDLLPHLEALAQQDASALAELDVLVNLAERAYTLNYTCPTFIDKPGIRITEGRHPVVEQVLNE
*** **         *           *     *    *       *     *     *   ** *                  *  *   ** *  *

(ATP-binding: LI-QP-GSGKST----L)
QTYIPNTIQMAEDTSIQLVTGPNMSGKSTYMRQLAMTAVMAQLGSYPAESAHLPIFDAIFTRIGAADDLVSGQSTFMVEMMEANNAISHATKNSLILFD  700
PF-IANPLNLSPQRRMLIITGPNMGGKSTYMRQTALIALMAYIGSVPAQKVEIGPIDRIFTRVGAADDLASGRSTFMVEMTETANILHNATEYSLVLMD
            *    ** ***** ******** *  * **  *** **       *  ***** **** *  ***** *     *  **      **

ELGRGTATYDGMALAQSIIEYIHEHIGAKTLFATHYHELTSLESSLQHLVNVHVATLEQDGQVTFLHKIEPGPADKSYGIHVAKIAGLPADLLARADKIL  800
EIGRGTSTYDGLSLAWACAENLANKIKALTFATHYFELTQLPEKMEGVANVHLDALEHGDTIAFMHSVQDGAASKSYGLAVAALAGVPKEVIKRARQKL
* **** ****  *           *   ****** ***          **  * *    *         **   ***  *  *  * *    ** *

TQLENQGTESPPPMRQTSAVTEQISLFDRAEEHPILAELAKLDVYNMTPMQVMNVLVELKQKL
RELESI---SPNAAATOVDGTQMSLLSVPEETSPAVEALENLDPDSLTPRQALEWIYRLKSLV
 **                  *   *     *    *       *
```

**Figure 29.3**   Comparison of mismatch repair proteins HexA of *S. pneumoniae* and MutS (lower) of *E. coli*. The amino-acid sequences of HexA (upper) and MutS (lower) are aligned to give maximum correspondence. Dashes indicate gaps produced by this alignment in one or the other sequence. Numbers on the right correspond to positions in the alignment and not to the polypeptide sequence. Amino termini of the polypeptides are at top left. Asterisks indicate identical amino-acid residues. A consensus sequence for ATP- or GTP-binding sites in proteins (Gill, Hatfull and Salmond, 1986) is shown in parentheses. Here dashes represent variable residues and symbols indicate amino acids most commonly found (>30% of sites); some (first and third G, and K) are almost invariant (>90% of sites). Either S or T, with approximately equal frequency, is found immediately following K. Various amino-acid residues with hydrophobic side-chains can occur in the positions of L and I in the consensus, as well as in the residue following the terminal L shown.

ncoding them, are compared. It is obvious that the proteins are homologous; 7% of their amino-acid residues are identical. This extent of homology ndicates that the two mismatch repair systems are not accidentally similar in roperties, but rather that they are derived from a common origin.

One highly conserved segment of HexA and MutS is of particular interest ecause it corresponds to a consensus sequence for an ATP- or GTP-binding ite in proteins (*Figure 29.3*). Inasmuch as a generalized mismatch repair ystem has to detect both a base mismatch and a strand break, which can be eparated by a considerable distance in the DNA, energy for movement of a mismatch correction monitor relative to the DNA may be provided by ATP ydrolysis.

Homology between HexA and MutS of *Salmonella typhimurium*, which has Mut system similar to *E. coli*, and the presence of a conserved ATP-binding ite were previously reported (Haber *et al.*, 1988; Priebe *et al.* 1988).

EVOLUTION OF MISMATCH REPAIR

n addition to the relationship between HexA of *S. pneumoniae* and MutS of *E. oli*, another curious bit of homology has been found between these species, .e. the homology of the Dam protein, which methylates GATC in *E. coli*, and he DpnM protein, which is part of the *Dpn*II restriction system of *S. pneumoniae* (Mannarelli *et al.*, 1985). The two proteins show 30% identity. These observations, together with other considerations, give rise to the scheme or evolution of generalized mismatch repair systems shown in *Figure 29.4*.

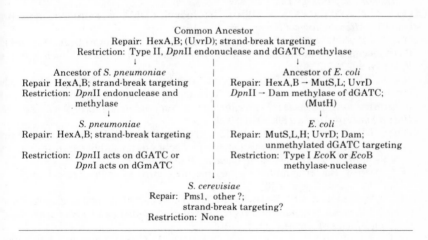

**Figure 29.4**   Proposed evolution of generalized mismatch repair and restriction enzyme systems in *S. pneumoniae*, *E. coli* and *S. cerevisiae*.

The ancestral cell common to prokaryotes and eukaryotes presumably had a mismatch repair system very similar to Hex. The bacterial ancestor also presumably had a Type II restriction system like *Dpn*II. Both systems were retained in the *S. pneumoniae* line, and an optional *Dpn*I restriction possibility was added later (Lacks *et al.*, 1987). In the *E. coli* line, the DpnM methylase of the *Dpn*II restriction system was recruited for use by the mismatch repair system. This methyl-dependent overlay appears to reduce spontaneous mutations by an additional factor of ten (Mannarelli *et al.*, 1985). With regard to restriction, the primitive Type II system was supplanted by the Type I *Eco*K and *Eco*B systems. *S. cerevisiae* (and other eukaryotic species) presumably inherited a mismatch repair system very much like Hex.

## Acknowledgements

I thank my colleagues in this work: T.S. Balganesh, S.D. Priebe, S.M. Hadi, J.D. Chen and B. Greenberg. I am grateful to P. Stanley and K.A. Stacey for sharing the nucleotide sequence of *E. coli muts* prior to publication. This research was conducted at Brookhaven National Laboratory under the auspices of the US Department of Energy Office of Health and Environmental Research. It was supported by US Public Health Service Grants AI14885 and GM29721 from the National Institutes of Health.

## References

ALBERTS, B. AND STERNGLANZ, R. (1977). Recent excitement in the DNA replication problem. *Nature (London)* **269**, 655–661.
BALGANESH, T.S. AND LACKS, S.A. (1985). Heteroduplex DNA mismatch repair system of *Streptococcus pneumoniae*: Cloning and expression of the *HexA* gene. *Journal of Bacteriology* **162**, 979–984.
CLAVERYS, J.P. AND LACKS, S.A. (1986). Heteroduplex DNA base mismatch repair in bacteria. *Microbiological Reviews* **50**, 133–165.
CLAVERYS, J.P., MEJEAN, V., GASC, A.M., GALIBERT, F. AND SICARD, A.M. (1981). Base specificity of mismatch repair in *Streptococcus pneumoniae*. *Nucleic Acids Research* **9**, 2267–2280.
CLAVERYS, J.P., MEJEAN, V., GASC, A.M. AND SICARD, A.M. (1983). Mismatch repair in *Streptococcus pneumoniae*: Relationship between base mismatches and transformation efficiencies. *Proceedings of the National Academy of Sciences of the United States of America* **80**, 5956–5960.
CLAVERYS, J.P., PRATS, H., VASSEGHI, H. AND GHERARDI, M. (1984). Identification of *Streptococcus pneumoniae* mismatch repair genes by an additive transformation approach. *Molecular and General Genetics* **196**, 91–96.
COX, E.C. (1976). Bacterial mutator genes and the control of spontaneous mutation. *Annual Review of Genetics* **10**, 135–156.
DOHET, C., WAGNER, R. AND RADMAN, M. (1985). Repair of defined single base-pair mismatches in *Escherichia coli*. *Proceedings of the National Academy of Sciences of the United States of America* **82**, 503–505.
DOHET, C., DZIDIC, S., WAGNER, R. AND RADMAN, M.(1987). Large non-homology in heteroduplex DNA is processed differently than single base pair mismatches. *Molecular and General Genetics* **206**, 181–184.
EPHRUSSI-TAYLOR, H. AND GRAY, T.C. (1966). Genetic studies of recombining DNA in pneumococcal transformation. *Journal of General Physiology* **49**(2), 211–231.
EPHRUSSI-TAYLOR, H., SICARD, A.M. AND KAMEN, R. (1965). Genetic recombination in DNA-induced transformation of pneumococcus. I. The problem of relative efficiency of transformation. *Genetics* **51**, 455–475.
GASC, A.M., GARCIA, P., BATY, D. AND SICARD, A.M. (1987). Mismatch repair during pneumococcal transformation of small deletions produced by site-directed

mutagenesis. *Molecular and General Genetics* 210, 369–372.

GHEI, O.K. AND LACKS, S.A. (1967). Recovery of donor deoxyribonucleic acid marker activity from eclipse in pneumococcal transformation. *Journal of Bacteriology* 93, 816–829.

GILL, D.R., HATFULL, G.F. AND SALMOND, G.P.C. (1986). A new cell division operon in *Escherichia coli. Molecular and General Genetics* 205, 134–145.

GLICKMAN, B.W. AND RADMAN, M. (1980). *Escherichia coli* mutator mutants deficient in methylation-instructed DNA mismatch correction. *Proceedings of the National Academy of Sciences of the United States of America* 77, 1063–1067.

GUILD, W.R. AND SHOEMAKER, N.B. (1976). Mismatch correction in pneumococcal transformation: donor length and hex-dependent marker efficiency. *Journal of Bacteriology* 125, 125–135.

HABER, L.T., PANG, P.P., SOBELL, D.I., MANKOVICH, J.A. AND WALKER, G.C. (1988). Nucleotide sequence of the *Salmonella typhimurium mutS* gene required for mismatch repair: homology of MutS and HexA of *Streptococcus pneumoniae. Journal of Bacteriology* 170, 197–202.

HATTMAN, S., KENNY, C., BERGER, L. AND PRATT, K. (1978). Comparative study of DNA methylation in three unicellular eucaryotes. *Journal of Bacteriology* 135, 1156–1157.

KORNBERG, A. (1980). *DNA Synthesis.* W.H. Freeman, San Francisco.

KRAMER, B., KRAMER, W. AND FRITZ, H.J. (1984). Different base/base mismatches are corrected with different efficiencies by the methyl-directed DNA mismatch-repair system of *E. coli. Cell* 38, 879–887.

LACKS, S. (1966). Integration efficiency and genetic recombination in pneumococcal transformation. *Genetics* 53, 207–235.

LACKS, S. (1970). Mutants of *Diplococcus pneumoniae* that lack deoxyribonucleases and other activities possibly pertinent to genetic transformation. *Journal of Bacteriology* 101, 373–383.

LACKS, S.A. (1988). Mechanisms of genetic recombination in gram-positive bacteria. In *Genetic Recombination* (R. Kucherlapati and G. Smith, Eds), pp. 43–85. American Society for Microbiology, Washington, DC.

LACKS, S. AND GREENBERG, B. (1977). Complementary specificity of restriction endonucleases of *Diplococcus pneumoniae* with respect to DNA methylation. *Journal of Molecular Biology* 114, 153–168.

LACKS, S.A., DUNN, J.J. AND GREENBERG, B. (1982). Identification of base mismatches recognized by the heteroduplex-DNA-repair system of *Streptococcus pneumoniae. Cell* 31, 327–336.

LACKS, S.A., MANNARELLI, B.M., SPRINGHORN, S., GREENBERG, B. AND DE LA CAMPA, A.G. (1987). Genetics of the complementary restriction systems *Dpn*I and *Dpn*II revealed by cloning and recombination in *Streptococcus pneumoniae.* In *Streptococcal Genetics* (J.J. Ferretti and R. Curtiss III, Eds), pp. 31–41. ASM Publications, Washington, DC.

LIEB, M. (1987). Bacterial genes *mutL, mutS,* and *dcm* participate in repair of mismatches at 5-methylcytosine sites. *Journal of Bacteriology* 169, 5241–5246.

LITMAN, R.M. (1961). Genetic and chemical alterations in the transforming DNA of pneumococcus caused by ultraviolet light and by nitrous acid. *Journal de Chimie Physique* 58, 997–1003.

LOPEZ, P., ESPINOSA, M., GREENBERG, B. AND LACKS, S.A. (1987). Sulfonamide resistance in *Streptococcus pneumoniae*: DNA sequence of the gene encoding dihydropteroate synthase and characterization of the enzyme. *Journal of Bacteriology* 169, 4320–4326.

LU, A.-L. AND CHANG, D.-Y. (1988). Repair of single base-pair transversion mismatches of *Escherichia coli in vitro*: Correction of certain A/G mismatches is independent of *dam* methylation and host *mutHLS* gene functions. *Genetics* 118, 593–600.

MANNARELLI, B.M., BALGANESH, T.S., GREENBERG, B., SPRINGHORN, S.S. AND

LACKS, S.A. (1985). Nucleotide sequence of the *Dpn*II DNA methylase gene o *Streptococcus pneumoniae* and its relationship to the *dam* gene of *Escherichia coli* *Proceedings of the National Academy of Sciences of the United States of America* **82** 4468–4472.

MARINUS, M.G. AND MORRIS, N.R. (1973). Isolation of deoxyribonucleic acic methylase mutants of *Escherichia coli* K-12. *Journal of Bacteriology* **114** 1143–1150.

MARTIN, B., PRATS, H. AND CLAVERYS, J.P. (1985). Cloning of the *hexA* mismatcl repair gene of *Streptococcus pneumoniae* and identification of the product. *Gen* **34**, 293–303.

MESELSON, M. (1988). Methyl-directed repair of DNA mismatches. In *The Recombination of Genetic Material* (K.B. Low, Ed.), pp. 91–113. Academic Press New York.

MITCHELL, M.B. (1955). Aberrant recombination of pyridoxine mutants o *Neurospora. Proceedings of the National Academy of Sciences of the United States of America* **41**, 215–220.

MODRICH, P. (1987). DNA mismatch correction. *Annual Review of Biochemistry* **56** 435–466.

MOSTACHFI, P. AND SICARD, A.M. (1987). Polarity of localized conversion ir *Streptococcus pneumoniae* transformation. *Molecular and General Genetics* **208** 361–363.

PRATS, H., MARTIN, B. AND CLAVERYS, J.P. (1985). The *hexB* mismatch repair gene o *Streptococcus pneumoniae*: characterization, cloning and identification of the product. *Molecular and General Genetics* **200**, 482–489.

PRIEBE, S.D., HADI, S.M., GREENBERG, B. AND LACKS, S.A. (1988). Nucleotide sequence of the *hexA* gene for DNA mismatch repair in *Streptococcus pneumoniae* and homology of *hexA* to *mutS* of *Escherichia coli* and *Salmonella typhimurium. Journal of Bacteriology* **170**, 190–196.

PUKKILA, P.J., PETERSON, J., HERMAN, G., MODRICH, P. AND MESELSON, M. (1983). Effects of high levels of DNA adenine methylation on methyl-directed mismatch repair in *Escherichia coli*. *Genetics* **104**, 571–582.

RADMAN, M. AND WAGNER, R. (1986). Mismatch repair in *Escherichia coli*. *Annual Review of Genetics* **20**, 523–538.

SHOEMAKER, N.B. AND GUILD, W.R. (1974). Destruction of low efficiency markers is a slow process occurring at a heteroduplex stage of transformation. *Molecular and General Genetics* **128**, 283–290.

SU, S.-S., LAHUE, R.S., AU, K.G. AND MODRICH, P. (1988). Mispair specificity of methyl-directed DNA mismatch correction *in vitro*. *Journal of Biological Chemistry* **263**, 6829–6835.

TIRABY, G. AND FOX, M.S. (1973). Marker discrimination in transformation and mutation of pneumococcus. *Proceedings of the National Academy of Sciences of the United States of America* **70**, 3541–3545.

TYE, B.-K., CHIEN, J., LEHMAN, I.R., DUNCAN, B.K. AND WARNER, H.R. (1978). Uracil incorporation: A source of pulse-labeled DNA fragments in the replication of the *Escherichia coli* chromosome. *Proceedings of the National Academy of Sciences of the United States of America* **75**, 233–237.

WELSH, K.M., LU, A.-L. AND MODRICH, P. (1987). Isolation and characterization of the *Escherichia coli mutH* gene product. *Journal of Biological Chemistry* **262**, 15624–15629.

WHITE, J.H., LUSNAK, K. AND FOGEL, S. (1985). Mismatch-specific postmeiotic segregation frequency in yeast suggests a heteroduplex recombination intermediate. *Nature (London)* **315**, 350–352.

WILLIAMSON, M.S., GAME, J.C. AND FOGEL, S. (1985). Meiotic gene conversion in *Saccharomyces cerevisiae*. I. Isolation and characterization of *pms1-1* and *pms 1-2*. *Genetics* **110**, 609–646.

ANOFSKY, C., COX, E.C. AND HORN, V. (1966). The unusual mutagenic specificity of an *E. coli* mutator gene. *Proceedings of the National Academy of Sciences of the United States of America* **55**, 274–281.

# 30
# Gene Conversion in *Streptococcus pneumoniae*

A.M. SICARD

Centre de Recherche de Biochimie et de Génétique Cellulaires du CNRS, 118 Route de Narbonne, 31062 Toulouse Cedex, France

## Introduction

Pneumococcus, officially known today as *Streptococcus pneumoniae*, has preoccupied bacteriologists since the turn of the century, as pneumonia, due to these bacteria, was a leading cause of death. A major advance in attempts to protect individuals from infection by using antiserum was the discovery, in pneumococcus in the early 1920s by Heidelberger and Avery, that the specific antigenic material within the bacterial capsule was not a protein but a polysaccharide (Heidelberger and Avery, 1923). The discovery in the early 1940s, by the Rockefeller bacteriologists, Avery, MacLeod and McCarty (1944) working on pneumococcus, that DNA was the biological substance that transmits genetic information opened the modern field of molecular genetics. Almost 20 years later, in the same organism, it was first found that mutations can be eliminated by a process of correction at the heteroduplex stage. More recently, additional correction systems were described in this organism. We will review here these processes that imply transfer of information from one strand of DNA to another one, i.e *gene conversion* in *Streptococcus pneumoniae*. An extended review of one of these correction processes, long-patch conversion, has been published recently (Claverys and Lacks, 1986).

## Long-patch conversion of mismatched bases

The most extensively studied process of gene conversion is the long-patch conversion of mismatched bases. An efficient way to create mismatched bases is by the bacterial transformation system. Pneumococcus is especially suited to experimental study since all cells are able to incorporate fragments of transforming DNA efficiently. Using cloned DNA, almost every bacterium can be transformed for a given marker (Claverys, Louarn and Sicard, 1981). One

*Genetic Transformation and Expression*
© Intercept Ltd, PO Box 716, Andover, Hants, SP10 1YG, UK

strand at random penetrates the cell and pairs with the homologous region of the recipient DNA. If the transforming DNA carries a mutation, the sequences will be mismatched along the non-complementary heteroduplex. It was first observed independently by several authors (Hotchkiss and Marmur, 1954; Lerman and Tolmach, 1957; Green, 1959; Litman and Ephrussi-Taylor, 1959) that the nature of the mutation will affect the transformation frequency. In this regard it was found that point mutations fall into four distinct classes with respect to their efficiency of transformation, defined by the ease with which they can be recombined into or out of a chromosome (Ephrussi-Taylor, Sicard and Kamen, 1965; Lacks, 1966). The differences can be as much as tenfold between the highest and the lowest efficiency classes.

Ephrussi-Taylor and Gray (1966) postulated that the poorly transforming heteroduplexes are recognized specifically and that this process eliminated the genetic material originating from the donor DNA. Although donor genetic material is destroyed preferentially, in about one-tenth of the events, the recipient genetic material is destroyed instead. A repair would then re-establish a double-stranded structure, copying from the persisting single strand. This excision–repair would transfer genetic information from one strand to the other, thus being a gene conversion. On the contrary, highly efficient markers are not excised at all and they are integrated. They can replicate, becoming homoduplex after one cell division. This type of transformation does not involve gene conversion. For some markers, only one of the two heteroduplexes is excised and converted. Several predictions from this model have been fulfilled:

1. Low-efficiency markers are destroyed by excision–repair (Shoemaker and Guild, 1974);
2. They are transmitted to all daughter cells about one cell division earlier than high-efficiency markers (Ephrussi-Taylor, 1966; Tiraby and Sicard 1973b);
3. Expression of the phenotype of low-efficiency markers is faster than for high-efficiency markers (Ephrussi-Taylor 1966; Claverys, Roger and Sicard, 1980) because for low-efficiency markers both strands contain the genetic information;
4. The frequency of mixed and pure clones after transformation by markers is consistent with a fast transmission of information to both strands (Louarn and Sicard, 1968);
5. The frequency of double unlinked low efficient–low efficient transformants is as expected for a fast transmission of information to both strands (Louarn and Sicard, 1969).

The length over which this conversion occurs has been estimated by genetic analysis of revertants at a locus that confers resistance to amethopterin (*amiA*). Some *amiA* revertants result from a substitution to a base different from that of the original wild type. When used as recipient in transformation these revertants reduce the recombination frequency of high-efficiency markers in proportion to the map distance separating the revertant site and the marker. It has been found that the conversion event concerns an average of at least

2000–3000 base pairs (Sicard and Ephrussi-Taylor, 1966; Sicard *et al.*, 1985a). Similar results were obtained by Lacks using double high efficient–low efficient mutants at the *malM* locus (Lacks, 1966), and by Gray and Ephrussi-Taylor at the *amiA* locus (Gray and Ephrussi-Taylor, 1967). Biochemical evidence for excision of a long sequence (several kbp) of DNA triggered by a low efficient mismatch was obtained by Méjean and Claverys (1984) using a cloned fragment of the *amiA* gene and re-extraction of the integrated fragment from the chromosome.

Support for an enzymatic process to excise and repair low efficient mismatched bases has come from the isolation of *hex* mutants, in which all single-site markers are transformed at the highest efficiency (Lacks, 1970). At least two genes (*hexA* and *hexB*) control this system (Claverys *et al.*, 1984; Martin, Prats and Claverys, 1985). They have been cloned (Balganesh and Lacks, 1985; Martin, Prats and Claverys, 1985; Prats, Martin and Claverys, 1985) and the purification of the gene products is in progress. An interesting property of *hex* genes is their antimutator effect. Tiraby and his co-workers demonstrated that the mutation rate of hex strains is higher than hex$^+$ strains (Tiraby and Fox, 1973; Tiraby and Sicard, 1973b). The increase of spontaneous reversions of mutations corresponding to transition can be as high as a hundredfold (Lacks, Dunn and Greenberg, 1982). Therefore it is likely that an enzymatic complex highly specific for some mismatched heteroduplexes is able to correct DNA by excising several thousand nucleotides around the recognized mismatch which serves as a signal.

The mechanism of preferential elimination of donor information by the Hex system is still obscure. Guild and Shoemaker (1976) proposed that, once triggered by a mismatched base-pair, the Hex-dependent complex would search for nicks and would degrade the donor DNA. Another model implying a double-strand break resulting from the conversion process (Tiraby and Fox, 1974) has been excluded (Guild and Shoemaker, 1976; Lefèvre, Claverys and Sicard, 1979).

Identification of the mismatched bases that are recognized and converted by the Hex system has been achieved by cloning and sequencing several mutants, wild type or revertants, either at the *amiA* locus (Claverys *et al.*, 1981; Claverys *et al.*, 1982; Claverys *et al.*, 1983) or at the *malM* locus (Lacks, Dunn and Greenberg, 1982). Taken together, efficiency of transformation can be correlated to all possible mismatches. Among single base changes, all transition mutations belong to the low-efficiency class, both mismatches A/C and G/T being equally poorly efficient due to excision and repair. Transversion mutations are more efficient because one or both mismatches are not well eliminated by the Hex system. When efficiency of individual strands could be measured (Claverys *et al.*, 1983), it was found that A/A and T/T mismatches are both partially excised. The majority of A/G and C/C mismatches are not at all excised, while some T/C and all G/G are excised. However, the neighbouring sequences may modulate the efficiency of some transversion mutations. For example, the same C/T mismatch is either not excised, or partially or fully excised, depending on the mutation (Gasc, Sicard and Claverys, 1989).

When two mismatches are separated by very few base pairs, we have observed some cases in which repair can be depressed. This interference is often found when a C/C mismatch that is not excised is close to a repairable mismatch. (*Table 30.1*). This suggests that the repair complex protein binds not only to repairable mismatches but also to some mismatches known to escape the repair system.

**Table 30.1**    Transformation efficiency of double mismatches

| Strains | Sequences | Mismatched heteroduplexes | $amiA$ transformants ml$^{-1}$ × 10$^5$ | $str-2$ transformants ml$^{-1}$ × 10$^6$ | Transformation efficiency |
|---|---|---|---|---|---|
| $amiA^+$(A1) | CCAGATTCAT | | | | |
| $amiA135$ | - - - - - - -AG- | $\frac{CA}{TC}$ and $\frac{GT}{AG}$ | 4·89 | 3·20 | 0·15 ± 0·02 |
| | | | 3·82 | 2·73 | 0·14 ± 0·93 |
| $amiA142$ | - - - -G- -A- - | $\frac{A--C}{C--T}$ and $\frac{T--G}{G--A}$ | 1·75 | 7·11 | 0·25 ± 0·03 |
| | | | 1·46 | 5·20 | 0·28 ± 0·04 |
| $amiA148$ | - - - -'- -C-A- - | $\frac{T-C}{G-T}$ and $\frac{A-G}{C-A}$ | 2·02 | 7·33 | 0·27 ± 0·03 |
| | | | 1·32 | 5·51 | 0·24 ± 0·03 |
| $amiA145$ | - - - - - - -A-C | $\frac{C-T}{T-G}$ and $\frac{G-A}{A-C}$ | 1·08 | 3·62 | 0·30 ± 0·04 |
| | | | 0·82 | 3·15 | 0·26 ± 0·03 |
| $amiA136$ | TG- - - - - - - - | $\frac{CC}{AC}$ and $\frac{GG}{TG}$ | 29·8 | 4·30 | 0·69 ± 0·09 |
| | | | 13·4 | 1·81 | 0·74 ± 0·07 |
| $amiA146$ | - - - - -G- A- - | $\frac{T-C}{C-T}$ and $\frac{A-G}{G-A}$ | 67·2 | 5·60 | 1·20 ± 0·12 |
| | | | 23·5 | 2·20 | 1·07 ± 0·10 |
| | | | | | |
| $amiA$+(B2) | CGTTTTAATG | | | | |
| $amiA126$ | - -TTTTT- -T | $\frac{T---G}{AA--A}$ and $\frac{A---C}{TT--T}$ | 3·69 | 1·15 | 0·32 ± 0·04 |
| | | | 1·49 | 4·95 | 0·30 ± 0·05 |

Wild-type bacteria were transformed by DNA carrying a double mutation and the reference marker $str-41$. Transformation efficiency is the ratio of amethopterin transformants to streptomycin transformants. Without interference, the predicted transformation efficiency is the efficiency of the best repaired single-site mutation: when both heteroduplexes are repaired this value is 0·15 on the average; when only one heteroduplex DNA is repaired this value is 1·20. Repair is inversely related to transformation efficiency. Sequences are written in the order 5' → 3' corresponding to the mRNA strand. (A1), wild-type sequence in the A1 fragment of the $amiA$ locus in the $amiA36$ region; (B2), wild-type sequence in the B2 fragment of the $amiA$ locus in the $amiA128$ region (Gasc et al., 1987).

The transforming ability of heterologies due to deletions depends on their length: small deletions, i.e. 93 base pairs at the *malM* locus (Lacks, Dunn and Greenberg, 1982), 34 base pairs at the *amiA* locus (Claverys *et al*., 1981), a six base-pair insertion at the *sul-d* locus (Lopez *et al*., 1987) or a five base-pair deletion at the *amiA* locus (Gasc *et al*., 1987), are transformed at the highest frequency, four and three base-pair deletions have an intermediate efficiency. Five mutants resulting from a ±1 base-pair change (Gasc and Sicard, 1986) or a two base-pair insertion (Claverys *et al*., 1983) are poorly efficient. Again, neighbouring sequences may modulate the efficiency of ±1 base-pair mutants because a spontaneous deletion of C/C gives an intermediate efficiency (Lacks, Dunn and Greenberg, 1982) and the same deletion at the autolysin locus is highly efficient (Lopez *et al*., 1986). No simple rule, such as G/C content, or Z-DNA, can explain the neighbour effect.

## Specialized conversion

We have studied an aberrant marker, *amiA36* that enhances recombination frequency when crossed with any other allele of the *amiA* gene. This effect is especially apparent for distances as short as 27 base pairs, where we observed 20% wild-type recombinants instead of the expected 1% (Lefèvre *et al.*, 1984). The mutation results from a C/G to A/T transversion in the sequence, i.e. from 5'. . . ATTCAT to 5' . . . ATTAAT. This hyper-recombination is due to a conversion of *amiA36* to wild type. This has been demonstrated in three-point crosses where it was found that the frequency of recombinants between outside markers was not increased when *amiA36* was in one of the molecules (Sicard *et al.*, 1985a). Since conversion can occur even for 27 base pairs, the observed hyper-recombination suggests that there is no co-conversion of these closely linked alleles (Sicard *et al.*, 1985). To estimate the length over which this event occurred, we have isolated two mutants located five bases away on either side and one mutant 12 bases away from *amiA36*. Hyper-recombination almost completely disappeared for the five-base markers and was maintained at half the usual value for the marker located 12 bases away from *amiA36*. This shows that the converting system involves an average of 10–12 bases, i.e. a turn of the DNA helix on either side of the signal.

Specialized conversion does not require the action of either hexA or hexB active genes (Lefèvre *et al.*, 1984). In an hex$^+$ recipient, when a nearby low-efficiency marker is crossed to *amiA36*, specialized conversion is drastically depressed (Lefèvre *et al.*, 1984). This further suggests that specialized conversion occurs at the heteroduplex stage, since the long-patch process also acts at this level.

If specialized conversion indeed occurs at the heteroduplex stage of recombination, we can ask the following question: Are the two possible heteroduplexes equally able to induce conversion? Using separated and cross-reannealed DNA strands, artificial heteroduplexes were constructed. It was found that only one heteroduplex was preferentially converted. The specialized conversion acts upon 5' . . . A . . . /3' . . . G . . ., changing A to C (Sicard *et al.*, 1985b). The reciprocal event, i.e. wild-type 5' . . . C to mutant 5' . . . A does not occur (Mostachfi and Sicard, 1987).

To determine the sequence required to trigger this conversion, site-specific mutagenesis has been used to create the same 5'ATTAAT mutation on another part of the *amiA* gene. Two-point crosses with nearby markers also showed a high level of conversion. Thus this six base-pair configuration is a sufficient signal for specialized conversion. Changing individual bases within this segment results in decreased conversion frequencies to levels that depend on the mutations (*Table 30.2*). Therefore specialized conversion is not restricted to the original six base-pair configuration but can be induced by related sequences, although at variable frequencies. Moreover, in my laboratory Franck Pasta has shown that homoduplex ATTAAT/TAATTA does not induce conversion.

Nothing is known about the molecular process leading to specialized conversion, but it could be the result of excision of a few bases close to the mutation. This model would be similar to the short-patch repair system of

**Table 30.2**  Recombination indices in transformation between the constructed mutants and other closely linked markers. Expected values would be 1, 1·2 and 6·6 for transformation by *amiA6*, *amiA141* and *amiA54* DNA respectively, in the absence of conversion. Underlined bases indicate a change from the sequence of *amiA36* (ATTAAT). *amiA136* is mutated six and seven bases on the left of *amiA36*, resulting from the double substitution: 5'. . . CTT CCA GAT → 5'. . . CTT TGA GAT

| Recipient strain | Donor DNA | | | |
|---|---|---|---|---|
| | *amiA6* | *amiA141* | *amiA54* | *amiA3*( |
| *amiA148* (A̲CTAAT) | 12 | 17 | 22 | 0 |
| *amiA142* (G̲TTAAT) | 7 | 8 | 21 | 0 |
| *amiA137* (ATTG̲AT) | 5 | 6 | 14 | 0 |
| *amiA135* (ATTAG̲T̲) | 7 | 8 | 12 | 0 |
| *amiA146* (AG̲TAAT) | 6 | 7 | 8 | 0 |
| *amiA145* (ATTAAC̲) | 1·6 | 1·6 | 2·5 | 0 |
| *amiA136* | 5 | 7 | 9 | 0·4 |

pyrimidine dimers after UV-irradiation of DNA. However, the UV repair system does not convert *amiA36* mutations since pneumococcal strains deficient in this process are still fully competent for conversion. An alternative hypothesis is that conversion results from the replacement of the mutant strand by the wild-type strand of the same polarity (Sicard *et al.*, 1985). If conversion occurs via an excision–repair process, we can predict a role for DNA polymerase. I.F. Pasta in my laboratory has tested this hypothesis using a pneumococcal *polI⁻* mutant provided by Paloma Lopez. In that strain specialized conversion is strongly depressed (one-fifth of the standard value). This suggests that specialized conversion requires an excision–repair mechanism.

**Elimination of deletions**

Deletions are neither recognized by the Hex system (Lacks, 1966) nor by the specialized conversion process. Is there another way to eliminate them during recombination? An answer to this question comes from the following observation: when fairly long deletions (more than a few hundred bases long) are carried on donor DNA to transform a recipient containing a linked point mutation, wild-type recombinants occur in large excess (Claverys, Lefèvre and Sicard, 1980). The frequency of these recombinants is the sum of recombinants expected from the distance between markers plus a 23% value (*Table 30.3*). The length of deletions that yields this value is from 200 base pairs to more than a few thousand base pairs. However, a smaller deletion of 76 base pairs (*amiA40*) yields only 7% excess wild-type recombinants. In three-factor crosses in which the deletion is located between two closely linked outside markers, we have found that the frequency of wild-type recombinants between these outside markers is not increased by the presence of this heterology (*Table 30.4*). This suggests that deletions are converted. Conversion occurs when markers are very close. This is exemplified in *Table 30.3*, part B. The length of this conversion event fluctuates between 20 and 100 bases outside the deletion. This fluctuation may be due to DNA base sequences. Conversion disappears when a mismatched base in the cross induces the Hex-directed long-patch conversion process (*Table 30.5*). This suggests that long heterologies resulting

**able 30.3** Recombination frequencies from reciprocal transformation involving deletions

| Recipient strain | Donor DNA | Recombination frequencies(%) | d (%) | Recipient strain | Donor DNA | Recombination frequencies(%) | d (%) |
|---|---|---|---|---|---|---|---|
| amiA22 | amiA6 | 18 | | amiA504 | amiA16 | 10·5 | |
| amiA6 | amiA22 | 18·1 | | amiA508 | amiA16 | 10·0 | |
| amiA502 | amiA22 | 19·8 | | amiA16 | amiA504 | 40·6 | |
| amiA22 | amiA502 | 42·3 | | amiA16 | amiA508 | 32·3 | |
| amiA22 | amiA505 | 39·7 | 21·2 | amiA16 | amiA510 | 31·2 | |
| | | | | amiA16 | amiA514 | 49 | 28·1 |
| amiA29 | amiA6 | 21 | | | | | |
| amiA502 | amiA29 | 18·9 | | amiA504 | amiA146 | 11·8 | |
| amiA29 | amiA502 | 40·6 | | amiA508 | amiA146 | 12·1 | |
| amiA29 | amiA505 | 48·4 | 25·6 | amiA146 | amiA504 | 40·4 | |
| | | | | amiA146 | amiA508 | 30·8 | |
| | | | | amiA146 | amiA514 | 32·7 | 24·3 |
| amiA20 | amiA6 | 7·4 | | amiA30 | amiA146 | 8·0 | |
| amiA6 | amiA20 | 8 | | amiA146 | amiA30 | 27·9 | 21·9 |
| amiA502 | amiA20 | 38·1 | | | | | |
| amiA20 | amiA505 | 42·5 | 29·5 | amiA509 | amiA16 | 1·3 | |
| | | | | amiA30 | amiA16 | 2·7 | |
| amiA24 | amiA6 | 8 | | amiA16 | amiA30 | 19·8 | 17·1 |
| amiA6 | amiA24 | 8·1 | | | | | |
| amiA502 | amiA24 | 8·1 | | amiA109 | amiA29 | 2·6 | |
| amiA24 | amiA502 | 26·9 | | amiA6 | amiA109 | 22·1 | 19·5 |
| amiA24 | amiA505 | 33·7 | 22·2 | | | | |
| | | | | amiA109 | amiA29 | 1·6 | |
| | | | | amiA29 | amiA109 | 26·4 | 24·8 |
| | | | | | | | |
| | | | | amiA109 | amiA22 | 3·5 | |
| | | | | amiA22 | amiA109 | 23·1 | 19·6 |
| **B** | | | | | | | |
| amiA28 | amiA511 | 1·9 | | amiA519 | amiA6 | 0·35 | |
| amiA511 | amiA28 | 10·9 | 9 | amiA6 | amiA519 | 4·30 | 3·95 |
| amiA28 | amiA16 | 11·9 | | amiA109 | amiA54 | 0·9 | |
| amiA16 | amiA28 | 20·8 | 8·9 | amiA54 | amiA109 | 5·1 | 4·2 |
| amiA28 | amiA1 | 7 | | amiA109 | amiA9 | 0·5 | |
| amiA1 | amiA28 | 23 | 16 | amiA9 | amiA109 | 11·3 | 10·8 |
| amiA28 | amiA23 | 6·3 | | amiA40 | amiA54 | 5 | |
| amiA23 | amiA28 | 18·6 | 12·3 | amiA54 | amiA40 | 12 | 7 |
| amiA578 | amiA74 | 1·7 | | amiA40 | amiA75 | 0·9 | |
| amiA74 | amiA578 | 11·4 | 10·3 | amiA75 | amiA40 | 7 | 7·1 |

n part A of the table the difference, *d*, between reciprocal crosses was homogeneous and equal to 23%. In part B he difference was smaller.

rom deletions are processed during the pairing steps (Lefèvre, 1986). The mechanism of conversion of deletion must be quite different from the pecialized conversion, since it was found that the former does not require an ctive polymerase I gene (F. Pasta, unpublished results). We propose that eterologies participate in heteroduplex DNA. During migration of donor JNA, at the level of the deletion, the parental homoduplex structure might be

**Table 30.4**  Recombination frequencies in crosses involving deletion *amiA109* and outside markers

| Recipient | Donor | AmiA$^+$/str-r $\times$ 100 |
|---|---|---|
| Three-point crosses with the double mutant *amiA109–amiA22* | | |
| *amiA54* | *amiA109–amiA22str41* | 2·4 |
| *amiA109–amiA22* | *amiA54str41* | 1·0 |
| *amiA6* | *amiA109–amiA22str41* | 7·5 |
| *amiA109–amiA22* | *amiA6str41* | 3·9 |
| Two-point crosses with *amiA109* or *amiA22* | | |
| *amiA54* | *amiA22str41* | 18·1 |
| *amiA22* | *amiA54str41* | 19·2 |
| *amiA22* | *amiA6str41* | 18·3 |
| *amiA6* | *amiA22str41* | 18·1 |
| *amiA109* | *amiA54str41* | 0·9 |
| *amiA54* | *amiA109str41* | 5·1 |
| *amiA109* | *amiA22str41* | 3·5 |
| *amiA22* | *amiA109str41* | 23·1 |
| *amiA109* | *amiA6str41* | 2·6 |
| *amiA6* | *amiA109str41* | 26·4 |

**Table 30.5**  Inhibition of conversion of deletions by excision–repair of mismatched bases

| Recipient strain | Donor DNA | Recombination frequencies (%) |
|---|---|---|
| hex*amiA24* | *amiA6* | 8 |
| hex*amiA24* | *amiA502* | 26·9 |
| hex*amiA24* | *amiA505* | 33·7 |
| hex$^+$*amiA24* | *amiA502* | 7·8 |
| hex$^+$*amiA24* | *amiA505* | 11·4 |
| hex$^+$*amiA502* | *amiA24* | 8·1 |
| | | |
| hex*amiA74* | *amiA578* | 11·4 |
| hex$^+$*amiA74* | *amiA578* | 2·8 |
| hex$^+$*amiA578* | *amiA74* | 1·7 |
| | | |
| hex*amiA6* | *amiA109* | 22·1 |
| hex$^+$*amiA6* | *amiA109* | 2·9 |
| hex$^+$*amiA109* | *amiA6* | 3·4 |
| | | |
| hex*amiA6* | *amiA519* | 4·30 |
| hex$^+$*amiA6* | *amiA519* | 0·24 |
| hex$^+$*amiA519* | *amiA6* | 0·35 |

Mutations *amiA6, amiA24, amiA74* are low-efficiency markers that are excised by the hex-mediated repair system; *amiA109, amiA502, amiA505, amiAa519* and *amiA578* are deletions.

reconstituted, thus yielding maximum pairing. Recipient and donor strands of identical polarity will be in contact, eventually leading to wild-type donor DNA by breakage and reunion (*Figure 30.1*).

Gene Conversion in S. pneumoniae    349

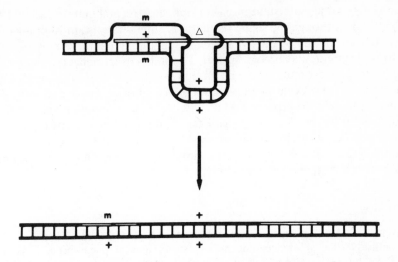

**Figure 30.1** Conversion of deletions. Double-strand chromosomal DNA carrying a point mutation (m) is unpaired when a single-strand donor molecule invades the recipient molecule (double line). Maximum pairing involves not only regions outside the deletion (△) but also the displaced strand of recipient DNA and the homologous recipient DNA. Breakage and ligation of single-strand DNA in the region of intersections (either one or both) between donor and recipient molecules will lead to converted wild-type recombinant. This recombinant molecule will be heteroduplex at the site of the point mutation (m) and wild-type homoduplex at the site of the deletion. After one cycle of chromosomal replication, wild-type colonies will be obtained.

**Significance of conversions**

The long-patch conversion system directed by *hex* genes acts in all natural pneumococcal isolates tested (Tiraby, Fox and Bernheimer, 1975) and in *Haemophilus influenzae* (Bagci and Stuy, 1979). Studies based on transfection assays with phage heteroduplexes first on *Bacillus subtilis* (Spatz and Trautner, 1970) and then on *E. coli* (White and Fox, 1974; Nevers and Spatz, 1975; Wildenberg and Meselson, 1975) show that an analogous process to the pneumococcal conversion is acting in those strains. Although the *E. coli* system requires the recognition of methylated sequences, it shares many similarities with the Hex system since the base specificity is nearly the same (Kramer, Kramer and Fritz, 1984; Dohet, Wagner and Radman, 1985). The mismatch specificity in two yeasts is also similar to the pneumococcal Hex system (Kohli *et al.*, 1984; White, Fogel and Lusnak, 1985). Therefore long-patch conversion is widespread. It is likely that it has been created and preserved during evolution to eliminate the most frequent spontaneous point mutations, such as ±1 base mutations and transitions, because pneumococcal and H. *influenzae hex* mutants behave as mutator alleles (Tiraby and Fox, 1973; Tiraby and Sicard, 1973a; Bagci and Stuy, 1979) as do the homologous *E. coli* genes *mut L*, *mut S* and *mut H* (Cox, 1976). The discarded mutations are precisely the same ones that are converted to wild type during recombination.

    The specialized conversion process described in pneumococcus has been found in several independent strains (Garcia, unpublished results). Moreover, there is an analogous system in bacteriophage λ recombination (Lieb, 1983; Lieb, 1985). Although the signal sequence is quite different, most of the other properties are shared by the two systems, suggesting that these more recently discovered systems may be widespread. The ability of specialized conversion to specifically convert mutant to wild type in families of related sequences may indicate a role in preventing these mutations (A/G) which are not recognized by the other repair processes. Likewise, potential spontaneous deletions occurring during errors of DNA synthesis might be eliminated by conversion. This is not restricted to pneumococcus since it has been observed in fungi (Hamza *et al.*, 1986) and may explain stimulation of recombination in λ-phage crosses (Lieb, Tsai and Deonier, 1984).

## References

AVERY, O.T., MACLEOD, C.M. AND MCCARTY, M. (1944). Studies on the chemical nature of the substance inducing transformation of pneumococcal types. I. Induction of transformation by a deoxyribonucleic acid fraction isolated from pneumococcus type III. *Journal of Experimental Medicine* **79**, 137–158.

BAGCI, H.L. AND STUY, J.H. (1979). A *hex* mutant of *Haemophilus influenzae*. *Molecular and General Genetics* **175**, 175–179.

BALGANESH, T.S. AND LACKS, S.A. (1985). Heteroduplex DNA mismatch repair system of *Streptococcus pneumoniae*: cloning and expression of the *hexA* gene. *Journal of Bacteriology* **162**, 979–984.

CLAVERYS, J.-P. AND LACKS, S. (1986). Heteroduplex DNA base mismatch repair in bacteria. *Microbial Reviews* **50**, 133–165.

CLAVERYS, J.-P., LEFÈVRE, J.C. AND SICARD, A.M. (1980). Transformation of *Streptococcus pneumoniae* with *S. pneumoniae* phage hybrid DNA: induction of deletions. *Proceedings of the National Academy of Sciences of the United States of America* **77**, 3534–3538.

CLAVERYS, J.-P., LOUARN, J.M. AND SICARD, A.M. (1981). Cloning of *Streptococcus pneumoniae* DNA: its use in pneumococcal transformation and in studies of mismatch repair. *Gene* **13**, 65–73.

CLAVERYS, J.-P., ROGER, M. AND SICARD, A.M. (1980). Excision and repair of mismatched base pairs in transformation of *Streptococcus pneumoniae*. *Molecular and General Genetics* **178**, 191–201.

CLAVERYS, J.-P., MÉJEAN, V., GASC, A.M., GALIBERT, F. AND SICARD, A.M. (1981). Base specificity of mismatch repair in *Streptococcus pneumoniae*. *Nucleic Acids Research* **9**, 2267–2280.

CLAVERYS, J.-P., MÉJEAN, V., GASC, A.M. AND SICARD, A.M. (1982). Relationship between base mismatches and integration efficiency in transformation of *Streptococcus pneumoniae*. In *Microbiology – 1982*. (D. Schlessinger, Ed.), pp. 248–252. American Society for Microbiology, Washington, DC.

CLAVERYS, J.-P., MÉJEAN, V., GASC, A.M. AND SICARD, A.M. (1983). Mismatch repair in *Streptococcus pneumoniae*: relationship between base mismatches and transformation efficiencies. *Proceedings of the National Academy of Sciences of the United States of America* **80**, 5956–5960.

CLAVERYS, J.-P., PRATS, H., VASSEGHI, H. AND GHERARDI, M. (1984). Identification of *Streptococcus pneumoniae* mismatch repair genes by an additive transformation approach. *Molecular and General Genetics* **196**, 91–96.

COX, E.C. (1976). Bacterial mutator genes and the control of spontaneous mutation. *Annual Review of Genetics* **10**, 135–156.

DOHET, C., WAGNER, R. AND RADMAN, M. (1985). Repair of defined single base-pair mismatches in *Escherichia coli*. *Proceedings of the National Academy of Sciences of* the United States of America **82**, 503–505.

EPHRUSSI-TAYLOR, H. (1966). Genetic recombination in DNA-induced transformation of pneumococcus. IV. The pattern of transmission and phenotypic expression of high and low-efficiency donor sites in the *amiA* locus. *Genetics* **54**, 211–222.

EPHRUSSI-TAYLOR, H. AND GRAY, T.C. (1966). Genetic studies of recombining DNA in pneumococcal transformation. *Journal of General Physiology* **49** (2), 211–231.

EPHRUSSI-TAYLOR, H., SICARD, A.M. AND KAMEN, R. (1965). The problem of relative efficiency of transforming factors. *Genetics* **51**, 455–475.

GASC, A.-M. AND SICARD, A.M. (1986). Frameshift mutants induced by quinacrine are recognized by the mismatch repair system in *Streptococcus pneumoniae*. *Molecular and General Genetics* **203**, 269–273.

GASC, A.-M., SICARD, A.M. AND CLAVERYS, J.-P. (1989). Repair of single-and multiple-substitution mismatches during recombination in *Streptococcus pneumoniae*. *Genetics* **121**, 29–36.

GASC, A.-M., GARCIA, P., BATY, D. AND SICARD, A.M. (1987). Mismatch repair during pneumococcal transformation of small deletions produced by site-directed mutagenesis. *Molecular and General Genetics* **210**, 369–372.

GRAY, T.C. AND EPHRUSSI-TAYLOR, H. (1967). Genetic recombination in DNA-induced transformation of pneumococcus. V. The absence of interference and evidence for the selective elimination of certain donor sites from the final recombinants. *Genetics* **57**, 125–153.

GREEN, D.M. (1959). A host specific variation affecting relative frequency of transformation of two markers in pneumococcus. *Experimental Cell Research* **18**, 466–480.

GUILD, W.R. AND SHOEMAKER, N.B. (1976). Mismatch correction in pneumococcal transformation: donor length and hex-dependent marker efficiency. *Journal of Bacteriology* **125**, 125–135.

HAMZA, H., KALOGEROPOULOS, A., NICOLAS, A. AND ROSSIGNOL, J.L. (1986). Two mechanisms for directional gene conversions. *Proceedings of the National Academy of Sciences of the United States of America* **83**, 7386–7390.

HEIDELBERGER, M. AND AVERY, D.T. (1923). Soluble specific substance of pneumococcus. *Journal of Experimental Medicine* **38**, 73–79.

HOTCHKISS, R.D. AND MARMUR, J. (1954). Double marker transformation as evidence of linked factors in desoxyribonucleate transforming agents. *Proceedings of the National Academy of Sciences of the United States of America* **40**, 55–60.

KOHLI, J., MUNZ, P., AEBI, R., AMSTUTZ, M., GYSLER, C., HEYER, W.D., LEHMANN, L., SCHUCHERT, P., SZANKASI, P., THURIAUX, P., LEUPOLD, U., BELL, J., GAMULIN, V., HOTTINGER, H., PEARSON, D. AND SÖLL, D. (1984). Interallelic and intergenic conversion in three serine tRNA genes of *Schizosaccharomyces pombe*. *Cold Spring Harbor Symposium on Quantitative Biology* **49**, 31–40.

KRAMER, B., KRAMER, W. AND FRITZ, H.J. (1984). Different base/base mismatches are corrected with different efficiencies by the methyl-directed DNA mismatch-repair system of *E. coli*. *Cell* **38**, 879–887.

LACKS, S. (1966). Integration efficiency and genetic recombination in pneumococcal transformation. *Genetics* **53**, 207–235.

LACKS, S. (1970). Mutants of *Diplococcus pneumoniae* that lack deoxyribonucleases and other activities possibly pertinent to genetic transformation. *Journal of Bacteriology* **101**, 373–383.

LACKS, S.A., DUNN, J.J. AND GREENBERG, B. (1982). Identification of base mismatches recognized by the heteroduplex DNA repair system of *Streptococcus pneumoniae*. *Cell* **31**, 327–336.

LEFÈVRE, J.C. (1986). *Mise en évidence et étude de deux phénomènes d'hyperrecombinaison chez* Streptococcus pneumoniae. Thèse d'Etat, Université Paul Sabatier, Toulouse , France.

LEFÈVRE, J.C., CLAVERYS, J.-P. AND SICARD, A.M. (1979). Donor deoxyribonucleic acid length and marker effect in pneumococcal transformation. *Journal of*

352    *DNA Repair*

*Bacteriology* **138**, 80–86.

LEFÈVRE, J.C., GASC, A.M., BURGER, A.C., MOSTACHFI, H. AND SICARD, A.M. (1984). Hyperrecombination at a specific DNA sequence in pneumococcal transformation. *Proceedings of the National Academy of Sciences of the United States of America* **81**, 5184–5188.

LERMAN, L.S. AND TOLMACH, L.J. (1957). Genetic transformation. I. Cellular incorporation of DNA accompanying transformation in pneumococcus. *Biochimica et Biophysica Acta* **26**, 68–82.

LIEB, M. (1983). Specific mismatch correction in bacteriophage lambda crosses by very short patch repair. *Molecular and General Genetics* **191**, 118–125.

LIEB, M. (1985). Recombination in the lambda repressor gene: evidence that very short patch (VSP) mismatch correction restores a specific sequence. *Molecular and General Genetics* **199**, 465–470.

LIEB, M., TSAI, M.M. AND DEONIER, R.C. (1984). Crosses between insertion and point mutations in λ gene *cI*: stimulation of neighboring recombination by heterology. *Genetics* **108**, 277–289.

LITMAN, R.M. AND EPHRUSSI-TAYLOR, H. (1959). Inactivation et mutation des facteurs génétiques de l'acide desoxyribonucléique du pneumocoque par l'ultraviolet et par l'acide nitreux. *Comptes Rendus de l'Academie des Sciences de Paris* **249**, 838–840.

LOPEZ, P., ESPINOZA, M., GREENBERG, B. AND LACKS, S. (1987). Sulfonamide resistance in *Streptococcus pneumoniae*: DNA sequence of the gene encoding dehydropteroate synthase and characterization of the enzyme. *Journal of Bacteriology* **169**, 4320–4326.

LOPEZ, R., SANCHEZ-PUELLES, J.M., GARCIA, E., GARCIA, J.L., RONDA, C. AND GARCIA, P. (1986). Isolation, characterization and physiological properties of an autolytic-deficient mutant of *Streptococcus pneumoniae*. *Molecular and General Genetics* **204**, 237–242.

LOUARN, J.M. AND SICARD, A.M. (1968). Transmission of genetic information during transformation in *Diplococcus pneumoniae*. *Biochemical and Biophysical Research Communications* **30**, 683–689.

LOUARN, J.M. AND SICARD, A.M. (1969). Identical transformability of both strands of recipient DNA in *Diplococcus pneumoniae*. *Biochemical and Biophysical Research Communications* **36**, 101–109.

MARTIN, B., PRATS, H. AND CLAVERYS, J.-P. (1985). Cloning of the *hexA* mismatch repair gene of *Streptococcus pneumoniae* and identification of the product. *Gene* **34**, 293–303.

MÉJEAN, V. AND CLAVERYS, J.-P. (1984). Effect of mismatched base pairs on the fate of donor DNA in transformation of *Streptococcus pneumoniae*. *Molecular and General Genetics* **197**, 467–471.

MOSTACHFI, P. AND SICARD, A.M. (1987). Polarity of localized conversion in *Streptococcus pneumoniae* transformation. *Molecular and General Genetics* **208**, 361–363.

NEVERS, P. AND SPATZ, H.C. (1975). *Escherichia coli* mutants *uvrD* and *uvrE* deficient in gene conversion of lambda heteroduplexes. *Molecular and General Genetics* **139**, 233–243.

PRATS, H., MARTIN, B. AND CLAVERYS, J.-P. (1985). The *hexB* mismatch repair gene of *Streptococcus pneumoniae*: characterization, cloning and identification of the product. *Molecular and General Genetics* **200**, 482–489.

SHOEMAKER, N. AND GUILD, W. (1974). Destruction of low efficiency markers is a slow process occurring at a heteroduplex stage of transformation. *Molecular and General Genetics* **128**, 283–290.

SICARD, A.M. AND EPHRUSSI-TAYLOR, H. (1966). Recombinaison génétique dans la transformation chez le pneumocoque. Etude des réversions au locus *amiA*. *Comptes Rendus de l'Academie des Sciences de Paris* **262**, 2305–2308.

SICARD, M., LEFÈVRE, J.C., MOSTACHFI, P., GASC, A.M., MÉJEAN, V. AND

CLAVERYS, J.-P. (1985a). Long- and short-patch gene conversions in *Streptococcus pneumoniae* transformation. *Biochimie* **67**, 377–384.

SICARD, M., LEFÈVRE, J.C., MOSTACHFI, P., GASC, A.M. AND SARDA, C. (1985b). Localized conversion in *Streptococcus pneumoniae* recombination: heteroduplex preference. *Genetics* **110**, 557–568.

SPATZ, H.C. AND TRAUTNER, T.A. (1970). One way to do experiments on gene conversion? Transfection with heteroduplex SPP1 DNA. *Molecular and General Genetics* **109**, 84–106.

TIRABY, G. AND FOX, M.S. (1973). Marker discrimination in transformation and mutation of pneumococcus. *Proceedings of the National Academy of Sciences of the United States of America* **70**, 3541–3545.

TIRABY, G. AND FOX, M.S. (1974). On the mechanism of the hex function in mutation and transformation of pneumococcus. *Mechanisms in recombination* (R. Grell, Ed.), pp. 225–236. Plenum Press, New York.

TIRABY, G. AND SICARD, A.M. (1973a). Integration efficiencies of spontaneous mutant alleles of *amiA* locus in pneumococcal transformation. *Journal of Bacteriology* **116**, 1130–1135.

TIRABY, G. AND SICARD, A.M. (1973b). Integration efficiency in DNA-induced transformation of pneumococcus. II. Genetic studies of mutants integrating all the markers with a high efficiency. *Genetics* **75**, 35–48.

TIRABY, G., FOX, M.S. AND BERNHEIMER, H. (1975). Marker discrimination in DNA-induced transformation of various pneumococcus strains. *Journal of Bacteriology* **121**, 608–618.

WHITE, R.L. AND FOX, M.S. (1974). On the molecular basis of high negative interference. *Proceedings of the National Academy of Sciences of the United States of America* **71**, 1544–1548.

WHITE, J.H., FOGEL, S. AND LUSNAK, K. (1985). Mismatch-specific post-meiotic segregation frequency in yeast suggests a heteroduplex recombination intermediate. *Nature* **315**, 350–352.

WILDENBERG, J. AND MESELSON, M. (1975). Mismatch repair in heteroduplex DNA. *Proceedings of the National Academy of Sciences of the United States of America* **72**, 2202–2206.

# 31
# DNA Repair is Required for Specialized Conversion in Pneumococcus

F. PASTA AND A.M. SICARD

Centre de Recherche de Biochimie et de Génétique Cellulaires du CNRS, 118 Route de Narbonne, 31062 Toulouse Cedex, France

Mismatch repair plays a central role in evolution to eliminate some spontaneous point mutations such as ±1 base mutations and transitions, as well as some long deletions (Sicard, 1987). Many mismatches resulting from base substitutions are eliminated by the major system controlled by the *hex* genes. In pneumococcus the mismatch A/G is very rarely repaired (*see* Claverys and Lacks, 1986, for a review). We have reported another repair process that is *hex*-independent and acts on this A/G mismatch in sequences related to ATT<u>A</u>AT/TAA<u>GT</u>A (Lefèvre *et al.*, 1984; Sicard *et al.*, 1985; Garcia *et al.*, 1988). This process involves only 10–12 bases, whereas the Hex system excises a few thousand bases. For that reason it was named 'localized conversion' in pneumococcus in contrast with the Hex-mediated long-patch conversion. A similar process has been described in *E. coli* as 'very short patch repair' (Lieb, 1983). As suggested by Lacks (Chapter 29, this volume), we will refer to 'specialized conversion' to emphasize the sequence specificity in contrast with other systems that are mismatch-dependent and almost entirely sequence-independent (Gasc, Sicard and Claverys, 1988).

The molecular process leading to specialized conversion could be the result of excision of a few bases close to the mutation followed by localized DNA synthesis (Sicard *et al.*, 1985). An alternative hypothesis could be that conversion might result from the replacement of the mutant strand by the wild-type strand of the same polarity. If conversion occurs via an excision repair process, we can predict the role of DNA polymerase I. In this chapter we will show that this is indeed the case, supporting the hypothesis of a localized repair process.

A polymerase-deficient strain has been obtained by insertion of the *cat* gene in the polymerase domain of the pneumococcal *polA* gene (P. Lopez *et al.*, Chapter 37, this meeting). We have introduced this mutation *polA::cat-28* into *Streptococcus pneumoniae amiA36 hex*, which carries the marker showing specialized conversion. This strain (*polA, amiA36hex*) was transformed by pneumococcal chromosomal DNA carrying the very closely linked marker *amiA6* (27 base pairs away from *amiA36*), and a reference marker *str-41*. Wild-type *amiA*⁺ recombinants were scored as described earlier (Sicard, 1964), as well as streptomycin-resistant transformants. In Table 31.1, it can be seen that the average frequency of recombinants is 5·1% in the cross involving the *polA* strain, whereas it is 23·3% when the *polA*⁺ strain is used. Therefore specialized conversion is strongly depressed in a *polA* mutant. This result supports the hypothesis of an excision–repair of a short stretch of bases.

**Table 31.1**  Effect of *polA* mutation on specialized conversion in pneumococcus

| Recipient strain | Donor DNA | *amiA*⁺ transformants/ml | *str-r* transformants/ml | Recombination frequencies (%) |
|---|---|---|---|---|
| *polA*⁺ *amiA36 hex* | *amiA6 str-41* | $4·90 \times 10^5$ | $2·10 \times 10^6$ | 23·3 |
| *polA amiA36 hex* | *amiA6 str-41* | $2·60 \times 10^4$ | $4·50 \times 10^5$ | 5·7 |
| *polA amiA36 hex* | *amiA6 str-41* | $2·50 \times 10^4$ | $5·40 \times 10^5$ | 4·6 |
| *polA amiA36 hex* | *amiA6 str-41* | $7·75 \times 10^4$ | $1·51 \times 10^6$ | 5·1 |

The frequency of recombination between *amiA6* and *amiA36* is calculated as the number of recombinants *amiA*⁺ over the number of *str-r*.

In the absence of specialized conversion, the expected value of the frequency of recombination should be 1% in such a cross. The reduction observed is not complete. It is unlikely that the residual conversion in the *polA* strain results from a leakiness of that mutation, since the mutant has been obtained by insertion, although the activity of the enzyme in the mutant strain is not known. Another possibility should be that polymerase III participates in DNA synthesis after excision. However, inhibitors such as 5-fluoro-uracil or novobiocin do not affect specialized conversion (Guillot, unpublished results). It might be that specialized repair is not only dependent on *polA* gene activity, but could require another minor pathway. It is interesting to note that similar results have been observed in *E. coli* for the very short patch repair that shares many similarities with the pneumococcal system (Radman, personal communication).

Such observations are in agreement with the proposal that specialized repairs triggered by some precise sequences have been preserved during evolution and might be found in a variety of organisms to protect against spontaneous mutations.

### Acknowledgement

We are very grateful to Dr Paloma Lopez for her gift of the *polA* mutant.

### References

CLAVERYS, J.P. AND LACKS, S. (1986). Heteroduplex DNA base mismatch repair in bacteria. *Microbiological Reviews* **50**, 133–165.

GARCIA, P., GASC, A.M., KYRIAKIDIS, X., BATY, D. AND SICARD, A.M. (1988). DNA sequences required to induce localized conversion in *Streptococcus pneumoniae* transformation. *Molecular and General Genetics* **214**, 509–513.

GASC, A.M., SICARD, A.M. AND CLAVERYS, J.P. (1988). Repair of single and multiple substitution mismatches during recombination in *Streptococcus pneumoniae*. *Genetics* **121**, 29–36.

LEFÈVRE, J.C., GASC, A.M., BURGER, A.C., MOSTACHFI, P. AND SICARD, A.M. (1984). Hyperrecombination at a specific DNA sequence in pneumococcal transformation. *Proceedings of the National Academy of Sciences of the United States of America* **81**, 5184–5188.

LIEB, M. (1983). Specific mismatch correction in bacteriophage lambda crosses by very short patch repair. *Molecular and General Genetics* **191**, 118–125.

SICARD, A.M. (1964). A new synthetic medium for *Diplococcus pneumoniae* and its use for the study of reciprocal transformation at the *ami*A locus. *Genetics* **50**, 31–44.

SICARD, A.M. (1987). Gene conversion in *Streptococcus pneumoniae*. *Microbiologia* **3**, 5–12.

SICARD, A.M., LEFÈVRE, J.C., MOSTACHFI, P., GASC, A.M. AND SARDA, C. (1985). Localized conversion in *Streptococcus pneumoniae* recombination: heteroduplex preference. *Genetics* **110**, 557–568.

# 32

# Excision–Repair and Mismatch–Repair in *Streptococcus pneumoniae*: Two Different Processes

ANNE-MARIE ESTEVENON* AND NICOLE SICARD[†]

* *UFR des Sciences Pharmaceutiques, Université Paul Sabatier, 35 Chemin des Maraîchers, 31062 Toulouse Cedex, France and* [†] *Centre de Recherche de Biochimie et de Génétique Cellulaires du CNRS, 118 Route de Narbonne, 31062 Toulouse Cedex, France*

## Introduction

Transformation efficiency in *Streptococcus pneumoniae* depends on the excision and correction of the donor DNA that forms heteroduplexes with recipient DNA (Ephrussi-Taylor and Gray, 1966). Excision–repair of mismatched bases has been extensively studied (Claverys and Lacks, 1986). A single mismatched base can trigger the excision of several kilobases of donor DNA. In *Escherichia coli*, pyrimidine dimers induced by UV-irradiation, as well as DNA adducts produced by various agents, are removed by the UvrABC excinuclease complex (Seeberg, Nissen-Meyer and Strike, 1976; Sancar and Rupp, 1983; Yeung *et al.*, 1983). Although differing from mismatch correction by the size of the excision patch and by the signal, it is of interest whether, in pneumococcus deficient in photoreactivation (Goodgal, Rupert and Herriott, 1957) and some SOS-like functions (Gasc *et al.*, 1980) but efficient in UV excision–repair (Estevenon and Sicard, 1989), there is any relationship between the mismatch–repair system and the repair of pyrimidine dimers similar to that described in *E. coli*. A direct approach to this problem is to test the repair capability of one system in mutants deficient in the other. Several pneumococcal mutants of the two genes, *hexA* and *hexB*, unable to correct mismatched bases have been isolated (Lacks, 1970; Tiraby and Sicard, 1973; Claverys *et al.*, 1984). They exhibit the same UV sensitivity as the wild-type strain but an estimation of their ability to repair pyrimidine dimers has so far not been made. UV-sensitive mutants have also been isolated which have a transformation efficiency similar to the efficiency of the parental strain (Lacks, 1970; Tiraby and Sicard, 1973). One of these mutants has been used in this study.

A rapid method for the detection of pyrimidine dimer excision *in vivo* has

*Genetic Transformation and Expression*
© Intercept Ltd, PO Box 716, Andover, Hants, SP10 1YG, UK

been developed, based on the detection of the remaining dimers in a plasmid after UV-irradiation and post-incubation of the host cells (Estevenon and Sicard, 1989). The use of this assay has enabled us to observe excision–repair in a mutant strain deprived of the correction system and to confirm the repair deficiency in a UV-sensitive mutant that is still able to repair mismatches, suggesting that there is some independence between the two processes.

## Materials and methods

### BACTERIAL STRAINS

*Streptococcus pneumoniae* R800 was used as the parental strain (Lefèvre, Claverys and Sicard, 1979). Strain R801 is a *hexB* mutant unable to excise mismatched bases, transforming all markers with the same high efficiency (Claverys *et al.*, 1984). Strain R402 is a UV-sensitive mutant, isolated after transfer of the UV-sensitive mutation 402 (Tiraby and Sicard, 1973) into R800. All the strains were transformed with pSP2 plasmid (Prats *et al.*, 1985). Transformants were selected on agar medium containing erythromycin at 4 μg ml$^{-1}$. Cultures of *S. pneumoniae* were grown at 37°C in complete medium (Prats *et al.*, 1985).

### UV-IRRADIATION OF BACTERIA

Exponentially growing bacteria (5·10$^7$ cells ml$^{-1}$) were harvested, washed and resuspended in the mineral buffer of a synthetic medium (Sicard, 1964). Suspensions of 50 ml were poured into a flat rectangular container giving a depth of 1·5 mm, and were irradiated with UV from a G1518 Sylvania germicidal lamp producing an incident dose rate of 2 J m$^{-2}$ s$^{-1}$. The cells were incubated for 1 hour.

### ISOLATION OF PLASMID DNA

Irradiated suspensions (2 × 50 ml) were centrifuged and the pellet lysed with 10 ml of the following solution: 0·15M NaCl, 0·015M EDTA, sodium dodecyl sulphate 0·02%, sodium desoxycholate 0·01% (Lefèvre, Claverys and Sicard, 1979). To denature the DNA, 10 ml of the same solution and 1·2 ml of 1N NaOH were added to the lysate. DNA was renatured by the addition of 3·7 ml of 0·55 M Tris, pH 7·5, and 2 M NaCl. After centrifugation, 25 ml of isopropanol was added to the supernatant to precipitate DNA for 1 hour at room temperature (Ish-Horowicz and Burke, 1981). Purification of plasmid DNA was performed by equilibrium centrifugation in caesium chloride. This purification is necessary for the accessibility of pyrmidine dimers in DNA to UV-endonuclease of *Micrococcus luteus*.

### DETERMINATION OF REMAINING PYRIMIDINE DIMERS

Pyrimidine dimers in plasmids were revealed as sites sensitive to UV-endonuclease which converts the covalently closed form to the open circular form.

Purified UV endonuclease from *M. luteus* was purchased from Applied Genetics Inc. and used as specified by the supplier, except that the concentration of the enzyme was 10 times higher. The assay was performed with an excess of enzyme. Treated and untreated samples (0·1–0·2 µg) of DNA were subjected to electrophoresis in 1% agarose gels, stained with ethidium bromide and the gels were photographed under short-wave UV light. The intensity of each plasmid band was measured from photographs by quantitative spectrophotometry (Hörz, Oefele and Schwab, 1981).

The percentage of the open circular (oc) form versus oc plus supercoiled monomer form (ccc), was calculated. The percentage in the untreated sample was subtracted from the percentage in the treated sample to eliminate the interference of breaks pre-existing before the treatment. The average number of nicks per molecule was calculated from the proportion of superhelical molecules remaining, assuming a Poisson distribution.

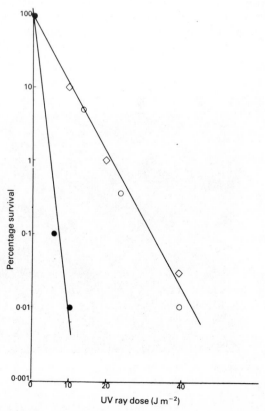

**Figure 32.1** Effect of UV on survival of pneumococcal strains. ◇, R800 (wild type); ●, R402 (UV-sensitive mutant); ○, R801 (*hexB*).

**Results and discussion**

SENSITIVITY TO UV RAYS

The survival curves of the parental strain, R800 and the two mutants, R80 (*hexB*) and R402 (UV sensitive) are shown in *Figure 32.1*. R402 exhibits a hig sensitivity to UV rays whereas the survivals of R800 and R801 are similar.

To verify that the UV sensitivity of R402 reflects a defect in excision–repai of pyrimidine dimers in the DNA, we measured the repair capability of th strains.

REPAIR CAPABILITY OF R800

The assay used was based on specific incision by UV endonuclease o pyrimidine dimers remaining on pSP2 DNA extracted from UV-irradiated cel after 1 hour post-incubation recovery (Estevenon and Sicard, 1989).

Assuming that $10 \text{ J m}^{-2}$ converts 0·041% of thymine residues to dimers, an that the relation is linear up to $80 \text{ J m}^{-2}$ (Seeberg and Strike, 1976), then 2 $\text{J m}^{-2}$ should give an average of 2 dimers per plasmid genome (9·2 kbp).

We have shown previously that for an increase in the incident dose from 20 t $40 \text{ J m}^{-2}$, the percentage of open circular form over the total plasmid DN decreases, whereas some superhelical forms appear, suggesting that pneumo coccal R800 might possess an excision–repair pathway to excise pyrimidin

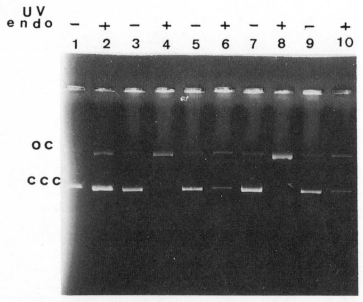

**Figure 32.2**    Incision of damaged pSP2 DNA extracted from UV-irradiated *S. pneumoniae* R80 The plasmid pSP2 has been either digested (+) or not (−) with UV endonuclease from *M. luteu* oc, Open circular DNA; ccc, covalently closed circular DNA; lanes 1–2, plasmid extracted fro unirradiated cells; lanes 3–4, irradiated cells ($20 \text{ J m}^{-2}$), no post-incubation; lanes 5–6, irradiate cells ($20 \text{ J m}^{-2}$), post-incubated for 1 h; lanes 7–8, irradiated cells ($40 \text{ J m}^{-2}$), no post-incubatio lanes 9–10, irradiated cells ($40 \text{ J m}^{-2}$), post-incubated for 1 h.

dimers formed after UV-irradiation (Estevenon and Sicard, 1989).

## REPAIR CAPABILITY OF R801

The repair capability of strain R801 *hexB*, which is isogenic to R800 except that it is deprived of the mismatch correction system, integrating all markers with the same high efficiency, was examined.

The results are presented in *Figure 32.2*. The incubation following an irradiation of 20 J m$^{-2}$ (lanes 3–6) reduced the oc form from 90% to 35%, which is similar to data obtained with the wild-type strain. Calculated from the Poisson distribution, 75% of the nicks have been repaired, the same repair efficiency as observed in the wild-type strain. The cell survival is 1% (*Figure 32.1*). A similar repair efficiency was observed following an irradiation of 40 J m$^{-2}$ (lanes 7–10), with a cell survival of 0·01%. These results show that the excision–repair process functions in the absence of mismatch correction, suggesting that the mechanisms for repairing modified DNA, either altered by the presence of dimers or by the presence of mismatched bases, might have different enzymatic requirements.

## REPAIR CAPABILITY OF R402

To confirm these findings, we examined the repair capability of the UV-sensitive strain, R402, which discriminates genetic markers in transformation at the same level as the wild-type strain (Tiraby, 1974).

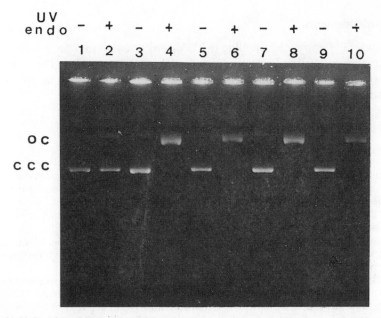

**Figure 32.3** Incision of damaged pSP2 DNA extracted from UV-irradiated *S. pneumoniae* R402. Details as for *Figure 32.2* apart from the UV doses: lanes 3–6, 10 J $^{-2}$; lanes 7–10, 20 J m$^{-2}$.

The results following irradiation doses of 10 and 20 J m$^{-2}$ are shown in *Figure 32.3*. The cell survival is 0·01% with 10 J m$^{-2}$ (*Figure 32.1*). The absence of excision–repair capacity is revealed by the persistence of the oc form in the plasmid after post-incubation and UV endonuclease treatment (*Figure 32.3* lanes 6 and 10). This explains the very high UV sensitivity of this mutant and indicates the absence of a relationship between the process of mismatch–repair and the repair of pyrimidine dimers.

The repair of mismatched bases has often been compared to the repair of UV lesions by excision. Our data suggest that in pneumococcus these processes are distinct, since mutants deficient in mismatch–repair can excise UV-induced pyrimidine dimers and conversely, a UV-sensitive mutant, unable to excise these products, repairs mismatched bases normally. However, it remains possible that some of the enzymes involved in the UV excision–repair system are also used in the mismatch–repair pathway. A complete comparison would imply the characterization of the whole enzymatic requirement for these systems and testing of all the mutants. A limitation is introduced by the failure of streptococcal plasmids to be established in a *polA*$^-$ mutant (F. Pasta, personal communication) as it is in an *E. coli polA*$^-$ mutant (Lacks *et al.*, 1986).

In *E. coli*, mismatched bases are repaired by the Mut H,L,S system, which is similar to the pneumococcal Hex system (Claverys and Lacks, 1986), and the Mut system differs from the Uvr-dependent mechanism. Moreover, in pneumococcus it is not excluded that the excision of pyrimidine dimers does not proceed through the Uvr-dependent system but through a specific DNA glycosylase, as observed in *M. luteus* (Carrier and Setlow, 1970; Haseltine *et al.*, 1980). Experiments are in progress to test this hypothesis.

## Acknowledgements

We thank G. Tiraby for providing the UV-sensitive mutant of *S. pneumoniae*. We are also grateful to B. Stevens for reading this manuscript. This work was supported by research funds from the Centre National de la Recherche Scientifique (LP n°8201).

## References

CARRIER, W.L. AND SETLOW, R.B. (1970). Endonuclease from *Micrococcus luteus* which has activity toward UV-irradiated DNA: purification and properties. *Journal of Bacteriology* 102, 178–186.

CLAVERYS, J.P. AND LACKS, S.A. (1986). Heteroduplex deoxyribonucleic acid base mismatch–repair in bacteria. *Microbiological Reviews* 50, 133–165.

CLAVERYS, J.P., PRATS, H., VASSEGHI, H. AND GHERARDI, M. (1984). Identification of *Streptococcus pneumoniae* mismatch–repair genes by an additive transformation approach. *Molecular and General Genetics* 196, 91–96.

EPHRUSSI-TAYLOR, H. AND GRAY, T.C. (1966). Genetic studies of recombining DNA in pneumococcal transformation. *Journal of General Physiology* 49(2), 211–231.

ESTEVENON, A.M. AND SICARD, N. (1989). Excision–repair capacity of UV irradiated strains of *E. coli* and *S. pneumoniae* estimated by plasmid recovery. *Journal of Photochemistry and Photobiology, B. Biology* 3, 185–192.

ᴊᴀsc, A.M., Sɪcᴀʀᴅ, N., Cʟᴀᴠᴇʀʏs, J.P. ᴀɴᴅ Sɪcᴀʀᴅ, A.M. (1980). Lack of SOS repair in *Streptococcus pneumoniae. Mutation Research* **70**, 157–165.

ᴊooᴅɢᴀʟ, S.H., Rᴜᴘᴇʀᴛ, C.S. ᴀɴᴅ Hᴇʀʀɪoᴛᴛ, R.M. (1957). Photoreactivation of *H. influenzae* transforming factor for streptomycin resistance by an extract of *E. coli* B. In *The Chemical Basis of Heredity* (W.D. McElroy and B. Glass, Eds). pp. 341–343. Johns Hopkins, Baltimore.

ᴀsᴇʟᴛɪɴᴇ, W.A., Goʀᴅoɴ, L.K., Lɪɴᴅᴀɴ, C.P., Gʀᴀғsᴛʀoм, R.H., Sʜᴀᴘᴇʀ, N.L. ᴀɴᴅ Gʀossмᴀɴ, L. (1980). Cleavage of pyrimidine dimers in specific DNA sequences by a pyrimidine dimer DNA glycosylase of *M. luteus. Nature* **285**, 634–641.

ᴏ̈ʀᴢ, W., Oᴇғᴇʟᴇ, K.V. ᴀɴᴅ Scʜᴡᴀʙ, H. (1981). A simple logarithmic amplifier for the photographic quantitation of DNA in gel electrophoresis. *Analytical Biochemistry* **117**, 266–270.

sʜ-Hoʀoᴡɪcᴢ, D. ᴀɴᴅ Bᴜʀᴋᴇ, J.F. (1981). Rapid and efficient cosmid vector cloning. *Nucleic Acids Research* **9**, 2989–2998.

ᴀcᴋs, S.A. (1970). Mutants of *Diplococcus pneumoniae* that lack deoxyribonucleases and other activities possibly pertinent to genetic transformation. *Journal of Bacteriology* **101**, 373–383.

ᴀcᴋs, S.A., Loᴘᴇᴢ, P., Gʀᴇᴇɴʙᴇʀɢ, B. ᴀɴᴅ Esᴘɪɴosᴀ, M. (1986). Identification and analysis of genes for tetracycline resistance and replication functions in the broad-host-range plasmid pLS1. *Journal of Molecular Biology* **192**, 753–765.

ᴇғᴇ̀ᴠʀᴇ, J.C., Cʟᴀᴠᴇʀʏs, J.P. ᴀɴᴅ Sɪcᴀʀᴅ, A.M. (1979). Donor DNA length and marker effect in pneumococcal transformation. *Journal of Bacteriology* **138**, 80–86.

ʀᴀᴛs, H., Mᴀʀᴛɪɴ, B., Poɢɴoɴᴇc, P., Bᴜʀɢᴇʀ, C. ᴀɴᴅ Cʟᴀᴠᴇʀʏs, J.P. (1985). A plasmid vector allowing positive selection of recombinant plasmids in *S. pneumoniae. Gene* **39**, 41–48.

ᴀɴcᴀʀ, A. ᴀɴᴅ Rᴜᴘᴘ, W.D. (1983). A novel repair enzyme: UVRABC excision nuclease of *E. coli* cuts a DNA strand on both sides of the damaged region. *Cell* **33**, 249–260.

ᴇᴇʙᴇʀɢ, E. ᴀɴᴅ Sᴛʀɪᴋᴇ, P. (1976). Excision repair of UV irradiated DNA in plasmolyzed cells of *E. coli. Journal of Bacteriology* **125**, 787–795.

ᴇᴇʙᴇʀɢ, E., Nɪssᴇɴ-Mᴇʏᴇʀ, J. ᴀɴᴅ Sᴛʀɪᴋᴇ, P. (1976). Incision of UV-irradiated DNA by extracts of *E. coli* requires three different gene products. *Nature* **263**, 524–525.

ɪcᴀʀᴅ, A.M. (1964). A new synthetic medium for *Diplococcus pneumoniae* and its use for the study of reciprocal transformations at the *amiA* locus. *Genetics* **50**, 31–44.

ɪʀᴀʙʏ, G. (1974). *Etude des mécanismes moléculaires responsables des efficacités de transformation chez* Diplococcus pneumoniae. Thesis, Université Paul Sabatier, Toulouse, France.

ɪʀᴀʙʏ, G. ᴀɴᴅ Sɪcᴀʀᴅ, A.M. (1973). Integration efficiency in DNA-induced transformation of Pneumococcus. II. Genetic studies of a mutant integrating all the markers with a high efficiency. *Genetics* **75**, 35–48.

ᴇᴜɴɢ, A.T., Mᴀᴛᴛᴇs, W.B., Oʜ, E.Y. ᴀɴᴅ Gʀossмᴀɴ, L. (1983). Enzymatic properties of purified *E. coli* uvrABC proteins. *Proceedings of the National Academy of Sciences of the United States of America* **80**, 6157–6161.

# Part IV

## Gene Cloning

# 33

# Cloning in *Streptomyces*: Some new Developments

TOBIAS KIESER

John Innes Institute and AFRC Institute of Plant Science Research, Norwich NR4 7UH, UK

## Introduction

Streptomycetes are non-pathogenic Gram-positive soil bacteria with hyphal growth. On agar media they first produce a compact mass of 'substrate mycelium' with a tough leathery consistency and a shiny surface. Later, vertical hyphae of 'aerial mycelium' are formed on top of the substrate mycelium, giving the colonies a furry appearance. This aerial mycelium can then differentiate into exo-spores which, unlike the endo-spores of *Bacillus*, are not particularly heat resistant, but can survive desiccation for long periods of time. In liquid cultures streptomycetes grow as large mycelial pellets and in most strains sporulation does not normally occur. Antibiotics and extracellular enzymes, which are important products of streptomycetes, are mostly formed late in the growth phase of a culture.

This chapter reviews some recent developments in the understanding of gene expression in *Streptomyces*, and of plasmid biology, together with new vectors and host strains which enhance our ability to clone genes in *Streptomyces*.

## Regulation of gene expression in *Streptomyces*

*Streptomyces coelicolor* A3(2), like many bacteria, utilizes RNA polymerase with several different sigma factors which specify the recognition of promoters of several different classes (Westpheling, Ranes and Losick, 1985; Buttner, Smith and Bibb, 1988). The gene for the extracellular agarase of *S. coelicolor* A3(2) is transcribed from four promoters, which are recognized by RNA polymerase holoenzyme forms containing at least three (and possibly four) different sigma factors (Buttner, Smith and Bibb, 1988). Multiple promoters have been identified upstream of several *Streptomyces* genes, while others have only a single promoter (e.g. extracellular amylase; Virolle and Bibb, 1988). The ratio of the RNA polymerases with different sigma factors may vary during the growth phase of a culture, but their precise roles are not yet clear.

*Genetic Transformation and Expression*
© Intercept Ltd, PO Box 716, Andover, Hants, SP10 1YG, UK

*whiG* mutants are blocked at the beginning of the conversion of aeria mycelium to spores. Sequence comparisons indicate that *whiG* most probabl encodes an additional sigma factor (K.F. Chater and C.J. Bruton, persona communication), which may be responsible for the co-ordinate transcriptiona regulation of sporulation genes that are scattered around the *S. coelicolo* A3(2) chromosome (Chater, 1972). Introduction of a multicopy plasmi containing the cloned *whiG* gene into strains leads to abundant prematur sporulation and also to sporulation in liquid medium, which does not normall occur with *S. coelicolor* A3(2).

*Streptomyces* DNA has a very high G+C content of about 72%, makin AT-rich codons very rare. One of these, the TTA (leu) codon, seems not to b used at all in the genes for primary metabolism in *S. coelicolor* A3(2). This wa discovered recently when the *bldA* gene product was found to be a tRNA-lik molecule. *bldA* mutations either changed the putative anticodon or disrupte proposed regions of base pairing. There is a small RNA which hybridizes to th *bldA* DNA and is specifically induced at the onset of aerial myceliun formation. Cloned genes which contain TTA codons are not expressed in *bld* mutants. This is evidence that *bldA* codes for the only TTA leucine tRN (Lawlor, Baylis and Chater, 1987; K.F. Chater, personal communication) *bldA* mutants are conditionally blocked at an early stage of the development o aerial mycelium and they lack the ability to form the different antibiotic produced by wild-type *S. coelicolor* A3(2). *bldA* mutants can form aeria mycelium and spores on some non-repressing carbon sources (e.g. arabinose o mannitol) but there are no known physiological conditions that can restor antibiotic biosynthesis. This suggests that *bldA* performs a purely regulator role in colony differentiation. The genes for the biosynthesis of actinorhodi and undecylprodigiosin, two antibiotics made by *S. coelicolor* A3(2), also seen to be free of TTA codons and thus regulated by *bldA* (E.P. Guthrie and A.-M Puglia, personal communications).

Streptomycetes have the ability to express genes from many differen bacteria, using their promoters and translational start signals. This is bein used for the expression of *Mycobacterium* genes, which are poorly transcribe in *E. coli* (Kieser *et al.*, 1986).

## Biology of the multicopy plasmid pIJ101

pIJ101 is a 8·9 kbp plasmid with a copy number of about 300 which can replicate in many *Streptomyces* strains. It is self-transmissible and promotes chromo somal recombination (fertility) in at least some of its hosts. Many useful cloning vectors have been derived from this plasmid (Kieser *et al.*, 1982; Hopwood *e. al.*, 1987; Kieser and Melton, 1988). The essential replication functions fertility determinants and two '*kil*' functions with their corresponding '*ki* override' (*kor*) functions have been located on the physical map of pIJ101 (Kieser *et al.*, 1982; Kendall and Cohen, 1987).

Deng, Kieser and Hopwood (1988) identified a new, non-essential function *sti* (for *s*trong *i*ncompatibility), on pIJ101, which is missing from most cloning vectors derived from pIJ101. Plasmids which lack *sti* accumulate single-

randed DNA, which is probably a replication intermediate, and they have a
opy number about one-third of that of the double-stranded form compared
ith pIJ101 and its derivatives that contain *sti*. Plasmids which lack *sti* are
nable to co-exist with plasmids that contain this sequence. Sti$^+$ plasmids,
hen introduced by transformation into strains containing resident Sti$^-$
lasmids, very efficiently eliminate these. This phenomenon is called 'strong
ncompatibility' to distinguish it from classical incompatibility where identical
r related plasmids are incompatible and dissimilar plasmids are compatible.
Pairs of plasmids derived from pIJ101, which either both possess *sti* in the
orrect orientation (Sti$^+$) or both lack *sti* or carry it in reverse orientation
Sti$^-$), can co-exist with each other at similar copy numbers.)

The DNA sequence, *sti*, which causes this 'strong incompatibility' was
ocalized on a DNA segment of about 200 bp that, as judged by its sequence,
oes not seem to code for a protein. The *sti* function is active only when present
n the natural orientation with respect to the basic replicon region of pIJ101.
he small size and the orientation dependence of the *sti* function indicate that it
 a signal that is recognized on the single-stranded form of the plasmids,
ossibly the main site where the synthesis of the second (lagging) DNA strand
 initiated during plasmid replication. (It is not known whether plasmids which
ick *sti* can convert single-stranded plasmid DNA to the double-stranded form
y utilizing secondary initiation sites, or whether they replicate via an
lternative mechanism without single-stranded intermediates.)

Analysis of a series of plasmids revealed no systematic correlation between
lasmid stability and the presence or absence of *sti*. There is also no indication
aat the single-stranded plasmid DNA might interfere with gene expression in
ose cases where the messenger RNA is complementary to the accumulated
ingle-stranded plasmid DNA.

The copy number of pIJ101 and its derivatives is influenced not only by the
resence or absence of *sti* but also by an additional *trans*-acting negative
egulator (*cop*) which probably acts on *sti*. Sti$^+$Cop$^-$ plasmids reach an
xtreme copy number of about 1000.

### IJ699, a multicopy positive selection plasmid vector for *Streptomyces*

Positive selection vectors give a high proportion of recombinant plasmids
without the penalty of reduced transformation frequency that results from the
se of dephosphorylated vector fragments. For shotgun cloning experiments
nd other applications it is preferable to dephosphorylate the target rather than
he vector DNA, to prevent the generation of multiple inserts. If most of the
ransformants resulting from such a cloning experiment are required to carry
nserts, a positive selection vector is needed. pIJ699, a plasmid vector which
ives positive selection for cloned DNA, was constructed using the replication
unctions of pIJ101 (*Figure 33.1*; Kieser and Melton, 1988). The selection for
nserts is based on the principle that plasmids with long uninterrupted perfect
alindromes (inverted repeats) are 'not viable' in bacteria (Collins, Volkaert
nd Nevers, 1982; Hagan and Warren, 1982). For cloning, pIJ699 is digested
vith *Bgl*II. This produces two fragments, one of which is the vector and the

372     *Gene Cloning*

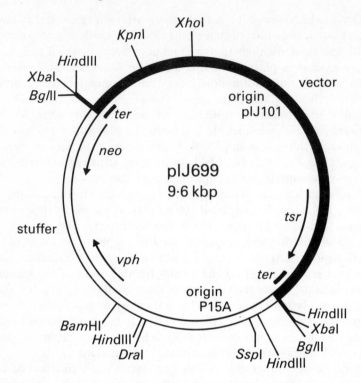

**Figure 33.1**   Restriction map of the *Streptomyces* positive selection vector pIJ699. pIJ699 is a *Bgl*II replacement vector for *Streptomyces*. Ligation of the *Bgl*II fragment labelled 'vector', which contains the origin of replication of the *Streptomyces* plasmid pIJ101, does not produce a 'viable plasmid because the fd terminator (*ter*) sequences in opposite orientation form an uninterrupted palindrome of about 350 bp. This means that there is positive selection for inserts. The 'stuffer' fragment, which contains an *E. coli* origin of replication of plasmid P15A, can be removed physically or inactivated with *Dra*I or *Ssp*I. *neo, tsr, vph*: resistance genes for kanamycin, thiostrepton and viomycin, respectively.

other is a 'stuffer', which is needed to keep the inverted repeat sequences apart. The vector fragment is separated from the 'stuffer' fragment and ligated with the DNA to be cloned. Plasmids with a fragment of cloned DNA, but not circularized vector fragments, give rise to thiostrepton-resistant transformants in *Streptomyces lividans*. The inverted repeat sequences contain a strong transcription terminator from the *E. coli* phage fd, which reduces transcriptional read-through both in and out of the cloned fragment. This improves the stability of many hybrid plasmids and facilitates the study of the regulation of cloned genes.

pIJ699 contains polylinkers that allow excision of the cloned fragments with *Hin*dIII or *Xba*I, two enzymes for which recognition sites occur infrequently in *Streptomyces* DNA. The polylinkers containing the cloning sites can be exchanged at will because perfect symmetry is the only requirement for positive selection.

A SCP2*-based low-copy-number vector, pIJ698, with inverted terminators analogous to pIJ699 has also been constructed. pIJ698 did not give good ositive selection for inserts because spontaneous deletions removing the ιverted repeats were too frequent. However, this plasmid may still be useful hen there is a need to clone DNA fragments between transcriptional ιrminators.

## Γ46, a recombination-deficient derivative of *S. lividans* 66 which improves the ιructural stability of hybrid plasmids

ι serious obstacle for gene-cloning experiments in *Streptomyces* (as in other osts) is that certain classes of plasmids are structurally unstable. In particular, ιfunctional vectors that contain replication origins for both *Streptomyces* and *. coli* seem to suffer from this problem and have therefore been little used for loning experiments. Tsai and Chen (1987) isolated strain JT46, a ιcombination-deficient derivative of *S. lividans* that reliably improves the ιructural stability of many recombinant plasmids. JT46 was isolated on the asis that it could maintain stably a plasmid with a tιndem duplication. Jnpublished experiments by H.M. Kieser, D. Henderson and D.A. Hopwood ιowed that JT46 is normal with respect to general homologous recombination f chromosomal genes, as measured both in conjugation and protoplast fusion xperiments. The use of JT46 as host strain, together with the introduction of ·anscription terminators to separate the *Streptomyces* replicon from the ιreign DNA (see above), allows the successful use of bifunctional vectors and ιus gives access to the well-developed and rapid *E. coli* cloning techniques, ιch as cosmid cloning and site-directed *in vitro* mutagenesis.

## ιte-specific cleavage of *Streptomyces lividans* DNA during electrophoresis in ιuffers contaminated with ferrous iron

)erivatives of *S. lividans* 66 are commonly used as host strains for gene cloning ι *Streptomyces*. *S. lividans* is closely related to *S. coelicolor* A3(2), genetically ιe most characterized streptomycete. The main advantage of using *S. lividans* ιather than *S. coelicolor* A3(2) as a host for gene cloning is that it does not ιestrict DNA isolated from other species.

In the past we and others experienced occasional difficulties in obtaining ιood DNA preparations from *S. lividans*. Preparations of plasmid and total )NA appeared to be partially degraded on agarose gels. It was generally ιssumed that endogenous nucleases, presumed to be active before the cells ιvere lysed, caused the problem.

Zhou *et al.* (1988) found that *S. lividans* DNA contains a modification which ιakes it susceptible to double-strand cleavage during electrophoresis in ·uffers contaminated with ferrous iron (which may be present in some batches ·f EDTA). The cleavage of the DNA is site-specific and the average fragment ιze resulting from limit digestion of total *S. lividans* DNA is about 6 kbp. DNA ιom *S. coelicolor* A3(2) and several other *Streptomyces* strains, and from *E. oli*, is not cleaved under the same conditions.

*S. lividans* DNA is degraded only during electrophoresis. Samples of ιlectrophoresis buffer from both the anode and the cathode tank were tested at different times before and during electrophoresis in buffer contaminated wit ferrous iron. The buffer from the anode reservoir became active a few minute after the start of electrophoresis, while the buffer in the cathode reservo became active only after about 30 min. This proved that, in addition to th ferrous iron, an agent produced at the anode was needed for the reaction. Th agent, possibly molecular oxygen, was produced in clean and contaminate buffer alike.

The active form of the ferrous iron is negatively charged, probably an EDT, complex. Complexes of ferrous iron and EDTA are known to cleav unmodified DNA in a reaction that depends on oxygen and the presence of reducing agent, such as DTT, whose concentration is critical (Hertzberg an Dervan, 1984). If too much of the reducing agent is present, it inhibits th reaction, probably by scavenging hydroxyl radicals which are believed to b involved. The activity is low but can be dramatically increased if th iron-EDTA complex is attached to the DNA. This has been achieved by linkin the complex covalently to intercalating agents, DNA-binding proteins c oligonucleotides (Dervan, 1986; Moser and Dervan, 1987 and reference therein). The site-specific cleavage of *S. lividans* DNA may be due to site-specific base modification, which acts as iron chelator.

A mutant strain, ZX1, which lacks the DNA modification, has been isolate from the recombination-deficient *S. lividans* strain JT46 (see above) afte nitrosoguanidine mutagenesis. No biological effect of the *S. lividans* DN/ modification has yet been found. In particular, there is no DNA restrictio associated with the *S. lividans*-specific DNA modification. ZX1 sporulate poorly and gave reduced expression of several cloned antibiotic resistanc determinants and of the tyrosinase gene. Analysis of the progency from protoplast fusion showed, however, that these effects were due to secondar mutations and not to the lack of DNA modification.

The discovery of the degradation of *S. lividans* DNA during electrophoresi is of practical importance because trace amounts of ferrous iron are likely t occur in EDTA. In most cases the amounts are so small that the effect is no obvious, especially when only small DNA molecules are handled. It may however, become important when dealing with large plasmids or larg chromosomal DNA fragments, such as those generated during chromosom mapping by pulsed-field gel electrophoresis.

**Conclusions**

The topics presented in this article touch only a fraction of the *Streptomyce* research that is in progress world-wide. They have been selected from the work which is actively pursued at the John Innes Institute, with special emphasis or the experiments the author has been involved in directly.

Cloning in *Streptomyces* is obviously essential for the fundamental study o the special properties of these unusual bacteria, and it may help the rationa improvement of antibiotic production. Streptomycetes will also prove useful for the production of foreign proteins, because they have the ability to secrete proteins directly into the growth medium where they are more likely to be

;oluble and folded correctly than inside the bacterial cells. These potential
applications of *Streptomyces* will certainly benefit from a better understanding
of the regulation of gene expression, and progress in the development of
cloning vectors and of host strains.

## Acknowledgements

I would like to thank all my colleagues who kindly provided unpublished
information and D.A. Hopwood for his help with the preparation of the
manuscript.

## References

BUTTNER, M.J., SMITH, A.M. AND BIBB, M.J. (1988). At least three different RNA
polymerase holoenzymes direct transcription of the agarase gene (*dagA*) of
*Streptomyces coelicolor* A3(2). *Cell* **51**, 599–607.
CHATER, K.F. (1972). A morphological and genetic mapping study of white colony
mutants of *Streptomyces coelicolor*. *Journal of General Microbiology* **72**, 9–28.
COLLINS, J., VOLKAERT, G. AND NEVERS, P. (1982). Precise and nearly-precise
excision of the symmetrical inverted repeats of Tn*5*; common features of
*recA*-independent deletion events in *Escherichia coli*. *Gene* **19**, 139–146.
DENG, Z., KIESER, T. AND HOPWOOD, D.A. (1988). 'Strong incompatibility' between
derivatives of the *Streptomyces* multi-copy plasmid pIJ101. *Molecular and General
Genetics* **214**, 286–294.
DERVAN, P.B. (1986). Design of sequence-specific DNA-binding molecules. *Science*
**232**, 464–471.
HAGAN, C.E. AND WARREN, G.J. (1982). Lethality of palindromic DNA and its use in
selection of recombinant plasmids. *Gene* **19**, 147–151.
HERTZBERG, R.P. AND DERVAN, P.B. (1984). Cleavage of DNA with
methidiumpropyl-EDTA-Iron(II): Reaction conditions and product analyses.
*Biochemistry* **23**, 3934–3945.
HOPWOOD, D.A., BIBB, M.J., CHATER, K.F. AND KIESER, T. (1987). Plasmid and
phage vectors for gene cloning and analysis in *Streptomyces*. *Methods in
Enzymology* **153**, 116–166.
KENDALL, K.J. AND COHEN, S.N. (1987). Plasmid transfer in *Streptomyces lividans*:
identification of a *kil-kor* system associated with the transfer region of pIJ101.
*Journal of Bacteriology* **169**, 4177–4183.
KIESER, T. AND MELTON, R.E. (1988). pIJ699, a multi-copy positive selection plasmid
vector for *Streptomyces*. *Gene* **65**, 83–91.
KIESER, T., HOPWOOD, D.A., WRIGHT, H.M., THOMPSON, C.J. (1982). pIJ101, a
multi-copy broad host-range *Streptomyces* plasmid: functional analysis and
development of DNA cloning vectors. *Molecular and General Genetics* **185**,
223–238.
KIESER, T., MOSS, M.T., DALE, J.W. AND HOPWOOD, D.A. (1986). Cloning and
expression of *Mycobacterium bovis* BCG DNA in *Streptomyces lividans*. *Journal of
Bacteriology* **168**, 72–80.
LAWLOR, E.J., BAYLIS, H.A. AND CHATER, K.F. (1987). Pleiotropic morphological
and antibiotic deficiencies result from mutations in a gene encoding a tRNA-like
product in *Streptomyces coelicolor* A3(2). *Genes and Development* **1**, 1305–1319.
MOSER, H.E. AND DERVAN, P.E. (1987). Sequence-specific cleavage of double helical
DNA by triple helix formation. *Science* **238**, 645–650.
TSAI, J.F.-Y. AND CHEN, C.W. (1987). Isolation and characterization of *Streptomyces
lividans* mutants deficient in intraplasmid recombination. *Molecular and General
Genetics* **208**, 211–218.

VIROLLE, M.-J. AND BIBB, M.J. (1988). Cloning, characterization and regulation of an alpha-amylase gene from *Streptomyces limosus*. *Molecular Microbiology* **2** 197–208.

WESTPHELING, J., RANES, M. AND LOSICK, R. (1985). RNA polymerase heterogeneity in *Streptomyces coelicolor*. *Nature (London)* **312**, 22–27.

ZHOU, X., DENG, Z., FIRMIN, J.L., HOPWOOD, D.A. AND KIESER, T. (1988) Site-specific degradation of *Streptomyces lividans* DNA during electrophoresis in buffers contaminated with ferrous iron. *Nucleic Acids Research* **16**, 4341–4352.

# 34

# A Method to Identify Gene Clones Encoding Staphylococcal Antigens Related to *Staphylococcus aureus* Infection

S. KOTHARI*, U. FORSUM[†] AND J.-I. FLOCK*

* Centre for Biotechnology, F82, and [†]Department of Clinical Bacteriology,
F71, Karolinska Institute, Huddinge University Hospital, S-14186 Huddinge,
Sweden.

## Introduction

Bacterial infections can be diagnosed either by cultivating the infectious agent taken from the site of infection or by monitoring the patient's antibodies against a well-defined bacterial antigen. For such a serological method to be useful for diagnostic purposes, a number of criteria concerning the antigen must be fulfilled. For example, the antigen must give rise to antibodies that can be detected with high sensitivity and specificity, and the immune response to the antigen must result in antibody formation early during infection. A non-infected healthy person should preferably have very low, or non-detectable titres. Also, it is, of course, important that the correlation between the infection and high antibody titres is as close to 100% as possible.

In the case of staphylococcal infections, serological testing of antibodies suffers from the lack of available antigens having most of the above-mentioned ideal characteristics. The main problem is that healthy persons also have antibodies against a large number of staphylococcal antigens (Bell, Pennington and Petrie, 1987). Often therefore, two samples have to be taken at a suitable interval to assess the increase in antibody titre during ongoing infection (Day *et al.*, 1980; Espersen and Hedström, 1981). The antigens used for routine diagnostic purposes are mainly teichoic acid and alpha-toxin (Granström, Julander and Möllby, 1983; Julander *et al.*, 1983), but others, such as peptidoglycan (Christensson *et al.*, 1985) and staphylokinase (Lack and Towers, 1962), have been tried.

To attempt to improve the situation, more staphylococcal antigens need to be tested for their suitability in serology. One approach has been to try one antigen after the other and, most often, either extracellular or surface-bound

*Genetic Transformation and Expression*
© Intercept Ltd, PO Box 716, Andover, Hants, SP10 1YG, UK

proteins have been tried. However, it is also possible that intracellular and other unidentified proteins could give rise to specific antibodies during the infection. We have therefore adopted a new approach to identify possible protein antigens for a further evaluation of their usefulness in diagnostic serology.

## Materials and methods

### STRAINS

*S. aureus* strain S127 was isolated from the blood of a patient with septicaemia who, 6 months later, suffered from endocarditis. The strain was isolated at the Department of Clinical Bacteriology, Huddinge University Hospital, Sweden.

*Escherichia coli*, Y1090 (r⁻, AMPʳ: Promega, Wisconsin, USA) was used as host strain for λ phage EMBL4 (Promega, Wisconsin, USA). The strain was propagated either in LB or NZCYM media (Maniatis, Fritsch and Sambrook, 1982) containing 100 µg ml⁻¹ ampicillin.

Lambda phage EMBL4 was propagated in the host strain Y1090, which had been grown overnight (O/N) at 37°C in NZCYM medium supplemented with 0·2% maltose and 100 µg ml⁻¹ ampicillin. Infection, large-scale preparation, *in vitro* DNA packaging and storage of bacteriophage has been described by Maniatis, Fritsch and Sambrook (1982).

### SOURCE OF SERA

From five *S. aureus*-infected patients, sera were selected randomly in terms of both sex and age. One serum included was from a patient taken during an early stage of endocarditis and was used for the initial screening of the DNA library. The patients were diagnosed as having osteomyelitis, septicaemia (acute) or endocarditis. Serum samples obtained from six healthy laboratory staff without any evidence of *S. aureus* infection were used as controls.

### DNA PREPARATION

*S. aureus* S127 was grown O/N at 37°C on 10% human blood agar plates. Cells were harvested in sterile PBS buffer, pelleted and resuspended in cold PBS three times. To cells were added 50 µg ml⁻¹ lysostaphin (Sigma, USA), 1 mg ml⁻¹ lysozyme and 20 µg ml⁻¹ RNase A (Boehringer, Mannhiem, FRG), and incubated at 37°C for 30 min. Proteins were extracted with equal volumes of Tris-saturated phenol : chloroform (1 : 1 ratio) and finally with chloroform. The DNA was precipitated from the aqueous phase with two volumes of ethanol, spooled, washed with 70% ethanol and dissolved in sterile 0·14 M NaCl.

Lambda phage EMBL4 DNA was prepared by the Kaslow method (Kaslow, 1986).

Gene Clones Encoding Staphylococcal Antigens 379

PREPARATION OF A S. AUREUS DNA LIBRARY

Restriction enzymes, T4 DNA ligase and alkaline phosphatase (Boehringer, Mannheim, FRG) were used according to suppliers' recommendations (unless specified otherwise).

A partial Sau3A digest of S. aureus DNA and a BamH1 digest of EMBL4 treated with alkaline phosphatase, were ligated in the ratio 1·5 : 1, respectively. The non-essential stuffer fragment of EMBL4 DNA was deleted completely, thus reducing the probability of wild types occurring and increasing the frequency of DNA recombinants.

Ligated DNA was packaged with Promega's (Wisconsin, USA) in vitro packaging system at 22°C for 2 h. To preserve phage titre, chloroform was added to a final concentration of 0·3% and the library was stored at 4°C. The phage titre of the library was approximately $10^8$ pfu $ml^{-1}$.

PLATING OF LIBRARY AND IMMUNOBLOTTING

Cells Y1090 were grown O/N in NZCYM medium containing 0·2% maltose and 100 µg $ml^{-1}$ ampicillin, pelleted and resuspended in sterile SM buffer (per litre: NaCl, 5·8 g; MgSO$_4$.7H$_2$O, 2 g; 1M Tris. HCl (pH 7·5), 50 ml; 2% gelatin, 5 ml) to $10^9$ cfu $ml^{-1}$. To 200 µl of bacteria were added $10^{3-4}$ pfu of phage library, and mixed. After 20 min at 20°C, 3 ml of 0·7% molten (45°C) NZCYM agar were added, mixed and poured onto duplicate 130 mm plates containing NZCYM agar with 100 µg $ml^{-1}$ ampicillin. Plates were incubated O/N at 37°C.

The Western blotting procedure was a slight modification of the methods described in Blake et al. (1984). Nitrocellulose filters (Schleicher & Schuell Co., FRG) were blocked by incubating for 10 min in buffer A (PBS buffer containing 1·5% Tween 20 and 0·002% Na azide). Filters were washed three times at two-minute intervals in buffer B (PBS containing 0·05% Tween 20). Human serum to be used in the Western blots was pre-adsorbed with E. coli proteins in the following way: a lysate of strain Y1090 was obtained by infecting $10^{10}$ cells with $10^8$ EMBL4 phage particles, incubated for 6 h at 37°C, and stored at 4°C (3 days maximum). 50 µl of this E. coli lysate was added to 50 ml human sera diluted 1/500 (or as specified) and mixed gently on a shaker for 2 h. The solution was spun at 5000 g, 15 min to reclarify and then added to the blots. This pre-incubation with crude E. coli lysates resulted in reduced background signal caused by antibodies present against E. coli.

All incubations with Western blot filters were performed under gentle agitation at either room temperature for 2 h or at 4°C O/N. After washing the filters five times at two-minute intervals in buffer B, the nitrocellulose papers were incubated for 2 h at 20°C with alkaline phosphatase conjugated polyvalent rabbit antihuman IgG, IgM and IgA antiserum (Dakopatts a/s, Copenhagen, Denmark). The immunoblots were then washed three times in buffer B and developed in substrate buffer containing 66 µl nitro blue tetrazolium (NBT) and 33 µl bovine calf intestinal phosphatase (BCIP) per 10 ml of AP buffer (100 mM Tris base, pH 9·5; 100 mM NaCl; 5 mM MgCl$_2$), as specified by Promega (Wisconsin, USA) for 30–45 min at 20°C.

SCREENING OF THE GENE LIBRARY

Plaque lifts were carried out with nitrocellulose papers left on the pre-dried phage plates for 30 min. The filters were then treated as described for the immunoblotting technique.

STABILIZATION OF PHAGE RECOMBINANTS

When phage recombinants were subsequently used in Western blot analysis, considerable instability problems were experienced. Thus it appeared that recombinant phages were lost, presumably due to deletions arising as a consequence of genetic instability caused by the presence of large foreign DNA inserts. To overcome both the instability problems and possible phage contamination, the positive clones were picked with sterile Pasteur pipettes and suspended in 100 µl SM buffer. Y1090 cells were reinfected with 10 µl aliquots, plated and rescreened with the same serum. Not all the plaques were positives, illustrating the presence of more than one type of phage. The positive plaques were picked and the above procedure repeated until all the plaques on a plate appeared positive.

PREPARATION OF *E. COLI*/PHAGE CELL LYSATE

Strain Y1090 was infected with either EMBL4 or recombinant phage and was grown up in 40 ml NZCYM (supplemented with 0·2% maltose and 100 µg ml$^{-1}$ ampicillin) at 37°C on a shaker, for 3·5–4 h, i.e. the time when cells were just beginning to lyse. To this culture was added trichloroacetic acid to a concentration of 10% w/v, mixed and stored on ice for 30 min to precipitate all the proteins in the culture. The precipitate was pelleted at 5000 g for 30 min at 4°C and washed three times in 10 ml acetone, before resuspending the pellet in 100 µl SDS loading buffer. The boiled samples were electrophoresed by SDS-PAGE on either large 15% gels or preformed 10–15% Phastgels (Pharmacia-LKB, Uppsala, Sweden). The proteins were transferred to nitrocellulose filters by electroblotting.

**Results**

Serum from a patient with acute endocarditis was used in a Western blot experiment with a staphylococcal total cell lysate as antigen. In a parallel lane, an *E. coli* lysate was run. Signals appeared at a large number of bands for the staphylococcal antigen as expected, but no signals at all in the *E. coli* antigen lane. This particular patient's serum was therefore considered suitable for screening of the gene bank due to the low background of *E. coli* antibodies. The situation was further improved by pre-adsorption of the serum with *E. coli* lysate (data not shown).

The gene bank was subjected to plaque lifting and immunoscreening with the serum. A large number of the plaques then appeared positive. In an attempt to eliminate all those clones encoding antigens against which healthy persons also have antibodies, the potential positive plaques were picked in a grid-fashion and lifted onto two parallel filters. One was rescreened with the endocarditis-serum and the other with serum from a healthy person. It was then found that several of the clones suffered from instability and impurities. Also, the strength of the signal varied from one serum to another and from one experiment to another. It was not possible by plaque screening alone to differentiate between, for example, weak signals and intermediate strong signals. Thus, parallel screening of the primarily identified candidates with both positive and negative sera is not reliable.

Instead, all candidates were first plaque purified to eliminate heterogeneity. Genetic stability also seems to be improved by repeated plaque purification. Only after this step were negative sera employed to eliminate all 'uninteresting' clones, using the Western blot technique. Although it may seem tedious, signals were much more specific in that the size of the antigen was also revealed. Furthermore, Western blotting was semiquantitative in that serial dilution of the serum could be made. This gave a relative serum titre to be used in comparisons between different antigen clones and between different groups of patients.

*Figures 34.1a* and *34.1b* show Western blots in which crude lysates of some of the λ clones were used and then screened with patient serum (*Figure 34.1a*) and serum from a healthy person (*Figure 34.1b*). In both cases sera were diluted 1/500. Amongst the clones tested, not all of them appeared positive with the endocarditis-serum, but even fewer were positive when using negative serum. Several such Western blots were run and probed with either patient sera (from patients with either acute *S. aureus*-septicaemia or endocarditis) or with negative sera. *Figure 34.2* shows such a series of Western blots. The clones chosen for this experiment were those showing the highest difference in response using the two groups of people in *Figures 34.1a* and *34.1b*. Again, dilution is only 1/500, which does not allow a quantitative estimation of serum titres. Therefore a serial dilution was made of the sera as shown in *Figure 34.3*. The sera used in *Figures 34.3a* and *34.3b* were from different sources. In *Figure 34.3a*, serum was obtained from a patient with acute septicaemia and confirmed positive blood culture. In *Figure 34.3b* serum from a 38-year-old healthy person was used. It is apparent that the patient's serum contains increased antibody titres (i.e. above 1/10 000 dilution) to all the clones tested except clone 26, in comparison to the control serum which has titres below 1/2500 dilution.

## Discussion

The above approach of cloning and isolating *S. aureus* genes that encode protein antigens is shown to accede to subsequent use in clinical serology. The four clones were genetically stable and the staphylococcal proteins were expressed in an *E. coli* host.

The clones 26 and 40 appear to be interesting in that almost all the sera from healthy persons tested lack complementary antibodies, while the majority of the patients had both the corresponding antibodies (*Figure 34.2*) and in high titres. At the same time, all the sera tested possessed antibody to the antigen

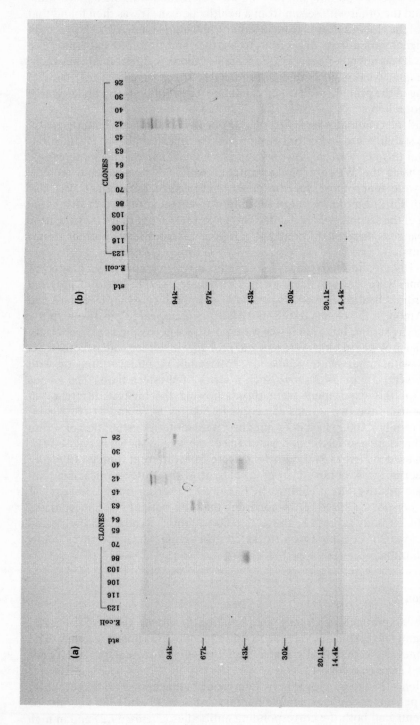

**Figure 34.1** Western blots of several clones. Probing was carried out with (a) endocarditis serum; (b) negative control serum.

# Healthy persons' sera (1/500)

| Sera | Clones | | | | |
|---|---|---|---|---|---|
| | 26 | 30 | 40 | 63 | |
| A | − | + | − | + | |
| B | − | + | − | + | |
| C | − | + | + | + | |
| D | − | + | − | + | |
| E | + | + | − | + | |

# Patients' sera (1/500)

| Sera | Clones | | | | |
|---|---|---|---|---|---|
| | 26 | 30 | 40 | 63 | |
| F | + | + | − | + | |
| G | − | + | + | + | |
| H | + | + | + | + | |
| I | + | + | + | + | |
| J | + | + | + | + | |

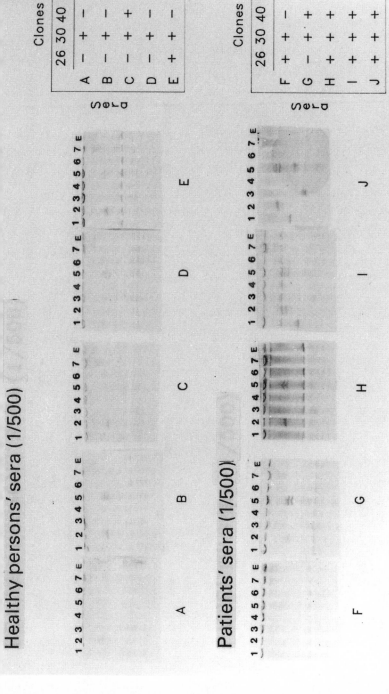

**Figure 34.2**    Western blots with sera from five patients and five negative control sera.

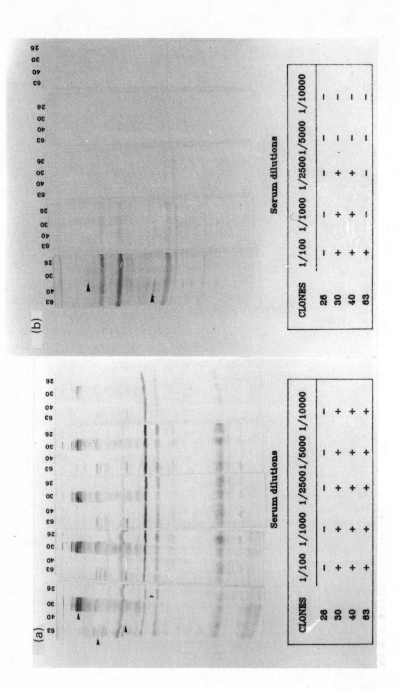

**Figure 34.3**    Western blot showing quantification of antibodies with serial dilution of (a) patient serum, (b) control serum.

encoded by clone 30, which shows that those antibodies are present in many people. The size of the antigens encoded by clones 26, 30, 40 and 63 are 95 kDa, 110 kDa, 48 kDa and 78 kDa, respectively. The antibody titres to three of the antigens were generally greater than 1/10 000 dilution in the patient serum. Such increases in antibody titres to staphylococcal antigens during infection is widely acknowledged and used currently in teichoic acid and alpha-toxin serology (Day *et al.*, 1980; Espersen and Hedstöm, 1981). With more clones it will no doubt be possible to identify antigens suitable for both clinical diagnosis and further understanding of the host–bacterial relationship.

## Acknowledgements

Grants were received for this work from Karolinska Institute's research fund.

## References

BELL, J.A., PENNINGTON, T.A. AND PETRIE, D.T. (1987). Western blot analysis of *S. aureus* antibodies present in human sera during health and disease. *Journal of Medical Microbiology* 23, 95–99.
BLAKE, M.S., JOHNSTON, K.H., RUSSELL-JONES, G.J. AND GOTTSCHLICH, E.C. (1984). A rapid, sensitive method for detection of alkaline phosphatase conjugated anti-antibody on Western blots. *Analytical Biochemistry* 136, 175–179.
CHRISTENSSON, B., ESPERSEN, F., HEDSTRÖM, S.Å. AND KORNVALL, G. (1985). Serological assays against *S. aureus* peptidoglycan, crude staphylococcus antigen and staphylolysin in the diagnosis of serious *S. aureus* infections. *Scandinavian Journal of Infectious Disease* 17, 1–7.
DAY, S.E.J., VASLI, K.K., RUSSELL, R.J. AND ARBUTHNOTT, J.P. (1980). A simple method for the study *in vivo* of bacterial growth and accompanying host response. *Journal of Infectious Disease* 2, 39–51.
ESPERSEN, F. AND HEDSTÖM, S.Å. (1981). Precipitating antibodies against staphylococcal septicaemia, investigated by means of quantitative immunelectrophoretic methods. *Acta Pathologica Microbiologica et Immunologica Scandinavica* 89, 261–266.
GRANSTRÖM, M., JULANDER, I. AND MÖLLBY, R. (1983). Serological diagnosis of deep *S. aureus* infection by ELISA for Staphylococcal hemolysins and teichoic acid. *Scandinavian Journal of Infectious Disease* 41, 132–139.
JULANDER, I.G., GRANSTRÖM, M., HEDSTRÖM, S.Å. AND MÖLLBY, R. (1983). The role of antibodies against alpha-toxin and teichoic acid in the diagnosis of staphylococcal infection. *Infection* 11, 77–83.
KASLOW, D.C. (1986). A rapid biochemical method for purifying lambda DNA from phage lysates. *Nucleic Acids Research* 14, 67.
LACK, C.H. AND TOWERS, A.G. (1962). Serological tests for staphylococcal infection. *British Medical Journal* 2, 1227–1231.
MANIATIS, T., FRITSCH, E.F. AND SAMBROOK, J. (1982). *Molecular Cloning: A Laboratory Manual*. Cold Spring Harbor Laboratory, New York.

# 35
# Development of a Gene Cloning System for Lactococci and Identification of a Gene Involved in Proteinase Maturation

J. KOK*, A.J. HAANDRIKMAN*, J.M.B.M. VAN DER VOSSEN*,
K.J. LEENHOUTS*, JAN MAARTEN VAN DIJL*, H. LAAN[†],
A.M. LEDEBOER[‡] AND GERARD VENEMA*

* Department of Genetics and [†] Department of Microbiology, University of Groningen, Kerklaan 30, 9751 NN Haren (Gn), The Netherlands and [‡] Unilever Research Laboratorium, Olivier van Noortlaan 120, 3133 AT Vlaardingen, The Netherlands

## Introduction

Lactococci (formerly lactic streptococci; Schleifer and Kilpper-Bälz, 1987) are used widely in the manufacture of fermented milk products, of which cheese is the most important. The increased economic importance of these organisms in the dairy industry and the scaling-up of the fermentations during the past decades has led to an intensification of research in the lactococci. Their prime functions during the manufacture of cheese are a rapid acid production through the conversion of lactose to lactate, and the formation of flavorous compounds. Rapid growth, necessary for rapid acid production, is completely dependent on the ability of these auxotrophic organisms to liberate essential amino acids from milk protein (casein). Moreover, the amino acids and peptides formed by this proteolysis are important determinants in cheese flavour and taste.

The observation that the proteolytic activity is an unstable trait in some strains of lactococci (Davies and Gasson, 1981; McKay, 1983) was the start of a project aimed at determining the genetical basis of this proteolytic instability and the isolation of the proteinase gene.

## Results and discussion

To be able to manipulate lactococci genetically, a host–vector system was developed based on a small cryptic *Lactococcus lactis* ssp. *cremoris* plasmid, which was able to replicate in *Bacillus subtilis* (Vosman and Venema, 1983; Kok, van der Vossen and Venema, 1984). The system is very versatile because

*Genetic Transformation and Expression*
© Intercept Ltd, PO Box 716, Andover, Hants, SP10 1YG, UK

the vectors constructed are replicated and expressed in *Lactococcus lactis*, *Bacillus subtilis* and *Escherichia coli*. Thus, the advanced recombinant DNA methodologies developed for the latter two organisms are available for genetic research in lactococci. This was demonstrated by the cloning in *B. subtilis* of a piece of DNA specifying the proteolytic activity of *L. lactis* ssp. *cremoris* Wg2 (Kok *et al.*, 1985). The resulting recombinant plasmid was transferred to a proteolytic-deficient strain of *L. lactis* and restored the ability of the *L. lactis* cells to grow rapidly in milk with concomitant rapid acid production. The gene products specified by the DNA fragment were identified both in *B. subtilis* and *L. lactis* with crossed immunoelectrophoresis, which proved that the structural gene for a proteinase had been cloned.

The nucleotide sequence of the entire DNA fragment was determined (Kok *et al.*, 1988b). The fragment, 6516 base pairs in length, carries two incomplete open reading-frames (ORFs) positioned in opposite directions (*Figure 35.1*). The longest ORF was sequenced completely using an overlapping piece of DNA. The complete ORF contained 1902 codons and was large enough to synthesize a protein of 200 kDa. A protein homology comparison revealed that three regions in the 200 kDa protein shared similarities with the active centre of subtilisins, serine proteinases produced by several bacilli (Smith *et al.*, 1968; Ottesen and Svendsen, 1970; Kraut, 1977) (*Figure 35.2*). In spite of the fact that 130 codons at the C-terminus were missing in the gene originally cloned, both the activity and the specificity of the truncated proteinase were unchaged. This was also the case with an *in vitro*-constructed deletion derivative of the proteinase, which lacked the C-terminal 343 amino acids (Kok *et al.*, 1988a).

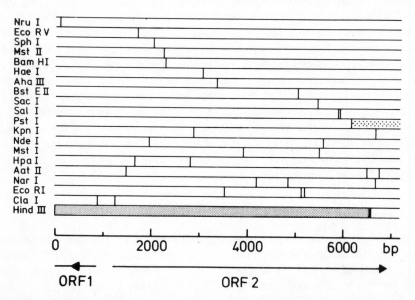

**Figure 35.1**    Restriction enzyme map of the DNA fragment specifying the proteolytic activity of *L. lactis* ssp. *cremoris* Wg2 as deduced from the nucleotide sequence. The positions of ORF1 and ORF2 are indicated by the arrows. The *Hind*III fragment originally cloned (Kok *et al.*, 1985) is shaded; the *Pst*I fragment used to extend the DNA sequence is stippled (Kok *et al.*, 1988b; courtesy of the American Society for Microbiology).

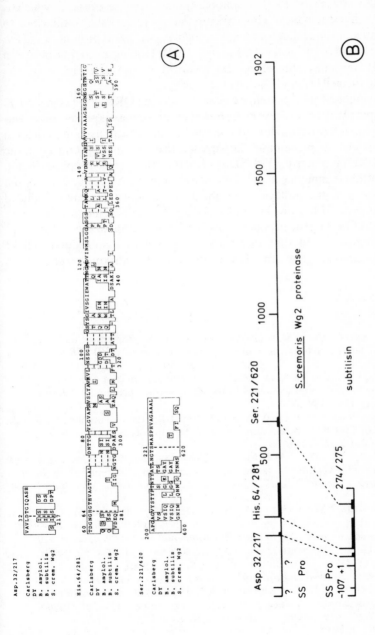

**Figure 35.2** Homology comparison. (A) Sequence homology of the *L. lactis* ssp. *cremoris* Wg2 proteinase and subtilisins Carlsberg, DY, *B. amyloliquefaciens* and *B. subtilis*. Sequences are from the NBRF protein bank, October 1986. Only amino acids that differ from the residues in the Carlsberg enzyme are shown, identical residues are boxed. Asp, His and Ser involved in the active site are indicated by vertical broken lines. The sequences forming the S1 specificity crevice are overlined. (B) The homologous regions from panel (A) (thick lines) were drawn to scale on a linear map of the whole proteinase and compared with a linear map of subtilisin. Numbers refer to amino-acid residues. SS, signal sequence; Pro, pro-sequence (Kok *et al.*, 1988b; courtesy of the American Society for Microbiology).

In cells carrying the entire proteinase gene, most of the proteinase is found attached to the cells. Deletions at the C-terminus result in the secretion of the proteinase into the culture medium. In the last 30 amino acids of the C-terminus, a stretch of 19 hydrophobic amino acids is present, which is flanked by charged residues. This structure shows remarkable similarities to membrane anchor sequences found in *Staphylococcus aureus* protein A and the type 6 M protein of *S. pyogenes* (Uhlen *et al.*, 1984; Hollingshead, Fischetti and Scott, 1986) and may, therefore, be involved in the attachment of the proteinase to the cell (Haandrikman *et al.*, 1989).

Cells carrying the entire proteinase gene but lacking ORF 1 (*see Figure 35.1*) are phenotypically Prt⁻. In these cells, however, proteinase is produced, as was shown with ELISA (enzyme-linked immunosorbent assay) using monoclonal antibodies against the proteinase. Apparently, the proteinase produced in the absence of ORF 1 is inactive. With SDS polyacrylamide gel electrophoresis and Western blotting techniques it was demonstrated that the inactive form of the proteinase has a higher molecular weight than the active enzyme (produced from the *prt* gene in the presence of ORF 1). It was concluded from these results that the ORF 1 gene product is involved in activation of the *L. lactis* ssp. *cremoris* proteinase and that this activation involves a molecular weight reduction of a large inactive form of the proteinase (Haandrikman *et al.*, 1989).

### References

DAVIES, F.L. AND GASSON, M.J. (1981). Reviews of the progress of dairy science; genetics of lactic acid bacteria. *Journal of Dairy Research* **48**, 363–376.
HAANDRIKMAN, A.J., KOK, J., LAAN, H., SOEMITRO, S., LEDEBOER, A.M., KONINGS, W.N. AND VENEMA, G. (1989). Identification of a gene required for maturation of an extracellular lactococcal serine proteinase. *Journal of Bacteriology* **171**, 2789–2794.
HOLLINGSHEAD, S.K., FISCHETTI, V.A. AND SCOTT, J.R. (1986). Complete nucleotide sequence of Type 6 M Protein of the group A Streptococcus. *Journal of Biological Chemistry* **261**, 1677–1686.
KOK, J.,VAN DER VOSSEN, J.M.B.M. AND VENEMA, G. (1984). Construction of plasmid cloning vectors for lactic streptococci which also replicate in *Bacillus subtilis* and *Escherichia coli*. *Applied and Environmental Microbiology* **48**, 726–731.
KOK, J., VAN DIJL, J.M., VAN DER VOSSEN, J.M.B.M. AND VENEMA, G. (1985). Cloning and expression of a *Streptococcus cremoris* proteinase in *Bacillus subtilis* and *Streptococcus lactis*. *Applied and Environmental Microbiology* **50**, 94–101.
KOK, J., HILL, D., HAANDRIKMAN, A.J., DE REUVER, M.J.B., LAAN, H. AND VENEMA, G. (1988a). Deletion analysis of the proteinase gene of *Streptococcus cremoris* Wg2. *Applied and Environmental Microbiology* **54**, 239–244.
KOK, J., LEENHOUTS, K.J., HAANDRIKMAN, A.J., LEDEBOER, A.M. AND VENEMA, G. (1988b). Nucleotide sequence of the cell wall proteinase gene of *Streptococcus cremoris* Wg2. *Applied and Environmental Microbiology* **54**, 231–238.
KRAUT, J. (1977). Serine proteases: structure and mechanism of catalysis. *Annual Reviews in Biochemistry* **46**, 331–358.
MCKAY, L.L. (1983). Functional properties of plasmids in lactic acid bacteria. *Antonie van Leeuwenhoek Journal of Microbiology and Serology* **49**, 259–274.
OTTESEN, M. AND SVENDSEN, I. (1970). The subtilisins. *Methods in Enzymology* **19**, 199–215.

SCHLEIFER, K.H. AND KILPPER-BÄLZ, R. (1987). Molecular and chemotaxic approaches to the classification of streptococci, enterococci and lactococci: a review. *Systematic and Applied Microbiology* **10**, 1–19.

SMITH, E.S., DE LANGE, R.J., EVANS, W.H., LANDON, M. AND MARKLAND, F.S. (1968). Subtilisin Carlsberg. V. The complete sequence; comparison with subtilisin BPN'; evolutionary relationships. *Journal of Biological Chemistry* **243**, 2184–2191.

UHLEN, M., GUSS, B., NILLSON, B., GATENBECK, S., PHILIPSON, L. AND LINDENBERG, M. (1984). Complete sequence of the staphylococcal gene encoding protein A. *Journal of Biological Chemistry* **259**, 1695–1702.

VOSMAN, B. AND VENEMA, G. (1983). Introduction of a *Streptococcus cremoris* plasmid in *Bacillus subtilis*. *Journal of Bacteriology* **156**, 920–921.

# 36

# Vectors for Cloning in Streptococci Derived from the Cryptic Pneumococcal Plasmid pDP1/pSMB1

GIANNI POZZI* AND PATRICIA M.-J. LIEVENS[†]

*Istituto di Microbiologia, Universita' di Verona, Strada Le Grazie, I-37134 Verona, Italy and [†]Istituto di Microbiologia, Universita' di Siena, Via Laterina, I-53100 Siena, Italy

## Introduction

Cryptic plasmids have been isolated from two different strains of *Streptococcus pneumoniae*; pDP1 (Smith and Guild, 1979) was found in D39S, a strain isolated by Avery in 1916 in New York, whereas pSMB1 (Coratza, Pozzi and Figura, 1983) was found in SMI7060, a strain isolated in Siena in 1980. Southern blot hybridization analysis and restriction mapping data indicated that pDP1 and pSMB1 are probably the same plasmid (Pozzi and Guild, unpublished results). pDP1/pSMB1 (3·2 kbp) was used to construct cloning vectors that could be used for cloning both in *S. pneumoniae* and *Streptococcus sanguis* (Pozzi and Guild, 1987; Pozzi *et al.*, 1987; Pozzi *et al.*, 1989). Restriction maps of pDP1/pSMB1 and its derivatives are presented in *Figure 36.1*.

## Cloning vectors

pDP23 (6·1 kbp) was constructed by joining pSMB1 and the staphylococcal plasmid pC194 (Horinouchi and Weisblum, 1982) at their single *Hin*dIII sites (Pozzi and Guild, 1987). pDP23 confers resistance to chloramphenicol when transforming competent streptococci.

pDP27 (4·5 kbp) carries the *cat* gene from the chromosomal elementt Ω6001 (Pozzi and Guild, 1988). A 1·2 kbp *Cla*I fragment containing the *cat* gene was subcloned in the single *Cla*I site of pDP1 (Priebe and Pozzi, in preparation). Chloramphenicol resistance is the selectable phenotype in *Streptococcus*.

pDP28 (7·8 kbp) is an *Escherichia coli–Streptococcus* shuttle vector. The *E. coli* plasmid pVA891 (Macrina *et al.*, 1983) was cut at the *Hin*dIII and *Sal*I sites, ligated to pSMB1 cut with the same enzymes, and the ligation mixture was used

*Genetic Transformation and Expression*
© Intercept Ltd, PO Box 716, Andover, Hants, SP10 1YG, UK

393

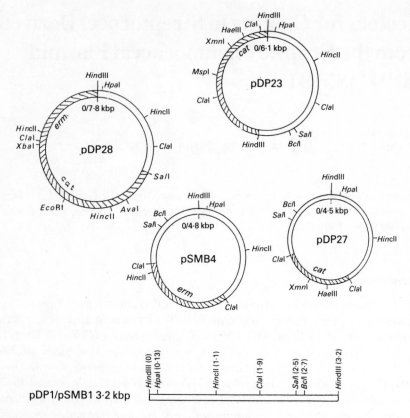

**Figure 36.1** Restriction maps of pDP1/pSMB1 and its derivatives. ☐ , DNA of pDP1/pSMB1; ▨ , DNA other than pDP1/pSMB1, *see* text.

to transform *S. pneumoniae*. The 2·5 kbp *Hind*III–*Sal*I fragment of pSMB1 was found to carry the information for plasmid replication in streptococci. pDP28 expresses chloramphenicol resistance in *E. coli*, and erythromycin resistance in streptococci (Pozzi *et al.*, 1987).

pSMB4 (4·8 kbp) was obtained by cloning in pSMB1 the chromosomal *erm* gene of *S. pneumoniae* GP1 (Pozzi *et al.*, 1989). A 1·6 kbp *Cla*I fragment containing the *erm* gene of the conjugative element ΩGP1 was cloned into the single *Cla*I site of pSMB1. pSMB4 confers resistance to erythromycin.

## Acknowledgements

This work was supported by grants 87.00600.52 and 87.00642.52 from the Consiglio Nazionale delle Ricerche.

## References

CORATZA, G., POZZI, G. AND FIGURA, N. (1983). A plasmid in a drug resistant clinical isolate of *Streptococcus pneumoniae*. *FEMS Microbiology Letters* **17**, 55–57.

HORINOUCHI, S. AND WEISBLUM, B. (1982). Nucleotide sequence and functional map of pC194, a plasmid that specifies inducible chloramphenicol resistance. *Journal of Bacteriology* **150**, 815–825.

MACRINA, F.L., EVANS, R.P., TOBIAN, J.A., HARTLEY, D.L., CLEWELL, D.B., AND JONES, K.R. (1983). Novel shuttle plasmid vehicles for *Escherichia–Streptococcus* transgeneric cloning. *Gene* **25**, 145–150.

POZZI, G. AND GUILD, W.R. (1987). Alkaline phosphatase inhibits cloning in *Streptococcus pneumoniae*. *FEMS Microbiology Letters* **41**, 309–311.

POZZI, G. AND GUILD, W.R. (1988). Two genes for chloramphenicol resistance common to staphylococci and streptococci. *European Journal of Epidemiology* **4**, 20–24.

POZZI, G., MUSMANNO, R.A., STELLINI, M. AND MOLINA, A.M. (1987). Transformation of *Streptococcus sanguis* Challis with a plasmid of *Streptococcus pneumoniae*. *FEMS Microbiology Letters* **48**, 189–194.

POZZI, G., STELLINI, M., MANCINI, R. AND CALDESI, F. (1989). Cloning of an *erm* gene from the chromosome of a clinical isolate of *Strepococcus pneumoniae*. *Microbios Letters*, in press.

SMITH, M.D. AND GUILD, W.R. (1979). A plasmid in *Streptococcus pneumoniae*. *Journal of Bacteriology* **137**, 735–739.

# 7

# The *polA* Gene of *Streptococcus pneumoniae* and the Enzyme it Encodes: Cloning, Expression, Function and Evolution

PALOMA LOPEZ*, SUSANA MARTINEZ[†], ASUNCION DIAZ*, MANUEL ESPINOSA* AND SANFORD A. LACKS[†]

Centro de Investigaciones Biológicas, Velazquez, 144–28006 Madrid, Spain *and [†] Biology Department, Brookhaven National Laboratory, Upton, NY 11973, USA*

## Introduction

DNA polymerase I (Pol I) of *Escherichia coli* has played an important role in elucidating the mechanisms of DNA replication and repair. Its three enzymatic activities, viz. DNA polymerase, 3'-exonuclease and 5'-exonuclease, and their roles in DNA replication and repair have been intensively investigated (Kornberg, 1980). We have cloned a gene encoding a similar DNA polymerase in *Streptococcus pneumoniae*, analysed the structure and expression of the gene, and purified and characterized the pneumococcal Pol I that it encodes. We have also examined cellular functions of the enzyme in *S. pneumoniae* and other bacterial hosts. Inasmuch as the Gram-positive *S. pneumoniae* and the Gram-negative *E. coli* are distantly related species, it is interesting to compare the structure and function of the Pol I proteins from these two sources.

## Cloning of the *S. pneumoniae polA* gene

The pneumococcal *polA* gene was cloned in an *S. pneumoniae*-cloning system using the vector pLS1 (Stassi *et al.*, 1981) to give the recombinant plasmid pSM22 (Martinez *et al.*, 1986). The *polA*-containing clone was identified on the basis of the increased exonuclease activity produced by this multicopy plasmid. In the DNase plate assay developed for screening nuclease mutants (Lacks, 1970), colonies containing pSM22 gave rise to zones of DNA hydrolysis, whereas the nuclease-defective host cells gave colonies devoid of zones. That the cloned nuclease corresponded to Pol I was indicated by the size of the polypeptide associated with the exonuclease activity, which was 100 kDa, as measured by renaturation within polyacrylamide gels after electrophoresis in

*Genetic Transformation and Expression*
© Intercept Ltd, PO Box 716, Andover, Hants, SP10 1YG, UK

the presence of sodium dodecylsulphate (Rosenthal and Lacks, 1977)
Presence of the *polA* plasmid also increased DNA polymerase activity in cell
extracts by ten- to twentyfold (*see*, for example, *Table 37.1*). When the *S.
pneumoniae polA* gene was placed in an *E. coli* vector with a T7 RNA
polymerase expression system, the pneumococcal Pol I was produced in
fivefold greater amount, and it corresponded to 5% of total cellular protein
(Martinez *et al.*, 1986).

### Purification and properties of *S. pneumoniae* Pol I

PURIFICATION PROCEDURE

Purified pneumococcal Pol I was prepared in milligram quantities from both
the *S. pneumoniae* and *E. coli* plasmid systems. Crude extracts obtained by
passage of the cells through a French pressure cell were fractionated by gel
filtration. In both cases a single peak of Pol I, measured both by its polymerase
and exonuclease activities, eluted at a position expected for a native protein of
100 kDa (unpublished results). It thus behaved similarly to the chromosomally
encoded enzyme (Lacks, 1970). After a second fractionation step, chromatography on heparin-agarose, the pneumococcal enzyme prepared from *E. coli*
was essentially pure. Contaminating polypeptides at this stage in the material
prepared from *S. pneumoniae* were eliminated by further fractionation by
chromatography on Q-sepharose and agarose gel filtration.

ENZYMATIC ACTIVITIES OF *S. PNEUMONIAE* Pol I

In addition to DNA polymerase activity, the purified pneumococcal enzyme
exhibits both 3'- and 5'-exonuclease activities. This was shown by its
preferential release of $^{32}$P from a linear duplex DNA substrate labelled
uniformly with [$^3$H]thymidine and with terminal nucleotide [$^{32}$P]phosphate at
either its 3'- or 5'-end (Lopez *et al.*, 1989).

PROTEOLYTIC SUSCEPTIBILITY OF *S. PNEUMONIAE* Pol I

Treatment of *S. pneumoniae* Pol I with small amounts of subtilisin gives rise to
two fragments approximately 68 kDa and 32 kDa in size (Lopez *et al.*, 1989).
The larger fragment retains DNA polymerase activity, and the smaller retains
exonuclease activity (unpublished results). Thus, the *S. pneumoniae* Pol I is
fragmented similarly to *E. coli* Pol I (Brutlag *et al.*, 1969; Klenow and
Henningsen, 1970), which gives rise to a 'Klenow' fragment of 70 kDa and a
smaller fragment of 35 kDa. The similar cleavage patterns indicate that the *S.
pneumoniae* and *E. coli* Pol I proteins share a similar domain structure.

N-TERMINAL AMINO-ACID SEQUENCE OF *S. PNEUMONIAE* Pol I

A sample of the purified Pol I prepared from *S. pneumoniae* was used to

:termine the N-terminal sequence of the protein in a gas-phase sequenator. he sequence found for the first 10 residues corresponded exactly to the :quence predicted from the first AUG codon in the mRNA transcript of the :ne (Lopez *et al.*, 1989).

**tructure and expression of the *polA* gene**

NA SEQUENCE OF THE *polA* GENE

. restriction map of pSM22 is shown in *Figure 37.1*. The nucleotide sequence 'as determined for both strands of DNA along a 2·8 kbp stretch of the agment from a *Dra*I site to the *Eco*RI site at the end of the insert, as indicated. he sequence itself has been reported elsewhere (Lopez *et al.*, 1989). A single irge open reading-frame consisting of 892 codons is present in the region :quenced. However, as discussed below, the mRNA transcript begins within iis open reading-frame, so that 477 amino-acid residues are encoded between anslation start and stop signals, as indicated in *Figure 37.2b*. The predicted iolecular weight of the Pol I polypeptide is 99 487.

IAPPING OF THE mRNA TRANSCRIPTS

1 nuclease mapping (Berk and Sharp, 1977) was used to determine both the eginning and end of mRNA transcripts of the *S. pneumoniae polA* gene Lopez *et al.*, 1989). RNA was prepared from *E. coli* and *B. subtilis* as well as om *S. pneumoniae*, all containing plasmids carrying the pneumococcal *polA* ene. Identical transcription start sites and similar termination sites were found i the three species. The results for *S. pneumoniae* are shown in *Figure 37.2*.

Situated upstream from the transcription start site (*Figure 37.2a*) is a :quence characteristic of prokaryotic promoters, with a −10 site identical to ie consensus and a −35 site deviating from it in three residues (Rosenberg and 'ourt, 1979). The transcripts terminate at nucleotides located near the 3'-end f a potential hairpin in the mRNA, which is underlined in *Figure 37.2c*. fairpins ending in a stretch of U residues frequently terminate prokaryotic iRNAs (Rosenberg and Court, 1979).

BSENCE OF A RIBOSOME-BINDING SEQUENCE

.s shown in *Figure 37.2a*, the mRNA begins only two nucleotides upstream om the translation start site. Thus, it lacks a ribosome-binding site composed f either the typical sequence (Shine and Dalgarno, 1975) or the atypical :quence possibly used by some streptococcal genes (de la Campa *et al.*, 1987). fevertheless, the amount of Pol I present in cells of *S. pneumoniae* is ppreciable. It has been calculated that a single copy of the *polA* gene in *S. neumoniae* gives rise to 500 molecules of Pol I in the cell (Lopez *et al.*, 1989).

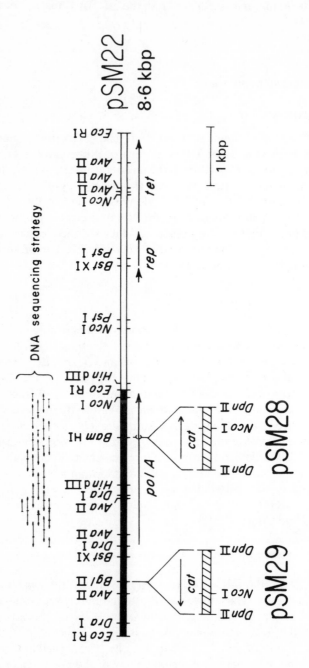

**Figure 37.1**   Map of plasmid pSM22, which contains the *polA* gene of *S. pneumoniae*, and related plasmids. Plasmid pSM22 is shown linearized at an *Eco*RI site. Open bar, pLS1 vector; solid bar, *S. pneumoniae* chromosomal insert. Positions of genes for plasmid replication and tetracycline-resistance functions are indicated. The strategy used for sequencing the *polA* gene is shown by the set of arrows, which indicate portions of the two strands that were read. (Not all restriction sites used are indicated on the map.) The position and orientation of inserts, which contain a *cat* gene that confers chloramphenicol resistance, in pSM22 to give pSM28 and pSM29 are also indicated.

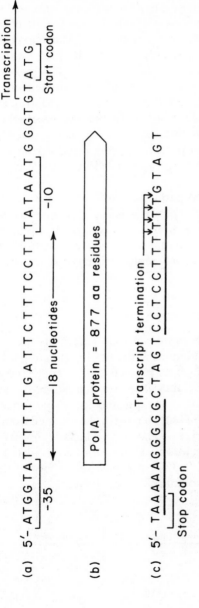

**(a)** 5′- ATGGTATTTTTTGATTCTTTCCTTTATAAT GGGTGTATG
   ‾‾‾‾‾           ‾‾‾     ‾‾‾‾‾‾
   -35   ←——— 18 nucleotides ———→  -10     Start codon
                        Transcription →

**(b)** ┌──────────────────────────────────┐
   │ PolA protein = 877 aa residues   &gt;
   └──────────────────────────────────┘

**(c)** 5′- TAAAAAGGGGGCTAGTCCTCCTTTTTTGTAGT
   ‾‾‾‾      ‾‾‾‾‾‾‾‾‾‾‾‾
   Stop codon
   Transcript termination ——→

**Figure 37.2** Transcription and translation signals for *polA* of *S. pneumoniae*. (a) Transcription promoter and start site, note proximity of mRNA transcription start site to translation start codon; (b) predicted size of *polA* protein product; (c) transcription terminator sequence and endpoints of mRNA. Underlined palindrome (beginning in translation stop codon) could form hairpin in RNA. Arrows indicate the most common end points found experimentally.

## Function and evolution of *polA* genes

### ROLES IN DNA REPLICATION AND REPAIR

The analysis of RNA from *B. subtilis* and *E. coli* cited above showed that thes hosts were able to transcribe the pneumococcal *polA* gene. The enhance production of DNA polymerase activity in these cases showed that the mRN/ was translated as well. In the case of *B. subtilis*, expression of the Pol I activit was approximately 30% of that in *S. pneumoniae* (Martinez *et al.*, 1987), and i *E. coli* expression was approximately 20% of that in *S. pneumoniae* (Lopez *al.*, 1987).

The pneumococcal Pol I enzyme is able to complement *polA*-defectiv mutants of *E. coli* (Lopez *et al.*, 1987) and *B. subtilis* (Martinez *et al.*, 1987), a indicated by its ability to confer resistance in these heterospecific hosts to DN/ damage by UV irradiation and exposure to methyl methanesulphonate However, multiple copies of the pneumococcal *polA* gene were required t achieve the same repair proficiency afforded by a single copy of the nativ gene.

In addition to its ability to participate in DNA repair functions, the Pol produced by the *S. pneumoniae* gene is able to complement a *polA* mutant of *E coli* in a plasmid replication function. This was shown by the ability of pSM22 t replicate just as well in a *polA* mutant of *E. coli* as in a *polA*⁺ strain, althoug the vector plasmid pLS1 could only replicate in a *polA*⁺ strain of *E. coli* (Lack *et al.*, 1986).

### MUTANTS OF *S. PNEUMONIAE polA*

No *polA* mutants of *S. pneumoniae* had heretofore been isolated. W constructed two insertion mutations in the *polA* region of pSM22 by insertin into the *Bgl*II and *Bam*HI sites, respectively, a *Dpn*II fragment of pJS. (Ballester *et al.*, 1986) carrying the *cat* gene of that plasmid, as shown in *Figur 37.1*. DNA polymerase activity was expressed normally from plasmid pSM29 which had the insert in the *Bgl*II site, but was not expressed from pSM28, whicl had the insert in the *Bam*HI site (*Table 37.1*). The latter insert was transferre into the *S. pneumoniae* chromosome by transformation (data to be publishec elsewhere). As seen in *Table 37.1*, polymerase activity in the mutant wa: reduced thirtyfold, yet the mutant cells were viable.

**Table 37.1**  Effect of insertion mutations on *polA* gene function in *Streptococcus pneumoniae*

| Chromosomal genotype | Plasmid present | Plasmid genotype | DNA polymerase Units*/mg protein | Relative activity |
|---|---|---|---|---|
| *polA*⁺ | none | — | 31 | (1·00) |
| *polA*⁺ | pSM28 | *polA::cat28* | 32 | 1·03 |
| *polA::cat28* | none | — | 1 | 0·03 |
| *polA*⁺ | pSM29 | *ins(cat)29* | 411 | 13·3 |

* One unit corresponds to one nmol of nucleotide incorporated into DNA per hour at 37°C.

COMPARISON OF Pol I PROTEINS FROM *S. PNEUMONIAE* AND *E. COLI*

Comparison of the predicted amino-acid sequences of the Pol I enzymes from *S. pneumoniae* and *E. coli* (Joyce, Kelley and Grindley, 1982) indicates that they are homologous along their entire length (Lopez *et al.*, 1989). This is evident from the dotmatrix plot comparing the protein sequences in *Figure 7.3*. The *E. coli* Pol I polypeptide appears to be divided into three structural and functional domains (Ollis *et al.*, 1985): the polymerase comprises most of the carboxyl-terminal half, a middle quarter corresponds to the 3'-exonuclease, and the amino-terminal third has 5'-exonuclease activity. The degree of similarity between the domains of the *S. pneumoniae* and *E. coli* Pol I proteins varies considerable; the proportion of identical residues is highest for the polymerase (49%), lowest for the 3'-exonuclease (29%), and intermediate for the 5'-exonuclease (36%) domains. Nevertheless, it seems safe to conclude that the *S. pneumoniae* and *E. coli polA* genes evolved from the same ancestral gene.

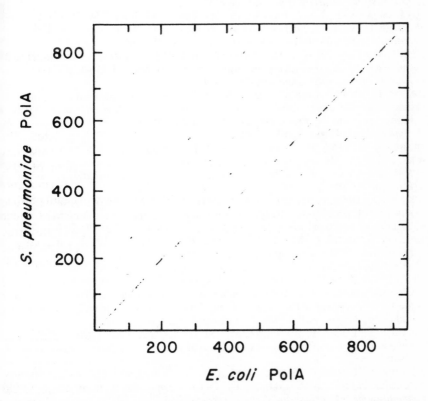

**Figure 37.3**   Dotmatrix comparison of DNA polymerase I proteins from *S. pneumoniae* and *E. coli*. The dotmatrix program used was provided by the Protein Identification Resource, National Biomedical Research Foundation, Georgetown University Medical Center. Points represent four or more identical amino-acid residues within a window of 15 residues.

**Acknowledgements**

Research at Brookhaven National Laboratory was under the auspices of the US Department of Energy Office of Health and Environmental Research; research at the Centro de Investigaciones Biológicas was under the auspices of the Consejo Superior de Investigaciones Cientificas. The work reported was supported in part by US Public Health Service grants AI14885 and GM29721 to S.A.L. by CSIC/CAICYT grant 608/501 to M.E., by award CCB-8609–041 to P.L. and S.A.L. from the US–Spain Joint Committee for Scientific and Technological Cooperation, and NATO grant 0119–88 to P.L. and S.A.L.

**References**

BALLESTER, S., LOPEZ, P., ALONSO, J.C., ESPINOSA, M. AND LACKS, S.A. (1986). Selective advantage of deletions enhancing chloramphenicol acetyltransferase gene expression in *Streptococcus pneumoniae* plasmids. *Gene* **41**, 153–163.

BERK, A.J. AND SHARP, P.A. (1977). Sizing and mapping of early adenovirus mRNAs by gel electrophoresis of S1 endonuclease-digested hybrids. *Cell* **12**, 721–732.

BRUTLAG, D., ATKINSON, M.R., SETLOW, P. AND KORNBERG, A. (1969). An active fragment of DNA polymerase produced by proteolytic cleavage. *Biochemical and Biophysical Research Communications* **37**, 982–989.

DE LA CAMPA, A.G., KALE, P., SPRINGHORN, S.S. AND LACKS, S.A. (1987). Proteins encoded by the *Dpn*II restriction gene cassette: two methylases and an endonuclease. *Journal of Molecular Biology* **196**, 457–469.

JOYCE, C.M., KELLEY, W.S. AND GRINDLEY, N.D.F. (1982). Nucleotide sequence of the *Escherichia coli polA* gene and primary structure of DNA polymerase I. *Journal of Biological Chemistry* **257**, 1958–1964.

KLENOW, H. AND HENNINGSEN, I. (1970). Selective elimination of the exonuclease activity of the deoxyribonucleic acid polymerase from *Escherichia coli* B by a limited proteolysis. *Proceedings of the National Academy of the Sciences of the United States of America* **65**, 168–175.

KORNBERG, A. (1980). *DNA synthesis*, 2nd edn. W.H. Freeman, San Francisco.

LACKS, S. (1970). Mutants of *Diplococcus pneumoniae* that lack deoxyribonucleases and other activities possibly pertinent to genetic transformation. *Journal of Bacteriology* **101**, 373–383.

LACKS, S.A., LOPEZ, P., GREENBERG, B. AND ESPINOSA, M. (1986). Identification and analysis of genes for tetracycline resistance and replication functions in the broad-host-range plasmid pLS1. *Journal of Molecular Biology* **192**, 753–765.

LOPEZ, P., MARTINEZ, S., DIAZ, A. AND ESPINOSA, M. (1987). *Streptococcus pneumoniae polA* gene is expressed in *Escherichia coli* and can functionally substitute for the *E. coli polA* gene. *Journal of Bacteriology* **169**, 4869–4871.

LOPEZ, P., MARTINEZ, S., DIAZ, A., ESPINOSA, M. AND LACKS, S.A. (1989). Characterization of the *polA* gene of *Streptococcus pneumoniae* and comparison of the DNA polymerase I it encodes to homologous enzymes from *Escherichia coli* and phage T7. *Journal of Biological Chemistry* **264**, 4255–4263.

MARTINEZ, S., LOPEZ, P., ESPINOSA, M. AND LACKS, S.A. (1986). Cloning of a gene encoding a DNA polymerase–exonuclease of *Streptococcus pneumoniae*. *Gene* **44**, 79–88.

MARTINEZ, S., LOPEZ, P., ESPINOSA, M. AND LACKS, S. (1987). Complementation of *Bacillus subtilis polA* mutants by DNA polymerase I from *Streptococcus pneumoniae*. *Molecular and General Genetics* **210**, 203–210.

OLLIS, D.L., BRICK, P., HAMLIN, R., XUONG, N.G. AND STEITZ, T.A. (1985). Structure of large fragment of *Escherichia coli* DNA polymerase I complexed with dTMP. *Nature* **313**, 762–766.

ROSENBERG, M. AND COURT, D. (1979). Regulatory sequences involved in the promotion and termination of RNA transcription. *Annual Review of Genetics* **13**, 319–353.

ROSENTHAL, A.L. AND LACKS, S.A. (1977). Nuclease detection in SDS-polyacrylamide gel electrophoresis. *Analytical Biochemistry* **80**, 76–90.

SHINE, J. AND DALGARNO, L. (1975). Determinant of cistron specificity in bacterial ribosomes. *Nature* **254**, 34–38.

STASSI, D.L., LOPEZ, P., ESPINOSA, M. AND LACKS, S.A. (1981). Cloning of chromosomal genes in *Streptococcus pneumoniae*. *Proceedings of the National Academy of Sciences of the United States of America* **78**, 7028–7032.

# Part V
## Gene Expression

# 38

# High-Level Expression of Proteins in *Escherichia coli*

GEOFFREY T. YARRANTON AND EDWINA M. WRIGHT

Department of Molecular Genetics, Celltech Ltd, 216 Bath Road, Slough, Berkshire, SL1 4EN, UK

## Introduction

*Escherichia coli* has been widely used as a host organism for the expression of heterologous proteins. The detailed understanding of the molecular mechanisms involved in plasmid replication and partition, transcription and translation, as well as the genetic definition of the major proteolysis pathways has greatly facilitated the development of efficient, stable expression systems. A typical expression vector, which was designed to overcome many of the deleterious effects on host cells of constitutive gene expression, is the dual-origin vector, pMG196 (*Figure 38.1*).

Although plasmid vectors and strong promoters can ensure efficient transcription and mRNA accumulation, the translation of heterologous mRNAs remains problematical. Several factors can affect the efficiency of mRNA translation including:

1. Shine–Dalgarno–AUG distance and base composition;
2. Secondary structure; and
3. Base sequence in the gene-coding sequence.

The first two parameters are well documented (Matteucci and Heyneker, 1983; Hui and de Boer, 1987), however, recent results suggest that the mRNA coding sequences can also influence ribosome binding, and that novel approaches need to be employed to overcome this.

Many mammalian proteins when over-expressed in *E. coli* accumulate as insoluble inclusion bodies (Itakura *et al.*, 1977; Marston *et al.*, 1984). This is probably due to the fact that most of these are naturally secreted proteins and correct folding does not occur in the reducing environment of the *E. coli* cell. Recent advances in the mechanisms of protein secretion in *E. coli* have demonstrated that several approaches are now available for the secretion of active proteins either into the periplasm or into the culture medium.

*Genetic Transformation and Expression*
© Intercept Ltd, PO Box 716, Andover, Hants, SP10 1YG, UK

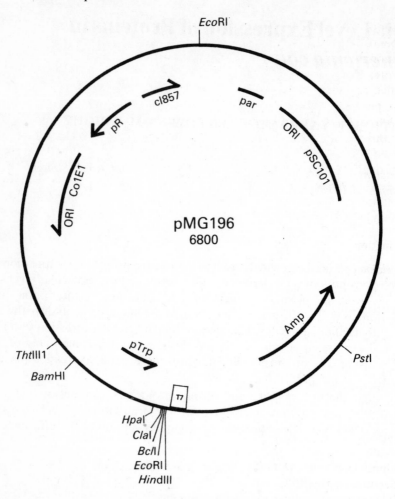

**Figure 38.1**    Dual-origin expression plasmid. This vector has a temperature-inducible copy number control allowing the separation of growth and production phases during fermentations, thereby overcoming problems of plasmid instability and the need for antibiotic selection (Wright, Humphreys and Yarranton, 1986).

The ability to manipulate and adapt *E. coli* as a host organism for the production of recombinant proteins makes its abandonment difficult when considering production systems.

**Dual-origin vector system (DOV)**

Expression vectors that have a constitutively high copy number are often found to be segregationally unstable, and the plasmid-bearing cells have a reduced growth rate. The kinetics of overgrowth of plasmid-free cells are exponential and a productive process cannot be achieved. To overcome these problems the dual-origin vector was developed (*Figure 38.1*). This vector comprised two origins of DNA replication, one derived from pSC101, which gives a copy number of 5 per cell, and a second origin derived from ColE1 but giving a copy number of 200–300 copies per cell. The ColE1 origin has been modified to give conditional expression through the replacement of the RNAII primer promoter by the pR promoter, under the control of the cI$^{857}$ temperature-sensitive repressor protein. At 30°C the plasmid has a low copy number (5 copies per cell) whereas after a shift to 37°C the copy number increases to 200–300 copies per cell. The expression of homologous or heterologous genes using this vector and the pTrp promoter has resulted in expression levels of between 10% and 40% total cell protein.

The dual-origin vector has been used on a large scale and its stability has been analysed in chemostat studies. More than 95% of the cells within the population retain the recombinant dual-origin vector after 150 generations in medium lacking selection.

### Translation of heterologous mRNA

The transcription of heterologous genes in *E. coli* can be readily achieved, but the factors affecting translation of heterologous mRNAs are less well defined. A region of homology [Shine–Dalgarno sequence (SD)] between the mRNA and 16S rRNA is well documented (Shine and Dalgarno, 1974), as is the need for an AUG initiation codon and a spacing of 6–10 bp between these elements. Wood *et al.* (1984) clearly demonstrated the effect of mRNA secondary structure on translation, where the sequestering of the AUG initiation codon in secondary structure inhibited translation.

Recently, heterologous mRNAs have been made that have no apparent secondary structure involving the SD or AUG, but which are still poorly translated (Schoner *et al.*, 1984). The inability to translate these messengers efficiently appears to be due to poor ribosome–mRNA interactions, and some evidence is accumulating for the involvement of sequences both upstream of the SD sequence and downstream of the initiation codon in these interactions.

### Influence of gene coding sequences on translation

Tissue inhibitor of metalloproteinases (TIMP) is a human protein of 20 kDa. The gene encoding this activity has been cloned and expressed in *E. coli* using the DOV (Docherty *et al.*, 1985). During vector construction different single-point mutations were introduced into the 5′ coding sequence of the gene (*Figure 38.2*). Surprisingly, the changes resulted in significantly different levels of protein accumulation (*Figure 38.3*). The altered levels of protein accumulation range from 1·6% to 7·4% of total protein. There are equivalent differences in labelled methionine incorporation in pulse-label experiments and in *in vitro* transcription–translation studies. An analysis of mRNA by Northern blot and by quantitative dot blotting demonstrated that the mRNAs are the same in size and quantity in all cases. Protein turnover experiments show no significant differences between the wild-type and mutant proteins, neither can codon bias account for the differences.

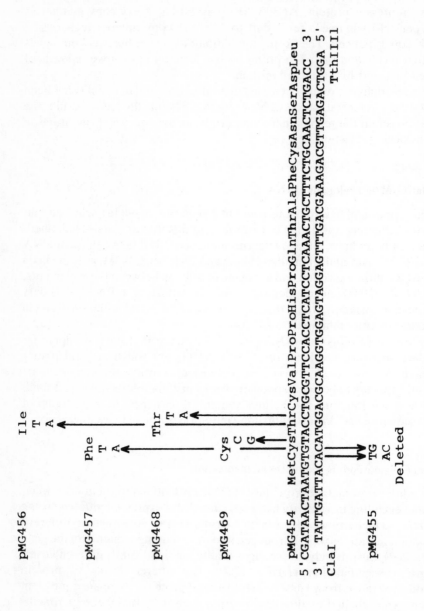

**Figure 38.2** Point mutations in the 5′ coding sequence of the *rec-TIMP* gene. Plasmid numbers (pMG) refer to the dual-origin expression vectors carrying the gene. The wild-type sequence is expressed from pMG454.

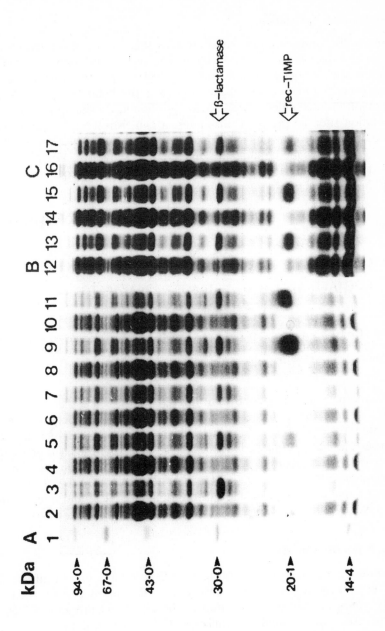

**Figure 38.3**   Polyacrylamide-SDS gel of total cell extracts. Total cell extracts were prepared from uninduced and induced cells. Lanes 2–17, alternatively uninduced and induced cells carrying plasmids pMG196 (lanes 2 and 3), pMG454 (lanes 4 and 5), pMG455 (lanes 6 and 7), pMG456 (lanes 8 and 9), pMG457 (lanes 10 and 11), pMG468 (lanes 12 and 13), pMG469 (lanes 14 and 15), pMG461 (lanes 16 and 17).

The conclusion from these data is that single bp changes in the 5' coding sequence of an eukaryotic gene can significantly affect the binding of *E. coli* ribosomes to the heterologous mRNAs.

## Improving mRNA translation

Since there are limitations on the alterations that can be made within the gene-coding sequence in order to enhance mRNA translation, alternative approaches are necessary. Schoner *et al.* (1984), using the bovine growth hormone gene (*bgh*) as a model, have shown that this heterologous mRNA is very poorly translated unless ribosomes are pre-bound at a site upstream of the *bgh* initiation site. To pre-bind ribosomes, a two-cistron expression system was used, in which an efficiently translated peptide sequence was immediately followed by a ribosome-binding site and the *bgh* sequence. For high-level expression of *bgh*, the translational stop for the peptide sequence had to overlap the SD sequence for *bgh* (*Figure 38.4*).

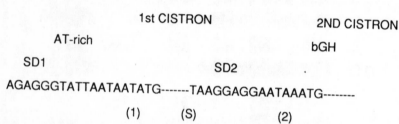

**Figure 38.4**    The two-cistron system (Schoner *et al.*, 1984). Translation is initiated at ATG (1), translates to the TAA(S) stop codon of the first cistron. Ribosomes terminating at S remain bound and reinitiate at ATG(2) of the second cistron.

An alternative solution to inefficient mRNA translation is that devised by McCarthy *et al.* (1986). This group have identified sequences in the 5' untranslated regions of several genes which apparently enhance mRNA translation. The initial sequence identified was that from the *atpE* gene, the general pattern comprising a U-rich sequence followed by an interrupted A-rich sequence; the *atpE* form is UUUUAACUGAAACAAA. Using this enhancing sequence, the production of interleukin-2 (IL2) and interferon-β (INFβ) have been increased by a factor of 6–10 (McCarthy *et al.*, 1986).

## Proteolysis of protein products

The accumulation of heterologous proteins in *E. coli* can be greatly influenced by the vector chosen and by the sensitivity of the product to proteolysis. Recently, we have used a combination of the DOV and protease-defective strains in order to accumulate efficiently (10% total cell protein) small polypeptides of 100 amino acids in length or smaller. Classically, these would have been made as fusion proteins and then subsequently cleaved *in vitro*. Using this technology we have successfully produced assembled active immunoglobulin FV fragments (Field, Yarranton and Rees, 1987).

## Protein secretion

Very few mammalian proteins are soluble and active when produced intracellularly in *E. coli*. Recently, progress has been made in the secretion of mammalian proteins into the periplasm or medium. The main requirement for such secretion is an N-terminal hydrophobic signal sequence derived from a bacterial secreted protein, e.g. OmpA, PhoA. Proteins produced in this way are soluble and active. However, secretion cannot always be achieved, and some proteins appear to contain regions which block membrane translocation. Secretion of complex eukaryotic proteins, e.g. immunoglobulin FAB and FV fragments, with assembly to give active product has recently been reported (Better *et al.*, 1988; Skerra and Pluckthun, 1988). The induction of gene expression appears to be critical in these expression/secretion systems, since over-expression leads to periplasmic leakage and eventually cell lysis.

An alternative *E. coli* secretion system, which allows true export into the culture medium, is that based on haemolysin A (HlyA) (Nicaud *et al.*, 1986). The secretion of HlyA requires two additional gene products (export functions) HlyB and HlyD. The HlyA protein is the 107 kDa haemolysin toxin and, although secreted, this lacks an N-terminal signal sequence. Secretion of HlyA is achieved using a C-terminal sequence, which, when fused onto other genes, allows them to be secreted in an export-dependent manner. Using this system, calf prochymosin protein has been secreted into the culture medium, even though the same protein with an N-terminal signal does not reach the periplasm. This offers the advantage of true secretion into the culture medium (Holland *et al.*, personal communication).

## Conclusion

*E. coli* offers an efficient and reliable host organism for the production of heterologous proteins. The detailed understanding of the production of heterologous proteins, involving the understanding of the molecular mechanisms of transcription, translation and plasmid biology, allow many problems associated with heterologous gene expression to be solved. The adaptation of homologous secretion systems to heterologous proteins is beginning to allow the production of a wide variety of active recombinant proteins.

## References

BETTER, M., CHANG, C.P., ROBINSON, R.R. AND HOROWITZ, A.H. (1988). *Escherichia coli* secretion of an active chimeric antibody fragment. *Science* **240**, 1041–1043.
DOCHERTY, A.J.P., LYONS, A., SMITH, B., WRIGHT, E.M., STEPHENS, P.E., HARRIS, T.J.R., MURPHY, G. AND REYNOLDS, J.J. (1985). Sequence of human tissue inhibitor of metalloproteinases and its identity to erythroid-potentiating activity. *Nature* **318**, 66–69.
FIELD, H., YARRANTON, G.T. AND REES, A.R. (1987). A functional recombinant immunoglobulin variable domain from polypeptides produced in *Escherichia coli*.

416     *Gene Expression*

In *Vaccines '88* (H. Ginsberg, F. Brown, R.A. Lermer and R.M. Chanock, Eds), pp. 29–34. Cold Spring Harbor Laboratory, New York.

HUI, A. AND DE BOER, H.A. (1987). Specialized ribosome system: Preferential translation of a single mRNA species by a sub-population of mutated ribosomes in *Escherichia coli. Proceedings of the National Academy of Sciences of the United States of America* **84**, 4762–4766.

ITAKURA, K., HIROSE, T., CREA, R., RIGGS, A.D., HEYNEKER, H.L., BOLIVAR, F. AND BOYER, H.W. (1977). Expression in *Escherichia coli* of a chemically synthesized gene for the hormone somatastatin. *Science* **198**, 1056–1063.

MCCARTHY, J.E., SEBALD, W., GROSS, G. AND LAMMERS, R. (1986). Enhancement of translational efficiency by the *Escherichia coli atpE* translational initiation region: its fusion with two human genes. *Gene* **41**, 201–206.

MARSTON, F.A.O., LOWE, P.A., DOEL, M.T., SCHOEMAKER, J.M., WHITE, S.Å. AND ANGAL, S. (1984). Purification of calf prochymosin (prorennin) synthesized in *Escherichia coli. Bio/technology* **2**, 800–804.

MATTEUCCI, M.D. AND HEYNEKER, H.L. (1983). Targeted random mutagenesis: the use of ambiguously synthesized oligonucleotides to mutagenize sequences immediately 5' of an ATG initiation codon. *Nucleic Acids Research* **11**, 3113–3121.

NICAUD, J.M., MACKMAN, N., GRAY, L. AND HOLLAND, I.B. (1986). The C-terminal, 23 kDa peptide of *E. coli* haemolysin 2001 contains all the information necessary for its secretion by the haemolysin (Hly) export machinery. *FEBS Letters* **204**, 331–335.

SCHONER, B., HSUING, H.M., BELAGAJE, R.M., MAYNE, N.G. AND SCHONER, R.G. (1984). Role of mRNA translational efficiency in bovine growth hormone expression in *Escherichia coli. Proceedings of the National Academy of Sciences of the United States of America* **81**, 5403–5407.

SHINE, J. AND DELGARNO, L. (1974). The 3'-terminal sequence of *Escherichia coli* 16S ribosomal RNA; complementarity to nonsense triplets and ribosome binding sites. *Proceedings of the National Academy of Sciences of the United States of America* **71**, 1342–1346.

SKERRA, A. AND PLUCKTHUN, A. (1988). Assembly of a functional immunoglobulin $F_v$ fragment in *Escherichia coli. Science* **240**, 1038–1041.

WOOD, C.R., BOSS, M.A., PATEL, T.P. AND EMTAGE, J.S. (1984). The influence of messenger RNA secondary structure on expression of an immunoglobulin heavy chain in *Escherichia coli. Nucleic Acids Research* **12**, 3937–3950.

WRIGHT, E.M., HUMPHREYS, G.O. AND YARRANTON, G.T. (1986). Dual-origin plasmids containing an amplifiable ColE1 *ori*: temperature-controlled expression of clonal genes. *Gene* **49**, 311–321.

# 39
# High-Level Expression in Vaccinia Virus

M. MACKETT

*Paterson Institute for Cancer Research, Christie Hospital and Holt Radium Institute, Wilmslow Road, Withington, Manchester, M20 9BX, England*

## Introduction

Poxviruses are characterized by their complex morphology, large double-stranded DNA genome and their cytoplasmic site of replication (reviewed by Moss, 1985). Vaccinia virus, the prototype orthopoxvirus, is the most intensively studied member of the poxvirus family and is widely known for its role as a vaccine in the smallpox eradication campaign. More recently, interest in vaccinia virus has been centred on its use as an expression vector and its possible use in recombinant live vaccines. This chapter will discuss factors affecting the level of expression of foreign genes in vaccinia and describe some attempts to obtain higher levels of the recombinant gene product.

Among the factors influencing the level of foreign gene product made by recombinant vaccinia viruses are the level of transcription of the gene, the stability of its mRNA, the efficiency of translation of the mRNA and the stability of the gene product itself. The only one of these factors that has been studied in any great detail is the level of transcription of the gene. *Figure 39.1* summarizes some of the salient features of transcription in vaccinia virus. The 187 kbp genome of vaccinia virus codes for over 100 different genes. Upon infection a subset of these genes is transcribed, capped and polyadenylated by enzymes packaged within the virus core. Consequently, this early phase of transcription is not prevented by inhibitors of protein or DNA synthesis. In contrast, late transcripts arise after DNA replication and require prior synthesis of vaccinia polypeptides.

Many early and late genes have been physically mapped and sequenced (Venkatessan, Gerhowitz and Moss, 1982; Rosel and Moss, 1985; Hangii, Bannworth and Stunnenberg, 1986; Lee-Chen and Niles, 1988; Lee-Chen *et al.*, 1988). In all cases the promoter region immediately upstream of the mRNA start site was found to be extremely rich in adenine and thymine. 5′ and 3′ deletions of several early and late promoters have shown that promoter function is contained within an approximately 30 bp fragment (Cochran, Puckett and Moss, 1985; Hangii, Bannworth and Stunnenberg, 1986; Berthelot

*Genetic Transformation and Expression*
© Intercept Ltd, PO Box 716, Andover, Hants, SP10 1YG, UK

417

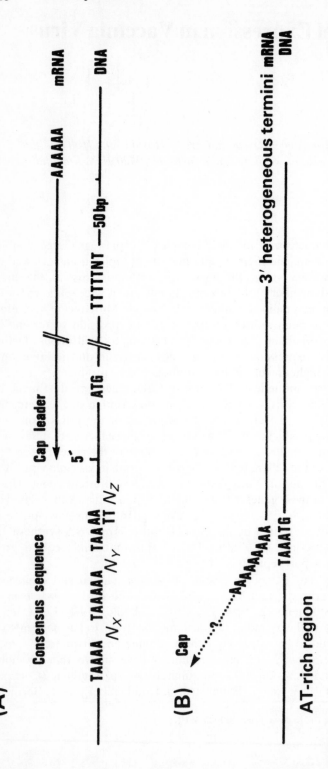

**Figure 39.1** Schematic representation of vaccinia virus transcription. (A) Early transcription occurs before DNA synthesis between 2 and 5 hours post-infection. $N_x$, $N_y$, $N_z$ refer to variable numbers of nucleotides where $x = 0$–4, $y = 0$–2 and $z = 6$–12. The upstream consensus sequence for early promoters suggested by Vassef (1987) is shown. Functional assays show that deletion of sequences 24–31 bases upstream of the mRNA start abolish promoter function (Cochran, Puckett and Moss, 1985; Weir and Moss, 1987b). TTTTTNT has been shown to be a signal for termination of early transcription (Rohrmann, Yuen and Moss, 1986). (B) Late transcription occurs after DNA synthesis. S1 nuclease analysis of late mRNA suggests that initiation of transcription occurs immediately upstream of the translational initiation start site. However, primer extension and oligonucleotide-protection studies indicate that late mRNAs contain a 5' poly A stretch of between 5 and 30 bases (Berthelot et al., 1987; Schwer et al., 1987). The question-mark indicates that other RNA sequences derived from vaccinia may also be present (Berthelot et al., 1987). Several groups have shown that mutation in the TAAAT motif abolishes late transcription.

*et al.*, 1987; Weir and Moss, 1987a, b). However, elements acting on transcription from a distance, analogous to eukaryotic enhancer sequences, cannot be completely ruled out. These vaccinia promoters do not resemble either their eukaryotic or prokaryotic counterparts, and conserved elements such as TATA-box or CAAT-box sequences are not present. Significant differences have also been observed between vaccinia early and late promoters. Vassef (1987) has proposed a consensus sequence for early promoters, which is shown in *Figure 39.1*. Late genes also contain a conserved sequence (TAAATG) immediately upstream of the translational initiation site. Mutation in the TAAAT motif drastically decreases transcription from the promoter (Hangii, Bannworth and Stunnenberg, 1986; Rosel *et al.*, 1986). A further surprising feature of late vaccinia messages is the presence of a poly A stretch of between 5 and 30 bases upstream of the ATG initiation site (Berthelot *et al.*, 1987; Schwer *et al.*, 1987) (*Figure 39.1*).

### Expression of foreign genes

Vaccinia virus has been used to express over 100 different genes as diverse as prokaryotic enzymes, eukaryotic growth factors, protozoan structural proteins and virus gene products. These recombinants have been used for a variety of purposes, including analysis of protein processing and transport in different cell types, the production of monoclonal and polyclonal sera, protection of animals against experimentally induced disease and the analysis of cell-mediated immunity to a variety of virus infections. As yet, however, little has been done to optimize expression of the foreign genes.

For high-level expression of genes in vaccinia it is necessary to use late promoters as they generally yield significantly higher levels of gene product. A complication of using early promoters is encountered when a foreign gene contains the sequence TTTTTNT. Rohrmann, Yuen and Moss (1986) have shown that 3' ends of RNA are formed by termination downstream of a regulatory signal, and that this control region includes all or part of the sequence TTTTTNT. Consequently, human papilloma virus type 16 L1-coding region was expressed only weakly by the 7·5 kDa promoter (which contains early and late elements) as it contained two consensus signals for termination of early transcription (Browne *et al.*, 1988). This complication can be avoided by using late virus promoters, and gives the added advantage of higher levels of expression. On the cautionary side, however, in some circumstances late promoters may be undesirable. Coupar and colleagues (1986) have shown that cells infected with a recombinant virus expressing influenza-A virus haemagglutinin (HA) under control of a late promoter were not recognized by HA-specific cytotoxic T lymphocytes (CTL) and the recombinant virus could not prime or stimulate HA-specific CTL. For analysis of CTL it may be necessary to use early promoters and eliminate consensus signals for early transcription termination. With a careful choice of oligonucleotides for *in vitro* mutagenesis, the amino-acid coding sequence can be maintained and the termination sequence altered.

We have attempted to assess the relative strengths of five different vaccinia virus promoters and one cowpox virus promoter using a transient expression system. The cowpox virus A-type inclusion body promoter is of particular interest as the gene product appears to be one of the most strongly expressed of all of the genes of orthopoxviruses, and can accumulate to form up to 4% of total cell proteins (Patel and Pickup, 1987; Funahashi, Sato and Shida, 1988). Recombinant plasmids containing the promoter regions of vaccinia virus genes ligated to the coding sequence of β-galactosidase were constructed (*Figure 39.2*). When the plasmids were introduced into vaccinia virus infected cells by transfection, assayable levels of β-galactosidase were produced (*Table 39.1*). Briefly, CV1 cells were infected with 20 pfu cell$^{-1}$ of wild-type virus and transfected with 20 μg of recombinant plasmid. After 24 hours cells were harvested, frozen and thawed three times, and assayed for β-galactosidase. The results in *Table 39.1* are expressed as relative amounts of β-galactosidase produced, the amount of enzyme produced from the TK plasmid being set at unity. As can be seen from the table, the late structural promoters (11K and 4b) produce significantly more β-galactosidase than the early promoters, the 11K gene promoter giving approximately twentyfold greater β-galactosidase than the 7·5K promoter (see footnote to *Table 39.2*). This is a slightly greater difference than if recombinant viruses are used rather than transient assays. A rather disappointing aspect of these results was the levels of β-galactosidase produced by the cowpox promoter. Inclusion of more upstream sequences or the use of cowpox virus may increase levels from this promoter.

**Table 39.1**　The relative strengths of six different orthopoxvirus promoters as determined by transient expression of β-galactosidase

| Promoter | Gene | Time of expression | Size (bp) | Relative amounts of β-galactosidase produced |
|---|---|---|---|---|
| TK | thymidine kinase | early | 550 | 1 |
| 19K | homologue to epidermal growth factor | early | 600 | 4 |
| 7·5K | gene of unknown function | early & late | 275 | 20 |
| 11K | structural phosphoprotein | late | 150 | 400 |
| 4b | major structural protein of core | late | 125 | 150 |
| Synthetic cowpox A | major inclusion body protein | late | 60 | 90 |

**Figure 39.2**

```
           EcoRI    SstI            SmaI      XbaI      SaII
(A)    pBLUE   GAATTCGAGCTCGGTACCCGGGGATCCTCTAGAGTCGAC...(cont.)
                     KpnI      BamHI
                              9th codon LacZ
               GTGCACGCATGCATCCCGTCGTT – β-galactosidase
                Pstl      Sphl
```

*cont'd*

**Figure 39.2** *cont'd*

```
                  5'
(B)       TK     TTTATTGTCATCATGAACGGC
                                    EcoRI
                 TTTATTGTCGACGGATCCCCGGGAATTC
                 Sa/I    BamHI  SamI
                         5' 5' 5'              DdeI
                              20              30
          19K    TATAAAATTCCCAA TCTT . . . / / . . . CTGAG . . . / / . . . ATGTCG
                              20
                 TATAAAATTCCCAATCTT . . ./ / . . .GCGGATCCAT
                                                  BamHI
                  5'
                             35    20
          7·5K   AAATATATTCTAATTTATTGC . . . / /GTAC/ / . . . ATG
          (early                        RsaI
          function)                          SmaI
                             35
                 AAATATATTCTAATTTATTGC . . . / /GGATCCCCGGGAATTC
                                           BamHI        EcoRI
                          S1 5'  5'  EcoRI
          11K    TTTTTTTCTATGCTATAAATGAATTC
                                   EcoRI    XhoI   BamHI    9th codon  LacZ
          pSC8, pSC20   TTTTTTTCTATGCTATAAATGAATTCCTCGAGGGATCCCGTC
          vAL1
                          5'S1
          4b     CGAATATAAATAATGGGAAGCCGTGGT
                 CGAATATAAATAAGATCT . . .
                                 Bg/II
                          SI   5'
Cowpox A-type    TTTTTTTATAATAAATGGAGG
inclusion        TTTTTTTATAAATATTGGATC
body promoter            SspI      BamHI
(2 60 bp oligonucleotides)
```

**Figure 39.2** Nucleotide sequences around the transcriptional initiation sites of the authentic and engineered vaccinia promoters used in transient expression of β-galactosidase. (A) The nucleotide sequence around the 5' end of the β-galactosidase gene we have used is shown. The large number of sites upstream of the translational initiation site of β-galactosidase greatly aided the construction of plasmids containing vaccinia. (B) Nucleotide sequences around the transcriptional initiation sites of several genes are shown. Sequences for the thymidine kinase, TK (Weir and Moss, 1983), the epidermal growth factor homologue gene, 19K (Venkatessan, Gershowitz and Moss, 1982), a gene coding for a 7·5 kDa protein of unknown function, 7·5 K (Cochran, Puckett and Moss, 1985), the 11 kDa structural phosphoprotein gene, 11K (Berthelot, Drillien and Wittek, 1985; Chakrabarti, Brechling and Moss, 1985; Hangii, Bannworth and Stunnenberg, 1986), the 4b core protein gene (Rosel and Moss, 1985) and the cowpox A-type inclusion body protein (Patel and Pickup, 1987; Funahashi, Sato and Shida, 1988) are shown. The top line of each pair indicates the authentic gene sequence and the 5' end of the mRNA as determined by nuclease S1 analysis. The bottom line shows the 3' end of the engineered promoter. The sizes of promoter fragments inserted in pBLUE are indicated in *Table 39.1*. In the cases of the TK, 19K, 7·5K, 4b and cowpox promoters the *Bam*HI site of pBLUE was used. The rest were constructed differently (Chakrabarti, Brechling and Moss, 1985). Gaps in the sequences are indicated by parallel lines with the number of missing nucleotides indicated.

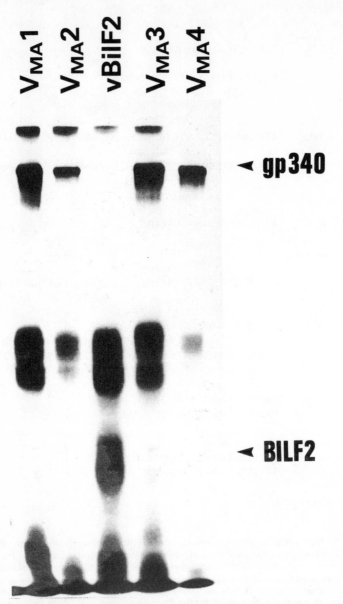

**Figure 39.3**   Effect of different vaccinia virus strains on yield of recombinant gene product. CV1 cells were infected with 30 pfu cell$^{-1}$ of recombinant viruses $V_{MA}1$–4 or vBILF2 and labelled with 25 $\mu$Ci ml$^{-1}$[$^3$H]glucosamine, electrophoresed on a 7·5% SDS-polyacrylamide gel, fixed and fluorographed. An autoradiograph is shown. $V_{MA}1$–4 were generated from the same plasmid construct, using different vaccinia virus strains such that they all express the Epstein–Barr virus (EBV) membrane antigen gp340/220 from the 7·5K promoter. $V_{MA}1$ is based on the laboratory strain WR, $V_{MA}2$ on the vaccine strain Wyeth (New York City Board of Health Strain), $V_{MA}3$ is based on the Copenhagen strain and $V_{MA}4$ on the IHD strain. vBILF2 was constructed to express the EBV open reading-frame BILF2 from the 7·5K promoter and was based on the laboratory strain WR.

The majority of recombinants have been generated from common laboratory strains of vaccinia virus such as WR or Copenhagen. We have constructed recombinants which express the Epstein–Barr virus (EBV) glycoprotein gp340 from the 7·5K promoter in four different virus strains. *Figure 39.3* shows the considerable difference in the expression obtained using these virus strains even though the cells were infected at identical multiplicities. As one might expect, the yield of gene product correlates well with the amount of virus produced by the different strains.

Levels of foreign gene product also depend on how well the virus replicates in the cell line used. *Figure 39.4A* shows the amount of β-galactosidase produced in several cell lines by a recombinant vaccinia virus which expresses the

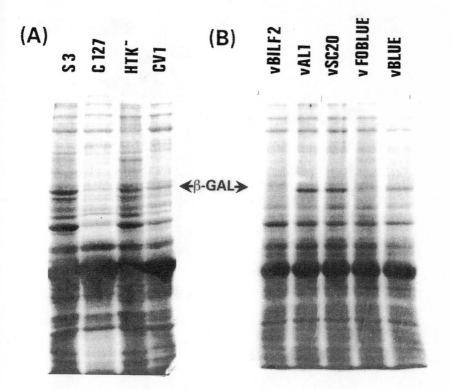

**Figure 39.4**  Expression of β-galactosidase by vaccinia virus recombinant infected cells using the 11K promoter. (A) Extracts of approximately $10^4$ mouse C127, HeLa S3, monkey kidney CV1 or HTK⁻143 cells infected with recombinant vAL1 at 30 pfu cell⁻¹ were electrophoresed on 7·5% SDA-polyacrylamide gels and proteins visualized by staining with Coomassie blue. The position of β-galactosidase is indicated. (B) CVI cells were infected at 30 pfu cell⁻¹ with vBILF2, vFOBLUE, vBLUE, vAL1 or vSC20, electrophoresed on 7·5% SDS-polyacrylamide gels and proteins visualized by staining with Coomassie blue. The position of β-galactosidase is indicated. All viruses expressed β-galactosidase from the 11K promoter; vSC20 (Buller *et al.*, 1988) contains two copies of β-galactosidase inserted within the 19K epidermal growth factor homologue gene, vFOBLUE expresses a β-galactosidase fusion protein with 19 amino acids of the foot-and-mouth disease virus antigenic peptide at the 5′ end of the fusion. vFOBLUE and vBLUE were generated using the Wyeth strain of vaccinia; vBILF2, vAL1 or vSC20 were generated using the WR laboratory strain of vaccinia. The transcriptional start sites and 5′ ends of the genes are indicated in the text.

β-galactosidase gene from the 11K promoter. *Figure 39.4B* shows β-galactosidase produced by a variety of other constructs using the 11K promoter. vBILF2-infected cells were included as a control. vSC20 contains two copies of the β-galactosidase gene inserted into the inverted terminal repeats interrupting the 19K epidermal growth factor homologue gene,

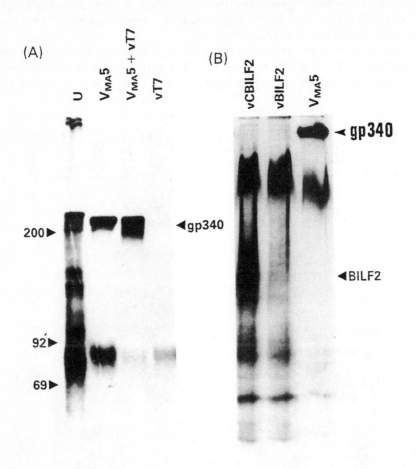

**Figure 39.5**   Expression of foreign genes in vaccinia virus using hybrid promoters. (A) CV1 cells infected with 10 pfu cell$^{-1}$ of $V_{MA}5$ (gp340/220 expression directed from 7·5K, T7 RNA polymerase fusion promoter) or vT7 (vaccinia virus which expresses T7 polymerase), or dually infected with 5 pfu cell$^{-1}$ of each virus, were labelled with 25 μCi ml$^{-1}$[$^3$H]glucosamine, electrophoresed on a 10% polyacrylamide gel, fixed and fluorographed. Molecular size markers were run in parallel and their positions are indicated. Track U was a labelled extract from uninfected cells. (B) CV1 cells infected, labelled and fluorographed as in (A). vBILF2 expresses the Epstein–Barr virus (EBV) open reading-frame BILF2 from the 7·5K promoter. vCBILF2 expresses the same open reading-frame from a hybrid promoter produced by fusing the 7·5K promoter with a 60 bp synthetic oligonucleotide corresponding to the cowpox virus A-type inclusion body promoter (*see Figure 39.2*). Molecular size markers were run in parallel and their position is indicated.

whereas vAL1 contains a single copy of the gene inserted into the thymidine kinase (TK) of the virus. vBLUE contains a single copy of β-galactosidase with the same 5' end as vSC20 inserted into the TK gene. However, a different strain (Wyeth) was used to generate the recombinant virus. These three recombinants illustrate the flexibility of the vaccinia system in that many virus strains can be used; insertion sites and the copy number of the foreign gene can be increased to give higher levels of expression. 25 kbp of foreign DNA can be inserted into vaccinia, thus allowing multiple copies of a single gene or many genes to be expressed in the same virus (Smith and Moss, 1983). A further point to be noted from *Figure 39.4B* is that the level of the β-galactosidase fusion protein is considerably decreased with respect to the authentic β-galactosidase. This may be due to a number of factors, such as stability of the fusion protein or even translational efficiency of the fusion mRNA. A more facile explanation that cannot be excluded fully is that the recombinant virus clone isolated has a concomitant mutation which affects virus viability. This is unlikely but possible.

We have also investigated the possibility of engineering higher levels of expression by ligation of two promoters to form stronger hybrid promoters. *Figure 39.5A* shows the effects of fusing a T7 RNA polymerase promoter with the 7·5K promoter. The T7 system developed by Fuerst and co-workers (Fuerst *et al.*, 1986; Fuerst, Earl and Moss, 1987) is based on the expression of a coliphage T7 RNA polymerase by a recombinant vaccinia virus. T7 RNA polymerase is a single-subunit enzyme with high catalytic activity and strict promoter specificity, ideal characteristics for controllable high-level expression. Two recombinant vaccinia viruses have been used; one expressed the T7 RNA polymerase gene, the other contained a foreign gene under control of a T7 promoter and transcription terminator. Expression of the foreign gene from the T7 promoter will occur only in cells infected with both viruses. *Figure 39.5A* shows the levels of EBV gp340 produced by a recombinant ($V_{MA}5$) that contains the T7, 7·5K hybrid promoter. In cells dually infected with $V_{MA}5$ and a vaccinia virus expressing the T7 RNA polymerase there was an approximately twofold increase in the expression of gp340 when compared with levels produced by $V_{MA}5$ alone. A greater increase was observed at 48 hours post-infection (data not shown). As yet it has not proved possible to isolate a single recombinant virus that expresses the T7 RNA polymerase and contains a T7 promoter. This difficulty, and the somewhat disappointing increase in gp340 expression when using the system, has led us to try several other fusions, one of which is shown in *Figure 39.5B*. We have fused a synthetic 50 bp oligonucleotide containing the cowpox A-type inclusion body promoter to the 7·5K promoter and used the hybrid promoter or the 7·5K promoter to express the EBV open reading-frame BILF2. As can be seen from *Figure 39.5B*, a substantial increase in BILF2 expressed by the hybrid promoter over the standard 7·5K promoter has been achieved.

*Table 39.2* shows the levels of expression so far achieved using vaccinia recombinants to express β-galactosidase, human immunodeficiency virus gp120 and hepatitis B virus surface antigen. It should be pointed out that none of these results has been optimized and these figures should be seen as the

**Table 39.2**    Estimated levels of foreign gene products produced by vaccinia recombinants*

| Promoter | Harvest time post-infection (h) | Gene | Level[†] (ng 3 × 10⁶ cells) | (mg litre⁻¹) |
|---|---|---|---|---|
| 7·5K | 24 | β-gal | 1 378 | 0·23 |
| 11K | 24 | β-gal | 10 944 | 1·823** |
| T7φ10 | 24 | β-gal | 5 358 | 0·89 |
| 7·5K | 48 | β-gal | 3 185 | 0·53 |
| T7φ10 | 48 | β-gal | 15 463 | 2·58 |
| T7φ10 | 48 | HbsAg | 3 970 | 0·66 |
| T7φ10 | 48 | HIV env | 3 000‡ | 0·5 |

β-gal, β-galactosidase; HbsAg, hepatitis B virus surface antigen; HIV env, human immunodeficiency virus envelope.
* Data synthesized from Fuerst, Earl and Moss (1987), Faulkner and Moss (1988).
[†] The level was derived from monolayers infected at 10 pfu cell⁻¹, except in the case of the 11K promoter where 7·5 pfu cell⁻¹ was used.
‡ Estimated as twice the figure quoted over a 24-hour period.
§ Assuming similar yields in HeLa S3 spinners cultured at 5 × 10⁵ cells ml⁻¹.
** Approximately equivalent to 3% of total cell protein.
Comparison of viruses expressing the chloramphenicol acetyltransferase (CAT) gene from the 7·5K or thymidine kinase (TK) promoters indicate that the 7·5K promoter is thirtyfold stronger than the TK promoter (Mackett, Smith and Moss, 1984). A fifteenfold difference was estimated using a transient assay system (Cochran, Puckett and Moss, 1985). A similar transient assay system suggested that the T7φ10 promoter was fifteenfold stronger than the 7·5K promoter (Fuerst *et al.*, 1986), whereas expression from recombinant viruses suggests a fivefold difference.

minimum levels attainable. We have shown that careful choice of vaccinia virus strains, cell lines and promoters can improve the yield of recombinant gene products. It is also possible to use hybrid promoters and multiple copies of the genes of interest to further improve expression. However, in order to rationally approach the obtaining of even higher levels it will be necessary to establish the function and relative importance of the unique features of vaccinia late transcripts. An understanding of the mechanism of generation of these features may also aid in optimizing the T7 system.

### Acknowledgements

I would like to thank Wendy Pelham and Sarah J. Morrissey for exceptional patience and excellent secretarial help. I am supported by the Cancer Research Campaign.

### References

BERTHELOT, C., DRILLIEN, R. AND WITTEK, R. (1985). One hundred base pairs of 5' flanking sequence of a vaccinia virus late gene are sufficient to temporally regulate late transcription. *Proceedings of the National Academy of Sciences of the United States of America* **82**, 2096–2100.
BERTHELOT, C., VAN MEIR, E., HEGGELER-BORDIER, B-TEN AND WITTEK, R. (1987). Vaccinia virus produces later mRNA's by discontinuous synthesis. *Cell* **50**, 153–162.
BROWNE, H.M., CHURCHER, M.J., STANLEY, M.A., SMITH, G.L. AND MINSON, A.C. (1988). Analysis of the L1 gene product of human papilloma virus type 16 by expression in a vaccinia virus recombinant. *Journal of General Virology* **69**, 1263–1273.
BULLER, R.M.L., CHAKRABARTI, S., MOSS, B. AND FREDRICKSON, T. (1988). Cell proliferative response to vaccinia virus is mediated by VGF. *Virology* **164**, 182–192.

High-Level Expression in Vaccinia Virus    427

CHAKRABARTI, S., BRECHLING, K. AND MOSS, B. (1985). Vaccinia virus expression vector: co-expression of β-galactosidase provides visual screening of recombinant virus plaques. *Molecular and Cellular Biology* **5**, 3403–3409.

COCHRAN, M.A., PUCKETT, C. AND MOSS, B. (1985). *In vitro* mutagenesis of the promoter region for a vaccinia virus gene: Evidence for tandem early and late regulatory signals. *Journal of Virology* **54**, 30–37.

COUPAR, B.E.H., ANDREW, M.E., BOTH, G.W. AND BOYLE, D.B. (1986). Temporal regulation of influenza haemagglutinin expression in vaccinia virus recombinants and effects on the immune response. *European Journal of Immunology* **16**, 1479–1487.

FAULKNER, F.G. AND MOSS, B. (1988). *Escherichia coli gpt* gene provides dominant selection for vaccinia virus open reading frame expression vectors. *Journal of Virology* **62**, 1849–1854.

FUERST, T.T., EARL, P.L. AND MOSS, B. (1987). Use of a hybrid vaccinia virus–T7 RNA polymerase system for expression of target genes. *Molecular and Cellular Biology* **7**, 2538–2544.

FUERST, T.R., NILES, E.G., STUDIER, F.W. AND MOSS, B. (1986). Eukaryotic transient-expression system based on recombinant vaccinia virus that synthesizes bacteriophage T7 RNA polymerase. *Proceedings of the National Academy of Sciences of the United States of America* **83**, 8122–8126.

FUNAHASHI, S., SATO, T. AND SHIDA, H. (1988). Cloning and characterisation of the gene encoding the major protein of the A-type inclusion body of cowpox virus. *Journal of General Virology* **69**, 35–47.

HANGII, M., BANNWORTH, W. AND STUNNENBERG, H.G. (1986). Conserved TAAAT motif in vaccinia virus late promoters: overlapping TATA box and site of transcription initiation. *EMBO Journal* **5**, 1071–1076.

LEE-CHEN, G.-J. AND NILES, E.G. (1988). Map positions of the 5' ends of eight mRNA's synthesised from the later genes in the vaccinia *Hin*dII D fragment. *Virology* **163**, 80–92.

LEE-CHEN, G.-J., BOURGEOIS, N., DAVIDSON, K., CONDIT, R.C. AND NILES, E.G. (1988). Structure of the transcription, initiation and termination sequences of seven early genes in the vaccinia virus *Hin*dII D fragment. *Virology* **163**, 64–79.

MACKETT, M., SMITH, G.L. AND MOSS, B. (1984). General method for production of, and selection of, infectious vaccinia virus recombinants expressing foreign genes. *Journal of Virology* **49**, 857–864.

MOSS, B. (1985). Replication of poxviruses. In *Virology* (B.N. Fields, D.M. Knipe, R.M. Chanock, J.L. Melnick, B. Roizman and R.E. Sharpe, Eds), pp. 658–703. Raven Press, New York.

PATEL, D.D. AND PICKUP, D.J. (1987). Messenger RNA's of a strongly-expressed late gene of cowpox virus contain 5'-terminal poly (A) sequences. *EMBO Journal* **6**, 3787–3794.

ROHRMANN, G., YUEN, L. AND MOSS, B. (1986). Transcription of vaccinia virus early genes by enzymes isolated from vaccinia virions terminates downstream of a regulatory sequence. *Cell* **46**, 1029–1035.

ROSEL, J. AND MOSS, B. (1985). Transcriptional and translational mapping and nucleotide sequence analysis of a vaccinia virus gene encoding the precursor of the major core polypeptide 4b. *Journal of Virology* **56**, 830–838.

ROSEL, J.L., EARL, P.L., WEIR, J.P. AND MOSS, B. (1986). Conserved TAAATG sequence at the transcriptional and translational initiation sites of vaccinia virus late genes deduced by structural and functional analysis of the *Hin*dIII H genome fragment. *Journal of Virology* **60**, 436–449.

SCHWER, B., VISCA, P., VOS, J.C. AND STUNNENBERG, H.G. (1987). Discontinuous transcription or RNA processing of vaccinia virus late messengers results in a 5' poly (A) leader. *Cell* **50**, 163–169.

SMITH, G.L. AND MOSS, B. (1983). Infectious poxvirus vectors have capacity for at least 25 000 base pairs of foreign DNA. *Gene* **25**, 21–28.

VASSEF, A. (1987). Conserved sequences near the early transcription start sites of vaccinia virus. *Nucleic Acids Research* **15**, 1427–1443.

VENKATESSAN, S., GERSHOWITZ, A. AND MOSS, B. (1982). Complete nucleotide sequence of two adjacent early genes located within the inverted terminal repetition. *Journal of Virology* **44**, 637–647.

WEIR, J.P. AND MOSS, B. (1983). Nucleotide sequence of the vaccinia virus thymidine kinase gene and the nature of spontaneous frameshift mutations. *Journal of Virology* **46**, 530–537.

WEIR, J.P. AND MOSS, B. (1987a). Determination of the promoter region of an early vaccinia virus gene encoding thymidine kinase. *Virology* **158**, 206–210.

WEIR, J.P. AND MOSS, B. (1987b). Determination of the transcriptional regulatory region of a vaccinia virus late gene. *Journal of Virology* **61**, 75–80.

0

# Expression of Human Prolactin in
# *Escherichia coli*

I.S. GILBERT, P.J. LOWRY AND D. SAVVA

Department of Physiology and Biochemistry, University of Reading,
Whiteknights, PO Box 228, Reading, RG6 2AJ, UK

## Introduction

Recent advances in recombinant DNA technology provide a means of producing fusion proteins in bacteria such as *Escherichia coli*. We are interested in expressing human prolactin in bacteria in the form of a fusion protein in an attempt to increase its immunogenicity. These fusion proteins could be used to produce high-affinity polyclonal and monoclonal antibodies.

Prolactin is a 199 amino acid polypeptide, with a molecular mass of 23 kDa. Prolactin acts mainly on the mammary gland, where it stimulates postpartum lactation. It is also involved in other aspects of pregnancy and has some physiological effects in men (Blackwell, 1985; Moltich, 1985). High-affinity antibodies to prolactin, for use in immunoassays, are useful tools in diagnosing patients with abnormal levels of serum prolactin. The antibodies available at present have been produced using human pituitary extracts (Hodgkinson and Lowry, 1981). The molecular biological approach would remove the need to handle human tissues and thus would provide a non-infectious source of prolactin, eliminating contact with viruses such as HIV and hepatitis; also, increased prolactin immunogenicity would produce antibodies of a higher affinity, resulting in more sensitive and faster immuno-detection systems.

Here we report the cloning and expression of three different fragments of human prolactin cDNA in *E. coli* using a pUR expression vector (Ruther and Muller-Hill, 1983). The clone phPRL1 contains a 800 bp prolactin cDNA fragment that codes for the complete 199 amino acid protein plus the 5' signal sequence and a portion of the 3' untranslated region. The clone phPRL5 contains a 580 bp prolactin cDNA fragment that codes for the signal sequence and the first 157 amino acids. The clone phPRL3 contains a 380 bp fragment that codes for amino acids 158–199 plus a portion of; the 3' untranslated region. Western blot analysis (Burnette, 1981) confirmed that the β-galactosidase–prolactin fusion proteins were immunoactive against antibodies raised against native prolactin.

Genetic Transformation and Expression
© Intercept Ltd, PO Box 716, Andover, Hants, SP10 1YG, UK

429

**Materials and methods**

Human prolactin cDNA fragments were obtained by carrying out specific restriction digests of the original pBR322 recombinant (*Figure 40.1*), kindly supplied by Dr J.A. Martial (Cooke *et al.*, 1981). These were then purified on a low-melting-point gel (Weislander, 1979) and ligated into pUR291 cleaved with the appropriate restriction enzymes (*see* Results). All restriction and ligation reactions were carried out according to the manufacturers' recommendations and were checked by gel electrophoresis.

Transformation of *E. coli* BMH 71–18 (Messing *et al.*, 1977) was performed using the calcium chloride method (Mandel and Higa, 1970). Transformants were plated on ampicillin-containing agar plates and screened using a radiolabelled prolactin cDNA probe (Grunstein and Hogness, 1975; Vogelstein and Feinberg, 1983). Plasmids from positive clones were isolated (Birnboim and Doly, 1979) and analysed.

The protein content of the positive clones was analysed by SDS polyacrylamide gel electrophoresis (Laemmli, 1970). Cultures (10 ml) were grown in Luria–Bertani (LB) broth for 2 hours at 37°C. Isopropyl-β-D-thiogalactopyranoside (IPTG) was added to a final concentration of 1 mM and the cultures grown for a further 2 hours at 37°C. After spinning at 10 000$g$ for 15 min the cells were washed in 1 ml of 10mM tris-HCl pH 7·5, 1mM ethylenediamine tetraacetic acid (EDTA) (TE) and recentrifuged. The cells were resuspended in 200 μl sample buffer (100mM tris-HCl pH 8·8, 4% SDS, 5mM EDTA, 15% sucrose, 10mM dithiothreitol and 0·005% bromophenol blue). Samples were boiled for 10 min and centrifuged in a microfuge for 5 min

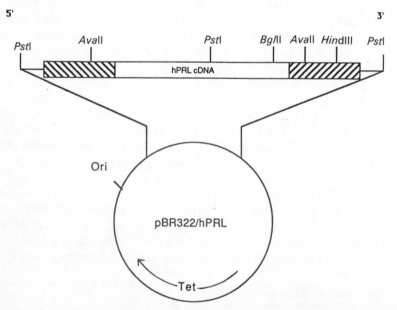

**Figure 40.1**   Partial restriction map of the recombinant plasmid pBR322/hPRL. The human prolactin cDNA is not shown to scale. ▨ , Signal sequence; ▭ , coding region of human prolactin cDNA; ▨ , 3′ untranslated region.

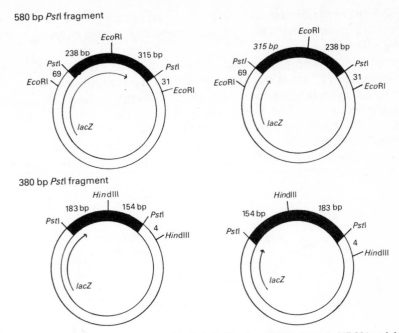

**Figure 40.2**   Possible recombinant plasmids after the ligation of *Pst*I-cleaved pUR291 and the 580 bp or 380 bp *Pst*I cDNA fragments. The prolactin cDNA is shaded and is not shown to scale.

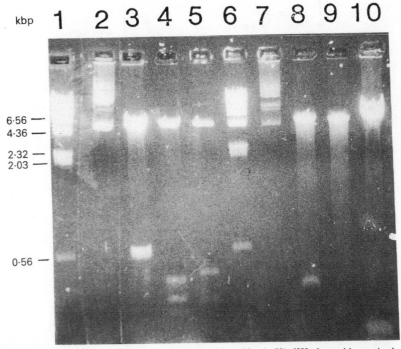

**Figure 40.3**   Restriction mapping of recombinant plasmids. 1, *Hin*dIII-cleaved bacteriophage λ DNA; 2, uncut pUR291; 3, phPRL5 × *Pst*I, 4, phPRL5 × *Eco*RI; 5, phPRL6 × *Eco*RI; 6, λ × *Hin*dIII; 7, uncut pUR291; 8, phPRL3 × *Pst*I; 9, phPRL3 × *Hin*dIII; 10, phPRL4 × *Hin*dIII.

to pellet any insoluble material. Aliquots (10 µl) of each sample were run on a 7·5% polyacrylamide-SDS gel with the appropriate protein molecular weight markers (Sigma).

Purification of the β-galactosidase fusion protein was carried out by affinity chromatography (Carroll and Laughon, 1985) on *p*-amino-benzyl-1-thio-β-D-galactoside agarose (Sigma). The purified samples were checked for homogeneity on SDS-PAGE gels and by Western blot analysis. Membrane-bound rabbit antihuman prolactin antibody (P2) was reacted with a goat antirabbit antibody (IgG H&L) linked to horseradish peroxidase and the antibody complex detected by the blue colour produced in the presence of 0·05% w/v 4-chloro-1-naphthol.

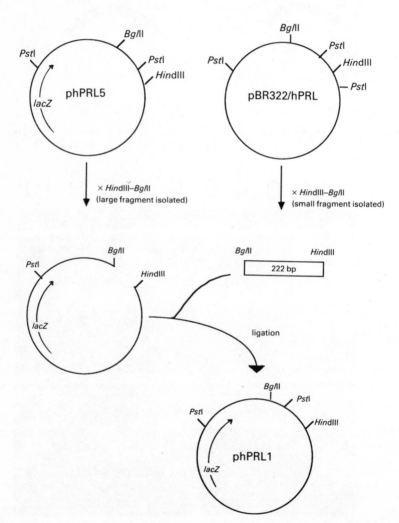

**Figure 40.4** Construction of plasmid phPRL1. The prolactin cDNA fragments are not shown to scale.

## Results and discussion

The construction of the recombinant plasmids involved using fragments produced from digestions of the original recombinant plasmid containing the prolactin cDNA (*Figure 40.1*). Plasmid was digested with the restriction enzyme *Pst*I to generate three fragments: the pBR322 segment and two smaller fragments of 580 bp and 380 bp. The 580 bp *Pst*I fragment codes for the 5′ signal sequence plus the first 157 amino acids. The 380 bp fragment codes for amino acids 158–199 plus a portion of the 3′ untranslated region. Both cDNA fragments were cloned into the *Pst*I site of the expression vector pUR291, which was chosen to ensure that the cloned cDNA fragment would be in the correct reading-frame for expression. The recombinant plasmids were cloned into *E. coli* BMH 71–18, and screened with a 700 bp *Ava*II–*Ava*II fragment of the prolactin cDNA (*Figure 40.1*) radiolabelled with $[\alpha-^{32}P]$dCTP to a specific activity of $2 \times 10^9$ cpm µg$^{-1}$ DNA. Plasmid DNA isolated from the transformed *E. coli* was analysed to verify whether the prolactin cDNA fragment was

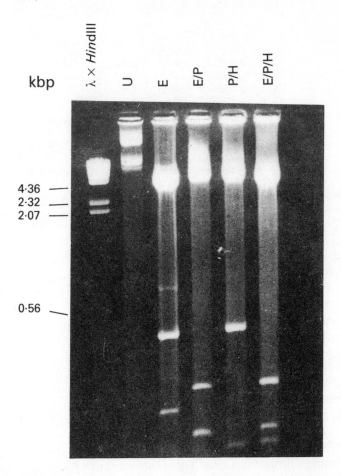

**Figure 40.5** Restriction mapping of plasmid phPRL1. E, *Eco*RI; P, *Pst*I; H, *Hin*dIII; U, uncut plasmid. Size markers are indicated in kbp.

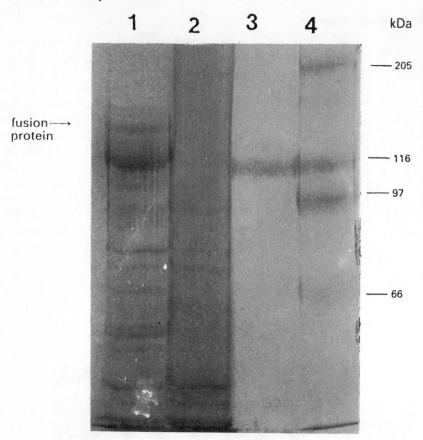

**Figure 40.6** SDS-PAGE gel showing fusion protein produced by cultures containing th recombinant plasmid phPRL1. 1, Total cellular protein from a culture containing phPRL plasmid; 2, total cellular protein from a culture of *E. coli* BMH 71–18; 3, β-galactosidase (11 kDa); 4, molecular size markers (205–29 kDa; Sigma).

inserted in the correct orientation (*Figure 40.2*). The results (*Figure 40.3* confirmed that phPRL3 and phPRL5 contain the appropriate fragments in th correct orientation. Plasmid phPRL5 contains the 580 bp fragment and plasmi phPRL3 contains the 380 bp fragment.

Construction of the recombinant plasmid containing the complete prolacti cDNA sequence involved using the newly formed phPRL5 plasmid. Th plasmid was digested with the restriction enzymes *Hin*dIII and *Bgl*II and th large DNA fragment (5·7 kbp) isolated from a low-melting-point agarose gel A 222 bp *Hin*dIII-*Bgl*II fragment was isolated from the original pBR32 recombinant (*Figure 40.1*); this was ligated into the linearized phPRL plasmid, as shown in *Figure 40.4*. Transformed *E. coli* BMH 71–18 wa screened with a radiolabelled 380 bp *Pst*I fragment of the prolactin cDNA Plasmid DNA isolated from positive clones was analysed to verify the presenc of the complete prolactin cDNA. The results shown in *Figure 40.5* confirm tha plasmid phPRL1 contains the complete cDNA sequence for prolactin.

The proteins synthesized by cultures containing the recombinant plasmid

re analysed by SDS-polyacrylamide gel electrophoresis. The results shown
*Figure 40.6* indicate that cultures containing plasmid phPRL1 produce a
otein band of a slower electrophoretic mobility than β-galactosidase; this
vel protein has a molecular mass of approximately 140 kDa, which is the
pected size for a β-galactosidase–prolactin fusion protein. Cultures
ntaining the plasmids phPRL3 and phPRL5 also produce proteins larger
an β-galactosidase (results not shown).

In order to verify that the fusion proteins contained the human prolactin,
estern blot analysis was performed on the total cellular protein, using the
o-antibody system as described on p. 432. The results (*Figure 40.7*) indicate
at the cells containing phPRL1 or phPRL5 produce a protein (molecular
ass approximately 140 kDa) that reacts with the prolactin antibody (P2) used.
owever, proteins produced by cells harbouring the phPRL3 clone do not
act with this particular antibody. These results confirm that the plasmids
PRL1 and phPRL5 do indeed express prolactin, or part of it, in the form of
galactosidase fusions. They also indicate that the epitope or epitopes
cognized by this antibody probably occur within the first 157 amino acids of
man prolactin.

A single-step affinity chromatography method was used to purify the fusion
otein coded for by phPRL1, as described on p. 432. The homogeneity of the
rified fusion protein was confirmed by SDS-PAGE and Western blot

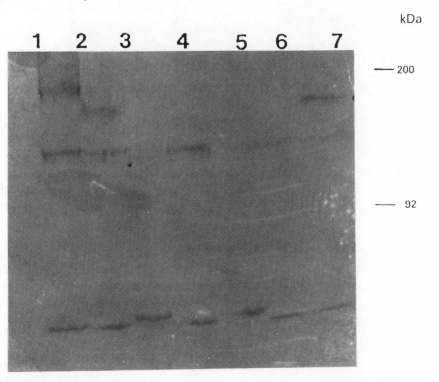

**Figure 40.7**   Western blot analysis of total cellular protein. The tracks are of *E. coli* BMH 71–18 containing: 1, pUR291 vector; 2, plasmid phPRL5; 3, plasmid phPRL6; 4, plasmid phPRL3; 5, plasmid phPRL4; 6, pUR291 vector; 7, plasmid phPRL1. Antibodies used were as stated on p. 432.

analysis. The photograph of the SDS-PAGE gel (*Figure 40.8*) shows that th
isolated fusion protein is homogeneous and has the expected molecular ma
for a protein comprising β-galactosidase and the complete prolactin sequenc
The results of the Western blot analysis (*Figure 40.9*) are in agreement wi
those obtained using the total cellular protein (*Figure 40.7*) in that the isolate
fusion protein is recognized by the antibody used.

The fusion protein produced by cultures harbouring phPRL1 will be used
raise polyclonal and monoclonal antibodies. These antibodies, and protei
coded for by plasmids containing smaller fragments of the prolactin cDNA, w
be used to map the epitopes on human prolactin.

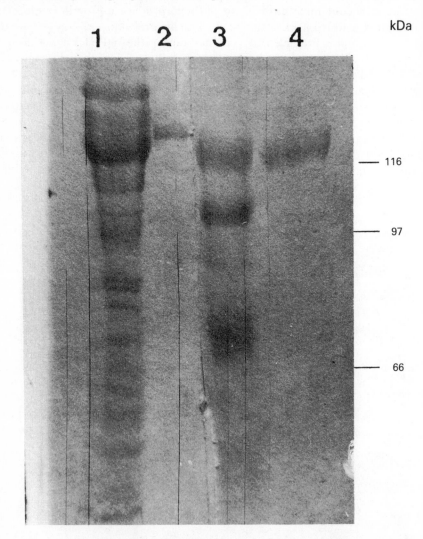

**Figure 40.8**   SDS-PAGE gel of isolated fusion protein stained with 0·1% Coomassie blue. 1, Tot
cellular protein from *E. coli* BMH 71–18 culture containing plasmid pUR291; 2, isolated fusi
protein coded by phPRL1; 3, molecular size markers (205–29 kDa); 4, β-galactosidase.

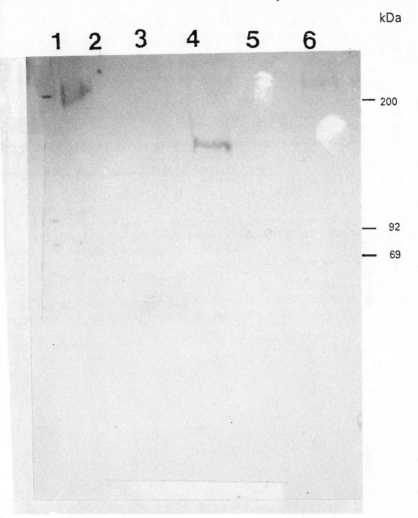

**Figure 40.9**   Western blot analysis of SDS-PAGE gel. 1 and 6, Molecular size markers; 2, β-galactosidase (116 kDa); 3 and 5, total cellular protein of *E. coli* BMH 71–18; 4, purified fusion protein. Antibodies used were as stated on p. 432.

## References

BIRNBOIM, H.C. AND DOLY, J. (1979). A rapid alkaline method extraction procedure for screening recombinant plasmid DNA. *Nucleic Acids Research* **7**, 1513–1518.
BLACKWELL, R.E. (1985). Diagnosis and management of prolactinomas. *Fertility and Sterility* **43**, 5–16.
BURNETTE, W.N. (1981). Western blotting. *Analytical Biochemistry* **112**, 195–203.
CARROLL, S.B. AND LAUGHON, A. (1985). Production and purification of polyclonal antibodies to a foreign segment of β-galactosidase fusion proteins. In *DNA cloning (a practical approach) Volume III* (D. Glover, Ed.), pp. 89–111, IRL Press, Oxford.

COOKE, N.E., COIT, D., SHINE, J., BAXTER, J.D. AND MARTIAL, A. (1981). Human prolactin; cDNA structural analysis and evolutionary comparisons. *Journal c Biological Chemistry* **256**, 4007–4016.

GRUNSTEIN, M. AND HOGNESS, D. (1975). Colony hybridisation. A method for the isolation of cloned DNA's that contain a specific gene. *Proceedings of the Nationa Academy of Sciences of the United States of America* **72**, 3961–3967.

HODGKINSON, S.C. AND LOWRY, P.J. (1981). Hydrophobic-interaction chromatogra phy and anion-exchange chromatography in the presence of acetonitrile *Biochemical Journal* **199**, 619–627.

LAEMMLI, U.K. (1970). Cleavage of structural proteins during the assembly of the heac of bacteriophage T4. *Nature* **227**, 680–686.

MANDEL, M. AND HIGA, A. (1970). Calcium dependent bacteriophage DNA infection. *Journal of Molecular Biology* **53**, 154–160.

MESSING, J., GRONENBORN, B., MULLER-HILL, B. AND HOFSCHNEIDER, H.-P. (1977). Filamentous coliphage M13 as a cloning vehicle: Insertion of a *Hin*dIII fragment of the *lac* regulatory region in the M13 replicative form *in vitro*. *Proceedings of the National Academy of Sciences of the United States of America* **74**, 3624–3646.

MOLTICH, M. (1985). Pregnancy and the hyperprolactinemic woman. *New England Journal of Medicine* **312**, 1364–1369.

RUTHER, U. AND MULLER-HILL, B. (1983). Easy identification of cDNA clones. *EMBO Journal* **2**, 1791–1794.

VOGELSTEIN, B. AND FEINBERG, A. (1983). A technique for radiolabelling restriction endonuclease fragments to a high specific activity. *Analytical Biochemistry* **132**, 6–13.

WEISLANDER, L. (1979). A simple method to recover intact high molecular weight RNA and DNA after electrophoresis separation. *Analytical Biochemistry* **98**, 305–312.

# 41
# Expression of Human Pro-Opiomelanocortin in *Escherichia coli*

T.S. GREWAL, P.J. LOWRY AND D. SAVVA

*Department of Physiology and Biochemistry, University of Reading, Whiteknights, PO Box 228, Reading, RG6 2AJ, UK*

## Introduction

The human pro-opiomelanocortin (POMC) is a precursor peptide of 241 amino acid residues; the initial translational product also contains a 26 amino acid signal sequence. Although the anterior and the neurointermediate lobes of the pituitary gland are the main sites for the expression and processing of POMC, it has also been detected in a number of other tissues, such as the human placenta, the reproductive organs (Bardin *et al.*, 1987) and the central nervous system.

The POMC precursor is enzymatically cleaved at pairs of basic amino acid residues by endoproteases to produce the various biologically active peptides (Loh, Birch and Castro, 1988). These include adrenocorticotropin hormone (ACTH(1–39)), ACTH(18–39), α-melanocyte-stimulating hormone (α-MSH), pro-γ-MSH, β-lipotropin (β-LPH), γ-LPH, β-MSH and β-endorphin; of all these peptides only ACTH has been assigned a distinct biological activity in man. With the aid of recombinant DNA technology we hope to express the POMC precursor and its derived peptides in *Escherichia coli*. This approach will allow us to obtain unlimited amounts of pure peptides for the production of high-affinity polyclonal and monoclonal antibodies. These antibodies will recognize the intact precursor together with the products of post-translational processing, which would therefore facilitate the study of complex biosynthetic pathways. Also, they could be utilized in radioimmunoassays (RIA) and immunoradiometric assays (IRMA) for the diagnosis of disorders of the hypothalamus–pituitary axis (West and Dolman, 1977).

Here we report the cloning and expression of a portion of the human POMC gene, corresponding to amino acids 59–241, as fused or unfused proteins.

## Materials and methods

A genomic POMC clone (pH-OX3) containing part of exonIII was kindly

*Genetic Transformation and Expression*
© Intercept Ltd., PO Box 716, Andover, Hants, SP10 1YG, UK

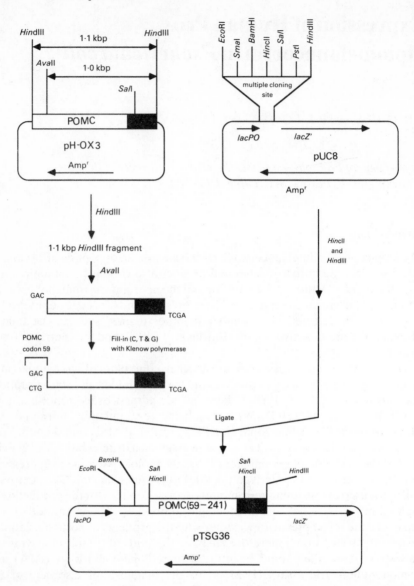

**Figure 41.1** Strategy used to clone a 1·0 kbp DNA fragment encoding amino acids 59–241 of the human POMC gene from pH-OX3 into pUC8.

provided by Professor J.L. Roberts (Mount Sinai Medical Center, New York). A 1·0 kbp DNA fragment coding for amino acids 59–241 was subcloned into the 5′ end of the *lacZ* gene in the expression vector pUC8 (Vieira and Messing, 1982) using the strategy shown in *Figure 41.1* to produce the recombinant plasmid pTSG36. This plasmid was then cleaved with the enzymes *Bam*HI and *Hin*dIII to release the POMC DNA which was then cloned into the 3′ end of the *lacZ* gene in the expression vector pUR291 (Ruther and Muller-Hill, 1983) to yield pTSG77, as shown in Figure 41.2. All restriction enzyme and ligation reactions were performed according to suppliers' recommendations.

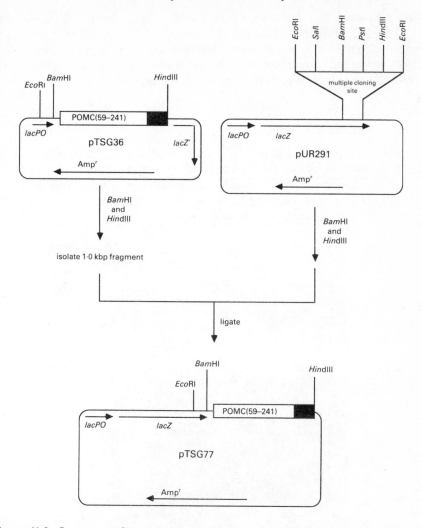

**Figure 41.2** Strategy used to generate a recombinant pUR291 vector expressing the β-galactosidase-POMC(59–241) fusion peptide.

Transformations of *E. coli* were carried out using the calcium chloride method (Mandel and Higa, 1970). The recombinant pTSG36 was used to transform *E. coli* CSR603 (Sancar and Rupert, 1978) and JM83 (Vieira and Messing, 1982), while plasmid pTSG77 was maintained in *E. coli* BMH71–18 (Messing *et al.*, 1977).

The proteins encoded by pTSG36 and pTSG77 were analysed using the maxicell procedure (Sancar, Hack and Rupp, 1979) and SDS-polyacrylamide gel electrophoresis (SDS-PAGE) (Laemmli, 1970), respectively.

Western blot analysis (Towbin, Staetelin, and Gordon, 1979) was used to check the antigenicity of the peptides produced by pTSG36 and pTSG77. The antibodies used were: antihuman γ-LPH (HA8), antihuman β-endorphin (BNS13), antihuman $γ_3$-MSH (SJ4 and Xavier), and antihuman ACTH(17–39)

442    *Gene Expression*

(CI); all antibodies were raised in rabbits, apart from the antihuman ACTH(1–24) (RW581B0) which was raised in sheep. Membrane-bound antigen–antibody complexes were detected using horseradish peroxidase (HRP) conjugated immunoglobins. All antibodies were kindly provided by Dr S. Jackson and Dr R. Woods (both in this department).

**Results and discussion**

Two plasmids (pTSG36 and pTSG77) were constructed. The cloning strategy used to produce them was designed so as to regenerate codon 59 of the POMC gene and to ensure the correct translational reading-frame. Both pTSG36 and pTSG77 plasmids were checked by restriction enzyme analysis to ensure that the constructs were correct (results not shown).

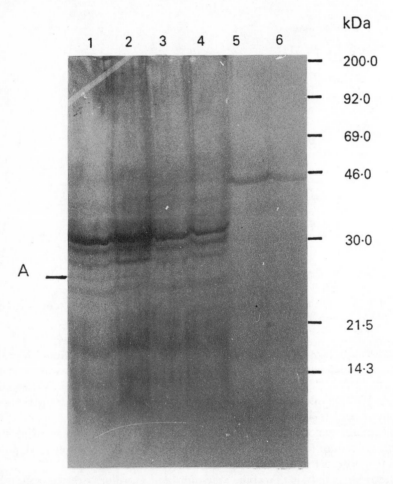

**Figure 41.3**  Autoradiograph of maxicell proteins separated on a 13·5% SDS-polyacrylamide gel. Cultures of *E. coli* CSR603 harbouring pTSG36 (1 and 2), pUC8 (3 and 4), or no plasmid (5 and 6) were labelled with 25 μCi of [35]S-methionine. The position of a novel 24 kDa peptide synthesized by pTSG36 is shown by A.

The proteins produced by maxicells harbouring pTSG36 were analysed by SDS-PAGE followed by autoradiography. The results (*Figure 41.3*) show that the recombinant plasmid directs the synthesis of a 24 kDa peptide; this is in close agreement with the expected molecular mass of POMC(59–241).

Analysis of total proteins from *E. coli* BMH71–18 harbouring pTSG77 indicates that this plasmid directs the synthesis of a 140 kDa $\beta$-galactosidase fusion peptide (*Figure 41.4*).

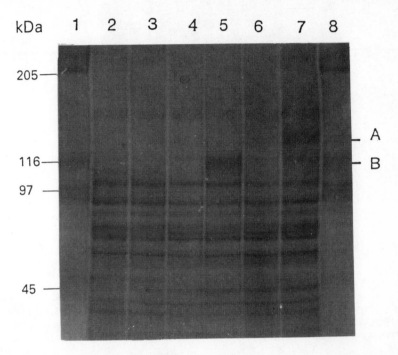

**Figure 41.4**   A 7·5% SDS-polyacrylamide gel of total cell proteins from *E. coli* BMH71–18 (2 and 3) harbouring pUR291 (4 and 5) or pTSG77 (6 and 7). Lanes 3, 5 and 7 represent cultures induced with 1mM IPTG. Protein molecular size markers are shown in 1 and 8. A and B show the positions of the 140 kDa $\beta$-galactosidase fusion peptide and $\beta$-galactosidase, respectively. The gel was stained with 0·2% (w/v) Coomassie blue.

Western blotting was used to establish whether these novel peptides produced by cultures containing pTSG36 or pTSG77 are recognized by antibodies raised against the processed POMC peptides. The results indicate that both the 24 kDa peptide (pTSG36) and the 140 kDa fusion protein (pTSG77) were recognized by the polyclonal sera HA8, BNS13, CI and RW581B0 but not by SJ4 and Xavier antihuman $\gamma_3$-MSH antibodies. A representative photograph of a Western blot is shown in *Figure 41.5*. The results are as expected since POMC(59–241) contains the coding regions for $\gamma$-LPH, $\beta$-endorphin and ACTH, while the $\gamma$-MSH region is not entirely contained within this fragment of POMC. Therefore, it can be concluded that the $\gamma_3$-MSH antibodies used in this investigation recognize epitopes at the amino terminus of $\gamma$-MSH, or that the $\beta$-galactosidase moiety exerted a steric hindrance effect.

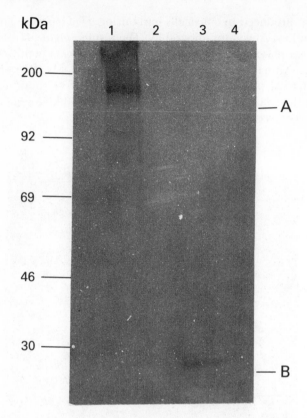

**Figure 41.5**  A Western blot of a 7·5% SDS-polyacrylamide gel incubated with antihuman ACTH(17–39). 1, *E. coli* JM83/pUC8; 2, JM83/pTSG36; 3, *E. coli* BMH71–18/pUR291; 4, BMH71–18/pTSG77. A and B indicate the position of the 140 kDa β-galactosidase–POMC(59–241) fusion protein, and the 24 kDa POMC(59–241) peptide, respectively.

The production of a β-galactosidase–POMC(59–241) fusion peptide has several advantages. First, the β-galactosidase fusion can be purified via a single step using *p*-aminobenzyl-1-thio-β-D-galactopyranoside affinity chromatography (Carroll and Laughon, 1985); since the fusion peptide retains β-galactosidase activity, its purification can be followed by a simple assay for the enzyme. Secondly, the β-galactosidase fusion protein provides some protection against degradation of the foreign portion of the peptide. Such degradation can be a major problem when trying to express foreign peptides in bacterial hosts. Another advantage of the fusion is that it acts as a hapten-carrier complex, which may elicit a stronger immunogenic response when used to raise polyclonal antibodies.

### References

BARDIN, C.W. CHEN, C.C., MORRIS, P.L., GERENDAI, I. BOITANI, C., LIOTTA A.S., MARGIORIS, A. AND KRIEGER, D. (1987). Proopiomelanocortin-derived peptides in testes, ovary and tissues of reproduction. *Recent Progress in Hormone Research* **43**, 1–28.

CARROLL, S.B. AND LAUGHON, A. (1985). Production and purification of polyclonal antibodies to a foreign segment of β-galactosidase fusion proteins. In *DNA Cloning, a Practical Approach, Volume III* (D. Glover, Ed.), pp. 89–111, IRL Press, Oxford.

LAEMMLI, U.K. (1970). Cleavage of structural proteins during assembly of the head of bacteriophage T4. *Nature* **227**, 680–686.

LOH, Y.P., BIRCH, N.P. AND CASTRO, M.G. (1988). Pro-opiomelanocortin and vasopressin converting enzyme in pituitary secretory vesicles. *Biochimie* **70**, 11–16.

MANDEL, M. AND HIGA, A. (1970). Calcium dependent bacteriophage DNA infection. *Journal of Molecular Biology* **53**, 154–160.

MESSING, J., GRONENBORN, B., MULLER-HILL, B. AND HOFSCHNEIDER, H. (1977). Filamentous coliphage M13 as a cloning vehicle: Insertion of a *Hind*III fragment of the *lac* regulatory region in the M13 replicative form *in vitro*. *Proceedings of the National Academy of Sciences of the United States of America* **74**, 3624–3646.

RUTHER, U. AND MULLER-HILL, B. (1983). Easy identification of cDNA clones. *EMBO Journal* **2**, 1791–1794.

SANCAR, A. AND RUPERT, C.S. (1978). Determination of plasmid molecular weights from ultraviolet sensitivities. *Nature* **272**, 471–472.

SANCAR, A., HACK, A.M. AND RUPP, W.D. (1979). Simple method of identifying plasmid-coded proteins. *Journal of Bacteriology* **137**, 692–693.

TOWBIN, H., STAETELIN, T. AND GORDON, J. (1979). Electrophoretic transfer of proteins from polyacrylamide gels to nitrocellulose sheets: Procedure and some applications. *Proceedings of the National Academy of Sciences of the United States of America* **76**, 4350–4354.

VIEIRA, J. AND MESSING, J. (1982). A new pair of M13 vectors for selecting either DNA strand of double-digest restriction fragments. *Gene* **19**, 269–276.

WEST, C.D. AND DOLMAN, L.I. (1977). Plasma ACTH radioimmunoassays in the diagnosis of pituitary–adrenal dysfunction. *Annals of the New York Academy of Science* **297**, 205–215.

# 42

# Induction of Levansucrase by Sucrose in *Bacillus subtilis*: Involvement of an Antitermination Mechanism Negatively Controlled by the PTS

D. LE COQ\*, A.M. CRUTZ\*, R. RICHTER\*, S. AYMERICH\*,
G. GONZY-TRÉBOUL[†], M. ZAGOREC\*, M.C. RAIN-GUION[†]
AND M. STEINMETZ\*

\* *Laboratoire de Génétique des Microorganismes, Institut National Agronomique, CBAI, 78850 Thiverval-Grignon, France and* [†]*Groupe Génétique et Membranes, Institut Jacques Monod, tour 43, 2 place Jussieu, 75005 Paris, France*

## Introduction

Sucrose induces at least three proteins in *B. subtilis* (Lepesant *et al.*, 1976): an intracellular sucrase (gene *sacA*), an extracellular levansucrase (gene *sacB*), and a sucrose-specific permease (EnzymeII[suc]; gene *sacP*) belonging to the phosphorylating transport system (PTS; for review *see* Postma and Lengeler, 1985). *sacP* and *sacA* appear to be organized in an operon and are not linked to *sacB* (Fouet *et al.*, 1987).

*sacB* regulation is beginning to be understood. The coding sequence is preceeded by a 400 bp regulatory region, called *sacR*, which contains the promoter and the targets for several regulators (*Figure 42.1*). A target for the products of the *sacU* and *sacQ* genes is located upstream from the promoter where these regulators, either directly or indirectly activate transcription initiation (Aymerich, Gonzy-Tréboul and Steinmetz, 1986; Zukowski and Miller, 1986; Henner *et al.*, 1987). A transcriptional terminator involved in *sacB* induction by sucrose is located just downstream from the promoter. Mutations or deletions altering this structure make *sacB* constitutive; the *sacB* promoter is constitutive but, in the absence of sucrose, transcripts are stopped at the terminator. It has therefore been proposed that *sacB* induction involves a novel type of transcriptional attenuation, modulated at the level of *sacR* by a sucrose-dependent regulator (Shimotsu and Henner, 1986; Steinmetz and Americh, 1986).

*Genetic Transformation and Expression*
© Intercept Ltd, PO Box 716, Andover, Hants, SP10 1YG, UK

**(a)**

**(b)**

```
BglC    MNMQITKILNNNVVVVIDDQQREKVVMGRGIGFQKRAGERINSSGIEKEYALSSHELNGR
        = = -=== = -== = -== ==- ==---= == ===- - - = === -
SacY    MKIKRILNHNAIVVK-DQNEEKILLGAGIAFNKKKNDIVDPSKIEKTFIRKDTPDYKQ


        LSELLSHIPLEVMATCDRIISLAQERLG-KLQDSIYISLTDHCQFAIKRFQQNVLLPNPL
        ==-= -= - -== = = =---= - - -== === = - -== ===
        FEEILETLPEDHIQISEQIISHAEKELNIKINERIHVAFSDHLSFAIERLSNGMVIKNPL
                       ↓                                  ↓
                       P                                  Y
        LWDIQRLYPKEFQLGEEALTII-DKRLGVQLPKDEVGFIAMHLVSA-QMSGNMEDVAGVT
        = -= ======== = -= == ==- -= ===- ===== -= - = = -=
        LNEIKVLYPKEFQIGLWARALIKDK-LGIHIPDDEIGNIAMHIHTARNNAGDMTQTLDIT


        QLMREMLQLIKFQFSLNYQEESLSYQRLVTHLKFLSWRILEHASINDSDESLQQAVKQNY
        --=---- -= = === =----== ======= = == - = - -= -
        TMIRDIIEIIEIQLSINIVEDTISYERLVTHLRFAIQHIKAGESIYELDAEMIDIIKEKF


        PQAWQCAERIAIFIGLQYQRKISPAEIMFLAINIERVRKEH
        = == = =- = =- ---= = =
        KDAFLCALSIGTFVKKEYGFEFPEKELCYIAMHIQRFYQRSVAR
```

**Figure 42.1**  (a) Organization of the regulatory region upstream from *sacB*. SD, Shine–Dalgarno; thick black arrow, start of transcription; thin black arrows, palindromic structure; broken line, target of the SacU and SacQ regulators (direct interaction with this target has not been demonstrated). (b) Homology between SacY and the BglC antiterminator of *E. coli*. '=' and '−' represent identical amino acids or conservative changes, respectively. The *sacS* constitutive mutations sequenced are indicated by arrows. The H→Y substitution was observed for two independent mutants.

The *sacS* locus, which is linked to neither *sacA* nor *sacB*, was identified by several kinds of mutations, some of which render both these genes constitutive (Lepesant *et al.*, 1976). This locus was cloned and shown to contain a gene coding for a positive regulator of *sacB* expression. It was observed that this positive regulator was no longer required for *sacB* expression when the *sacR* terminator was inactivated by mutation. Therefore it was suggested that *sacS* encoded an antiterminator that interacts with the *sacR* transcript (Aymerich and Steinmetz, 1987).

### Structure of the *sacS* locus: the *sacX* and *sacY* genes

The *sacS* locus was recently sequenced and shown to contain two open reading-frames (ORF), *sacX* (460 codons) and *sacY* (280 codons), which might constitute an operon (Steinmetz *et al.*, 1988; Zukowski *et al.*, 1988; Zukowski *et*

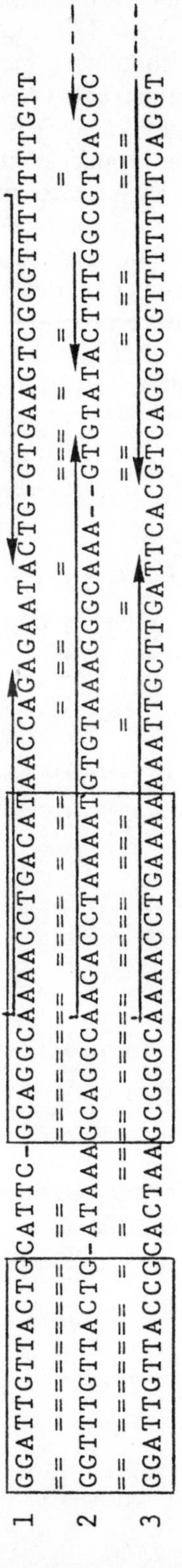

```
1  GGATTGTTACTGCATTC-GCAGGCAAAACCTGACATAACCAGAGAATACTG-GTGAAGTCGGGTTTTTTTGTT
   ==  ========== ==  ======== ==== == ||  ||   ||  ===  || || === ||
2  GGTTTGTTACTG-ATAAAGCAGGCAAGACCTAAAATGTGTAAAGGGCAAA--GTGTATACTTTGGCGTCACCC
   == ======== ||  ===== ===== ==== ==     || ||       ||  || ||  |||  |||
3  GGATTGTTACCGCACTAAGCGGGCAAAACCTGAAAAAAATTGCTTGATTCACGTCAGCGCCGTTTTTTTCAGGT
```

**Figure 42.2**  Homology between *term1* (1) or *term2* (3), the two *E. coli* terminators involved in the *bgl* operon regulation, and the *B. subtilis sacR* terminator (2). '=' represents identical nucleotides.

*al.*, in preparation). *sacY*, downstream from *sacX*, encodes the putative antiterminator. The direct interaction of SacY with *sacR* is very likely since it was recently shown that a plasmid containing *sacY* could stimulate the expression of a *sacR::lacZ* fusion in *E. coli* (Aymerich and Steinmetz, unpublished results). As shown in *Figure 42.1*, SacY is highly homologous with an *E. coli* putative antiterminator, the product of the *bglC* gene (Schnetz, Toloczyki and Rak, 1987). BglC probably interacts with two terminators that show sequence homology with the *sacR* terminator (Mahadevan and Wright, 1987; Schnetz, Toloczyki and Rak, 1987) (*Figure 42.2*). The *bgl* operon was also negatively controlled by the product of the *bglS* gene that encodes EnzymeII$^{bgl}$. Convincing arguments were proposed suggesting that, in the absence of inducer, BglS inhibited the BglC antiterminator through a direct interaction (Mahadevan, Reynolds and Wright, 1987).

```
1 MDFEQISCSLLPLLGGKENIASAAL-ATRLRLVLVDDSLADQQAIGKVEGVKGCFRNAGQMQIIFGTGVVNKVY
  =     == = === == =       ====  = --- =  = == = =  == ===== ======-=
2 MH-KEIAKELLLLAGGKNNIISISHCTTRLRFDVKDETKIDIHAIENLQGVQGTFFRYGLFQIIFGAGVVNKIY
  = == == =- = === ==== == ==== -===-=== -= = == = = - ====== =-====-
3 MDYKETAKRLIELLGGKENIISAAHCATRLRLVMKDESKIDQAQVEELDGVKGAFSSSGQYQIIFGTGLVNKVP

1 AAFTQAAGISES-SKSEAADIAAKKLNPFQRIARLLSNIFVPIIPAIVASGLLMGLLGMVKTYGWVDPGNAIYI
  =           = -===  =- == ========== ========--==-=  =
2 KEVVHVWETAPSEEPVNHQKKASRKLNPAAAFAKTLSDIFVPIIPAITASGLLMGLIGMIKVFHNFAAGSPWIK
  -       ==  ===== ====== ========== ===========-=== == =  = -
3 DAFSKEAD-IEREEHVNHQDAAKEKLNPAARFAKTLSNIFVPIIPAIVASGLLMGLLGMINAFHWMSKDSALLQ

1 MLDMCSSAAFIILPILIGFTAAREFGGNPYLGATLGGILTHPALTNAWGVAAGFH-TMNFFGFEIAMIGYQGTV
  ===  ==  === ====== == =====  = ==== = =-==== =   -     -- = =-=====--
2 MLDLVSSTAFILLPILVGFSAARQFGSNPYLGAVIAGLLTHPDLLDPSMLGGKTPSSLDIWGLHIPMMGYQGSM
  -==- == ==== ====- - ======== === == ==  = =  = = - =
3 LLDMFSSAAFIFLPILIGFSASKEFGSNPYLGAVIGGIMIHPNLLNPWGLAEEQL-ITCIFSDLISLFSATGNC

1 FPVLLAVWFMSIVEKQLRRAIPDALDLILTPFLTVIISGFIALLIIGPAGRALGDGISFVLSTLISHAGWLAGL
  =-== = = -== = = -=  = ==-=== = ======- -===-= == -= -- - === ==
2 IPILLSVFVMRKIEKLLKSIVPKSLDVVIIPFITVMVTGCLALIVMNPAASIIGQIMTQSIVYIYDHAGIAAGA
  =          =---- ==-===-== -= = =  = === -= = -====== == =
3 YPCPACGVCDEQGREMDEKSGSTCGDLLVTPFVTVIVTGFVAFIAIGPLGRALGSGITVALTYVYDHAGFVAGL

1 LFGGLYSVYVITGIHHSFHAVEAGLLGNPSIGVNFLLPIWAMANVAQGGACLAVWFKTKDAKIKAITLPSAFSA
  ==== == =--=== ==- = === == -= ========== === === -= = ==  -=
2 LFGGIYSTIVLSGLHHSFYAIEATLLANPHVGYNFLVPIWSMANVAQGGAGLAVFLKTKQSSLKKIALPASLTA
  -=== == ======= == == -= ==  =  = ===== ==-  ==  = ===== -=
3 IFGGTYSLIVLTGVHHSFHAIEAGLIAD--IGKNYLLPIWSMANVAQGGAGLAVFFMAKKAKTKEIALPAAFSA

1 MLGITEAAIFGINLRFVKPFIAALIGGAAGGAWVVSVHVYMTAVGLTAIPGMAIVGASSLLNYIIGMVMPLASP
  === = -===-==- --=== = ==== === == = =  === == - == =-- =- =
2 FLGIVEPIVFGVNLKLIRPFIGAAIGGAIGGAYVVAVQVVANSYGLTGIPMISIVLPFGAANFVHYMIGFLIAA
  ==== ===== ==== === === ==== === =  == === = === = =-=== =  ===
3 FLGITEPVIFGVNLRYRKPFIAAMIGGALGGAYVVFTHVAANAYGLTGIPMIAIAAPFGFSNLIHYLIGMAIAA

1 LRC---SLVLKYKTDAE
  -       -= = -= = =
2 VSAFIATLFLGFKEETE
  ======= - =- =
3 VSAFIAAFVMKINEDEERKK
```

**Figure 42.3** Homology between EnzymesII$^{suc}$. ScrA (1), SacX (2) and SacP (3). '=' and '—' represent identical amino acids or conservative changes, respectively.

The SacX protein shows strong homologies with the products of *sacP* and another gene encoding an EnzymeII$^{suc}$, *scrA* (Ebner and Lengeler, 1988) (*Figure 42.3*). These homologies and unpublished observations suggest that *sacX* encodes a second *B. subtilis* EnzymeII$^{suc}$. Since the *sacP* mutants do not grow on sucrose, the *sacX* contribution to sucrose permeation would be very low in a wild-type strain but might play a regulatory role. Insertion of transposon Tn917 into *sacX* renders *sacB* constitutive. In the *sacX::Tn917* mutant, the *sacY* gene was expressed from a relatively strong promoter present within the transposon. This constitutivity decreased markedly if the strain carrying the insertion was transformed by a multicopy plasmid bearing a functional *sacX* gene (*Table 42.1*). This suggests that the product of *sacX* exerts a negative control on levansucrase induction (Aymerich and Steinmetz, 1987; Steinmetz *et al.*, unpublished results).

**Table 42.1** *sacB* phenotypes associated with different mutations

| Relevant genotype | *sacB* phenotype |
|---|---|
| wild type | inducible |
| *sacX*::Tn917 | constitutive |
| *sacX*::Tn917, p(*sacX*)* | weakly constitutive |
| *ptsI*::Tn917 | constitutive |
| △*sacY* | negative |
| *ptsI*::Tn917, △*sacY* | negative |

\*  p(*sacX*), replicative multicopy plasmid bearing the *sacX* gene.

### Cloning and characterization of *sacS* constitutive mutations

We have cloned and characterized the mutations from previously isolated *sacS* mutants that constitutively expressed levansucrase. These mutations were mapped by transformation, using a collection of plasmids containing different parts of *sacS*. We then used a *B. subtilis–E. coli* shuttle plasmid to clone *in vivo* the *sacS* mutant locus. This was done by a conversion event, which was detected by the loss of an antibiotic resistance (*Figure 42.4*). Ten independent *sacS* constitutive mutations were mapped and all but one were localized in the *sacY* gene. Preliminary results suggest that the only exception was not a point mutation. Three of the mutations have been sequenced and have been shown to be mis-sense point mutations; one to a serine to proline substitution at position 73 and the other two to an identical histidine to tyrosine substitution at position 99 (*Figure 42.1*).

### Involvement of the PTS in *sacB* induction

It had been previously observed that *B. subtilis ptsI* mutants deficient in the EnzymeI of the PTS constitutively expressed *sacB*. This property allowed the selection of an insertion of transposon Tn917 into *ptsI* and subsequent cloning of this chromosomal region (Gonzy-Tréboul and Steinmetz, 1987). This region contains four ORFs in the same orientation and in the following order: *orfG*, *ptsX, ptsH* and *ptsI*. The products of *ptsX* and *orfG* are strongly homologous to

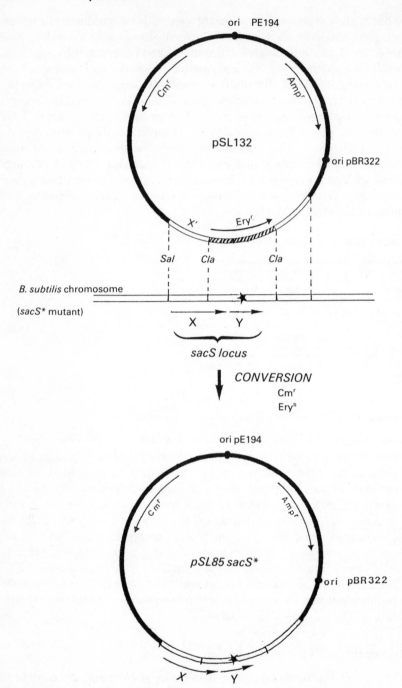

**Figure 42.4** Cloning of *sacS* mutations by selecting a conversion event. The *sacS* mutant is transformed by pSL132 and Cm$^r$ Ery$^s$ clones selected. The resulting plasmid, (pSL85*sacS*), was extracted and introduced in *E. coli*. The star symbolizes the mutation. Plasmid pSL132 is a derivative of pSL42 (Aymerich and Steinmetz, 1987) with the origin of replication of pE194 and a *Cla*I fragment in *sacS* replaced by an erythromycin-resistance gene.

the products of enteric *crr* and *ptsG* genes, respectively (Gonzy-Tréboul *et al.*, 1989), and additional data suggest that *orfG* and *ptsX* encode the glucose-specific EnzymeII–EnzymeIII pair (unpublished results).

Strains harbouring a *ptsI*::Tn*917* insertion (or a *ptsI* deletion) constitutively express *sacB*, however, this constitutivity is abolished by the introduction of a *sacY* deletion (Steinmetz *et al.*, 1988). Therefore, a *sacY* deletion is epistatic on the *ptsI* insertion.

## Phenotype of *sacX* mutations

Since most of the *sacS* constitutive mutations affected *sacY*, we constructed two *sacX* mutations and introduced them in the *B.subtilis* chromosome. The first corresponded to a frameshift mutation (a *ClaI* site, in the middle of *sacX*, filled in by Klenow polymerase) and the second to an in-frame deletion (deletion from codon 240 to codon 452). The corresponding mutants expressed *sacB* at a low constitutive level and were slightly overinducible. This constitutive *sacB* expression was some tenfold lower than that observed in the *sacY* constitutive mutant. This low level of constitutivity could be due to a polar effect on *sacY* expression. We therefore constructed *sacX–ptsI* double mutants and observed that they expressed *sacB* constitutively at the (high) level observed in a *ptsI* mutant. Since *ptsI* controls *sacB* via *sacY*, this result makes it unlikely that the *sacX* mutations have a polar effect on *sacY* expression.

## Discussion

A model is proposed on the basis of:

1. The homology between SacX and two EnzymesII$^{suc}$;
2. The homologies at several levels with the regulation of the *E. coli bgl* operon; and
3. Our observations concerning the involvement of the PTS.

The SacX protein is a functional but minor EnzymeII$^{suc}$ with a mainly regulatory role. In the absence of sucrose, this integral membrane protein would be fully phosphorylated by the PTS and, in this phosphorylated form, would inhibit the antiterminator function of SacY. Sucrose would be taken and phosphorylated at least partially via SacX. Consequently, dephosphorylated SacX would no longer inhibit the SacY antiterminator. A mutation in *ptsI* would prevent phosphorylation of SacX and render *sacB* constitutive (*Figure 42.5*).

However, some of our observations indicate that the situation is more complex. In the case of the *bgl* system of *E. coli*, a majority of constitutive mutations affect the negative regulator (BglS/EnzymeII$^{bgl}$) and are *trans*-recessive, while only rare *trans*-dominant constitutive mutations affect the BglC antiterminator (Mahadevan, Reynolds and Wright, 1987). In our case, 10 *sacS* constitutive mutations were mapped and all but one localized in *sacY*, the structural gene of the antiterminator. The effect of a multicopy plasmid bearing *sacX* and the phenotype of the *sacX* mutants point towards a negative role for

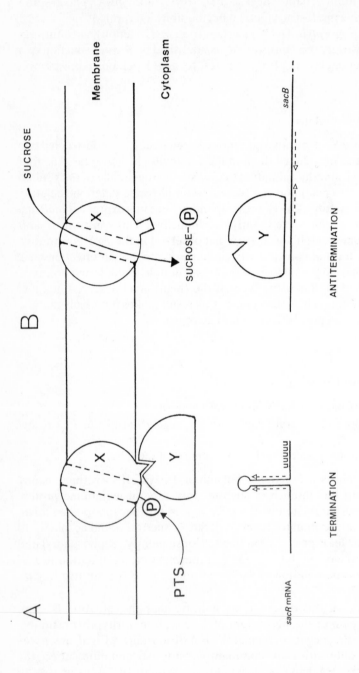

**Figure 42.5**   A model for *sacB* induction by SacX and SacY. It is proposed that SacX is a functional EnzymeII$^{\text{suc}}$ inserted in the membrane. The PTS phosphorylates SacX (A) and the resulting phosphorylated EnzymeII inhibits the SacY antiterminator. In presence of sucrose in the medium (B), this sugar is used as a phosphoryl acceptor and concomitantly internalized. This results in SacX dephosphorylation and a consequential relief of SacY inhibition, which could then interact with nascent *sacR* transcript and prevent termination. P, phosphoryl residue; X and Y, the SacX and SacY proteins, respectively. This model suggests that phosphorylated SacX can sequester SacY. A variant can be proposed: SacX could phosphorylate (and inactivate) SacY. As discussed in the text, some results suggest that in addition to SacX, a second protein could inhibit SacY.

this gene. However, the *sacX* mutants are weakly constitutive, far less so than the *sacY* constitutive mutants. This shows that the selection of the constitutive mutants was largely biased and suggests that *sacY* is negatively controlled by a second protein in addition to SacX. Mutations in *sacY* could render its product insensitive to both of these synergistic negative regulators. This second regulator would also be dependent on both the PTS and sucrose, since the *ptsI* mutations render *sacB* fully consitutive and sucrose overinduces the *sacX* mutants.

## Acknowledgement

We are very grateful to Mark Zukowski and his collaborators for helpful information and discussions.

## References

AYMERICH, S. AND STEINMETZ, M. (1987). Cloning and preliminary characterization of the *sacS* locus from *Bacillus subtilis* which controls the regulation of the exoenzyme levansucrase. *Molecular and General Genetics* **208**, 114–120.

AYMERICH, S., GONZY-TRÉBOUL, G. AND STEINMETZ, M. (1986). 5'-non-coding region *sacR* is the target of all identified regulation affecting the levansucrase gene in *Bacillus subtilis*. *Journal of Bacteriology* **166**, 993–998.

EBNER, R. AND LENGELER, J.W. (1988). Sucrose-specific EnzymeII$^{scr}$ of the bacterial phosphotransferase system: nucleotide sequence of the gene *scrA* from pUR400. *Molecular Microbiology* **2**, 9–17.

FOUET, A., ARNAUD, M., KLIER, A. AND RAPPOPORT, G. (1987). *Bacillus subtilis* sucrose-specific EnzymeII of the phosphotransferase system. Expression in *Escherichia coli* and homology to EnzymesII from enteric bacteria. *Proceedings of the National Academy of Sciences of the United States of America* **84**, 8773–8777.

GONZY-TRÉBOUL, G. AND STEINMETZ, M. (1987). Phosphoenolpyruvate: sugar phosphotransferase system of *Bacillus subtilis*: cloning of the region containing the *ptsH* and *ptsI* genes and evidence for a *crr* like gene. *Journal of Bacteriology* **169**, 2287–2290.

GONZY-TRÉBOUL, G., ZAGOREC, M., RAIN-GUION, M.C. AND STEINMETZ, M. (1989). Phosphoenolpyruvate: sugar phosphotransferase system of *Bacillus subtilis* – nucleotide sequence of *ptsX*, *ptsH* and the 5'-end of *ptsI* and evidence for a *ptsHI* operon. *Molecular Microbiology* **3**, 103–112.

HENNER, D.J., YANG, M., BAND, L., SHIMOTSU, H., RUPEN, M. AND FERRARI, E. (1987). Genes of *Bacillus subtilis* that regulate the expression of degradative enzymes. In *Fifth International Symposium on the Genetics of Industrial Microorganisms* (M. Alacevic, D. Hranuelli and Z. Toman, Eds), pp. 81–90. Academic Press, New York.

LEPESANT, J.A., KUNST, F., PASCAL, M., LEPESANT-KEJZLAROVA, J., STEINMETZ, M. AND DEDONDER, R. (1976). Specific and pleiotropic regulatory mechanisms in the sucrose system of *B. subtilis* 168. In *Microbiology 1976* (D. Schlessinger, Ed.), pp. 58–69. American Society for Microbiology, Washington, DC.

MAHADEVAN, S. AND WRIGHT, A. (1987). A bacterial gene involved in transcription antitermination: regulation at a rho-independent terminator in the *bgl* operon of *E. coli*. *Cell* **50**, 485–494.

MAHADEVAN, S., REYNOLDS, A.E. AND WRIGHT, A. (1987). Positive and negative regulation of the *bgl* operon of *E. coli*. *Journal of Bacteriology* **169**, 2570–2578.

POSTMA, P.W. AND LENGELER, J.W. (1985). Phosphoenolpyruvate: carbohydrate phosphotransferase system of bacteria. *Microbiological Reviews* **49**, 232–269.

SCHNETZ, K., TOLOCZYKI, C. AND RAK, B. (1987). The β-glucoside (*bgl*) operon of *Escherichia coli* K-12: Nucleotide sequence, genetic organization and possible evolutionary relationship to regulatory components of two *Bacillus subtilis* genes. *Journal of Bacteriology* **169**, 2579–2590.

SHIMOTSU, H. AND HENNER, D. (1986). Regulation of the *Bacillus subtilis sacB* gene: sucrose modulates expression via an attenuation mechanism, the *sacU* and *sacQ* genes regulate the steady-state mRNA level. *Journal of Bacteriology* **168**, 380–388.

STEINMETZ, M. AND AYMERICH, S. (1986). Analyse génétique de *sacR*, régulateur en *cis* de la synthèse de la lévane-saccharase de *Bacillus subtilis*. *Annales de Microbiologie de l'Institut Pasteur (Paris)* **137A**, 3–14.

STEINMETZ, M., AYMERICH, S., GONZY-TRÉBOUL, G. AND LE COQ, D. (1988). Levansucrase induction by sucrose in *Bacillus subtilis* involves an antiterminator. Homology with the *Escherichia coli bgl* operon. In *The Fourth International Conference on Genetics and Biotechnology of Bacilli* (A.T. Ganesan and J.A. Hoch, Eds), pp. 11–15. Academic Press, New York.

ZUKOWSKI, M. AND MILLER, L. (1986). Hyperproduction of an intracellular heterologous protein in a *sacU*[h] mutant of *B. subtilis*. *Gene* **46**, 247–255.

ZUKOWSKI, M., MILLER, L., COGSWELL, P. AND CHEN, K. (1988). An inducible expression system based on sucrose metabolism genes of *Bacillus subtilis*. In *The Fourth International Conference on Genetics and Biotechnology of Bacilli* (A.T. Ganesan and J.A. Hoch, Eds), pp.17–22. Academic Press, New York.

# 43

# Cloning and Characterization of *Bacillus subtilis* Transcription Units Involved in Synthesis of the ATP-Dependent Dnase

JAN KOOISTRA, BEN VOSMAN AND GERARD VENEMA

*Department of Genetics, University of Groningen, Kerklaan 30, 9751 NN Haren(Gn), The Netherlands*

## Introduction

In *Escherichia coli* three genes, *recB, recC* and *recD*, encoding proteins with molecular masses of 135 kDa, 125 kDa and 58 kDa, respectively (Hickson and Emmerson, 1981; Amundsen *et al.*, 1986), are involved in the synthesis of ATP-dependent Dnase(ADD). *E. coli recB recC* mutants show a reduced recombination in conjugation and generalized transduction and are impaired in the ability to repair DNA damage (Clark, 1973).

The data concerning the composition of the *Bacillus subtilis* ADD enzyme are contradictory. Doly and Anagnostopoulos (1976) have reported that the enzyme consists of five different subunits with molecular masses of 81 kDa, 70 kDa, 62 kDa, 52 kDa and 40 kDa, whereas Chestukhin *et al.* (1972) reported that the enzyme is composed of only two subunits with molecular masses of 130 kDa and 155 kDa. The ADD-deficient *recE5* mutant of *B. subtilis* (Doly, Masarman and Anagnostopoulos, 1974) exhibited reduced transformation with chromosomal DNA and was also poorly transducible.

To study the role of the ADD enzyme in recombination in *B. subtilis*, we attempted to clone and characterize the genes encoding the *B. subtilis* ADD subunits.

## Materials and Methods

In general, the materials and methods used have been described elsewhere (Kooistra, Vosman and Venema, 1988).

### *IN VITRO* TRANSCRIPTION/TRANSLATION

*In vitro* transcription and translation from plasmid DNA was performed with

458     *Gene Expression*

the aid of the 'Prokaryotic DNA-directed translation kit' (Amersham International plc, UK) as recommended by the manufacturer. After the reaction, samples (8 μl) were electrophoresed on an SDS-polyacrylamide (7·5%) gel according to Laemmli (1970). Samples were heated for 10 min at 100°C before being applied to the gel. Molecular size marker proteins consisted of the ¹⁴C-methylated proteins: lysozyme (14·3 kDa), carbonic anhydrase (30 kDa), ovalbumin (46 kDa), bovine serum albumin (69 kDa), phosphorylase b (92·5 kDa) and myosin (200 kDa) (Amersham International). Electrophoresis was conducted at room temperature for about 2·5 hours at a constant current of 25 mA. After electrophoresis the gel was dried in a Gel Slab Dryer (model 483 Biorad Laboratories) and then autoradiographed by overlaying with a Kodak XAR-5 film.

## Results and discussion

### ISOLATION OF ADD-DEFICIENT MUTANTS

By insertional mutagenesis of a *B. subtilis* 8G5 strain (Bron and Venema, 1972) with the plasmid pHV60 (Michel, Niaudet and Ehrlich, 1983), mutants were isolated which were deficient in transformation and showed an increased sensitivity to mitomycin-C(MC) as compared to that of the wild-type strain. A number of these mutants lacked ATP-dependent DNase activity.

### ISOLATION OF A PLASMID CONTAINING *add* NUCLEOTIDE SEQUENCES

With the aid of one of the mutants, obtained by insertion into the chromosome of pHV60 containing chromosomal *Eco*RI fragments, a plasmid was isolated that contained *add*-specific sequences. The DNA of this mutant was digested with *Pst*I and, after ligation, was transformed into an *E. coli* JM83 (Vieira and Messing, 1982). From the resulting tetracycline-resistance (Tcʳ) transformants, a plasmid was isolated (plasmid pKV42) that contained a 4·2 kbp *Eco*RI–*Pst*I chromosomal DNA fragment. When pKV42 DNA was transformed into *add*-deficient mutants, *add-71* and *add-72* (C. Anagnostopoulos, personal communication), transformants with a wild-type Add⁺ phenotype were formed, showing that the chromosomal fragment contained *add*-specific sequences. However, after transformation of an *add-5* mutant (i.e. *recE5*; Doly, Sasarman and Anagnostopoulos, 1974; C. Anagnostopoulos, personal communication) with pKV42, none of the transformants showed a wild-type Add⁺ phenotype, indicating that, in contrast to the *add-71* and *add-72* mutations, the sequence altered in the *add-5* mutation was not present on the 4·2 kbp *Eco*RI–*Pst*I fragment. It appears, therefore, that the *Eco*RI–*Pst*I fragment does not contain the entire region involved in ADD-synthesis.

### SCREENING OF A *B. SUBTILIS* CHROMOSOMAL DNA BANK IN λ EMBL4

To isolate a larger DNA fragment than the 4·2 kbp *Eco*RI–*Pst*I fragment, a genome bank in phage λ EMBL4, containing 12–17 kbp *Eco*RI fragments of

he *B. subtilis* chromosome, was screened with plasmid pKV42 as a probe. The
ecombinant phage hybridizing with this probe contained a 13·3 kbp *Eco*RI
hromosomal DNA fragment. This fragment was inserted into the *Eco*RI site
·f the kanamycin-resistance (Km$^r$) plasmid, pGV1, which can replicate both in
:. *coli* and *B. subtilis* (Vosman *et al.*, 1987). This resulted in plasmid pGV133.
When pGV133 DNA was used to transform mutants containing *add-5, add-71*
·r *add-72*, transformants with the wild-type Add$^+$ phenotype were formed,
ndicating that all three *add* mutations are located within the sequence
ontained on this 13·3 kbp *Eco*RI fragment.

LOCALIZATION OF AN *add* TRANSCRIPTION UNIT

n order to determine whether the 13·3 kbp *Eco*RI fragment contained an
entire *add* transcription unit, various restriction fragments of the 13·3 kbp
*Eco*RI fragment (*Figure 43.1*) were subcloned into pUC9 or pUC19 (Vieira
and Messing, 1982), together with a fragment containing the erythromycin-
esistance marker (Em$^r$) derived from pE194 (Iordanescu, 1977). A wild-type
strain of *B. subtilis* was transformed with these plasmids and Em$^r$ transformants
elected. Because these plasmids contain no *B. subtilis* replicon the resulting
Em$^r$ transformants must have arisen by integration into the host chromosome
>y a Campbell-like recombination between homologous DNA on the plasmid.
The Em$^r$ transformants were tested for sensitivity to MC. Em$^r$ transformants
hat were as resistant to MC as the wild-type strain, and which therefore had an
ADD-proficient phenotype, contained a plasmid with either one end of the
ranscription unit or no part of the transcription unit at all. Em$^r$ transformants
hat were more sensitive to MC than the wild-type strain, and which had an
ADD mutant phenotype, contained a plasmid with a DNA fragment that was
nternal to the transcription unit. *Figure 43.1* summarizes the results and shows
hat one end of the *add* transcription unit was located on a *Sph*I(1)–*Hin*dIII(2)
ragment and the other end on the *Xba*I(2)–*Sma*I fragment. Therefore, the
3·3 kbp *Eco*RI fragment contained an entire *add* transcription unit, which was
ocated between the left-hand *Sph*I site and the right-hand *Sma*I site (*Figure
3.1*). The *add* transcription unit is flanked by a unique *Eco*RI site on the left and
unique *Sma*I site on the right. This 7·7 kbp *Eco*RI–*Sma*I fragment was inserted
nto plasmid pGV1, resulting in plasmid pGV77.

COMPLEMENTATION IN AN *add* DELETION MUTANT

o examine whether plasmid pGV77, containing the *add* transcription unit,
ould complement a mutant in which the entire transcription unit was deleted,
n *add* deletion mutant was constructed. The *Sph*I(1)–*Sph*I(3) fragment was
eplaced by a fragment containing the Cm$^r$ gene from pC194 (Iordanescu,
975). When this *add* deletion mutant was transformed with plasmid pGV77,
ne resulting Km$^r$ transformants were as resistant to MC as the wild-type strain.
his indicates that plasmid pGV77 can complement the *add* deletion mutant
nd must contain the entire *add* transcription unit in an intact form.

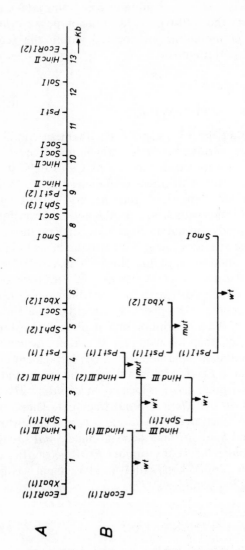

**Figure 43.1** Restriction map of the 13·3 kbp *Eco*RI fragment and localization of the *addA* transcription unit. (A) Restriction map of the 13·3 kbp *Eco*RI fragment. (B) Restriction fragments inserted into pUC plasmids for transformation of a *B. subtilis* wild-type Add⁺ strain. The fragments that transformed the recipient to an Add⁻ phenotype are indicated by *mut*, those which did not, by *wt*.

ETERMINATION OF THE *add* GENE PRODUCT

he gene product of the *add* transcription unit was identified in an *in vitro* anscription/translation system using plasmid pGV77. The results (*Figure 43.2*) ow that plasmid pGV77 encodes a protein with a Mr of approximately 150 Da, which is not produced by plasmid pGV1. Several other smaller bands were tected, which may represent breakdown products of the 150 kDa protein, ossibly due to proteolytic activity in the *E. coli* transcription/translation stem. The observation that plasmid pGV77 specified a protein of approximately 150 kDa, is in good agreement with the data of Chestukhin *et al.* 972).

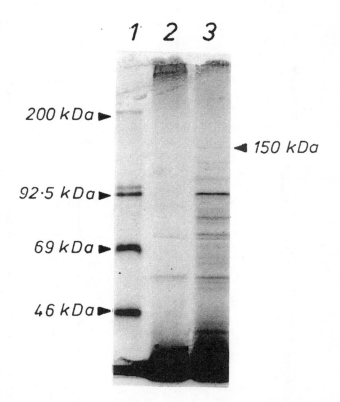

**gure 43.2** *In vitro* transcription/translation of pGV77. The proteins formed by *in vitro* anscription/translation were labelled with [35]S-methionine, separated by PAGE and autoradiog- phed. Lane 1, molecular size markers; lane 2, proteins formed from plasmid pGV1; lane 3, oteins formed from plasmid pGV77, containing the cloned *addA* transcription unit.

APPING OF THE *add* MUTATIONS

he *add-5, add-71* and *add-72* mutations were mapped to determine whether ey were located in the same transcription unit. It was found that wild-type, dd⁺ transformants were formed when all three *add* mutants were ansformed with DNA of pGV1 carrying the *Xba*I(1)–*Xba*I(2) fragment

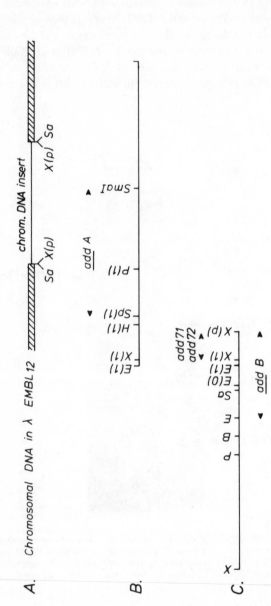

**Figure 43.3**   Cloning of the *addB* transcription unit. (A) *B. subtilis* chromosomal DNA (*Sau*3A fragments) in phage λ EMBL12. The chromosomal DNA fragments were inserted into the *Bam*HI site of phage λ EMBL12, in which they are flanked by unique *Xba*I and *Sal*I sites. (B) The 13·3 kbp *Eco*RI fragment (*Figure 43.1*) containing the *addA* transcription unit. (C) Chromosomal DNA fragment in phage λ EMBL12 hybridizing with the *Eco*RI(1)–*Hind*III(1) fragment. B,E, H,P, S, Sp and X represent *Bam*HI, *Eco*RI, *Hind*III, *Pst*I, *Sal*I, *Sph*I and *Xba*I sites, respectively.

*Figure 43.1*). Add⁺ transformants were recovered when an *add-5* mutant was transformed with plasmid pHV60, carrying the *PstI*(1)–*PstI*(2) fragment, and then both *add-71* and *add-72* mutants were transformed with plasmid pHV60, carrying the *EcoRI*(1)–*HindIII*(1) fragment. From these results it can be concluded that the *add-5* mutation is located between the *PstI*(1) and *XbaI*(2) sites (designated *addA*), and *add-71* and *add-72* mutations are located between the *XbaI*(1) and the *HindIII*(1) sites on the cloned fragment. This implies that the *add-71* and *add-72* mutations are not located in the *addA* transcription unit, but are located in a second *add* transcription unit, designated *addB*.

CLONING OF THE *addB* TRANSCRIPTION UNIT

The *addB* transcription unit was identified in a *B. subtilis* genome bank of 2–17 kbp *Sau3A* fragments in phage λ EMBL12 (Natt and Scherer, 1986) by screening with plasmid pHV60, carrying the *EcoRI*(1)–*HindIII*(1) fragment (*Figure 43.1*). One recombinant phage hybridizing with this probe contained two *XbaI* fragments of 1·2 kbp and 9·0 kbp. Transformation of mutants *add-71* or *add-72* with plasmid pGV1 carrying the 1·2 kbp *XbaI* fragment produced ADD proficient Kmʳ transformants, indicating that the *add-71* and *add-72* mutations were located between the *XbaI*(1) and the *XbaI*(p) sites (*Figure 43.3*). The *XbaI*(1) site corresponded to the *XbaI*(1) site on the 13·3 kbp *EcoRI* fragment (*Figure 43.1*). The *XbaI*(p) site was not present on the chromosome, and most probably represents an *XbaI* site in λ EMBL12 (*Figure 43.3*). A similar analysis as that of the *addA* transcription unit showed that one end of the *addB* transcription unit was located between the *XbaI*(1) and *XbaI*(p) sites, and the other was located between the *EcoRI*(0) and *EcoRI*(1) site (*Figure 43.3*). The *addB* transcription unit is therefore flanked by a unique *SalI* site on the left and a unique *HindIII* site (*HindIII*(1)) on the right.

Note

Some of the results have been published in *Journal of Bacteriology* **170**, 4791–4797.

References

AMUNDSEN, S.K., TAYLOR, A.F., CHAUDHURY, A.M. AND SMITH, G.R. (1986). *Rec*D: The gene for an essential third subunit of exonuclease V. *Proceedings of the National Academy of Sciences of the United States of America* **83**, 5558–5562.

BRON, S. AND VENEMA, G. (1972). Ultraviolet inactivation and excision repair in *Bacillus subtilis*. I. Construction and characterization of a transformable eightfold-auxotrophic strain and two ultraviolet-sensitive derivatives. *Mutation Research* **15**, 1–10.

CHESTUKHIN, A.V., SHEMYAKIN, M.F., KALININA, N.A. AND PROZOROV, A.A. (1972). Some properties of ATP-dependent deoxyribonucleases from normal and *rec* mutant strains of *Bacillus subtilis*. *FEBS Letters* **24**, 121–125.

CLARK, A.J. (1973). Recombination deficient mutants of *Escherichia coli* and other bacteria. *Annual Review of Genetics* **7**, 67–86.

DOLY, J. AND ANAGNOSTOPOULOS, C. (1976). Isolation, subunit structure and properties of the ATP-dependent deoxyribonuclease of *Bacillus subtilis*. *European Journal of Biochemistry* **71**, 309–316.

DOLY, J., SASARMAN, E. AND ANAGNOSTOPOULOS, C. (1974). ATP-dependent deoxyribonuclease in *Bacillus subtilis* and a mutant deficient in this activity. *Mutation Research* **22**, 15–23.

HICKSON, I.D. AND EMMERSON, P.T. (1981). Identification of the *Escherichia coli recB* and *recC* gene products. *Nature* **294**, 578–580.

IORDANESCU, S. (1975). Recombinant plasmid obtained from two different, compatible staphylococcal plasmids. *Journal of Bacteriology* **124**, 597–601.

IORDANESCU, S. (1977). Relationships between cotransducible plasmids in *Staphylococcus aureus*. *Journal of Bacteriology* **129**, 71–75.

KOOISTRA, J., VOSMAN, B. AND VENEMA, G. (1988). Cloning and characterization of a *Bacillus subtilis* transcription unit involved in ATP-dependent DNase synthesis. *Journal of Bacteriology* **170**, 4791–4797.

LAEMMLI, U.K. (1970). Cleavage of structural protein during the assembly of the head of bacteriophage T4. *Nature* **227**, 680–685.

MICHEL, B., NIAUDET, B. AND EHRLICH, S.D. (1983). Intermolecular recombination during transformation of *Bacillus subtilis* competent cells by monomeric and dimeric plasmids. *Plasmid* **10**, 1–10.

NATT, E. AND SCHERER, G. (1986). EMBL12, a new lambda replacement vector with sites for *Sal*I, *Xba*I, *Bam*HI, *Sst*I and *Eco*RI. *Nucleic Acids Research* **14**, 7128.

VIEIRA, J. AND MESSING, J. (1982). The pUC plasmids, an M13mp7–derived system for insertion mutagenesis and sequencing with synthetic universal primers. *Gene* **19**, 259–268.

VOSMAN, B., KOOISTRA, J., OLIJVE, J. AND VENEMA, G. (1987). Cloning in *Escherichia coli* of the gene specifying the DNA-entry nuclease of *Bacillus subtilis*. *Gene* **52**, 175–183.

# 4
# Development of a pUB110-Derived Vector for Post-Exponential Phase Expression in Bacillus subtilis

G. DAXHELET AND P. HOET

Microbiology and Genetics Unit, University of Louvain Medical School,
ICP-UCL 7449, 75 Avenue Hippocrate, 1200 Brussels, Belgium

## Introduction

Plasmid pGR71 (Goldfarb, Doi and Rodriguez, 1981; Goldfarb, Rodriguez and Doi, 1982), constructed by combining the *Staphylococcus aureus* plasmid pUB110, the *E. coli* plasmid pBR350 (referred to as pBR322 in later publications; Lin *et al.*, 1985), and the *cat* (chloramphenicol-resistance) gene of transposon Tn9, can replicate and express kanamycin-resistance in *B. subtilis* and *E. coli*. Chloramphenicol resistance, however, is not expressed because the promoter activating the *cat* gene of Tn9 was deleted. The insertion of a sequence allowing the expression of this gene would therefore identify a promoter functional in *B. subtilis*.

The aim of the present work was to clone promoters of the virulent *B. subtilis* phage 2C into shuttle vector pGR71. The genome of phage 2C (closely related to SP01, SP82 and Øe) is a double-stranded DNA molecule of about 100 mDa with long redundant ends. It contains an unusual base, hydroxymethyluracil (HMU), instead of thymine (T). Viral coded enzymes promote the synthesis of HMU, to the detriment of T, in the course of infection (Hemphill and Whiteley, 1975; Coene, Hoet and Cocito, 1983; Hoet, Coene and Cocito, 1983). The virus-promoted formation of different cofactors addressing the core subunit of RNA polymerase to specific viral promoters explains the cascade gene regulation operating during the replication cycle (Losick and Pero, 1981; Geiduschek and Ito, 1982; Doi and Wang, 1986). The philosophy underlying our approach was that viral promoters, being able to provide their own genes with a selective advantage over cellular genes, would strongly promote the expression of downstream cistrons.

The results obtained did not match our expectations. When 2C phage DNA sequences were cloned in pGR71, activation of the *cat* gene was observed,

*Genetic Transformation and Expression*
© Intercept Ltd, PO Box 716, Andover, Hants, SP10 1YG, UK

however, no viral sequences were recovered in the chimeric vector. Furthe investigation led to the discovery of a silent plasmid promoter endowed wit unexpected properties, including its ability to induce gene expression in *I subtilis* during post-exponential growth. This promoter did not function in *I coli*.

## Materials and methods

### BACTERIA, PHAGE AND PLASMIDS

Strains SB202 (*trpC2, his-2 tyr-1, aro-2*) and GSY908 (*argC4, hisA1, recE4*) o *B. subtilis* were used as hosts in transformation experiments with bot competent cells (Anagnostopoulos and Spizizen, 1961) and protoplasts (Chan and Cohen, 1979). Phage 2C DNA was prepared as previously describe (Hoet, Fraselle and Cocito, 1976). *E. coli* K12 strain C600 (*thr-1, leu-6, thi-I supE44, lacY1, tonA2*) was transformed according to Dagert and Ehrlic (1979). DNA concentration was 30 µg ml$^{-1}$ for transformation of *E. coli* an protoplasts of *B. subtilis*, and 100 µg ml$^{-1}$ for transformation of competent *B subtilis* cells. Plasmids pGR71 and △pGR71, which are able to replicate in bot *B. subtilis* and *E. coli*, were extracted and purified either by hydroxylapatit column chromatography (Niaudet and Ehrlich, 1979) or by the minilysat method (Birnboim and Doly, 1979). Chromosomal DNA was purified from *B subtilis* as described by Marmur (1961).

### RECOMBINANT DNA TECHNIQUES

Restriction endonucleases and other enzymes, purchased from Boehringe (Mannheim, W. Germany) were used according to Maniatis, Fritsch an Sambrook (1982). BAL31-promoted deletions were obtained as follows pGR71 plasmid (6 µg), previously linearized with *Xba*I, was incubated fo different lengths of time at 30°C with 0·6 unit of BAL31 exonuclease in 100 µl o 20mM Tris-HCl pH 7·2, 400mM NaCl, 12·5mM MgCl$_2$, 12·5mM CaCl$_2$, 1mM EDTA. After 1, 3, 5, 8, 11 and 14 min, 15 µl aliquots were withdrawn an EGTA (final concentration 20mM) was immediately added to stop th reaction. Under these conditions, the rate of hydrolysis was about 200 b min$^{-1}$. After *Hin*dIII hydrolysis, filling-in of protruding ends with Klenov DNA polymerase in the presence of the 4 dNTP and ligation with T4 DN/ ligase, the DNA was transformed into *B. subtilis* protoplasts.

### CAT ACTIVITY AND WESTERN BLOTS OF CELL EXTRACTS

Chloramphenicol acetyl transferase (CAT) activity was measured an expressed as nmoles of acetylated chloramphenicol min$^{-1}$ mg protein$^{-1}$ Plasmid-harbouring strains were grown in LB medium containing 10 µg ml$^{-}$ each of kanamycin and chloramphenicol. Cells were washed with 1M NaCl 50mM Tris HCl pH 7·9, centrifuged, suspended in 200 µl 100mM Tris HCl pH 7·9 0·5mM phenylmethylsulphonylfluoride (PMSF), 50µM dithiothreitol and 0·:

g ml$^{-1}$ lysozyme. This suspension was incubated in ice for 30 min, sonicated r 30 sec (60 W) and centrifuged in an Eppendorf microfuge for 15 min. CAT tivity in the supernatant was determined spectrophotometrically, as escribed by Shaw (1975). Total protein content was determined by the ethod of Bradford (1976).

For Western blots, cell extracts were electrophoresed in a 12·5% olyacrylamide-SDS gel, transferred to a nitrocellulose membrane, pre- eated with bovine serum albumin, and then reacted with rabbit antibodies ised against purified CAT from *E. coli* (Sigma Chem., Deisenhofen, W. jermany). These were visualized by a horseradish peroxidase-conjugated cond antibody (Promega, Madison WI, USA). Molecular size markers were ectrophoresed in the same gel.

## Results

### LONING OF PHAGE 2C DNA AND *BACILLUS SUBTILIS* CHROMOSOMAL DNA IN HE PROMOTER-PROBE PLASMID pGR71

lasmid pGR71 carries a promoterless *cat* gene from transposon Tn*9*. It is not xpressed in *B. subtilis* or *E. coli*. The structural gene is preceded by a hine–Dalgarno sequence, which is recognized by *E. coli* but not by *B. subtilis* ibosomes (Goldfarb, Rodriguez and Doi, 1982). The insertion upstream of the at gene of a fragment activating the gene in *B. subtilis* would need to provide a ranscription initiation site and a Shine–Dalgarno sequence, leading to a fusion eptide.

The genomes of *B. subtilis* and phage 2C were digested with *Hin*dIII. Phage C DNA yielded 35–40 *Hin*dIII-fragments of sizes ranging from 10 to less than kbp. To both samples, equal amounts of *Hin*dIII-linearized pGR71 (a unique *Hin*dIII site is located upstream of the *cat* gene; *Figure 44.1*) and ligase were dded, and the mixtures were incubated for 16 h at 9°C. The same ligation nixtures were used to transform competent cells and protoplasts of *B. subtilis* B202. Additional experiments were carried out with GSY908, a *recE4* mutant f *B. subtilis*, to prevent the intergration of cloned chromosomal DNA into the ost genome. Km$^r$ colonies were screened for resistance to 5 and 20 μg ml$^{-1}$ of hloramphenicol. Cm$^r$ *B. subtilis* colonies were obtained after transformation vith chimeric plasmids containing 2C DNA (*Table 44.1*). In all cases the clones narboured plasmids reduced in size (5–6·2 kbp) with respect to native pGR71 8·4 kbp). Deletion of sequences located upstream to the *cat* structural gene nad occurred: they extended, in most cases, beyond the *Bam*H1 site and involv- d the pUB110 moiety of pGR71 (*Figure 44.1*). Southern hybridization with ick-translated [$^{32}$P]2C DNA, which was performed under standard conditions s well as at low stringency, was unable to identify viral sequences within the recombinant plasmids (results not shown). No *B. subtilis* chromosomal DNA nsertion had occurred in these deletion derivatives, as substantiated by nybridization experiments (results not shown). The deleted plasmids were referred to as △pGR71.

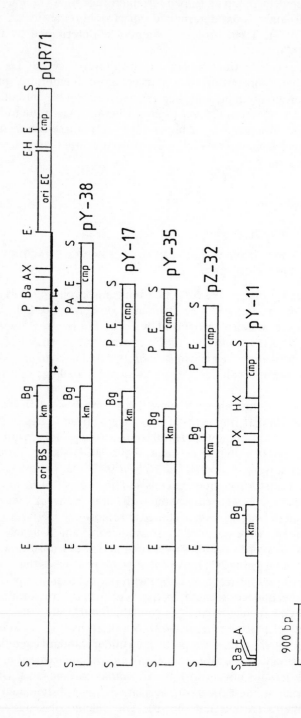

**Figure 44.1**  Restriction maps of pGR71 and pGR71-derived plasmids. To facilitate comparison, the plasmids are aligned according to the single *Sal*I site, which is present in all of them. Symbols: *ori*EC and *ori*BS, replication origins of pBR322 and pUB110 (Lin *et al.*, 1985); Cmp and Km, genes conferring resistance to chloramphenicol and kanamycin; →, starting points of pUB110 ORFS (McKenzie *et al.*, 1986; Semon *et al.*, 1987). Restriction sites: S, *Sal*I; E, *Eco*RI; Bg, *Bgl*II; P, *Pvu*II; Ba, *Bam*HI; A, *Ava*I; X, *Xba*I; H, *Hind*III. The pUB110 moiety of pGR71, is shown by a heavy line.

**Table 44.1**   Number of *B. subtilis* Km and Cm resistant recombinants after transformation with hybrid plasmids pGR71–2C or pGR71–*B. subtilis* chromosomal DNA

| Transforming DNA | Number of colonies | | Mode of transformation* |
|---|---|---|---|
| | Km$^r$ | Cm$^r$ | |
| pGR71 | 450 | 0 | c |
| | 3000 | 0 | p |
| pGR71–2C | 369 | 41 | c |
| | 3500 | 317 | p |
| pGR71–*B. subtilis* | 80 | 3 | c |
| | 1600 | 49 | p |

* c, competent cells; p, protoplast.

By contrast, cloning of segments of *B. subtilis* chromosome produced recombinant plasmids that were larger than the original pGR71. From 11 out of 20 recombinant plasmids, a restriction fragment was liberated by cleavage with *Hind*III, Southern hybridization of such recombinant plasmids with nick-translated [$^{32}$P]-chromosomal DNA of *B. subtilis* confirmed the insertion of chromosomal segments into the unique *Hind*III site of the cloning vector.

The level of resistance to chloramphenicol, conferred by the two classes of recombinants, was determined (*Table 44.2*): it can be seen that the $\Delta$pGR71 plasmids provide a much higher minimal inhibitory concentration than plasmids having inserted promoter sequences from the host chromosome.

PLASMID PROMOTER SEQUENCES ACTIVATE THE CHLORAMPHENICOL ACETYL TRANSFERASE GENE; RESTRICTION MAPPING OF THE $\Delta$pGR71 PLASMIDS

The experiments described in the previous section suggest an activation of the *cat* gene by a deletion bringing a plasmid promoter close to the gene itself. This possibility was verified by endonuclease cleavage of pGR71. Accordingly, the latter was linearized with *Xba*I, incubated for an increasing length of time with BAL31 exonuclease and cleaved with *Hind*III (*see* p. 466 and the pGR71 map in *Figure 44.1*). The protruding ends of the cleaved plasmids were filled by the use of DNA polymeraseI (Klenow fragment) and ligated. *B. subtilis* SB202 protoplasts were transformed with the BAL31-restricted plasmid and Km$^r$ transformants yielded 12 Cm$^r$ colonies.

These data provide evidence for an activation of the silent *cat* gene that occurred when *B. subtilis* was transformed either with chimeric pGR71–2C plasmids (*in vivo* deletions leading to $\Delta$pGR71) or with BAL31 exonuclease-treated pGR71 (*in vitro*-produced deletions). From both groups, five recombinant colonies were chosen for restriction mapping of their plasmids. In *Figure 44.1*, the restriction map of $\Delta$pGR71 plasmids (obtained *in vivo* with chimeric pGR71–2C DNA) shows deletions extending within the pUB110 part of the chimeric plasmid pGR71. In addition to deletions, complex rearrangements have occurred. As shown for some recombinant plasmids (*Figure 44.1*), pUB110 sequences located between the *Bgl*II site (within the Km$^r$ gene) and the *Eco*RI site, were deleted in plasmids pY17, pY35 and pZ32. This *Bgl*II–*Eco*RI fragment was shorter in these recombinant plasmids, than in the original pGR71. pY11 was the smallest among the deletion plasmids produced *in vivo*: it had suffered extensive deletions and complex

rearrangements. All plasmids retained a *Pvu*II restriction site upstream of th
*cat* gene.

## CHARACTERIZATION OF THE NOVEL △pGR71 PROMOTERS: COMPARISON WITH *B. SUBTILIS* CHROMOSOMAL PROMOTERS

Data in the previous section has revealed the activation of a *cat* gene by
plasmid promoter of △pGR71. Its properties were compared to those carrie
by *B. subtilis* chromosomal DNA, inserted in the pGR71 promoter-prob
plasmid.

As shown in *Table 44.2*, recombinant △pGR71 plasmids provided muc
higher levels of resistance to Cm than the pGR71–*B. subtilis* recombinants
Moreover, data in *Figure 44.2* indicate that △pGR71 recombinants expresse
the *cat* gene mainly during the post-exponential phase of growth and afforde
variable levels of resistance toward chloramphenicol. Similar growth-relate
CAT-activities were obtained with the BAL31-derived plasmids. In contrast
the *cat* gene was expressed in the pGR71–*B. subtilis* recombinants at a lowe
but constant level during all phases of growth.

**Table 44.2**   Level of chloramphenicol resistance of *B. subtilis* colonies containing pGR71-derive
plasmids

| Minimal inhibitory concentration (in µg ml⁻¹) | Number of colonies resistant to given amount of Cm | |
|---|---|---|
| | △pGR71 | pGR71–*B. subtilis* DNA |
| < 90 | 10 | 50 |
| 90–100 | 25 | 10 |
| 100–110 | 12 | 3 |
| 110–120 | 19 | |
| 120–130 | 65 | |
| 130–140 | 32 | |
| 140–150 | 12 | |
| 150–160 | 23 | |
| 160–170 | 21 | |
| 170–180 | 11 | |
| 180–190 | 54 | |
| 190–200 | 10 | |
| > 200 | 23 | |

Surprisingly, △pGR71 plasmids did not allow expression of Cmʳ in *E. coli*.
This was shown by extracting plasmids from chloramphenicol-resistant *B.
subtilis* recombinants and screening Kmʳ-transformed *E. coli* colonies for Cmʳ.
The inability to express the chloramphenicol resistance in *E. coli* could be due
to an impairment either of transcription or of translation. Dot-blot RNA
hybridizations (not shown) indicated that CAT expression in *E. coli* was
prevented by lack of transcription in this host. This was further confirmed by
the absence, in recombinant *E. coli* extracts, of both chloramphenicol
acetyltransferase activity and CAT protein (SDS-PAGE, data not shown).

In contrast, pGR71–*B. subtilis* plasmids expressed both Km and *cat* genes in
*E. coli*, in agreement with previous observations (Goldfarb, Dci and
Rodriguez, 1981).

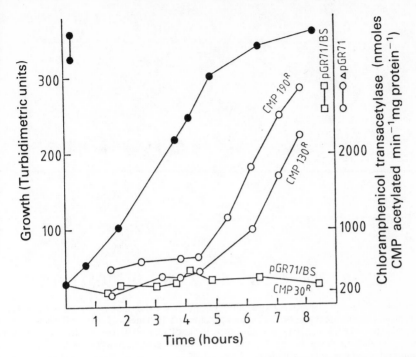

**Figure 44.2** Relationship between the synthesis of chloramphenicol acetyltransferase and the growth phase of recombinant strains. Recombinant *B. subtilis* plasmids, pY17, conferring resistance to 190 μg ml$^{-1}$ (CMP 190$^R$); pY38, conferring resistance to 130 μg ml$^{-1}$ (CMP 130$^R$); pGR71–*B. subtilis*, conferring resistance to 30 μg ml$^{-1}$ (pGR71/BS; CMP 30$^R$). Symbols: –•– cell growth (Turbidimetric Klett Units); –○–, plasmids pY17 and pY38; –□–, pGR71–BS. Specific activities of CAT are expressed in nmoles of acetylated chloramphenicol min$^{-1}$ mg protein$^{-1}$.

SIZE OF THE CAT FUSION PROTEIN IN *B. SUBTILIS*, CARRYING ΔpGR71 PLASMIDS

Expression of the *cat* gene of pGR71 as a consequence of plasmid rearrangements, entails the adequate positioning of a promoter sequence and of a ribosome binding site, leading to the production of a fusion protein (Goldfarb, Rodriguez and Doi, 1982). Hence, the size of the CAT protein in different recombinant plasmids was analysed by SDS-PAGE electrophoresis and immunoblotting of transferred proteins with anti-CAT antibodies. It can be seen (*Figure 44.3*) that the size of the fused CAT-protein is similar in different recombinant clones, sampled at three points of their growth curve. By comparison with the native *cat* gene product (Goldfarb, Rodriguez and Doi, 1982), this size would correspond to the addition of about 25 amino acids, corresponding to 75 bp. These data suggest that the translation initiation site is at a similar location in the different recombinants. This has to be confirmed by determination of the amino-terminal sequence of the CAT-fusion proteins.

SEARCH FOR pUB110 TEMPORALLY REGULATED PROMOTERS

All ΔpGR71 plasmids had maintained a *Pvu*II site upstream of the *cat*

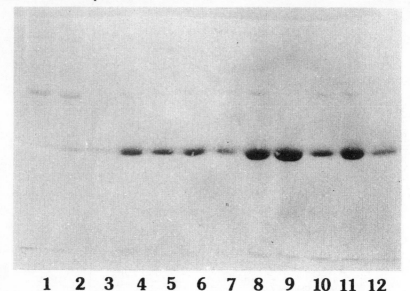

**1   2   3   4   5   6   7   8   9   10 11 12**

**Figure 44.3**   Western blot analysis with anti-CAT antibodies of *B. subtilis* extracts. Cells had been transformed with pGR71 (lanes 1, 2, 3) and plasmids pY38 (lanes 4, 5, 6), pY17 (lanes 7, 8, 9) and pY35 (lanes 10, 11, 12). Samples were taken at Klett Units of 130 (lanes 1, 4, 7, 10), 300 (lanes 2, 5, 8, 11) and 355 (lanes 3, 6, 9, 12) and processed as described (*see* 466–7). The major band visualized by anti-CAT antibodies has a $M_r$ of 23 500.

structural gene (*Figure 44.1*), suggesting that specific nucleotide sequences had been shifted appropriately in order to provide gene expression in the different recombinants. Since pUB110 has been sequenced, a computer search was carried out for putative promoter sequences recognized by *B. subtilis* sigma factors. *Table 44.3* reports these data, pointing to overlapping sequences possibly recognized by sigma-43 and sigma-29 in close proximity to the *Pvu*II site (position 1055; McKenzie *et al.*, 1986). A putative ribosome-binding site (around nucleotide 859; $\triangle G$ for interaction with 16S RNA: $-9\cdot8$ kcal, calculated according to Tinoco *et al.*, 1973) is 12 nucleotides away from a potential translation initiation codon (TTG).

**Discussion**

Instability is a well-established feature of plasmids in *B. subtilis* and represents a major limitation to genetic engineering with this host. The cloning experiments described in the present work represent an extreme example in which phage 2C DNA could not be cloned into bifunctional plasmid pGR71. The stability of the vector itself in *B. subtilis* is unquestionable. Indeed, chimeric plasmids carrying chromosomal *B. subtilis* DNA sequences were replicated and maintained without major rearrangements, in experiments performed in other laboratories (Goldfarb, Doi and Rodriguez, 1981) and in ours (*Table 44.1*).

The mechanisms underlying the 2C-induced plasmid deletion and rearrangements in *B. subtilis* are unclear. They do not seem to involve preferred

**Table 44.3**  Location and nature of putative promoter sequences in pUB110 (in the vicinity of its *Pvu*II site), possibly recognized by *B. subtilis* sigma factors

| Sigma factor | Consensus sequences (Doi and Wang, 1986) | | | Sequences found in pUB110 (McKenzie *et al.*, 1986) | | | |
|---|---|---|---|---|---|---|---|
| | $-10$ | $-35$ | Spacing | $-10$ | $-35$ | Start position $-10/-35$ | Spacing |
| $\sigma^{43}$ | TATAAT | TTGACA | 17–19 | TATGAT* | TTGACC | 945/972 | 20 |
| | | | | TAGAAT | TTTACA | 1057/1081 | 18 |
| $\sigma^{29}$ | CATATT | TTNAAA | 14–15 | AATATT | TTGAAA | 932/949 | 10 |
| | | | | CATATG | CTAAAA | 1077/1096 | 14 |
| $\sigma^{32}$ | TANTGNTTNTA | AAATC | 14–15 | TATTGATTACA | AAATG | 922/934 | 7 |
| $\sigma^{37}$ | GGAATTNTTT | AGGATTTNA | 11–15 | TGAGTTTTTT | AGGGTTTAA | 1372/1390 | 9 |

* Nucleotides, different from the consensus sequence, are underlined.

recombination sites, as shown by the different sizes and restriction maps (*Figure 44.1*) of the resulting pGR71 plasmids. The observed rearrangements might be due to alignment of regulatory sequences with respect to the structural gene to be expressed: such a shifting step is likely to have been imposed by the selection procedure.

The inability of foreign genes (freely translated in *E. coli*) to be expressed in *B. subtilis* has been repeatedly observed: it is due to a block of transcription and translation steps (McLaughlin, Murray and Rabinowitz, 1981; Goldfarb, Rodriguez and Doi, 1982; Moran *et al.*, 1982). The present work relates the unique situation in which cloned genes are efficiently expressed in *B. subtilis*, but not in *E. coli*.

The simplest interpretation of our data is that some deletions have repositioned in front of the structural gene Shine–Dalgarno and promoter sequences, the latter of which is recognized by a RNA polymerase sigma factor mainly during post-exponential *B. subtilis* growth. This would explain the post-exponential increase of CAT activity in recombinant cells (*Figure 44.2*); and the inability of *E. coli* to recognize these promoter sequences. In fact, *B. subtilis* has several minor sigma factors (for a review, *see* Doi and Wang, 1986), one of which might be responsible for our findings. Minor sigma factors are believed to control developmental genes in both lytic phage and sporulation cycles of *B. subtilis*. Activation of the *cat* gene might be due to the fortuitous positioning of promoter sequences carried by the pUB110 moiety of pGR71, after deletion of intervening plasmid sequences.

The present study reports the location and sequence of promoters and ribosome-binding site, found in the vicinity of the *Pvu*II site of the pUB110 sequence. We are currently determining experimentally which sequences regulate post-exponential *cat* gene expression of ΔpGR71 plasmids. Experiments are now in progress to use them for temporally regulated expression of foreign genes in *B. subtilis*.

### Acknowledgements

G. Daxhelet is a predoctoral fellow of IRSIA. P. Hoet is senior research associate of the National Fund for Scientific Research (Belgium). This work was initiated with the help of a NATO grant for international collaboration in research, awarded to R.H. Doi, University of California, Davis (USA) and to Philippe Hoet, Brussels. The help of R.H. Doi and his associates in carrying out experiments and in preparing the manuscript is kindly acknowledged by P. Hoet. BAL31-derived plasmids were obtained by S. Ryckaart and J.C. Vanderelst during a course in Molecular Genetics (School of Pharmacy, University of Louvain, Brussels). Critical reading of the manuscript by M. Coene is acknowledged, as well as the technical assistance of P. Rensonnet. Research was supported by grant 3.4549.81 from the Fund for Medical Scientific Research.

### References

ANAGNOSTOPOULOS, C. AND SPIZIZEN, J. (1961). Requirement for transformation in *Bacillus subtilis*. *Journal of Bacteriology* **81**, 741–746.

BIRNBOIM, H.C. AND DOLY, J. (1979). A rapid alkaline extraction procedure for screening recombinant plasmid DNA. *Nucleic Acids Research* **7**, 1513–1523.

BRADFORD, M.M. (1976). A rapid and sensitive method for the quantification of microgram quantities of protein utilizing the principle of protein-dye binding. *Analytical Biochemistry* **72**, 248–254.

CHANG, S. AND COHEN, S.N. (1979). High frequency transformation of *Bacillus* protoplasts by plasmid DNA. *Molecular and General Genetics* **168**, 111–115.

COENE, M., HOET, P. AND COCITO, C. (1983). Physical map of virus 2C-DNA. Evidence for the existence of large redundant ends. *European Journal of Biochemistry* **132**, 69–75.

DAGERT, M. AND EHRLICH, S.D. (1979). Prolonged incubation in calcium chloride improves the competence of *E. coli* cells. *Gene* **6**, 23–28.

DOI, R. AND WANG, L.F. (1986). Multiple procaryotic ribonucleic acid polymerase sigma factors. *Microbiological Reviews* **50**, 227–243.

GEIDUSCHEK, E.P. AND ITO, J. (1982). Regulatory mechanisms in the development of lytic bacteriophages in *Bacillus subtilis*. In *The Molecular Biology of the Bacilli* (D. Dubnau, Ed.), pp. 203–245. Academic Press, New York.

GOLDFARB, D.S., DOI, R.H. AND RODRIGUEZ, R.L. (1981). Expression of Tn9-derived chloramphenicol resistance in *Bacillus subtilis*. *Nature* **293**, 309–311.

GOLDFARB, D.S., RODRIGUEZ, R.L. AND DOI, R.H. (1982). Translational block to expression of the *E. coli* Tn9-derived chloramphenicol resistance gene in *Bacillus subtilis*. *Proceedings of the National Academy of Sciences of the United States of America* **79**, 5886–5890.

HEMPHILL, H.E. AND WHITELEY, H.R. (1975). Bacteriophages of *B. subtilis*. *Bacteriological Reviews* **39**, 257–315.

HOET, P., COENE, M. AND COCITO, C. (1983). Comparison of the physical maps and redundant ends of the chromosomes of virus 2C, SP01, SP82. *European Journal of Biochemistry* **132**, 63–67.

HOET, P., FRASELLE, G. AND COCITO, C. (1976). Recombinational-type transfer of viral DNA during bacteriophage 2C replication in *Bacillus subtilis*. *Journal of Virology* **17**, 718–726.

LIN, C.-K., GOLDFARB, D., DOI, D.H. AND RODRIGUEZ, R.L. (1985). Mutations that affect the translation efficiency of Tn9-derived *cat* gene in *Bacillus subtilis*. *Proceedings of the National Academy of Sciences of the United States of America* **82**, 173–177.

LOSICK, R. AND PERO, J. (1981). Cascades of sigma factors. *Cell* **25**, 582–584.

MCKENZIE, M., HOSHINO, T., TANAKA, T. AND SUEOKA, N. (1986). The nucleotide sequence of pUB110: some salient features in relation to replication and its regulation. *Plasmid* **15**, 93–103.

MCLAUGHLIN, J.R., MURRAY, C.L. AND RABINOWITZ, J.C. (1981). Unique features in the ribosome binding site sequence of the Gram-positive *Staphylococcus aureus* β-lactamase gene. *Journal of Biological Chemistry* **256**, 11283–11291.

MANIATIS, T., FRITSH, E.F. AND SAMBROOK, J. (1982). *Molecular Cloning: A Laboratory Manual*. Cold Spring Harbour Laboratory Press, New York.

MARMUR, J. (1961). A procedure for the isolation of deoxyribonucleic acid from microorganisms. *Journal of Molecular Biology* **3**, 208.

MORAN, P.C., LANG, N., LEGRICE, F.J., LEE, G., STEPHENS, M., SONENSHEIN, A.L., PERO, J. AND LOSICK, R. (1982). Nucleotide sequences that signal the initiation of transcription and translation in *Bacillus subtilis*. *Molecular and General Genetics* **186**, 339–346.

NIAUDET, B. AND EHRLICH, S.D. (1979). *In vitro* genetic labeling of *Bacillus subtilis* cryptic plasmid pHV400. *Plasmid* **2**, 48–58.

SEMON, D., RAO MOVVA, N., SMITH, T.F., EL ALAMA, M. AND DAVIES, J. (1987). Plasmid-determined bleomycin resistance in *Staphylococcus aureus*. *Plasmid* **17**, 46–53.

SHAW, W.V. (1975). Chloramphenicol acetyltransferase from chloramphenicol-resistant bacteria. *Methods in Enzymology* **43**, 737–755.

TINOCO, I., BORER, P.N., DENGLER, B., LEVINE, M.D., UHLENBECK, O.C., CROTHERS, D.M. AND GRALLA, J. (1973). Improved estimation of secondary structure in ribonucleic acids. *Nature (New Biology)* **246**, 40–41.

# 45
# Peptide Antibiotic Biosynthesis Genes: Organization of the Gramicidin S and Tyrocidine Synthetase Genes of *Bacillus brevis*

GERHARD MITTENHUBER, MICHAEL KRAUSE AND
MOHAMED A. MARAHIEL

*Institut für Biochemie und Molekulare Biologie, Technische Universität Berlin,
Franklinstr. 29, D-1000 Berlin 10, FRG*

## Introduction

The biosynthetic pathway of the cyclic decapeptide antibiotics gramicidin S and tyrocidine (*Figure 45.1*) has been studied extensively during the past 20 years. These examples of non-ribosomal peptide biosynthesis were thought to be remnants of an evolutionary primitive peptide synthesis mechanism (Lipmann, 1971; Lipmann, 1975). The principles of non-ribosomal peptide biosynthesis are presented and discussed in numerous reviews (Laland and Zimmer, 1973; Kurahashi, 1974; Katz and Demain, 1977; Kleinkauf and von Döhren, 1983).

The production of peptide antibiotics in *Bacillus* seems to be associated with the onset of morphological differentiation (Schaeffer, 1969). Mutants that are blocked in the earliest stage (stage 0) of the sporulation process are highly pleiotrophic (Piggot and Coote, 1976; Losick, Youngman and Piggot, 1986). *spo0A* and *spo0B* mutants are also defective in protease and antibiotic production (Brehm and Hoch, 1973). However, it has been shown recently that antibiotic production, although sporulation-associated, is not *per se* a necessary event for sporulation to proceed (Modest *et al.*, 1984; Marahiel *et al.*, 1987). Since a number of post-exponentially induced genes (e.g. α-amylase, serine protease and antibiotic synthetase genes) other than those involved in the endospore formation of *Bacillus* have been cloned, it becomes easier to attempt to unravel the complex relationship between their expression and the onset of sporulation (Hoch and Setlow, 1985). In order to provide a basis for studying the molecular genetics of antibiotic production in *Bacillus*, we have recently cloned the ornithine-activating domain of the *grsB* gene and the entire structural *tycA* gene in *E. coli* (Krause *et al.*, 1985; Marahiel, Krause and

*Genetic Transformation and Expression*
© Intercept Ltd, PO Box 716, Andover, Hants, SP10 1YG, UK

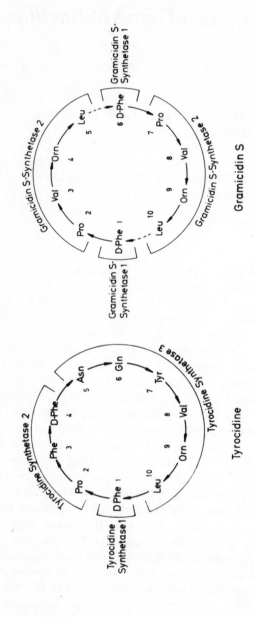

**Figure 45.1**   Structure of gramicidin S and tyrocidine. The brackets embrace substrate amino acids which are incorporated in the peptide antibiotic by the action of gramicidin S synthetases 1 and 2 (GrsA and GrsB) or of tyrocidine synthetases 1, 2 and 3 (TycA, TycB and TycC), respectively. Gramicidin S is produced by *B. brevis* ATCC 9999 whereas the closely related strain *B. brevis* ATCC 8185 synthesizes tyrocidine.

Skarpeid, 1985). The regulation of *tycA* expression in *B. subtilis* was studied extensively (Marahiel *et al.*, 1987). To this chapter we focus on the organization of peptide antibiotic biosynthetic genes from *B. brevis*.

**Results and discussion**

Due to the lack of artificial transformation techniques for the antibiotic-producing *B. brevis* strains, we were not able to clone the peptide synthetase genes by complementation of well-characterized, antibiotic-deficient mutants (Marahiel *et al.*, 1979; Saito, 1982; Modest *et al.*, 1984). The availability of polyclonal antibodies directed against GrsB, which also recognize tyrocidine synthetases and of immune serum directed against GrsA, enabled us to clone *grsB* and *grsA* genes in *E. coli*. The vectors we used were either expression plasmids or bacteriophage vectors that accept large DNA fragments. It was necessary to choose a cloning vehicle that is specific for large inserts because peptide synthetases are large proteins with a molecular mass ranging from 120 to 440 kDa. Therefore, DNA up to 10 kbp in length must encode those proteins. The following scheme led to successful cloning of peptide antibiotic biosynthetic genes:

1.  Partial *Sau*3A digestion of chromosomal DNA isolated from *B. brevis*; ligation into *Bam*HI-cut pUR2–Bam (Rüther, 1980; Krause *et al.*, 1985) or EMBL3 (Frischauf *et al.*, 1983). Transformation of plasmids in *E. coli* HB101 (Boyer and Roulland-Dussoix, 1969) or *in vitro* packaging of bacteriophage DNA and infection of *E. coli* LE392 (Maniatis, Fritsch and Sambrook, 1982).
2.  Identification of positive clones by modified *in situ* immunoassay (Helfman *et al.*, 1983, Krause *et al.*, 1985) using either GrsA or GrsB antibodies.
3.  Analytical protein preparations from induced or phage-infected *E. coli* cells. Immunodetection of antigenic proteins by Western blotting (Towbin, Staehelin and Gordon, 1979) (*see Figure 45.2*).
4.  Large-scale protein preparations and determination of antibiotic synthetase specific activities by monitoring the activation of substrate amino acids ([$^{32}$P]ATP–PPi exchange reaction). This activation step is the first reaction in a series catalysed by these multifunctional enzymes (Kleinkauf and von Döhren, 1983).

The determination of enzymatic activities related to antibiotic synthesis clarified the nature of the cloned gene products. Several features of recombinant DNA clones obtained using this strategy are summarized in *Table 45.1*.

pMK2 and pBT2 (*Table 45.1*) are recombinant plasmids constructed in the vector pUR2-Bam. pMK2 encodes the ornithine-activating domain of the *grsB* gene (Krause *et al.*, 1985), whereas pBT2 harbours the *tycA* structural gene (Marahiel, Krause and Skarpeid, 1985).

By the use of the bacteriophage vector EMBL3 the clone EMBL315 was identified. EMBL315 (*Figure 45.3A*) encodes the GrsA protein and contains, at the far right end, the 5'-end of the *grsB* structural gene, as deduced from

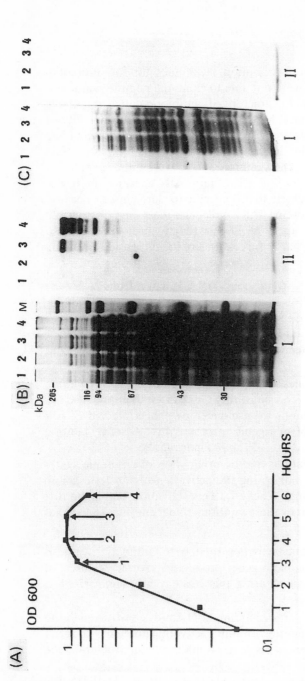

**Figure 45.2** Analysis of *E. coli* cells infected with clone EMBL25–1. (A) A single positive plaque was resuspended in 1 ml of phage buffer (Maniatis, Frisch and Sambrook, 1982). 100 µl of this suspension and 100 µl overnight culture of *E. coli* LE392 were incubated at 37°C in 5 ml NZCYM medium with vigorous aeration. The growth of the culture and the subsequent lysis of the host cells were monitored by measuring the OD$_{600}$. At the times indicated (1–4) 1 ml of the culture was removed and the cells were spun down. A crude extract was prepared from the culture medium and from the cells. (B) Analysis of infected cells. Proteins [an equivalent to 0·5 ml of culture harvested at the times indicated in (A)] were separated by SDS-PAGE on a 7·5% gel. One part of the gel was stained with Coomassie Blue R (I), the proteins of the other part were transferred to nitrocellulose sheets (II) (Towbin, Staehelin and Gordon, 1979). The detection of immunoreactive proteins was performed using GrsB antibodies and subsequently, by an incubation step with [$^{125}$I]-labelled protein A followed by autoradiography. One hour after the entry into the stationary growth phase a 190 kDa immunoreactive protein appears (lane 3). The intensity and the quantity of this band increases during lysis (lane 4). The same phenomenon can be observed with a protein around 120 kDa. Further analyses showed that the 190 kDa protein represents the TycB protein whereas the 120 kDa protein was identified as the TycA protein. The immunoreactive bands in the range from 140 to 180 kDa can be interpreted as degradation products of the 190 kDa protein. (C) Analysis of the culture supernatant. Proteins which were present in the culture medium at the times indicated in (A) (1–4) were precipitated with two volumes of acetone, subjected to SDS-PAGE, and analysed by Coomassie Blue R staining and Western blotting as described in (B). (I) shows the stained gel, (II) the autoradiogram of the blot. Due to the lysis of host cells, *E. coli* as well as phage-encoded proteins accumulated in the supernatant, but no immunoreactive protein can be detected in the medium. This observation indicates that the cloned gene products are linked to cell wall or membrane components of the infected cells.

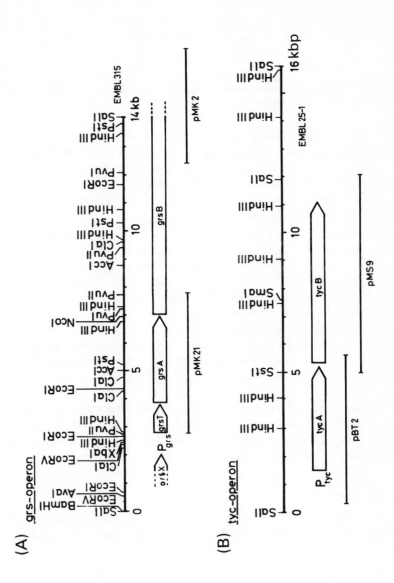

**Figure 45.3**   The diagram depicts the organization of gramicidin S (A, *grs*-operon) and tyrocidine (B, *tyc*-operon) biosynthesis genes. The *grs*-operon contains in addition to the synthetase genes *grsA* and *grsB* the open reading-frame, *grsT*, which encodes a 29 kDa protein homologous to fatty acid thioesterases (Krätzschmar, Krause and Marahiel, 1989). In the *tyc*-operon the genes *tycA* and *tycB* are clustered and co-transcribed from a promoter located in front of the *tycA* gene (Mittenhuber, Weckermann and Marahiel, 1989). The locations of the P$_{grs}$ and P$_{tyc}$ promoters are indicated.

**Table 45.1**    Antibiotic biosynthesis genes expressed in *E. coli*

| Clone designation | Origin | Size of immunoreactive proteins | Enzymatic activation of | Represents enzyme |
|---|---|---|---|---|
| pMK2 | genomic DNA | 155 kDa | L-Orn | GrsB |
| EMBL315 | genomic DNA | 120 kDa | D-Phe | GrsA |
| pMK21 | EMBL315 | 120 kDa | nd | GrsA |
| pBT2 | genomic DNA | 120 kDa | D-Phe | TycA |
| EMBL25-1 | genomic DNA | 190 kDa | L-Pro | TycB |
|  |  | 120 kDa | D-Phe | TycA |
| pMS9 | EMBL25-1 | 190 kDa | nd | TycB |

nd, not determined. In all cases, except in the analysis of clones EMBL315 and pMK21, GrsB antibodies were used for immuno-detection. The Western blot of EMBL315- and pMK21-encoded proteins was performed using GrsA antibodies. The organization of the genes *grsA* and *grsB*, as well as of *tycA* and *tycB*, is shown in *Figure 45.3*.

Southern blot experiments using pMK2 as a probe (Krause and Marahiel, 1988). The construction of subclones (*see Figure 45.3A*) from EMBL315, in which the *grsA* gene is deleted at the 3'-end and which therefore produce truncated immunoreactive proteins, as well as sequencing studies revealed that the *grsA* and *grsB* genes are clustered and transcribed as an operon (Krätzschmar, Krause and Marahiel, 1989).

We also investigated the organization of tyrocidine biosynthesis genes. As shown in *Figure 45.3B*, the genes encoding the tyrocidine synthetases 1 and 2, *tycA* and *tycB*, were also found to be clustered within the 16 kbp insert of the recombinant phage EMBL25-1. A detailed primary publication on cloning, expression and organization of the tyrocidine biosynthesis genes is in press (Mittenhuber, Weckermann and Marahiel, 1989).

Gene clustering has also been reported for most of the antibiotic synthetase genes studied so far from the genus *Streptomyces* (Malpartida and Hopwood, 1984; Chater and Bruton, 1985; Fayerman, 1986; Malpartida and Hopwood, 1986; Distler *et al.*, 1987; Fishman *et al.*, 1987; Motamedi and Hutchinson, 1987).

Studies on identification and characterization of the promoters which drive the post-exponential transcription of antibiotic biosynthesis genes in Gram-positive bacteria will increase our knowledge about regulatory events that are involved in antibiotic production at the onset of sporulation.

**Acknowledgements**

We thank H. Kleinkauf for continuous support and P. Zuber for comments on the manuscript. This work was supported by the Deutsche Forschungsgemeinschaft (Sfb9, Teilprojekt D6).

**References**

BOYER, H.W. AND ROULLAND-DUSSOIX, D. (1969). A complementation analysis of the restriction and modification of DNA in *Escherichia coli*. *Journal of Molecular Biology* **41**, 459–472.

BREHM, S.P. AND HOCH, J.A. (1973). Phenotypic negative sporulation mutants of *Bacillus subtilis*. *Journal of Bacteriology* **115**, 1063–1070.

CHATER, K.F. AND BRUTON, C.J. (1985). Resistance, regulatory and production genes for the antibiotic methlylenomycin are clustered. *EMBO Journal* 4, 1893–1897.

DISTLER, J., BRAUN, C., EBERT, A. AND PIEPERSBERG, W. (1987). Gene cluster for streptomycin biosynthesis in *Streptomyces griseus*: analysis of a central region including the major resistance gene. *Molecular and General Genetics* 208, 204–210.

FAYERMAN, J.T. (1986). New developments in gene cloning in antibiotic producing microorganisms. *Bio/technology* 4, 786–788.

FISHMAN, S.E., COX, K., LARSON, J.L., REYNOLDS, P.A., SENO, E.T., YEN, W.K., VAN FRANK, R. AND HERSHBERGER, C.L. (1987). Cloning genes for the biosynthesis of a macrolide antibiotic. *Proceedings of the National Academy of Sciences of the United States of America* 84, 8248–8252.

FRISCHAUF, A.M., LEHRACH, H., POUSTRA, A. AND MURRAY, N. (1983). Lambda replacement vectors carrying polylinker sequences. *Journal of Molecular Biology* 170, 827–842.

HELFMAN, D.M., FERAMISCO, J.R., FIDDES, I.C., THOMAS, G.P. AND HUGHES, S.H. (1983). Identification of clones that encode chicken tropomyosin by direct screening of a cDNA library. *Proceedings of the National Academy of Sciences of the United States of America* 80, 31–35.

HOCH, J.A. AND SETLOW P. (EDS) (1985). *Molecular Biology of Microbial Differentiation*. ASM, Washington DC.

KATZ, E. AND DEMAIN, A.L. (1977). The peptide antibiotics of bacilli: chemistry, biogenesis and possible functions. *Bacteriological Reviews* 41, 449–474.

KLEINKAUF, H. AND VON DÖHREN, H. (1983). Peptides. In *Biochemistry and Genetic Regulation of Commercially Important Antibiotics* (L.C. Vining, Ed.), pp. 95–145. Butterworths, Boston.

KRÄTZSCHMAR, J., KRAUSE, M. AND MARAHIEL, M.A. (1989). *Journal of Bacteriology*, in press.

KRAUSE, M. AND MARAHIEL, M.A. (1988). Organisation of the biosynthesis genes for the peptide antibiotic gramicidin S. *Journal of Bacteriology* 170, 4669–4674.

KRAUSE, M., MARAHIEL, M.A., VON DÖHREN, H. AND KLEINKAUF, H. (1985). Molecular cloning of an ornithine activating fragment of the gramicidin S-synthetase 2 gene from *Bacillus brevis* and its expression in *Escherichia coli*. *Journal of Bacteriology* 162, 1120–1125.

KURAHASHI, K. (1974). Biosynthesis of small peptides. *Annual Review of Biochemistry* 43, 445–459.

LALAND, S.G. AND ZIMMER, T.L. (1973). The protein thiotemplate mechanism synthesis for the peptide antibiotics produced by *Bacillus brevis*. *Essays in Biochemistry* 9, 31–57. Academic Press, New York.

LIPMANN, F. (1971). Attempts to map a process evolution of peptide biosynthesis. *Science* 173, 875–884.

LIPMANN, F. (1975). The search of remnants of early evolution in present day metabolism. *Biosystems* 6, 234–238.

LOSICK, R., YOUNGMAN, P. AND PIGGOT, P.J. (1986). Genetics of endospore formation in *Bacillus subtilis*. *Annual Review of Genetics* 20, 625–669.

MALPARTIDA, F. AND HOPWOOD, D.A. (1984). Molecular cloning of the whole biosynthetic pathway of a *Streptomyces* antibiotic and its expression in a heterologous host. *Nature* 309, 462–464.

MALPARTIDA, F. AND HOPWOOD, D.A. (1986). Physical and genetic characterisation of the gene cluster for the antibiotic actinorhodin in *Streptomyces coelicolor* A3(2). *Molecular and General Genetics* 205, 66–73.

MANIATIS, T., FRITSCH, E.F. AND SAMBROOK, J. (1982). *Molecular Cloning: A Laboratory Manual*. Cold Spring Harbor Laboratory Press, New York.

MARAHIEL, M.A., KRAUSE, M. AND SKARPEID, H.J. (1985). Cloning of the tyrocidine synthetase 1 gene from *Bacillus brevis* and its expression in *Escherichia coli*. *Molecular and General Genetics* 201, 231–236.

MARAHIEL, M.A., DANDERS, W., KRAUSE, M. AND KLEINKAUF, H. (1979). Biological role of gramicidine S in spore functions: Studies on gramicidin S-negative mutants

of *Bacillus brevis* ATCC 9999. *European Journal of Biochemistry* **99**, 49–55.
MARAHIEL, M.A., ZUBER, P., CZEKAY, G. AND LOSICK, R. (1987). Identification of the promoter for a peptide antibiotic biosynthesis gene from *Bacillus brevis* and its regulation in *Bacillus subtilis*. *Journal of Bacteriology* **169**, 2215–2222.
MITTENHUBER, G.M., WECKERMANN, R. AND MARAHIEL, M.A. (1989). *Journal of Bacteriology*, in press.
MODEST, B., MARAHIEL, M.A., PSCHORN, W. AND RISTOW, H. (1984). Peptide antibiotics and sporulation: Induction of sporulation in asporogenous and peptide-negative mutants of *Bacillus brevis*. *Journal of General Microbiology* **130**, 747–755.
MOTAMEDI, H. AND HUTCHINSON, C.R. (1987). Cloning and heterologous expression of a gene cluster for the biosynthesis of tetracenomycin C, the anthracycline antitumor antibiotic of *Streptomyces glaucescens*. *Proceedings of the National Academy of Sciences of the United States of America* **84**, 4445–4449.
PIGGOT, P.J. AND COOTE, J.G. (1976). Genetic aspects of bacterial endospore formation. *Bacteriological Reviews* **40**, 908–962.
RÜTHER, U. (1980). Construction and properties of a new cloning vehicle, allowing direct screening for recombinant plasmids. *Molecular and General Genetics* **178**, 475–477.
SAITO, Y. (1982). Some characteristics of gramicidin S-synthetase obtained from mutants of *Bacillus brevis* which could not form D-phenyalanyl-L-prolyl-diketopiperazine. In *Peptide Antibiotics* (H. Kleinkauf and H. von Döhren, Eds), pp. 195–207. Walter de Gruyter, Berlin.
SCHAEFFER, P. (1969). Sporulation and the production of antibiotics, exoenzymes and exotoxins. *Bacteriological Reviews* **33**, 48–71.
TOWBIN, H., STAEHELIN, T. AND GORDON, J. (1979). Electrophoretic transfer of proteins from polyacrylamide gels to nitrocellulose sheets: procedure and applications. *Proceedings of the National Academy of Sciences of the United States of America* **76**, 4350–4354.

# 46
# Molecular Control of the *Bacillus pumilus* *cat-86* Chloramphenicol-Resistance Gene in *Bacillus subtilis* and *Escherichia coli*

D.J. BLACKBOURN, A.K. WINSTON AND C.R. HARWOOD

*Microbial Technology Group, Department of Microbiology, The Medical School, Newcastle upon Tyne, NE2 4HH, UK*

## Introduction

The chloramphenicol (Cm)-resistance gene, *cat-86* (Harwood, Williams and Lovett, 1983), from *Bacillus pumilus* has been cloned into the kanamycin-resistant *Staphylococcus aureus* plasmid pUB110 as pPL608, with a promoter from bacteriophage SPO2 (Williams, Duvall and Lovett, 1981). A shuttle plasmid pCH100, has been constructed from derivatives of pBR322 and pPL608 to elucidate details of the mechanisms controlling induction of *cat-86* (Harwood, Bell and Winston, 1987). This construct shows a twentyfold induction in *Bacillus subtilis*, but low, non-inducible levels of CAT activity in *Escherichia coli*. The control of expression of *cat-86* is proposed to reside primarily at the level of translation.

However, an element of control at the level of transcription cannot be ruled out since Duvall, Williams and Lovett (1984) found that induction of *cat-86* resulted in a concomitant increase in *cat* mRNA levels. These changes in *cat-86* mRNA levels may be due to the presence of a potential transcription terminator site upstream of *cat-86* (Ambulos, Mongkolsuk and Lovett, 1985).

The inducibility of *cat-86* is independent of promoter used to express *cat-86* (Williams, Duvall and Lovett, 1981; Mongkolsuk, Ambulos and Lovett, 1984) and, as a result of gene-replacement studies, neither *cat-86* nor its gene product are involved in Cm inducibility.

Control of *cat-86* has been found to reside in a 144 bp region 5' to the start of the structural gene (Mongkolsuk, Ambulos and Lovett, 1984). A 14 bp complementary repeat sequence, which extends over the *cat-86* ribosome-binding site (RBS), is believed to sequester the RBS by the formation of an energetically stable stem-loop in transcripts initiated upstream of the inverted

*Genetic Transformation and Expression*
© Intercept Ltd, PO Box 716, Andover, Hants, SP10 1YG, UK

repeats (Duvall *et al.*, 1983). Destabilization of the stem-loop would then permit translation initiation by allowing base-pairing between 16S rRNA and the *cat-86* Shine–Dalgarno sequence.

In the present study we report the use of an *in vitro* transcription system (Melton *et al.*, 1984) to generate *cat* mRNA for use in an *E. coli in vitro* translation system, and confirm the results of physiological studies that only deletion derivatives in the region of the stem-loop can be translated efficiently in *E. coli*.

## Methods

CONSTRUCTION OF pCH100 AND DELETION DERIVATIVES

The construction of pCH100 and its deletion derivatives was described previously (Harwood, Bell and Winston, 1987).

MEASUREMENT OF ENZYME ACTIVITY

The expression of *cat-86* in strains containing pCH100 and its deletion derivatives was determined in *B. subtilis* and *E. coli* after growth in the presence or absence of 25 μg Cm ml$^{-1}$ culture. Chloramphenicol acetyltransferase (CAT) activity was determined using the colorimetric assay of Shaw (1975) and protein was determined by the dye-binding assay of Bradford (1976).

*IN VITRO* TRANSCRIPTION

The Riboprobe Gemini vectors pGEM-1 and pGEM-2 (Melton and Krieg, 1984) were used to synthesize *cat-86* messenger RNA. These vectors contain both T7 and SP6 promoters separated by a multiple cloning site (MCS) containing 11 unique restriction sites; pGEM-2 has the multiple cloning site in the opposite orientation to pGEM-1. Transcripts were analysed on denaturing polyacrylamide gels.

*IN VITRO* TRANSLATION

An *E. coli* cell-free translation kit (Amersham International) was used to translate *in vitro*-generated mRNA. Translation products were analysed by SDS-polyacrylamide gel electrophoresis.

## Results

*In vitro* transcription of non-deleted fragments of *cat-86* by T7 polymerase produced more than one main species of mRNA. When the template was linearized with *Bam*HI downstream from the *cat-86* gene, two transcripts were obtained: one terminating at the end of *cat-86* and the other terminating 5′ to the start of the gene (*Figure 46.1*). These findings are consistent with the results

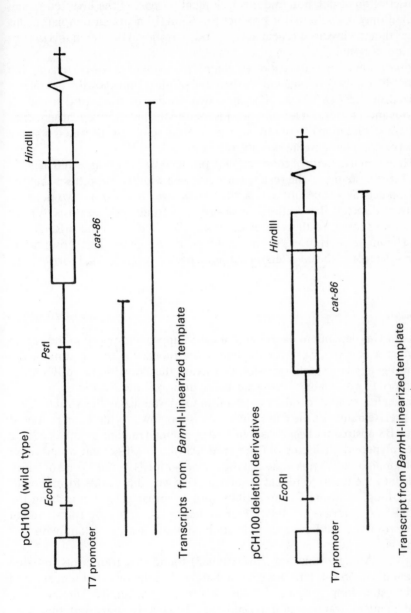

**Figure 46.1**   The main transcripts produced by *in vitro* transcription of *cat-86* located on pCH100 and deletion derivatives.

Ambulos, Mongkolsuk and Lovett (1985) obtained from *cat-86* transcription using SP6 polymerase, and suggest that the inverted repeat sequence in this region may act as a transcriptional as well as a translational barrier.

Transcription of deletion mutants lacking all or part of the inverted repeat generated only a single major product for *Bam*HI-linearized template. This confirms that the inverted repeat acts as a transcriptional barrier in this *in vitro* transcription system.

Transcription of pCH100 *cat-86* fragments cloned into pGEM-2 to generate antisense RNA also produced more than one product (not shown). Templates linearized at the *Eco*RI site generated two species of transcript: a run-off transcript and a transcript terminating just before the inverted repeat sequence (in the sense direction). In contrast, the deletion mutants generated a single species corresponding to the run-off transcript.

The functional activity of *cat-86* mRNA produced *in vitro* was tested in an *E. coli* cell-free system and the results correlate well with the hypothesis that the stem-loop acts as a translational barrier. Messenger RNA from two deletion derivatives directed the synthesis of a protein of the same size as CAT. In contrast, no protein of the size of CAT was detected when the mRNA was derived from transcription of the wild-type *cat-86* gene. This observation confirms the role of the inverted repeat sequence as a translational barrier in *E. coli*.

### Discussion

Control of Cm-dependent expression of *cat-86* appears to reside in the region containing a pair of inverted complementary repeats 5′ to the start of the structural gene. The stable stem-loop structure that forms in the mRNA has been shown to act as a barrier to translation in *E. coli* and *B. subtilis*, with the former lacking a Cm-dependent mechanism for destabilizing this structure.

The precise nature of the Cm-inducibility is unknown. It has been proposed that an RBS upstream of *cat-86* is followed by an open reading-frame encoding a short polypeptide. Binding of Cm to the 50S ribosomal subunit would cause the ribosome to stall in this region of the *cat* leader mRNA, the 3′-end of which extends into the inverted repeat sequence. This would preclude formation of the stem-loop, allowing Cm-free ribosomes to initiate translation from the *cat-86* RBS (Alexieva *et al.*, 1988). Our studies involving *in vitro* translation of mRNA from the wild type and deletion mutants are consistant with this hypothesis.

Ambulos, Mongkolsuk and Lovett (1985) found that transcripts initiated upstream of *cat-86* can terminate immediately 3′ to the inverted repeats, and that the stem-loop formed in the RNA is structurally similar to a rho-independent transcription terminator. Thus it is suggested that Cm-inducible expression of *cat-86* may include a level of transcriptional control, and that Cm addition to cells may partially relieve transcription termination at the stem-loop. The results of *in vitro* transcription studies in the present investigation correlate well with those of Ambulos and colleagues (1985). Furthermore, it may be significant that transcription using T7 polymerase to produce antisense RNA is terminated in the stem-loop region. Analysis of the sequence of the *cat-86* antisense RNA stem-loop also reveals structural similarities to a rho-independent transcription terminator.

## References

ALEXIEVA, Z., DUVALL, E.J., AMBULOS, N.P., KIM, U.J. AND LOVETT, P.S. (1988). Chloramphenicol induction of *cat-86* requires ribosome stalling at a specific site in the leader. *Proceedings of the National Academy of Sciences of the United States of America* **85**, 3057–3061.

AMBULOS, N.P., JR, MONGKOLSUK, S. AND LOVETT, P.S. (1985). A transcriptional termination signal immediately precedes the coding sequence for the chloramphenicol-inducible plasmid gene *cat-86*. *Molecular and General Genetics* **199**, 70–75.

BRADFORD, M.M. (1976). A rapid and sensitive method for quantitation of microgram quantities of protein utilising the principle of protein-dye binding. *Analytical Biochemistry* **72**, 248–254.

DUVALL, E.J., WILLIAMS, D.M. AND LOVETT, P.S. (1984). Regulatory regions that control expression of two chloramphenicol-inducible *cat* genes cloned in *Bacillus subtilis*. *Journal of Bacteriology* **158**, 784–790.

DUVALL, E.J., WILLIAMS, D.M., LOVETT, P.S., RUDOLPH, C., VASANTHA, N. AND GUYER, M., (1983). Chloramphenicol-inducible gene expression in *Bacillus subtilis*. *Gene* **24**, 171–177.

HARWOOD, C.R., WILLIAMS, D.M. AND LOVETT, P.S. (1983). Nucleotide sequence of a *Bacillus pumilus* gene specifying chloramphenicol acetyltransferase. *Gene* **24**, 163–169.

HARWOOD, C.R., BELL, D.E. AND WINSTON, A.K. (1987). The effects of deletions in the leader sequence of *cat-86*, a chloramphenicol-resistance gene isolated from *Bacillus pumilus*. *Gene* **54**, 267–273.

KRIEG, P.A. AND MELTON, D.A. (1984). Functional messenger RNAs are produced by SP6 *in vitro* transcription of cloned cDNAs. *Nucleic Acids Research* **12**. 7057–7070.

MELTON, D.A., KRIEG, P.A., REBAGLIATI, M.R., MANIATIS, T., ZINN, K. AND GREEN, M.R. (1984). Efficient *in vitro* synthesis of biologically active RNA and RNA hybridization probes from plasmids containing a bacteriophage SP6 promoter. *Nucleic Acids Research* **12**, 7035–7056.

MONGKOLSUK, S., AMBULOS, N.P., JR AND LOVETT, P.S. (1984). Chloramphenicol-inducible gene expression in *Bacillus subtilis* is independent of the chloramphenicol acetyltransferase structural gene and its promoter. *Journal of Bacteriology* **160**, 1–8.

SHAW, W.V. (1975). Chloramphenicol acetyltransferase from chloramphenicol resistant bacteria. *Methods in Enzymology* **43**, 737–754.

WILLIAMS, D.M., DUVALL, E.J. AND LOVETT, P.S. (1981). Cloning restriction fragments that promote expression of a gene in *Bacillus subtilis*. *Journal of Bacteriology* **146**, 1162–1165.

# 47

# Cloning in the *glp* Regulon of *Bacillus subtilis*

CHRISTINA HOLMBERG AND BLANKA RUTBERG

Department of Microbiology, University of Lund, Sölvegatan 21, S-223 62 Lund, Sweden

In *Bacillus subtilis*, utilization of glycerol requires two specific enzymes. In the first step, glycerol is phosphorylated to glycerol-3-phosphate (G3P) by glycerol kinase. In the second step, G3P is converted to dihydroxyacetone phosphate (DHAP) by a NAD-independent G3P-dehydrogenase. DHAP then enters the glycolytic pathway. Four genes involved in glycerol metabolism have been identified (Lindgren and Rutberg, 1974). The *glpT* gene codes for G3P permease, the *glpK* gene codes for glycerol kinase and the *glpD* gene codes for G3P dehydrogenase. The fourth gene, *glpP*, codes for a protein that is required for expression of the *glpT, glpK* and *glpD* genes. The *glp* genes constitute a regulon (Lindgren and Rutberg, 1976).

The *glp* regulon is repressed by glucose and induced by glycerol. G3P is the true inducer. The regulation is complex. Rather little is known about glucose (or catabolite) repression in bacteria outside the enterics, both with regard to mechanisms and to effector molecules involved. In order to improve our understanding of the regulation of the *glp* regulon, we have started to clone its component genes. Plasmid pHV32 (Niadet, Goze and Ehrlich, 1982) can replicate in *Escherichia coli* but not in *B. subtilis*. It expresses chloramphenicol resistance in both bacteria. This plasmid was integrated into the *B. subtilis* chromosome close to *glpK* and *glpD*. The vector with adjacent chromosomal DNA was excised using different restriction endonucleases. Hybrid plasmids were then regenerated in *E. coli*. Plasmids were obtained that carried wild-type alleles of *glpK* and glpD mutations. One such plasmid, pLUM20, generated by cleavage with *Cla*I, was further characterized. It carries a 3·5 kbp insert of chromosomal *B. subtilis* DNA. The relative order of *glpK* and *glpD* in the insert was determined by creating a series of deletions in the insert using nuclease *Bal*31 and testing for the presence of *glpK* and *glpD* markers.

A physical map of the *glpK–glpD* region of the *B. subtilis* chromosome was established by Southern blotting, using pLUM20 as a probe. These experiments, together with restriction enzyme analysis of the insert, showed

*Genetic Transformation and Expression*
© Intercept Ltd, PO Box 716, Andover, Hants, SP10 1YG, UK

that it had suffered a 200 bp deletion, including the *Cla*I site used to generate pLUM20. All attempts so far to clone the region containing this *Cla*I site have resulted in inserts carrying deletions that include this site. The insert in pLUM20 was subcloned in a low copy mutant of pUB110 called pUB110*cop-1* (this plasmid was a kind gift from Dr J.C. Alonso). The resulting plasmid could complement a *glpK* mutation in a *recE4* background, but it could not complement a *glpD* mutation. It is possible that the deletion in pLUM20 extends into the *glpD* gene.

Further work is oriented towards defining the control regions of *glpK* and *glpD*. We will also attempt to isolate the remaining known (and unknown) genes of the *glp* regulon.

### Acknowledgement

This work was supported by grants from the Swedish Medical Research Council, Emil and Vera Cornells Foundation and Kungliga Fysiografiska Sällskapet.

### References

LINDGREN, V. AND RUTBERG, L. (1974). Glycerol metabolism in *Bacillus subtilis:* Gene–enzyme relationships. *Journal of Bacteriology* **119**, 431–442.

LINDGREN, V. AND RUTBERG, L. (1976). Genetic control of the *glp* system in *Bacillus subtilis. Journal of Bacteriology* **127**, 1047–1057.

NIAUDET, B., GOZE, A. AND EHRLICH, S.D. (1982). Insertional mutagenesis in *Bacillus subtilis*: mechanism and use in gene cloning. *Gene* **19**, 277–284.

# Part VI
## Protein Secretion

48

# *agr*: A Complex Locus Regulating Post-Exponential Phase Exoprotein Synthesis in *Staphylococcus aureus*

R. NOVICK, J. KORNBLUM, B. KREISWIRTH, S. PROJAN
AND H. ROSS

The Public Health Research Institute, 455 First Ave., New York, NY 10016, USA

## Introduction

Gram-positive bacterial pathogens have in common the ability to elaborate and secrete toxins, enzymes and other exoproteins. These proteins, many of which are involved in infectivity, are not essential for the basic processes of cell growth and division, and may thus be regarded as accessory proteins. Indeed, many are genotypically variable in that they are produced by some strains but not by others, and some are components of variable genetic elements such as plasmids, transposons and temperate phages. For the most part, these exoproteins are typical secondary metabolites, being produced in laboratory cultures only after the cessation of active exponential growth (Coleman 1967; Coleman, Jakeman and Martin, 1978), and it has been known for some time, on the basis of pleiotropic exoprotein-defective mutants, that they are co-ordinately regulated. It is our view that this regulation involves a metabolic toggle switch that is set for accessory protein synthesis at the end of exponential phase and that when a new growth cycle is initiated (e.g. by dilution into fresh medium) the switch is reset for the synthesis of exponential-phase proteins. Although neither the nature of the switch nor the identity of any metabolic factors involved is known, it is likely that the regulatory system involved is similar to other known global switching systems in bacteria and probably consists of a complex multigenic pathway.

In *Staphylococcus aureus*, spontaneous pleiotropic mutations affecting post-exponential phase exoprotein production (Exp⁻ mutations) have been described by several laboratories (Katsuno and Kondo, 1973; Yoshikawa *et al.*, 1974; Bjorklind and Arvidson, 1980); commonly, these mutations block the synthesis of the following proteins: serine protease, nuclease, lipase, fibrinolysin, α-haemolysin, β-haemolysin, δ-haemolysin, enterotoxin B and

*Genetic Transformation and Expression*
© Intercept Ltd, PO Box 716, Andover, Hants, SP10 1YG, UK

toxic shock syndrome toxin-1 (TSST-1), whereas production of certain other exoproteins, including protein A and coagulase, is increased (Bjorklind and Arvidson, 1980; Recsei *et al.*, 1985). One such pleiotropic exoprotein-deficient mutation is a Tn*551* insertion isolated by Pattee and co-workers (Mallonee, Glatz and Pattee, 1982), and referred to as *hla* on the basis of its α-haemolysin-negative phenotype. Studies of the mutant strain revealed that its α-haemolysin structural gene is intact (O'Reilly *et al.*, 1986), and that its pleiotropic regulatory phenotype is correlated with a lack of mRNA corresponding to the genes whose expression is blocked (Recsei *et al.*, 1985; Peng *et al.*, 1988). Consequently, with the concurrence of Pattee (P.A. Pattee, personal communication), we have re-designated the gene *agr* (*accessory gene regulator*). A similar Tn*551* insertion has recently been described by Arvidson and co-workers (Morfeldt *et al.*, 1988). We have undertaken a molecular biological investigation of the *agr* locus and its role in the regulation of post-exponential phase exoprotein production in *S. aureus* and have previously reported the cloning and sequencing of a gene that complements the *agr⁻* defect of strains containing the above-mentioned Tn*551* insertion (Peng *et al.*, 1988). The cloned gene, henceforth referred to as *agrA* on the basis of results presented below, is transcribed from a weak constitutive promoter and complements only partially the Tn*551*-induced defect. In this paper, we present additional sequencing and subcloning data that identify a second gene, *agrB*. *agrB* is upstream of *agrA* and is transcribed from a strong promoter that is activated by AgrA and is also temporally regulated. This promoter gives rise to a 3·5 kbp transcript that includes *agrA* as well as *agrB*, suggesting that the *agr* operon is regulated by autogenous activation.

## Materials and methods

### BACTERIAL STRAINS AND PLASMIDS

All of the *S. aureus* strains used are derivatives of NCTC8325, an *agr*⁺ wild type. RN450, our standard host strain, is 8325 cured of three prophages, φ11, φ12 and φ13. Note that the elimination of φ13 activates the expression of β-haemolysin (Coleman *et al.*, 1986). Substrains of RN450 vary in their exoprotein expression from laboratory to laboratory; our extant laboratory strain is partially defective; RN6390 is a fully active RN450 derivative and ISP546 is the original *agr*::Tn*551* strain isolated and kindly provided by P. Pattee. RN4220 is a derivative of RN450, also partially defective in exoprotein expression, that is able to accept *E. coli* DNA (Kreiswirth *et al.*, 1983). RN6734, RN6751 and RN6654 are φ13 lysogens of RN6390, RN4220 and ISP546, respectively. In *Table 48.1* are listed the plasmids used, including those newly constructed. pSK265 (kindly provided by S. Khan) is a derivative of pC194 (Horinouchi and Weisblum, 1982) with the polylinker region of pUC18 inserted at its unique *Hin*dIII site pSA0802 is a derivative of pC194 that is thermosensitive for replication (Iordanescu and Surdeanu, 1983), kindly provided by S. Iordanescu.

**Table 48.1**  Plasmids

| Plasmid | Description | Source or Reference |
|---|---|---|
| pSK265 | pC194::pUC19 polylinker (PL) | Jones and Khan (1986) |
| pWN2018 | pC194::*ori* ColE::*bla*::pUC18 PL | Wang *et al.* (1987) |
| pWN2019 | pC194::*ori* ColE1::*bla*::pUC19 PL | Wang *et al.* (1987) |
| pRN3032 | p2258::*blaZ401*::*cad-52*::*seq-36* | Novick *et al.* (1979a) |
| pRN6677 | pSA0802::pUC18::*agr*-a0 | This work |
| pRN6584 | pSK265::*agr*-a4 | Peng *et al.* (1988) |
| pRN6585 | pSK265::*agr*-a6 | Peng *et al.* (1988) |
| pRN6661 | pSK265::*agr*-a12 | Peng *et al.* (1988) |
| pRN6662 | pSK265::*agr*-a14 | Peng *et al.* (1988) |
| pRN6664 | pSK265::*agr*-a17 | Peng *et al.* (1988) |
| pRN6599 | pWN2019::*agr*-a8 | Peng *et al.* (1988) |
| pRN6598 | pWN2018::*agr*-a8 | Peng *et al.* (1988) |
| pRN6671 | pSK265::*agr*-a20 | This work |
| pRN6672 | pSK265::*agr*-a21 | This work |
| pRN6673 | pSK265::*agr*-a26 | This work |
| pRN6674 | pSK265::*agr*-a27 | This work |
| pRN6599 | pWN2019::*agr*-a8 | Peng *et al.* (1988) |
| pRN6675 | pWN2019::*agr*-a25 | This work |
| pRN6676 | pWN2019::*tst*-t1 | This work |

MEDIA AND GROWTH CONDITIONS

CY broth (Novick and Brodsky, 1972) was used for liquid cultures, shaken at 37°C and monitored turbidimetrically with a Klett–Summerson photoelectric colorimeter read at 540 nm. GL agar (Novick and Brodsky, 1972) was supplemented with antibiotics as indicated. Tetracycline (Tc), chloramphenicol (Cm) and erythromycin (Em) were used at 5 µg ml$^{-1}$.

Protoplast transformation was performed according to the method of Chang and Cohen (1979) as modified for *S. aureus* (Novick *et al.*, 1984). Transduction was with phage 80α as described (Novick, 1967). Plasmid copy numbers were determined by fluorimetric densitometry of ethidium bromide-stained agarose gels (Projan and Novick, 1986). Plasmid stability was assessed by scoring the cultures used for exoprotein measurements for retention of the plasmid Cm$^r$ marker.

ANALYSIS OF EXOPROTEINS

β-lactamase was assayed colorimetrically using nitrocefin as substrate (O'Callaghan *et al.*, 1972); α-haemolysin was assayed by serial dilution of supernatants using 0·5% whole defibrinated rabbit blood as substrate. Samples were incubated for 90 min at 37°C, then held at 4°C for 30 min. Activity was determined by reading the samples turbidimetrically (Klett–Summerson colorimeter, red filter) and interpolating to calculate the 50% lysis point. Activities (haemolytic units—HU) are expressed as the reciprocal of the dilution giving 50% lysis. Although β-haemolysin inhibits the activity of α-haemolysin on sheep-blood agar plates, no such inhibition was observed in the Tris-saline buffer used for the α-haemolysin titrations.

RESTRICTION MAPPING AND CLONING

Restriction endonucleases were purchased from Boehringer Mannheim

Biochemicals and were used as described by the manufacturer. Restriction mapping and fragment isolations were performed with ethidium bromide–CsC purified plasmid DNA samples (Novick *et al.*, 1979b; Novick *et al.*, 1985). For molecular cloning, specific fragments were eluted from polyacrylamide gels, phenol extracted, and ethanol precipitated. For ligation, samples were combined in approximately equimolar ratios and incubated for 16–24 hours at 14°C at a DNA concentration of at least 10 μg ml$^{-1}$ and a ligase concentration of 40 units ml$^{-1}$. Cloning with pBR322, pUC18 and M13 in *E. coli* was performed as described by Maniatis, Fritsch and Sambrook (1982). *E. coli* clones were verified by restriction analysis and by blot hybridization (Southern, 1975) as required. DNA sequencing was by the dideoxynucleotide methods of Sanger and co-workers (Sanger, Nicklen and Coulson, 1977; Sanger *et al.*, 1980) using M13*mp*10, M13*mp*11 clones and various synthetic oligonucleotide primers purchased from Pharmacia and from Genetic Designs. Northern and Southern blot hybridizations were performed according to standard procedures (Southern, 1975; Thomas, 1980).

**Results**

CLONING OF *agr*

Strain RN4256 (Kreiswirth *et al.*, 1983) was constructed in connection with an earlier study of the toxic shock syndrome toxin (Kreiswirth *et al.*, 1983) by transforming a naturally occurring toxic shock strain, RN4282, for erythromycin resistance (Em$^r$) with DNA from ISP546, the original Tn*551*-induced *agr$^-$* strain isolated by Pattee and co-workers (Mallonee, Glatz and Pattee, 1982). A segment of chromosomal DNA from RN4282 containing the site of the Tn*551* insertion in RN4256 was cloned in two stages. In the first stage, a *Bgl*II fragment containing one end of the transposon and about 3 kbp of flanking sequences was cloned from RN4256 to pBR322 in *E. coli* using the transposon as probe. In the second stage, the first clone was used to probe a λ library prepared from RN4282, which contains the functional *agr* determinant. Phage DNAs prepared from three positive plaques were restriction mapped and shown to have a common central region and different end points, suggesting that they were a true representation of the native chromosomal region (Peng *et al.*, 1988). Subcloning from one of these phage clones to pUC18 in *E. coli* yielded a 6·1 kbp *Eco*RI–*Bgl*II fragment which contained the Tn*551* insertion site. Attempts to clone this fragment to *S. aureus* using the vector pSK265 were unsuccessful; evidently the complete *agr* determinant is detrimental or lethal at the high gene dosage obtained with pSK265 (80–100 copies per cell). Most recently, we have succeeded in cloning the a0 fragment in *S. aureus* using pSA0802, a pC194 derivative that is thermosensitive for replication (Iordanescu and Surdeanu, 1983). This clone could be maintained at 37°C, a temperature at which the vector exists at 1–2 copies per cell but not at 32°C, a temperature at which the vector exists at about 15 copies per cell. This clone has *agr* activity in RN4220 and its analysis is currently in progress. A series of subclones containing fragments derived from a0 have been prepared and

# *agr* clone

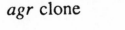

a21          a6          a10          none

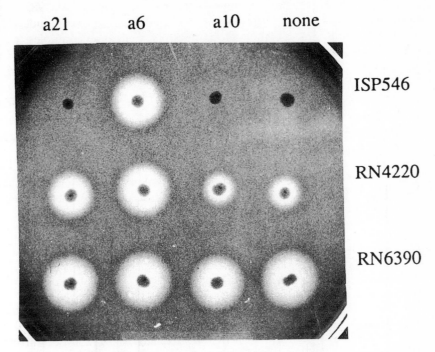

ISP546

RN4220

RN6390

**Figure 48.1**   Haemolytic activity of *S. aureus* strains. Strains were spotted on sheep-blood agar and incubated for 24 h at 37°C. Host strains are indicated at right, all φ13 lysogens; the indicated *agr* fragments correspond to pSK265 clones listed in *Table 48.1*.

analysed in some detail. This analysis consisted in testing for the ability to complement the *agr* defects in RN4220, RN4256 and ISP546. The effect of each clone on the *agr* activity of RN6390 was also evaluated. To simplify the analysis, we used φ13 lysogens of each of the three host strains and scored them for haemolytic activity on sheep-blood agar (α-haemolysin is the only detectable haemolysin in φ13 lysogens of strains of the 8325 series). Verification for other exoproteins is in progress. Typical results are shown in *Figure 48.1* and summarized in *Figure 48.2*. Restriction fragments in the *agr* regions are numbered in series, in the order of cloning, using the letter 'a' to indicate *agr*. As can be seen in *Figure 48.2*, the smallest fragment with *agr* activity in ISP546 (φ13) is a17, an 824 bp *Hinc*II–*Tth*111I fragment that includes the Tn*551* insertion site. A second functional region, active in RN4220 but not in ISP546 is located within a 3·9 kbp *Pvu*II fragment (a21). Deletion analysis (*see* below) in conjunction with sequencing data suggest that this second region is clearly separate from the first one and is located, at least in part, between the *Bst*N1 and *Pst*I sites (see a25, a26 and a27). On the basis of these results plus transcription analysis (*see* below) we elected to determine the nucleotide sequence of the entire 6·1 kbp region. Sequencing was by the dideoxynucleotide method (Sanger, Nicklen and Coulson, 1977) using

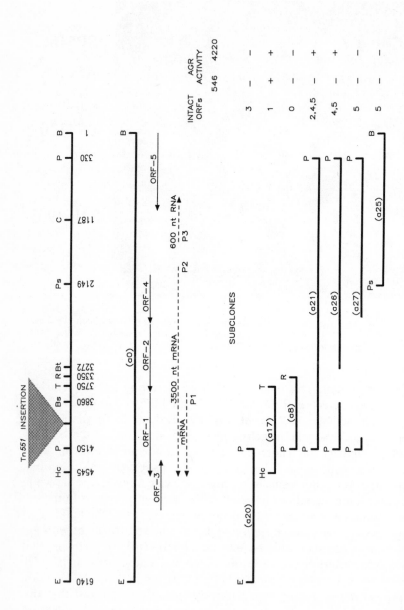

**Figure 48.2**   Characterization of the *agr* operon. The upper line represents chromosomal DNA of the *agr* operon in ISP546. The Tn*551* insertion and important restriction sites are shown. The five major ORFs and their orientations are indicated by solid arrows, and the known RNA transcripts by dashed arrows. Line drawings, below, indicate the extent of subclones. The intact ORFs contained within each subcloned fragment and their *agr* activities in ISP546 and RN4220 are listed. Restriction enzyme abbreviations are: B, *Bgl*II; Bs, *Bst*NI; Bt, *Bst*EII; C, *Cla*I; E, *Eco*RI; Hc, *Hinc*II; P, *Pvu*II; Ps, *Pst*I; R, *Rsa*I; T, *Tth*111I.

synthetic oligonucleotides as primers with M13 subclones of various fragments in both orientations. Approximately 4·7 kb have been sequenced to date (*see Figure 48.3*). Analysis of this 4·7 kb sequence revealed four major open reading-frames, ORF-1, ORF-2, ORF-4 and ORF-5, read from right to left, and a part of a fifth, ORF-3, read from left to right, as indicated in *Figure 48.2*. We also determined the sequence of the chromosome–Tn*551* junction in the original pBR322 clone, and this sequence showed that the transposon had inserted in ORF-1 near the N-terminus. The *agr* subclones were examined for the presence of these various ORFs as shown in *Figure 48.2*. The presence of the intact ORF-1 plus about 90 nt 5′ to the putative translational start (fragment a17) was necessary and sufficient for the restoration of *agr* activity in strains containing the original Tn*551* insertion, as determined by the production of α-haemolysin in RN6654, and the same was true for RN4256 with respect to TSST-1 production (kindly analysed by P. Schlievert). ORF-1 is therefore designated *agrA*. Although all clones containing *agrA* complemented the Tn*551*-induced *agr* defect, in no case was the activity restored to the full wild-type level. Possible explanations for this lack of full complementation are discussed below. Clones containing the left-hand 2 kbp of the a0 fragment (such as a20) had no detectable activity, nor did this region enhance the activity of *agrA*. Although the sequence of this region is incomplete, it is considered likely that all of ORF-3 is included in a20 simply on the basis of size. There is, in any case, no evidence at present that the ORF-3 region is or is not involved. On the other hand, the a21 clone, inactive in RN6654 (*see Figure 48.1*) showed significant *agr* activity in RN6751 [RN4220 (φ13)]. Typical results are illustrated in *Figure 48.1*, which shows α-haemolysin activity on sheep-blood agar for several *agr* subclones in several host strains. As noted, RN4220 is a nitrosoguanidine-induced mutant of RN450 selected for its ability to accept *E. coli* DNA (Kreiswirth *et al.*, 1983). On the basis of its weak expression of α-haemolysin and other exoproteins (Peng *et al.*, 1988), it appears to have a leaky exoprotein defect (Exp⁻). Since RN4220 shows complementation by *agrA* clones, the mutation is likely to affect this gene; the activity of a21 in this strain suggests that there is a second functional component of the *agr* system and that RN4220 is defective in the expression of this component also. This component was localized by deletion mapping to the ORF-4 region. Deletions were generated by digesting the pSK265::*agr*-a21 clone with *Bst*EII and *Bst*NI, and transforming *S. aureus* RN4220 with this linear DNA with non-matching ends. Deletions were mapped by Southern blotting with an oligonucleotide probe that covers the 3′ terminus of the ORF-4 reading frame. Typical examples, a26 and a27, are depicted in *Figure 48.2*; from this analysis, it is tentatively concluded that ORF-4 is a functional component of the a21 fragment. ORF-4 is henceforth referred to provisionally as *agrB*.

TRANSCRIPTION ANALYSIS

Northern blotting experiments, performed with strand-specific probes derived from various *agr* subclones, revealed a major 3·5 kbp transcript read from right to left and starting to the right of the *Pst*I site (Peng *et al.*, 1988) and a second, much smaller, transcript reading from left to right and traversing the *Cla*I site at

```
2701                                                                                              2801
TATTATTATAATGTATTTTGTCAAAATCAAATGGTATTCTATTTTGTTGATTATGAGTTCGCAGATTATTCTATACTGTGCTAACTACATGTATATAGTTATATATGCATATATCACCAAAATTTCTGATAGTATATTTGTAATATTCCCTAGCTTTTTTGTAGTTTATGTGACTATTAG
eIleIleIleMetTyrPheValLysIleLysTrpTyrSerIleLeuLeuIleMetSerSerGlnIleIleLeuTyrCysAlaAsnTyrMetTyrIleValIleTyrAlaTyrIleThrLysIleSerAspSerIlePheValIlePheProSerPhePheValValTyrValThrIleSe

AccI            2901                                                                                              3001
TATACTATTCTCATATATAATAAATAGAGTTCTCAAAAAAATTAGCACACCATATCTAATACTAAACAAAGGATTTTTAATAGTTATTTCGACTATCTTACTGCTTACTTTTTCATTATTTTTCTTTTATTCACAAATAAACTCGGATGAAGCTAAAGTAATAAGGCAGTATTCTTTATT
rIleLeuPheSerTyrIleIleAsnArgValLeuLysLysIleSerThrProTyrLeuIleLeuAsnLysGlyPheLeuIleValIleSerThrIleLeuLeuLeuThrPheSerLeuPhePhePheTyrSerGlnIleAsnSerAspGluAlaLysValIleArgGlnTyrSerLeuPh

                                            3101                                                                                              3201
TTATTGGTATCACTATATTTTAAGTATATTAACATTGTATTCTCAATTTCTCCTTAAAGAGATGAAATATAAACGTAATCAAGAAGAAATTGAAACCTATTATGAATATACATTGAAGATTGAAGCTATCAACAACGAAATGCGCAAGTTCCGTCATGATTATGTCAATATCTTAACGAC
eTyrTrpTyrHisTyrIleLeuSerIleLeuThrLeuTyrSerGlnPheLeuLeuLysGluMetLysTyrLysArgAsnGlnGluGluIleGluThrTyrTyrGluTyrThrLeuLysIleGluAlaIleAsnAsnGluMetArgLysPheArgHisAspTyrValAsnIleLeuThrTh

                                   BstNI                  3301                                     BsmI                                              3401
ACTTTCAGAATACATTCGAGAAGATGACATGCCTGGCCTACGTGATTATTTCAATAAAAATATTGTACCTATGAAAGACAATTTACAAATGAATGCTATAAAATTAAATGGTATCGAGAATCTTAAAGTACGTGAAATTAAAGGCTTAATTACTGCGAAAATTTTACGTGCACAAGAAAT
rLeuSerGluTyrIleArgGluAspAspMetProGlyLeuArgAspTyrPheAsnLysAsnIleValProMetLysAspAsnLeuGlnMetAsnAlaIleLysLeuAsnGlyIleGluAsnLeuLysValArgGluIleLysGlyLeuIleThrAlaLysIleLeuArgAlaGlnGluMe

                                                                ClaI                  3501
GAATATTCCGATTAGTATCGAAATACCCGATGAAGTAAGTAGCATTAACTTGAATATGATCGATTTAAGTCGCAGTATTGGTATTATTCTTGATAATGCAATTGAGGCATCAACTGAAATTGATGACCCTATCATTCGCGTTGCATTTATTGAAAGTGAAAATTCAGTAACGTTTATTGT
tAsnIleProIleSerIleGluIleProAspGluValSerSerIleAsnLeuAsnMetIleAspLeuSerArgSerIleGlyIleIleLeuAspAsnAlaIleGluAlaSerThrGluIleAspAspProIleIleArgValAlaPheIleGluSerGluAsnSerValThrPheIleVa

3601                              BsmI                                                                    3701
TATGAATAAATGCGCTGATGATATACCACGCATTCATGAATTGTTCCAAGAAAGTTTTTCTACTAAAGGTGAAGGTCGTGGTTTAGGTCTATCAACTTTAAAAGAAATTGCTGATAATGCAGACAATGTCTTATTAGATACAATTATCGAAAATGGTTTCTTTTATTCAAAAAGTTGAAA
lMetAsnLysCysAlaAspAspIleProArgIleHisGluLeuPheGlnGluSerPheSerThrLysGlyGluGlyArgGlyLeuGlyLeuSerThrLeuLysGluIleAlaAspAsnAlaAspAsnValLeuLeuAspThrIleIleGluAsnGlyPhePheTyrSerLysSer...

                        S.D
                        3801                                                              BstEii                            3901
TTATTAACAACTAGCCATAAGGATGTGAATGTATGAAAATTTTCATTTGCGAAGACGATCCAAAACAAAGAGAAAACATGGTTACCATTATTAAAAATTATATAATGATAGAAGAAAAGCCTATGGAAATTGCCCTCGCAACTGATAATCCTTATGAGGTGCTTGAGCAAGCTAAAAATA
                        ORF-1 (agrA) MetLysIlePheIleCysGluAspAspProLysGlnArgGluAsnMetValThrIleIleLysAsnTyrIleMetIleGluGluLysProMetGluIleAlaLeuAlaThrAspAsnProTyrGluValLeuGluGlnAlaLysAsnM

                                             4001                                                                                         4101  AccI
TGAATGACATAGGCTGTTACTTTTTAGATATTCAACTTTCAACTGATATTAATGGTATCAAATTAGGCAGTGAAATTCGTAAGCATGACCCAGTTGGTAACATTATTTTCGTTACGAGTCACAGTGAACTTACCTATTTAACATTTGTCTACAAAGTTGCAGCGATGGATTTTATTTTTA
etAsnAspIleGlyCysTyrPheLeuAspIleGlnLeuSerThrAspIleAsnGlyIleLysLeuGlySerGluIleArgLysHisAspProValGlyAsnIleIlePheValThrSerHisSerGluLeuThrTyrLeuThrPheValTyrLysValAlaAlaMetAspPheIlePheL

         PvuII                                                   4201                                                                                              4301
AAGATGATCCAGCTGAATTAAGAACTCGAATTATAGACTGTTTAGAAACTGCACATACACGCTTACAATTGTTGTCTAAAGATAATAGCGTTGAAACGATTGAATTAAAACGTGGCAGTAATTCAGTGTATGTTCAATATGATGATATTATGTTTTTTGAATCATCAACAAAATCTCACA
ysAspAspProAlaGluLeuArgThrArgIleIleAspCysLeuGluThrAlaHisThrArgLeuGlnLeuLeuSerLysAspAsnSerValGluThrIleGluLeuLysArgGlySerAsnSerValTyrValGlnTyrAspAspIleMetPhePheGluSerSerThrLysSerHisA

                                                                                    4401
GACTCATTGCCCATTTAGATAACCGTCAAATTGAATTTTATGGTAATTTAAAAGAACTGAGTCAATTAGATGATCGTTTCTTTAGATGTCATAATAGCTTTGTCGTCAATCGCCATAATATTGAATCTATAGATTCGAAAGAGCGAATTGTCTATTTTAAAAATAAAGAACACTGCTATG
rgLeuIleAlaHisLeuAspAsnArgGlnIleGluPheTyrGlyAsnLeuLysGluLeuSerGlnLeuAspAspArgPhePheArgCysHisAsnSerPheValValAsnArgHisAsnIleGluSerIleAspSerLysGluArgIleValTyrPheLysAsnLysGluHisCysTyrA

4501                                                HincII                                            4601
CATCGGTGAGAAACGTTAAAAAAATATAATAAGATAATAAAGTCAGTTAACGACGTATTCAATTGTAAATCTTGTTGGATTTTAACAAGATAACTAGCAAATGCACTGTATAGCTGGCTTTTTAATTTTATTAACAAAATTAAATATGACGCGTGAATTAAAAAATGATGTAACGTCTCT
laSerValArgAsnValLysLysIle

TTGTAT
```

**Figure 48.3** Nucleotide sequence of the *agr* region. The sequenced region extends from the *Bgl*II site (position zero in *Figure 48.2*) to the *Acc*I site, position 4·68). The region between nucleotides 2881–4686 has been previously sequenced (Peng *et al*., 1988); the newly determined sequence (1–2880) is 85% double-stranded with some ambiguity between positions 2460 and 2505 owing to G–C compression. The predicted amino-acid sequences and probable translational start points are given for the four significant open reading-frames ORF-1 (3813–4526), ORF-2 (2342–3775), ORF-4 (1776–2342) and ORF-5 (3–806), reading from right to left. The fifth (ORF-3, not shown) starts beyond the known sequence and reads in from the left, terminating at position 4388.

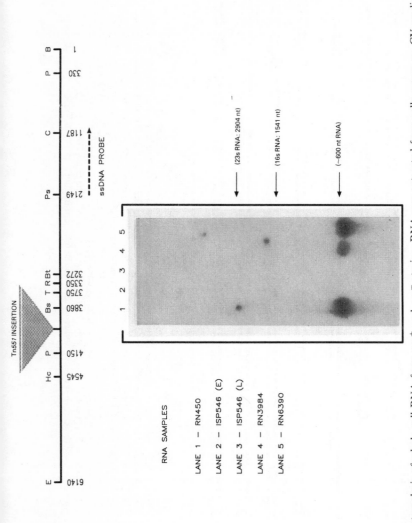

**Figure 48.4** Northern blot analysis of whole cell RNA from *agr*⁺ and *agr*⁻ strains. RNA was extracted from cells grown on CY medium in the presence of guanidinium thiocyanate and purified by the method of Chirgwin *et al.* (1979). Each RNA sample was heat-denatured and electrophoresed on 1·0% agarose containing 20mM morpholinopropane sulphonic acid, pH 7·0, 2·2 M formaldehyde and ethidium bromide (1 μg ml⁻¹). RNA was transferred to nitrocellulose using the Pharmacia VacuGene blotting system, baked for two hours at 80°C and then pre-hybridized and hybridized at 55°C. The hybridization probe was single-stranded DNA from an M13 clone containing the 962 bp *Psr*I–*Cla*I fragment (dashed line), which was labelled by the primer extension method using the M13 Hybridization Primer (BM), α-[³²P]dATP and Klenow fragment of DNA polymerase I. ISP546 (E) refers to RNA isolated from a mid-exponential phase cells, whereas ISP546 (L) refers to RNA isolated from early stationary phase cells. The concentration of the RNA samples was: RN450, 6 μg; ISP546 (E), 14 μg; ISP546 (L), 31 μg; RN3984, 7 μg and RN6390, 2 μg.

position 1·2. The small rightward transcript, as well as the larger leftward one, was absent in ISP546, the *agrA*::Tn*551* strain, as shown in *Figure 48.4*. Similar transcripts have been detected in strain V8 by Arvidson and co-workers (Morfeldt *et al.*, 1988), who also reported that the major leftward transcript was absent in *agr⁻* strains.

GENE FUSION ANALYSIS

In a preliminary attempt to analyse promoter function in the *agr* region, we utilized a promoter-probe vector, pWN2019, that we have recently developed for gene fusion analysis (Wang *et al.*, 1987). This vector contains the pUC18 polylinker in either orientation followed by a promoterless derivative of the *S. aureus* plasmid pI258 *bla* gene. Thus far, we have cloned the a8 and a25 fragments as well as a 960 bp *Bam*HI–*tst*(tl) fragment containing part of the TSST-1 gene (*tst*) plus 5′ flanking sequences (Kreiswirth *et al.*, 1983) to these vectors and found all three to have promoter activity. The a8 fragment was cloned in both orientations and found to express β-lactamase only in the orientation appropriate for *agrA* transcription (Peng *et al.*, 1988). The a25 fragment has thus far been cloned in only the orientation appropriate for *agrB* transcription. β-lactamase production by the active fusion derivatives was measured in ISP546, RN4220 and RN6390, and the results are presented in *Figure 48.5*. The active a8 fusion produced 1–2 units of enzyme mg$^{-1}$ dry weight in all three strains. These activities are rather low—about 0·05% of that seen with a constitutive mutation of the native β-lactamase expression system (Novick and Richmond, 1965), were unaffected by the presence of an active *agr* determinant and showed no change during the transition from exponential to post-exponential phase. Activities of both a25 and tl were very low in ISP546, high in RN6390 and intermediate in RN4220. These activities were temporally regulated in RN6390 and RN4220 but not in ISP546, suggesting that *agrA* is a key component of the temporal regulation system.

**Table 48.2**   Activity ratios

|  | Native | | *bla* fusion | | |
|---|---|---|---|---|---|
|  | α-haemolysin | TSST-1 | *agr*:P1 | *agr*:P2 | *tst*:P1 |
| RN6390/ISP546 | >1000 | | 1·7 | 13 | 19 |
| RN4282/RN4256 | | >150 | | | |
| RN4220/ISP546 | >9 | | | 2·8 | 1·6 |
| ISP546(*agrA*)/ISP546 | >12 | | | | |
| RN4256(*agrA*)/RN4256 | | >4 | | | |
| RN6390(sta)/RN6390(exp) | 35 | | 2 | 8·1 | 23 |
| RN4220(sta)/RN4220(exp) | | | 1·3 | 4·5 | >10 |
| ISP546(sta)/ISP546(exp) | | | 1·6 | 2·2 | 1·8 |

sta, Stationary phase; exp, exponential phase.

An important question with gene fusions is that of how well the fusion reflects the activity of the native gene. This question was addressed by comparing ratios of activity of the fusion product with those of native exoproteins. This comparison is presented in *Table 48.2*, from which the following conclusions can be drawn:

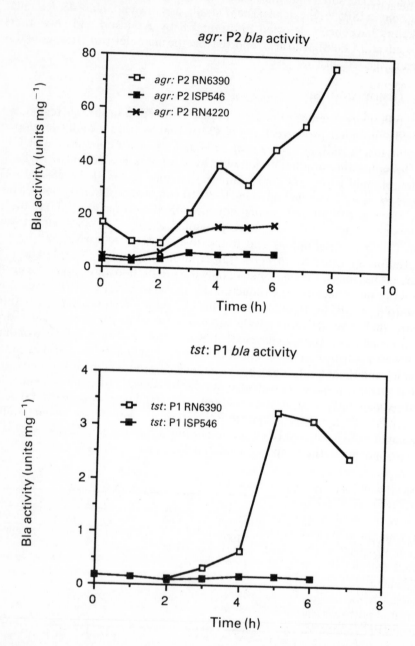

**Figure 48.5**  Production of β-lactamase by gene fusion strains. Cells were grown in CY broth at 37°C with shaking, starting in early exponential phase at about $10^8$ ml$^{-1}$ and reaching early stationary phase, at about $5 \times 10^9$ ml$^{-1}$. β-Lactamase was measured on unfractionated samples taken at the indicated time points. *agr*:P2 corresponds to fragment a25 cloned to pWN2019; *tst*:P1 corresponds to fragment *tst*-t1 cloned to the same vector. Each line on the graph corresponds to the β-lactamase activity of the indicated host strain carrying the *agr*:P2 or *tst*:P1 fusion.

1.  The activities of native exoproteins are more sensitive to *agr* than is any of the *bla* fusions. In particular, the fusions have significant activity in *agr*::Tn*551* strains.
2.  The complemented *agr*::Tn*551* mutation is considerably less efficient than the native chromosomal configuration with respect to the expression of α-haemolysin and TSST-1.
3.  *agr*:P2 and *tst*:P1 *bla* fusions show no temporal regulation in ISP546.
4.  Temporal regulation of the *agr*:P2 transcript is weaker than that of native exoproteins.

Since these *bla* fusions are purely transcriptional, differences between these and the native proteins could reflect a component of post-transcriptional regulation; alternatively, they could reflect differences in the expression of plasmid-carried v. chromosomal genes.

## Discussion

The data presented in this report demonstrate that *agr* is a *trans*-activator of a series of exoprotein genes that are expressed during the post-exponential phase of growth in *S. aureus*. The cloned *agr* determinant contains at least five separate reading frames, of which we have shown two to be involved in *agr* activity; these have accordingly been designated *agrA* and *agrB*, respectively. Three promoters have also been identified, a weak constitutive promoter, *agr*:P1, that is just 5' to *agrA*, and two much stronger *agr*-sensitive divergent promoters. One of these, *agr*:P2, is used to initiate a 3·5 kbp transcript that probably traverses *agrA* as well as *agrB*. The other, *agr*:P3, traverses a region whose role in the regulatory system is thus far unknown. *agr*:P2 and *agr*:P3 are inactive in strains containing a Tn*551* insertion in *agrA*, suggesting that they are activated by the *agrA* product. A key finding in the attempt to understand the functional organization of this system is the *agr* activity of the *agrB*-containing a21 fragment in RN4220. RN4220 has a partial *agr*-defect that is complemented by *agrB* as well as by *agrA* clones, indicating that *agrB* is a component of the system. Given that the *agrB* promoter is activated by the *agrA* product, the most economical of many possible hypotheses for RN4220 is that of a single leaky mutation in *agrA*. Consistent with this hypothesis is the reduced activity of *agr*:P2 in RN4220 and the lack of *agrB* activity in ISP546, which has a complete *agrA* defect. It would follow from this hypothesis that *agrB* acts subsequently to *agrA* in the activation of exoprotein expression. Our working model, then, has *agrA* transcribed by a weak constitutive promoter and activated post-transcriptionally by an unknown metabolic signal generated at the end of exponential growth. In the absence of AgrA activity, the regulated genes would be expressed at very low basal constitutive levels. The *agrA* product would then activate transcription from *agr*:P2 and *agr*:P3, which has two consequences: production of AgrB and auto-amplification of the *agrA* transcript. The role of the *agr*:P3 transcript has yet to be defined. The auto-amplification of AgrA would result in a burst of synthesis of AgrB and of the regulated exoproteins. This is, indeed, what is observed and it accomodates nicely the need of the cell to achieve rapid high-level expression of the

508     *Protein Secretion*

exoproteins at a time when cellular metabolism is rapidly declining. This autogenous induction system should be compared with classical enzyme induction in which enzyme synthesis is tied to cell growth (after one generation the enzyme concentration is half-maximal, after two, three-quarters, etc.) and which, consequently, would not be at all suitable for the post-exponential phase. In our hands, post-exponential phase synthesis comes to a halt soon after stationary phase has been reached; upon re-entry into exponential phase, the system would be switched off because the metabolic signal that activates the *agrA* function would no longer be present. Note that implicit in this model is a possible explanation for the failure of *agrA* clones to restore fully the exoprotein phenotype of the Tn*551*-containing strains: the auto-activation circuit, which would require co-transcription of *agrA* and *agrB*, is broken when the two components are in *trans*. In the light of all of the presently available data, it would appear that the *agr* system has both transcriptional and post-transcriptional regulatory components. Thus the auto-activation circuit is transcriptional as is the *agr*-specific activation and repression of the various exoprotein genes (Recsei *et al.*, 1985; Janzon, Löfdahl and Arvidson, 1986). Activation of the temporal switch would appear to be post-transcriptional as the local *agrA* promoter, *agr*:P1, does not show temporal regulation. This inference brings to mind a number of earlier observations of inhibition of post-exponential phase exoprotein synthesis by translation inhibitors, such as macrolide antibiotics, and by limitations by the availability of certain amino acids (Kihara and Snell, 1955). These observations will doubtless be of increasing significance as our understanding develops.

**Acknowledgement**

We thank L. Janzon and S. Ardvison for helpful discussions and for communication of unpublished data. This work was supported by a grant from the Aaron Diamond Foundation (to R.P.N.) and by NIH grant 5 RO1 AI22159–03 (to R.P.N.)

**References**

BJORKLIND, A. AND ARVIDSON, S. (1980). Mutants of *Staphylococcus aureus* affected in the regulation of exoprotein synthesis. *FEMS Microbiology Letters* 7, 203–206.
CHANG, S. AND COHEN, S.N. (1979). High frequency of transformation of *Bacillus subtilis* protoplasts by plasmid DNA. *Molecular and General Genetics* 168, 111–115.
CHIRGWIN, J., PRZABYLA, A., MACDONALD, R. AND RUTTER, W. (1979). Isolation of biologically active ribonucleic acid from sources enriched in ribonuclease. *Biochemistry* 18, 5294–5299.
COLEMAN, D.C., ARBUTHNOTT, J.P., POMEROY, H.M. AND BIRKBECK, T.H. (1986). Cloning and expression in *Escherichia coli* and *Staphylococcus aureus* of the beta-lysin determinant from *Straphylococcus aureus*: evidence that bacteriophage conversion of beta-lysin activity is caused by insertional inactivation of the beta-lysin determinant. *Microbial Pathogenesis* 1, 549–564.
COLEMAN, G. (1967). Studies on the regulation of extracellular enzyme formation by *Bacillus subtilis*. *Journal of General Microbiology* 49, 421–431.

Regulation of Exoprotein Synthesis in S. aureus 509

COLEMAN, G., JAKEMAN, C. AND MARTIN, N. (1978). Patterns of extracellular protein secretion by a number of clinically isolated strains of *Staphylococcus aureus*. *Journal of General Microbiology* **107**, 189–192.

HORINOUCHI, S. AND WEISBLUM, B. (1982). Nucleotide sequence and functional map of pC194, a plasmid that specifies inducible chloramphenicol resistance. *Journal of Bacteriology* **150**, 815–825.

IORDANESCU, S. AND SURDEANU, M. (1983). Isolation and complementation of temperature-sensitive replication mutants of *Staphylococcus aureus* plasmid pC194. *Molecular and General Genetics* **191**, 201–206.

JANZON, L., LÖFDAHL, S. AND ARVIDSON, S. (1986). Evidence for a coordinate transcriptional control of alpha-toxin and protein A synthesis in *Staphylococcus aureus*. *FEMS Microbiology Letters* **33**, 193–198.

JONES, C.L. AND KHAN, S.A. (1986). Nucleotide sequence of the enterotoxin B gene from *Staphylococcus aureus*. *Journal of Bacteriology* **166**, 29–33.

KATSUNO, S. AND KONDO, M. (1973). Regulation of staphylococcal enterotoxin B synthesis and its relation to other extracellular proteins. *Japanese Journal of Medical Science and Biology* **26**, 26–29.

KIHARA, H. AND SNELL, E.E. (1955). Peptides and bacterial growth. III. Relation to inhibitions by thienylalanine, ethionine, and canavanine. *Journal of Biological Chemistry* **212**, 83–94.

KREISWIRTH, B., LÖFDAHL, S., BETLEY, M., O'REILLY, M., SCHLIEVERT, P., BERGDOLL, M. AND NOVICK, R.P. (1983). The toxic shock syndrome exotoxin structural gene is not detectably transmitted by a prophage. *Nature* **305**, 709–712.

MALLONEE, D.H., GLATZ, B. AND PATTEE, P. (1982). Chromosomal mapping of a gene affecting Enterotoxin A production in *Staphylococcus aureus*. *Applied Environmental Microbiology* **43**, 397–402.

MANIATIS, T., FRITSCH, E.F. AND SAMBROOK, J. (1982). *Molecular Cloning: A Laboratory Manual*. Cold Spring Harbor Laboratory Press, New York.

MORFELDT, E., JANZON, L., ARVIDSON, S. AND LÖFDAHL, S. (1988). Cloning of a chromosomal locus (*exp*) which regulates the expression of several exoprotein genes in *Staphylococcus aureus*. *Molecular and General Genetics* **211**, 435–440.

NOVICK, R. (1967). Properties of a cryptic high-frequency transducing phage in *Staphylococcus aureus*. *Virology* **33**, 155–166.

NOVICK, R.P. AND BRODSKY, R.J. (1972). Studies on plasmid replication: plasmid incompatibility and establishment in *Staphylococcus aureus*. *Journal of Molecular Biology* **68**, 285–302.

NOVICK, R.P. AND RICHMOND, M.H. (1965). Nature and integrations of the genetic elements governing penicillinase synthesis in *Stephylococcus aureus*. *Journal of Bacteriology* **90**, 467–480.

NOVICK, R.P., EDELMAN, I., SCHWESINGER, M.D., GRUSS, A.D., SWANSON, E.C. AND PATTEE, P.A. (1979a). Genetic translocation in *Staphylococcus aureus*. *Proceedings of the National Academy of Sciences of the United States of America* **76**, 400–404.

NOVICK, R.P., MURPHY, E., GRYCZAN, T.J., BARON, E. AND EDELMAN, I. (1979b). Penicillinase plasmids of *Staphylococcus aureus*: restriction–deletion maps. *Plasmid* **2**, 109–129.

NOVICK, R.P., ADLER, G.K., PROJAN, S.J., CARLETON, S., HIGHLANDER, S., GRUSS, A., KHAN, S.A. AND IORDANESCU, S. (1984). Control of pT181 Replication. I. The pT181 copy control function acts by inhibiting the synthesis of a replication protein. *EMBO Journal* **3**, 2399–2405.

NOVICK, R.P., PROJAN, S.J., KUMAR, C., CARLETON, S., GRUSS, S., HIGHLANDER, S.K. AND KORNBLUM, J. (1985). Replication control for pT181, an indirectly regulated plasmid. In *Plasmids in Bacteria* (D.R. Helinski, S.N. Cohen, D.B. Clewell, D.A. Jackson and A. Hollaender, Eds), pp. 299–320. Plenum Press, New York.

O'CALLAGHAN, C.H., MORRIS, A., KIRBY, S.M. AND SHINGLER, A.H. (1972). Novel method for detection of β-lactamases by using a chromogenic cephalosporin substrate. *Antimicrobial Agents and Chemotherapy* **1**, 283–288.

O'REILLY, M., DE AZEVADO, J.C., KENNEDY, S. AND FOSTER, T.J. (1986). Inactivation of the alpha-haemolysis gene of *Staphylococcus aureus* 8325–4 by site-directed mutagenesis and studies on the expression of its haemolysins. *Microbial Pathogenesis* **1**, 125–138.

PENG, H., NOVICK, R.P., KREISWIRTH, B. AND SCHLIEVERT, P. (1988). Cloning, characterization and sequencing of an accessory gene regulator (*agr*) in *Staphylococcus aureus. Journal of Bacteriology* **170**, 4365–4372.

PROJAN, S.J. AND NOVICK, R.P. (1986). Incompatibility between plasmids with independent copy control. *Molecular and General Genetics* **204**, 341–348.

RECSEI, P., KREISWIRTH, B., O'REILLY, M., SCHLIEVERT, P., GRUSS, A. AND NOVICK, R.P. (1985). Regulation of exoprotein gene expression by *agr*. In *The Staphylococci* (J. Jeljaszewicz, Ed.), pp. 701–706. Gustav Fischer Verlag, Stuttgart.

SANGER, G., NICKLEN, S. AND COULSON, A.R. (1977). DNA sequencing with chain-terminating inhibitors. *Proceedings of the National Academy of Sciences of the United States of America* **74**, 5463–5467.

SANGER, F., COULSEN, A., BARRETT, G., SMITH, A. AND ROE, B. (1980). Cloning in single-stranded bacteriophage as an aid to rapid DNA sequencing. *Journal of Molecular Biology* **143**, 161–178.

SOUTHERN, E. (1975). Detection of specific sequences among DNA fragments separated by gel electrophoresis. *Journal of Molecular Biology* **98**, 503–517.

THOMAS, P.S. (1980). Hybridization of denatured RNA and small DNA fragments transferred to nitrocellulose. *Proceedings of the National Academy of Sciences of the United States of America* **77**, 5201–5204.

WANG, P.Z., PROJAN, S.J., LEASON, K. AND NOVICK, R.P. (1987). Translational fusion with a secretory enzyme as an inducer. *Journal of Bacteriology* **169**, 3082–3087.

YOSHIKAWA, M., MATSUDA, F., NAKA, M., MUROFUSHI, E. AND TSUNEMATSU, Y. (1974). Pleiotropic alteration of activities of several toxins and enzymes in mutants of *Staphylococcus aureus. Journal of Bacteriology* **119**, 117–122.

# 49
# The Exoprotein Regulatory Region *exp* of *Staphylococcus aureus*

STAFFAN ARVIDSON*, LARS JANZON*, SVEN LÖFDAHL[†]
AND EVA MORFELDT[†]

* Department of Bacteriology, Karolinska Institute, S-104 01 Stockholm,
Sweden and [†] Department of Bacteriology, National Bacteriological
Laboratory, S-105 21 Stockholm, Sweden

## Introduction

*Staphylococcus aureus* produces a large number of extracellular proteins. More than 25 different exoproteins have been identified; about 10 have been characterized as toxins while those remaining are mostly non-toxic hydrolytic enzymes (*see* Arvidson, 1983). Also, bacterial surface proteins, such as protein A, clumping factor and fibronectin-binding protein, belong to the group of extracellular proteins in the sense that they have passed through the cytoplasmic membrane.

Co-ordinated control of exoprotein synthesis has been suggested on the basis of the observation that production is strictly synchronized and appears mainly during the post-exponential or stationary phase of growth (Abbas-Ali and Coleman, 1977; Coleman and Abbas-Ali, 1977).

Previous studies in our laboratory have demonstrated that the production of at least nine of these extracellular proteins (*see Table 49.1*) is controlled by a chromosomal locus, called *exp* (Björklind and Arvidson, 1980). Mutants of *exp* are characterized by a decreased production of alpha-toxin, serine protease, metallo-protease, staphylokinase, nuclease, acid phosphatase and leucocidin, and a simultaneous increase in the production of protein A and coagulase. The total extracellular protein production by a spontaneous *exp* mutant, K6812–1 and the corresponding wild-type strain, *S. aureus* V8, is shown in *Figure 49.1*. There was no difference in the rate of exoprotein production during exponential growth between the two strains but the dramatic increase in production by the wild type during post-exponential growth phase was not observed in the mutant. This suggests that *exp* may be involved in the growth-rate-dependent regulation of exoprotein production. Analysis of alpha-toxin and protein A mRNAs by DNA–RNA hybridization revealed that the regulation of these two exoproteins was at the level of transcription (Janzon, Löfdahl and Arvidson, 1986).

*Genetic Transformation and Expression*
© Intercept Ltd, PO Box 716, Andover, Hants, SP10 1YG, UK

**Table 49.1**    Extracellular proteins regulated by *exp*

alpha-toxin
beta-toxin (Recsei *et al.*, 1986)
pyrogenic toxin (TSST-1) (Recsei *et al.*, 1986)
leucocidin
nuclease
phosphatase
serine protease
metallo-protease
staphylokinase
staphylocoagulase*
protein A*

* Negative control.

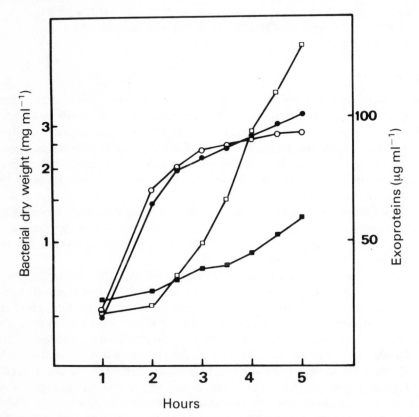

**Figure 49.1**    Bacterial dry weight (circles) and extracellular protein formation (squares) of *S. aureus* strain V8 (open symbols) and one *exp* mutant, K6812–1 (closed symbols) in brain–heart infusion medium.

## Results and discussion

In order to clone the *exp* locus, an insertional mutant (WA250) of *S. aureus* strain 8325-4 (Novick, 1967) with a typical Exp⁻ phenotype was isolated using the transposon Tn*551* (Morfeldt *et al.*, 1988). A restriction map of the cloned DNA is shown in *Figure 49.2*. Northern blot hybridization experiments, using as probes different restriction fragments of the cloned DNA, revealed two

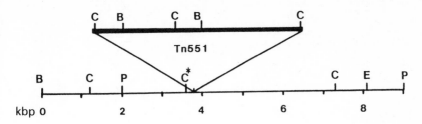

**Figure 49.2** Restriction map of the combined cloned chromosomal DNA of the *exp* region, including Tn*551* as it would appear in WA250. The thin line represents chromosomal DNA and the heavy line TN*551* DNA. Restriction site designations are: B, *Bgl*II; C, *Cla*I; E, *Eco*RI; P, *Pst*I; C*, a *Cla*I site that is methylated in *Escherichia coli*.

major RNAs of approximately 3·0 and 0·5 kbp, which were both absent in the insertional mutant, WA250 (Morfeldt *et al.*, 1988; *Figure 49.3*). The Tn*551* insert was located in the DNA sequence coding for the 3·0 kb RNA, indicating that the transcription of the 0·5 kb RNA is affected by a gene coded for by the larger RNA. The close vicinity of the two RNAs and their co-ordinate control suggests that they are both involved in the regulation of exoprotein production. They were therefore designated EXPA and EXPB for the 3·0 and the 0·5 kb RNA respectively. Since the same RNAs were also totally depressed in the spontaneous *exp* mutant, it was concluded that the insertional mutation was in the same locus (Morfeldt *et al.*, 1988).

Recsei *et al.* (1986) have described an insertional mutation with Tn*551* in a chromosomal locus called *agr* for accessory gene regulation. This mutation resulted in the same pleiotropic effects on exoprotein production as the *exp* mutation (*see Table 49.1*) and was also shown to affect the expression of several intracellular proteins in stationary phase bacteria. Northern blot hybridization experiments showed that both the EXPA and EXPB RNAs were totally depressed in this mutant also, suggesting that *agr* is identical to *exp* (Morfeldt *et al.*, 1988).

On the basis of the Northern blot experiments mentioned above, it was concluded that both RNAs extended into the 950 bp *Cla*I–*Pst*I fragment to the left of the site of insertion of Tn*551*. By using single-stranded probes of this fragment, it was shown that EXPA and EXPB were transcribed in opposite directions, starting within the 950 bp fragment. In order to map the promoters and to determine the extension of EXPB, a DNA fragment of approximately 2 kbp was sequenced. Primer extension experiments revealed that the transcription start points were 187 bases apart (*Figure 49.4*). Both start points are preceded by typical −10 and −35 boxes. 517 bases downstream from the EXPB transcription start point an inverted repeat, with a calculated free energy of −14·7 kcal mole$^{-1}$ was found. The repeat is immediately followed by a stretch of six T's and is probably the transcription terminator of EXPB. This is in agreement with the estimated size of 510 bases of the EXPB transcript. In the case of EXPA only the first 1200 bases were determined.

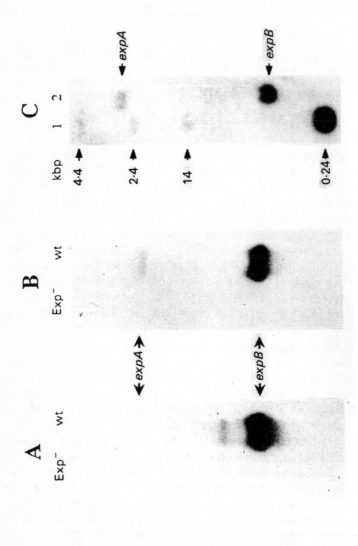

**Figure 49.3**    Northern blot. Equal amounts of RNA from *S. aureus* WA250 (Exp⁻) and the wild type 8325-4 (wt) were separated on a denaturing agarose gel and hybridized with the 1·2 kbp *Bg*III–*Cla*I (panel A) and the 950 bp *Cla*I–*Pst*I (panel B) chromosomal fragments. Panel C: Size determination of *expA* and *expB* transcripts. A RNA size marker (lane 1) was run together with RNA extracted from *S. aureus* 8325-4 (lane 2) on a denaturing agarose gel and hybridized with a mixture of λ-DNA and the 950 bp *Cla*I–*Pst*I fragment.

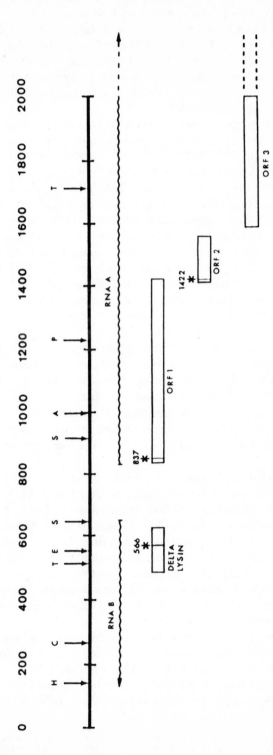

**Figure 49.4** Map of the sequenced part of the *exp* region in *S. aureus*. The thick line represents a restriction map as derived from the nucleotide sequence. H. *Hae*III; C. *Cla*I; T. *Taq*I; E. *Eco*RV; A. *Aco*I; P. *Pst*I; S. *Sau*3AI. Wavy lines indicate the transcripts of *expA* and *expB*, respectively. Open reading-frames (ORF) are indicated by open boxes. Translation initiation sites are indicated by stars, and the numbers above are the positions of the first bases in the initiation codons.

The sequences of the two transcripts were translated in all three reading-frames. As shown in *Figure 49.4*, EXPB contains a short open reading-frame (ORF) of 45 amino acids. The deduced amino-acid sequence was compared with the NBRF Protein Data Bank, which revealed that the 26 carboxy-terminal residues of the ORF were identical with the sequence of delta-lysin from *S. aureus* (Fitton, Dell and Shaw, 1980). Delta-lysin is an extracellular protein, produced by most *S. aureus* strains, with a cytolytic activity against all kinds of cells (Möllby, 1983).

This suggested that *expB* is not involved in the regulation of exoprotein production but is just an exoprotein gene regulated by *expA*. However, insertional inactivation of EXPB, using a temperature-sensitive plasmid, pRN8103 (Novick, Edelman and Löfdahl, 1986), containing an internal EXPB fragment (*Figure 49.5*), resulted in a mutant, WA350, with a phenotype similar to that of the *expA* mutant—with a decreased production of alpha-toxin, metallo-protease and serine protease and a simultaneous increase in protein A production. In the case of alpha-toxin and protein A the effect was at the level of mRNA. Since the level of EXPA transcript was not affected, this means that the inactivation of EXPB was responsible for the effects on exoprotein production. In the EXPB mutant two truncated forms of the EXPB transcript were formed (containing the first 383 bases of the gene), which should permit the production of delta-lysin. Delta-lysin was indeed produced, although at a slightly reduced level as compared to the wild type. This suggests that it is not the translational product of EXPB that is important but that the EXPB transcript itself might have a role in exoprotein gene regulation. Revertants that were selected for loss of tetracycline resistance coded by the inserted plasmid had all regained the wild-type characteristics.

The role of delta-lysin in the production of extracellular proteins is not yet known. However, since delta-lysin seems to have the ability to form pores in lipid bilayers (Freer, Birkbeck and Bhakoo, 1984), a role in protein secretion may be suggested.

In the part of EXPA sequenced so far, three different open reading-frames, preceded by proper Shine–Dalgarno sequences, were found. In the case of the third reading-frame, no known initiation codon was seen (*Figure 49.4*).

An interesting finding was that the Tn*551* insertion in EXPA was located in the middle of the RNA. The fact that no *expA* transcript was seen in this mutant suggests that the insertion resulted in the production of an extremely unstable RNA. Alternatively, Tn*551* may inactivate a cistron that is involved in the autoregulation of EXPA transcription. This was supported by preliminary results showing that the EXPA promoter fused to the *cat-86* gene on a plasmid was not expressed in the EXPA mutant WA250.

In conclusion, we have shown that at least two different genes are involved in the regulation of exoprotein synthesis in *S. aureus*. One of the genes, *expA*, seem to be a positive regulator of EXPB, whereas EXPB controls the expression of at least four exoproteins, acting both as an activator (of the alpha-toxin gene) and a repressor (of the protein A gene) directly or indirectly.

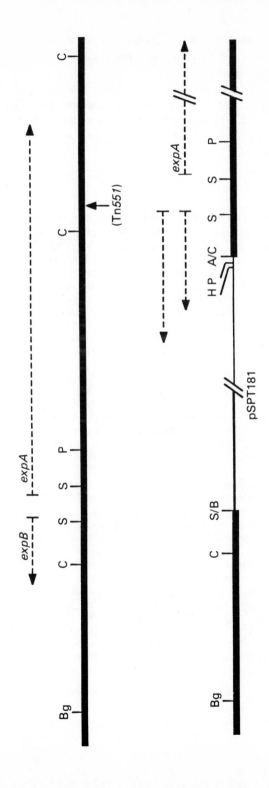

**Figure 49.5**  Inactivation of EXPB. Homologous recombination over the 350 bp *Cla*I–*Sau*3AI fragment subcloned in pSPT181 (pRN8103 + pSP64) and the chromosome of *S. aureus* 8325-4 results in strain WA350, with the plasmid integrated in the chromosome. Thin lines represent vector DNA and heavy lines staphylococcal DNA. In pSPT181 the pSP64 part is represented by the line of intermediate width and the pRN8103 part by the thinner line. Abbreviations: A, *Acc*I; B, *Bam*HI; Bg, *Bgl*II; C, *Cla*I; H, *Hin*dIII; P, *Pst*I; S, *Sau*3AI (only *Sau*3AI sites within the 950 bp *Cla*I–*Pst*I fragment are indicated). The *expA* and *expB* transcripts are indicated by dotted arrows and the two hybrid transcripts from the *expB* promoter in WA350 by asterisks. The site of insertion of Tn*551* in WA250 is marked by a vertical arrow.

**Note**

Since the *exp* locus studied by us has turned out to be identical to the *agr* locus described by Novick and co-workers, in this book the following should be pointed out to avoid confusion:

The EXPA transcript is the same as the major *agr* transcript from the P2 promoter; and the gene *expA* refers to the gene inactivated by Tn*551*, and is identical to *agrA*. The EXPB transcript is the same as the transcript from the promoter P3 and should not be mixed up with the *agrB* gene that is part of the polycistonic *agr* transcript.

**References**

ABBAS-ALI, B. AND COLEMAN, G. (1977). The characteristics of extracellular protein secretion by *Staphylococcus aureus* (Wood 46) and their relationships to the regulation of alpha-toxin. *Journal of General Microbiology* **92**, 277–282.

ARVIDSON, S. (1983). Extracellular enzymes from *Staphylcoccus aureus*. In *Staphylococci and Staphylococcal Infections, Volume 2* (C.S.F. Easmon and C. Adlam, Eds), pp. 745–808. Academic Press, New York.

BJÖRKLIND, A. AND ARVIDSON, S. (1980). Mutants of *Staphylococcus aureus* affected in the regulation of exoprotein synthesis. *FEMS Microbiology Letters* **7**, 203–206.

COLEMAN, G. AND ABBAS-ALI, B. (1977). Comparison of the pattern of increase in alpha-toxin and total extracellular protein by *Staphylococcus aureus* (Wood 46) grown in media supporting widely differing growth characteristics. *Infection and Immunity* **17**, 278–281.

FITTON, J.E., DELL, A. AND SHAW, W.V. (1980). The aminoacid sequence of the delta-haemolysin of *Staphylococcus aureus*. *FEBS Letters* **115**, 209–212.

FREER, J.H., BIRKBECK, T.H. AND BHAKOO, M. (1984). Interaction of staphylococcal delta-lysin with phospholipid monolayers and bilayers. In *Bacterial Protein Toxins* (Alouf *et al.*, Eds), pp. 181–189. Academic Press, London.

JANZON, L., LÖFDAHL, S. AND ARVIDSON, S. (1986). Evidence for a coordinate transcriptional control of alpha-toxin and protein A in *Staphylococcus aureus*. *FEMS Microbiology Letters* **33**, 193–198.

MÖLLBY, R. (1983). Isolation and properties of membrane damaging toxins. In *Staphylococci and Staphylococcal Infections, Volume 2* (C.S.F. Easmon and C. Adlam, Eds), pp. 619–669. Academic Press, London.

MORFELDT, E., JANZON, L., ARVIDSON, S. AND LÖFDAHL, S. (1988). Cloning of a chromosomal locus (*exp*) which regulates the expression of several exoprotein genes in *Staphylococcus aureus*. *Molecular and General Genetics* **211**, 435–440.

NOVICK, R.P. (1967). Properties of a cryptic high-frequency transducing phage in *Staphylococcus aureus*. *Virology* **33**, 155–166.

NOVICK, R.P., EDELMAN, I. AND LÖFDAHL, S. (1986). Small *Staphylococcus aureus* plasmids are transduced as linear multimers that are formed and resolved by replicative processes. *Journal of Molecular Biology* **192**, 209–220.

RECSEI, P., KREISWIRTH, B., O'REILLY, M., SCHLIEVERT, R., GRUSS, A. AND NOVICK, R.P. (1986). Regulation of exoprotein gene expression in *Staphylococcus aureus* by agr. *Molecular and General Genetics* **202**, 58–61.

# 50

# Protein Secretion in *Bacillus subtilis*: Characterization of Randomly Selected Signal-Sequence-Coding Regions

HILDE SMITH, ANNE DE JONG, JAN MAARTEN VAN DIJL, SIERD BRON AND GERARD VENEMA

*Department of Genetics, University of Groningen, Kerklaan 30, 9751 NN Haren (Gn), The Netherlands*

## Introduction

Several advantageous properties make bacilli useful for the production of many valuable proteins. In particular, the ability of bacilli to secrete large amounts of exoenzymes into the culture medium (Priest, 1977) makes these organisms attractive for the synthesis of foreign gene products on an industrial scale. Moreover, fundamental research on the mechanism of protein secretion in Gram-positive bacteria is important from a scientific point of view. Most proteins secreted by prokaryotic (Gram-positive and Gram-negative bacteria) and eukaryotic cells are initially synthesized as precursors containing an N-terminal extension or signal peptide (Watson, 1984). The signal peptide is required for protein export and is removed during or after translocation of the protein across the cellular membrane. Generally, signal sequences are composed of three different regions: an N-terminal region of 2–8 amino acids, containing one or more positively charged amino acids; a hydrophobic core, 9–18 amino acids long; and a region of approximately 4–6 amino acids defining the cleavage region (Silhavy, Benson and Emr, 1983). In order to optimize the secretion of proteins by bacilli, a better understanding of the specific elements within signal peptides that are required for optimal function is desirable. Our approach was to select and analyse the signal sequences of proteins that are encoded by the *Bacillus subtilis* chromosome naturally. A comparison of these sequences with respect to the efficiency of protein secretion might help to define more clearly the parameters affecting the translocation mechanism.

*Genetic Transformation and Expression*
© Intercept Ltd, PO Box 716, Andover, Hants, SP10 1YG, UK

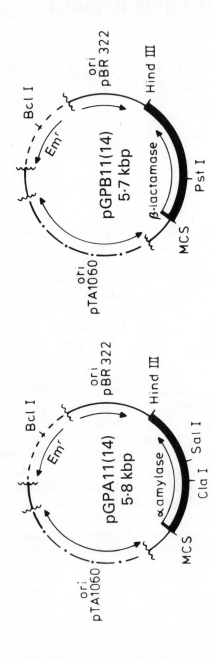

**Figure 50.1**  pGPA14 and pGPB14 are bifunctional *E. coli–B. subtilis* vectors, containing the erythromycin-resistance gene from pE194, the origin of replication from pUC13 and a 1·6 kbp fragment from the cryptic *B. subtilis* plasmid pTA1060, containing the replication functions. In addition, the plasmids contain a truncated α-amylase gene from *B. licheniformis*, or a truncated β-lactamase gene from *E. coli*, respectively. For details, *see* text and Smith *et al.* (1987).

**Results and discussion**

SIGNAL-SEQUENCE SELECTION VECTORS

Two vectors were constructed (pGPA14 and pGPB14) that could be used to 'fish' for signal sequences from the *B. subtilis* chromosome (*Figure 50.1*). These vectors contained the coding regions for the α-amylase of *Bacillus licheniformis* (Gist-brocades NV, European patent application 8320106.9, 1983; Yuuki *et al.*, 1985) and the TEM-β-lactamase of *Escherichia coli* (Sutcliff, 1978), respectively. However, the genes lacked their ribosomal-binding site, start codon and a functional signal sequence. pGPA14 lacks the coding region for the first 26 N-terminal amino acids of the signal peptide, but still contains the original processing site. In pGBP14 the entire signal sequence had been removed (Palva *et al.*, 1982; Smith *et al.*, 1987). The truncated genes are preceded by a multiple cloning site.

SELECTION OF SIGNAL SEQUENCE FROM *B. SUBTILIS* DNA

Both vectors were used as probes to 'fish' for signal sequences from the *B. subtilis* chromosome by shotgun cloning restriction fragments into the multiple cloning sites. Transformants which restored protein secretion were selected in *E. coli* either by their ability to form halos on plates containing starch, or by their resistance to ampicillin. Positive clones were obtained with efficiencies varying from 0·02–0·5% of the total number of transformants. To study whether the plasmids obtained in *E. coli* would also result in protein export in *B. subtilis*, a random selection of recombinant plasmids was used to transform *B. subtilis* cells. The transformants obtained were subsequently analysed for their ability to secrete α-amylase or β-lactamase to the culture supernatants. *Table 50.1* shows that considerable amounts of α-amylase or β-lactamase were present in the culture supernatants of *B. subtilis* cells containing the recombinant plasmids. These results indicate that the selected export regions functioned both in *E. coli* and in *B. subtilis*.

**Table 50.1** Amounts of α-amylase and β-lactamase in the culture supernatants of various *B. subtilis* clones

| A | | B | |
|---|---|---|---|
| Plasmid | α-amylase activity (U ml$^{-1}$) | Plasmid | β-lactamase activity (U ml$^{-1}$) |
| pSPA2 | 525 | pSPB4' | 630 |
| pSPA8 | 345 | pSPB8' | 800 |
| pSPA9 | 45 | pSPB9' | 16 |
| pSPA12 | 270 | pSPB19' | 230 |
| pSPA13 | 154 | pSPB20 | 585 |
| pSPA26 | 3·5 | pSPB23 | 9 |
| pSPA31 | 60 | pSPB28 | 17 |
| pSPA42 | 3·6 | pSPB32 | 78 |

*B. subtilis* cultures were grown in TY medium (for α-amylase assay) or in minimal medium (for β-lactamase assay). The α-amylase and β-lactamase activities were determined as described previously (Smith *et al.*, 1987; Smith *et al.*, 1988).

## INTERCHANGEABILITY OF EXPORT FUNCTIONS

To test whether the selected signal sequences were interchangeable, we next examined whether the export signals picked up with the α-amylase vector would function in the β-lactamase vector, and vice versa. The results are shown in *Table 50.2*. All constructed pSPB-A plasmids, which contain the β-lactamase gene preceded by inserts originally selected with the α-amylase probe vector conferred resistance to ampicillin in *E. coli* and caused high levels of β-lactamase activity in *B. subtilis*. Moreover, α-amylase activity could be measured in the supernatants of *B. subtilis* cells containing pSPA-B plasmids. These results show that the selected regions were interchangeable between the two target proteins. However, a comparison of *Table 50.2A* and *Table 50.1B* showed that in *B. subtilis* the relative order of levels of α-amylase activities obtained with the original pSPA vectors, and those of β-lactamase obtained with the interchanged pSPB-A vectors, were not identical. Since no differences at the transcriptional and translational level could exist, and the same export signals were used, these results suggest that, in addition to the signal sequences, the mature parts of the proteins contributed to the amounts of protein secreted. The same conclusion can be drawn from the reciprocal experiment in which the α-amylase gene was preceded by inserts originally selected in the β-lactamase probe vector.

**Table 50.2** Interchangeability of export signals

| | A | | | B |
|---|---|---|---|---|
| Plasmid | *E. coli* Amp$^r$ | *B. subtilis* β-lactamase activity (U ml$^{-1}$) | Plasmid | *B. subtilis* α-amylase activity (U ml$^{-1}$) |
| pSPB-A2 | 300 | 20000 | pSPA-B4′ | 123 |
| pSPB-A8 | 275 | 495 | pSPA-B8′ | 16 |
| pSPB-A9 | 275 | 2900 | pSPA-B9′ | 82 |
| pSPB-A12 | 10 | 34 | pSPA-B19′ | 12 |
| pSPB-A13 | 300 | 4200 | pSPA-B20 | 40 |
| pSPB-A26 | 5 | 880 | pSPA-B23 | 57 |
| pSPB-A31 | 100 | 720 | pSPA-B28 | 37 |
| pSPB-A32 | 20 | 710 | pSPA-B32 | 96 |

The level of resistance to ampicillin was defined as the maximal concentration of ampicillin to which 100% of the cells were resistant. *B. subtilis* cultures were grown in TY medium (for α-amylase assay), or in minimal medium (for β-lactamase assay). The α-amylase and β-lactamase activities were determined as described previously (Smith *et al.*, 1987; Smith *et al.*, 1988).
Abbreviation: Amp$^r$, ampicillin resistance.

## PROPERTIES OF THE SELECTED EXPORT SIGNALS

To learn more about the nature of the cloned export functions, the nucleotide sequences of 16 randomly selected inserts were determined. All nucleotide sequences, and consequently all deduced amino-acid sequences, appeared to be different. Moreover, none seemed to be identical to known *B. subtilis* signal sequences. The estimated number of exported proteins in *B. subtilis* is 20–30 (Priest, 1977). We estimate that at least 50 different signals were picked up by our selection procedure, suggesting that in *E. coli* and *B. subtilis* a considerable number of sequences not normally involved in protein secretion can functionally replace natural signal sequences. This could indicate that the specificity of signal-sequence recognition in these organisms is rather low.

Recently, a comparable system for the selection of signal sequences was described by Kaiser and co-workers (1987), using the eukaryotic yeast invertase probe gene. These authors showed that in yeast, also, many more or less random sequences were functional as export signals.

The hydrophobicity characteristics of a number of the derived signal peptides are shown in *Figure 50.2*. For comparison the hydrophobicity plots of the signal peptides of the wild-type α-amylase and β-lactamase are included. The cloned regions showed the general characteristics of natural signal

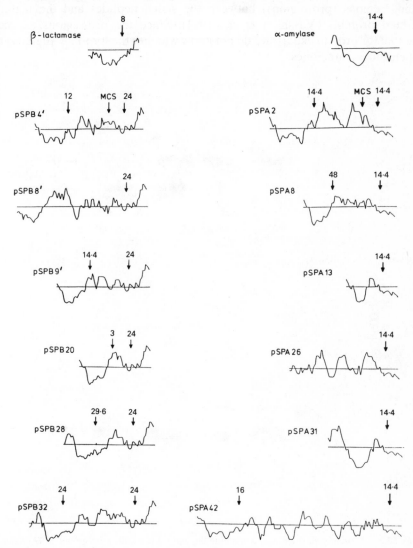

**Figure 50.2** Hydrophobicity patterns were predicted according to Hopp and Woods (1981) and plotted against the amino-acid sequences. Hydrophilic regions were plotted above, and hydrophobic regions below, the horizontal lines. Arrows indicate the positions of potential signal peptidase cleavage sites. Numbers refer to the processing probabilities, according to von Heÿne (1983).

peptides, including a basic N-terminal region followed by a hydrophobic core. Moreover, as calculated according to the rules of von Heÿne (1983), the hydrophobic core in a considerable number of clones was followed by a potential signal peptidase cleavage site. Of interest is the observation that a number of the signal sequences contained large open reading-frames between the potential cleavage sites and the fusion points with the probe genes. In this respect these signal sequences are comparable to those of the proteases secreted by bacilli, which are synthesized as preproenzymes containing large coding regions (pro-regions) between the signal peptides and the mature secreted proteins (Vasantha *et al.*, 1984). Since the pro-regions are not essential for protein export, we do not know whether the 'pro-like' regions are dispensible in our clones.

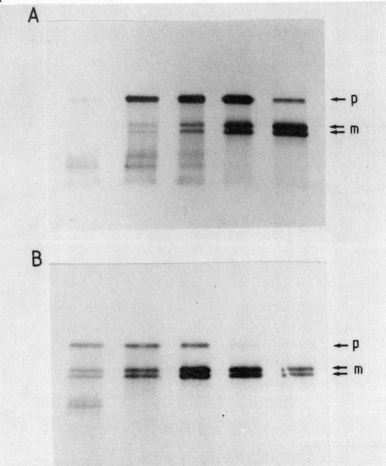

**Figure 50.3**   *B. subtilis* 8G-5 cultures containing the various plasmids were grown in S7 medium (Vasantha and Freese, 1980) to log-phase at 37°C. Cells were starved for methionine for about 30–45 min at 37°C. Proteins were labelled by incubating the cultures with $^{35}$S-methionine for 30 sec. Immediately after the pulse, further incorporation of radioactivity was prevented by the addition of an excess of non-radioactive methionine. Subsequently, samples were withdrawn at 0, 15, 30, 60 and 120 sec after the addition of the chase. After immunoprecipitation, samples were applied to a 12·5% SDS-PAA gel. (A) Cells labelled at 37°C; (B) cells labelled at 25°C. p, pre-β-lactamase; m, mature β-Lactamase.

EFFICIENCIES OF EXPORT FUNCTIONS

We have used enzymatic activities in the culture supernatants to characterize the various *B. subtilis* clones. These activities are affected not only by the efficiencies of the signal sequences but also by the efficiencies of their promoter and ribosome-binding sequences, which were different in most of the clones. Therefore, to analyse the efficiencies of the signal sequences, pulse–chase experiments were performed. *Figure 50.3* shows the results of such experiments with *B. subtilis* cells containing pSPB-A2.

At 37°C a rapid processing of pre-β-lactamase to mature product was observed (*Figure 50.3A*). Under these conditions the pre-β-lactamase had a half-life of about 30 sec. Surprisingly, two bands of similar molecular size appeared near the position of mature β-lactamase. Presumably, the pre-β-lactamase encoded by pSPB-A2 was processed at two different but close sites, which are used with similar efficiencies. At 25°C (*Figure 50.3B*) the rate of processing was reduced and the half-life was increased to approximately 50 sec. As shown in *Figure 50.4*, this temperature effect was even more dramatic at 17°C (half-life 244 sec). In conclusion, these results show that:

1.  The precursor is progressively processed to the mature protein as a function of time; and
2.  The rate of processing is strongly temperature dependent.

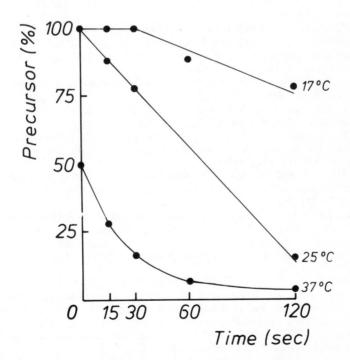

**Figure 50.4**  Kinetics of processing of β-lactamase encoded by pSPB-A2 in *B. subtilis*. The processing of pre-β-lactamase encoded by pSPB-A2 was analysed by pulse–chase labelling as described for *Figure 50.3*. The relative amounts of precursor and mature β-lactamase were estimated by densitometric scanning of the autoradiograms.

Moreover, pulse–chase experiments with *B. subtilis* cells containing pSPB-A1?
and pSPB-A42 revealed (results not shown) that the rates of processing varie?
considerably among the various clones. The half-life of the precursor of th?
pre-β-lactamase encoded by pSPB-A13 was very high: 225 sec at 37°C, wherea?
the precursor encoded by pSPB-A42 had a half-life of 78 sec at 37°C. We do no?
as yet know the cause(s) of these differences. In the near future we hope that a?
comparison of the various cloned export signals with respect to their
efficiencies of processing will help to define more clearly the relationship?
between signal peptide structure and function.

## Acknowledgements

We thank Elsevier Science Publishers for the reproduction of *Figure 50.2*.
Funding for the project of which this work is a part was provided by
Gist-brocades NV, Delft, The Netherlands.

## References

HOPP, T.P. AND WOODS, K.R. (1981). Prediction of protein antigenic determinants from amino acid sequences. *Proceedings of the National Academy of Sciences of the United States of America* **47**, 3824–3828.

KAISER, C.A., PREUSS, D., GRISAFI, P. AND BOTSTEIN, D. (1987). Many random sequences functionally replace the secretion signal sequence of yeast invertase. *Science* **235**, 312–317.

PALVA, I., SARVAS, M., LEHTOVAARA, P., SIBAKOV, M. AND KAARIAINEN, L. (1982). Secretion of *Escherichia coli* β-lactamase from *Bacillus subtilis* by the aid of α-amylase signal sequence. *Proceedings of the National Academy of Sciences of the United States of America* **79**, 5582–5586.

PRIEST, F.G. (1977). Extracellular enzyme synthesis in the genus *Bacillus*. *Bacteriological Reviews* **41**, 711–753.

SILHAVY, T.J., BENSON, S.A. AND EMR, S.D. (1983). Mechanisms of protein localization. *Microbiological Reviews* **47**, 313–344.

SMITH, H., BRON, S., VAN EE, J. AND VENEMA, G. (1987). Construction and use of signal sequence selection vectors in *Escherichia coli* and *Bacillus subtilis*. *Journal of Bacteriology* **169**, 3321–3328.

SMITH, H., DE JONG, A., BRON, S. AND VENEMA, G. (1988). Characterization of signal-sequence-coding regions selected from the *Bacillus subtilis* chromosome. *Gene* **70**, 351–361.

SUTCLIFF, J.G. (1978). Complete nucleotide sequence of the *Escherichia coli* plasmid pBR322. *Cold Spring Harbor Symposia on Quantitative Biology* **43**, 77–90.

VASANTHA, N. AND FREESE, E. (1980). Enzyme changes during *Bacillus subtilis* sporulation caused by deprivation of guanine nucleotides. *Journal of Bacteriology* **144**, 1119–1125.

VASANTHA, N., THOMPSON, L.D., RHODES, C., BANNER, C., NAGLE, J. AND FILPULA, D. (1984). Genes for alkaline protease and neutral protease from *Bacillus amyloliquefaciens* contain a large open reading frame between the regions for signal sequence and mature protein. *Journal of Bacteriology* **159**, 811–819.

VON HEŸNE, G. (1983). Patterns of amino acids near signal-sequence cleavage sites. *European Journal of Biochemistry* **133**, 17–22.

WATSON, M.E.E. (1984). Compilation of published signal sequences. *Nucleic Acids Research* **12**, 5145–5164.

YUUKI, T., NOMURA, T., TEZUKA, H., TSUBOI, A., YAMAGATA, H., TSUKAGOSHI, N. AND UKADA, S. (1985). Complete nucleotide sequence of a gene coding for heat-nd pH-stable α-amylase of *Bacillus licheniformis*: comparison of the amino acid equence of three liquefying α-amylases deduced from the DNA sequence. *Journal f Biochemistry* **98**, 1147–1156.

# 51

# Secretion in *Bacillus subtilis*: Interaction of Levansucrase::β-Galactosidase Hybrids with Secretory Apparatus

M. ZAGOREC, M. STEINMETZ AND H. HESLOT

*Laboratoire de Génétique des Microorganismes, Institut National Agronomique, CBAI, 78850 Thiverval-Grignon, France*

## Introduction

The Gram-positive bacterium *Bacillus subtilis* is known to secrete several proteins into the culture medium; however, there is little information on the secretory apparatus in this organism. An 'S complex' was described and isolated as a complex of four proteins, some of them interacting with ribosomes (Caulfield *et al.*, 1984, 1985). An immunological cross-reactivity was described between one component of this complex and a 60 kDa protein belonging to a similar molecular complex characterized in *Staphylococcus aureus* (Adler and Arvidson, 1984), however, the precise involvement in secretion of both complexes has not been elucidated. Furthermore, no secretory mutant has yet been described in *B. subtilis*: several loci such as *sacU* or *sacQ* were identified (Kunst *et al.*, 1974) by mutations which increased or lowered expression of a set of secreted proteins, but it was subsequently shown that these mutations acted at the level of genes transcription rather than at a secretion step (Aymerich, Gonzy-Tréboul and Steinmetz, 1986; Shimotsu and Henner, 1986).

In the Gram-negative bacterium *Escherichia coli*, the use of hybrid proteins containing the NH$_2$-end of periplasmic or outer-membrane proteins fused to the cytoplasmic β-galactosidase (*see* Bankaitis *et al.*, 1985) allowed selection of secretory mutants. We used the *sacB* gene of *B. subtilis* to construct *sacB::lacZ* fusions and investigate the effects of their expression. *sacB* encodes an extracellular levansucrase (LS) which is secreted during exponential growth. LS synthesis is induced by sucrose (Le Coq *et al.*, Chapter 42, this volume). It was shown that LS was synthesized as a precursor from which signal peptide is cleaved to lead to a membrane-processed form, which was subsequently secreted in the medium (Petit-Glatron, Benyahia and Chambert, 1987). Like *sacB*, the constructed *sacB::lacZ* fusions are sucrose inducible and controlled

*Genetic Transformation and Expression*
© Intercept Ltd, PO Box 716, Andover, Hants, SP10 1YG, UK

by the *sac* regulatory loci. Strong expression of these fusions results in ce death.

## Results

*sacB::lacZ* fusions were constructed by BAL31 deletions generated from the unique *Hind*III site of pLS153*lacZ* (*Figure 51.1*). Ligation mixtures were used to transform a *B. subtilis* strain carrying the replicative plasmid pHV1201△. Resulting plasmids were maintained in this strain by recombination with pHV1201△ (*Figure 51.1A*). The transformants constitute a collection of fusions which could be introduced in various strains. Twenty-three construc- tions were used to transform the strain QB112 by integration into the chromosome at the *sacB* locus (*Figure 51.1B*). This strain is a *sacU32* mutant which produces high levels of LS (Chambert and Petit-Glatron, 1984). *sacU* is a *trans*-acting locus that acts on *sacB* transcription (Aymerich, Gonzy-Tréboul and Steinmetz, 1986). In the selected transformants, one copy of hybrid *sacB::lacZ* and one copy of wild-type *sacB* gene were present, each being sucrose inducible. The plasmid pLG131 (Aymerich, Gonzy-Tréboul and Steinmetz, 1986), in which *lacZ* is directly fused to the initiator ATG of *sacB*, was used as a standard. Transformants were tested for growth on media with or without sucrose. Two fusions (the corresponding transformants were called GM454 and GM456) appeared to produce a slight sucrose sensitivity, as compared to the control strain (GM421), which contained an integrated copy of pLG131. This sensitivity was less clear cut than the lethality phenomenon described in the case of *E. coli* strains expressing similar fusions. Starting from GM421, GM454 and GM456, strains containing spontaneously amplified constructions were selected by growth in the presence of increasing amounts of chloramphenicol. In the corresponding strains (GM422, GM455 and GM457, respectively) several copies of *lacZ* or *sacB::lacZ* were present. It appeared

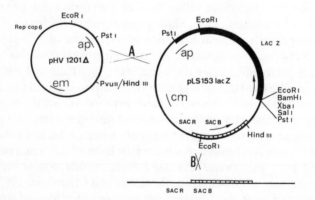

**Figure 51.1**  Strategy used for *sacB::lacZ* fusion construction. Deletions were generated with BAL31 from the unique *Hind*III site of pLS153*lacZ* and ligated to the *Sal*I site. (A) Plasmids carrying *sacB::lacZ* fusions could be maintained as a replicative form by recombination with the homologous part of pHV1201△. (B) Fusions can be introduced into the chromosome by recombination at the *sacR–sacB* locus. (*sacR* is the 400 bp region containing the *sacB* promoter and targets for the *trans*-acting regulatory *sac* loci; Le Coq *et al.*, Chapter 42, this volume.)

at the strains GM455 and GM457 were clearly sucrose sensitive whereas the standard strain GM422 was not. Thus expression of the fusions contained in transformants GM454 and GM456 seemed to affect growth of the cells.

Strong expression of the fusions in strains GM455 and GM457 carrying amplified constructions was lethal. These strains were studied further to determine whether the sucrose sensitivity was due to an interaction of fusion protein with the secretion apparatus. *Figure 51.2* shows growth curves of strains carrying amplified fusions grown on C medium containing glucose. The strains carrying the *sacB::lacZ* fusions showed a sucrose sensitivity about two hours after sucrose addition. After three hours, β-galactosidase activity was determined. This enzyme was never observed in culture supernatants and appeared only in the sucrose-induced cells. LS activity was also assayed in the culture supernatants (*Table 51.1*). It was observed that in strains carrying

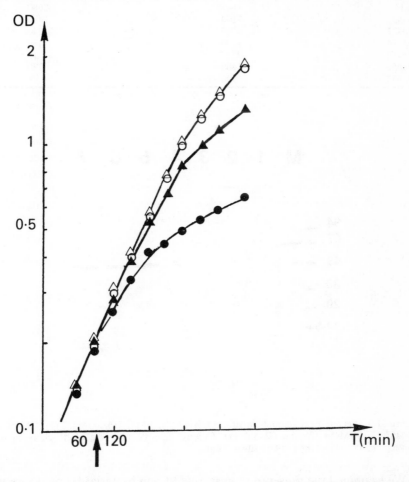

**Figure 51.2**  Growth curves of strains GM455 (circles) and GM457 (triangles) carrying several copies of the *sacB::lacZ* fusions. Bacteria were grown in liquid C medium containing glucose (open symbols). The arrow indicates sucrose (2% w/v) addition (closed symbols). Standard strain GM422 grown with or without sucrose shows the same growth curve as GM455 or GM457 grown without sucrose induction. Growth was monitored by optical density at 600 nm.

fusions LS activity was decreased as compared to untransformed QB112. This decrease was more significant in strains containing amplified constructions; in strain GM455, LS activity was 0·3–0·5% of that assayed in QB112. This suggested that expression of the fusions interfered with LS secretion and/or expression. Such a drastic effect was not observed in strain GM422, suggesting that *lacZ* expression *per se* did not interfere. Low LS activities in culture supernatants of strains expressing one or several copies of the fusions were correlated with the amount of secreted LS, determined by polyacrylamide gel electrophoresis of supernatants (*Figure 51.3*).

**Table 51.1**    β-galactosidase activity assayed in bacterial extracts and LS activity in the culture supernatants

| Strain | β-galactosidase Miller unit $ml^{-1}OD_{600}^{-1}$ | LS activity $mUnit\, ml^{-1}OD_{600}^{-1}$ |
|---|---|---|
| QB112 | — | 2680 |
| GM421 | 1100 | 2480 |
| GM422 | 6100 | 2240 |
| GM454 | 1100 | 180 |
| GM455 | 2524 | 10 |
| GM456 | 400 | 720 |
| GM457 | 920 | 75 |

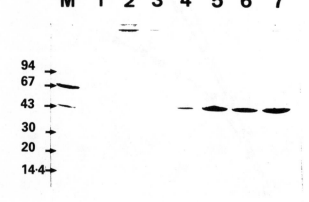

**Figure 51.3**    Secreted LS amounts in strains QB112 (7), GM421 (6), GM422 (5), GM456 (4), GM457 (3), GM454 (2) and GM455 (1). Culture supernatants were electrophoresed on a polyacrylamide gel and the proteins silver stained.

We examined the presence of unsecreted LS in bacteria. LS precursor was detected immunologically in bacterial extracts by Western blotting (*Figure 51.4*). We observed that in strains expressing *sacB::lacZ* fusions (GM455 and GM457) unprocessed LS precursor was accumulated, whereas in strain GM422 or QB112, only the processed form was detectable (this form is also present in strains carrying fusions). This precursor accumulation was very low in the case of GM455 after three hours of sucrose induction. This suggests that unsecreted LS might be proteolysed or that the secretion inhibition could exert a negative-feedback effect on LS synthesis.

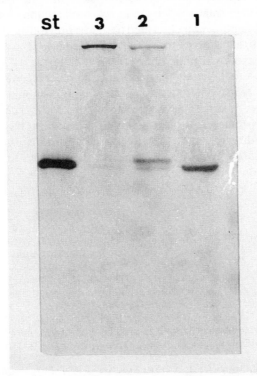

**Figure 51.4** Immunodetection of LS precursor in strains GM422 (1), GM457 (2) and GM455 (3). Supernatant of a culture of the strain QB112 was used as a standard for mature LS (st). Bacterial extracts were separated by polyacrylamide gel electrophoresis, electrotransferred onto nitrocellulose membrane and detected with antiserum raised against purified LS (a kind gift of M.F. Petit-Glatron and R. Chambert).

Thus, expression of the *sacB::lacZ* fusions led to inhibition of LS secretion. This phenomenon was more pronounced as expression of the fusions increased. It was accompanied by accumulation of LS precursor in the bacteria and resulted in cell death. The fusion present in strains GM454 and GM455 led to a more drastic sucrose sensitivity and a stronger secretion inhibition. DNA sequencing showed that the fusions harboured by GM454 and GM456 contained the first 216 and 191 codons of *sacB*, respectively (including the 29 codons corresponding to signal peptide).

**Conclusions**

Inhibition of LS secretion, accompanied by a lethality phenomenon caused by a strong expression of some *sacB::lacZ* fusions, was observed in *B. subtilis*. This could be the consequence of interaction between fusion proteins and components of the secretion apparatus. This interaction might, for example, cause a congestion of secretion apparatus, which becomes lethal for the cells.

The sucrose sensitivity caused by expression of these fusions should permit isolation of sucrose-resistant mutants. Preliminary results showed that such sucrose-resistant mutants can be isolated. These mutants may be affected in sucrose regulation or transport, or could also be secretion mutants.

The lethality phenomenon described here was previously observed in *E. coli* for a set of exported proteins fused to β-galactosidase (Bassford, Silhavy and Beckwith, 1979; Beckwith and Silhavy, 1983; d'Enfert and Pugsley, 1987). But it appeared that a *sacU* genetic background and several copies of fusions were needed in *B. subtilis* to obtain a similar phenotype. It should be noted that the two constructions described here were also lethal for *E. coli*, despite the fact that the *sacB* promoter is not highly expressed in this organism. Our observations indirectly and tentatively suggest that the Gram-positive bacterium *B. subtilis* might be less sensitive than *E. coli* to congestion of its secretion apparatus.

## References

ADLER, L.A. AND ARVIDSON, S. (1984). Immunological cross-reaction between proteins supposed to be involved in protein secretion in *Staphylococcus aureus* and *Bacillus subtilis. FEMS Microbiology Letters* **23**, 17–20.

AYMERICH, S., GONZY-TRÉBOUL, G. AND STEINMETZ, M. (1986). 5'-noncoding region *sacR* is the target of all identified regulation affecting the levansucrase gene in *Bacillus subtilis. Journal of Bacteriology* **166**, 993–998.

BANKAITIS, V.A., RYAN, J.P., RASMUSSEN, B.A. AND BASSFORD, P.J., JR (1985). The use of genetic techniques to analyze protein export in *Escherichia coli*. In *Current Topics in Membranes and Transport, Volume 24*, pp. 105–150. Academic Press, New York.

BASSFORD, P.J., SILHAVY, T.J. AND BECKWITH, J.R. (1979). Use of gene fusion to study secretion of maltose-binding protein into *Escherichia coli* periplasm. *Journal of Bacteriology* **139**, 19–31.

BECKWITH, J. AND SILHAVY, T.J. (1983). Genetic analysis of protein export in *Escherichia coli*. In *Methods in Enzymology, Volume 97*, pp. 3–40. Academic Press, New York.

CAULFIELD, M.P., HORIUCHI, S., TAI, P.C. AND DAVIS, B.D. (1984). The 64-kilodalton membrane protein of *Bacillus subtilis* is also present as a multiprotein complex on membrane-free ribosomes. *Proceedings of the National Academy of Sciences of the United States of America* **81**, 7772–7776.

CAULFIELD, M.P., FURLONG, D., TAI, P.C. AND DAVIS, B.D. (1985). Secretory S complex of *Bacillus subtilis* forms a large, organized structure when released from ribosomes. *Proceedings of the National Academy of Sciences of the United States of America* **82**, 4031–4035.

CHAMBERT, R. AND PETIT-GLATRON, M.F. (1984). Hyperproduction of exocellular levansucrase by *Bacillus subtilis*: examination of the phenotype of a *sacU* strain. *Journal of General Microbiology* **130**, 3143–3152.

D'ENFERT, C. AND PUGSLEY, A.P. (1987). A gene fusion approach to the study of pullulanase export and secretion in *Escherichia coli. Molecular Microbiology* **1**, 159–168.

KUNST, F., PASCAL, M., LEPESANT-KEJZLAROVA, J., LEPESANT, J.A., BILLAULT, A. AND DEDONDER, R. (1974). Pleiotropic mutations affecting sporulation conditions and the synthesis of extracellular enzymes in *Bacillus subtilis* 168. *Biochimie* **56**, 1481–1489.

PETIT-GLATRON, M.F., BENYAHIA, F. AND CHAMBERT, R. (1987). Secretion of *Bacillus subtilis* levane sucrase: a possible two step mechanism. *European Journal of Biochemistry* **163**, 379–387.

SHIMOTSU, H. AND HENNER, D.J. (1986). Modulation of *Bacillus subtilis* levane sucrase gene expression by sucrose and regulation of the steady state mRNA level by *sacU* and *sacQ* genes. *Journal of Bacteriology* **168**, 380–388.

# 52

# Use of the Signal Peptide from Subtilisin Carlsberg for Export of Protein G from *Bacillus subtilis*

PER EGNELL AND JAN-INGMAR FLOCK

*Center for BioTechnology, F82, Karolinska Institute, Huddinge University Hospital, S-14186 Huddinge, Sweden*

## Introduction

Subtilisin Carlsberg is an extracellular serylprotease produced from *Bacillus licheniformis*. The gene was cloned (Jacobs *et al.*, 1985) and the sequence then revealed that, like subtilisin BPN from *B. amyloliquefaciens* (Wells *et al.*, 1983), there is an N-terminal region of 76 amino acids, the pro region, between the signal sequence and the mature protein. The pro region is thought to be autocatalytically processed, resulting in release of the mature protein from the membrane (Power, Adams and Wells, 1986). The signal peptide has been used in a fusion to the staphylococcal protein A gene, resulting in secretion of protein A (Vasantha and Thompson, 1986a). However, when the pro region between the signal sequence and the protein A gene was also included, processing of the signal sequence only occurred and the pro region fused to protein A was found extracellularly (Vasantha and Thompson, 1986b).

We have made a gene fusion between protein G, which is an extracellular protein, with the signal sequence, pro region and an N-terminal fragment of native subtilisin Carlsberg. Protein G is a surface protein found in group G streptococci and which binds to IgG in a similar way to protein A from *Staphylococcus aureus* (Björck and Kronvall, 1984).

## Materials and methods

### BACTERIAL STRAINS AND GROWTH METHODS

*E. coli* strain JM109, *B. subtilis* 168 and *B. subtilis* DB104 (Kawamura and Doi, 1984) were used as bacterial hosts. Bacteria were grown at 37°C in LB broth and kept on LB agar plates. When required, chloramphenical was added

*Genetic Transformation and Expression*
© Intercept Ltd, PO Box 716, Andover, Hants, SP10 1YG, UK

at 5 mg $1^{-1}$, kanamycin at 20 mg $1^{-1}$. *B. subtilis* strains were grown in a rich broth medium to improve cell yield.

## PLASMID CONSTRUCTIONS

Restriction endonucleases and other enzymes were used according to the suppliers' recommendations. Transformation of *E. coli* was carried out as described by Hanahan (1983). Transformation of *B. subtilis* was carried out as described by Arwert and Venema (1973). Plasmid DNA was prepared by a modified alkaline extraction method as described by Kieser (1984). Oligonucleotides were synthesized on a 380D DNA synthesizer (Applied Biosystems Inc., CA).

## CELL FRACTIONATION AND PROTEIN PURIFICATION

*B. subtilis* was grown in rich medium in an orbital shaker at 240 r.p.m. to late log phase. The cultures were made 1mM in *p*-methylsulphonylfluoride (PMSF) and chilled on ice. Cells were then centrifuged at 11 500 *g* for 20 min at 4°C. After centrifugation the supernatant was centrifuged once again as described above. The supernatant was then applied directly onto an IgG-Sepharose column (Pharmacia, Uppsala, Sweden) or stored at −20°C until used. The pellet was washed once with PBSP centrifuged, resuspended in PBSP (50 mM phosphate buffer, pH 7·3 with 0·15M NaCl and 1mM PMSF) (1/10 of original volume) containing lysozyme (40 µg ml$^{-1}$), incubated at 37°C for 30 min and centrifuged (40 000 *g*, 20 min). The crude membrane fraction was resuspended in PBSP (1/10 of original volume) containing 10mM $MgCl_2$ and treated with DNase (10 µg ml$^{-1}$) for 15 min at 37°C and centrifuged (40 000 *g*, 20 min).

The membrane pellet was dissolved in PBSP (1/10 original volume) containing 1% Triton X-100, and incubated for 30 min at 37°C. After centrifugation (40 000 *g* for 30 min at 4°C) the supernatant was diluted tenfold with PBSP (4°C) and applied to an IgG-Sepharose column (Pharmacia, Uppsala, Sweden). After elution with 0·5M acetate buffer, pH 2·7 from the IgG column, the IgG-binding protein was desalted on a NAP column (Pharmacia) and lyophilized. The IgG-binding protein from the supernatant was further purified on a Superose-12 column (Pharmacia) in a FPLC system.

## PROTEIN SEQUENCING

The IgG-binding protein from the membrane and supernatant fractions were purified as described above, and 1 nmol of each was subjected to sequence analysis on a 470 A protein sequencer (Applied Biosystems Inc., CA).

## PROTEIN ANALYSIS AND WESTERN BLOTTING

SDS-polyacrylamide gels and Western blotting were used to analyse gene expression. The primary antibodies used in Western blots were polyclonal antibodies raised against subtilisin Carlsberg in rabbit. The secondary antibodies used were alkaline-phosphatase conjugated goat antirabbit IgG (Dakopatts, Copenhagen, Denmark). For quantification of protein G, a modified inhibition ELISA test was used. Microtitre plates were coated with human IgG at 750 ng 100 $\mu l^{-1}$ then followed by a secondary coating with 5% skimmed milk powder in PBS with 0·05% Tween 20. Samples were added and incubated for 1 h at room temperature. After washing, alkaline-phosphatase conjugated protein A (Pharmacia) was added at 200 ng 100 $\mu l^{-1}$. Incubation was allowed for 1 h at room temperature. After washing, alkaline-phosphatase substrate (*p*-nitro-phenyl phosphate tablets; Sigma, MO, USA) was added. Absorption was monitored at 450 nm. Competition between protein G and protein A was determined with standardized protein G from Pharmacia.

## Results

### EXPRESSION OF SUBTILISIN

The gene for subtilisin Carlsberg was cloned in *E. coli* but no detectable expression was found (Jacobs *et al.*, 1985 and unpublished observations). We therefore inserted the gene with its own ribosomal-binding sequence in the *Bam*HI site of plasmid pUB110, such that the promoter for open reading-frame β, described by McKenzie *et al.* (1986), transcribes the subtilisin gene. Subtilisin was then produced and exported at about 2–20 ng $ml^{-1}$. This promoter does not seem to be sufficiently strong to drive the expression of a commercially interesting protein.

### FUSION OF SUBTILISIN C-TERMINUS TO CHLORAMPHENICOLACETYL TRANSFERASE (CAT) N-TERMINUS

In order to increase the expression level, a promoter from the *E. coli* phage T5, described by Melin and Dehlin (1987) and functional in *B. subtilis*, was employed. In plasmid pT28, described by Melin and Dehlin (1987), the T5 promoter was inserted upstream of the *cat-86* gene from *B. pumilus* (Williams, Duvall and Lovett, 1981). A 3′-coding part of *cat-86* gene was substituted in this plasmid with a 3′-coding part of the subtilisin gene in the same reading-frame, resulting in a completely non-functional protein. An antisera raised against native subtilisin was used to detect this fusion protein in a Western blot. It was then found that the molecular mass corresponded to a non-processed form, i.e. the signal sequence and/or the pro region of subtilisin remaining on the fusion protein. The amount found was around 0·7 μg $ml^{-1}$ of bacterial culture. All the protein was found to be membrane bound and none was extracellular, either due to lack of secretion or complete proteolytic degradation extracellularly (data not shown).

Attempts were made to place the T5 promoter upstream of a non-truncated non-fused subtilisin gene, without success. The T5 promoter could only be used in combination with truncated subtilisin.

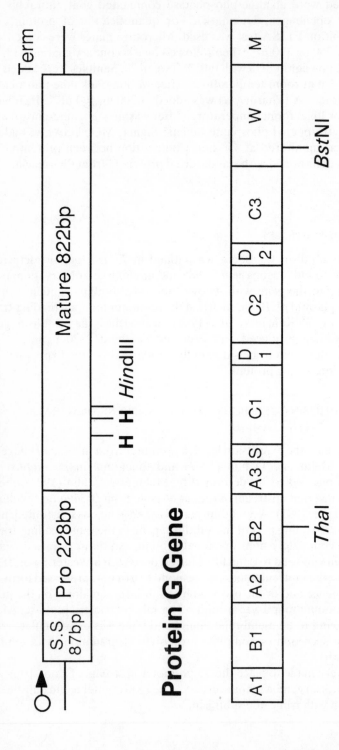

**Figure 52.1** Schematic drawing of the subtilisin Carlsberg gene and the protein G gene. Regions in the protein G gene have the same designations as in Guss *et al.* (1986) with the same letter for repetitious regions. C-regions are IgG binding.

# SUBTILISIN–PROTEIN G FUSION IN pTG100

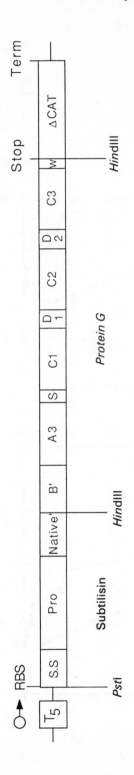

**Figure 52.2** Fusion between the subtilisin and the protein G genes. The region between *Tha*I and *Bst*N1 (*see Figure 52.1*) was inserted into the first of the *Hind*III sites in the subtilisin gene.

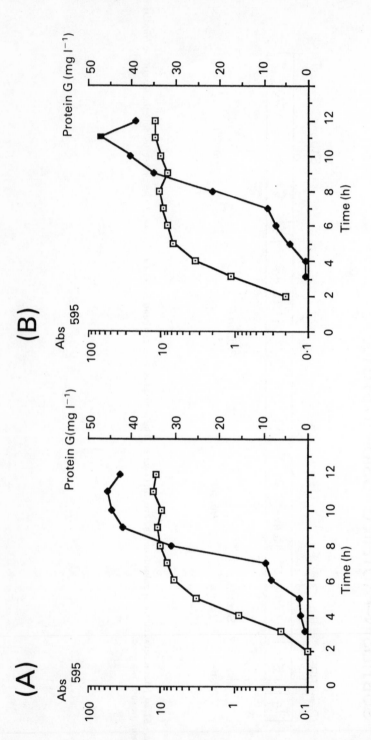

**Figure 52.3**   Growth curves and production of protein G from (A) *B. subtilis* 168 and (B) DB104, with plasmid pTG100 encoding the subtilisin–protein G fusion protein. Growth curve, —□—; protein G production, —■—.

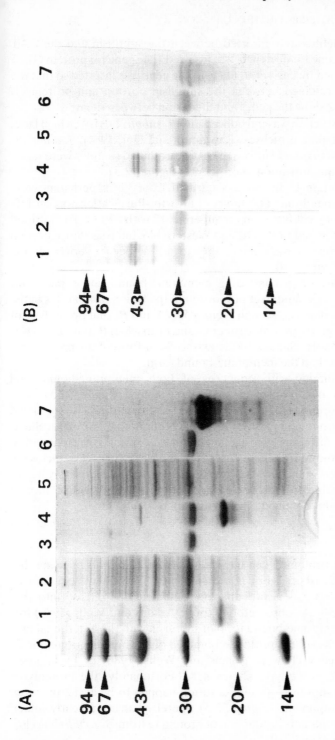

**Figure 52.4** Polyacrylamide gel of subtilisin–protein G samples, Coomassie stained. Lanes: 0, molecular size markers; 1, membrane fraction from DB104 purified on IgG Sepharose; 2, crude supernatant fraction from DB104; 3, supernatant fraction from DB104 purified on IgG Sepharose followed by gel filtration; 4, membrane fraction from 168 purified on IgG Sepharose; 5, crude supernatant fraction from 168; 6, supernatant fraction from 168 purified on IgG Sepharose followed by gel filtration; 7, protein G purchased from Pharmacia. (B) Western blot of the gel shown in (A).

PRODUCTION OF SUBTILISIN-PROTEIN G FUSION

At a *Hin*dIII site deliberately inserted between the subtilisin and the CAT coding regions, the gene for protein G was inserted. The gene for protein G had previously been cloned by Guss *et al.* (1986). The gene was inserted so that the reading frame was retained between the subtilisin portion and protein G. *Figures 52.1* and *52.2* show the genes and the fusion between them.

The plasmid construction was introduced into *B. subtilis* DB104, which lacks both neutral and alkaline proteases (Kawamura and Doi, 1984), and into *B. subtilis* 168. Both strains were cultivated in rich broth and samples were taken at various times for quantification of protein G (*Figure 52.3*).

The subtilisin–protein G fusion was purified from the supernatants and extracted from the membrane at 7 hours of growth. Purification was on IgG Sepharose followed by gel filtration on Superose-12 with FPLC. The purified protein was then subjected to PAGE and Western blot analysis. Since protein G binds to any serum, it was unnecessary to use a specific serum for the Western blotting (*Figure 52.4*).

It was found that, when comparing membrane-bound and supernatant fractions of protein G, a significant proportion of the fusion protein was in the membrane fraction. It can be seen in *Figures 52.4A* and *B*, that proteolysis of the protein was minimal in the crude supernatant, even when *B. subtilis* 168 was used as a host. The molecular size of the extracellular form of the protein was considerably smaller than the membrane-bound form.

The N-terminal amino-acid sequences of both membrane-bound and extracellular forms of the protein were determined (*Figure 52.5*). The membrane-bound form was correctly processed at the natural site for signal peptidase with the pro region of subtilisin at the N-terminus. The extracellular form showed three different cleavage sites, none of which corresponded to processing at the pro-mature junction. Rather, the cleavage occurred close to the subtilisin–protein G junction, thus resulting in protein G completely free of subtilisin. No detectable proteolytic cleavage occurred at any other position of protein G. The amount obtained ranged from 10 to 50 mg $l^{-1}$.

**Discussion**

We have shown that protein G can be secreted from *B. subtilis* by using the gene for subtilisin Carlsberg from *B. licheniformis*. The signal sequence is properly processed but this is probably not sufficient for release into the medium of the protein. As observed by Power, Adams and Wells (1986) for subtilisin BPN′, a membrane-bound form of subtilisin with the N-terminal pro region is found. Release of the protein is obtained only when the pro region is cleaved autocatalytically (Power, Adams and Wells, 1986) or by another proteolytic cleavage, as we have shown here. Fortunately, the proteolytic cleavage sites in the subtilisin–protein G fusion happen to be at the junction between the two components (*Figure 52.5*), thereby leaving a nearly intact protein G in the supernatant. Production of protein G from *B. subtilis* has also been reported by Fahnstock (1987).

An interesting observation is that the proteolytic behaviour of strains DB104

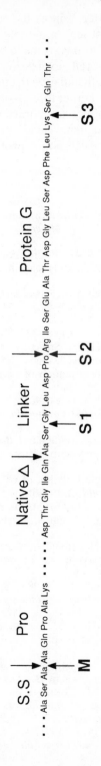

**Figure 52.5**    Amino-acid sequences at proteolytic sites of subtilisin–protein G fusion protein. Arrows show proteolytic cuts to generate the N-termini that were determined. M is the site in the membrane fraction and S1, S2 and S3 the sites in forms isolated from extracellular medium. Both strains DB104 and 168 showed identical proteolytic sites.

and 168 does not seem to differ, since the generated N-termini of subtilisin–protein G in the two strains are identical and the proteolytic degradation from either of the two strains seems to be minimal. We therefore conclude that, provided the overall expression can be improved by optimization of the promoter strength and growth conditions, this system may be useful for export of protein G and other foreign proteins from *B. subtilis*. It is plausible that the mode of secretion, a temporary retainment of the protein on the membrane followed by subsequent release, may in some way make the fusion protein less accessible to some cell-bound proteases.

## References

ARWERT, F. AND VENEMA, G. (1973). Transformation in *Bacillus subtilis*. Fate of newly introduced transforming DNA. *Molecular and General Genetics* **123**, 185–198.

BJÖRCK, L. AND KRONVALL, G. (1984). Purification and some properties of streptococcal protein G, a novel IgG binding reagent. *Journal of Immunology* **133**, 969–974.

FAHNSTOCK, S. (1987). Secretion of streptococcal protein G by *B. subtilis*. *Presentation at the 4th International Conference on Genetics and Biotechnology of Bacilli, San Diego*.

GUSS, B., ELIASSON, M., OLSSON, A., UHLÉN, M., FREJ, A.-K., JÖRNVALL, H., FLOCK, J.-I. AND LINDBERG, M. (1986). Structure of the IgG-binding regions of streptococcal protein G. *EMBO Journal* **5**, 1567–1575.

HANAHAN, D. (1983). Studies on transformation of *Escherichia coli* with plasmids. *Journal of Molecular Biology* **166**, 557–580.

JACOBS, M., ELIASSON, M., UHLÉN, M. AND FLOCK, J.-I. (1985). Cloning, sequencing and expression of subtilisin Carlsberg from *Bacillus licheniformis*. *Nucleic Acids Research* **13**, 8913–8926.

KAWAMURA, F. AND DOI, R. (1984). Construction of a *Bacillus subtilis* double mutant deficient in extracellular alkaline and neutral proteases. *Journal of Bacteriology* **160**, 442–444.

KIESER, T. (1984). Factors affecting the isolation of CCC DNA from *Streptomyces lividans* and *Escherichia coli*. *Plasmid* **12**, 19–36.

MCKENZIE, T., HOSHIMO, T., TANAKA, T. AND SUEOKA, N. (1986). The nucleotide sequence of pUB110: Some salient features in relation to replication and its regulation. *Plasmid* **15**, 93–103.

MELIN, L. AND DEHLIN, E. (1987). Functional comparison of an early and a late promotor active DNA segment from coliphage T5 in *Bacillus subtilis* and in *E. coli*. *FEMS Microbiology Letters* **41**, 141–146.

POWER, S.D., ADAMS, R.M. AND WELLS, J.A. (1986). Secretion and antoproteolytic maturation of subtilisin. *Proceedings of the National Academy of Sciences of the United States of America* **83**, 3096–3100.

VASANTHA, N. AND THOMPSON, L.D. (1986a). Secretion of a heterologous protein from *Bacillus subtilis* with the acid of protease signal sequence. *Journal of Bacteriology* **165**, 837–842.

VASANTHA, N. AND THOMPSON, L.D. (1986b). Fusion of pro region of subtilisin to staphylococcal protein A and its secretion by *Bacillus subtilis*. *Gene* **49**, 23–28.

WELLS, J.A., FERRARI, E., HENNER, D., ESTELL, D.A. AND CHEN, E.Y. (1983). Cloning, sequencing and secretion of *Bacillus amyloliquefaciens* subtilisin in *Bacillus subtilis*. *Nucleic Acids Research* **22**, 7911–7925.

WILLIAMS, D., DUVALL, E. AND LOVETT, P. (1981). Cloning restriction fragments that promote expression of a gene in *Bacillus subtilis*. *Journal of Bacteriology* **146**, 1162–1165.

# 53
# Kinetics of Protein Export from *Bacillus subtilis*

R.D. COXON, A.R. ARCHIBALD AND C.R. HARWOOD

*Microbial Technology Group, Department of Microbiology, The Medical School, Newcastle upon Tyne, NE2 4HH, UK*

## Introduction

The ability of *Bacillus subtilis* to secrete substantial amounts of various proteins into the growth medium is well known (Priest, 1977). This characteristic has been exploited commercially for the production of several homologous extracellular enzymes, notably α-amylase and alkaline and neutral proteases (Priest, 1989). Advances in molecular biological techniques have led to an interest in the *Bacillus* export system for the expression and secretion of foreign cloned gene products (Sarvas, 1986). However, since the mechanisms involved in this highly efficient secretion system are only poorly understood, characterization of the processes involved is an essential prerequisite for the optimization of secretion.

To date, investigations on the secretion of extracellular proteins have generally focused on the process by which these proteins are translocated across the cytoplasmic membrane (Randall and Hardy, 1984). In Gram-negative organisms this is the sole 'export' process for proteins, which are then not able to cross the outer membrane and hence they are referred to as periplasmic proteins. Strains of *Bacillus*, like other Gram-positive bacteria, do not possess an outer membrane and, therefore, the cytoplasmic membrane has been regarded as the major physical barrier to protein secretion. However, external to the cytoplasmic membrane, bacilli possess a thick wall composed of peptidoglycan and associated anionic heteropolymers, such as teichoic or teichuronic acids. The wall confers strength and shape on the bacterial cell in addition to being a biochemically active environment in its own right. It might reasonably be expected that the physical properties of the wall, in particular its porosity and charge, would have some influence on the passage of proteins from the inner to outer wall surface, and on the release of proteins from the outer surface into the surrounding fluid.

We have studied the kinetics of protein export by *B. subtilis* in batch culture and have shown that, whereas some proteins are exported immediately upon

*Genetic Transformation and Expression*
© Intercept Ltd, PO Box 716, Andover, Hants, SP10 1YG, UK

synthesis, others are delayed in their appearance in the supernatant. This delay is typically of the order of three-quarters to one generation time.

A variety of *B. subtilis* strains have been studied, including one deficient in major extracellular proteases. The effect of a protease deficiency is pertinent to the stability of exoproteins in the supernatant and also to the integrity of the wall itself.

## Materials and methods

### BACTERIAL STRAINS

Derivatives of *B. subtilis* strain 168 were used throughout. Strains DB104 (*hisA4, aprA3, nprR2, nprE18*) and DB102 (*hisA4, nprR2, nprE18*), were kindly provided by R. Doi (Kawamura and Doi, 1984), and BR151 (*trpC2, metB10, lys3*) by P.S. Lovett.

### KINETICS OF EXPORT

The kinetics of protein export were monitored by administering a pulse (0·05–7·5 $\mu$Ci ml$^{-1}$ final concentration) of $^{14}$C- or $^3$H-phenylalanine or $^{35}$S-methionine to early exponential-phase batch cultures growing at 37°C and 200 r.p.m. in shake flasks containing a minimal salts medium supplemented with 2% glucose and trace elements. Under these conditions all of the strains examined grew with a doubling time of approximately 60 min.

The appearance of labelled proteins in the supernatant was detected by precipitation with trichloracetic acid (TCA) and scintillation counting, using a toluene-based high Triton X-100 scintillant. Supernatant samples were also loaded onto SDS-polyacrylamide gels (SDS-PAGE) either directly, or after TCA precipitation, depending on the specific activity of the labelled exoproteins. The gels were dried and analysed by fluorography.

Samples were taken throughout exponential growth and into early stationary phase. Growth was monitored by taking optical density readings at 660 nm. The level of the intracellular enzyme isocitrate dehydrogenase in the supernatant was determined as a means of monitoring cell lysis.

## Results

In all the strains of *B. subtilis* studied, labelled extracellular protein appeared in the supernatant within 20 min of label addition. The export of these particular proteins was, therefore, very rapid. the kinetics of export for strain BR151 (*Figure 53.1*) and the extracellular protease-deficient strain DB104 (*Figure 53.2*), show that proteins continued to appear in the supernatant for up to 60 minutes, or one generation time, after the addition of the pulse. Therefore, although a proportion of the exoproteins passed rapidly through and were released from the cell membrane and wall, others were delayed in their appearance in the supernatant. The kinetics of export of four representative proteins are shown in *Figure 53.3*.

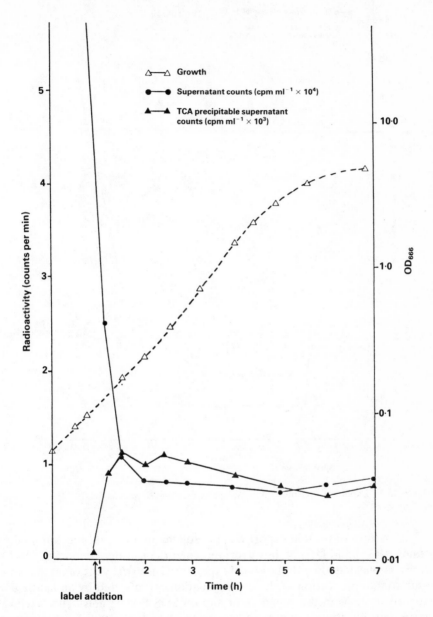

**Figure 53.1** Export of $^{14}$C pulsed-labelled proteins from *B. subtilis* BR151 (*trpC2, lys3, metB10*).

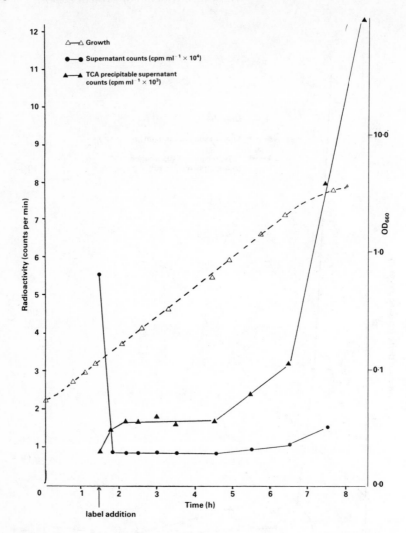

**Figure 53.2** Export of $^{14}$C pulsed-labelled proteins from *B. subtilis* DB104 (*hisA4*, *nprR2*, *nprE18*, *aprA3*).

This pattern of protein export was the sole mode of secretion exhibited by strains BR151 and DB104; however, the kinetics of protein export by DB104 were complicated towards the end of exponential growth by the onset of lysis of a substantial proportion of the cell population, as reflected by an increase in labelled proteins in the supernatant and on SDS-PAGE gels. This lysis was confirmed by the presence of isocitrate dehydrogenase in the culture supernatant (*Table 53.1*). Thus any further release of labelled protein to the supernatant after 200 min following label addition was likely to be the result of cell lysis.

Pronounced cell lysis was a feature of DB104 and an isogenic intermediate strain, DB102, that lacks neutral protease only (data not shown). Since these proteases would normally moderate the activity of the autolytic enzymes

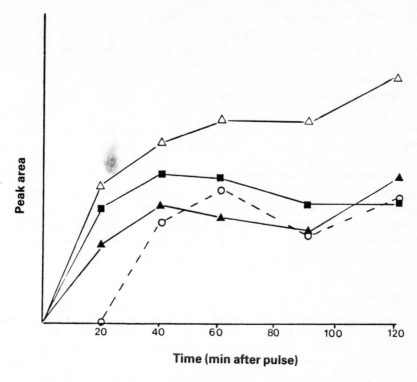

**Figure 53.3** Export kinetics of representative proteins from DB104, determined by measurement of relative peak areas from fluorograms of SDS-PAGE.

**Table 53.1** Release of isocitrate dehydrogenase (ICDH) from strains of *B. subtilis*

| Time post-labelling (min) | Supernatant ICDH as a percentage of total cell activity | |
| --- | --- | --- |
| | BR151 | DB104 |
| 60 | nd* | 0 |
| 160 | nd | 0·6 |
| 380 | nd | 22·2 |

\* nd, not detected.

(Joliffe, Doyle and Streips, 1980), premature autolysis may be an intrinsic problem of protease-deficient strains developed to reduce inactivation of heterologous gene products.

## Conclusions

In all the strains of *B. subtilis* studied, labelled extracellular protein appeared in the supernatant within 20 min, or approximately 0·33 of a generation time, of label addition. The export of these proteins is, therefore, rapid. In strains DB104 and BR151, however, a significant proportion of the secreted proteins does not appear in the supernatant until at least 40 min after labelling. After this point, no new species of labelled protein appear in the supernatant (data not shown), although the extracellular concentration of many of these proteins continues to increase for up to 60 min, or approximately one generation, after labelling. We are carrying out experiments to determine whether the delayed proteins are associated with the cell membrane or the wall. It is possible that some proteins interact with components of cell wall during synthesis and are only released into the surrounding medium as this material reaches the outer surface of the wall by inside-to-outside growth (Merad *et al.*, 1989).

Measurements of the kinetics of protein export by strain DB104 were complicated by the onset of lysis of substantial proportions of the cell population towards the end of exponential growth. This lysis was confirmed by the presence of isocitrate dehydrogenase, an intracellular enzyme, in the culture supernatant. Thus any further release of labelled protein to the supernatant, subsequent to 200 minutes following label addition, is likely to be of the intracellular products of cell lysis. Cell lysis appears to be more pronounced in strains DB104 and DB102 than in strain BR151, presumably because their deficiency in extracellular proteases results in an inability of these enzymes to moderate the activity of autolytic enzymes.

## References

JOLIFFE, L.K., DOYLE, R.J. AND STREIPS, U.N. (1980). Extracellular proteases modify cell wall turnover in *Bacillus subtilis*. *Journal of Bacteriology* **141**, 1191–1208.

KAWAMURA, F. AND DOI, R.H. (1984). Construction of a *Bacillus subtilis* mutant deficient in extracellular alkaline and neutral proteases. *Journal of Bacteriology* **160**, 442–444.

MERAD, T., ARCHIBALD, A.R., HANCOCK, I.C., HARWOOD, C.R. AND HOBOT, J.A. (1989). Cell wall assembly in *Bacillus subtilis*: visualization of old and new wall material by electron microscopic examination of samples stained selectively for teichoic acid and teichuronic acid. *Journal of General Microbiology* **135**, 645–655.

PRIEST, F.G. (1977). Extracellular enzyme synthesis in the genus *Bacillus*. *Bacteriological Reviews* **41**, 711–753.

PRIEST, F.G. (1989). Products and applications. In *Biotechnology Handbooks 2: Bacillus* (C.R. Harwood, Ed.) pp. 293–320. Plenum, New York.

RANDALL, L.L. AND HARDY, S.J.S. (1984). Export of protein in bacteria. *Microbiological Reviews* **48**, 290–298.

SARVAS, M. (1986). Protein secretion in bacilli. *Current Topics in Microbiology and Immunology* **125**, 103–125.

# 54

# Secretion of Heterologous Proteins by *Corynebacterium glutamicum*

WOLFGANG LIEBL*, KARL HEINZ SCHLEIFER* AND
ANTHONY J. SINSKEY[†]

* *Lehrstuhl für Mikrobiologie, Technische Universität München, Arcisstr. 21,
D-8000 München 2, FRG and* [†] *Department of Biology, Massachusetts Institute
of Technology, Cambridge, MA 02139, USA*

## Introduction

Corynebacteria are used extensively in biotechnology for the large-scale production of primary metabolites such as amino acids and nucleotides. The recent construction of cloning vectors and the development of transformation systems for two closely related non-pathogenic species within the coryneform group, i.e. *Corynebacterium glutamicum* (Katsumata *et al.*, 1984; Yoshihama *et al.*, 1985) and *Brevibacterium lactofermentum* (Santamaria *et al.*, 1984; Smith *et al.*, 1986) have opened the field for the investigation of gene expression and regulation in these bacteria and allow the development of novel strategies for the improvement of industrial strains.

The understanding of the molecular biology of coryneform bacteria, however, is still poor and topics such as heterologous gene expression and protein export by corynebacteria have hardly been studied to date. The analysis of the expression of characterized foreign genes in *C. glutamicum* not only defines the limits of using this host organism for the production of various heterologous proteins, but also can be an approach for investigating the possible structure of coryneform expression signals and can thus provide clues about the probable structure of corynebacterial promoters and secretion signals.

In this chapter we report the introduction of three different staphylococcal genes encoding the exported proteins lipase (from *Staphylococcus hyicus*), heat-stable nuclease and protein A (both from *Staphylococcus aureus*) into *C. glutamicum*, and discuss the observations made when analysing the expression of the corresponding proteins.

*Genetic Transformation and Expression*
© Intercept Ltd, PO Box 716, Andover, Hants, SP10 1YG, UK

**Bacterial strains and methods**

*C. glutamicum* strains ASO19 and E12 (Yoshihama *et al.*, 1985; Follettie and Sinskey, 1986) were used as corynebacterial cloning hosts.

The cloning vector pWST1 is a *C. glutamicum–E. coli* shuttle vector, which is derived from pWS124 (Batt, Shanabruch and Sinskey, 1985) and carries the *Escherichia coli trp* a terminator followed by a series of useful cloning sites. Plasmid constructions were usually carried out in *E. coli*, and subsequently transferred to *C. glutamicum*. For details concerning the experimental procedures *see* the results section.

**Results and discussion**

PROTEIN A

Protein A is a protein that binds selectively to the $F_c$ region of certain immunoglobulins (Langone, 1982). It is produced as an extracellular or cell wall bound polypeptide by most strains of *S. aureus*. The expression of protein A has been studied in several different bacterial species, including *E. coli*, *Bacillus subtilis* and several coagulase-negative staphylococci (Uhlén *et al.*, 1984; Nilsson *et al.*, 1985). In most cases, however, the expression of the plasmid-encoded gene was rather low when compared to the chromosomal protein A gene, *spa*, of *S. aureus*.

A deletion derivative of the protein A gene encoding a truncated form of protein A but still possessing the complete promoter region was isolated from plasmid pRIT5 (Nilsson, Abrahamsen and Uhlén, 1985) on an approximately 1·1 kbp *Taq*I fragment and inserted into *C. glutamicum–E. coli* shuttle vector pWST1. The resulting plasmid, pWPA7 (*see Figure 54.1*), was transformed into protoplasts of *C. glutamicum* ASO19. In a Western blotting experiment, culture supernatant of strain ASO19/pWPA7 was separated on a SDS-polyacrylamide gel, whereafter the exoproteins were transferred to a nitrocellulose membrane and probed with alkaline-phosphatase-conjugated antigoat IgG (from rabbit, Sigma). However, only a very weak band of size approximately 31 kDa (the predicted size of the truncated protein A) was detected by virtue of its ability to react with the enzyme-linked IgG (data not shown).

The reason for this obviously poor expression of extracellular protein A is not yet clear, but could lie in poor promoter recognition by the host strain or problems with the export of a protein with unusual structural features as found in protein A and therefore improper localization of the protein in the cytoplasm or cell wall of *C. glutamicum*. Further experiments will be necessary to elucidate which of the factors, transcription, translation or export, is limiting for the production of protein A by *C. glutamicum*.

*S. HYICUS* LIPASE

The staphylococcal plasmid pLipPS1 (a kind gift from F. Götz, Tübingen, FRG) was used as a source for a foreign lipase gene. This plasmid contains the

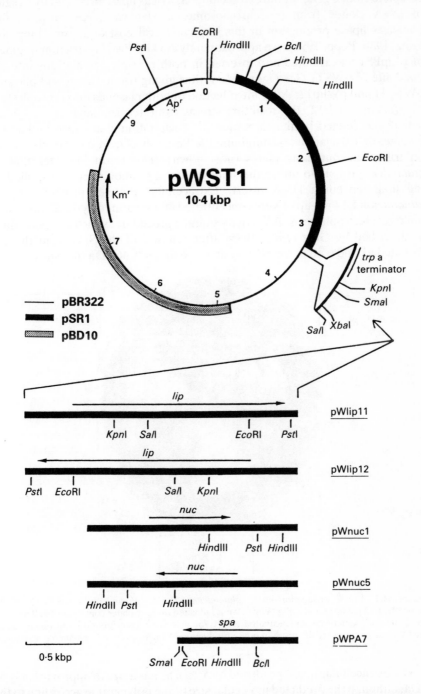

**Figure 54.1**   Derivatives of pWST1 carrying various staphylococcal exoprotein genes. The *Sma*I site of pWST1 was used as the cloning site for all of the constructions. The DNA inserts are shown as horizontal bars, the relative orientation of the genes is indicated with arrows. Abbreviations: *spa*, staphylococcal protein A gene; *lip*, *S. hyicus* lipase gene; *nuc*, staphylococcal nuclease gene.

complete cloned gene for the extracellular *S. hyicus* lipase preceded by a region of DNA cloned from the chromosome of *Staphylococcus carnosus* that enhances lipase production in this staphylococcal host organism (Liebl and Götz, 1986; Popp, 1986). An approximately 2·5 kbp *Pvu*II restriction fragment of pLipPS1 was isolated and inserted in both possible orientations into the *Sma*I site of pWST1 (*see Figure 54.1*), thus giving rise to the hybrid plasmids pW1ip11 and pWlip12. After introduction of both plasmids into protoplasts of *C. glutamicum* E12, the resulting strains exhibited similar levels of lipase activity, as judged by the formation of precipitation zones surrounding the colonies on LB agar plates containing 1% Tween 80 (*Figure 54.2*) or clear halos on tributyrin-containing plates (not shown). This result indicates that *C. glutamicum* is able to utilize the staphylococcal promoter region supplied on the lipase-encoding DNA insert. Extracellular proteins produced by *C. glutamicum* E12/pWlip12 were concentrated and separated by SDS polyacrylamide gel electrophoresis. An activity staining procedure, which was performed as described by Götz *et al.* (1985) after removal of the SDS from the gel, revealed a band with lipase activity at approximately 46 kDa (not shown).

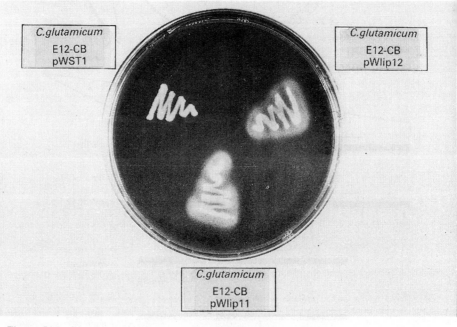

**Figure 54.2** Lipase production by *C. glutamicum*. The *C. glutamicum* strains E12/pWST1 (control), E12/pWlip11 and E12/pWlip12 were indicated on agar plates containing 1% Tween 80 and 15 µg ml$^{-1}$ kanamycin and incubated at 30°C for 36 h. Turbid precipitation zones surrounding the bacterial colonies are the result of lipase production by the respective *C. glutamicum* strains.

The extracellular lipase produced by *S. hyicus* has a size of approximately 50 kDa, although the predicted molecular size of the polypeptide according to the nucleotide sequence of the chromosomal lipase gene is 71 kDa (Götz *et al.*, 1985). This discrepancy of sizes makes the occurrence of post-translatory, probably post-secretory processing of the initially synthesized peptide likely.

The expression of *S. hyicus* lipase has also been analysed in *S. carnosus*. In his host, the majority of lipase found in the culture supernatant has a molecular weight of approximately 86 kDa and is not processed (Götz *et al.*, 1985). Finally, in the non-related host *C. glutamicum* the lipase appears extracellularly as a 46 kDa form, which compares reasonably well with the size of the enzyme produced by the original host organism *S. hyicus*. Thus, a similar form of processing of extracellular lipase seems to take place with *C. glutamicum* as host as with *S. hyicus*. This observation was surprising since *S. carnosus*, which is more closely related to *S. hyicus*, is not capable of performing this kind of processing.

STAPHYLOCOCCAL NUCLEASE

Staphylococcal nuclease is the third exoenzyme we chose for the analysis of secretion of foreign proteins by *C. glutamicum*. This enzyme is produced by most strains of *S. aureus*, a fact which is reflected by the observation that the cloned nuclease gene can be used as a specific DNA probe for the identification of *S. aureus* (Liebl *et al.*, 1987). Plasmid pNuc1 (manuscript in preparation) which carries the nuclease gene cloned from pFOG301 (a gift from D. Shortle; Shortle, 1983) in the staphylococcal vector pCA43 (Kreutz and Götz, 1984) served as the source for the staphylococcal nuclease gene. An approximately 1·9 kbp *EcoR*V fragment of pNuc1 was inserted into the *Sma*I site of pWST1. The resulting constructs, pWnuc1 and pWnuc5 (*see Figure 54.1*), were

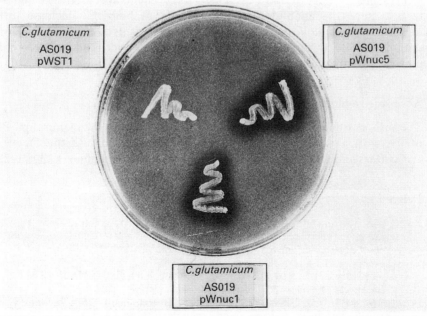

**Figure 54.3** Production of staphylococcal nuclease by *C. glutamicum*. DNase agar plates (Oxoid) containing 15 µg ml$^{-1}$ kanamycin were inoculated with the *C. glutamicum* strains ASO19/pWST1 (control), ASO19/pWnuc1 and ASO19/pWnuc5 and incubated at 30°C for 36 h. Strains with DNA-hydrolyzing activity develop clear halos against a white background upon precipitation of residual DNA in the plate with 1N hydrochloric acid.

transformed into protoplasts of *C. glutamicum* ASO19. The extent of extracellular nuclease production by the plasmid-containing *C. glutamicum* strains was estimated with a simple plate assay using DNase agar (Oxoid; *Figure 54.3*). The level of nuclease activity found with *C. glutamicum* is higher than the level produced upon introduction of the gene into certain coagulase-negative staphylococcal strains (unpublished data).

As in the case of the lipase gene described above, the relative orientation of the nuclease gene in the vector pWST1 does not significantly influence the production of staphylococcal nuclease by *C. glutamicum*. Analysis of the culture supernatant of *C. glutamicum* ASO19/pWnuc5 by SDS-polyacrylamide gel electrophoresis and an activity staining procedure revealed that, in liquid media containing 2% tryptone, 0·5% yeast extract and 1% sodium chloride, two enzymatically active nuclease species with molecular sizes of approximately 17 kDa and 20 kDa, respectively, are produced (manuscript in preparation).

It has been shown that in culture supernatants of the native host, *S. aureus*, varying amounts of a large nuclease form, termed 'nuclease B', with a 19 amino acid amino-terminal extension can be found in addition to the mature 'nuclease A' (Davis *et al.*, 1977). With *B. subtilis* strains carrying the staphylococcal nuclease gene, pulse–chase experiments have shown that the first nuclease species appearing in the culture supernatant is an approximately 20 kDa protein, which co-migrates with staphylococal nuclease B. This nuclease form is rapidly processed in *B. subtilis* supernatant to yield a smaller nuclease A-like form (Miller, Kovacevic and Veal, 1987). Experiments are currently under way to determine the amino-terminal sequences of both the nuclease forms secreted by *C. glutamicum* ASO19/pWnuc5. The results of these investigations should provide information about the signal peptide and post-secretory processing of the staphylococcal nuclease precursor by *C. glutamicum*.

### Acknowledgements

The authors would like to thank Mrs H. Huber for typing the manuscript. Part of the work described above was sponsored by a grant of the Deutsche Forschungsgemeinschaft (DFG) awarded to W. Liebl (grant no. Li 398/1–2).

### References

BATT, C.A., SHANABRUCH, W.S. AND SINSKEY, A.J. (1985). Expression of pAM 1 tetracycline resistance gene in *Corynebacterium glutamicum*: segregation of antibiotic resistance due to intramolecular recombination. *Biotechnology Letters* 7, 717–722.

DAVIS, A., MOORE, I.B. PARKER, D.S. AND TANIUCHI, H. (1977). Nuclease B. *Journal of Biological Chemistry* 252, 6544–6553.

FOLLETTIE, M.T. AND SINSKEY, A.J. (1986). Recombinant DNA technology for *Corynebacterium glutamicum*. *Food Technology* 40, 88–94.

GÖTZ, F., POPP, F., KORN, E. AND SCHLEIFER, K.H. (1985). Complete nucleotide sequence of the lipase gene from *Staphylococcus hyicus* cloned in *Staphylococcus carnosus*. *Nucleic Acids Research* 13, 5895–5906.

KATSUMATA, R., OZAKI, A., OKA, T. AND TURUYA, A. (1984). Protoplast transformation of glutamate-producing bacteria with plasmid DNA. *Journal of Bacteriology* **159**, 306–311.

KREUTZ, B. AND GÖTZ, F. (1984). Construction of *Staphylococcus* plasmid vector pCA43 conferring resistance to chloramphenicol, arsenate, arsenite and antimony. *Gene* **31**, 301–304.

LANGONE, J.J. (1982). Protein A of *Staphylococcus aureus* and related immunoglobulin receptor produced by streptococci and pneumococci. In *Advances in Immunology, Volume 32* (F.J. Dixon and H.G. Kunkel, Eds), pp. 157–252. Academic Press, New York.

LIEBL, W. AND GÖTZ, F. (1986). Studies on lipase directed export of *Escherichia coli* β-lactamase in *Staphylococcus carnosus*. *Molecular and General Genetics* **204**, 166–173.

LIEBL, W., ROSENSTEIN, R., GÖTZ, F. AND SCHLEIFER, K.H. (1987). Use of staphylococcal nuclease as DNA probe for *Staphylococcus aureus*. *FEMS Microbiology Letters* **44**, 179–184.

MILLER, J.R., KOVACEVIC, S. AND VEAL, L.E. (1987). Secretion and processing of staphylococcal nuclease by *Bacillus subtilis*. *Journal of Bacteriology* **169**, 3508–3514.

NILSSON, B., ABRAHAMSEN, L. AND UHLÉN, M. (1985). Immobilization and purification of enzymes with staphylococcal protein A gene fusion vectors. *EMBO Journal* **4**, 1075–1080.

NILSSON, B., HOLMGREN, E., JOSEPHSON, S., GATENBECK, S., PHILIPSON, L. AND UHLÉN, M. (1985). Efficient secretion and purification of human insulin-like growth factor I with a gene fusion vector in staphylococci. *Nucleic Acids Research* **13**, 1151–1162.

POPP, F. (1986). *Molekularbiologische Charakterisierung der Lipasegens aus* Staphylococcus hyicus *Kloniert in* Staphylococcus carnosus. Ph.D. thesis, Lehrstuhl für Mikrobiologie, Technische Universität München, Munich, FRG.

SANTAMARIA, R., GIL, J.A., MESAS, J.M. AND MARTIN, J.F. (1984). Characterization of an endogenous plasmid and development of cloning vectors and a transformation system in *Brevibacterium lactofermentum*. *Journal of General Microbiology* **130**, 2237–2246.

SHORTLE, D. (1983). A genetic system for analysis of staphylococcal nuclease. *Gene* **22**, 181–189.

SMITH, M.D., FLICKINGER, J.L., LINEBERGER, D.W. AND SCHMIDT, B. (1986). Protoplast transformation in coryneform bacteria and introduction of an α-amylase gene from *Bacillus amyloliquefaciens* into *Brevibacterium lactofermentum*. *Applied and Environmental Microbiology* **51**, 634–639.

UHLÉN, M., GUSS, B., NILSSON, GÖTZ, F. AND LINDBERG, M. (1984). Expression of the gene encoding protein Ain *Staphylococcus aureus* and coagulase-negative staphylcocci. *Journal of Bacteriology* **159**, 713–719.

YOSHIHAMA, M., HIGASHIRO, K., RAO, E.A., AKEDO, M., SHANABRUCH, W.G., FOLLETTIE, M.T., WALKER, G.C. AND SINSKEY, A.J. (1985). Cloning vector system for *Corynebacterium glutamicum*. *Journal of Bacteriology* **162**, 591–597.

# 55

# Analysis and Use of the Serum-Albumin-Binding Domains of Streptococcal Protein G

MARGARETA ELIASSON, PER-ÅKE NYGREN AND
MATHIAS UHLÉN

*Department of Biochemistry and Biotechnology, The Royal Institute of
Technology, S-100 44 Stockholm, Sweden*

Streptococcal protein G (*Figure 55.1C*) is an IgG-binding receptor with a molecular mass of 63 kDa as predicted from the sequence of the corresponding gene (Olsson *et al.*, 1987). Here we show that a truncated recombinant protein of 22 kDa (*Figure 55.1B*) still has IgG-binding capacity and also interacts specifically with human serum albumin (HSA) (Nygren *et al.*, 1988). This demonstrates that protein G is a bifunctional receptor. To investigate the structures needed for IgG- and albumin-binding, different parts of the receptor molecule (*Figures 55.1A* and *55.1D*) were produced in *Escherichia coli*, using a coupled expression/secretion system. Affinity chromatography, using IgG or HSA immobilized on Sepharose, showed that the two binding activities are structurally separated. From these experiments, it was concluded that a region of 64 amino-acid residues is sufficient for albumin-binding. The structure of this part of the protein suggests either a divalent or a trivalent binding capacity. The specific interaction to albumin was used to purify heterologous proteins by affinity chromatography to yield pure fusion proteins (*Figures 55.1E* and *55.1F*) in a one-step procedure. This novel affinity system might be useful as a tool to facilitate protein immobilization and purification.

## References

NYGREN, P.-Å., ELIASSON, M., PALMCRANTZ, E., ABRAHMSÉN, L. AND UHLÉN, M. (1988). Analysis and use of the serum albumin binding domains of streptococcal protein G. *Journal of Molecular Recognition* 1(2), 69–74.
OLSSON, A., ELIASSON, M., GUSS, B., NILSSON, B., HELLMAN, U., LINDBERG, M. AND UHLÉN, M. (1987). Structure and evolution of the repetitive gene encoding streptococcal protein G. *European Journal of Biochemistry* 168, 319–324.

*Genetic Transformation and Expression*
© Intercept Ltd, PO Box 716, Andover, Hants, SP10 1YG, UK

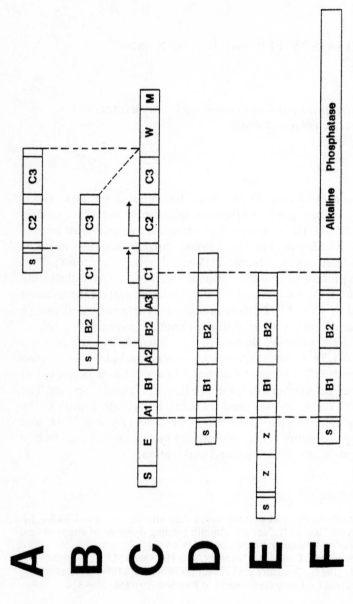

**Figure 55.1**   Schematic drawings of Streptococcal protein G and the protein-G-derived proteins encoded by the different plasmids used in the study. The proteins are encoded by pC2C3 (A), pEG (B), the native *spg* gene (C), pB1B2 (D), pZZB1B2 (E) and pNP-1 (F). Different regions of protein G are indicated with bold letters. The NH$_2$-termini of the two truncated forms of protein G, that resulted from restarts in the heterologous host *E. coli*, are indicated by arrows. The lines originating at protein G show the parts subcloned in the different plasmid constructs. The promoter, signal peptide (S) and first six amino acids of Staphylococcal protein A were used in the expression of subcloned fragments. The protein-A-derived synthetic Z domains constitute the NH$_2$-terminal part of the fusion protein encoded by pZZB1B2. The 52 extra COOH-terminal amino acids of the protein encoded by pB1B2 result from the plasmid vector. In plasmid pNP-1 the gene encoding alkaline phosphatase, derived from *E. coli*, is fused to the gene coding for the albumin-binding domains of protein G. The enzymatic activity of alkaline phosphatase is retained in the fusion protein. ((A–E) Nygren *et al.*, 1988, (F) Swedish Patent Application 8800378–5.)

# 56

# Primary Sequence of an IgA-Binding Protein from *Streptococcus pyogenes*: Relation to Streptococcal M Proteins

ELISABET FRITHZ*, LARS-OLOF HEDÉN* AND
GUNNAR LINDAHL[†]

* *Department of Microbiology, University of Lund, S-223 62 Lund, Sweden and* [†] *Department of Medical Microbiology, University of Lund, S-223 62 Lund, Sweden*

The gene for an IgA receptor protein (Arp) from *Streptococcus pyogenes* was cloned in *Escherichia coli* and shown to be expressed as a protein with a molecular mass of about 45 000 Da which binds radiolabelled IgA. The nucleotide sequence was determined by the Sanger dideoxy chain termination method. The deduced amino-acid sequence corresponds to a protein of 44 kDa with a 41 amino acids signal sequence extensively homologous to those found in streptococcal M proteins. The 45 kDa protein observed on SDS-polyacrylamide gels corresponds to the processed form of the protein and is located in the periplasmic space. The aberrant gel migration observed may be associated with the unusual amino-acid composition of the protein. A matrix comparison shows that there are three internal repetitive sequences in the C-terminal portion of the molecule. When the corresponding amino-acid sequences are compared to the repetitive sequences found in other bacterial surface proteins, a striking similarity to streptococcal M proteins is found. The most C-terminal part of the molecule is highly homologous to the corresponding region in protein G and streptococcal M proteins. The presence of this conserved region is not unexpected, and it is probably involved in anchorage of the molecule to the cell membrane.

A schematic presentation of the coding region for protein Arp is given in *Figure 56.1*. The data presented show that protein Arp is the first example of a protein with properties common to both M proteins and Ig receptors, as illustrated in *Figure 56.2*.

*Genetic Transformation and Expression*
© Intercept Ltd, PO Box 716, Andover, Hants, SP10 1YG, UK

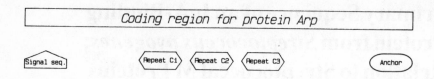

**Figure 56.1**    Schematic presentation of the coding region for protein Arp.

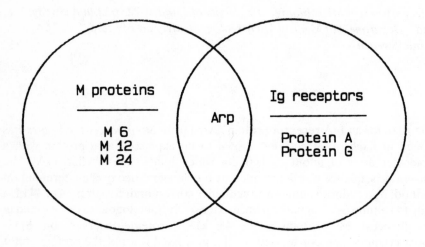

**Figure 56.2**    Protein Arp has properties in common with both streptococcal M proteins and Ig receptors.

# Index